SIR NICHOLAS HARRIS NICOLAS was born in 1799, and served in the Royal Navy in the Mediterranean from 1808 to 1816 under Admiral Duckworth and Lord Exmouth. Retired on half-pay at the end of the Napoleonic Wars, he turned to antiquarian and literary pursuits after a brief legal career, compiling and editing a large number of scholarly works. This seven-volume annotated compilation of Nelson's correspondence was originally published by Henry Colburn between 1844 and 1847, and was to be followed by his ambitious *A History of the British Navy, from the Earliest Times to the Wars of the French Revolution*, but when he died in France in 1848, only the first two volumes, covering up to the year 1422, had been completed.

THE

DISPATCHES AND LETTERS

OF

VICE ADMIRAL

LORD VISCOUNT NELSON

WITH NOTES BY

SIR NICHOLAS HARRIS NICOLAS, G.C.M.G.

THE FIFTH VOLUME.

JANUARY 1802, TO APRIL 1804.

CHATHAM PUBLISHING

LONDON

Published in 1998 by
Chatham Publishing,
1 & 2 Faulkner's Alley, Cowcross Street,
London EC1M 6DD

Chatham Publishing is an imprint of
Gerald Duckworth and Co Ltd

First Published in 1845
by Henry Colburn

ISBN 1 86176 052 3

A catalogue record for this book is available
from the British Library

Printed and bound in Great Britain by
Redwood Books, Trowbridge, Wiltshire

PREFACE.

Some explanation of the contents of this Volume seems necessary, because many of the public documents in it are of rather a different description from those that preceded them, and Lord Nelson's private correspondence was partly with different persons, and on different subjects from his former Letters. Though equally illustrative of his character, occasionally treating of important topics, and forming valuable materials for Naval, and sometimes for General History, they have not the vivid interest of either his previous or his subsequent correspondence, being written while he was on half-pay, or during the monotony of a blockade. They exhibit Nelson, however, in a new position; and the admiration which was bestowed on his matchless exploits, will now be given to the wonderful energy and zeal which he displayed as Commander-in-Chief in the Mediterranean; and the Public will learn for the first time, what were the multiplied duties of an Officer holding that most important post.

The period over which this portion of Nelson's Dis-

patches and Letters extend, is from the 1st of January
1802, to the 30th of April 1804. At the commencement of 1802, though still commanding the Squadron
for the defence of the English Coast, LORD NELSON
was on leave of absence, and resided at Merton. On the
10th of April 1803, he was permitted to strike his flag;
and he remained on shore during the Peace of Amiens,
about twelve months. His correspondence while on half-
pay, was not very extensive; and the most remarkable
Letters are those to the Lord Mayor and Sheriffs of London,
again expressing his dissatisfaction with the conduct of
the City, respecting the Battle of Copenhagen; and to
Mr. Addington, the Prime Minister, urging the inade-
quacy of his income to support his rank, and the unfair-
ness of his pension being limited to £2000 per annum,
he having, besides his other services, gained two Battles,
while Lords St. Vincent and Duncan, who had fought
only one, had each a pension of £3000. But his pension
was never increased.

His mind, while on shore, was as fully devoted to the
service of his Country, as when commanding her Fleets;
and there are several remarkable manifestations at this
time, of his attention to his profession. During a tour
into Wales, being struck with the value of the Forest
of Dean in supplying timber for the Navy, he submitted
his observations to Mr. Addington, and it is believed
that his suggestions were adopted. In December 1802,
he drew up a paper on the Island of Malta; and he
soon after sent to the Earl of St. Vincent, then First
Lord of the Admiralty, a Plan for manning the Navy.

In the first Parliament after the Union, he seconded the Address; he spoke, on several occasions, in 1802, in the House of Lords, on professional subjects, particularly on the Bill for an Inquiry into Naval Abuses; and he afterwards gave his evidence before the Commissioners appointed to investigate that subject, respecting the misapplication of Prize money by Prize agents.

On the renewal of hostilities with France, LORD NELSON was selected for the command in the Mediterranean; and he hoisted his flag in the Victory, at Spithead, on the 18th of May 1803. The supposed necessity of reinforcing Admiral Cornwallis's Squadron off Ushant with that Ship (which was only given to NELSON after some remonstrances on his part, and he had said, with wounded pride, " I trust I can take a French Admiral as well as any of them") exposed him to the annoyance of removing at sea into the Amphion frigate, which conveyed him to Malta, and thence, on the 8th of July, to his Squadron off Toulon.

His public correspondence in the Mediterranean, was chiefly with Sir John Acton and Mr. Hugh Elliot (British Minister at Naples, and a brother of Lord Minto, who had sailed from England with Lord Nelson) on the state of Naples and Sicily, and particularly as to the safety of the Royal Family, an object always uppermost in his thoughts; with the Turkish Government, the Barbary Powers, the British Ambassador at Constantinople, and with our Minister at the Court of the King of Sardinia; with the Secretary for the War Department, on the affairs of the various States in the Mediterranean; with the Admiralty, on matters connected with his Squadron; with the Officers of the Dockyards at Malta and Gibraltar, the Storekeepers at those places, and the Vice-consuls at Barcelona and Rosas, about *matériel* and provisions for the Fleet, especially with the view of promoting the health and comfort of the Crews; and with various Officers, for the protection of our Trade, in appointing the necessary Convoys, &c.

It would be difficult to select any of these Letters as more interesting or more important than the rest; since they all bear in a greater or less degree upon each other, and must be read in connexion, to be properly understood and appreciated. The paper which he sent to Mr. Addington in June, 1803, containing his views respecting Gibraltar, Algiers, Malta, Sicily, Sardinia, Rome, Tuscany, Genoa, and the Morea, was so able as to obtain the marked approbation of the Government, accompanied by a request that he would in future direct his observations on Political subjects at once to the Secretary of State for the War Department.

In LORD NELSON'S opinion, it was of the utmost importance that Great Britain should obtain a cession of Sardinia; and the soundness of that opinion, which he repeated over and over again to every person of the least Political influence, is not likely to be disputed by any one who remembers the central position of that Island, its admirable harbours, and the necessity of watching the Enemy's Squadron at Toulon.

His Letters to the Dey of Algiers, and his instructions

to Captain Keats when that Officer was sent to demand
satisfaction for the Dey's treatment of the British Consul,
and for other insults to this Country, as well as the
prudence with which he proposed to defer retaliating,
until he could strike an effective blow, are very
characteristic.

LORD NELSON's private Letters are mostly to the Duke
of Clarence, the Earl of St. Vincent, Mr. Addington,
Lord Minto, Admiral Lord Radstock, Mr. Hugh Elliot,
Mr. Rose, Sir Alexander Ball, General Villettes,
Mr. Davison, his brother Dr. Nelson, Lady Hamilton,
and his daughter, now Mrs. Horatia Nelson Ward. No
part of the Editor's task was so difficult as to decide
upon the course which he ought to follow with respect
to the Letters to Lady Hamilton. It was his original
intention to omit those Letters altogether; but this was
found inexpedient, because, after the separation from
Lady Nelson, they describe NELSON's private feelings
more fully and more naturally than any of his other
Letters. It was, however, impossible to reprint those Letters exactly as they occur, on account of some personal
and other objectionable allusions in them; and still more,
because it would not have been proper, under any circumstances, to republish coarse and offensive expressions,
without being sure that they exist in the originals. He
has, therefore, printed every part of the Letters in question
except paragraphs, or entire Letters of that description,
and except those terms of endearment and affection,
which that person ought not to have called forth.

It may be right to anticipate the objection that many of the Letters in this Volume are on small details, while some are little more than acknowledgments of Orders from the Admiralty. These Letters have been selected from numerous others of a similar kind; and the reason for printing them, is that the one class exhibits NELSON'S extraordinary attention to everything connected with his Squadron, and affords to unprofessional readers an idea, not only of his zeal, but of the manner in which Ships of War are governed and regulated; while the other class shows the duties he was directed to perform, and explains many of his subsequent Letters and proceedings.

The "Orders" to his Captains, which often exhibit the sagacity and vigour of his mind, are, it is submitted, necessary for the comprehension of his plans, as manifested in the disposition of his Squadron. The "Order-Book" of the Duke of Wellington has properly been published ; and if selections from the "Orders" of NELSON had not been inserted, this collection would have been imperfect.

Two more Volumes will complete the Work, which has unavoidably been extended beyond the original design, in consequence of the unexpected accession of materials.

1st December, 1845.

CONTENTS.

LETTERS.

1802.

1802, *continued.*

1803.

1803, *continued.*

1803, *continued.*

1803, *continued.*

1803, *continued.*

1803, *continued.*

1803, *continued.*

1803, *continued.*

1803, *continued.*

1803, *continued.*

1804.

1804, *continued.*

1804, *continued.*

1804, *continued.*

1804, *continued.*

1804, *continued.*

1804, *continued.*

CONTENTS.

1804, *continued.*

ANALYSIS

OF THE

LIFE OF NELSON,

FROM JANUARY 1802 TO APRIL 1804.

YEAR.	MONTH.	FACTS.
1802.		
—	January 1st to April 9th	VICE-ADMIRAL OF THE BLUE, Commanding in Chief a Squadron employed between Orfordness and Beachy Head ; but on leave, and residing at Merton, in Surrey.
—	— 10th	Struck his Flag.
1803.	to May 15th	On half-pay. In July and August 1802, he made a tour into Wales, and returned to Merton early in September 1802. On the 23rd of November, 1802, he seconded the Address in the House of Lords, in the first Parliament after the Union.
—	— 16th	Appointed COMMANDER - IN - CHIEF in the Mediterranean.
—	— 18th	Hoisted his Flag on board H. M. Ship *Victory*, Captain Samuel Sutton, at Spithead.
—	— 20th	Sailed from Spithead in company with the *Amphion*, Captain Thomas Masterman Hardy.
—	— 21st	Off the Start, captured a Dutch Merchant Ship.
—	— 23rd	Off Ushant. Shifted his Flag to the *Amphion*, and proceeded in her to the Mediterranean.
—	June 3rd	Arrived at Gibraltar.
—	— 4th	Sailed from Gibraltar.
—	— 15th	Arrived at Malta.
—	— 17th	Sailed from Malta.
—	— 19th	Off Messina.
—	— 25th	Off Capri, in the Bay of Naples.

YEAR.   MONTH.   FACTS.

1804, *continued* ....VICE-ADMIRAL OF THE BLUE.

— July 1st ....Off Monte Christo.

— — 8th ....Joined the Fleet, consisting of nine Sail of
                          the Line, one Frigate, and one Sloop, off
                          Toulon.

— — 30th   ⎧ The *Victory* having joined the `Fleet, he
        to   ⎪ again hoisted his Flag on board that Ship,
— October 30th   ⎨ taking with him Captain Hardy.
                    ⎩ Off Toulon.

— — 31st............Anchored at the Madalena Islands, Sardinia,
                          with the Squadron.

— November 10th.........Sailed from the Madalena Islands.

        to   ⎫
— December 9th   ⎬ ...Off Toulon.
                    ⎭

— — 10th ......Anchored with the Fleet in the Gulf of Palma,
                          on the South side of Sardinia

— — 19th ......Sailed from Palma.

        to   ⎫
— — 23rd   ⎬ ...Off Toulon.
                    ⎭

— — 24th ......Anchored at the Madalena Islands.

1804. January 4th ....Sailed from the Madalena Islands with the
                          Squadron.

        to   ⎫
— — about 14th   ⎬ ...Off Toulon.
                    ⎭

— — 17th   ⎫
        to   ⎬ ...Off Algiers.
— — 19th   ⎭

— — 22nd ....Off Toulon.

— — 26th ....Anchored at the Madalena Islands with the
                          Squadron.

— February 1st ....Sailed from the Madalena Islands with the
                          Squadron.

— — 8th ....Anchored at the Madalena Islands.

— — 19th ....Sailed with the Squadron from the Madalena
                          Islands.

— — to   ⎫
                    ⎬ ...Off Toulon.
—· March 23rd   ⎭

— — 24th ....Anchored with the Squadron at the Madalena
                          Islands.

— April 3rd ....Sailed from the Madalena Islands.

        to   ⎫ ...Off Toulon. On the 23rd of April, he was pro-
— — 30th   ⎬   moted to be a VICE-ADMIRAL OF THE
                    ⎭   WHITE.

LETTERS

LETTERS.

1802—ÆT. 43.

TO CAPTAIN SUTTON, H.M. SHIP AMAZON.

[Autograph, in the possession of Captain Ives Sutton.]

Merton, January 6th, 1802.

My dear Sutton,

I send you the order, but I do not think it will be useful to the men. I feel much obliged for Captain Owen's kind offer about Connor, and if he is employed I shall gladly accept his offer; but I see so little of any of the Admiralty people, and they tell me nothing, that I am as ignorant of any arrangements as you can possibly conceive. I cannot get my *discharge*. I asked yesterday : my answer was, ' No person of any rank is to be discharged.' It is very cold, even here, and I have been laid up with swelled face. Yesterday, I went to London for two hours, the first time for a month. I can readily conceive your desire to be paid off, and, from the little I hear, it cannot be long. Remember us kindly to the Lutwidges, Commodore Sutton, and all our friends about you. Say, in your next, how poor Langford is. Bedford has been very ill, and I fear cannot yet venture out, for we asked him to come and see us. As probably I shall not return to *Deal*, I think I may venture to have my papers and cot sent to London : therefore, I will request you to send them by the waggon directed to 23 Piccadilly, and tell me when they are sent. I trust you will forgive my giving you all this trouble, and believe me ever, my dear Sutton, your much obliged,

NELSON AND BRONTE.

We all join in wishing you every happiness in the present year.

TO JOHN JULIUS ANGERSTEIN, ESQ., CHAIRMAN OF THE
COMMITTEE OF THE PATRIOTIC FUND.

[From a Copy in the Nelson Papers.]

My dear Sir,   Merton, January 15th, 1802.
I will send to the Medusa directly for a Return of Wounded:
they must have been near forty. We are all obliged by your
humane attention to us Seamen, and none more than, my dear
Sir, your most obedient servant,

NELSON AND BRONTE.

TO CAPTAIN SUTTON, H.M. SHIP AMAZON.

[Autograph, in the possession of Captain Ives Sutton.]

Merton, January 15th, 1802.
My dear Sutton,
Many thanks for the trouble you have taken with my
things. You may rely that I will write to either the Board
or some one of the Members, if that is the best mode of obtaining success for Mr. Caie, your Surgeon. We are sorry
that anything should disturb the comfort of our good friends
the Lutwidges, but we hope sincerely it will end well. But
it can answer no good end their fretting for the unhappy
young man.[1] The story I never heard, but suppose he has
killed some other young man: if so, many have done so
before him. I saw Lord St. Vincent yesterday; he looked
very ill and much altered for the worse. Remember me
kindly to the Commodore, and the good Admiral and Mrs.
Lutwidge, in which cordially joins this party with, dear Sutton,
your much obliged,

NELSON AND BRONTE.

[1] Lieutenant Henry Thomas Lutwidge, of the Resistance, nephew of Admiral
Skeffington Lutwidge, was supposed to have caused the death of a drunken seaman, in
January 1802, by striking him with the tiller of the launch, to compel him to give
up the oar which he was incapable of using. The blow, intended for the arm, fell on
his head, and the man died the next morning. Though there were strong reasons
for believing that his death was produced by apoplexy, a Jury returned a verdict of
wilful murder, and Mr. Lutwidge was tried at the Assizes at Winchester, on the 13th
of March. Being found guilty of manslaughter, he was sentenced to pay a fine of
£100, and to three months' imprisonment. The particulars are fully given in the
Naval Chronicle, vol. vii. p. 252. He became a Retired Commander in November
1830.

TO CAPTAIN SUTTON, H.M. SHIP AMAZON.

[Autograph, in the possession of Captain Ives Sutton.]

Merton, January 21st, 1802.

My dear Sutton,

Doctor Harness[2] assures me in writing, that Mr. Caie shall be employed whenever the Amazon is paid off: therefore, whenever that takes place, he may present himself to Dr. H.; Langford, poor fellow! is with us: I much fear he is still far from well. Lord St. Vincent went into Essex on Sunday to avoid the Birth-day, and I believe is not yet returned to London, although only fifty minutes drive. I cannot yet obtain my discharge. Make our kindest regards to the Lutwidges and all friends, and believe me ever, my dear Sutton, your obliged and attached,

NELSON AND BRONTE.

What a gale!

TO THE RIGHT HONOURABLE HENRY ADDINGTON.

[Autograph, in the Sidmouth Papers.]

My dear Sir,　　　　　　　　　Merton, January 31st, 1802.

I received yesterday from Lord Elgin the Letters and Ribbon sent herewith, and I have to request that you will have the goodness to lay them before the King, in order that I may know his Royal pleasure as to wearing the Ribbon. This mark of regard from the Sultan has made a strong impression on my mind, as it appears that the Battle of Copenhagen has been the cause of this new Decoration from the Porte.

If his Majesty should from regard to the Sultan, or honour to me, intend to place the Ribbon on me, I am ready to attend His commands; but I own, my dear Sir, that great as this honour would be, that it would have its alloy, if I cannot at the same time wear the Medal for the Battle of Copenhagen, the greatest and most honourable reward in the power of our Sovereign to bestow, as it marks the personal services of, my dear Sir, your most obliged,

NELSON AND BRONTE.

[2] Vide vol. i. p. 473.

TO CAPTAIN SUTTON, H.M. SHIP AMAZON.

[Autograph, in the possession of Captain Ives Sutton.]

My dear Sutton,   Merton, February 6th, 1802.

I beg you will thank Captain Cochrane for his advice about the thrashing machine, which I will most certainly send out. I have had very good accounts from Bronté. I wish you were all paid off, but that cannot be done till the Definitive Treaty, which I fancy will not be long. The weather has been very severe. I saw Lord St. Vincent yesterday: he looks very unwell. The history of Medals for Copenhagen he has promised me shall be brought before the Cabinet Council. The Grand Signior has sent me a Red ribbon and Medal for the Battle of Copenhagen, with a very flattering letter. All here join in every good wish with your ever obliged,   NELSON AND BRONTE.

Best regards to the good Admiral, and Mrs. Lutwidge, and the Commodore.

TO CAPTAIN SUTTON, H.M. SHIP AMAZON.

[Autograph, in the possession of Captain Ives Sutton.]

Merton, February 9th, 1802.

My dear Sutton,

As Allen,[3] my servant, leaves me to-morrow, I wish him to be discharged from the Amazon. I believe it can be done by ticket, so that he can go and get his wages. Was he discharged from Medusa with his original entry? I send Doctor H.'s note, which you may give Mr. Caie. All here join in best regards with, dear Sutton, your much obliged,

NELSON AND BRONTE.

TO JOHN JULIUS ANGERSTEIN, ESQ.

[From a Copy in the Nelson Papers.]

Merton, February 17th, 1802.

My dear Sir,

Captain Johnson,[4] promoted for the Battle of Copenhagen, was in that Action Lieutenant of the Edgar, and lost his left

---

[3] Vide vol. i. p. xxv.

[4] Captain Joshua Johnson: he died a Commander, about 1831.

arm. He has therefore requested of me a letter to you, in order that he may receive the proportion of the subscription set apart for him. Captain Johnson is also a very excellent Officer, and a good man. In nine days from the loss of his arm, he did his duty again as First Lieutenant of the Ship. Such spirit in the Service is never to be overcome. Believe me, my dear Sir, your much obliged,

NELSON AND BRONTE.

TO CAPTAIN SIR THOMAS TROUBRIDGE, BART., ADMIRALTY.

[Autograph, in the possession of Colonel Davison.]

Merton, February 17th, 1802.

My dear Troubridge,

I doubt much if all the Admirals and Captains will subscribe to poor dear Miller's monument; but I have told Davison, that whatever is wanted to make up the sum, I shall pay. I thought of Lord St. Vincent and myself paying £50 each; some other Admirals may give something, and I thought about £12 each for the Captains who have served with him in the Actions of Cape St. Vincent and the Nile, would about do the business; for if we desire too much, it will not do. The spirit of liberality seems declining; but when I forget an old and dear friend, may I cease to be your affectionate,

NELSON AND BRONTE.

TO CAPTAIN SIR EDWARD BERRY.

[From a Copy in the Nelson Papers.]

Merton, February 18th, 1802.

My dear Sir Edward,

You are perfectly right that I have not the smallest interest at the Admiralty, to get poor Mr. Hooper[5] confirmed; I remember him very well. Why Mr. Davis is not confirmed, I cannot comprehend, as it was his name I gave to Admiral Pole; but I can do nothing. Lord St. Vincent once told me all the Baltic promotions should be confirmed. I think it

---

[5] Apparently Lieutenant William Read Hooper, who obtained that rank in 1802, and died about 1809.

very hard to keep you at Yarmouth, but *nothing* is to be said, for who can know anything but the Board of Admiralty? The time was, the present Lords did not think the Admiralty infallible in their judgments. Sir William and Lady Hamilton join in every good wish for your speedy release, with, my dear Sir Edward, your most sincere friend,

NELSON AND BRONTE.

I beg my best respects to Admiral Dickson.

TO THE RIGHT HONOURABLE HENRY ADDINGTON.

[Autograph, in the Sidmouth Papers.]

Merton, February 23rd, 1802.

My dear Sir,

I was happy to see by the Papers of this day, that Miss Addington was better, and I assure you I can readily conceive the anguish of a parent for the fear of losing a beloved child, and beg that no thought of anything on my account may agitate or intrude itself on your mind. Your brother [6] will tell you of what passed between him and me the other day; but I know your friendship, and want no intervening person, be his rank ever so high. When I feel that the honours of others are entrusted to me, then I am as firm as a rock; any inattentions or mortifications to myself, I can and do bear with, I trust, becoming humility. I am, in a word, truly sensible of all your friendship for me. I send you a letter I received on Saturday; it is not necessary to show it to the King, but as really a matter of curiosity, he may like to read it. If I can judge of the feelings of others by myself, there can be no Honours bestowed upon me by Foreigners, that do not reflect ten times on our Sovereign and Country. Believe me, my dear Sir, with every kind and good wish for yourself and family, your much obliged and faithful,

NELSON AND BRONTE.

[6] The Right Honourable John Hiley Addington: he died in June 1818.

TO EVAN NEPEAN, ESQ., ADMIRALTY.

[From a Copy in the Admiralty.]

Merton, February 24th, 1802.

Sir,

My Agents having acquainted me that my name is not on the Half-pay list from July to January 1800, I have to request that you will state to their Lordships, that I having, through Lord Keith, obtained their Lordships' permission to return home, by either sea or land, for the benefit of my health, which had been very much shattered by my exertions in the Mediterranean, I therefore left the Fleet, the 13th July, and arrived at Yarmouth, November 6th, when finding my health very much improved by the journey overland, I offered my services, which were accepted; and as soon as the San Josef was commissioned, I was directed to proceed to Plymouth, and hoist my Flag on board her: I have therefore to request that either whole or half-pay may be ordered me. I am, Sir, your most obedient servant,   NELSON AND BRONTE.

TO LIEUTENANT LAYMAN.[7]

[From Marshall's "Naval Biography," vol. iii. p. 324.]

Merton, Surrey, March 1st, 1802.

My dear Sir,

I have been favoured with your letter, requesting I would state the nature of the services you had been employed in from the St. George. That you were always ready to go on every service, I am sure; for the only favour you ever asked of me, was to be sent on all services of danger and difficulties: and I always understood you acquitted yourself as an able Officer and Seaman. You were in the Isis at the Battle of Copenhagen, and Captain Walker gave me a high character of the conduct of the Officers and men of the St. George. Believe me to be fully sensible of all your merits; and I have no scruple in saying, that if your interest does not get you promoted, at any future time when I may be employed, I shall be happy in receiving you, for I am your sincere friend,

NELSON AND BRONTE.

[7] Afterwards a Commander: he will be frequently mentioned.

TO CAPTAIN SUTTON, H.M. SHIP AMAZON.

[Autograph, in the possession of Captain Ives Sutton.]

My dear Sutton,   Merton, March 8th, 1802.

I do not believe that there will be a War, but if there is, nothing shall be wanting on my part to have you with me, should I be employed; but I own my interest at the Admiralty is not very great, and very few situations in which I could be employed, can offer. But be assured, if I am employed, that you shall, if in my power, assuredly be with me, for I am, dear Sutton, truly your attached friend, and much obliged,   NELSON AND BRONTE.

Sir William and Lady Hamilton desire their best regards, and give all ours to Admiral and Mrs. Lutwidge.

TO CAPTAIN SUTTON, H.M. SHIP AMAZON.

[Autograph, in the possession of Captain Ives Sutton.]

My dear Sutton,   Merton, March, 1802.

Mr. Tooley[8] is to be made a Lieutenant, whenever promotion takes place. Why he was discharged from the St. Albans is not very clear; but it appears, from his own account, not very criminal. If you see no objection, can you enter him in the Amazon as anything, acting or Mid. ? He is recommended by Mr. William Perry,[9] late a Surgeon in the Navy, and an old Ship and Messmate of Commodore Sutton. I have wrote you this day. Ever yours most truly,

NELSON AND BRONTE.

TO THE RIGHT HONOURABLE HENRY ADDINGTON.

[Autograph, in the Sidmouth Papers. On the 20th of March 1802, Lord Nelson was stated in the "London Gazette" to have obtained His Majesty's permission to accept and wear the Order of the Crescent.]

My dear Sir,   23, Piccadilly, March 25th, 1802.

I send you a letter which I received last night from the true daughter of Maria Theresa, and also one which Lady Hamilton received; they will serve to show you her Majesty's great soul, and that she sees things in their true point of view.

---

[8] Vide vol. iv. p. 524: he was drowned in November 1808, coming on shore from Spithead, being then a Lieutenant, and Agent for Transports.

[9] Vide vol. iv. p. 524.

I did not fail to tell her, in your own words, that your attention to the interests of the King of Naples had occasioned
much difficulty in the arrangement of the Definitive Treaty;
and I never fail to express what is true, that *you* are truly
sensible of the loyalty of the King of Naples in their attachment to this Country. Ever, my dear Sir, your attached,

NELSON AND BRONTE.

Lady Hamilton allows me also a letter of February 6th,
which speaks so fully that I wish you to read it with attention.
She is a Monarch deserving of all our regards and services.

TO ALEXANDER DAVISON, ESQ., ST. JAMES'S SQUARE.

[Autograph, in the possession of Colonel Davison.]

My dear Davison,　　　　　　Merton, 30th March, 1802.

I send you a letter from my Father. You will see his
statement of his money in the Funds, or rather, which he has
a right to receive interest for during his life. I was in the
House last night, and voted for the payment of the Civil List,
that you might get paid the *enormous* sum of £152 18s. 10d.!
Lord Moira's sentiments I admired most exceedingly, and
hope that the Public will be made to understand better the
Civil List, and not to fancy that *all* goes into the King's
pocket. Lord Moira said enough to suggest a plan of the
sort, very simple. So far from the King having given away
too much, I think he has been by far too parsimonious.
On Thursday I shall see you. Ever, my dear Davison, your
obliged,　　　　　　　　　　NELSON AND BRONTE.

TO CAPTAIN FYERS,[1] ROYAL ARTILLERY.

[From White's "Life of Nelson," p. 222.]

My dear Sir,　　　　　　　Merton, April 8th, 1803.

Colonel Suckling has just told me that he has the pleasure
of knowing you, and that you had given him reason to believe
that you intended favouring me with a visit before your
going into Scotland. My relation also tells me, that he has
seen a proof print of your drawing of the Danish Line, which

---

[1] Captain Peter Fyers. An account of the services of this Officer, (now a
Major-General, and a Companion of the Bath,) who was wounded in the attack on
the Flotilla at Boulogne, and served at Copenhagen, is given in White's "Life of
Nelson." p. 216.

we are all very anxious should come out. It can give offence to no party. Sir Hyde, Fremantle, Colonel Stewart, Doyle, &c., are all inquiring why it is not out. Therefore, I have to request you will be so good as to tell me who your engraver is, and also the name and abode of your friend who has the management of the Print. It will, I am sure, do well. I am glad to hear you suffer no inconvenience from the wound in your thigh. You would regret sincerely the loss of poor Parker. Langford, I am fearful, will lose his leg. He is still confined by bones continually coming away. With every good wish, believe me, my dear Sir, your much obliged,

NELSON AND BRONTE.

TO CAPTAIN SUTTON, H.M. SHIP AMAZON.

[Autograph, in the possession of Captain Ives Sutton.]

My dear Sutton,   Merton, April 10th, 1802.

I have this moment received an order to strike my Flag, *and come on shore.* I hope soon you will be at liberty, and nobody will be happier to see you than your friends at Merton. I suppose I must be discharged this day with my retinue. I am very anxious to keep Charles[2] afloat, and I wish you would turn your eyes round to any Ship that is to be kept in commission—if going abroad the better, and a good man who will do justice by the lad. But few, very few, will take that care of him which you have been good enough to do, and for which we are most truly thankful; and believe me ever your much obliged,   NELSON AND BRONTE.

TO LIEUTENANT-COLONEL SUCKLING.

[From " The Athenæum."]

My dear Suckling,   April 15th, 1802.

Many thanks for your kind present of oysters. I yesterday saw Colonel Yorke,[3] and he has promised me that he will take the first opportunity of removing you into a *permanent* and better situation. I left a memorandum with him, that Norwich would be most desirable after Chatham; but he really seemed disposed to do everything which we can desire. Ever yours faithfully,   NELSON AND BRONTE.

[2] Charles Connor.
[3] The Right Honourable Charles Yorke, then Secretary at War, afterwards First Lord of the Admiralty.

TO JOHN M'ARTHUR, ESQ.

[Original, in the possession of Mrs. Conway.]

Merton, April 23rd, 1802.

My dear Sir,

I am very sorry that you could not meet us at Cockburn's[4] next Tuesday, as I was in hopes that everything relative to our Vado prize-money could have been settled. The amount of the Corn-ship, and the other, a Corn-vessel, was, when I was in England, latter end of '97, or beginning of '98, brought into the funds in our names. Has Marsh and Creed had the receiving the dividends, or have you received? Be so good as to send me a line here, that I may get it on Monday, or I shall not be able to open my mouth to much purpose. You are right, the Corn-vessel was taken by Agamemnon alone; but Cockburn, and I fancy some others, share for her—the other was taken by Southampton: her nett amount, £923 sterling, as my head tells me, for I am at this moment writing from memory. The Corn-ship was £100 nett. Write all you know on these subjects. I beg my best regards to Mr. Hood, and believe me, my dear Sir, your most obedient servant,

NELSON AND BRONTE.

TO JOHN M'ARTHUR, ESQ.

[Original, in the possession of Mrs. Conway.]

Merton, April 28th, 1802.

My dear Sir,

I should have answered your letter sooner, but for the event of the death of my dear Father.[5] I had thought that the money was done something with in our joint names. I had always told Cockburn and others concerned so; but your accounts, of course, will put that matter right. I saw Cockburn yesterday; but we could do nothing, as you had not sent me the account how much the amount of the St. Antonio de Padua amounted to, and how much the other. Pray let me have it as soon as possible with the particulars, that a distribution

---

[4] Captain, now the Right Hon. Sir George Cockburn, G.C.B., so often mentioned.

[5] The Reverend Edmund Nelson died at Bath on the 26th of April 1802, in his seventy-ninth year.

may take place. I beg my best respects to Mr. Hood; and
believe me, dear Sir, most faithfully yours,

NELSON AND BRONTE.

I have been, and am very unwell, and these Prize concerns
torment me; for they will think I have been using the money.
Write me what you know.

TO SIR BROOKE BOOTHBY, BART.

[From a Copy in the Nelson Papers.]

Merton, Surrey, May 1st, 1802.

My dear Sir,

I feel very much flattered by your kind remembrance of our
truly pleasant party at Hamburgh, and I can assure you that
it would give Sir William, Lady Hamilton, and myself, much
pleasure, could we meet here, where I have made a very
small purchase, and live retired, although we live so near
London; for I hate the noise, bustle, and falsity of what is
called the great world.

We are now at peace with all the world, except Lord
Grenville, Windham, and that party: they see that destruction to the Country from it which I cannot. I am the friend
of Peace without fearing War; for my politics are to let France
know that we will give no insult to her Government, nor will
we receive the smallest. If France takes unfair means to
prevent our trading with other Powers under her influence,
this I consider the greatest act of hostility she can show us;
but if Buonaparte understands our sentiments, he will not
wish to plunge France in a new war with us. Every man in
France, as well as in this Country, is wanted for commerce;
and powerful as he may be, France would pull him down for
destroying *her* commerce, and the war in this Country would
be most popular against the man who would destroy *our* commerce. I think our Peace is strong if we act, as we ought,
with firmness, and allow France to put no false constructions
on the words, or on omissions in the Treaty. But for what
am I getting into politics? I am truly sorry for Dumourier;
but, alas! it is not in my power to assist him. If his Country
receives him, he will be the worst enemy we ever found, for
he must hate us for our treatment of him. No man can fear

to be suspected of falseness if he is really well-intentioned, which, from my heart, I believe Dumourier was.

Lady Hamilton desires me to say every kind thing for her. She is one that never forgets an old friend, and to be grateful, which is more, than can be said of an old acquaintance of yours. With every good wish, believe me, my dear Sir Brooke, your most obliged friend,　　　　NELSON AND BRONTE.

TO HERCULES ROSS, ESQ.

[Autograph, in the possession of Horatio Ross, Esq.]

My dear Friend,　　　　　　　Merton, May 3rd, 1802.

I should certainly have seen you long before this time, but for my own state of health, and the irreparable loss I have sustained in a beloved parent. I have seen Davison for a moment, and he will be happy to be known to you. He tells me Sir Alured Clarke has settled all the money concerns about your nephew;[6] but he will explain this matter to you when you meet. If your other avocations in the great Town will allow you time to drive to Merton, we shall be truly happy to see you. Lady Hamilton desires her compliments, and believe me, ever yours most truly,

NELSON AND BRONTE.

TO HERCULES ROSS, ESQ.

[Autograph, in the possession of Horatio Ross, Esq.]

My dear Friend,　　　　　　　Merton, May 6th, 1802.

We shall be very glad to see you and Dr. Moseley[7] on Monday. I am better, but still much indisposed, but ever your obliged friend,　　　　NELSON AND BRONTE.

TO JOHN M'ARTHUR, ESQ.

[Original, in the possession of Mrs. Conway.]

My dear Sir,　　　　　　　Merton, May 7th, 1802.

I am favoured with your letter and account. The Corn-ship, Madonna del Rosario, was taken by Agamemnon *alone*. I share with some other Captains, but *no Ship*. The other,

---

[6] Vide vol. iv. p. 348. General, afterwards Field-Marshal, Sir Alured Clarke, K.B. commanded the Troops which captured the Cape of Good Hope.

[7] Vide vol. i. p. 7.

Captain Cockburn can tell you who shares for her; Agamemnon, Meleager, and, I believe, Southampton, and there may be others. Charges can be but little, as the money was paid nett, everything deducted. When I am a little better, I will meet you at Cockburn's. Suppose I say Wednesday next, at 10 o'clock in the morning, if that day will suit Cockburn. You had better write to Wolseley[8] about the other. I believe I have some concern in it, but I am not certain. I am, dear Sir, yours most faithfully,

NELSON AND BRONTE.

TO SIR JOHN SINCLAIR, BART.

[From the " Sinclair Correspondence," vol. i. p. 189.]

Sir,   Merton, May 13th, 1802.

My state of health absolutely prevents my having the pleasure of dining with the Society for encouraging the Fisheries, for no purpose can be more truly patriotic, and deserving the attention of every friend of his Country. I had purposed yesterday doing myself the honour of calling upon you—but I was, to my sorrow, prevented—as I wish much to be personally known to a gentleman of your great and useful knowledge, and who so candidly carries it into effect for the benefit of his Country. I have the honour to be, Sir, with the highest respect, your most obliged and obedient servant,

NELSON AND BRONTE.

TO CAPTAIN SUTTON, H.M. SHIP AMAZON.

[Autograph, in the possession of Captain Ives Sutton.]

My dear Sutton,   Merton, May 29th, 1802.

As I know your wish to get clear of the Amazon as soon as you can, I have asked Captain Shepard, of the Phœbe, to take Charles Connor with him up the Mediterranean, not *the other*.[9] We shall never forget your kindness, and I shall repay your pecuniary goodness with many thanks. Hoping very soon to see you at Merton, I am ever, my dear Sutton, your obliged friend,   NELSON AND BRONTE.

---

[8] Captain, afterwards Admiral William Wolseley, *Vide* vol. i. p. 350, *et passim.*
[9] Mr. Banti.

TO CAPTAIN SIR EDWARD BERRY.

[From a Copy in the Nelson Papers.]

Merton, June 8th, 1802.

My dear Sir Edward,

I sent your Case[1] to a friend of mine, Doctor Fisher, of the Commons, and send you his Opinion; therefore I suppose you will direct your Agent to set about the needful. My evidence can be taken, as it is the most proper, with all the circumstances from first to last. All here join in good wishes for your health, and believe me ever, yours most faithfully,

NELSON AND BRONTE.

TO JOHN M'ARTHUR, ESQ.

[Autograph, in the possession of Mrs. Conway.]

Merton, June 11th, 1802.

My dear Sir,

Captain Middleton and Cockburn share with me for the Corn-ship. I know nothing of the two Ships sharing, (unless in sight.) The Tartan sold by Pollard, I suppose was shared. Cockburn knows more of these things than I can recollect at this moment. Ever yours faithfully,

NELSON AND BRONTE.

TO MRS. BOLTON.

[Autograph in the possession of James Young, Esq., of Wells.]

Merton, June 11th, 1802.

My dear Sister,

Here is £100, which I shall pay you on the 11th June, for three years, towards the education of your children; by that time, other things may turn up, and this is a trifle in case you may [want] any little thing going through London. All I desire is, that you would not say or write me a syllable on the subject, for I am sorry I cannot do more, being truly your most affectionate brother,

NELSON AND BRONTE.

[1] Relating to Prize money.

TO . . . . . .

[Autograph in the possession of J. Wilde, Esq.]

June 16th, 1802.

With Lord Nelson's compliments, and shall always be happy in rendering any assistance in his power, to so worthy a family.

TO ADMIRAL THE EARL OF ST. VINCENT, K.B.

[Autograph in the possession of Vice-Admiral Sir William Parker, Bart., G.C.B.]

Merton, June 16th, 1802.

My dear Lord,

My young friend Collier[2] would go to the Devil for promotion (or he would not be acknowledged by me): therefore, if you think there is a better chance in the West Indies, and will have the goodness to give him a letter to Admiral Totty, he will jump into a Packet, and carry it out to Totty, and take the chance of losing a month's time. But if you think it better to go to that healthy station, Halifax, he will join Leander this night. Collier is a good young man, and will do credit to your kindness towards him. I am ever, my dear Lord, yours most faithfully,

NELSON AND BRONTE.

TO CAPTAIN SUTTON, H.M. SHIP AMAZON.

[Autograph in the possession of Captain Ives Sutton.]

Merton, June 18th, 1802.

My dear Sutton,

I am so totally ignorant of what is going on at the Admiralty, that I cannot say why Amazon is kept in the Downs, or why, if you choose it, you should not be superseded; but I suppose no Captain would wish to take your Ship merely to pay her off. Lady Hamilton and myself cannot thank you enough about C. Connor, and Captain Shepard will take him when his Ship is nearly ready for sea, or the Amazon re-

---

[2] The present Commodore Sir Francis Augustus Collier, C.B., K.C.H.: he was made a Lieutenant in April 1803.

moved from her present station. I shall accept your kind offer of fitting Charles out. Mr. Banti must return home when you are removed. His family are going to Italy. I need not say how happy we shall be to receive you at Merton, for I am ever your much obliged,

NELSON AND BRONTE.

Sir William and Lady Hamilton's compliments.

TO LADY COLLIER.

[Autograph, in the possession of Commodore Sir Francis Augustus Collier, K.C.H.]

Merton, June 18th, 1802.

Dear Madam,

I send you a letter to Admiral Totty. I shall write to Duckworth on Monday. I am more sure of Totty, if the Admiralty will give him an opportunity. I assure you I regard your son for his own worth, and I am certain he will ever do credit to himself, which is the most grateful return to his sincere friend,

NELSON AND BRONTE.

TO THE RIGHT HONOURABLE THE LORD MAYOR.

[From a Copy in the Nelson Papers.]

Merton, June 21st, 1802.

My Lord,

A few days past, I saw in the Newspapers that a Motion had been made in a Court of Common Council, to thank me for my conduct in taking the command of a Force destined to prevent any designs our Enemies might have of approaching the City of London, but which Motion stands over for some future Court. I have therefore to entreat that your Lordship will use your influence that no such Motion may be brought forward.

There is not, my Lord, one individual in the world who appreciates the honour of having their conduct approved by the City of London, higher than myself. I was desired to take the Command in question in a very indifferent state of health, as I was flattered with the opinion that it would keep

quiet the minds of all in London, and the Coast between
Beechy-Head and Orfordness. This would have been a sufficient
reason for me to have laid down my life, much less to suffer
a little from ill-health ; and, my Lord, His Majesty's Government gave me such a powerful Force, that the gallant Officers
and Men I had the honour to command, almost regretted that
the Enemy did not make the attempt of Invasion. Therefore,
you see, my Lord, I have no merit—I only did my duty with
alacrity, which I shall always be ready to do when directed.

But, my Lord, if any other reason was wanting to prevent
the City of London from thanking me for only showing an
alacrity in stepping forth in time of danger, it is this—not
four months before I was appointed to this Command, I had
the happiness of witnessing, under all its circumstances, the
most hard-fought Battle, and the most complete Victory (as far
as my reading goes) that ever was fought and obtained by the
Navy of this Country. This Battle, my Lord, had not the
honour of being approved in the way which the City of
London has usually marked their approbation : therefore, I
entreat that you will use your influence that no Vote of approbation may ever be given to me for any services since the 2nd
of April, 1801 ; for I should feel much mortified when I re-
flected on the noble support I that day received, at any
honour which could separate me from them, for I am bold
to say, that they deserve every honour and favour which a
grateful Country can bestow.

I entreat your Lordship's indulgence for thus expressing
my feelings, and again request that the intended Motion of
Thanks may be withdrawn. I trust your Lordship will give
[me] full credit for the high estimation in which I hold the
City of London, and with what respect I am your Lordship's
most obedient humble servant,

NELSON AND BRONTE.

TO THE REV. MR. COMYN.[4]

[Autograph in the possession of Page Nicol Scott, Esq.]

My dear Sir,　　　　　　　Merton, June 24th, 1802.

I send you the Chancellor's letter, and most sincerely congratulate you on your preferment, which to a person who has conducted himself so prudently in pecuniary affairs will make you truly comfortable. Mr. Thom[5] died on Monday. Ever yours faithfully,

NELSON AND BRONTE.

If you set off on Monday morning, I suppose it will do; but of that you must be the judge when the patent may be out, for I would not lose a moment in getting possession. Upon recollection of what you told me of the Post-Office, I have thought it best to send you an express, which I shall pay for, and you have only to give the man a receipt, and, if you like it, half-a-crown.

TO LADY COLLIER.

[Autograph, in the possession of Commodore Sir Francis Augustus Collier, K.C.H.]

Merton, July 3rd, 1802.

Dear Madam,

I grieve for the death of Admiral Totty[6] in every respect, but under all circumstances I think you will do right to ask Lord St. Vincent to send out Francis to Totty's successor, and

---

[4] Mr. Comyn was Lord Nelson's Chaplain in the Vanguard, at the Nile, and was one of his Domestic Chaplains. The preferment alluded to was the Rectory of Bridgeham, in Norfolk, and it appears to have been obtained in fulfilment of a promise made to him three years before, which Mr. Comyn thus mentioned in a letter to his wife, dated—"Foudroyant, Naples Bay, 4th August, 1799. I have now to communicate a circumstance that occurred last night at supper. Lord Nelson drank to me, with his wishes for a good Living. Lady Hamilton promised to write a letter to the Lord Chancellor, Lord Loughborough, signed by Lord Nelson and Sir William Hamilton, stating my situation as his Lordship's Chaplain in the Battle of the Nile. This interest, no doubt will have the desired effect, as the Lord Chancellor is well known to Sir William and the party."—*Aytograph*, in the possession of Robert Cole, Esq.

[5] Apparently "the Reverend and learned James Thom, Rector of Southacre in Norfolk," who died on the 20th June.

[6] He died in the command of the Leeward Islands Station, on the 2nd of June,

propose his going with General Grinfield, whose protection
will be useful in promoting Francis's interest with any Admiral on that Station.   When I know who the Admiral is, I
will certainly write to him.   I am truly sorry for the accident
which has happened to your other son, but I hope a cold
climate will restore him.   I have the honour to be with every
good wish, your Ladyship's most obedient servant,

NELSON AND BRONTE.

TO THE RIGHT HONOURABLE THE EARL OF CLANRICARDE.[7]

[Autograph in the possession of Miss Shee.]

Merton, July 3rd, 1802.

My dear Lord,

I am afraid that I got so decisive an answer about Mr.
Henry that but very little hopes are to be expected from the
present Admiralty; I trust you will believe that if the business
rested with me, I would contrive some mode of bringing Mr.
H. again into the service.   Not having seen the Minutes of
the Court Martial, I can form no judgment of what can be urged
in Mr. H.'s memorial for restoration to his rank, as I was not in
the Baltic when he was tried.   Two ways are open : one a Memorial to the King, stating all the favourable circumstances of
his case—which Memorial is referred to the Admiralty :   the
other is, as you propose, to get some Admiral to make him
from the station of Midshipman; but then it lays with the
Admiralty to confirm him, and the present Board have given
their opinion; and as to claims, Lord St. Vincent told me that
he conceives that no Officer has *any* claim for *any* services.
Lord Henry Paulet is just paying off his Ship, and if he will
join me in any further application, I shall readily embrace
every occasion of doing what you would wish me, for I am,
my dear Lord, with the greatest truth, your much obliged and
sincere friend,

NELSON AND BRONTE.

I beg my kindest regards to Sir Erasmus Gower,[8] when you
see him.

[7] Vide vol. ii. p. 238.

[8] A Rear-Admiral of the Red. Memoirs of this veteran Officer, who became a full
Admiral, are given in the Naval Chronicle, voi. iv. p. 257, and vol. xxx. p. 265.

TO ALEXANDER DAVISON, ESQ.

[Autograph, in the possession of Colonel Davison. The date of the year does not occur to this Letter, and it may possibly have been written in 1801; but as it appears to have accompanied some Memoranda on the subject, which were certainly written in 1802, it is assigned to that year. Mr. Davison possessed considerable influence in the City of London, and Lord Nelson was accustomed to communicate to him his expectations and wishes on any subject connected with the Corporation, or the City Companies. It must be flattering to the City of London to perceive the very high value which Nelson attached to its approbation.]

Boxhill, July 9th, 7 P.M. [1802.]

(A very pretty place, and we are all very happy.)

My dear Davison,

If the Victory of the 2nd *was real,* the Admirals, Officers, and Men, who fought and obtained the Victory, are from custom entitled to the Thanks of the City of London. Custom has never gone back to the first *causers* of Victories, but simply to the *Victors.* Lord St. Vincent had no thanks given him for the Victory of the Nile, and Sir Hyde Parker, except being nearer the scene of action, had no more to do with that of Copenhagen than Lord St. Vincent. I cannot object to any thanks or rewards being bestowed on any man; but I have a fair claim, from custom to be alone considered through the *whole* of the Battle, as the Commander of the Ships fighting. The Thanks of Parliament went only to Sir Hyde's conduct in *planning,* not for the *fighting;*[9] therefore, I look forward with confidence to a Sword from the City of London; and their Thanks, and the Freedom in a Gold Box, to Admiral Graves. The City of London has never yet failed noticing Sea Victories, and I trust, as the first commercial City in the world, never will. I remember, a few years back, on my noticing to a *Lord Mayor,* that if the City continued its gene-

---

[9] " Resolved, *nem. diss.,* That the Thanks of this House be given to Admiral Sir Hyde Parker, for the able and judicious disposition made by him of the Force under his command, by which the Danish Ships of War forming the Line of Defence of the Harbour of Copenhagen were taken or destroyed, on the 2nd of April, 1801. Resolved, *nem. diss.,* That the Thanks of this House be given to Vice-Admiral Lord Nelson, K.B.; Rear-Admiral Graves, and Colonel Stewart, commanding his Majesty's 40th Regiment of Foot, and a Corps of Riflemen; and to the several Captains and Officers of the Fleet under the command of Admiral Sir Hyde Parker, for their bravery and gallant conduct on the said most glorious occasion; and that Admiral Sir Hyde Parker do signify the same to them," &c.—*Lords' Journals,* vol. xliii. p. 101; *Commons' Journal,* vol. lvi. p. 285.

rosity, we should ruin them by their gifts, his Lordship put his hand on my shoulder and said—*aye, the Lord Mayor of London said*—' Do you find Victories, and we will find rewards.' I have since that time found *two complete Victories.* I have kept my word, and shall I have the power of saying that the City of London, which exists by Victories at Sea, has not kept its promise—a promise made by a Lord Mayor in his robes, and almost in the Royal presence? I have a fair and honourable claim: my part of the honourable contract has been now doubly fulfilled. We shall dine in Piccadilly, Saturday, five o'clock, and Lady Hamilton and Sir William beg that you will come to us; and ever believe me, my dear Davison, your obliged and affectionate, NELSON AND BRONTE.

MEMORANDUM.

[Autograph, in the possession of Colonel Davison.]

[Apparently written about July, 1802.]

From the very particular situation in which the Honourable Lieutenant-Colonel Stewart, with the Troops under his command, were placed on board the Fleet under the command of Sir Hyde Parker, for they certainly did not belong to any of the Ships, therefore they were borne as supernumeraries, and they cannot be considered merely as passengers, therefore they must, in fairness, be considered as connected with the services of the Fleet, and as the situation is entirely new, and being truly sensible that the Army shared with us the toils and dangers of the Expedition, we do, therefore, (as the proclamation for the distribution of Prize-money, nor any joint Expedition is in the smallest degree similar to the present,) as a mark of our high sense of the services of the Honourable Colonel Stewart and the Army, agree to give up a proportion of the Admirals' one-eighth of Prize-money, so as to make Colonel Stewart's share of Prize-money equal to that of a Junior Flag-Officer; and we hereby authorize our Agent, Alexander Davison, Esq., to take from the one-eighth due to the class of Admirals such a sum as will make Colonel Stewart's share equal to a Junior Flag-Officer; and we are of opinion that the Field Officers of the 49th Regiment ought to share with the Captains of the Navy, and the other classes according to their rank with the Navy.

TO CAPTAIN SUTTON, H.M. SHIP AMAZON.

[Autograph, in the possession of Captain Ives Sutton.]

Merton, July 12th, 1802.

My dear Sutton,

Many thanks for your kindness to Connor, and I will write to Captain Shepard this day; and when you return, or will have the goodness to send me Connor's and Banti's account, I will pay them with many thanks. I think you will like the trip to the Baltic—at all events, it is better than being kept as you have been. We shall always be happy to receive you at Merton. Foley was with us this morning; he is in perfect health. I have only to wish you a pleasant voyage, and to beg you to be assured that I am ever, your much obliged friend,

NELSON AND BRONTE.

TO THE REVEREND MR. YONGE,[8] TORRINGTON, DEVON.

[Autograph, in the possession of the Rev. W. G. Cokesley, of Eton College. In the months of July and August, 1802, Lord Nelson, accompanied by Sir William and Lady Hamilton, made a tour into Wales. Passing through Oxford, he was created an honorary Doctor of Laws; and was admitted to the Freedoms of the Corporations of Monmouth, Hereford, and Worcester, on visiting those Cities.

Lord Nelson was received at Swansea with every mark of distinction, and on the 17th of August, a Paper was printed and circulated throughout the Town, apparently taken from a Letter which he had written to the Portreeve:—

"To the Corporation and Inhabitants of Swansea, and of the Neighbourhood, at the particular instance and request of LORD NELSON. I have the honour to communicate to you his Lordship's most grateful and sincere thanks for his flattering reception amongst you, and to assure you that the favours you have conferred upon him will never be effaced from his memory—that the remembrance of them will descend with him to his grave. That he feels the distinguished marks of regard and applause not so much on his own account as for what the example of their being so bestowed on him might afford to the rising generation. 'That their endeavours to serve their Country and probably to succeed in it, as he had been flattered, had fallen to his lot, would be as amply encouraged and rewarded, and their names recorded with posterity amongst those who had deserved well of it.' Thomas Morgan, Portreeve, August 17th, 1801."

At Monmouth, on the 19th of August, he made a speech, the concluding paragraph of which should be engraved on the heart of every young Officer in both Services:—

"I beg leave to return you my most respectful thanks, for the honour done me in drinking my health, and also for the acknowledgment of the important Public

---

[8] Apparently the Father of Mrs. Nelson, afterwards Countess Nelson.

services you are pleased to say I have rendered my Country. It was my good fortune
to have under my command some of the most experienced Officers in the English
Navy, whose professional skill was seconded by the undaunted courage of British
Sailors; and whatever merit might attach itself to me, I must declare, that I had only
to show them the Enemy, and Victory crowned the standard. The British Navy has
received a large portion of public applause; but, however well deserved, it should be
told, that the same valour and sense of duty would have marked the conduct of the
British Army, had it been placed in such situations as would have afforded it an
equal opportunity of displaying its National courage; but it has unluckily happened that the same good fortune, in this instance, did not occur, or we should
have had equal reason for praising its heroism and Public services. When the
English Army was sent to Egypt, it was the opinion of many intelligent characters that
it would be destroyed. For my own part, I never thought so; for wherever British
Soldiers have been opposed to those of France, they have uniformly conquered
them. In my own person I have received an overflowing measure of the Nation's
gratitude—far more than I either merited or expected; because the same success
would have crowned the efforts of any other British Admiral, who had under his
command such distinguished Officers, and such gallant Crews. And here let me
impress it on the mind of every Officer in the Service, that to whatever quarter of
the Globe he may be destined, whether to the East or West Indies, to Africa, or
America, the eyes of his Country are upon him; and so long as Public men, in
Public stations, exert themselves in those situations, to fulfil the duty demanded
from them by the Public, they will always find the British Nation ready to heap
upon them the utmost extent of its gratitude and its applause."—*Naval Chronicle*,
vol. xx. p. 110.]

Llandovery, July 28th, 1802.

Dear Sir,

I am much obliged by your letter telling me of the death
of Dr. Harward,[1] which I received ere our departure from
Merton, and I sent to Mr. Addington. What the result of
the application may be I know not; but be it as it may we all
feel equally obliged to you. We are so far on our journey to
Milford, and shall return in August. We all desire our best
compliments to Mrs. Yonge, and beg you to believe me, your
much obliged,

NELSON AND BRONTE.

MEMORANDA RESPECTING THE FOREST OF DEAN.

[Autograph, in the Sidmouth Papers. The following Observations respecting the
Forest of Dean having occurred to Lord Nelson during his Tour, he communicated
them to the Prime Minister:]

[About August, 1802.]

The Forest of Dean contains about 23,000 acres of the
finest land in the Kingdom, which, I am informed, if in a high

---

[1] Doctor Charles Harward, Dean of Exeter, who died on the 15th of July, 1802. It
would seem that Lord Nelson applied to Mr. Addington to appoint his brother, Doctor
Nelson, to the vacant Deanery, but, if he did so, the request was not complied with.

state of cultivation of oak, would produce about 9200 loads of
timber, fit for building Ships of the Line, every year—that
is, the Forest would grow in full vigour 920,000 oak trees.
The state of the Forest at this moment is deplorable; for,
if my information is true, there is not 3500 load of timber in
the whole Forest fit for building, and none coming forward.
It is useless, I admit, to state the causes of such a want of
timber where so much could be produced, except that, by
knowing the faults, we may be better enabled to amend ourselves.

First, the generality of trees, for these last fifty years, have
been allowed to stand too long. They are passed by instead
of removed, and thus occupy a space which ought to have
been re-planted with young trees.

Secondly, that where good timber is felled, nothing is
planted, and nothing can grow *self* sown; for the deer (of
which now only a few remain) bark all the young trees. Vast
droves of hogs are allowed to go into the woods in the autumn;
and if any fortunate acorn escapes their search, and takes root,
then *flocks* of sheep are allowed to go into the Forest, and they
bite off the tender shoot. These are sufficient reasons why
timber does not grow in the Forest of Dean.

Of the waste of timber, in former times, I can say nothing;
but of late years, it has been, I am told, shameful. Trees cut
down in swampy places, as the carriage is done by contract,
are left to rot, and are cut up by people in the neighbourhood.
Another abuse *is the* Contractors, as they can carry more
measurement, are allowed to cut the trees to their advantage
of carriage, by which means the invaluable crooked timber is
lost for the service of the Navy. There are also—another
cause of the failure of timber—a set of people called Forest
Free Miners, who consider themselves as having a right to dig
for coal in any part they please. These people, in many
places, inclose pieces of ground, which is daily increasing by
the *inattention,* to call it by no worse name, of the *Surveyors,*
Verderers, &c., who have the charge of the Forest.

Of late years, some *apparently* vigorous measures were taken
for preserving and encouraging the growth of timber in the
King's Forests, and part of the Forest of Dean has been enclosed; but it is so very ill attended to, that it is little, if
anything better than the other part.

There is another abuse which I omitted to mention. *Trees* which die of themselves are considered as of no value. A gentleman told me, that in shooting *on foot*, for on horseback it cannot be seen, hid by the fern, which grows a great height, the trees of fifty years growth, fit for buildings, fencing, &c., are cut just above ground entirely through the *bark:* in two years the tree *dies*, and it becomes either a *perquisite*, or is allowed to be taken away by favoured people. These shameful abuses are probably [not] known to those high in power; but I have gathered the information of them from people of all descriptions, and perfectly disinterested in telling me, or knowing that I had any view in a transient inquiry. But, knowing the abuses, it is for the serious consideration of every lover of his Country, how they can either be done away, or, at least, lessened—perhaps, a very difficult or impossible task.

If the Forest of Dean is to be preserved as a useful Forest for the Country, strong measures must be pursued. First, the *Guardian* of this support of our Navy, must be an intelligent honest man, who will give up his time to his employment: therefore, he must live in the Forest, have a house, a small farm, and an adequate salary. I omitted to mention that the expense of a Surveyor of Woods, as far as relates to this Forest, to be done away: *Verderer*, as at present, also. The Guardian to have proper *Verderers* under him who understand the planting, thinning, and management of timber trees. These places should be so comfortable, that the fear of being turned out should be a great object of terror, and, of course, an inducement for them to exert themselves in their different stations. The first thing necessary in the Forest of Dean is to plant some acres of acorns; and I saw plenty of *clear fields* with *cattle* grazing in my voyage *down* the *Wye*. In two years, these will be fit for transplanting.

N.B.—I am aware that objections have been made to the transplanting of oak. I am not knowing enough in this matter to say how far this is true, when so young as two to five, or six years. The next thing is to be careful to thin the trees; for more timber is lost by being too fearful of cutting down, than by badly thinning. A tree from ten years of age ought, by a scale given to me by a very able man, to be as follows, viz.:—

Number of trees that such land as the Forest of Dean may contain at different periods from their being first set:—

Trees distant from each other. Feet.	Years after been set. Number.	Number of Trees in an acre.	Number of Trees to be thinned.
6	10	1200	—
10	20	430	770
15	40	190	240
20	60	100	90
25	80	60	40
30	100	45	15

In forty years, these Forests will produce a great value of timber fit for many uses in the Navy—indeed all, except for Ships of the Line.

If, on a due consideration, it is found not to be practicable for Government to arrange a plan for growing their own timber, then I would recommend at once selling the Forests, and encourage the growth of oak timber. I calculate, that taking away the 3500 load of timber at present fit for cutting, (or be it more or less,) that the Forest of Dean will sell for £460,000. I am sensible that what I have thrown together upon paper is so loose, that no plan can be drawn from it ; but if these facts, which I have learnt from my late tour, may be in the least degree instrumental in benefiting our Country, I shall be truly happy.

A few Thoughts on encouraging the Growth of Oak Timber, drawn from conversations with many gentlemen in my late tour :

First, The reason why timber has of late years been so much reduced has been uniformly told me, that, from the pressure of the times, gentlemen who had £1000 to £5 worth of timber on their estates, although only half-grown, (say fifty years of age,) were obliged to sell it to raise temporary sums, (say to pay off legacies.) The owner cannot, however sorry he may feel to see the beauty of his place destroyed, and what would be treble the value to his children annihilated, help himself. It has struck me forcibly, that if Government could form a plan to purchase of such gentlemen the growing oak, that it would be a National benefit, and a great and pleasing accommodation to such growers of oak as wish to sell.

My knowledge of this subject, drawn from the conversation of gentlemen in the oak countries, I think, would almost obviate all difficulties. Of myself, I own my incompetence to draw up a plan fit for public inspection; but all my gathered knowledge shall be most cheerfully at the service of some able man.

TO THE REVEREND DIXON HOSTE.

[Autograph, in the possession of Captain Sir William Hoste. On the 15th of July 1802, the " London Gazette," announced the King's permission to Lord Nelson " to accept and wear the Ensigns of Knight Grand Commander of the Equestrian Secular and Capitular Order of St. Joachim, into which he had been elected by a General Chapter of the Order at Westenbourg." Vide vol. iv. p. 510.]

Milford, August 3rd, 1802.

My dear Sir,

I had a letter from William, dated Malta, June 24th. He was perfectly well, but very anxious to return to England, and I hope the Greyhound's turn will soon arrive, when you will receive one of the best young Men and Sea-officers in Europe. I am, dear Sir, your most obedient servant,

NELSON AND BRONTE.

TO THE RIGHT HONOURABLE SIR JOHN EAMER.

[From a Copy in the Nelson Papers.]

Private.   Merton, 8th September, 1802.

My dear Sir John,

I can assure you that I should dine with you in your private capacity with the greatest pleasure; but it is impossible, as I am sure you are sensible of, that Lord Nelson can receive any mark of distinction from the Chief Magistrate of the City of London, the conduct of the brave Captains, Officers, and Men, who so bravely fought, died, and conquered in the Battle of Copenhagen not having had the honour of the approbation of the City of London, in their Corporate capacity. Whatever my demerits might have been on that glorious day, I am bold to say, that British valour never shone more conspicuously, or more successfully, than on the 2nd of April, 1801. Whenever, my dear Sir John, you cease to be Chief Magistrate of the City of London, name your day, and I will dine with you with satisfaction; but never till the City of London think justly of the merits of my brave Companions of the 2nd of April, can I, their Commander, receive any attention from the City of London. Believe me, my dear Sir John, your much obliged,

NELSON AND BRONTE.

TO ALEXANDER DAVISON, ESQ., SWANLAND HOUSE, NORTHUMBERLAND.

[Autograph, in the possession of Colonel Davison.]

Merton, September 11th, 1802.

My dear Davison,

I called at your house, and was glad to find that you left London free from the gout; and I hope that the fine fresh air of Swanland has kept you in perfect good health; but I own myself selfish enough to wish you in St. James' Square, for at your breakfast I heard all that was going on in the great world, and it was a central place where any one could meet me. We have had rather a longer tour than was at first intended; for Merton was not fit to receive us, Dods being so very ill, even at death's door, the work went on so very slowly. It is not even yet finished. Our tour has been very fine and interesting, and the way in which I have been every where received most flattering to my feelings; and although some of the higher powers may wish to keep me down, yet the reward of the general approbation and gratitude for my services is an ample reward for all I have done; but it makes a *comparison* fly up to my mind, not much to the credit of some in the higher Offices of the State. Axe's estate is not yet paid for, the papers not being yet forthcoming. Pray, in whose hands is the money received from Tucker placed, and have I the power of drawing for it, or must you give an order? I saw Nepean; the Earl, &c., are on a visitation to the Dock-yards. As to political news, I have seen nobody who could tell me anything except Mr. Addington for a moment, and the only thing he told me was, that the receipts at the Custom

House and Excise Office were never so great as at present.
Pray God they may continue! The fall of the Funds is considered as a trick to ruin Lord Carrington's house,[9] and that
they will fall to 65, and rise immediately to 75 after the loan
is paid in, which will be in November, and that Peace or War
has nothing to do with them. Lady Hamilton desires to join
me in every kind and good wish for yourself and family
with, my dear Davison, your truly faithful and affectionate
friend,

NELSON AND BRONTE.

Sir William is gone to Windsor.

TO ALEXANDER DAVISON, ESQ.

[Autograph, in the possession of Colonel Davison.]

Merton, September 20th, 1802.

My dear Davison,
I feel very much obliged by your kind and truly affectionate
letter. You are right about the Country; for London seems
absolutely deserted, and so hot and stinking that it is truly
detestable. I will not say what I feel about your bankers, for
to a generous mind it would feel distressing. It is a rare
instance of friendship, and such as I can never forget. We are
fixed here till next year, and it is not impossible but we may
make a Northern visit, and we shall have much pleasure in
visiting Swanland House.
We have had several of our friends drop off. Poor Dods is
gone, and our house not finished. I have not heard who is to
carry on his business. You who have built so fine a house to
make his fortune in. What a change! *How short sighted we are!*
I have also lost Mr. Græfer, my governor of Bronté: he died
August 7th. It embarrasses me a little, but I endeavour to
make the best of things, and it may possibly turn out to my
pecuniary advantage. I have his full account of my estate;
rather more than £3000 a year nett, and increasing every year
in value. General Acton has taken possession of everything

---

[9] The well-known Banking-house of Smith, Payne, and Smith.

for me, and is behaving very friendly.   Sir William and Lady
Hamilton desire their kind compliments; and believe me, my
dear Davison, your obliged and affectionate friend,

NELSON AND BRONTE.[1]

TO WILLIAM MOBBS, ESQ.

[From a Copy.]

Merton, September 28th, 1802.

Sir,

The having my conduct approved by every description of
my Countrymen, cannot but be highly flattering, and I beg
leave to return my sincere thanks for the honour they have
done me in electing me an Honorary Member of their Society;
and I can only hope that the name of the Club, *Odd*, from
having *honour for their pilot*, and *truth for their rudder*, will
not soon be lost, by every man in the Kingdom adhering to
those principles.   With every sentiment of respect, I am,
Sir, your much obliged and obedient servant,

NELSON AND BRONTE.

TO CAPTAIN SUTTON.

[Autograph, in the possession of Captain Ives Sutton.]

Merton, October 11th, 1802.

My dear Sutton,

Your Steward has called upon me for my influence to get
him a place.   Alas, I have not the smallest interest to get any
place, however small!   Will you come and see us to-morrow?
We have a bed for you, and we shall be very happy to receive
you at Merton, and I am ever, my dear Sutton, your obliged
friend,

NELSON AND BRONTE.

---

[1] To this Letter, Lady Hamilton added a few lines, expressing her concern for
Mr. Dods' death, and saying they would do anything to assist his widow.   She
expressed her regret that Mr. Davison would not be with them on the 29th, " to
keep the Hero of Heroes' birth-day;" and added that they had had "a most charming
tour," which would cause " some of the enemies of the greatest man alive to burst"
with envy.

TO ALEXANDER DAVISON, ESQ., SWANLAND HOUSE,
NORTHUMBERLAND.

[Autograph, in the possession of Colonel Davison.]

Merton, October 20th, 1802.

My dear Friend,

I am really so very little in the world, that I know little, if anything, beyond [what] Newspaper reports say respecting our conduct on the affairs of the Continent. It is true, I have seen Mr. Addington and Lord St. Vincent several times; but our conversations are like Swift's and Lord Oxford's.[1] Yet it was not difficult to discover, that *We* felt our importance in the scale of Europe degraded, if Buonaparte was allowed to act as he has lately done ; and that it was necessary for us to speak a dignified language; but when, where, or to whom all this was to be done I know no more than your ploughman. By the meeting of Parliament many things must come forth. I asked Lord St. Vincent a few days past when the Holstein[2] was to be paid for, and the stores. He said that Lord Hawkesbury had requested him to let this stand until the Dutch business was finished; and, what was odd, Lord St. Vincent seemed to agree with me that it would have been better to have given us £100,000 as a gift in lieu of Head-money, Ships, &c. &c. *Apropos,* I have had an offer for the purchase of the brass guns;[2] you have the account of those I sent to Woolwich,

---

[1] " 'Tis (let me see) three years and more
        (October next it will be four)
        Since Harley bid me first attend,
        And chose me for an humble friend ;
        Would take me in his coach to chat,
        And question me of this and that :
        As " What's o'clock?" and " How's the wind ?"
        " Whose chariot's that we left behind?"
        Or gravely try to read the lines
        Writ underneath the country signs ;
        Or, " Have you nothing new to-day
        From Pope, from Parnell, or from Gay ?"
        Such tattle often entertains
        My Lord and me as far as Staines,
        As once a-week we travel down
        To Windsor, and again to Town ;
        Where all that passes *inter nos*
        Might be proclaimed at Charing-Cross ! "

[2] Taken at Copenhagen.

and have you got those left at Yarmouth, and aboard several Ships which I sent you an account of? I called the last [time] I was in Town at your house, but Mr. Bowring was out, and the other Clerk told me he supposed Mr. Cutler managed all the Prize business. Sir William and Lady Hamilton desire to be kindly remembered. We had the pleasure of dining in company with Mr. Gosling a few days ago. Ever, my dear Davison, I am your obliged and faithful friend,

NELSON AND BRONTE.

TO SAMUEL FORD, ESQ.

[From the "Gentleman's Magazine," vol. lxxvi. p. 304.]

Merton, October 24th, 1802.

Sir,

I feel much honoured by the polite invitation you have (by the direction of the Chairman and Committee of the Constitutional Livery of London,) sent me; and I am very sorry to be so situated, that it is out of my power to accept it. I have farther to request that you will have the goodness to present my compliments to the Chairman and Committee. I return the ticket of admission, and I am, with great respect, Sir, your much obliged and humble servant,

NELSON AND BRONTE.

TO THE RIGHT HONOURABLE THE LORD MAYOR ELECT, AND SHERIFFS OF LONDON.

[From a Copy in the Nelson Papers.]

Merton, November 8th, 1802.

Lord Nelson returns his most respectful compliments to the Lord Mayor Elect, and the Sheriffs, and is most exceedingly sorry that it is not in his power to do himself the honour and pleasure of dining with them at Guildhall on Lord Mayor's day, for the following reasons;

Lord Nelson having waited with the greatest patience until every individual who had rendered the smallest service to the Country had been marked by the City of London, wrote a letter to the Lord Mayor, (Sir John Eamer,) stating his sorrow that those under his command, who fought the most bloody Battle, and obtained the most complete Victory of any Naval Battle in this, or, Lord Nelson believes, in any War, had not had the honour to receive from the great City of London the same mark of approbation as had been bestowed on others; but Lord Nelson being advised of the impropriety of pointing out what the City of London ought to have done, wrote another letter to the Lord Mayor, desiring to withdraw his letter.

But Lord Nelson's sentiments being precisely the same, and feeling for the situation of those brave Captains, Officers, and Men, who so bravely fought, profusely bled, and obtained such a glorious, complete, and most important Victory for their King and Country, cannot do himself the honour and happiness of meeting his Fellow-Citizens on the 9th of November.

Lord Nelson flatters himself that the Lord Mayor Elect, and the Sheriffs, will approve of his feelings on this occasion, and consider that if Lord Nelson could forget the services of those who have fought under his command, that he would ill deserve to be so supported as he always has been.

TO CAPTAIN GEORGE MURRAY.

[Autograph, in the possession of George Murray, Esq.]

Merton, November 10th, 1802.

My dear Murray,

We shall be very happy to see you on Friday, as Thursday does not suit Captain Domett. I can assure you that at all times I am ever glad to see you, for I never shall forget your gallant support of me at the Battle of Copenhagen, and I thank you for taking the trouble of driving seven miles to make me a visit; for, could you believe it, there are those who I thought were my firm friends, some of near thirty years' standing—who have never taken that trouble! I am ever, my dear Murray, your obliged and faithful,

NELSON AND BRONTE.

TO CAPTAIN SIR EDWARD BERRY.

[From a Copy in the Nelson Papers.]

Merton, November 27th, 1802.

My dear Sir Edward,

We feel infinitely obliged by your kind present of a brace of fine pheasants. I should have answered your kind present sooner, but I have been taken up by business in Town. My cause is now to be brought before the Court of King's Bench,[3] and another year may pass away. The Judges being two and two, a new trial was necessary, or an appeal on my part to another, allowing judgment to be given against me : but I now begin to think that justice will carry it against power. Sir William and Lady Hamilton desire their kind compliments and believe me ever, yours most faithfully,

NELSON AND BRONTE.

TO CAPTAIN PAGE,[4] H.M. SHIP CAROLINE.

[From " The United Service Journal" for October 1839.]

Merton, December 2nd, 1802.

My dear Sir,

A young man of the name of Coleman, of the Close, at Norwich, recommended to me by Mr. Wyndham, was with me in the St. George, 90, in the Baltic, and paid off from her. He is eighteen months at sea, and I will thank you to take him; but I have nothing to do with his pecuniary concerns, and only beg leave to suggest the practice now followed, of parents lodging the money in the Captain's or Agent's hands, before the Captain advances money for them, and what he may never have repaid him. I again thank you for your kindness in taking the lad for me, and am ever your much obliged,

NELSON AND BRONTE.

---

[3] His lawsuit with the Earl of St. Vincent, before mentioned.
[4] Captain Benjamin William Page, now an Admiral of the Blue.

TO THE RIGHT HONOURABLE HENRY ADDINGTON.

[Autograph, in the Sidmouth Papers.]

Merton, December 4th, 1802.

My dear Sir,

I send you my thoughts respecting Malta, made as they flow, from my pen, but with the less diffidence, as I feel that you do not consider my thoughts (on paper) as impertinent intrusions on your time, but as the well meaning of your sincere and attached,

NELSON AND BRONTE.

ON MALTA.

It must never belong to France—England does not want it. If Russia will not guarantee Malta, then a new negotiation must be set on foot, and we must hold fast until it is settled. But if Russia will guarantee Malta, then it will become a serious consideration in the new state of the Order, whether it can be carried into effect. Malta is materially changed since the Treaty of Amiens, by Spain having (in breach of that Treaty) taken away a great part of that revenue which was to support the expenses of the Order, and if one power can do it, another can do the same, and the Order of Malta, unable to maintain itself, falls of course.

N.B.—It is easy to see from whose advice Spain has acted; other Countries may follow the same advice.

The Order of Malta cannot, in keeping the fortifications in repair, ships, galleys, &c., be kept up for less than the former revenue, and by the introduction of the new Langue, the pride of Spaniards will not allow them, nor even the Italians, to enter into the Order; and they brought a vast accession of flowing wealth to the Order, which now will fail.

Under these circumstances, it becomes a consideration what can be done with it to accord to the spirit of the Treaty of Amiens, that neither France or England shall possess it.

The King of the Two Sicilies is the acknowledged Lord of the Island, even the Maltese, after the destruction of the Order, in their addresses style themselves his Subjects; therefore, on the face of the act, there could be no objection to giving it to him; but the consideration is, how a weak State can keep it out of the power of so powerful a one as France—only by guarantees that the King of the Two Sicilies shall hold Malta on the same terms as the Order, (if it is possible that it shall always be neutral,) and tied up by the guarantee that on no consideration of exchange of territory shall it be given up. The Emperor of Russia having guaranteed all the King of Naples' Dominions last year, will not probably object to do the same for Malta. It is so much the interest of the King of the Two Sicilies to keep Malta from France, (for he would lose Sicily if he gave it up) that I think him, under guarantees, the most proper person to have it. France could not object by the spirit of the Treaty of Amiens, to its being placed, (the Order not being possible to be restored,) in the King of Naples' hands under the same restrictions, and this Country would save £300,000 a year, and by as far as human faith and fore-sight can go, keep Malta out of the hands of France.

The King of Naples can wish for neither France or Eng-land to possess Malta. By the first, he must lose Sicily : by the latter, he may be involved in a war about Malta, should France and England go to war; and this, in my opinion, could be the only rational inducement for the King of Naples to pay the great expenses of holding Malta.

If neither of these plans can be accomplished, we have no choice but to keep Malta.

NOTE.—When I was instructed by Lord Grenville to con-sider the Emperor of Russia as Grand Master of the Order, in my correspondence with him on the situation of Malta, I represented to him the tyranny of the Order over the Inha-bitants, and presumed to recommend, in order that they should be reconciled to the return of the Order, that he would direct them to be assured that they should be eligible to be elected to any Office in the Island. He directly ordered his Minister at Naples to go to Malta, and to assure this boon to the Inhabitants; and Chevalier Italinski went and returned in one of our Ships. This, perhaps, considering the pride of the Knights, was all that could be obtained. The Spaniards already term the Maltese Langue, the Shopkeeper Langue.

TO HERCULES ROSS, ESQ.

[Autograph in the possession of Horatio Ross, Esq.]

Merton, December 16th, 1802.

My dear Friend,

Your letter is gone to Colonel Brownrigg,[5] with one from myself, this morning. The moment I get his answer you shall have it. I know not that I have any influence with His Royal Highness, but I will without difficulty, to show my readiness to oblige you, being truly your most obliged and faithful friend,

NELSON AND BRONTE.

TO HERCULES ROSS, ESQ.

[Autograph, in the possession of Horatio Ross, Esq.]

St. James's-square, Tuesday Morning.

My dear Friend,

I am extremely sorry, but it is absolutely out of my power to be in Harley Street this morning, as I am obliged to go in the City on business, which will admit of no excuse, for my new purchase depends on it. I can therefore only wish you, which I do from my heart, health and every blessing which the Deity can bestow, and believe me, my dear friend, ever your most affectionate and faithful,

NELSON AND BRONTE.

TO MR. JAMES FITTLER.

[Autograph, in the possession of J. Wild, Esq. On the 21st of December, 1802, Lord Nelson made the following Speech on the Bill for a Naval Inquiry into abuses. After mentioning the confidence that might be placed in the authoritative inquiry of the Commissioners, he said: " My Lords, in the absence of my noble friend who is at the head of the Admiralty, I think it my duty to say a few words to your Lordships in regard to a Bill, of which the objects have an express reference to the interests of my profession as a Seaman. It undoubtedly originates in the feeling of the Admiralty, that they have not the power

---

[1] Lieutenant-Colonel, afterwards Sir Robert Brownrigg, Bart., G.C.B., then Military Secretary to his Royal Highness the Duke of York, Commander-in-Chief.

to remedy certain abuses which they perceive to be the most injurious to the Public service. Every man knows that there are such abuses; and I hope there is none among us who would not gladly do all that can be constitutionally effected to cor-rect them. Yet, if I had heard of any objection of weight urged against the measure in the present Bill, I should certainly have hesitated to do aught to promote its progress through the forms of this House. But I can recollect but one thing with which I have been struck, as possibly exceptionable in its tenour. It authorizes the Commissioners to call for and inspect the books of Merchants who may have had transactions of business with any of the Boards or Prize-agents into whose conduct they are to inquire. But the credit of the British Merchant is the support of the commerce of the world; his books are not lightly, nor for any ordinary purpose, to be taken out of his own hands; the secrets of his business are not to be too curiously pried into. The books of a single Merchant may betray the secrets, not only of his own affairs, but of those with whom he is principally connected in business, and the reciprocal confidence of the whole Commercial world may, by the authoritative in-quiry of these Commissioners, be shaken. All this, at least, I should have feared as liable to happen, if the persons who are named in the Bill had not been men whose characters are above all suspicion of indiscretion or malice. I may presume it to be the common conviction of the Merchants, that in such hands they will be safe; since they have made no opposition to the Bill in its former progress, and since they have offered no appearance against it by counsel, at your Lordship's bar; and truly, my Lords, if the Bill be thus superior to all objections, I can affirm, that the necessities, the wrongs of those who are employed in the Naval service of their Country, most loudly call for the redress which it proposes. From the highest Admiral in the service to the lowest cabin-boy that walks the street, there is not a man but may be in distress, with large sums of wages due to him, of which he shall, by no diligence of request, be able to obtain payment: there is not a man, whose entreaties will be readily answered with aught but insults, at the proper places for his application, if he come not with particular recommendations to a preference. From the highest Admiral to the meanest Seaman, whatever the sums of Prize-money due to him, no man can tell when he may securely call any part of it his own. A man may have £40,000 due to him in Prize-money, and yet be dismissed without a shilling, if he ask for it, at the proper Office, without particular recommendation. Are these things to be tolerated? Is it not for the interest—is it not for the honour of the Country, that they should not be as speedily as possible redressed? I should be as unwilling as any man to give an over-weening preference to the interests of my own Profession; but I cannot help thinking, that under all the circumstances of the affair, your Lordships will be strongly disposed to advance this Bill into a law, as speedily as may be consistent with the order of your proceedings, and with due pru-dence of deliberation." His Lordship also, on the third reading of the Bill, on the following day, expressed his desire that the necessary inquiries into the flagrant abuses by Prize-agents, might be made the subject of a separate act; observing at the same time, that there might be instances in which the delay of payment resulted from unavoidable accidents.—*Clarke and M'Arthur*, 8vo Ed., vol. ii. p. 458.]

Merton, December 21st, 1802.

Sir,

I have received your most beautiful print of the Battle of the Nile, and if you will be so good as to let me know the price of the print, I will try and get some of them sold; but

I fear the time for such events being interesting is past. I beg your acceptance of the £25 sent herewith; and I am, Sir, with every good wish for the sale of your print, your most obliged and obedient servant,

NELSON AND BRONTE.

TO THOMAS POLLARD, ESQ., LEGHORN.[6]

[Autograph, in the possession of John Luxford, Esq.]

Merton, Surrey, January 21st, 1803.

My dear Pollard,

I feel very much obliged by your kind letter of November 26th, and for your offer of service, and I will trouble you to send me two cases of Florence wine; not sweet wine, but that which is known in this Country as *Florence* wine. I think you judge quite right to see how Tuscany is settled, before you get into much business. Sir William and Lady Hamilton join me in every good and kind wish to you and Mrs. Pollard; and I am ever your much obliged and faithful friend,

NELSON AND BRONTE.

TO ADMIRAL THE EARL OF ST. VINCENT, K.B.

[Autograph, in the possession of Vice-Admiral Sir William Parker, Bart., G.C.B.]

Merton, January 26th, 1803.

My dear Lord,

Captain (Major) Weir, who you have given the retirement of the Marines to, was with me this morning, and truly thankful for your kind reception of him when he arrived in England. We all know him to be a worthy, good man, and a most excellent Officer. He was, for the benefit of the King's Service, and at the request of Colonel Graham, appointed to the rank of Major. His whole conduct in raising a Maltese Corps, and his merits at Porto Ferraio, are fully known to you. What he wishes, as a *feather* in his cap, is, to have his Brevet rank, given by me, confirmed by the Admiralty, that he may be called Major in future. As this will not be any

[6] Vide vol. i. p. 350, *passim.*

expense to the State, but a high gratification to a most deserving Officer, I hope that your Lordship will find no difficulty in complying with his wishes, and in so doing you will also much oblige your faithful and affectionate,

NELSON AND BRONTE.

TO ADMIRAL THE EARL OF ST. VINCENT, K.B.

[Autograph, in the Sidmouth Papers.]

23, Piccadilly, January 28th, 1803.

My dear Lord,

As your indifferent state of health will, I fear, prevent your coming to Town for some time, I write to your Lordship on a subject which we once entered upon, but which you desired to defer till the Dutch Ships were paid for, when you would settle our Copenhagen business with Lord Hawkesbury. I am now, by desire of several Captains, asking your Lordship if any decision has taken place on this business? If you refer me to Lord Hawkesbury, as the proper Minister for this business, or any other Minister, I shall address myself to him (or them;) or if you think that a Public letter to the Secretary of the Admiralty is the proper channel, I will write one to him. It is near two years since that Battle was fought. I own myself exactly of the same opinion as when I wrote to you from the Baltic, that under all the peculiar circumstances of the case—*no war with Denmark*, therefore no condemnation could take place—that it would be better to give a gratuity for our services. I said (I believe) £100,000 was as little as could be offered. You differed from me, but wrote me that you would recommend a large price to be given for the Holstein. You will, my dear Lord, see the situation I am placed in, and excuse my reverting to you to advise me in what channel I shall proceed, to bring our Copenhagen prize business to a close. With every kind wish for the re-establishment of your health, believe me yours most faithfully,

NELSON AND BRONTE.[8]

[8] The following Memorandum occurs on this Letter:—"Lord St. Vincent settled with Lord Nelson that Lord St. Vincent would tell Mr. Addington on Friday last that £65,000 would satisfy Lord Nelson for the Ships and Stores taken at Copenhagen, exclusive of the £30,000 Head-money already paid—the above sum to include the Holstein, brass Cannon, and other Stores, landed in our Arsenals.—N. AND B. February 25th, 1803."

TO ALEXANDER DAVISON, ESQ.

[Autograph, in the possession of Colonel Davison.]

My dear Davison,   23, Piccadilly, February 8th, 1803.

I have longed, for an age, to write you a line; for no one [can] have more felt for the distress you must have suffered than us of this house. Miss Davison was so good as to send us word that William[9] was better. I trust that you will now soon be enabled to travel, and that I shall very soon have the pleasure of shaking you by the hand. Your kind offer I feel most sensibly; but at present I have no wants; and I hope soon to be in that state of complete independence, which you so really wish. But 'A friend in need is a friend indeed' is an old adage, but not the less true, and I am truly thankful and grateful for all your kindness. I am just got to work on the Copenhagen business, and I hope to get from Mr. Addington 50 or £60,000 for the Captors, including the Holstein. Sir Hyde has given up the management of this matter to me. At another Board, they are still disputing; but the Secretary and myself are feeling towards each other as we ever ought (I do not choose to mention names.) Yesterday, I was at Colonel Despard's[1] trial, subpœnaed by him for a character. I think the plot deeper than was imagined; but as to the extent, nothing except the *Guards* has come out. I have been, and am, very bad in my eyesight, and am forbid writing; but I could not resist. Lady Hamilton joins me in kind respects to Mrs. Davison, and to the boys every good wish; and believe me ever, my dear Davison, your most faithful and affectionate friend,   NELSON AND BRONTE.

[9] Mr. Alexander Davison married, in February 1788, Harriet, daughter of Robert Gosling, Esq., the Banker in Fleet Street, by whom he had three sons—viz., Colonel Hugh Percy Davison, (to whom the Editor is indebted for the Letters to his father,) Lieutenant Colonel Sir William Davison, K.H., (twins,) and Alexander, who died young; and three daughters, Elizabeth, who married General White; Dorothy, who married Captain Samuel Edward Widdrington, R.N., of Newton Hall, K.T.S.; and Harriet, who died unmarried. Mr. Alexander Davison died, at Brighton, in his eightieth year, in December 1829.

[1] On the 7th of February, Lord Nelson appeared as a Witness on the trial of Colonel Despard for high treason, when he deposed that he had served with the prisoner on the Spanish Main and at the attack of Fort St. Juan, in 1780, [vide vol. i. p. 34*,] and that he bore the character of a brave Officer and honourable and loyal man. Lord Chief Justice Ellenborough, adverting to this testimony, observed, that it had been given by "a man on whom to pronounce an eulogy were to waste words."

TO ALEXANDER STEPHENS, ESQ.

[From a Copy in the possession of the Right Honourable John Wilson Croker.]

23, Piccadilly, February 10th, 1803.·

Sir,

By your letter, I believe that you wish to be correct in your History,[2] and therefore wish to be informed of a transaction relative to Naples. I cannot enter at large into the subject to which you allude. I shall briefly say, that neither Cardinal Ruffo, or Captain Foote, or any other person, had any power to enter into any Treaty with the Rebels—that even the Paper which they signed was not *acted* upon, as I very happily arrived at Naples, and prevented such an infamous transaction from taking place; therefore, when the Rebels surrendered, they came out of the Castles as they ought, without any honours of War, and trusting to the judgment of their Sovereign. *I put aside, and sent them notice of it, the infamous* Treaty, and the rebels surrendered, as I have before said. If you attend to that Mrs. Williams' book, I can assure you that nearly all relative to Naples is either destitute of foundation, or falsely represented. I am, Sir, &c.

NELSON AND BRONTE.

I must beg leave to warn you to be careful how you mention the characters of such excellent Sovereigns as the King and Queen of Naples. If you wish to have any conversation with me on the subject, I shall be at home any morning at 10 o'clock.

TO ADMIRAL THE EARL OF ST. VINCENT, K.B.

[Autograph, in the possession of Vice-Admiral Sir William Parker, Bart., G.C.B.]

23, Piccadilly, February 28th, 1803.

My dear Lord,

I take the liberty of inclosing some ideas of mine relative to our Seamen. My reasons for committing them to paper are stated in the first lines of my Paper. I have sent a copy of

------

[2] " History of the Wars of the French Revolution," 2 vols. 1803. *Vide* vol. iii. p. 520.

them to Mr. Addington. Probably you have arranged similar, or better plans, for obtaining the same much to be desired object. If so, they will have the fullest support of, my dear Lord, your most faithful and affectionate,

NELSON AND BRONTE.

PLAN FOR MANNING THE NAVY.

[Original, in the possession of Vice-Admiral Sir William Parker, Bart., G.C.B.]

February, 1803.

At a time when, I have been repeatedly told, the Seamen, notwithstanding their good pay, and abundance of the very best provisions, manifest a reluctance to enter into the Naval Service, it becomes, in my humble opinion, a duty for people conversant with the manners and disposition of Seamen, to turn their thoughts on the mode of inducing the Seamen to be fond, and even desirous of serving in the Navy, in preference to the Merchant Service. Their pay and provisions cannot possibly be improved from what they are at present; but, I think, a plan could be brought forward to Register the Certificates given to Seamen; and a form of Certificate to be general, and filled according to regulations issued by the Admiralty under the authority of an Act of Parliament. The greatest good would result, from such a regulation to the Seamen, who are by hundreds in distress in London, for want of Certificates authenticating their persons; for want of which so many wrong Seamen have been paid, that neither the Pay-Office, nor any Prize-Agent, will venture to pay the Seaman his just due; and the benefit to the Seamen producing good characters, &c. never been concerned in mutinies, or deserted, &c., would much benefit them in getting good berths in the Merchant Service.

When we calculate by figures on the expense of raising Seamen, I think it is said, £20 per man, that 42,000 Seamen deserted during the late War, the loss in money, in that point alone, amounts to £840,000; without taking into consideration the greater expense of raising more men—and certainly not so good as those who have been used to the King's Naval Service. I shall therefore propose, that every

Seaman who has served faithfully five years in War, and by
his Certificates never been concerned in mutinies, nor deserted, shall receive every New Year's Day, or on the King's
birth-day, the sum of two guineas; and if he serves eight years,
shall have four guineas, exclusive of any pension for wounds.
It may appear, at first sight, for the State to pay, an enormous
sum; but when it is considered that the average life of a Seaman is, from *old* age finished, at forty-five years, he cannot
many years enjoy the annuity; to assist the paying which,
the interest of the money saved by their not deserting would
go very far, and perhaps as the Merchants give large wages
in War, a tax might be imposed, when wages are above such
a sum. It would answer one of these two purposes, either
making the increase of wages, in the Merchant's Service,
beneficial to those who serve their King and Country in the
Navy; or, by keeping down the Merchants' wages, render
desertion the less desirable. Much, very much, can be said,
and is necessary to be considered on this subject; but the
more I think of it, the easier it appears to me to be put in
practice. Prize-money to be as regularly paid in London,
Portsmouth, Plymouth, &c. as Seamen's wages: this is so easy
and simple, that a very few days would, in my opinion, complete such a plan.

But the great thing necessary to guard against is desertion;
for notwithstanding all I have proposed, to induce Seamen to
serve faithfully, yet a sum of money, and liquor, held out to
a Seaman, are too much for him: he allows himself to be
seduced and hid, he first becomes fearful of apprehension,
and then wishes and exerts himself to get out of the Country in the Merchant's employ. It will be found, (if necessary
to be inquired into at the Navy-Office,) and I know it, that
whenever a large Convoy is assembled at Portsmouth, and
our Fleet in Port, not less than 1000 men desert from the
Navy; and I am sure that one-third of this number, from
loss of clothes, drinking, and other debaucheries, are lost by
death to the Kingdom. I shall only relate one fact, of a
thousand, which could be brought forward: a Ship, from
London, clears at Gravesend for her voyage to India. Amongst
other Papers, the names of her crew and number are necessary; the names, qualities, &c., are properly filled up, the

Ship, to a common observer, is fully manned; but the fact is this, the Ship is navigated to Portsmouth by Ticket-men, (men who are protected from the impress for some cause or other.) The Owner or Captain sends to Portsmouth, (to crimps,) I have been told in one instance as far as fifty men —twenty-five able Seamen, fifteen ordinary, and ten lands-men, the bounty being, of course, different according to their qualifications; the Ticket-men leave the Ship, the deserters to take up the names, and away they go.

Knowing the case, an Act of Parliament would, if not entirely, very nearly prevent this infamous conduct; the regu-lation, I think, would be very plain and easy. I am sensible that no plan for these very important purposes can be matured by any one head, much less by mine; but as the ideas flow from a pure source, and a sincere desire to benefit our King and Country, I submit them, with deference, to much wiser and abler men than

NELSON AND BRONTE.

TO CAPTAIN PAGE, H. M. SHIP CAROLINE.

[From "The United Service Journal" for October 1839.]

Piccadilly, March 4th, 1803.

My dear Sir,

A friend of mine has requested me to write you a line, recommending his godson, Mr. Robert Fausset,[3] to your notice, which I therefore take the liberty of doing. I hope you like the Caroline; and, go where you will, you have the sincere good wishes of all your friends at Merton, and of none more cordially than your much obliged,

NELSON AND BRONTE.

This young Officer became a Lieutenant in October 1809, and died in that rank between 1816 and 1820.

TO THE RIGHT HONOURABLE HENRY ADDINGTON.

[Autograph, in the Sidmouth Papers.]

Sir,   London, March 8th, 1803.

I feel very great reluctance in troubling you with any personal concerns of mine, but I am really compelled to it, by circumstances,[4] which, when explained, will, I think, convince you, that I cannot do otherwise; and knowing the value of your time, I will do it as shortly as I can.

His Majesty was graciously pleased, on account of my services in the Battle of the Nile, to bestow on me the high honour of a Peerage of Great Britain, and to recommend it to

---

[4] Lord Nelson submitted for Mr. Addington's consideration the following statement of his property and income, which shows how necessary it was that he should receive the same pecuniary reward as had been given to the other Admirals who had gained a Victory. No increase of Pension was, however, granted to him.

" LORD NELSON'S INCOME AND PROPERTY.

My Exchequer Pension for the Nile £2000	0	0
Navy Pension for loss of one arm and one eye 923	0	0
Half-pay as Vice-Admiral 465	0	0
Interest of £1000 3 per Cents. 30	0	0
£3418	0	0

OUTGOINGS OF LORD NELSON.

To Lady Nelson £1800	0	0
Interest of money owing 500	0	0
Pension to my Brother's Widow 200	0	0
To assisting in educating my Nephews 150	0	0
Expenditure 2650	0	0
Income 3418	0	0
For Lord Nelson . . 768	0	0

Therefore, Lord Nelson is *free* of House-rent, but has to pay charities necessary for his station in life, taxes, repairs, servants, and to live upon £768 per annum.

PROPERTY OF LORD NELSON.

Merton House, land, plate, and furniture £20,000 0 0
In 3 per Cents, £1000 Stock.

DEBTS.

By Mortgage on Merton, to assist in the purchase . . 6000	0	0
Fitting out for the Baltic, and again for my Command on the Coast, in Summer 1801 . . . . } 4000	0	0
£10,000	0	0

Real Property of Lord Nelson, £10,000.
In Three per Cents, £1000 Stock."

Parliament to enable him to grant a Pension of £2000 a-year
to me, and eventually for two lives after mine.   In the former
part of the Message for that purpose, his Majesty expresses
a desire to bestow on me the Pension, and to *the two next
succeeding heirs male of my body*.   But in the recommendatory
part of the Message the words are, ' to consider of a proper
method of enabling his Majesty to grant the same, and of
extending, securing, and settling such annuity to the said
Rear-Admiral Lord Nelson, and *to the two next persons on
whom the title of Baron Nelson, &c. shall descend, in such manner
as shall be thought most effectual for the benefit of the said Lord
Nelson and his family*."[5]

The grant was made to me and the two next succeeding
heirs male of my body, which was probably done without an
attentive consideration of the whole of the Message.   But it
was then of no importance to me, as the grant followed the
Title; but as His Majesty has since been graciously pleased to
confer upon me the Title of a Viscount,[6] with the remainder to
my brother and nephews, (failing issue of my own,) I must entreat that you will lay me at his Majesty's feet, and that you
will have the goodness to express to him, in the most dutiful
manner, my humble hope that, as I have not had the good
fortune to acquire sufficient wealth to put it in my power to
enable my nephews to support in any degree the rank of a
Peer, to which they may eventually succeed, his Majesty will
be graciously pleased to take such measures as he shall think
necessary, for continuing the Pension in the manner it appears
to have been his Majesty's gracious intention it should have
been originally granted.

In making this application to you, Sir, it is but fair that I
should apprise you that Lord St. Vincent is in the same situation, I believe, with myself; but I know of no other case at
all similar, as Lord Duncan has male issue.   And I also beg
leave to state that both Lord St. Vincent and Lord Duncan

---

[5] The copy of the Message in vol. ii. p. 79, is not accurately stated; it was in
the words quoted by Lord Nelson.

[6] It is remarkable that Lord Nelson should have mistaken the limitation of his
Viscountcy, which was confined to the heirs male of his own body.   It was the
Barony of Nelson of the Nile and *of Hilborough*, granted in August 1801, that was
to devolve (on failure of his own male issue) on his brother and nephews.   Vide
vol. iv. p. 540.

had a grant from the Irish Parliament of £1000 a-year, which, from not having been recommended by Government here, was not bestowed upon me. I presume to make only one remark : Was it, or not, the intention of his Majesty's Government to place my rewards for services lower than Lord St. Vincent or Lord Duncan ? I had the happiness to be a sharer of the glory of the 14th of February ; and I had the honour to command the Fleet which gained the Victory of the Nile, which, till that of Copenhagen, was, I believe, the most complete one ever obtained. I have the honour to be, &c.

NELSON AND BRONTE.

TO ADMIRAL THE EARL OF ST. VINCENT, K.B.

[Autograph, in the possession of Vice-Admiral Sir William Parker, Bart., G.C.B.]

Admiralty, Saturday, [March, 1803.]

My dear Lord,

My old Shipmate, and one who your Lordship has been very good to, Captain Richard Williams,[7] is desirous of returning to his old post of Regulating at Belfast, and has this moment requested of me to say *one* word for him, which is, that giving him that appointment will much oblige yours most faithfully,

NELSON AND BRONTE.

TO LADY COLLIER.

[Autograph, in the possession of Commodore Sir Francis A. Collier, K.C.H.]

March 21st, 1803.

Dear Madam,

I am very happy to hear that your good son is made a Lieutenant. His commission should be enclosed to Sir Evan Nepean, requesting him to move the Lords of the Admiralty for the confirmation : a letter, also, to Lord St. Vincent, asking him to confirm Francis, will be proper. I am sorry to be obliged to be from home to-morrow, but sensible of the honour intended me ; and I am your Ladyship's most obedient servant,

NELSON AND BRONTE.

---

[7] Captain Williams was made a Post-Captain in June 1799, and died about 1815. Lord Nelson's request appears to have been complied with.

TO CAPTAIN GEORGE MURRAY,[8] H.M.S. SPARTIATE, PLYMOUTH.

[Autograph, in the possession of George Murray, Esq.]

March 22nd, 1803.

My dear Murray,

Many thanks for your kind letter. As far as my knowledge goes, we are in the same state of uncertainty as to War
or Peace, as when you left London. The plan is still for us
eventually to embark in the Amphion. Sam. Sutton is to fit
out the Victory for us, which I am very glad of, as she will be
well fitted. My best regards to all friends, and every good
wish towards you, from your most faithful,

NELSON AND BRONTE.

Sir William and Lady Hamilton desire their kind regards.

MEMORANDUM.

[Autograph, in the possession of Vice-Admiral Sir William Parker, Bart., G.C.B.]

March 24th, 1803.

Lord Nelson requests the kindness of Lord St. Vincent to
send to the Mediterranean a very near connexion of his,

---

[8] This distinguished Officer won Lord Nelson's admiration and friendship by the
gallant manner in which, in command of the Edgar, he led the Squadron to the
attack of Copenhagen. On being appointed Commander-in-Chief in the Mediterranean, Lord Nelson determined on having Captain Murray as Captain of the Fleet,
but he hesitated to accept the situation, saying, the nature of its duties often led to
disagreements between the Admiral and First Captain, and that he should be very
unwilling to risk a diminution of the regard and respect which he entertained
for his Lordship. Lord Nelson, however, assured him that under no circumstances
would he forget the intimacy which subsisted between them; "and that even
should anything go contrary to his wishes, he would waive the rank of *Admiral*,
and explain or expostulate with him as his *friend* Murray." Captain Murray, accordingly, became his First Captain; and was made a Rear-Admiral of the Blue
on the 23rd of April, 1804. After the return of the Squadron to England, Rear-
Admiral Murray was induced, from his private affairs, to leave the Victory; and
when, on going off Cadiz, in July 1805, other Captains applied for the vacancy,
Nelson's reply was, that, " if ever he had another Captain of the Fleet, it must be
Murray;" and he sailed without one. See the Memoir of Admiral Murray, in the
Naval Chronicle, vol. xviii. pp. 189, 190. On the extension of the Order of the
Bath, in January 1815, Vice-Admiral Murray was nominated a Knight Commander,
and he died a Vice-Admiral of the Red, on the 28th of February, 1819.

Captain William Bolton,[9] a Master and Commander; and Lord Nelson also recommends Captain Frederick Langford[1] to Lord St Vincent's notice and protection.

***

TO CAPTAIN SIR EDWARD BERRY.

[Autograph, in the possession of Lady Berry.]

Piccadilly, March 26th, 1803.

My dear Sir Edward,

I have only a moment to answer your questions—War or Peace? Every person has a different opinion. I fear perhaps the former, as I hope so much the latter. If War, I go to the Mediterranean in Hardy's Frigate: the Victory is to be my Ship[2]—Sam Sutton to fit her out. You know how happy I should be to have you in any Fleet I command, particularly on the day of Battle: I should be sure of being well supported. You must judge for yourself about applying for employment; but I should think you will have no fears for a Ship being forced upon you. In Peace, Mids. may be difficult to get on board Ship; but our establishment, even if blessed Peace continues, will be large. You will be truly sorry to hear that good Sir William is, I fear, very near his last breath: he is all but gone. You may readily conceive Lady Hamilton's and my feelings on such an occasion: indeed, all London is interested. Ever, my dear Sir Edward, yours most sincerely,

NELSON AND BRONTE.

Reports say, but I know not how truly, that changes are in agitation.

[9] Captain William Bolton, eldest son of the Rev. William Bolton, brother of Thomas Bolton, Esq., who married Susannah, Lord Nelson's eldest sister. He was at that time engaged to his first cousin, Catherine Bolton, Lord Nelson's niece, whom he married on the 18th of May, 1803, the evening before the Installation of Knights of the Bath, when Captain Bolton was Knighted, as a qualification to act as Lord Nelson's Proxy at the Ceremony. Sir William Bolton was Posted on the 10th of April 1805, and died on the 16th of December 1830.

[1] Vide vol. iv. p. 467.

[2] The Victory was selected for Lord Nelson's Flag Ship, but it was doubtful whether she would be ready at the time he was to proceed to the Mediterranean. He did, however, sail in her, under the command of his friend, Captain Samuel Sutton, accompanied by the Amphion, Captain Thomas Masterman Hardy.

TO LADY COLLIER.

[Autograph, in the possession of Commodore Sir Francis A. Collier, K.C.H.]

Merton, March 30th, 1803.

Madam,

Although Lord St. Vincent, or those under him, have not had the attention to answer your letter, yet I can have no doubt that they will confirm your son.[3] A note to Troubridge, or Markham,[4] or Sir Evan Nepean, will draw an answer, and, I doubt not, a favourable one. It is no use writing Lord St. Vincent again on the subject. With every kind wish for Francis, I am your Ladyship's most obedient servant,

NELSON AND BRONTE.

TO MRS. BOLTON, CRANWICH.

[Autograph, in the possession of James Young, Esq., of Wells.]

Wrote last Saturday, and forgot.
Merton, March 30th, 1803.

My dear Sister,

I have strongly memorandumed Lord St. Vincent for Captain Bolton to be sent to the Mediterranean, and if we unfortunately have a War, his promotion may be looked upon as sure, and as he is likely to be related, my interest for his welfare must increase. I really believe him to be a most excellent young man. Dear Sir William is *very*, *very* bad: he can't, in my opinion, get over it, and I think it will happen very soon. You will imagine Lady Hamilton's and my feelings on the occasion; indeed, all London is interested in the fate of such a character. Kind regards to all at Cranwich; and believe me ever, your most affectionate brother.

NELSON AND BRONTE.[5]

---

[3] Mr. Collier's commission as Lieutenant was dated on the 11th of April 1803.

[4] Captains Sir Thomas Troubridge and John Markham, both Lords of the Admiralty.

[5] To this letter, Lady Hamilton added—" I have only to say, dearest Mrs. Bolton, Sir W. was so ill yesterday, he could not live, we thought; to-day he is better. I am worn out, but ever yours affectionately, E. H."

THE EXAMINATION OF VICE-ADMIRAL LORD VISCOUNT NELSON,
DUKE OF BRONTE, TAKEN UPON OATH, BEFORE THE COM-
MISSIONERS OF NAVAL INQUIRY, ON THE 1ST OF APRIL,
1803.

[From a Copy in the Admiralty. The passages in brackets are written in the
margin by Lord Nelson himself.]

From my own knowledge and experience I am warranted
in observing that Prize Money does not get into the pockets
of the Captors so expeditiously as it ought, and in many
instances not at all : great sums of money having been lost by
the failure of Agents. I am of opinion that Prize Agents
should be appointed by the Captors as at present, but that at
the time of registering their Powers of Attorney in the Admiralty and Vice Admiralty Courts, they should give *security* in
the sum of two or three thousand pounds, for the purpose of
securing a faithful discharge of their duty and excluding improper persons from acting as Agents. [To keep out bad
characters, but not exclude men of small fortune with good
characters.] That Government should establish a general
Prize Agency Office in London, and an Agent or Receiver at
each of the Foreign Stations. That no Prize Money or Prize
Goods should be liable to the Debts of Agents. That if the
Agents make the distribution within three months from the
day of the condemnation, they should be allowed the full
commission of five per cent, and at the expiration of that
period, deliver into the Prize Office (or if abroad to the Receiver) an Account of Sales, and pay over the amount of
unclaimed shares remaining in their hands. That if the Prize
shall have been disposed of and distribution made not in
three months, the Agent shall deliver an Account of Sales to
the Prize Office or Receiver as aforesaid, and pay over the
whole of the nett proceeds with a deduction of
from the rate of the commission allowed him, unless he shall
have been prevented making distribution by the absence of
the Ship on service, in which case, should her return into Port
be soon expected by the Commander-in-Chief, the Prize
Agent shall, on a certificate from him to that effect, be allowed
a further time of six weeks for making such distribution.

If the Prize or the whole of the goods shall not be sold, he should pay over the amount of the money in his hands, and give his reasons for not having sold the whole, which if satisfactory, a further time not exceeding three months should be allowed him to dispose of the remainder. If in that time he does not finally close his Accounts, or give good and sufficient reasons to the Prize Office or Receiver for not doing so, he should then be allowed only two and a half per cent., and be subject to penalties or the business taken out of his hands. [In order that they should not run up most enormous bills, which is the case at present; and for many other good reasons.]

The Agent's commission should be calculated upon the nett,[6] and not upon the gross amount of the proceeds of Prizes.

In cases of Appeal no distribution should be made until a *final* decision; [I have known this happen;] and in the event of the Decree being reversed, the Claimants should only be entitled to the nett proceeds; [Government to do what is right beyond this sum, the sentence being reversed being the cause of the additional expense;] and the Captor exonerated from all expenses incurred by the erroneous decisions of the Judges who are appointed by Government. All Neutral property whether captured by the King's Ships or by Privateers should be lodged in the hands of the Officers appointed by Government until final decision, [to prevent the present iniquitous conduct of Privateers.[7]]

The Agents of the Navy, Victualling, and Sick and Hurt Boards abroad should be directed to take up the money necessary for the carrying on the Naval Service from the Receiver of Prize Money. The Treasurer of the Navy to be at the head of the Prize Board.

---

[6] In the Copy of this Paper in Clarke and M'Arthur, vol. i. p. 369, the following note is said to have been added to this paragraph in Lord Nelson's own hand, but it does not occur in the copy in the Admiralty:—" Every Merchant is content with two and a half per cent. on the gross, and therefore, surely, Agents may be well contented with five per cent. on the nett."

[7] " To the great distress of Neutral Powers."—*Ibid.*

TO CAPTAIN MURRAY.

[Autograph, in the possession of George Murray, Esq.]

My dear Murray,   April 2nd, 1803.

I have this day seen both Mr. Addington and Lord St. Vincent, and as they were not expediting my departure, I take for granted that we are not more Warlike (except, I hope, in our preparations) than when I wrote you. Report says, and, I believe, truly, that we wait the issue of a Courier from Russia. Buonaparte has, we know, tried for Russia, and I fear successfully, by an offer of Hanover. If Russia sides against us, we shall, I suppose, give up the point; if otherwise, we have the only chance of Buonaparte giving way, which I do not much credit, but you shall know the moment I know anything. I have this day finished our Copenhagen business; they have been squabbling out of what fund we were to be paid. Apropos, most heartily I congratulate you on the return of this day;[8] and no man sets a more just value on your gallantry and important services than myself. I have yesterday delivered my opinion on conducting Prize business in future. I hope it will meet the approbation of the Service. The Commissioners must *make it their own,* or of what use are the Commissioners? We are on the eve of losing dear Sir William. I much doubt his holding twenty-four hours longer —our dear Lady is dreadfully afflicted—remember us kindly to Louis, and believe me ever yours, most faithfully and affectionately,   NELSON AND BRONTE.

Make our best compliments to Lord Keith[9] and all our friends about you, George Campbell, Sir Edward Pellew, &c.

TO CAPTAIN SAMUEL SUTTON, 312, OXFORD STREET.

(If not in Town, to be sent to him.)

[Autograph, in the possession of Captain Ives Sutton.]

Monday, April 4th, 1803.

My dear Sutton,

Markham desires me to tell you that the Victory will be commissioned on the 7th or 8th. I have sent a list of six

---

[8] The Anniversary of the Battle of Copenhagen.
[9] Commander-in-Chief at Plymouth.

Lieutenants, which will be enough to begin with. The
Master I have sent for, and name the Surgeon who is in the
Amphion. Poor dear Sir William is just gone; but I will see
you, being truly yours,

NELSON AND BRONTE.

TO SIR EVAN NEPEAN, BART., ADMIRALTY.

[Original, in the Admiralty.]

London, 6th April, 1803.

Sir,

I beg to enclose you a letter from Mr. John Scott, Purser
of His Majesty's Ship Royal Sovereign, requesting, for the
reasons therein mentioned, to be removed from that Ship into
any one in Ordinary. I have therefore to request you will
lay the same before the Lords Commissioners of the Admiralty, and to move their Lordships to comply with Mr.
Scott's [9] request, and grant him leave of absence to attend me
as Secretary accordingly. I am, &c.,

NELSON AND BRONTE.

TO ALEXANDER DAVISON, ESQ., ST. JAMES'S SQUARE.

[Autograph, in the possession of Colonel Davison.]

Wednesday, 11 o'clock, [6th April, 1803.]

My dear Davison,

Our dear Sir William died at ten minutes past ten, this
morning, in Lady Hamilton's and my arms, without a sigh or
a struggle. Poor Lady Hamilton is, as you may expect,
desolate. I hope she will be left properly; but I doubt. Ever
yours most affectionately,

NELSON AND BRONTE.

TO GEORGE G. MILLS, ESQ.

[Autograph, in the possession of Mrs. Conway.]

April 6th, 1803.

My dear Sir,

Having just lost my dear friend Sir William Hamilton I
can only answer your kind letter respecting Mr. Moore,

---

[9] Mr. John Scott, who was killed by Lord Nelson's side, at Trafalgar.

as he is to go into the Victory, which will be commissioned on
Saturday next, at Chatham. Mr. Moore should be there, and
if he will apply to Lord Proby in my name, I am sure he will
discharge him into the Victory, and he should join her as soon
as possible, for those who distinguish themselves most in fitting
out the Ship, will be first on my list for promotion. Mr. Moore
and I shall become acquainted in due time, and he has *no*
business in London. On board the Victory, at Chatham, is
the proper place for him to be fixed. I am, dear Sir, most
faithfully yours,

NELSON AND BRONTE.

TO HIS ROYAL HIGHNESS THE DUKE OF CLARENCE.

[From Clarke and M'Arthur, vol. ii. p. 312.]

6th April, 1803.

Your Royal Highness knows that you have a right to command me; and it was my full intention, when the thing was
fixed for my going, to have offered my services to you.[1] All that
I know officially is, that the Cabinet, through the mouth of the
First Lord of the Admiralty, have named me for the Command
in the Mediterranean, that it might be necessary for me to
go out in a Frigate, and that the Victory should follow. I am
truly impressed with all your goodness to me. I assure you,
I shall endeavour to merit the continuance of that friendship,
which you have been pleased to honour me with for upwards
of twenty-three years. My dear friend, Sir William Hamilton,
died this morning: the world never lost a more upright and
accomplished gentleman. I am, &c.

NELSON AND BRONTE.

[1] His Royal Highness appears, from the following letter to Lord Nelson, to have
placed a young gentleman under his protection:—

" Bushy House, Friday Evening.

" My dear Lord,

" Pike, the youngster who you are so good as to take on board the Victory, says
he wants his pay, which, he informs me, by some new regulation, he cannot receive
without your Lordship's interference. I am truly happy to embrace this opportunity of repeating to you how sincerely I am, and ever must be, dear Nelson, your
best friend, WILLIAM."—*Autograph*, in the Nelson Papers.

TO CAPTAIN MURRAY.

[Autograph, in the possession of George Murray, Esq.]

April 13th, 1803.

My dear Murray,

I think you will get into a scrape with the Earl was I to talk to him about your quitting your Ship at this moment, but I will speak to Troubridge. It was first intended that you should be Captain of the Victory—then it was thought better you should go out with me, and you thought it better to take Spartiate till I was certain of going. You are fixed as fate my First Captain, and it is only on that score that I can speak to the Earl soon, if nothing is decided soon as to Peace or War, to beg that you may not be sent out of the way, and then, if you authorize me, I will mention to him that if the Spartiate is wanted to go to sea, that you submit to him whether it would not be better to give her up—there are scores wanting her. I congratulate you on the birth of a son;[2] if one of his names is not *Baltic*, I shall be very angry with you indeed—he can be called nothing else. Lady Hamilton is very low, but desires her kind regards and good wishes, and believe me ever, yours most truly,

NELSON AND BRONTE.

Kind regards to Louis.[3]

TO CAPTAIN SAMUEL SUTTON.

[Autograph, in the possession of Captain Ives Sutton.]

April 16th [1803.]

My dear Sutton,

Many thanks for your letter. I yet hope the Victory will not make more than a Spithead voyage. I hear to-day that Mr. Grayson, who was Boatswain of the Theseus, late of the Hercule, invalided for a hurt side a few months ago, is appointed Boatswain of the Victory. He applied for my interest to get him a Seventy-four in ordinary, and being, I believe, a

[2] He was born on the 2nd of April, the anniversary of the Battle of Copenhagen.

[3] Captain Louis of the Conqueror, at Plymouth. *Vide* vol. iii. p. 90.

good man, I recommended him to Mackellar. I mention this circumstance to show you that he is not belonging to me : therefore, you will act by him as he deserves. With every good wish, I am most truly yours,

NELSON AND BRONTE.

TO HIS ROYAL HIGHNESS THE DUKE OF CLARENCE.

[From Clarke and M'Arthur, vol. ii. p. 312.]

April 17th, 1801.

I agree with your Royal Highness most entirely, that the son of a Rodney⁴ ought to be the protégé of every person in the Kingdom, and particularly of the Sea-Officers: had I known that there had been this claimant, some of my own Lieutenants must have given way to such a name, and he should have been placed in the Victory—she is full, and I have twenty on my list; but whatever numbers I have, the name of Rodney must cut many of them out. I am well aware that in my Prize plan, Lawyers must remove all the difficulties that will occur in the completion. Much, very much, is necessary to be considered on every part of it, but I think many objections would be overcome by a temperate and serious discussion. I was told the difficulties were insurmountable, or nearly so. My answer was, ' As the thing is necessary to be done, the more difficulties, the more necessary to try to remove them.' I am, &c.

NELSON AND BRONTE.

TO THE RIGHT HONOURABLE HENRY ADDINGTON.

[Autograph, in the Sidmouth Papers. On the 22nd of April, Lord Nelson, with his friends, Lords Minto and Hood, and Lord Hotham, appeared as Witnesses to the character of Captain Macnamara, on his trial for killing Colonel Montgomery in a duel.]

April 23rd, 1803.

The Pensions to the Admirals St. Vincent, Duncan, and Nelson, were, I suppose, either granted for the great Victories they obtained over the Enemy, or for enabling them to support

---

⁴ Lieutenant the Honourable Edward Rodney, youngest son of Admiral Lord Rodney: he was made a Commander in April 1805; Posted in January 1806 ; and died in November 1828.

the dignity of the Peerage, to which his Majesty was pleased to raise them for their Victories, for which their private fortunes were not supposed equal. If Earl St. Vincent obtained the Pension of £2000 a-year in Great Britain, and £1000 a-year in Ireland, for the Victory off Cape St. Vincent, and Viscount Duncan for that off Camperdown, Lord Nelson trusts, that in any comparison, the Victory off the Nile was equal to either of the others; and, therefore, in strict justice, his Pension should have been equal to the other two noble Admirals.

If it is said that the Pensions are not given for the Victories, but to enable the noble Admirals to support their ranks in the Peerage, then Lord Nelson trusts that his wants will be found superior to either of the others ; for Earl St. Vincent, at the time his Pension was granted, had realized not a less sum than £100,000, and Viscount Duncan, not less than £50,000; whereas Lord Nelson, at the time his Pension of £2000 a-year was granted, had not realized £5000 ; therefore, why Lord Nelson should have had £1000 a-year less Pension than either of the two noble Admirals, is unaccountable. This comparison is only made to the Battle off the Nile. Since which time Lord Nelson was, by his Majesty, raised to the dignity of a Viscount, for his services in commanding his Majesty's Fleet, when the great, important, and decisive victory off Copenhagen was obtained, but no Pension was given with this accession of Title.

Nelson and Bronte.

TO LADY COLLIER.

[Autograph, in the possession of Commodore Sir Francis Augustus Collier, K.C.H.]

19, Piccadilly, April 24th, 1803.

Madam,

If Francis's hopes of promotion only arise from Commodore Hood's[5] not having Officers recommended to him, he will very soon find his mistake. The present Admiralty will recommend him more than he can provide for, with those who have served with him, if he was to stay seven years abroad.

---

[5] Sir Samuel Hood. *Vide* vol. iii. p. 90.

However, I can have no objection to write to him in favour of your son; but I must apprise you, that Captain Hood never offered to take even a Midshipman for me. With every good wish for Francis, I am your Ladyship's most obedient servant,

NELSON AND BRONTE.

TO CAPTAIN SUTTON, H.M. SHIP VICTORY.

[Autograph, in the possession of Captain Ives Sutton.]

April 28th, 1803.

My dear Sutton,

A Barge I like much better than a Cutter for my ease, and I have wrote to the Comptroller about the cabin, (it was done to the San Josef.) When the Victory gets to Spithead, and if Lord St. Vincent does not give you the Amphion, which I think would be a hard case, no exertion of mine shall be wanting in getting you a good Ship; and I shall feel real regret if you should suffer for fitting out the Victory, to oblige, my dear Sutton, your much attached,

NELSON AND BRONTE.

TO THE RIGHT HONOURABLE SIR WILLIAM SCOTT.

[Autograph, in the possession of William Chisholm, Esq.]

19, Piccadilly, May 2nd, 1803.

My dear Sir,

You was so kind as to put in your pocket my crude ideas on the situation of our Navy respecting the Seamen.[6] The importance of the subject every one must admit, and woful experience tells us that something must be done on the occasion.

I am sensible that my abilities are unequal to the task; but I should do injustice to my own feelings, and, I think, betray the confidence which has so often been reposed in me, was I not to bring them forward. One good effect must result from it, that in proving them bad, better will be brought forward. The mainspring of all my plan is, that of Certificates fully

6 *Vide* p. 44, *ante.*

descriptive of the persons; the very greatest good must result from it. Names cannot be changed, as the gratuity will be looked forward to, therefore desertion will be less frequent, and easier detected. Pay, Prize-money, &c. &c., could rarely be paid to wrong persons; the Seaman would have his money without the very great difficulty he meets with at present, and many executions would be avoided by the almost impossibility of the fraud of personification being committed, (two, alas! suffered last week for this crime.) If, my dear Sir William, you think, as I do, that something should be attempted at these times to make our Seamen, at the din of War, fly to our Navy, instead of flying from it, I am sure it could not be brought forward by any one so ably as yourself; and if my feeble endeavours in so great a cause can be of the least use, I shall be too happy in offering my assistance.

Will you allow me, any morning that you will appoint, to call upon you at your house to converse on this subject? and I beg you to believe me, my dear Sir, your most obedient and faithful servant,

NELSON AND BRONTE.

Long before this Armament, the Paper was delivered to Mr. Addington and Lord St. Vincent; but I suppose they have not time to attend so much to this subject as, in my opinion, it merits.

TO CAPTAIN SUTTON, H.M. SHIP VICTORY, CHATHAM.

[Autograph, in the possession of Captain Ives Sutton.]

May 6th, 1803.

My dear Sutton,

You are to have the Utrecht's Ship's company, and I have fixed for your having the Amphion; and you know [how] anxious I am to meet your wishes. Should it be War, my things will be sent from London to the Victory immediately. Ever yours most faithfully,

NELSON AND BRONTE.

TO ALEXANDER DAVISON, ESQ., ST. JAMES'S SQUARE.

[Autograph, in the possession of Colonel Davison.]

Private.   9 P.M. [Friday Evening, 6th May, 1803.]
My dear Davison,

I am ordered to prepare for departure. I will see you when I return from Merton. Ever yours most affectionately,

NELSON AND BRONTE.

TO ADMIRAL THE EARL OF ST. VINCENT, K.B.

[Autograph, in the possession of Vice-Admiral Sir William Parker, Bart., G.C.B.]

9 P.M., May 6th, 1803.

My dear Lord,

I have had my tradesmen, and ordered my things. I am going to Merton in the morning, to settle matters there. Government cannot be more anxious for my departure than I am, if a War, to go; and I trust in God to return in Peace. Will you send for George Murray? I shall be ready before other things are prepared. All I ask is not to go to Portsmouth until I carry my orders, and that Amphion is ready with my cot, &c., to start. When I return, I will call at the Admiralty. Ever, my dear Lord, &c.,

NELSON AND BRONTE.

TO ADMIRAL THE EARL OF ST. VINCENT, K.B.

[Autograph, in the possession of Vice-Admiral Sir William Parker, Bart., G.C.B.]

May 8th, 1803.

My dear Lord,

The inclosed is for Captain Hardy to prepare my stock, but not to embark it till farther orders. Ever, my dear Lord, yours most faithfully,   NELSON AND BRONTE.

Captain Hoste[7] delivers this letter. He is just paid off, but very anxious to serve, if a War, and with me; and I should be truly happy to have him.

[7] Afterwards Captain Sir William Hoste, so frequently mentioned, (vide vol. i. p. 355.) On the 22nd of January, 1803, when commanding the Greyhound at Gibraltar, he said, in a letter to his father at Godwick, "I have not received Lord

TO CAPTAIN SUTTON, H. M. SHIP VICTORY.

[Autograph in the possession of Captain Ives Sutton.]

London, May 12th, 1803.

The d——d Pilots have run the Raisonable aground: take great care of scant winds in sands. [?]

My dear Sutton,

I suppose Bell will supply my wine. An application must be made to the Treasury for the quantity of wine and spirits for you as Captain of the Victory; for they are very particular about the allowing it to be brought over. The Vessel is not yet fixed upon by the Admiralty. You had better write to the Treasury for the quantity, and say that you will direct it to be sent in the Vessel with Lord Nelson's. Ever yours, faithfully,

NELSON AND BRONTE.

Write me when you think the Victory can sail from the Nore, that I may send my things to Portsmouth or Sheerness.

TO ADMIRAL THE EARL OF ST. VINCENT, K.B.

[Autograph, in the possession of Vice-Admiral Sir William Parker, Bart., G.C.B.]

Private.   May 12th, 1803.

My dear Lord,

Your mention of the Victory remaining some time in England, so much according with what I am told of Lord Keith's saying that he was to have her for the present—induces me to hope that if the Victory is ready, or as soon as she is, that I

Nelson's letter, but I am happy to hear he is well, and sincerely do I hope he is happy also. I had a Mameluke sword given me in Egypt, which I got mounted, and sent it to him as a present; for so much am I indebted to him, that though now I am independent of his services, I shall never forget that it was through him I am so. Had War broke out, and Lord Nelson been Commander-in-Chief, I should have considered myself particularly fortunate for many reasons, though I confess I am better pleased matters stand as they do, for in case of War, the Lord knows when I should have seen old Godwick." On the 28th of February, Captain Hoste wrote, " Pray give my best respects to Lord Nelson when you see or write to him. I hope most truly, if ever War takes place, I may belong to the Squadron he commands."—*Memoirs of Captain Sir William Hoste*, vol. i. pp. 197, 201. Captain Hoste was not again employed until November 1804, when he was appointed to the Eurydice, and afterwards placed under Lord Nelson's command.

may have her; for all my things, servants, wines, &c. &c.,
are ordered to be sent to her, be where she will—even my
sheep, poultry, hay, corn, and every comfort are ordered to
her. But if Lord Keith, or any other man is to have her, for
a given time, I must un-order all these things. I trust, my
dear Lord, that I can take a French Admiral as well as any of
them, and have as much chance of falling in with one. I
will call this morning for one moment on this subject. Ever,
my dear Lord, yours faithfully,

NELSON AND BRONTE.

TO THE RIGHT HONOURABLE GEORGE ROSE.

[Autograph in the possession of the Right Hon. Sir George Rose, G.C.H.]

May 15th, 1803.

My dear Sir,

I was with Mr. Addington this morning ; and as we conversed on the subject of the extension of my Annuity, and
also on the extraordinary thing of my not receiving the Irish
Pension, as was done for Lords St. Vincent and Duncan, I
said that I had conversed much with you on the subject, and
that I was sure that you thought it was a mistake my not
having it, and that you would tell him so ; therefore, the
favour I have to beg of you is, to tell Mr. Addington, that it
was a mistake giving me less than other Officers; and if Mr.
Addington wants an additional inducement to do me justice,
your· kind friendship may put in, that I got nothing as a
reward for Copenhagen, &c. Your friendship may do much
for me ; and I am ever, my dear Sir, your obliged and faithful,

NELSON AND BRONTE.

TO CAPTAIN SUTTON, H. M. SHIP VICTORY.

[Autograph, in the possession of Captain Ives Sutton. Early in 1803, his Majesty directed that the Knights Elect of the Order of the Bath should be Installed ;
and several Chapters and Conventions of the Knights were held, to arrange the
proceedings, many of which Lord Nelson attended. (*Vide* the Additional MS.,
No. 6237, in the British Museum.) The Installation took place on the 19th of
May, the day on which Lord Nelson sailed for the Mediterranean, and he was represented by Captain Sir William Bolton. His Esquires were, his nephews, Horatio Nelson (afterwards Viscount Trafalgar) and Thomas Bolton (afterwards
second Earl Nelson), and John Tyson, his old Secretary.]

Admiralty, May 17th, 1803.

My dear Sutton,

If you can get my things on board the Victory, pray lose no time: part will be at Portsmouth. I hope by the time you receive this letter, that the waggon will have arrived. Lord Gardner,[8] of course, will give you Boats. If you can get twelve good sheep, some hay, and fowls and corn, it will do no harm, for I may yet go out in the Victory. Ever yours faithfully,

NELSON AND BRONTE.

TO SIR EVAN NEPEAN, BART., ADMIRALTY.

[Original, in the Admiralty. " Monday, 16th May, 1803, A.M. Received my appointment from the Lords Commissioners of the Admiralty, as Commander-in-Chief of his Majesty's Ships and Vessels employed and to be employed on the Mediterranean Station. On the 17th, made several necessary public arrangements previous to my leaving Town; and about 4 A.M. on Wednesday morning, the 18th, set out from London for Portsmouth, where I arrived on that day, about ½ past Noon. Thursday, 19th May, P.M. (*i.e.*, the afternoon of the 18th.) About ½ past 3, hoisted my Flag on board his Majesty's Ship Victory. Saluted Admiral Lord Gardner's Flag on board the Endymion, with thirteen guns, which was returned with an equal number."—Victory's *Log*, in the Nelson Papers.]

Portsmouth, 18th May, 1803.

Sir,

You will be pleased to acquaint the Lords Commissioners of the Admiralty, that I arrived here about one o'clock this afternoon, and have hoisted my Flag on board his Majesty's Ship Victory. Captain Sutton informs me that she will be in every respect ready for sea on Friday morning. I am, &c.

NELSON AND BRONTE.

TO ADMIRAL THE EARL OF ST. VINCENT, K.B.

[Autograph, in the possession of Vice-Admiral Sir William Parker, Bart., G.C.B.]

May 18th, 3 P.M. [1803.]

My dear Lord,

As the Victory will be ready, Captain Sutton tells me, to sail on Friday morning at daylight, (and I am trying to make

---

[8] Admiral Lord Gardner, Commander-in-Chief at Portsmouth.

that to-morrow night,) I have, on many accounts, thought it
best to hoist my Flag in her.   If Admiral Cornwallis wants
her—which it is very improbable according to what I have
heard—but if he does, I shall remove nothing from the
Frigate but my cot: and, therefore, be gone in five minutes.
You may rely, my dear Lord, that nothing shall be left
undone by me, by a vigorous and active exertion of the force
under my command, to bring about a happy Peace.   I am
ever, my dear Lord, your most obliged and faithful,

NELSON AND BRONTE.[9]

TO ADMIRAL THE EARL OF ST. VINCENT, K.B.

[Autograph, in the possession of Vice-Admiral Sir William Parker, Bart., G.C.B.]

My dear Lord,   May 19th, 1803.

This will be presented to you by my nephew, Sir William
Bolton, and now he stands in so near a situation to me, it
must be my anxious wish to get him employed, and with me,
and promoted.   If the Devil stands at the door, the Victory
shall sail to-morrow forenoon.[1]   Keep your health, my dear
Lord, and ever believe me your most obliged and affectionate,

NELSON AND BRONTE.

TO THE RIGHT HONOURABLE ADMIRAL LORD GARDNER,
COMMANDER-IN-CHIEF AT PORTSMOUTH.

[Autograph, in the possession of Mr. Empson.]

My dear Lord,   May 20th, 1803, 3 P.M.

However I felt on reading the order[2] you showed me this
morning, yet I am not of a disposition to complain; for if I

---

[9] In reply to this Letter, Lord St. Vincent wrote to him on the next day—" I
very much lament your detention at Portsmouth, equally unpleasant to you and
injurious to the Public Service . . . . Your Lordship has given so many proofs
of transcendent zeal in the Service of your King and Country, that we have only to
pray for the preservation of your invaluable life, to insure everything that can be
achieved by mortal man."—Tucker's *Memoirs of the Earl of St. Vincent*, vol. ii.
p. 239.

[1] " Portsmouth, 20th May, 1803.   Such was the anxiety of Lord Nelson to embark, that yesterday, to every one who spoke to him of his sailing, he said, ' I cannot before to-morrow, and that's an age.'   This morning, about ten o'clock, his
Lordship went off in a heavy shower of rain, and sailed with a Northerly wind."—
Naval Chronicle, vol. ix. p. 421.

[2] Apparently respecting the Crew of the Victory.

got safe to the Mediterranean, my mind was made up to dismantle some Ship of War, for I believe the honour of the Country ought not to be risked by having the Victory half manned. But the more I felt, the more truly am I sensible of your Lordship's goodness; and thanking you sincerely, and wishing you, my dear Lord, health and happiness, believe me your much obliged and obedient servant,

NELSON AND BRONTE.

TO ADMIRAL THE EARL OF ST. VINCENT, K.B.

[Autograph, in the possession of Vice-Admiral Sir William Parker, Bart., G.C.B.]

My dear Lord,   May 20th, 1803.
You may rely that I shall be off Brest as expeditiously as possible, and there wait for Admiral Cornwallis. I am mad at losing a moment of this wind, but I cannot help myself. She is to be paid at eight o'clock, and I shall be on board at nine. Ever, my dear Lord, yours most faithfully,

NELSON AND BRONTE.

Many thanks for your kind letter by the Post. May every blessing attend you, and may we *soon* meet in *Peace*.

TO SIR EVAN NEPEAN, BART., ADMIRALTY.

[Original, in the Admiralty. "Friday, 20th May, A.M. About 10, the Right Hon. Lord Viscount Nelson, Captain George Murray, Captain of the Fleet, and Lieutenant Pearce, Signal Officer, &c., came on board. Saturday, 21st (*i. e.*, the afternoon of the 20th.) Unmoored Ship, and weighed. Made sail out of Spithead, through St. Helens, when H. M. Ship Amphion joined, and proceeded to sea in company with us."—Victory's *Log*. On board the Victory were embarked, Mr. Hugh Elliot, who had been appointed Minister at Naples, the brother, and Captain (now Rear-Admiral) the Honourable George Elliot, the son of Lord Minto, who was permitted to serve with Lord Nelson as a Volunteer.

On the 18th of May, 1803, Lord Nelson received the following Orders from the Admiralty:—

" Whereas by our Commission, bearing date the 16th instant, we have appointed your Lordship Commander-in-Chief of his Majesty's Ships and Vessels employed and to be employed in the Mediterranean; you are hereby required and directed to proceed forthwith to Portsmouth, and, hoisting your Flag on board his Majesty's Ship Amphion, make the best of your way to the Island of Malta, where you may expect to find Rear-Admiral Sir Richard Bickerton; and on meeting the Rear-Admiral, take him and the Ships and Vessels there, as well as in the Mediterranean, under your command. On your Lordship's arrival at Malta, you are to lose no time in concerting with Sir Alexander Ball, his Majesty's Commissioner at that Island, such arrangements as may be necessary with a view to the protection and security of that Island ; you are then to proceed off Toulon, with such part of the Squadron under your command as you may judge to be adequate to the service, and take such a position as may, in your Lordship's opinion, be most proper for enabling you to take, sink, burn, or otherwise destroy, any Ships or Vessels belonging to France, or the Citizens of that Republic, and also for detaining and sending into Port any Ships or Vessels belonging to the Batavian Republic, or the Citizens thereof, that you may happen to fall in with. Your Lordship is to be very attentive to the proceedings of the French at Genoa, Leghorn, and other Ports on that side of Italy, for the purpose of gaining the most early information of any armaments that may be forming there, either with a view to an attack upon Egypt, or any other part of the Turkish Dominions, or against the Kingdoms of Naples and Sicily, or the Islands of Corfu ; and in the event of your having reason to believe that any such plan shall be in contemplation, your Lordship is to exert your best endeavours to counteract it, and to take, sink, burn, or destroy any Ships or Vessels which may be so employed ; as well as to afford to the Sublime Porte and his Sicilian Majesty and their subjects, any protection or assistance which may be in your power, consistently with a due attention to the other important objects entrusted to your care.

" As it is highly important that your Lordship should be watchful of the conduct of the Court of Spain in the present moment, you are to direct your attention to the Naval preparations that may be making in the several Ports of that Kingdom in the Mediterranean, as also at Cadiz, and to take every practicable means of obtaining, from time to time, all the intelligence you may be able to collect on that subject. Your Lordship is to take care that no interruption be offered by any of the Ships or Vessels under your command to any Spanish Ships of War or Trade, while they conduct themselves in a manner becoming a Neutral Nation ; but, at the same time, your Lordship is to understand, that however desirable it may be to avoid any measure of hostility against that Country, you are not to suffer any Squadron of Spanish Ships of War to enter a French Port, or to form a junction with any Squadron, or Ships or Vessels of that, or the Batavian Republic. Your Lordship is also to be careful not to infringe the Neutrality of other Powers, so long as their conduct towards his Majesty and the commerce of his Subjects shall be actuated by a similar principle. And whereas there is reason to believe that some of the French Line of Battle Ships which have recently been employed in conveying Troops to the French West India Islands may, on their return to Europe, attempt to proceed to the Ports in the Mediterranean ; your Lordship is to detach such part of the Squadron under your command as you can spare from other more important services, as soon as possible, to Gibraltar, with orders to the Senior Officer of such Detachment, after obtaining the best information he may be able to collect at that place, to take such a position as he may conceive to be most convenient, with a view to the intercepting the said Ships, and any others belonging to the French or Batavian Republics, which may attempt to pass or repass the Straits ; and your Lordship is to apprise the Senior Officer, from time to time, of your movements, to the end that no delay that can be prevented may take place in the furnishing your Lordship with any orders or instructions which we may have occasion to send you, for the further regulation of your conduct ; and, finally, you are to transmit to our Secretary, for our information, frequent accounts of your proceedings, and every intelligence you may have obtained, proper for our knowledge. Given under our hands, the 18th May 1803,—St. Vincent, Ph. Stephens, T. Troubridge."

On the 15th of May, Lord Nelson was directed by the Admiralty " to detain and bring into Port all Ships and Vessels belonging to the Batavian Republic, there to remain until his Majesty's further pleasure shall be signified respecting them ;" giving " directions to the Officers to whom the charge of such Ships or Vessels may be entrusted, to take all possible care that no embezzlement of any kind whatever do take place, as they will answer the contrary at their peril."

On the 17th of May, Lord Nelson was informed that the King had directed Letters of Marque and Reprisals to be issued against the Ships and Vessels of the French Republic ; and he was directed to use his " best endeavours to seize or destroy all Ships and Vessels belonging to the French Republic, or to any persons being Citizens of the said Republic, or inhabiting within any of the Territories thereof, you may be able to fall in with accordingly, and to give the like directions to all the Captains and Commanders of his Majesty's Ships and Vessels under your command."—*Originals*, in the possession of the Right Hon. John Wilson Croker.]

Sir,   Victory, at Spithead, 20th May, 1803.

I was honoured with your letter, sent by a Messenger at half-past four yesterday, at half-past one this morning; and I beg leave to assure you that I hold it impossible for any Officer, under such orders as their Lordships' to me, to designedly miss Admiral Cornwallis off Brest. Their Lordships may rely on my strict obedience to their orders, and I rely with confidence on their liberal constructions of my actions. The Victory shall sail the moment she is paid. I have the honour to be, &c.   NELSON AND BRONTE.

TO SIR EVAN NEPEAN, BART., ADMIRALTY.

[Original, in the Admiralty.]

Sir,   Victory, off the Start, 21st May, 1803.

You will please to acquaint the Lords Commissioners of the Admiralty, that I have this morning detained a Dutch Merchant Ship from Surinam, laden with cocoa, coffee, and sugar, and sent her into Plymouth. I am, Sir, &c.

NELSON AND BRONTE.

TO THE CAPTAIN OF ANY OF HIS MAJESTY'S SHIPS WHICH THE AMPHION MAY MEET AT SEA, OR IN CAWSAND BAY.

[Letter-Book.]

Sir,   Victory, off the Start, 21st May, 1803.

It is my directions that you take charge of the Dutch Ship under the charge of Captain Hardy, and see her safe into

Plymouth: or if this letter should be delivered to any Ship in Cawsand Bay, it is my directions that the Senior Officer there take charge of her; and it is my positive directions that the Amphion is not detained one moment. Great care is to be taken that none of her cargo is embezzled, [for,] as the Admiralty order expresses, you will answer it at your peril. I am, Sir, &c.

NELSON AND BRONTE.

TO ADMIRAL THE EARL OF ST. VINCENT, K.B.

[Autograph, in the possession of Vice-Admiral Sir William Parker, Bart., G.C.B. " Monday, 23rd (*i. e.*, Tuesday, 22nd, P.M.)   At 5, Ushant Light House, N.E. b E. seven miles. Standing off and on off Ushant. Joined H.M. Ships Sirius and Amphion." "Tuesday, 24th May (*i. e*, 23rd May, P.M.)   At 4, saw two strange Sail, S.E. b E., which proved to be H.M. Ships Naiad and Hazard; hove to; at 7-40, out Boats. The Admiral shifted his Flag to the Amphion. At 7-50, Lord Nelson came on board the Amphion, and hoisted his Flag, and made sail. At 10, lost sight of the Squadron."—*Log.*]

My dear Lord,   May 22nd, 1803, Noon, close to Ushant.

I am looking out for Cornwallis. I think we must see him before one, if he is this side the Saints, and I hope that he will not want the Victory. I am very comfortably placed here. I forgot to mention Mr. Barrillier to you. If Sir John Henslow[3] goes off, could he not be more generally usefully employed than at Milford? I have cleared the Victory for to carry a raft fifty feet by fourteen. It can be done with ease, and a passage can be had in the place where the double hammocks are stowed. I hope one will be built and tried: answer the purpose intended with my head.

3 P.M.—We are inside Ushant, but where is Cornwallis? However, I shall block up Brest till he comes to liberate me.

½ past 5.—In sight of Saint Matthew's. Murray says, if the Fleet was off Brest, that they must be seen. Blows strong at North. What a wind for carrying us to Portugal.

6 P.M.—Just got hold of the Sirius. Captain Prowse[4] tells me, that the Admiral is cruizing W.N.W. from the Saints' Bridge twenty leagues. I have demonstrated the Victory off Brest, and am now going to seek the Admiral in the ocean.

[3] Surveyor of the Navy: he died, aged eighty-six, in September, 1815.

[4] Captain William Prowse: he died a Rear-Admiral, and a Companion of the Bath, in March 1826.

May 23rd.—You will, by my letter to the Admiralty, see how much ground we have traversed in search, and if I do not find him by six o'clock, if the weather will allow me [to] shift myself into the Amphion, and leave the Victory to look for Cornwallis. I am clear, by his conduct, that there can be nothing in Brest to demand his attention. It blows very strong, and a heavy sea. I doubt the possibility of my getting out of the Ship, whether I meet him or not.

6 P.M.—Captain Neve[5] is on board. He supposes the Admiral ten leagues off Ushant: therefore there is no looking for him, and I am embarking in the Amphion. God bless you, and ever believe me yours most faithfully,

NELSON AND BRONTE.

TO LADY HAMILTON.

[Extract from the " Letters of Lord Nelson to Lady Hamilton," vol. i. p. 108.]

May 22nd, [1803.]   Eight o'clock in the Morning.

My dearest Emma,

We are now in sight of Ushant, and shall see Admiral Cornwallis in an hour. I am not in a little fret, on the idea that he may keep the Victory, and turn us all into the Amphion. It will make it truly uncomfortable; but I cannot help myself. We are very comfortable. Mr. Elliot is happy, has quite recovered his spirits : he was very low at Portsmouth. George Elliot is very well; say so to Lord Minto. Murray, Sutton—in short, every body in the Ship, seems happy ; and, if we should fall in with a French Man-of-War, I have no fears but they will do as we used to do. Hardy is gone into Plymouth, to see our Dutchman safe. I think she will turn out a good Prize. Gaetano[6] desires his duty to Miledi! He is a good man, and, I dare say, will come back; for I think it cannot be a long War : just enough to make me independent in pecuniary matters. If the wind stands, on Tuesday we shall be on the Coast of Portugal; and, before next Sunday, in the Mediterranean. To Mrs. Cadogan say every kind thing ; to good Mrs. Nelson, the Doctor, &c. &c. If you like,

------

[5] Captain Robert Jenner Neve, of the Hazard : he was Posted in 1806, and died about 1815.

[6] His Steward.

you may tell him about the entailing of the Pension : but perhaps he will be so much taken up with Canterbury,[7] that it will do for some dull evening at Hilborough.

I shall now stop till I have been on board the Admiral. . . . . I shall direct to Merton, after June 1st. Therefore, as you change, make Davison take a direction to Nepean ; but I would not trouble him with too many directions, for fear of embroil.

May 23rd.

We were close in with Brest yesterday, and found by a Frigate that Admiral Cornwallis had a Rendezvous at sea. Thither we went ; but to this hour cannot find him. It blows strong. What a wind we are losing! If I cannot find the Admiral by six o'clock, we must all go into the Amphion, and leave the Victory, to my great mortification. So much for the wisdom of my superiors. I keep my letter open to the last, for I still hope ; as, I am sure, there is no good reason for my not going out in the Victory. I am just embarking in the Amphion—cannot find Admiral Cornwallis. May God in Heaven bless you, prays your most sincere

NELSON AND BRONTE.

Stephens's publication[8] I should like to have. I have left my silver seal ; at least, I cannot find it.

TO SIR EVAN NEPEAN, BART., ADMIRALTY.

[Original, in the Admiralty.]

Sir,   Victory, at Sea, 23rd May, 1803, ½ past 6 o'clock P.M.

I send you the track and proceedings of the Victory since she rounded Ushant yesterday afternoon. It is perfectly certain that not even a Frigate was inside of us ; nor could Admiral Cornwallis have made inside Ushant his Station from Wednesday last, for on that day the Sirius, Captain Prowse, was inside Ushant, and not finding Admiral Cornwallis returned to Plymouth to know how to proceed, when he received from Admiral Dacres the Rendezvous of the Admiral, W.N.W. of

---

[7] Dr. Nelson was gazetted as a Prebendary of Canterbury, on the 24th of May, 1803.

[8] "History of the Wars of the French Revolution," 2 vols. 4to, 1803. *Vide* p. 43, *ante*, and vol. iii. p. 521.

the Saint's Bridge, twenty leagues, latitude 48° 04″, longitude 6° 35″ W. You will see, by our track, that at half-past six o'clock this morning we were on the Rendezvous, with the two Frigates, they looking out on different bearings all night. At seven saw a Dogger, which the Sirius spoke; at eight, saw two other Sail bearing S.S.E., spoke a Brig from Bordeaux; from this time till noon steering E.S.E., which makes an East course good, the wind being at N.N.E. blowing strong. Supposing Admiral Cornwallis to have been yesterday noon on his Rendezvous, he must have drifted to the Southward; therefore, allowing for a reasonable drift, he must be as far to the Southward as ourselves at noon—viz., 47° 41″. I think, with this wind, it is impossible he could keep his head to the Westward, he would certainly make Southing with his Westing; therefore I think he must be inshore, unless, for some reason totally beyond my guess, he has judged it proper to avoid the French Coast.

In this case, I have my choice to take the Victory or Frigate. I am decidedly of opinion that I ought, under all the circumstances of the case, to proceed in the Victory; for either Admiral Cornwallis has found the French Fleet ready for sea so insignificant, that it was not an object to block up Brest very close, in which case he could not want a First-rate, which would remove the objection of the Admiralty to my taking the Victory; or, the Admiral has judged it proper to go off the Coast, in which case I do not think I ought to leave the Victory. Yet, as I feel from your Letter of the 19th May, ' on no account to pass Admiral Cornwallis, so as to run any chance of his being deprived of the services of the Victory, if he should judge it necessary to detain her,' I shall, therefore, contrary to my judgment, leave the Victory to look out for one week for Admiral Cornwallis; and if Captain Sutton does not fall in with him, to return to Plymouth for further orders. I am proceeding in the Amphion, in the execution of the important instructions to me. I am, Sir, &c.

NELSON AND BRONTE.

P.S.—Enclosed is Captain Murray's report, for their Lordships' information.

TO ADMIRAL THE HONOURABLE WILLIAM CORNWALLIS, COMMANDER-IN-CHIEF.

[Letter-Book.]

Victory, at Sea, 23rd May, 1803, ½ past 6 o'clock P.M.

Sir,

I have the honour to transmit you the directions of the Admiralty for my joining you off Brest; but as I have not been so fortunate as to meet you, and the whole business of the Mediterranean waiting my arrival, I have judged it proper to shift my Flag to the Amphion, and to proceed in her. If you have no commands for the Victory, I trust you will order her to join me without a moment's loss of time. I am, Sir, with great regard, your obedient humble servant,

NELSON AND BRONTE.

TO ADMIRAL HIS ROYAL HIGHNESS THE DUKE OF CLARENCE.

[From Clarke and M'Arthur, vol. ii. p. 313.]

Off Cape Finisterre, 26th May, 1803.

Your Royal Highness will have heard that I sailed in the Victory to join Admiral Cornwallis off Brest; but as I could not find him on his Rendezvous, or near Brest, and having a fair wind, I determined on embarking in the Amphion, and proceeding to the Mediterranean, leaving the Victory to follow, if Admiral Cornwallis did not want her assistance. I now wish I had not persevered so long in looking for him, for I have lost the fair wind. I never could fancy that our assistance would be wanted.

NELSON AND BRONTE.

TO THE RESPECTIVE CAPTAINS AND COMMANDERS OF HIS MAJESTY'S SHIPS AND VESSELS ON THE MEDITERRANEAN STATION.

[Order-Book.]

Amphion, off Cape Finisterre, 30th May, 1803.

The Lords Commissioners of the Admiralty having acquainted me in consequence of a Letter of the 17th instant, from the Right Hon. Lord Hobart, one of His Majesty's

Principal Secretaries of State, that His Majesty had been pleased to order Letters of Marque and Reprisals, to be issued against the Ships and Vessels of the French Republic, You are therefore hereby required and directed to use your best endeavours to seize or destroy all Ships and Vessels belonging to the French Republic, or to any persons being Citizens of the said Republic, or inhabiting within any of the Territories thereof, you may be able to fall in with, accordingly.

NELSON AND BRONTE.

TO THE RESPECTIVE CAPTAINS AND COMMANDERS OF HIS MAJESTY'S SHIPS AND VESSELS ON THE MEDITERRANEAN STATION.

[Order-Book.]

Amphion, off Cape Finisterre, 30th May, 1803.

The Lords Commissioners of the Admiralty having acquainted me, in consequence of a letter of the 15th instant, from the Right Hon. Lord Hobart, one of His Majesty's Principal Secretaries of State, that from the measures lately adopted by the French Government, there is too much reason to apprehend that the Batavian Republic will be forced to take part with the French in hostility against this Country, and at the same time signified His Majesty's pleasure that directions should be given for detaining and bringing into Port all Ships and Vessels belonging to the Batavian Republic, You are therefore hereby required and directed, on falling in with any Ships or Vessels of the said Republic, to detain and bring them into Port, there to remain until His Majesty's farther pleasure shall be signified respecting them. In the event of your detaining any Ship or Vessel of the above description, it is the orders of the Lords Commissioners of the Admiralty, that the most positive directions are given to the Officers to whom the charge of such Ships or Vessels may be entrusted, to take all possible care that no embezzlement of any kind whatever do take place, as they will answer the contrary at their peril.

NELSON AND BRONTE.

TO THE RESPECTIVE CAPTAINS AND COMMANDERS OF HIS MAJESTY'S SHIPS AND VESSELS ON THE MEDITERRANEAN STATION.

[Order-Book.]

Amphion, off Cape Finisterre, 30th May, 1803.

Pursuant to instructions from the Lords Commissioners of the Admiralty, you are hereby required and directed on no account whatever to interrupt any Spanish Ships or Vessels of War which you may fall in with, nor to molest the Trade of his Catholic Majesty. It is also their Lordships' particular direction that you do not infringe on the Neutrality of any Power in Amity with Great Britain.

NELSON AND BRONTE.

TO ADMIRAL THE RIGHT HONOURABLE LORD RADSTOCK.

[Autograph, in the possession of Rear-Admiral Lord Radstock, C.B.]

My dear Lord,　　　　　　Off Lisbon, June 2nd, 1803.

You may rely that I shall not omit anything in my power to be useful to your son:[8] when he has served his time he shall come directly into the Victory. You had, my dear Lord, only to tell me where he was placed, to be sure of my attention; and if he is not a good young man, I am sure he will not be like his Father. We have had a long passage, having had to go off Brest, and since which time foul winds. With every kind wish, believe me, my dear Lord, ever your most obliged and attached,　　　　　　NELSON AND BRONTE.

TO ADMIRAL HIS ROYAL HIGHNESS THE DUKE OF CLARENCE.

[From Clarke and M'Arthur, vol. ii. p. 313. " Saturday, 4th June, (i. e., Friday, 3rd June, P.M.,) at 6·30, boarded a French Brig under French colours ; took possession. At 9·30, came to, in Gibraltar Bay."—Amphion's Log.]

June 3rd, 1803.

Having buffeted with a foul wind and nasty sea, we are now entering the Straits, and I hope to anchor at Gibraltar before dark. As they knew nothing of the War being abso-

---

[8] The Honourable George Granville Waldegrave, now Rear-Admiral Lord Radstock, C.B.

lutely begun here, I am much hurried, being very anxious to
join the Fleet as soon as possible ; this must apologize for the
shortness of my letter.   Buonaparte's brother Jerome passed
from Martinique a few days ago in a Ship of the Line.   I
am, &c.

NELSON AND BRONTE.

TO EDWARD POWNALL, ESQ., NAVAL STORE-KEEPER AT
GIBRALTAR.

[Order-Book.]

Amphion, in Gibraltar Bay, 3rd June, 1803.

Whereas it is essentially necessary for the good of his
Majesty's Service, that the most strict attention is paid to the
preservation and issue of every description of Naval Stores
committed to your charge ; You are therefore hereby required
and directed to pay due attention to the preservation of the
Stores committed to your charge accordingly ; and on no account or consideration whatever, to supply any of his Majesty's
Ships or Vessels under my command with Naval Stores, without being furnished with the Boatswain's and Carpenter's
Supplies, Expenses, and Remains, by the Commander of the
Ship or Vessel making such demand.   You are then only to
complete their remains to four months, agreeable to the establishment.   It is also my particular directions that you do
not on any account supply those of his Majesty's Ships or
Vessels which may arrive from England with Stores of any
kind, unless it shall be to replace articles which (from accidents
in bad weather) may have been rendered unserviceable on the
passage.

NELSON AND BRONTE.

TO CAPTAIN SUTTON, H.M. SHIP VICTORY.

[Autograph, in the possession of Captain Ives Sutton.]

My dear Sutton,   Gibraltar, June 4th, 1803.

You will not anchor here, but proceed and join me as expeditiously as possible on the Rendezvous : if no place is
mentioned, of course Malta.   I recommend making the South
end of Sardinia and also Maretimo in Sicily—this Island is

bold, too, inside or out.　Mr. Atkinson[9] will keep you clear of the Esquerques, but after you are past Maretimo, do not keep too near Sicily for the shoals lie out five or six miles.　Hoping for a quick sight of you, believe me, dear Sutton, yours most sincerely,

NELSON AND BRONTE.

Hardy has made your fortune.[1]

TO THE RIGHT HONOURABLE HENRY ADDINGTON.

[Autograph, in the Sidmouth Papers.]

Amphion, Gibraltar, June 4th, 1803.

My dear Sir,

We arrived here in the night, and as the news of actual War had not reached this place, I am anxious to get to the Fleet.　Mr. Elliot has been so good as to send a Messenger to Madrid to get information respecting Spain, but although our Consul at Cadiz expects that there must be a War with Spain, yet I do not find that any particular activity prevails in their Naval Arsenal at Cadiz.　They have just got two rich Ships from Manilla.　You may rely on my activity in getting off Toulon, when all will go on smoothly.　Buonaparte's brother Jerome passed from Martinique a few days ago in a Ship of the Line.　It would have been pleasant to have laid a little salt on his tail, but I hope to do it yet.　Believe me ever, my dear Sir, your most attached and faithful friend,

NELSON AND BRONTE.

TO SIR EVAN NEPEAN, BART., ADMIRALTY.

[Original, in the Admiralty.]

Amphion, in Gibraltar Bay, 4th June, 1803.

Sir,

You will please to acquaint the Lords Commissioners of the Admiralty of my arrival here last night, and that I have directed the Tourterelle to proceed, according to the orders her Commander has received from Sir Richard Bickerton, to

---

[9] Master of the Victory.
[1] Alluding, jocularly, to the capture of the French Brig.

Cork, and from thence to England, taking under his protection the Abundance Store-ship, and the Trade bound his way. And, as I have received information that the Enemy have Cruizers off Cape Trafalgar, I have left orders for the Resistance, on her arrival here from Lisbon, to proceed with the Tourterelle and convoy her twenty or twenty-five leagues to the Westward of Cadiz, or the Strait's Mouth—calling for the Trade from Cadiz, should he be informed by the Consul that there are any there. After executing these orders, to return and cruize between Cape Trafalgar and Cape Spartel, occasionally calling at Gibraltar for further orders. You will farther inform their Lordships, that I am getting under weigh in the Amphion to proceed to Malta, and shall take the Maidstone with me—having left the Bittern to cruize between Europa Point and Ceuta, to keep the communication open with the Coast of Barbary. I am, Sir, &c.

NELSON AND BRONTE.

TO THE RESPECTIVE OFFICERS OF GIBRALTAR YARD.

[Order-Book.]

Amphion, in Gibraltar Bay, 4th June, 1803.

You are hereby required and directed to put the Gun and Flat-bottomed Boats in a state of service, as well as to fit the Guerrier Sheer-hulk for the reception of thirty or forty Officers, and three hundred common men ; and for the better expediting the above services, you are to enter twelve Shipwrights on the Garrison establishment till completed.

NELSON AND BRONTE.

TO CAPTAIN THE HONOURABLE PHILIP WODEHOUSE,[2] H.M. SHIP RESISTANCE.

[Order-Book.]

Amphion, in Gibraltar Bay, 4th June, 1803.

Having directed Captain Simpson[3] of the Tourterelle to follow the order of Rear-Admiral Sir Richard Bickerton of

[2] Vide vol. iv. p. 504.
[3] The present Captain John Simpson, who was posted in December 1809.

the 4th ultimo, and, in addition, to take the Abundance Store-
ship, together with such Trade as may be bound from hence
to the United Kingdom, You are hereby required and directed
to proceed with his Majesty's Ship under your command,
and accompany the Tourterelle and her Convoy, from twenty
to twenty-five leagues to the Westward of Cadiz, or the
Straits' Mouth. Having so done, return, and cruize between
Cape Trafalgar and Cape Spartel, for the protection of the
Trade, and annoyance of the Enemy, calling occasionally at
Gibraltar, which is recommended to be done, when the wind
is to the Eastward, that you may return again to your station,
unless you should find orders there to the contrary, and to
afford every assistance required by his Excellency Lieutenant-
General Sir Thomas Trigge. Having directed the Bittern
to cruise for the purpose of keeping the communication open
between Gibraltar and the Coast of Barbary, you are at
liberty to give her Commander such directions as you may
find necessary for the more effectual execution of this service.
In case you should receive information of importance, necessary for me to know, you will either proceed yourself, or send
the Bittern, to join me at Malta, or to the Rendezvous I may
hereafter send you. In the event of not receiving such
Rendezvous, you are to make the South end of Sardinia, and
the Island of Maretimo, in Sicily, where it is probable you
may fall in with some Cruizer, which will give you information where I am.

NELSON AND BRONTE.

TO HIS EXCELLENCY SIR JOHN ACTON, BART.

[From a Copy, in the possession of Vice-Admiral Sir William Parker, Bart.,
G.C.B. "Sunday, 5th June (*i. e.* Saturday, 4th, P.M.) At 4, weighed and made
sail, in company with H.M. Ships Maidstone and Bittern. At 5, saw a strange
Frigate under French colours ; gave chace and cleared for action: it proved to be
the Tourterelle. A.M. (Sunday, 5th June,) at 6·30, brought to the Vrow Agneta,
Dutch Brig; took possession of her, and made sail. At 10·30, brought to the
Silvain, French Brig, took possession of her, and sent them both to Malta."]

June 10th, 1803.

My dear Sir John,
  Writing as I do, it is impossible that I can know anything
of the situation of the Kingdom of the Two Sicilies, and par-

ticularly that of Naples, but I can readily conceive that it
must be very unpleasantly situated; for if it goes too far,
either on one side or the other, unpleasant circumstances may
arise.   Indeed, there is a chain of difficulties; but, without
a compliment, I know nobody at this trying moment so able
to steer the Vessel of State, for the benefit of our good Sovereigns, as your Excellency.   As I bring Mr. Elliot with me,
it is not for me to enter very deeply into Political subjects, yet it is right, as far as the purport of my orders go,
to touch upon them.   The words of my orders are—viz.,
'Your Lordship is to be very attentive in observing if the
French have any design of attacking the Kingdoms of Naples
or Sicily, and your Lordship is to exert yourself to counteract
it, and to take, sink, burn, or destroy any Ships or Vessels
which may be so employed, and to afford to his Sicilian
Majesty, and his Subjects, all the protection and assistance
which may be in your power, consistently with a due attention
to the other important objects intrusted to your care.'   No
orders, my dear Sir John, can be clearer or fuller, and I do
assure you that the last words of Mr. Addington to me were,
'Take every possible care of their Sicilian Majesties, for the
King considers them as the most faithful Allies that he has
ever had;' and there is not in the Ministry a difference of
opinion on this point, as Mr. Elliot will more fully explain
than it would be proper for me to do, as he is going to you;
but of him, your Excellency may be assured that he goes to
you with the kindest and best wishes for the welfare of the
Two Sicilies, and the honour of their Majesties.   You will
readily believe how desirous I am to pay my duty to the King,
Queen, and the Royal Family, and I am using force upon
myself to keep away; for I think it likely, was I to fly to
Naples, which I am so much inclined to do, that the French
might turn it to some plea against those good Sovereigns:
but, should the time come when your Excellency might wish
to talk with me, or think it right for me to pay my respects, I
shall attend your summons with the greatest pleasure.   This
being a letter of business, I shall conclude with assuring you
that I am ever devoted, both by duty and inclination, to the
service of their Sicilian Majesties, and, my dear Sir John,
your Excellency's most obliged and faithful friend,

NELSON AND BRONTE.

TO HIS EXCELLENCY SIR JOHN ACTON, BART.

[From a Copy, in the possession of Vice-Admiral Sir William Parker, Bart., G.C.B.]

June 10th, 1803.

My dear Sir John,

Although I am sure it is totally unnecessary for me to introduce the brother of Lord Minto to your Excellency, yet Mr. Elliot has desired me to do it, that you may be assured his sentiments are precisely the same as his noble brother's, for the general safety of all Italy, and particularly for that of the Two Sicilies. Mr. Elliot and myself both concur on the advantages which must accrue, could the Kingdoms of Naples and Sicily be kept perfectly Neutral, but we doubt of the French allowing the advantage of such a Neutrality; and, therefore, although it may not be in the power of Great Britain to keep the French Troops out of the Kingdom of Naples, yet that [it] is perfectly easy for us to keep them out of Sicily, which if they were once to get a footing in, it would be totally lost for ever. Therefore we must naturally look on this object, and never allow the possibility of such an event happening, so ruinous to their Majesties, and disadvantageous to Great Britain. I am confident that you will, my dear Sir John, see these objects in the same point of view as we do, and concur with Mr. Elliot on what may be most advantageous to both our Countries. Feeling all the inclination as I used to do, to be serviceable to their Sicilian Majesties, I shall only assure you, my dear Sir John, that I wish to prove myself your most sincerely attached friend,

NELSON AND BRONTE.

TO HIS SACRED MAJESTY THE KING OF THE TWO SICILIES.

[From a Copy in the Sidmouth Papers.]

June 10th, 1803.

Sire,

I am confident that your Majesty will readily believe how desirous I must be to pay my humble duty at Naples; but consideration for the situation of your Majesty, and your Kingdom of Naples at this moment prevents me from following my inclinations, as I have fully set forth in my letter to General Acton; but I beg leave to assure your Majesty, that one great reason for my being appointed Commander-in-Chief of the British Fleet in the Mediterranean, was my known attachment to your Majesty, the Queen, and Royal Family, and my ardent wish for maintaining the true honour of your Majesty, and the safety and welfare of your Kingdoms.

The sentiments of his Britannic Majesty will be much better expressed by his Representative, Mr. Elliot, than I could possibly find words for, but your Majesty's good faith and attachment to the British Nation are known and acknowledged by the whole Nation.

It only remains for me to apologize for addressing a letter to your Majesty; but, from your former goodness to me, I cannot resist assuring your Majesty how devotedly I am your most grateful, attached, and faithful servant,

NELSON AND BRONTE.

TO HER SACRED MAJESTY THE QUEEN OF THE TWO SICILIES.

[From a Copy in the Sidmouth Papers.]

June 10th, 1803.

Madam,

Your Majesty's never-failing goodness and condescension toward me, makes me take the liberty of addressing a letter to you by Mr. Elliot, the brother of Lord Minto; and I am confident that your Majesty will find him, both from his duty and inclination, a most firm friend to the true honour of the King, your Majesty, and Royal Family.[7]

[7] A translation of this letter in the Elliot Papers, contains the following passages not in the English copy. After the words "Royal Family,—" Je ne parlerai pas de moi, je n'ai pas besoin de renouveller mes protestations, je suis connu et je ne saurois changer." Before the paragraph beginning, "I saw Prince Castelcicala," &c.,—"J'ai quitté Lady Hamilton le 18 Mai, et si attachée à votre Majesté qu'elle sacrifieroit volontiers sa propre existence pour conserver la votre. Votre Majesté n'a jamais eu une amie plus sincère, plus attachée, et plus vraie que votre chère Emma. Vous apprendrez avec chagrin que le bon Chevalier Hamilton ne l'a pas autant avantagé du côté de sa fortune, que l'état de ses affaires le lui aurait permis. Il a legué ses biens à ses parens, mais elle fera toujours honneur à sa memoire, quoique la plûpart de ses amis blame ses dernieres dispositions." In Lord Nelson's letter to Lady Hamilton, written early in July, he quotes (in English) this paragraph in his letter to the Queen of Naples. *Vide* p. 118, *post*.

I do not go to Naples at present, for reasons which I have wrote to General Acton, but shall be truly happy to pay my humble duty when it may be judged more convenient than at this moment. I saw Prince Castelcicala[8] the evening before I set off. He is most zealously attached to the service of his good Sovereign; but I trust, at this moment, he sees things in a darker point of view than the event will justify. With the most fervent prayers for the health of your Majesty and the Royal Family, be assured that I am your most devoted, humble servant, NELSON AND BRONTE.

TO HIS EXCELLENCY MR. JACKSON, MINISTER AT TURIN.

[From Clarke and M'Arthur, vol. ii. p. 314.]

[About 10th June, 1803.]

As far as I can, consistently with my duty to our own King, I will take care that no unpleasant circumstances shall happen to cause the French to be insolent to those good Sovereigns. You, Sir, will be so good as to tell me your opinion of the situation of Sardinia. If the King wished it, and the people would support their Sovereign, I should feel bound to afford them not only every assistance in my power, but to recommend a body of Troops, say 3000, to aid so just a cause. My movements, you know, must materially depend on the sentiments and exertions of other Powers: my Naval line of duty is perfectly simple; but I should feel happy in a more extended sense of duty to aid and assist his Majesty's faithful Allies. I am, &c., NELSON AND BRONTE.

TO CAPTAIN RICHARD HUSSEY MOUBRAY, H. M. SHIP MAIDSTONE.[9]

[Order-Book. " Saturday, 11th June. At 8, brought to, and hoisted out the Boats; Hugh Elliot, Ambassador, left the Ship, and went on board the Maidstone."
—*Amphion's Log*.]

Amphion, at Sea, 11th June, 1803.

You are hereby required and directed to receive on board his Majesty's Ship under your command, his Excellency

---

[8] The Neapolitan Minister in London.

[9] Afterwards Vice-Admiral Sir Richard Hussey Hussey, G.C.M.G., K.C.B.: he died on the 6th of November 1842.

Hugh Elliot, Esquire, his Majesty's Envoy Extraordinary and Minister Plenipotentiary, (together with his *suite,*) and proceed with him to Naples, with the utmost possible dispatch, affording his Excellency every necessary accommodation during the passage. After having landed him and his suite at the above-mentioned place, you are to wait for his Excellency's dispatches; but on no account to remain at Naples longer than seven days from the time of your arrival. You are then to return and join me on the Rendezvous herewith transmitted, without a moment's loss of time; unless from unforeseen circumstances Mr. Elliot should tell you it is necessary to proceed direct to Malta.

NELSON AND BRONTE.

TO HIS EXCELLENCY WILLIAM DRUMMOND, ESQ.

[Autograph Draft, in the possession of the Reverend Henry Girdlestone.]

[About 11th June, 1803.]

Sir,

I beg leave to inform your Excellency of my arrival in the Mediterranean, as Commander-in-Chief of his Majesty's Fleet in these seas, and I think it also proper to inform your Excellency, that one article of my instructions is as follows—viz., ' Your Lordship is to be very attentive to the proceedings of the French in Italy, in case they should have in view any attack upon Egypt, or any other part of the Turkish Dominions.'

Your Excellency will have the goodness to assure the Sublime Porte of my readiness to contribute all in my power to the prosperity of the Ottoman Empire; and to preserve it from the invasion of an ambitious and restless Government, and I have only to be informed how I can render them most service, to make that a cheerful part of my duty.

I have taken the liberty of writing to the Grand Vizir and Capitan Pasha, to assure them of the same, which, considering my personal close connexion with the Sublime Porte, I hope your Excellency will not disapprove of. I should be glad to be informed of the state of Albania—whether the Government at Constantinople thinks there is any probability of the

French trying to realize one of their schemes, of making the Morea a Greek Republic. I think if we can establish a mode of communication through Mr. Spiridion Foresti, it would be the quickest way, unless any event of very great importance should call for a Ship being sent direct to Constantinople. The time an express by land will take from Corfu to Constantinople, will be desirable for me to know. Mr. Elliot, your successor at Naples, came out with me, and I have just put him into a Frigate, and sent him to Naples, whilst I am making my voyage to Malta, from whence I shall, as soon as possible, get with the Fleet off Toulon, from whence I shall do myself the honour of writing you. I have the honour to be, &c.

NELSON AND BRONTE.

TO HIS HIGHNESS THE CAPITAN PACHA.

[Autograph draught, in the possession of the Rev. Henry Girdlestone.]

June 14th, 1803.

Sir,

The restless ambition of the Person who, for the misfortune of mankind, still rules in the Government of France, has called me forth from my repose once more to arms, and the King, my Master, has thought it proper to appoint me Commander-in-Chief of his Fleet in the Mediterranean. I trust that the Ottoman Empire will be allowed to remain tranquil, and not again be unjustly invaded; but should any attempt be made by the French to carry such an object into execution, I have the honour to inform your Highness, that I am instructed to use every means to prevent it, and to afford to the Sublime Porte and its Subjects, every assistance in my power. This is a part of my instructions, which I should feel real pleasure in obeying, as it would not only enable me to evince my gratitude to his Imperial Majesty, but also afford me the pleasure I have so long desired, of being personally known to your Highness, and of assuring you that I am, with the greatest respect and attachment, your Highness's most obedient and faithful humble servant,

NELSON AND BRONTE.

TO THE ILLUSTRIOUS GOVERNMENT OF THE REPUBLIC OF THE SEVEN ISLES.

[From a Copy in the possession of Page Nicol Scott, Esq. ".Thursday, 16th, (*i. e.* Wednesday, 15th, P.M.) At 4, came to in the harbour of Valetta. Returned a salute to the Garrison with 17 guns. At 4·30, returned a salute to an American Commodore with 17 guns. At 5, saluted Sir Alexander John Ball, Bart., with 13 guns. A.M. [16th] Sailed H.M. Ships Anson and Stately, and Spider Brig. Friday, 17th June, 4, A.M. unmoored and hove short; employed warping out of the harbour of Malta. At 8, got out, filled and made sail. Joined H.M. Ship Phœbe.' —*Amphion's Log.*]

Malta, June 16th, 1803.

Illustrious Gentlemen,

Having received orders from the Great King, my Master, to afford every protection and assistance (consistent with the other great objects of my instructions) to the Republic of the Seven Isles, I therefore beg leave to inform you of it, and to assure you how ready I shall be at all times when called upon, to afford that assistance. Mr. Foresti will more fully convey my sentiments of respect to the Illustrious Government, and I have only to assure you of my sincere wishes for your happiness and prosperity, and that I am, with the highest respect, Illustrious Gentlemen, your most obedient, humble servant,

NELSON AND BRONTE.

TO SPIRIDION FORESTI, ESQ., CORFU.

[Autograph Draught, in the possession of the Reverend Henry Girdlestone.]

[About 16th June, 1803.]

Sir,

Being appointed Commander-in-Chief of his Majesty's Fleet in the Mediterranean, I have to request that you will acquaint the Government of the Republic of the Seven Islands of it, and to assure them that I am instructed (which I shall most willingly obey) to afford them all the protection and assistance in my power, should the French attempt any invasion of their Territory, or molestation to their commerce. You will also have the goodness to deliver my letter to the Government, [and] you will, of course, let me know the situation of that infant Republic, whether you think it will be able to maintain its independence, and whether the generality of the people are attached to it; and whether, in your opinion, they wish for a change or dissolution of the present Government; and whether the whole, or any party, would wish to give themselves up to France; and if that they wish to remain as they are, would they take up arms to defend themselves against the French? Your accurate knowledge of those Islands, and the character of every individual on them, will enable you to give me such answers as will assist me to regulate my conduct. You will believe that I must have all the inclination to render them service, when I recollect the very elegant compliment made me by the Island of Zante.[9] I have, &c.   NELSON AND BRONTE.

TO CAPTAIN WILLIAM EDWARD CRACRAFT,[1] H.M. SHIP ANSON.

[Order-Book.]

Amphion, in Valetta Harbour, 16th June, 1803.

Whereas I have received information that the French have a Squadron of Frigates in the Archipelago, You are hereby required and directed to take his Majesty's Ship Stately, (whose Captain has orders to put himself under your command,) and proceed with all possible dispatch, and cruize between Cape Matapan and the South-West end of Candia, from fifteen to twenty leagues off the Island of Cerigo, for the protection of the commerce of his Majesty's Subjects, and the destruction and annoyance of that of the Enemy. You are to continue on this station for the space of one month; and at the expiration thereof, to return to the harbour of Valetta for further orders. In the event of not finding any here, you are to take such position for the protection of our commerce, and annoyance of that of the Enemy, as you shall from circumstances judge most proper, taking care to leave with the Senior Officer at this place, or with his Excellency Sir Alexander John Ball, Bart., [notice] where you may be found, and afterwards not to be absent from Valetta Harbour more than fourteen days at a time.   NELSON AND BRONTE.

[9] *Vide* vol. iv. p. 151.
[1] He died at Chichester, in 1810, while commanding the Sea Fencibles on the Coast of Sussex.

TO SIR EVAN NEPEAN, BART., ADMIRALTY.

[Original, in the Admiralty.]

Amphion, at Sea, 17th June, 1803, 9 o'clock A.M.

Sir,

You will please to acquaint the Lords Commissioners of the Admiralty, that I left Gibraltar on the 4th instant, at 4 o'clock, P.M., with his Majesty's Ship Maidstone, after having ordered the Bittern and La Tourterelle on the service mentioned in my letter to you of that date. On the 11th, in latitude 37° 12″ North, I dispatched the Maidstone to Naples, with his Excellency Mr. Elliot, his Majesty's Minister at that Court; and on the 15th, about 4 o'clock in the afternoon, I arrived at Malta, from whence Rear-Admiral Sir Richard Bickerton, with the Ships and Vessels under his command, sailed on the 18th of May last, and I am now on my way to join him. I am, Sir, &c.

NELSON AND BRONTE.

TO SIR EVAN NEPEAN, BART., ADMIRALTY.

[Original, in the Admiralty.]

Amphion, at Sea, 17th June, 1803.

Sir,

I herewith transmit you for the information of the Lords Commissioners of the Admiralty, the copy of a letter from Captain Moubray, of his Majesty's Ship Maidstone,[2] which was delivered me by the Lieutenant sent in with the Vessel therein mentioned, on the morning of the 17th instant, as the Amphion was getting under weigh from Malta. I am, Sir, &c.

NELSON AND BRONTE.

P.S.—There are several large cases of Antiquities on board L'Arabe, brought from Athens, said to be for Buonaparte for the French Republic.

---

[2] Acquainting Lord Nelson with the capture of L'Arabe, a French Brig of eight small guns and fifty-eight men, on the 14th of June, off the Island of Faro.

TO SIR EVAN NEPEAN, BART., ADMIRALTY.

[Original, in the Admiralty.]

Amphion, at Sea, 17th June, 1803.

Sir,

You will please to acquaint the Lords Commissioners of the Admiralty, that on examining the state of His Majesty's Yard at Gibraltar, it was found necessary to have the Gun and Flat-bottomed Boats (of which there are only three) put in a state for service, and the Guerrier Sheer-hulk fitted for the reception of thirty or forty Officers and three hundred other Prisoners. I therefore ordered the Naval Storekeeper to enter twelve Shipwrights on the Garrison establishment, until the above work was completed. And I beg leave to suggest to their Lordships the propriety of appointing a Lieutenant, Purser, and other proper Officers to the said Sheer-hulk,— the Governor having offered to keep a constant Guard on board for the safety of the Prisoners.

I also submit the propriety of a similar Establishment at Malta. I have for the present appointed the Madras, whose men Sir Richard Bickerton has drafted on board the Fleet. I am, Sir, &c.

NELSON AND BRONTE.

TO CAPTAIN SUTTON, H. M. SHIP VICTORY.

[Autograph, in the possession of Captain Ives Sutton.]

Amphion, June 18th, 1803.

My dear Sutton,

You will find my Rendezvous off Toulon, where I am sure you will join me as soon as you can. Ever yours, most truly,

NELSON AND BRONTE.

The Amphion is one of the nicest Frigates I have seen— not so large as Amazon, but has every good quality.

TO HIS EXCELLENCY SIR JOHN ACTON, BART.

[From a Copy in the Admiralty.]

Faro of Messina, June 19th, 1803.

Sir,

This morning I met the Cyclops, Captain Fyffe,[3] and your Excellency will believe what displeasure it gave me to find, that when his Ship was in the Bay of Naples at anchor, that he should commit such a breach of Neutrality as sending his Boats to capture any Vessel coming into the Port; however, I am glad that Captain Fyffe immediately restored one, and when the other arrives at Malta, I have ordered her to be released; for as I would not suffer the French to break the Neutrality of any Power with impunity, so I will never suffer such an improper thing to be done by any of His Majesty's Ships under my command. I have the honour to be, &c.,

NELSON AND BRONTE.

TO HIS EXCELLENCY SIR JOHN ACTON, BART., NAPLES.

[From a Copy in the Admiralty.]

June 19th, 1803.

Private.

My dear Sir John,

I have wrote you a Public letter as it may be necessary to show it to the French Minister at Naples, that he may take a hint relative to Neutrality, but I am most exceedingly displeased with the conduct of the Cyclops and Experiment. I entreat you, my dear Sir John, to be assured of my sincere and affectionate good wishes (and, if necessary, exertions) for the happiness of our good Sovereigns. I pray you to assure them of my eternal attachment; and do you believe me, with the greatest truth, your most sincere and faithful friend,

NELSON AND BRONTE.

[3] Captain John Fyffe: in 1806, he commanded the Reindeer, fought a gallant action with two French Brigs, and was Posted in October 1807. Captain Fyffe died in March, 1835.

TO HIS EXCELLENCY HUGH ELLIOT, ESQ.

[Autograph in the Elliot Papers.]

Private.   Off Messina, June 19th, 1803.

My dear Sir,

As I am sending a line to General Acton, for the very reprehensible conduct of two of our Ships taking Vessels when they were at anchor in the Port of Naples, and intend, if possible, sending it on, though at Messina, I cannot refrain from giving you a line, merely to say that we arrived at Malta on Wednesday afternoon, the 15th. We were received with enthusiasm by the Maltese. Having put things in train, I left it the 17th at daylight. We spoke your Brig from Athens going in. I am going towards Capri, where I hope to find your letters. I cannot write what I wish, but all is smooth at Malta. General Villettes is well disposed to attend to my requisitions. Doctor Scott, and all on board, are well, and desire their kind remembrances, and I beg you to believe me ever yours most faithfully,

NELSON AND BRONTE.

TO THE COMMANDING OFFICER OF H.M. SHIPS AT MALTA.

[Letter-Book.]

Amphion, June 20th, 1803.

Sir,

If the Merchants at Messina want protection for their Ships from thence to Malta to go home with the Convoy, you will send either the Charon or Experiment for them. I have desired the Merchants to fix the day they will be ready, but the Convoy is not to be detained if they are not ready. I am, Sir, &c.,

NELSON AND BRONTE.

TO SIR EVAN NEPEAN, BART., ADMIRALTY.

[Original, in the Admiralty. On Monday, the 20th June, the Niger joined, and, with the Amphion, passed through the Faro, and was joined by the Phœbe. On the 21st, Lord Nelson sent the Boats to board a Ship, which proved to be a Greek Vessel.—*Amphion's Log.*]

Amphion, off Strombolo, 22nd June, 1803.

Sir,

Mr. Falcon, our Consul at Algiers, having by his representation made to Lord Pelham,[4] been sent away in a very improper manner (supposing it a Civil Court) from Algiers, for the commission of an offence in his house which never will be forgiven by a Moor,[5] I have not, as I have done to the States of Tunis and Tripoli, sent any civil message or notification of my arrival in these Seas; it must depend on the wisdom of Administration what line of conduct they mean to pursue, for, as is known to many Lords of your Board, our conduct must be decisive, whether it is under all circumstances to force the present Consul on the Dey, or to submit to the Dey's having another Consul named. The two Jews mentioned by Mr. Falcon I know are entirely in the French interest, indeed they are known partners in Mercantile houses at Marseilles; how far our Government would go in insisting on the banishment of these Jews, it must determine: all I wish and submit to their Lordships with great respect is, that if the business is left to me, my orders may be decisive. The insolence of the Dey's Cruizers is beyond whatever I have known, and if we give up one tittle of what we originally demand, we shall always be troubled with his insolence. The striking a sudden blow on his numerous Cruizers is the only way we have of bringing him to terms. Should the business be left to me, I shall go to Algiers, and if the Dey refuses a complete acquiescence in our demands, instantly take all his Cruizers.

As Mr. Falcon has sent triplicates of his letter to Lord Pelham, and as it is a business the Cabinet, and not the Admiralty Board, must settle, I have not thought it necessary

---

[4] Secretary of State for Foreign Affairs.

[5] Two Moorish women were discovered in Mr. Falcon's house at Algiers. This affair was the subject of many subsequent Letters.

to send you a copy of Mr. Falcon's letter to Lord Pelham, but enclose you a copy of his letter of the 4th ultimo to me, for their Lordships' information.　I am, Sir, &c.,

NELSON AND BRONTE.

TO HIS EXCELLENCY HUGH ELLIOT, ESQ.

[Autograph, in the Elliot Papers.]

June 25th, [1803,] off Capri.

Wrote before the Maidstone joined.[5]

My dear Sir,

I did myself the pleasure of writing you a line from Messina, under cover to Sir John Acton: I am now anxiously looking out for the Maidstone; for my passage has been so long—nine days from Malta—that I am miserable at not having joined the Fleet, when so much depends on my arrival to make the necessary arrangements.　I shall not touch on the politics of Italy, or fancy what the French are after at Genoa and Leghorn.　That I expect from your Excellency.

I cannot sufficiently reprobate the Paper that our Consul and Merchants have been weak enough to sign at Leghorn, if what I have is the true account.　The moment they were detained Prisoners of War, then the whole matter ended.　It was not necessary for them to give any opinion or any pledge, beyond what Prisoners on parole usually give.　I send the Niger with this letter—she is not to anchor; and if she does not join me in twenty-four hours, or less, from her leaving me, she must follow me off Toulon; for I cannot stay another moment.

I wrote to General Acton from Messina reprobating the conduct of the Cyclops, in sending her Boats, when at anchor in the Bay of Naples, to board and capture French Vessels. One, I find, was given up, and the other I have ordered, if she arrives at Malta; for as I would not suffer the French to do it with impunity, so I will not allow any Ship under my command to break any Neutrality, much less that of Naples,

---

[5] When off Capri, at 10 A.M., on the 25th of June, Lord Nelson recalled the Maidstone and Redbridge from Naples, and they joined the Amphion at noon.— *Log.*

whose situation I commiserate from the very bottom of my
soul.

Your Excellency will, I am sure, say every kind thing for
me to Sir John Acton, and be assured that I am, with the
highest respect, your Excellency's most obedient and faithful
servant,   NELSON AND BRONTE.

Noon.—The Maidstone just joined, and I am looking at
dear Naples, if it is what it was ; God send me good news !

TO HIS EXCELLENCY HUGH ELLIOT, ESQ.

[Autograph, in the Elliot Papers.]

No. 1.

My dear Sir,   M., June 25th, [1803,] off Capri,

I have read your letter, and those of General Acton's, with
much attention ; and it could not cost me one minute's reflection, under all the peculiar circumstances of the Two
Sicilies, what line of conduct I would pursue at the present
moment, (but this must be subject to change, as the French
may alter their conduct,) Great Britain having nothing else
in view than the preservation of the Two Sicilies. It is a
most important point to decide (the French having invaded
the Kingdom, although with a pretence not just or honourable,) when Sicily ought to be placed in a state of security.
For the present, I am content to say that Messina need not be
taken possession of ;[6] but the strictest watch must be kept by
Sir John Acton, that we are not lulled into a fatal security,
and thus lose both the Kingdoms. If the French assemble a
greater number of Troops than usual at Brindisi, Otranto, and
Tarento, or assemble any number of large Boats at those
places, particularly Tarento, then I think that not a moment

------

[6] In a Letter from Lord Hobart, Secretary of State for the War Department,
to Major-General Villettes (vide vol. i. p. 378,) or the Officer commanding the
Troops in Malta, dated on the 17th of May, 1803, his Lordship said, "if Lord
Nelson, in the prosecution of his instructions, judged it expedient to take possession
of the Citadel and Fort of Messina, and should apply to you for the cô-operation
of a detachment of the Troops under your command, you are to comply with his
application, provided that the force which you shall so detach do not exceed 2000
men, and that the said force can be spared from Malta without evident risk to the
security of that Island."—*Copy*, in the possession of the Right Honourable John
Wilson Croker.

should be lost to secure Sicily. In a small degree we risk it every day, in hopes of preserving the Kingdom of Naples; but for the present moment I am, if Sir John Acton coincides with me, induced to participate in the risk. I shall instantly send two Ships of War to cruise off Cape Spartavento, and towards the Gulf of Tarento, to give a check to the movements of Troops by sea. By land I cannot judge of the time, but a few Boats would very soon bring over from Reggio some thousands of Troops; nor could all the Navy of Europe prevent the passage, the current running seven miles an hour. Therefore I shall only observe again, that to save for the moment Naples, we risk the two Kingdoms, and General Acton must join me in this heavy responsibility. Every defence against such a voyage by sea shall be taken. With respect to securing an asylum, and safe retreat to the Royal Family at this moment, I will leave a Frigate, and either a Ship of the Line or Frigate shall always be at Naples. With respect to the other part of Sir John Acton's letter, we have ever thought the same, in which most cordially has coincided Lord Minto, that not less than 10,000 men should be kept for the service of the Mediterranean.

The moment I get off Toulon, I shall send a Vessel to England, and something to Naples to replace the Phœbe, and everything shall be stated most fully. Your Excellency will have the goodness to assure their Majesties and Sir John, that as it is my orders, so it will ever be a most cheerful part of my duty, to do everything for the personal security of the Royal Family, and for the security of their Kingdoms, and I assure your Excellency that it will be my pride to co-operate with you in this desirable work, for I am ever, with the greatest respect, &c.

NELSON AND BRONTE.

TO HIS EXCELLENCY SIR JOHN ACTON, BART.

[From a Copy in the Elliot Papers.]

My dear Sir John,　　　　　　　Off Capri, June 25th, 1803.

Your Excellency having done me the honour to call upon me for my sincere opinion, I have given it to the best of my judgment, and with a view to all the different circumstances of the case, viz.—that the French having made a (false) pretence for taking possession of Pescaro, Brindisi, Otranto, and Tarento, would, if Great Britain was to secure Sicily from their insatiable grasp, probably come to Naples; and thus the King (God bless him) lose one of his Kingdoms. In this view I have given my opinion for the present moment, to his Excellency Mr. Elliot, who will, if you please, give your Excellency a copy of my letter and opinion. In forming it, I have endeavoured to conform to the spirit of my instructions —to do everything in my power, for the security of the dominions of his Sicilian Majesty.' I am as anxious as your Excellency can be, to run every reasonable risk for the preservation of the Royal authority over the rest of the Kingdom of Naples; but both you and myself are bound to take care that the probability of the loss of two Kingdoms, does not outweigh the momentary honour of ruling (by ' la grace de la Republique Française') over a great part of one of them; and we must always recollect, that although Naples may be lost, Sicily is secure; but if Sicily is lost, so is Naples. I will not trouble your Excellency with combating the reasoning of such a Power as France, and with such an Army at your door. Will not Russia support our guarantee? The honour of Monarchs is fled. My dear Sir John, you have my opinion; and I am ready, jointly with your Excellency, to run the risk of Sicily for a short time, till we can form some further ideas of their plans, by the movements of their Troops. On this I must rely on your Excellency. If the French approach near enough to Naples to make prisoners the Royal Family, then all is lost; for then the struggle would be, shall the French or English get Sicily? If the English got it in possession, the French would not believe (or pretend so) but that the King gave his approbation, and they would treat him accordingly. If his Majesty gave the French possession, it would be lost for ever, and the King would hold Naples *durante bene placito.*

I am aware of the difficulty of deciding, but as an honest man, and with the best judgment which God has given me, I think your Excellency should not advise his Majesty to run too much risk of his person falling into the hands of the

French.   Everything else which I could urge on this important subject, will so naturally suggest themselves to you, that it would be presumptuous to say more.   A Ship of War—and, generally, of the Line—shall, on some pretence or other, always be in the Bay of Naples, to prevent that worst of all accidents, the loss of the Royal Family.

The Prince, as Viceroy, could not be of half the importance as the King; for his Royal Highness is still only a Subject.   I entreat your Excellency to lay me at their Majesties' feet; and to declare most solemnly, that to save their persons from falling into the hands of the French, I would lay down my life; and I beg your Excellency to believe me, with the highest respect, &c.

NELSON AND BRONTE.

P.S.—I do not presume to write to their Majesties at this moment, having stated my free thoughts to your Excellency and Mr. Elliot, but I feel truly sensible of their Majesties' good opinion of my zeal and activity, and which it shall ever be my pride to merit.

TO HIS EXCELLENCY SIR JOHN ACTON, BART.

[From a Copy in the Elliot Papers.]

Private.   June 25th, 1803, off Capri.

My dear Sir John.

If I know myself, it is to know, that the more my friends are in distress, the more I am anxious to serve them.   A mouse assisted a lion, which is the only comparison I can make in arrogating to myself the power of assisting a King of the House of Bourbon; and I am sorry to say, the only one who has strictly preserved his honour, or dignity, and fidelity to his Allies, and I shall feel proud in aiding you, my dear Sir John, in saving these two fine Kingdoms, and Mr. Elliot will join us most cordially in this good work.   All we must take care of is, not to run the risk of Sicily, beyond the line of prudence; on this point we rely, (as the Seamen's phrase is,) on your Excellency's look-out.   You must be aware of our distance, and be in time.   I will, if you send to

me off Toulon, either attend myself, or send Sir Richard
Bickerton.[6] Declarations are to come from our Officers, that
the authority of his Majesty is in no one respect to be
abridged; and if my counsel can have weight, I should recommend, at the risk of a War with all the Barbary States, to
liberate the Sicilian Flag from their insolence. I assure you
I would only ask for three months' War to put them in order;
not by attacking Algiers, but taking all their Cruisers. I am
going off Toulon, and from thence shall send a Vessel direct
to England. It has been my plan to have 10,000 disposable
Troops in the Mediterranean; this is also Lord Minto's, and
his Excellency Mr. Elliot's. I shall write to you from off Toulon,
and ever believe me, with the truest esteem, your Excellency's
most obedient and faithful friend,

NELSON AND BRONTE.

Give my respects to Lady Acton, and I shall be happy in
making my bow, and seeing your little ones, when it may be
judged prudent. I only beg that you will not apologize for
your English writing; very few write English so well. I am
not surprised that the King will not part with your Excellency; if he did, adieu this Kingdom. Faithful servants are
not to be parted with at this time. I shall send a Squadron
to look after Genoa and Leghorn.

N. AND B.

I have wrote to your Excellency from Messina, respecting
the conduct of the Frigates who sent their Boats after the
French Vessels.

TO HIS EXCELLENCY HUGH ELLIOT, ESQ.

[Autograph, in the Elliot Papers.]

No. 2.

My dear Sir,   June 25th, 1803.
I am so anxious to answer your Excellency's letter, that I
have only touched on the most important part of it, jointly

----

[6] Rear-Admiral Sir Richard Bickerton, Bart., second in command, with his Flag
(White at the mizen) in the Kent. This able Officer died an Admiral of the Red,
and a Knight Commander of the Bath, in February 1832.

with Sir John Acton. I shall not, therefore, repeat to him my letter No. 1; but request of you to show it him, and, if he wishes it, a copy. I have given my opinion to the best of my judgment, under all the circumstances. Had I only to consider, Is Sicily safe at this moment? I should say, *No.* But let it be recollected, that I am called upon not to entirely lose Naples by my opinion, but to try, with that important object in view, to save Sicily. I have arranged with General Villettes to have 2000 men ready for service; and I shall write secretly to have them in momentary preparation. If Sir John Acton, without choosing to run too great a risk for Sicily, chose to send to me off Toulon, I would attend myself, if possible, this very important service. I am very anxious to join the Fleet; for I must place a Squadron between Elba and Genoa, to prevent that Expedition from moving, and also to send some Ships to the Straits' Mouth, and to keep enough to watch the Ships in Toulon, of whose force or readiness for service I am totally ignorant. These are all important objects, but nothing when compared with the security of the Sicilies. I am ever, your Excellency's most faithful and obedient servant,

　　　　　　　　　　　　　　NELSON AND BRONTE.

TO HIS EXCELLENCY HUGH ELLIOT, ESQ.

[Autograph, in the Elliot Papers.]

　　　　　　　　　　　　　　June 25th, off Capri [1803.]

My dear Sir,

I send you an order which, when necessary, you will deliver to the Commander of any King's Ship in the Bay of Naples. I will never trust the Royal Family; but if you think it right to send away the Ship with any dispatches to me, you must judge of the propriety of it. You may rely on my care of you by water. Toulon is my Rendezvous, but I very much doubt if any Neapolitan Vessel will come off that place. If they *really* do come, they are changed. Ever, my dear Sir, yours faithfully,

　　　　　　　　　　　　　　NELSON AND BRONTE.

TO THE SENIOR CAPTAIN OF HIS MAJESTY'S SHIPS IN THE BAY OF NAPLES.

[Autograph in the Elliot Papers.]

Amphion, off Capri, 26th June, 1803.

Most secret and confidential.

You are hereby required and directed, on this order being delivered to you, to receive on board, or to convoy them if they embark on board one of their own Ships, the King, Queen, and Royal Family of Naples, to Palermo, or such other place as the King may choose to proceed to; and you will afford every protection and assistance to all those who may wish to follow their Majesties, (and that they approve of.) And you will also receive his Majesty's Minister and suite, and afford such other protection as is in your power, to all British Subjects and their property, as the urgency of the case may require.

NELSON AND BRONTE.

TO HIS EXCELLENCY HUGH ELLIOT, ESQ.

[Autograph, in the Elliot Papers.]

No. 3.   June 26th, 7 A.M., [1803.]

My dear Sir,

Calms have prevented my sending off the Phœbe to you yesterday; and I have to request that your Excellency will make all due allowances for the language which I may have used, and for not having put my opinion more concise than it appears at present; but as it flowed from the unlettered pen of a Seaman, you must receive it, my whole opinion resting in these few words—*that we must not risk Sicily too far in trying to save Naples; therefore, General Acton, yourself, and myself, must keep a good look-out.*

When the French General comes to Naples, the business will be clear; for if he insists on our being shut out of the Ports of the Kingdom, their plan is decided, and we must not lose time. Ever, my dear Sir, yours most truly,

NELSON AND BRONTE.

TO CAPTAIN HENRY RICHARDSON,[7] H. M. SHIP JUNO.

[Order-Book.]

Amphion, off Capri, 26th June, 1803.

Whereas, the French have taken possession of Pescara, Brindisi, Otranto, and Tarento, and it being apprehended that they will convoy their Troops along shore either into Sicily, or the Coast of Calabria opposite to it, you are therefore hereby required and directed (notwithstanding former orders) to proceed with his Majesty's Ship under your command, and cruize very diligently off Cape Spartivento and on the Coast towards Tarento, for the purpose of intercepting any French Troops, which I have reason to believe will be attempted to be convoyed along shore; and in the event of your falling in with them, to take, sink, burn, and destroy them, without regard to their being in any Ship or Vessel bearing a Neutral Flag. You are to continue on this service until you are relieved, or receive my further orders, acquainting me as opportunity may offer of your proceedings.

NELSON AND BRONTE.

N.B.—A Sloop of War will be sent to you soon.

TO SIR EVAN NEPEAN, BART., ADMIRALTY.

[Original, in the Admiralty.]

Amphion, off Capri, 26th June, 1803.

Sir,

I received letters from their Excellencies Mr. Elliot and General Acton yesterday afternoon, and as the French have declared their intention, and begun to put in execution, the taking possession of Pescara, Brindisi, Otranto, and Tarento, and as it must ever be uncertain what further measures they may take for the entire subjugation of the whole Kingdom of Naples, I have thought it right to send a Frigate to lay in the Bay of Naples, in order to secure a retreat to our Minister and the English and their property, and others who may unhappily again want the protection of his Majesty's

---

[7] Captain Richardson will be frequently mentioned.

Flag; and, under the present circumstances, the Bay of Naples will never be left without a Ship of war.

I have also sent directions for a Frigate and Sloop of War to cruize from Cape Spartavento towards Tarento, with orders, if the French move coastways in Vessels, to take, sink, or destroy them, without any regard for their being embarked in Ships bearing the Neutral Flag; thus having arranged everything in my power for the service of Naples and Sicily, I am now on my way off Toulon, where Sir Richard Bickerton very judiciously proceeded with the Fleet, the moment he was certain of hostilities. I am, Sir, &c.

NELSON AND BRONTE.

TO CAPTAIN CHARLES MARSH SCHOMBERG, H.M. SHIP MADRAS, OR THE SENIOR OFFICER OF H. M. SHIPS AND VESSELS AT MALTA.

[Order-Book.]

Amphion, off Capri, 26th June, 1803.

Whenever General Villettes, commanding his Majesty's Troops at Malta, shall require any assistance for convoying a body of Troops to Sicily, you are hereby required and directed to take, if wanted, (for such service only) every man from the Transports or Merchant-Vessels at Malta, and afford Major General Villettes all the assistance in your power, for the purpose of convoying the Troops above-mentioned from Malta to Sicily, taking particular care that the men are returned to their respective Ships the moment this service is performed, of which you will acquaint the men when taken from their Ships.

NELSON AND BRONTE.

TO MAJOR-GENERAL VILLETTES, MALTA.

[Autograph, in the possession of J. B. Heath, Esq.]

June 26th, 1803.

Secret and confidential,

My dear General,

I have had my communication with Naples, and a melancholy one it has been. The French have taken possession of

Pescara, Brindisi, Otranto, and Tarento, on a pretence that we were to evacuate Malta as they did Naples; but as we have not done so, they resume their former position in the Kingdom of Naples. The King is fully sensible of the injustice of the French, and although he would, I am sure, be very glad for us to secure Messina, yet he thinks that the moment we possess ourselves of Messina, that moment the French would march to Naples. Thirteen thousand is the force of the French, spread over 200 miles of country; therefore, for the present moment, I have consented not to push our occupying Messina, till we see what further steps the French will take; for the King hopes to retain still the rest of his Kingdom of Naples. But the moment any appearance is made of further invasion, we shall be desired secretly to go to Messina, and, if we had the Troops, to have garrisoned Naples and Gaëta. I assure you, under all the circumstances which have been laid before me, I have had a difficult task to form my opinion. The sum of it is this: to keep a strict look out on every movement and language of the French, and not to risk Sicily beyond the line of prudence, in order to allow the King for a short time to rule over part of the Kingdom of Naples; and for the King to recollect that if Sicily is lost, so is Naples; but that Naples being lost, is more likely to be regained by securing Sicily. The whole purport of my letters goes not further than this.

With respect to the Neapolitan Troops, General Acton told Mr. Elliot that he hoped by this time that the Neapolitan Troops had arrived in Sicily. I have the same reasons for wishing them kept back, as I had when at Malta—' a fear that they will fancy themselves stronger at Messina and Sicily than they really are, and therefore defer calling for our assistance so soon as I could wish;' therefore, I still wish those Troops kept back. If General Acton sends for them, we must submit; but at present we need not find means of sending them away. With respect to the 2000 men, or such a number as you can spare for the service of Messina, I earnestly request that they may be held in constant readiness, for you may very likely be sent to from one moment to another.

The distance is so short, that it would not be necessary to wait for baggage, &c.; I would take care that the Garrison

should want for no comfort in my power. The first appearance of the 2000 men, or as near as possible to that number,
would have a very happy effect, and much encourage the
Sicilians in resisting even French influence; which is all I
hope that ever they will be able to attempt in that Island:
and if it should be necessary, a part afterwards can be withdrawn.

I shall send a Vessel to England, the moment I get off
Toulon; and as both the Spider and the Redbridge come to
me directly, they will bring your dispatches: for if even the
first Vessel is sailed, ... through one seems the only safe
mode of communication with England. I am, my dear General, with the greatest respect, your most faithful servant,

NELSON AND BRONTE.

TO THE RIGHT HONOURABLE HENRY ADDINGTON.

[Autograph, in the Sidmouth Papers.]

Amphion, June 28th, 1803, between Sardinia and Naples.

My dear Sir,

Knowing how very much you are pressed for time, I shall,
as briefly as possible, consistent with telling you, as a friend,
my sentiments on all the topics which I shall necessarily touch
upon, with that sincerity which becomes me to you, be my
opinion right or wrong.

I shall only say one word of GIBRALTAR, on which I had a
serious conversation with Sir Thomas Trigge, on the impropriety of placing Dillon's Regiment[8] as part of the Garrison of
Gibraltar. When we reflect how that Regiment is composed,
and that fifty men, the usual Guard at Land Port Gate, by
being corrupted, might lose the place, who shall say Gibraltar
is secure with those Troops? If it is said, do not trust them with
the Guard, then you show your distrust, and, naturally, they
become your enemies. The Regiment of Rolle is a fine Corps,
and will serve faithfully; but I would not trust them at Gibraltar.

The next point I come to is ALGIERS. Mr. Falcon the
Consul having sent home his own account of the transaction,

---

[8] That regiment, like De Rolle's, was formed entirely of Foreigners.

it rests with Government to determine what steps are to be taken. All that I entreat, if the matters are left to me to settle, [is] that our demands for satisfaction be fixed; for if we give way in the smallest thing, the insolence of the Dey will but increase. Whatever the wisdom of Government directs shall be attended to. The alternative must be instantaneous War on a refusal to our demands, or an entire acquiescence. Mr. F. thinks that the Dey never will receive him. *He* knows best the reasons why he thinks so.

MALTA.—I arrived there the 15th of June, in the evening. The French Minister, General Vial, had left it in a Ragusa Vessel in the morning. The Maltese are in the highest spirits, and sincerely hope that they will now be never separated from England. My opinion of Malta, as a Naval station for watching the French in Toulon, is well known; and my present experience of what will be a three weeks' passage, most fully confirms me in it. The Fleet can never go there if I can find any other corner to put them in: but having said this, I now declare, that I consider Malta as a most important outwork to India, that it will ever give us great influence in the Levant, and indeed all the Southern parts of Italy. In this view, I hope we shall never give it up. I carried out orders from Lord Hobart, that General Villettes was to hold 2000 men at my requisition, if they could be spared from the defence of Malta, for the service of Sicily. The language of General Villettes was natural: 'The Garrison appointed for Malta is not more than on the most economical number of men was judged sufficient; and, looking to the assistance of the Maltese in case of a siege, that these numbers of British troops were only sufficient for the ordinary duties, and that, when the Neapolitan Troops went away, (and he was ordered to send them away,) the duty would be very severe; that the addition of Maltese Troops, when trained and formed, would be little better than a well-formed Militia; and, however much they undoubtedly would assist, yet they could not be counted as British Troops; however, that he should not hesitate in providing 1200 men, and a Corps of Artillery, to be under the command of General Oakes, a most excellent Officer, for the service of Messina, whenever I might call for them:' and the General wished that I should mention this conversation, when

I had any opportunity of communicating with Ministers, (but which opportunity I never can have, but in this private, confidential way.) Sir Alexander Ball thinks, that if half the Troops were gone on other services, particularly to Sicily, that the Maltese would defend the Island, against any force the French could send, supported by our Fleet. Truth probably lays between; but, my dear Sir, these sort of orders should never be left discretionary. You make an Officer responsible for the safety of the place, yet tell him in the same breath, ' Send away so many men, if you can spare them without evident risk.' The conduct of the Officer must be naturally to secure himself from the very great responsibility thrown upon him by such an order.

SICILY.—The state of Sicily is almost as bad as a civilized Country can be. There are no Troops fit to be called such, with a scarcity of corn never known, and of course bread so dear that the lower class of People are discontented. The Nobles are oppressors, and the middle rank wish for a change; and although they would prefer us to the French, yet I believe they would receive the French, rather than not change from the oppression of the Nobles. The Citadel of Messina is strong and in good order, but with a few miserable Troops badly paid, if paid at all; therefore, what could be expected from them? A French Frigate has been there lately, a French Aide-de-camp to the Grand Master, and, lastly, General Vial: they have good eyes, and many at Messina are seduced by them; and if the Neapolitan Troops at Malta were removed there, I fear we should find more enemies and the French more friends. (On these Troops I shall touch in another place.)

On the 17th, at daylight, I left Malta; on the 20th, I passed the Faro of Messina. The lower class of Boat-people came on board with fruit, &c.—their expressions were strong, and ought to be received with caution, yet with their hearts in their hands, you may gather sentiments to form a pretty accurate opinion. ' Viva il Rè! Viva Inglesé! When will the English come back to Messina?' On asking them if they had any Jacobins in the City, ' Yes, the gentry who wear their hats so—on one side the head'—vide Bond-street loungers. On the 25th, I was at the entrance of the Bay of Naples, where I had appointed the Frigate which carried Mr.

Elliot to Naples to join me. I send you copies of my letters
to Sir John Acton, the King and Queen, with their answers,
Mr. Elliot's, and likewise those I have sent to Lord St.
Vincent, for him to lay them before the Cabinet. Here
it is necessary to observe to you, that a Sea-Officer cannot
hold any official correspondence but with the Secretary of
the Admiralty, without an order for that purpose, which is
often given : therefore, I have certainly irregularly sent them
to Lord St. Vincent, as a Cabinet Minister—conceiving they
are on subjects which the Board of Admiralty can have
nothing to do with, much less the Clerks of that Office,
through whose hands they must pass. When you, my dear
Sir, take into your consideration all the letters sent me, with
the liberal conduct towards my judgment, I trust that you
will agree with me, that under all circumstances at this moment, I did right to give the opinion which I have done;
but I stand open to the correction of the Cabinet. I felt that
it was our wish to make Naples feel that we were her true
friends, and sincerely wished to preserve as much as possible
for her, and not to hasten the loss of any part of the Kingdom
of Naples.

SARDINIA is declared Neutral, but that no Foreign Troops
would be allowed to land. I wish they may keep off the
French. We have no Troops to assist them, if they wanted
our assistance. This reminds me of a word about more Troops
for Naples: should the King of Naples, which is most probable,
be obliged to quit his Capital and retire to Palermo, what
General Acton suggests would be attended with the very
happiest consequences,—the possession of Gaëta, a very strong
fortified Frontier Town, with a fine Bay and Port, the country
people hostile to inveteracy against the French : 1500 British
would secure this post, and always give us an entry into the
country. I am not Military man sufficient to say how long our
Troops could hold St. Elmo and the other Castles at Naples;
but they would give that energy to the people, which might,
and probably would be attended with the happiest effects. I
regret the necessity of withdrawing the last part of that fine
Egyptian Army, and am aware of the influence it will have
on the timid Council of Naples.

ROME.—By a letter from Mr. Jackson, his Majesty's Minister to the King of Sardinia, of June 17th, he says:—'I have seen the Secretary of State of this Government, and his Eminence told me there was no doubt that this State would be suffered to remain Neuter, and, consequently, that the Ships of the belligerent Powers will be received in the Ports of the Pope's States.' This may be the case for the moment; but if we were to receive the least advantage by it, I am sure we should be turned out as heretofore.

TUSCANY.—It is difficult to know how to consider this State; they are not our friends, and it would, perhaps, be hard to consider them as enemies. Yet why should France use them against us, and we are to suffer Leghorn to enjoy its commerce for the advantage, ultimately, of the French? for it is they who receive the fruits of the Tuscan labour and commerce. And as the French have declared Leghorn in a state of siege, I can see no impropriety of considering it so likewise, and for our Government to place it in a state of blockade whilst the French remain in it. This is for the wise and grave consideration of our Government.

GENOA OR LIGURIA.—The same as the Italian Republic; it is France as much as Toulon; it has not even a name of independence. Therefore I shall, as far as I see at this present moment, have no hesitation in considering all Genoese Vessels as French. Everything at Genoa is French; therefore I hope that not a moment will be lost in declaring Genoa so considered. The blockade of Genoa ought to be declared instantly; if not, it will be what it always has been, the granary of the South of France, and the North part of Italy, which will be much distressed by such a measure, and I hope it will induce the Piedmontese, Genoese, &c., to rise against the French. Be that as it may, I do not think that we ought to allow the French Armies and friends to be maintained and enriched by our not blockading all the Genoese Ports. I therefore hope that this will instantly be done. The Imperial and Greek flag are filling it and Leghorn with corn.

MOREA.—It is perfectly clear that the French are at work in that Country, either to prepare for their own reception, or to induce the Greeks to revolt against the Porte, and either way, it is a chain for their getting again to Egypt. If the French or their friends conquer the Morea, Egypt would be the

price of returning it, unless by an alliance with the Mamelukes they can possess both.   This brings to my mind the
Bey, who is going to England to solicit our justice against
Turkish oppression.   It appears very clear that the Territory
assigned them in Upper Egypt, will not maintain them and
their flocks.   Government will know how to steer between
the Turks and Mamelukes.

July 2nd.   To this long letter, I shall only beg to call your
attention, for what purpose the French are collecting such an
Army in Italy, where at present there can be no prospect of
an Army able to face them: 13,000 are in the Kingdom of
Naples, 8000 are at this moment in Leghorn, 6000 marched
in on the 28th June, the other parts of Italy are filling with
Troops, even drawing them from Switzerland.   The objects
must be the conquest of Naples, (perhaps Sicily,) and certainly getting over to the Morea; therefore I regret the
removal of our Egyptian Army, which in any of these enter-
prises, have kept the French in check: for I am sure they
are afraid of that Army, and the Italians have the greatest
confidence in it, and would make a struggle in their mountains; and time gained to us would be very desirable.

July 9th.—I joined our Fleet yesterday.   With the casual
absence of one or two Ships, we shall be always seven Sail of
the Line; and as the French have at least seven—I believe
nine—nearly ready, we are in hopes that Buonaparte may be
angry, and order them out, which, I have no doubt, will put
our Ships in high feather; for I never knew any wants after
a Victory, although we are always full of them before.   I will
only [add,] that no endeavours of mine shall be wanted to gain
one more, for I am worn up; and be assured that I am ever,
my dear Sir, your most faithful and attached friend,

                                        NELSON AND BRONTE.

TO HIS EXCELLENCY HUGH ELLIOT, ESQ.

[From a Copy in the Elliot Papers.]

Secret and private.   June 29th, 1803.
  My dear Sir,
    I have answered hastily your letters, and I think that you
can work on General Acton's mind to call upon us secretly in

time to save Sicily.   A reason is fully sufficient for all Europe, and the King of Naples, by his Protest, has paved the way for securing Sicily.   He has the words put into his mouth.   The English will hold Messina, whilst the French hold any part of the Kingdom of Naples ; but I well know, and so do you, that the French would assuredly march to Naples.   They have, unhappily, the upper hand for land forces.   With respect to the Neapolitan Troops at Malta, General Villettes has orders to send them home, but I have requested him to keep the secret, and not to send them ; for if they got into Messina, they would certainly not keep the French out one moment, and it would give a good excuse for not asking us to secure Messina.   Indeed, I wish General Acton to tell us secretly— ' Secure Sicily for us.'   The more he scolds us jointly with the French, the better.   It is a nice point for him; for if he abuses us too much, the French will kindly offer him assist- ance.   Further, with respect to the Neapolitan Troops at Malta, the General tells me, that with the absence of the 2000 Neapolitan Troops, and the 2000 British, that he will be hard pressed to do the duty of the Garrison.   These are points for your consideration.   If you talk on this subject with Sir John, and he makes a point of the Neapolitan Troops being taken from Malta, could it not be managed to have our Troops go to Messina with them? and then they would remain under the orders of General Oakes[9] who is the Officer destined to command at Messina—an excellent Soldier, and a good Man. I have done.   Ever yours faithfully,

NELSON AND BRONTE.

TO CAPTAIN THOMAS M. HARDY, H.M. SHIP AMPHION.

[Order-Book.]

Amphion, off Monte Christo, 1st July, 1803.

Whereas the Government of the Republic of Genoa (or Ligurian Republic) has, by its conduct in adopting the wishes of the French Minister at that place as acts of their own Government, become hostile to Great Britain, you are there-

---

[9] Afterwards General Sir Hildebrand Oakes, Baronet, G.C.B., and Lieutenant- General of the Ordnance : he died in September 1822.

fore hereby required and directed to seize and detain all Ships, Vessels, and property belonging to the Republic of Genoa (or Ligurian Republic), or to any of its Subjects, which you may fall in with, and send them into Port, there to remain (under the same particular instructions as the detained Ships or Vessels belonging to the Batavian Republic, mentioned in my order to you of the 30th May last)[1] until I shall receive directions from the Lords Commissioners of the Admiralty respecting them.

NELSON AND BRONTE.

TO SIR EVAN NEPEAN, BART., ADMIRALTY.

[Original, in the Admiralty.]

Sir,   Amphion, off Monte Christo, 1st July, 1803.

From the following extract of a letter, dated June 14th, from Mr. Jackson, at Rome, his Majesty's Minister to the King of Sardinia, viz. :

'The Measures which have been adopted at Genoa against us, are the work of this Government, at the requisition of the French Minister, as well as the Italian Republic, which gives Letters of Marque against our Vessels. In Tuscany the Government has wisely refused to act. I just hear that at Genoa the French Minister required 5000 Troops of the Government, which replied that they had but 2000, which were at his service: it is supposed they will be sent out of the Republic, and Genoa be garrisoned with French Troops.'

In every point of view in which I have been able to see Genoa, I can only consider her as a part of France, and as such I have directed her Shipping to be seized and detained till I receive further orders from their Lordships ; and, with due deference to the wisdom of Government, I would earnestly recommend that Genoa should be declared a Blockaded Port, and thus cut off all supplies for the Southern parts of France and the Northern parts of Italy; it will make the Inhabitants severely feel the baneful effects of French fraternity, and in case of a co-operation with some of the Continental Powers, will make them ready to throw off the French yoke.   Much

---

[1] Vide p. 76, ante.

more could be urged on the propriety of this measure, but it would be presumptuous in me to say more.

The Blockade, for to have its full effect should be declared in England, as was done in February 1800, and all the Genoese Ports should be declared blockaded, and especially Port Especcia, which will otherwise be amply supplied from Leghorn, and through it the Italian Republic.

With respect to a blockade of Leghorn, the French having declared it in a state of siege, Government must decide how far we should have the complaisance to consider it otherwise, and not blockade it. The loyal Government, it is true, does nothing, but the French do everything, treating it as a conquered Country, even to hoisting the French Flag on the same staff as the Tuscan; the latter Flag of course is to save themselves, and the former to enable them in Tuscany to be hostile to us; such conduct deserves that Leghorn should be considered as blockaded whilst the French Troops remain in it, and that it is hostile to Great Britain. I am, Sir, &c.,

NELSON AND BRONTE.

TO ADMIRAL THE EARL OF ST. VINCENT, K.B.

[Autograph in the possession of Vice-Admiral Sir William Parker, Bart., G.C.B.]

Amphion, off Monte Christo, July 2nd, 1803.

My dear Lord,

Having wrote everything relative to every Ship in the Fleet, and of Naval matters, I do not think that the Papers I send you herewith are necessary to be laid before the Board of Admiralty, but if your Lordship thinks they are, then I beg that you will have the goodness to give them to Sir Evan Nepean for that purpose; but that if you agree with me, you will either lay them before the Cabinet, or send them to one of his Majesty's Principal Secretaries of State. I am ever, my dear Lord, your most faithful, humble servant,

NELSON AND BRONTE.

TO THE RIGHT HONOURABLE EARL MOIRA.

[From Clarke and McArthur, vol. ii. p. 319.]

2nd July, 1803.

Another great plan of Buonaparte's is now perfectly clear; he will attempt the Morea, either by assisting the Greeks in an insurrection against the Porte, or this may be done in concert with Russia. On this important subject we are both agreed, that it is very probable those two Powers may have in view, by concert, the downfall of the Turkish Empire in Europe. Candia and Egypt would, of course, if this plan is followed, be given to the French, when, sooner or later, farewell India! But even supposing Russia has nothing to do with this plan, it would equally answer Buonaparte's purpose of alarming the Porte, to do it by the Greeks, or by assisting Ali Vizir in throwing off his dependence on the Porte; he would be equally ready to suppress or support even rebellion, provided the reward, Egypt, were the same. That is his great object at present, and for it he would sacrifice either Greeks, Russians, or Turks. We know he is not very scrupulous in the honourable means of accomplishing his darling object. Every State in Italy, except Naples, is at this moment as much France, as France itself, and in all things is obedient to his nod. And for fear that the Spanish Family, in *his* Kingdom of Etruria, should appear to the world not sufficiently degraded, he has ordered, and they fly on the same Flag-staff, both French and Tuscan colours to be hoisted. At Genoa, they literally obey the order of his Minister; a few days ago, he desired of the Government 5000 Troops—they answered that they had only 2000, but that they were very much at his service. My firm opinion is, that the Mediterranean will again be an active scene; and if Ministers do not look out, I shall have the Brest Fleet to pay me a visit; for as the Army can only be moved by the protection of a superior Fleet, that Fleet they will try to have, and a month's start of us would do all the mischief. I am, &c.,

NELSON AND BRONTE.

TO ADMIRAL THE EARL OF ST. VINCENT, K.B.

[Autograph, in the possession of Vice-Admiral Sir William Parker, Bart., G.C.B.]

Amphion, July 4th, 1803, 20 Leagues W.N.W. of Cape Corse.

My dear Lord,

Never was such miserably long passages, or any man more anxious to join the Fleet. Sailing from Gibraltar the 4th of June, it was the 15th in the afternoon when we arrived at Malta. Having found that Sir Richard Bickerton had sailed on the 18th of May, to cruise between Naples and Sicily, I left Malta on the next night, but it was the 25th before I got off Capri, where I had appointed the Maidstone (who carried Mr. Elliot to Naples) to join me. Having received the letters which I have sent you, and answered them, it was, notwithstanding all our exertions, last night before I could get round Cape Corse.

The large French Army that is assembling in Italy must be placed there ready for a remove, whenever they have Fleet enough to keep us from looking them in the face; and although I know that can only be for a very short space of time, yet much may be done before reinforcements can arrive. Your Lordship knows what Admiral Bruix might have done, had he done his duty, and they may buy their experience. The 6000 Men marched with nine Generals into Leghorn on the 28th of June, can only be for embarkation. I look upon Naples as lost, unless we can have Troops to defend the Castles of Naples (the City) and Gaeta. In that case, the peasantry would, I believe, defend their mountains, and at least it would give a check to the movements of the French, and give us time to get a Fleet into the Mediterranean. You will see how fearful the Court of Naples is of our securing Sicily; for they know, and so do we, that the moment we take possession of Messina, they would make a conquest of Naples, unless we have Troops, as I before mentioned; and you will observe General Acton lays much stress on them. I shall write to Acton very soon; but my Lord, if I say too much, even of probabilities of what may happen, the Cabinet of Naples takes fright, and entreat us to do nothing; if, on the other hand, they are not a little alarmed, they will think themselves so safe, that if we act, they will attribute all their losses to us; and losses they will have I much fear. However, no exertion of mine shall be wanting to bring the Fleet to Action the moment it is in my power; and I shall endeavour to keep such a look-out at the Mouth of the Straits, that I may fight one or the other, before they can form a junction. I shall only assure you that I will do my best, let what will happen, and endeavour to approve myself worthy the high honour of this Command. I again request that you will have the goodness to let my nephew, Sir William Bolton, come to me in a Sloop of War. George Elliot will go into the Termagant as you desired, Captain Stuart[1] being Captain of the Kent; and be assured, my dear Lord, that I shall be anxious to follow closely every wish of yours, and that I am, my dear Lord, your most faithful and obliged,

NELSON AND BRONTE.

I am looking out very sharp for the Victory.

TO LADY HAMILTON.

[Extract from "Letters of Lord Nelson to Lady Hamilton," vol. i. p. 113.]

[5th July, 1803.]

My dearest Emma,

Although I have wrote letters from various places, merely to say, ' Here I am, and ' There I am,' yet, as I have no doubt but that they would all be read, it was impossible for me to say more than ' Here I am, and well:' and I see no prospect of any certain mode of conveyance, but by sea; which, with the means the Admiralty has given me, of small Vessels, can be but seldom.

Our passages have been enormously long. From Gibraltar to Malta, we were eleven days; arriving the fifteenth in the evening, and sailing in the night of the sixteenth—that is, three in the morning of the seventeenth—and it was the twenty-sixth before we got off Capri, where I had ordered the Frigate which carried Mr. Elliot to Naples, to join me. I

---

[1] Captain John James Stuart, second son of Lord Nelson's friend, General the Honourable Sir Charles Stuart, K.B. (vide vol. i.) : he died Captain of H. M. Ship Saldanha, at Lough Swilly, in Ireland, on the 19th of March, 1811.

send you copies of the King and Queen's letters. I am
vexed that she did not mention you! I can only account for
it by hers being a political letter.

When I wrote to the Queen, I said[2]—' I left Lady Hamilton, the eighteenth of May; and so attached to your Majesty,
that I am sure she would lay down her life to preserve yours.
Your Majesty never had a more sincere, attached, and real
friend, than your dear Emma. You will be sorry to hear that
good Sir William did not leave her in such comfortable circumstances as his fortune would have allowed. He has given
it amongst his relations. But she will do honour to his
memory, although every one else of his friends call loudly
against him on that account.'

I trust, my dear Emma, she has wrote you. If she can
forget Emma, I hope God will forget her! But, you think,
that she never will or can. Now is her time to show it. You
will only show the King and Queen's letters to some few particular friends. The King is very low; lives mostly at Belve-
dere. Mr. Elliot had not seen either him or the Queen, from
the 17th, the day of his arrival, to the 21st. On the next
day, he was to be presented.

I have made up my mind, that it is part of the plan of that
Corsican Scoundrel to conquer the Kingdom of Naples. He
has marched thirteen thousand men into the Kingdom, on the
Adriatic side; and he will take possession, with as much
shadow of right, of Gaeta and Naples: and, if the poor King
remonstrates, or allows us to secure Sicily, he will call it War,
and declare a conquest. I have cautioned General Acton,
not to risk the Royal Family too long; but Naples will be
conquered, sooner or later, as it may suit Buonaparte's convenience. The Morea, and Egypt, are likewise in his eye. An
Army of full seventy thousand men are assembling in Italy.

Gibbs and Noble[3] are gone to Malta. I am, you may
believe, very anxious to get off Toulon, to join the Fleet.
Sir Richard Bickerton went from off Naples, the day I left
Gibraltar. We passed Monte Christo, Bastia, and Cape
Corse, yesterday; and are now moving, slowly, direct for
Toulon. What force they have, I know not; indeed, I am

---

[2] Vide p. 84, ante.   [3] Two English Merchants at Palermo.

totally ignorant : some say nine Sail of the Line, some seven, some five.　If the former, they will come out ; for we have only the same number, including Sixty-fours, and very shortly manned.　However, I hope they will come out, and let us settle the matter.　You know I hate being kept in suspense.

July 8th.

I left this hole, to put down what force the French have at Toulon.　Seven Sail of the Line ready, five Frigates, and six Corvettes.　One or two more in about a week.　We, to-day, eight ·Sail of the Line—to-morrow, seven ; including two Sixty-four gun Ships.

You will readily believe how rejoiced I shall be to get one of your dear, excellent letters, that I may know everything which has passed since my absence.　I sincerely hope that Mr. Booth has settled all your accounts.　Never mind, my dear Emma, a few hundred pounds, which is all the rigid gripe of the law, not justice, can wrest from you.　I thank God that you cannot want ; (although that is no good reason for its being taken from you :) whilst I have sixpence, you shall not want for fivepence of it !　But you have bought your experience that there is no friendship in money concerns, and your good sense will make you profit of it.　I hope the Minister has done something for you.　But never mind, we can live upon bread and cheese.　Independence is a blessing ; and although I have not yet found out the way to get Prize money—what has been taken has run into our mouths—however, it must turn out very hard if I cannot get enough to pay off my debts, and that will be no small comfort.

I have not mentioned my Bronté affairs to Acton, as yet ; but if Naples remains much longer, I shall ask the question. But I expect nothing from them.　I believe even Acton wishes himself well and safely removed.　I think from what I hear, that the King's spirits are so much depressed, that he will give up the reins of Naples, at least, to his Son, and retire to Sicily.　Sir William, you know, always thought that he would end his life so.　Certainly, his situation must be heart-breaking !　Gaetano returned in the Frigate.　I believe he saw enough of Naples.　He carried his family money ; and Mr. Falconet (Gibbs being absent) will pay Mr. Greville's pension to Gaetano's family.　I have now [sent] Gaetano to the post: and he desires to present his duty; and to tell you that Mr. Ragland, from Sir William's death, will not pay any more pensions, without orders from Mr. Greville. Vincenzo has had none paid. He is very poor; keeps a shop. His son wanted, I find, to come in the Frigate to me. I cannot afford to maintain him, therefore I shall give no encouragement. Old Antonio was allowed a carline a day; that is, now, not paid. Sabatello lives with Mr. Elliot. Nicolo, and Mary Antonia have left Mr. Gibbs, for some cause; Gaetano says, be believes, for *amore*. Francesca has two children living, and another coming. She lives the best amongst them, like *gallant homme*. Pasqual lives with the Duke Monteleone; and Joseph, with the old Russian. Your house is a hotel; the upper parts are kept for the Marquis, the owner. Mr. Elliot has taken the house of the Baillé Franconi, on the Chaia. Doctor Nudi inquired kindly after us; and all the women at Santa Lucia expected, when they saw Gaetano, that you was arrived. Bread never was so dear; everything else in plenty. The wages not being raised, Gaetano says the poor of England are a million times better off. So much for Gaetano's news. He desires his duty to Signora Madre, and remembrances to Mary Ann, Fatima, &c.

July 8th.

We joined, this morning, the Fleet. The men in the Ships are good; but the Ships themselves are a little the worse for wear, and very short of their complements of men. We shall never be better; therefore, let them come; the sooner the better. I shall write a line to the Duke,[4] that he may see I do not forget my friends; and I rely, my dearest Emma, on your saying every kind thing for me to the Doctor, Mrs. Nelson, Mrs. Bolton, Mr. and Mrs. Matcham, Mrs. Cadogan, whose kindness and goodness I shall never forget. You will have the goodness to send the inclosed as directed; and be assured that I am, to the last moment of my life, your most attached, faithful, and affectionate,

NELSON AND BRONTE.

---

4 The Duke of Hamilton.

TO ADMIRAL HIS ROYAL HIGHNESS THE DUKE OF CLARENCE.

[From Clarke and M'Arthur, vol. ii. p. 313.]

Off Monaco, July 5th.

I arrived at Gibraltar on the 3rd, in the night, and sailed on the 4th of June. On the 15th I reached Malta, and left it at three o'clock on the morning of the 17th. It was the 25th before I got off Naples, where I was glad to find that Sir Richard Bickerton had, on the 4th of June, steered for Toulon. Owing to the frequent calms at this season in the Mediterranean, we have not yet joined Sir Richard, but I hope to see them to-morrow. Reports say that the Fleet is in very good order as to discipline, but miserably off in respect to numbers; we have only to hope that the French will soon give us an opportunity of trying our strength with them. It is perhaps very difficult for any one to say what are the plans of Buonaparte: he is assembling a very large Army in Italy, and has already placed 13,000 men in the Kingdom of Naples. I think it can only be with a view to conquer it, when it may, on some pretence or other, suit his convenience. The Morea, and ultimately Egypt, are in his view: therefore his assembling so many Troops in Italy—they say full 80,000—can only be for the purpose of removing them across the Adriatic. With this idea, I fully expect that the French Fleet from Brest will assuredly come into the Mediterranean, to protect this Army across the water, and alongshore from Genoa, Leghorn, &c. which are full of Troops. We must keep a good look out, both here and off Brest; and if I have the means, I shall try and fight one party or the other, before they form a junction. I am, &c.

NELSON AND BRONTE.

TO ADMIRAL THE EARL OF ST. VINCENT, K.B.

[Autograph, in the possession of Vice-Admiral Sir William Parker, Bart., G.C.B. "Friday, 8th July, A.M., at 2-43 saw the Fleet. At 4 30, made the Private signal with a gun. At 4-40, repeated ditto, which was answered. At 6-30 bore up, and returned the salute with eleven guns to Sir Richard Bickerton, Bart. At 7, joined the Fleet, consisting of nine Sail of the Line, one Frigate, and two Sloops; viz., Kent, Donegal, Gibraltar, Superb, Belleisle, Triumph, Agincourt, Monmouth, Renown, Medusa, Termagant, and Weazle. At Noon, entrance of Toulon, N.E. B. N."—Amphion's Log.]

Amphion, off Toulon, July 8th, 1803.

My dear Lord,

I joined the Fleet this morning, and as far as outside show goes, they look very well ; but they complain of their bottoms, and, as you will see, are very short of men. The Blonde, which sails for England with the Convoy, takes hers this day from the Triumph and Agincourt. Sir Richard Bickerton had put Captain Burn,[5] of the Blonde Troop-Ship, into her, in room of Captain Stuart, removed to the Kent, in the room of Captain O'Brien,[6] invalided. If the reports which I hear from Gore[7] are true, that Whitby[8] is going home, I shall—as I take for granted an arrangement is made for Captain Stuart— desire Sir Richard Bickerton to select his own Captain, till the pleasure of the Admiralty is known, and appoint a Lieutenant to act in the vacancy. Captain George Elliot, of course, goes directly into the Termagant.

By the Toulon report, your Lordship will see that we are not very superior, if anything, in point of numbers ; for it seems uncertain whether there are not more than the seven clearly in a state of forwardness. My reports from Italy say nine, five Frigates, and some Corvettes ;—Formidable, Scipion, Berwick, Swiftsure, Hannibal, Jemappes, two Ships seen by the Raven off Minorca the latter end of April, supposed those seen by the Dragon on her passage home ; one Ship seen by a Merchant-Ship off Cape de Gatte.

Seven of the Line and five Frigates are clearly to be seen, with two Admirals and a Commodore, and a Commodore in the Frigate. However, your Lordship may rely that I shall make the best of what I have ; but you will see that I cannot detach any Ships of the Line for the Straits' Mouth. The

---

[5] Captain John Burn : he died a Commander in February 1813.

[6] Captain Edward O'Brien : he became a Rear-Admiral, and died in December 1808.

[7] Captain John Gore, of the Medusa, who will be frequently mentioned, afterwards Vice-Admiral Sir John Gore, K.C.B., G.C.H. : he died in August 1836.

[8] Captain John Whitby, eldest son of the Rev. Thomas Whitby, of Creswell Hall, near Stafford. Writing to Admiral Cornwallis some months afterwards, Lord Nelson said, "As my old acquaintance and Shipmate, Captain Hargood, is not arrived, I have directed Whitby to remain a short time in the Belleisle, in order to reap the harvest of all his toils. He has had up-hill work in her, and I should wish him to enjoy the fruit alongside a Frenchman. I assure you I am not singular in regretting the loss of Whitby from our little Squadron: it is universal."—*Clarke and M'Arthur.* Captain Whitby died on the 7th of April, 1806.

Monmouth and Agincourt sail very ill, and in these times are hardly to be reckoned. I cannot send them to watch either Genoa or Leghorn; and if these gentry should come forth, I shall want all the Seventy-fours. The Triumph's bowsprit is in such a dangerous state, that I am sending her to Gibraltar, to get either a new one, or her present one repaired; and from thence she will soon join me with a Westerly wind. Malta is out of the question; with all my anxiety I have been three weeks.

Sir Richard Bickerton has requested of me to mention to your Lordship that he is very desirous of remaining in the Mediterranean. I can, of course, have no objection; on the contrary, I have always heard him spoken of very highly as an Officer. Ever, my dear Lord, I am your obliged and faithful,   NELSON AND BRONTE.

Poor Captain Burn, who Sir Richard speaks very highly of, has requested of me to mention him to you, in hopes you will give him a good Sloop.

July 9th.—There are, Captain Staines[9] says, two Sail of the Line under Sepet, in the Bight, which, as Gore only looked over Isthmus, he could not see.

TO ALEXANDER DAVISON, ESQ.

[Autograph, in the possession of Colonel Davison.]

My dear Davison,   Amphion, off Toulon, July 8th, 1803.
This will, I hope, find you at Swarland, and relieved from the cruel state in which your anxiety to oblige your friends [has placed you.] I assure you not a day has passed that I have not thought of you, and I shall rejoice to hear that you are got quit of this embarrassment.[1] Of myself I can say that you have not a more sincere, attached friend in the world, and that includes all I could say. I only joined the Fleet this day, and I find that the French in Toulon are equal to me at this moment; but I do not think they will come out till they have a greater superiority. If they do, I shall be agreeably disappointed. The event, I trust, although we are miserably

---

[9] Vide p. 139, post.   [1] Vide p. 143, post.

short of men, would be glorious, and hasten a Peace; which that it may soon do, is the sincere prayer of, my dear Davison, your most obliged, faithful, and affectionate friend,

NELSON AND BRONTE.

I have not made my fortune by Prizes yet.

TO JAMES CUTFORTH, ESQ., AGENT VICTUALLER, GIBRALTAR.

[Letter-Book.]

Sir,   Amphion, off Toulon, 8th July, 1803.

Having received information from the Victualling Board, that several Ships laden with Provisions have been ordered to Gibraltar, I am to desire you will send two of them here immediately, (should a Man-of-War be coming this way,) otherwise have them in readiness to accompany the Triumph, whose Captain is directed to take them under his protection. You are to be particularly careful to send as near as possible the regular proportions of each species of provisions in the said Victuallers, and continue to do so on all future occasions, when it can be done consistent with the Service. You are to send as much wine as you can conveniently, but on no account spirits. I am, Sir, &c.

NELSON AND BRONTE.

TO SIR EVAN NEPEAN, BART., ADMIRALTY.

[Original, in the Admiralty.]

Sir,   Amphion, off Toulon, 8th July, 1803.

You will please to acquaint the Lords Commissioners of the Admiralty, that I arrived off here yesterday forenoon, and was joined by Rear-Admiral Sir Richard Bickerton, with his Majesty's Ships named in the margin.[9]

Captain Gore, of the Medusa, having reconnoitred the harbour of Toulon, yesterday, acquaints me that there are seven Sail of the Line in the Inner and Outer Roads, fully rigged, or nearly so, together with five Frigates, and six or seven Corvettes, in the same state of forwardness, and that there is

---

[9] Kent, Donegal, Superb, Belleisle, Triumph, Renown, Gibraltar, Monmouth, Agincourt, Medusa, Weazle, Termagant. Maidstone rejoined the 25th June; Niger joined the 20th June; Raven joined the 2nd July.

reason to believe there is one or two Sail of the Line in the Arsenal. There is an Admiral's Flag at the main, a Rear-Admiral, and Commodore in a Line-of-Battle Ship, and a Commodore in one of the Frigates. I shall take a very early opportunity of sending a Frigate off the harbour of Toulon, in order to ascertain their state of forwardness, and watch their motions accordingly. I am, Sir, &c.

NELSON AND BRONTE.

TO ADMIRAL HIS ROYAL HIGHNESS THE DUKE OF CLARENCE.

[From Clarke and M'Arthur, vol. ii. p. 314.]

July 9th, 1803.

I joined the Fleet yesterday, and it was with much sorrow that I saw your Royal Highness's friend, Captain Keats,[1] looking so very ill; but he says he is recovering. I have such a high respect for his character, that I should be happy in doing all in my power to promote it. He is too valuable an Officer for the King's Service to lose. The French Fleet is seven or nine Sail of the Line, nearly ready for sea, five Frigates, and some Corvettes. We have only to wish for their coming out, it would remove most of our fancied wants, we have few real ones, except the sight of the French Fleet, which would give much pleasure to your Royal Highness's attached and devoted servant,

NELSON AND BRONTE.

TO ADMIRAL THE EARL OF ST. VINCENT, K.B.

[Autograph, in the possession of Vice-Admiral Sir William Parker, Bart., G.C.B.

July 9th, 1803.

My dear Lord,

I have wrote Troubridge about your intentions for the Ambuscade,[2] and for any other Ships of War which may be

---

[1] Afterwards Admiral Sir Richard Keats, G.C.B.

[2] The Ambuscade French Frigate was captured by the Victory, Captain Samuel Sutton, on the 28th of May, 1803, in latitude 45° 40′ N., longitude 6° 10′ W. She was formerly an English Frigate of the same name, which she still continued to bear when again taken into our Navy.

taken. I have received nothing officially from Sutton (nor privately) relative to the capture; and I hope that you will approve of my plan for getting such Prizes in a state for sea. Your Lordship knows that the Harbour of Malta is well adapted for such an arrangement, even if it extended to twenty Sail of the Line. Ever, my dear Lord, yours most faithfully,

NELSON AND BRONTE.

TO MAJOR-GENERAL VILLETTES.

[Autograph, in the possession of J. Wilde, Esq.]

Off Toulon, July 9th, 1803.

My dear General,

I have this moment ordered the Phœbe, who is at Naples, to receive on board immediately any money there may be there for the service of Malta. The Active is just arrived, and I have an immediate opportunity of obeying your commands, which it will always give me the sincerest pleasure to attend to. The French in Toulon are not, it appears a match for us just yet. I have not heard a word from England since I left it. Sir Richard Bickerton going to Malta, renders my writing the less necessary, for I find him a very intelligent and correct Officer. When I shall see you, the French must determine; but I am, my dear General, ever yours most faithfully,

NELSON AND BRONTE.

INSTRUCTIONS TO REAR-ADMIRAL SIR RICHARD BICKERTON, BART.

[From a Copy, in the possession of James Young, Esq., of Wells.]

Amphion, off Toulon, July 10th, 1803.

Lord Nelson requests Sir Richard Bickerton, to attend to the following Memoranda:—

The Convoy to be dispatched for England as soon as possible, and the Mameluke Bey[3] to be ordered a passage in one of the Ships, and all invalided men to be sent home. The destination of the Ships cruizing to be changed, if Sir Richard

---

[3] Mahomed Bey Elfi. Vide p. 111, ante.

finds that circumstances have altered which induced me to place them on their several stations. A French Vessel having been captured by the Cyclops and Experiment, I fear in violation of the Neutral Port of Naples, I beg that you will make such inquiries as the case may require; and if you find that she has been improperly taken, you will order her to be released to the Master and her Crew, giving the Vessel a passport to Naples. If any unforeseen circumstance should arise, Lord Nelson has that perfect confidence in the judgment of Sir R. Bickerton, that there can be no doubt but that whatever arrangement he may think proper to make, will be approved of.

NELSON AND BRONTE.

MEMORANDA.

[Autograph, in the possession of James Young, Esq., of Wells.]

[About 10th July, 1803.]

The Bey to be sent to England with the Convoy. The Commissary for prisoners, if necessary to be appointed. The Buoys to be laid down in the Harbour's mouth.[4] The Master-Attendant to have a Boat and six men, and a Coxswain, allowed for his use, to be entered in the Dock-yard. The Ambuscade's stores to be received into the Naval Storehouses, and taken care of, and the Ship to be taken care of by the Officers of the Yard. An awning to be kept spread over her in the day, and her decks and sides to be wetted every evening, and when the business of the Fleet will admit. She is to be caulked, her bends blacked and painted, and rigging put in order. 500 Maltese, if possible, to be raised. A bounty of   dollars to be given for those who have served in the Navy before;   dollars for those who have never been at sea: to serve three years, if the War lasts so long. To be paid half their wages to their families, and when they are paid off, to be paid their wages at Malta, and not to be sent out of the Mediterranean station without their consent.

⁴ Valetta.

TO CAPTAIN HENRY RICHARDSON, H. M. SHIP JUNO.

[Letter-Book.]

Amphion, off Toulon, 10th July, 1803.

Sir,

In addition to my order to you of the 26th ultimo,[4] I am to desire, should you, from information, find the Enemy are not likely to convoy their Troops along shore into Sicily, or the Coast of Calabria opposite to it, immediately, that you will stretch occasionally with his Majesty's Ship (and Sloop named in the margin[5]) under your command into the entrance of the Adriatic, for the purpose of protecting the Trade of his Majesty's Subjects, and the annoyance and destruction of that of the Enemy; paying, however, strict regard to the order of the 26th ultimo, above-mentioned. I am, Sir, &c.

NELSON AND BRONTE.

TO THE OFFICERS OF HIS MAJESTY'S YARD AT MALTA.

[Order-Book.]

Amphion, off Toulon, 10th July, 1803.

Captain Sutton, of his Majesty's Ship Victory, having captured the French Frigate Ambuscade, and sent her into Malta, You are hereby required and directed to receive the stores of every description belonging to the said Ship, into his Majesty's Store-houses under your charge, and to be very careful that no embezzlement of any kind takes place; and you are, as early as convenient, to value the hull, masts, rigging and stores of the said Ship; and in order that the strictest regard may be had to a faithful and just statement thereof you are to take to your assistance the Carpenter of his Majesty's Ship Kent, and any person or persons that you may think necessary on the occasion. After such valuation has been made, you are to take charge of the Ship, stores, &c., and put her in a proper condition for being Commissioned, with as much expedition as possible.

NELSON AND BRONTE.

[4] Vide p. 103, ante.   [5] Morgiana.

TO HIS EXCELLENCY HUGH ELLIOT, ESQ.

[Autograph, in the Elliot Papers.]

Amphion, off Toulon, July 11th, 1803.

My dear Sir, .

I joined the Fleet the 8th, in the morning, having had nothing but calms and contrary winds. The French have seven Sail of the Line, nearly ready for sea, five Frigates and six or seven Corvettes. I believe from other observations of the Enemy's Fleet, and calculations, that there are nine Sail of the Line, unless some are gone to sea, which I do not believe. I dispatched all our letters to England on the 9th, in which, I stated everything relative to this Country. It is perfectly clear to me that if our reports are true of Troops collecting at Leghorn and Genoa, these can only be for embarkation in a Fleet which may be expected there. I must not say too much; for, God knows, I -wish from my heart every security to the Kingdom of Naples, but I expect to hear of the French demanding to garrison Gaeta, the consequence of which would be great. I would not be thought for a moment to see Fear. beyond what is necessary—therefore, I will not say more about securing Sicily than I have done. I send the Superb, 74, Captain Keats, one of the very best Officers in his Majesty's Navy. I have directed him to remain fourteen days at Naples, and if you represent by letter that it is, from extraordinary circumstances, necessary that he should remain longer, Captain Keats has directions to acquiesce. But, I trust, your Excellency will not do this, unless such necessity does exist; for you will recollect that I am left with six Sail of the Line opposed to seven or nine—in which number are two 64-gun Ships. But I take every responsibility to show my attention to the safety of the Royal Family of Naples. I have not heard a word from England since we left it. I have the honour to be, &c.,

NELSON AND BRONTE.

TO HIS EXCELLENCY HUGH ELLIOT, ESQ.

[Autograph, in the Elliot Papers.]

Private.   July 11th, 1803.

My dear Sir,

George[6] took possession of his Sloop yesterday, and if you can send him some little matters, they will be acceptable to young housekeepers—not bulky articles, for Captain Keats could not receive them. Give me leave to introduce Captain Keats to your particular notice. His health has not been very good, but I hope he will soon recover; for his loss would, I assure you, be a serious one to our Navy, and particularly to me ; for I esteem his *person* alone as equal to *one* French 74, and the Superb and her Captain equal to two 74-gun Ships : therefore, if it is not necessary, you will not keep him; for another Ship will be on her way to Naples, at the time I guess she will be near her departure ; and, although I should be glad to see the French out, even six to nine, yet these are odds which, although I should not avoid, yet ought not to be seeking.

The Victory is at Malta. She has taken the Ambuscade French Frigate, and two or three Ships from St. Domingo ; but with my usual luck for Prize-money, they belong to Admiral Cornwallis,[7] and not to me. Captain Murray, Hardy, Doctor Scott,[8] Mr. Scott,[9] and all your friends here, join in every good wish for your health, with, my dear Sir, yours most faithfully,

NELSON AND BRONTE.

A little tea, sugar, and a few hams, is all Captain Keats can take for George, and all that is necessary to send him.

---

[6] Captain the Honourable George Elliot, who was appointed to the command of the Termagant.

[7] Having been captured within the limits of Admiral Cornwallis' Station.

[8] The Reverend Alexander John Scott, Chaplain of the Victory, whom Lord Nelson generally called " Doctor," though he did not take that Degree until after the battle of Trafalgar. An interesting Memoir of this learned and accomplished person was published by his daughter and son-in-law in 1842, entitled, " Recollections of the Life of the Reverend A. J. Scott, Lord Nelson's Chaplain," which contains many interesting anecdotes of Nelson."

[9] Lord Nelson's Secretary.

TO THE RIGHT HONOURABLE GEORGE ROSE.

[Autograph, in the possession of the Right Honourable Sir George Rose, G.C.H.]

Amphion, off Toulon, July 12th, 1803.

My dear Sir,

I find your young friend is Lieutenant of the Acasta Frigate, who is in the Channel, not that at this moment I have any chance of being useful to him; but I shall always bear him in mind.

The French in Toulon are busy fitting out: they have, at least seven—I believe nine—Sail of the Line, five Frigates, six or seven Corvettes, ready, or nearly so, for sea. We wish them out, that we may make a beginning. What diabolical plans they are after in Italy, time must show us; but I think that Egypt is their great object. To keep their hands in, they may take Naples, try for Sicily and Sardinia—certainly, the Morea, Seven Isles, and Egypt. *Live and see.* All our Egyptian Army is gone, and we never wanted 10,000 Troops more than at this moment, which might save Naples, Sicily, the Morea, and Egypt, by assisting and giving confidence to the Inhabitants. Our friend the Reverend Mr. Scott is very much recovered since he came out; but I have told him, that, at this moment, I cannot address a letter to Mr. Addington for him. With every sentiment of respect and friendship, believe me ever, my dear Sir, your much obliged and faithful friend,

NELSON AND BRONTE.

I have not heard one word from England since I sailed, May 20th.

TO SIR EVAN NEPEAN, BART., ADMIRALTY.

[Original, in the Admiralty.]

Amphion, off Toulon, 12th July, 1803.

Sir,

As there is no Agent Victualler attached to the Fleet under my command, and as most of the supplies of fresh beef and other necessary refreshments for the Ships' Companies, must be procured from Sardinia, Barbary, or, clandestinely, from

Spain, where Victualling or other Bills are not negotiable; and
as the great distance from Malta or Gibraltar renders the
getting such refreshments from those places, in a regular manner, absolutely impossible; and at all seasons, from the length
of passage to Malta, must ever preclude a very frequent intercourse, I, therefore, beg leave to submit to their Lordships,
(if they do not judge proper to appoint an Agent Victualler
to the Fleet,) the propriety of lodging Public money on board
the Fleet, for the purpose of paying for the fresh beef and
vegetables which may be appropriated for this service, provided, but on *no account otherwise*, that their Lordships will
give orders that the simple receipt from the Captain of the
Ship, to whom any sum or sums of money is given, for the
payment of such fresh supplies, may be a sufficient Voucher
for the disbursement of such money, and a full discharge from
any impress against me. And as this measure will attach a
responsibility upon the Captains who may be sent for procuring
fresh beef, &c., for the Fleet, I also beg that their Lordships
will exonerate them from the charge, and direct the Victualling
Board not to impress their Accounts for such purchases, provided the Vouchers for them are regular and correct, and that
the usual forms in procuring provisions have been duly attended
to, and executed accordingly.

I shall on all occasions, where live cattle, &c., are purchased
for the individual Ship, or Fleet, direct the Captains to send
their Masters on shore with their respective Pursers, to ascertain the prices and quality thereof, and shall direct that every
pound of beef, vegetables, &c., so purchased, may be weighed
on its coming on board, and entered in the Log-Book immediately, and that the Signing Officers shall examine the Vouchers
with that Book, previous to their putting their signatures to
them, in order that every species of fraud (should any be
intended) may be detected, and the possibility of doing
wrong prevented, as much as possible. I am, Sir, &c.

                              NELSON AND BRONTE.

TO ADMIRAL THE EARL OF ST. VINCENT, K.B.

[Autograph, in the possession of Vice-Admiral Sir William Parker, Bart., G.C.B.]

My dear Lord,   Amphion, July 12th, 1803.

From our being shut out of almost every place where our
bills will be taken for beef, &c., &c., and there being no Agent-
Victualler like Mr. Heatly, who would find the Fleet in everything, in all parts that we used to send to, we are absolutely in
distress for money to purchase in Sardinia, or anywhere else,
where bullocks, &c., can be had for *money*, but where our bills
are useless.   But, although Sir Richard Bickerton very handsomely, for the good, in every sense of the word, of his Majesty's
Service, took up 10,000 dollars, and issued to the Fleet, yet
the forms of Office I know so far from applauding his conduct,
will distress him most probably to get his Accounts cleared of
this impress.   Troubridge told me, when I asked him for a
floating Agent-Victualler, who would pay all things in all
places, 'Mr. Wilkie[1] is a very clever man ; he will arrange
everything ; he will get you things from everywhere.'   *Now*,
the direct contrary is the fact.   Mr. Wilkie will have nothing
to do with supplying the Fleet anywhere but *at* Malta.   No,
not even to send a man who might make some arrangement for our getting bullocks and refreshments from Sardinia, or from the Bay of Rosas, or other parts of Spain ;
from his management, I thought he could have managed our
intercourse with Spain, even clandestinely. I certainly hate to
have anything to do with the management of money ; but if the
Admiralty will sanction my drawing for a sum of money, and
will give orders that the *simple* receipt of the Captain for so
much Public money, shall be a clear and sufficient discharge
for me, in that case, I will take this task upon me.   I know
some people are preparing for fleecing us, and, without we
have money to go to market, so they must.

The Ships having come out on the expectation of a three
weeks' cruise, I am, in turn, sending them into Port, to prepare for a War cruize.   Many of the Ships have much scurvy
in them, but onions and lemons I hope will eradicate that
complaint, and a sight of the French Squadron twenty leagues

---

[1] Mr. Peter Wilkie, Agent-Victualler at Malta.

at sea will cure all our complaints, which, that it may very soon do, is the sincere wish of, my dear Lord, your most faithful,   NELSON AND BRONTE.

Mr. Fulton, who has been recommended to you and myself by poor Locker,[2] has just been with me. He is Acting-Purser of the Gibraltar, in the room of Mr. Grant; and requests me to intercede with your Lordship that in case Mr. Grant does not come out, he may be confirmed for her.

TO SIR EVAN NEPEAN, BART., ADMIRALTY.

[Original, in the Admiralty.]

Sir,   Amphion, off Toulon, 12th July, 1803.

Several Prisoners having been sent to Malta in the French Prizes captured by his Majesty's Ships and Vessels on this Station, and put in quarantine in Valette harbour, and there being no Commissary or person at that place authorized by Government to take charge of such Prisoners, or to supply them with provisions, you will please to acquaint the Lords Commissioners of the Admiralty, that I have appointed a Mr. Chapman to act as Commissary of Prisoners till some person shall be appointed from England, or he receives further orders from me, which I hope will meet their Lordships' approbation. This gentleman (who I have not seen) belonged to the Secretary of State's Office, and was sent to Malta by Lord Hobart, to act *pro tempore* as Secretary to the Civil Commissioner, and is recommended to me by Sir Alexander Ball. I am, &c.

                                    NELSON AND BRONTE.

TO SIR EVAN NEPEAN, BART., ADMIRALTY.

[Original, in the Admiralty.]

Sir,   Amphion, off Toulon, 12th July, 1803.

Inclosed is an extract of a Memorandum, sent by Rear-Admiral Sir Richard Bickerton to Malta, (who is gone to that place to make good the defects of the Kent,) for the raising five hundred Maltese for his Majesty's Navy. The bounty

---

[2] His old friend, Commodore Locker.

to be given is left blank for the Rear-Admiral (after he has
consulted with Sir Alexander Ball on the subject) to determine.

I am, therefore, to request you will please to lay the
inclosure above-mentioned before the Lords Commissioners
of the Admiralty for their consideration; and if they approve
thereof, that directions may be given for the payment and due
execution thereof accordingly.　I am, Sir, &c.

　　　　　　　　　　　　　　　NELSON AND BRONTE.

TO SIR EVAN NEPEAN, BART., ADMIRALTY.

[Letter-Book.]

Amphion, off Toulon, 12th July, 1803.

　Sir,
A number of Midshipmen belonging to his Majesty's Ships
and Vessels under my command, who have served their time,
and are desirous to pass for Lieutenants, have requested my
permission to go to England for that purpose, in order that
they may be in the way of promotion.　You will be pleased
to acquaint their Lordships, that I have not thought proper
to comply with their request, until I shall be informed whether
this regulation is to be considered in force, and whether those
Midshipmen who have served their time, and are desirous to
pass for Lieutenants, shall be discharged from their Ships, and
sent to England to pass their examination accordingly.　I beg,
with due deference, to observe to their Lordships the great hardship and inconvenience which this measure subjects the Midshipmen to, and may be attended with great disadvantage to
his Majesty's Service in these seas.　I am, Sir, &c.,

　　　　　　　　　　　　　　　NELSON AND BRONTE.

TO ADMIRAL THE EARL OF ST. VINCENT, K.B.

[Autograph, in the possession of Vice-Admiral Sir William Parker, Bart., G.C.B.]

Off Toulon, July 13th, 1803.

　My dear Lord,
The Monmouth and Agincourt are certainly, for the men
they have, most extraordinarily well-manned Ships; but, in

point of sailing, the Britannia was, in her last days, a flyer
compared to them.   I verily believe, that a French Seventy-
four, main-topsail to the mast, would beat them in turning to
windward; but their men would be a sufficient number,
filled up with landsmen, to man a Three-decker : therefore, if
the Admiralty direct particular Ships to be sent home, when
others are sent out, I hope these two will be amongst the first.
When a Winter's cruize comes, they never can keep company
with the Squadron.   Ever, my dear Lord, yours faithfully,

NELSON AND BRONTE.

TO THE RIGHT HONOURABLE HENRY ADDINGTON.

[From Clarke and M'Arthur, vol. ii. p. 320.]

Off Toulon, 16th July, 1803.

I send you some Papers relative to, and some Letters from,
Odessa, a Russian Port in the Black Sea, of which the Duke
de Richelieu is Governor.   You will know much better than
I can tell you, how this emigrant Duke has been courted
by Buonaparte through his Minister in Russia.   We must
recollect that he is a Frenchman, and his ultimate views probably turn in getting back some of his estates in France.   It
appears odd it should so happen, that a Frenchman should be
appointed Governor of a place where the French are to have so
much intercourse.   From all I have heard before I left England,
I cannot help thinking that Russia and France understand each
other about the Turkish Dominions.   If so, Egypt will be the
price; this Mr. Bourgoin is a very clever fellow, and knows
his business; I take him to be nephew to the Minister who
was in Denmark.   The French trade in the Levant did not
answer in the Peace;—all the letters I have say so (more than
100), and many houses in Marseilles have stopped payment.
Forgive my suggestions, but they will naturally obtrude
themselves, I meant merely to send the Papers.   I am, &c.,

NELSON AND BRONTE.

TO CAPTAIN JAMES HILLYAR,[1] H. M. SHIP NIGER.

[Order Book.]

Amphion, off Toulon, 20th July, 1803.

You are hereby required and directed to proceed immediately with his Majesty's Ship Niger under your command towards Genoa and Leghorn, and endeavour by every means in your power, to ascertain the number of Troops that are collected at those places, and in their vicinity, and whether there are any Vessels assembling for their embarkation. You are also to use your utmost endeavours to obtain such intelligence of the Enemy's movements and intentions, as you may judge necessary for my information. You are also to endeavour to find out whether the Hannibal or any French Frigates are in the harbours of Genoa, Leghorn, Porto Ferraio, or St. Fiorenzo. Having so done, you are to return and join me on my Rendezvous off this place, in fourteen or sixteen days from the time you shall leave the Fleet on the above service.

NELSON AND BRONTE.

TO ADMIRAL THE EARL OF ST. VINCENT, K.B.

[Autograph, in the possession of Vice-Admiral Sir William Parker, Bart., G.C.B.]

Amphion, July 21st, 1803.

My dear Lord,

As the Medusa is going to Gibraltar, and to look out to the Westward of the Straits, I send my letters to take their chance of a conveyance to England. It is not in my power to send any Line of Battle Ships to the Westward, for your Lordship will know that I am endeavouring to keep the generality of them patched up for the service here. The strength of the N.W. gales does not seem to have diminished since we were here last. I expect Victory about the end of the month, for less than a three weeks' passage from Malta is not to be expected at this season. The Redbridge Schooner I ordered to sail July 1st, and she is not arrived: Lieutenant ——— is, I believe, a very bad tool, besides, to work with.

---

[1] Afterwards Rear-Admiral Sir James Hillyar, K.C.B., K.C.H.: he died in July 1843.

I am keeping the Fleet West from Cape Sicie from ten to fifteen leagues, to intercept anything which may come from the Westward, and two Frigates are off the Harbour. Ever, my dear Lord, wishing you health and comfort, I am your most faithful servant,

NELSON AND BRONTE.

I do not think the Toulon Squadron will move till joined by something from Brest.

TO CAPTAIN JOHN GORE, H.M. SHIP MEDUSA.

[Order-Book.]

Amphion, off Toulon, 21st July, 1803.

Whereas there is reason to believe that a Squadron of the Enemy's Ships of War are coming from the West Indies or from Brest, to join the Fleet in Toulon; You are, therefore, hereby required and directed to take your route from Cape Spartel towards Madeira, from thence to Cape St. Vincent, and to Cape Spartel, and to use every possible endeavour to gain such intelligence of the Enemy's movements and intentions as you may judge necessary for my information, which you are to forward to me by a Sloop of War from Gibraltar; but should you fall in with an Enemy's Squadron steering for the Mediterranean, you are in that case to join me on my Rendez-vous off Toulon without a moment's loss of time, sending a Boat into Gibraltar to acquaint any of the Squadron which may be there with such information, that if of the Line they may join me immediately. You are to continue on this service till further orders, returning to Gibraltar at the expiration of six weeks from the time of your leaving Cape Spartel, if you should not have gained any information which might make it necessary for my being acquainted with it before that time.

NELSON AND BRONTE.

TO CAPTAIN THOMAS STAINES,[2] H. M. SLOOP CAMELEON.

[Order-Book.]

Amphion, off Toulon, 25th July, 1803.

You are hereby required and directed to proceed immediately with his Majesty's Sloop Cameleon, under your command, to Barcelona, and on your arrival there, deliver the Public letter you will herewith receive, addressed to his Britannic Majesty's Consul-General at that place, where you are to remain for the space of twelve hours for his answer, and afterwards return and join me, on my Rendezvous off this place, with the utmost possible dispatch. You are not to salute the Fort of his Catholic Majesty, unless you receive a positive assurance that an equal number of guns will be returned, and that every hospitality is shown you, which, from the Peace and subsisting good understanding between the two Monarchs, we have every reason to demand and expect.

NELSON AND BRONTE.

TO HIS EXCELLENCY HUGH ELLIOT, ESQ.

[Autograph, in the Elliot Papers.]

My dear Sir,　　　　Amphion, July 26th, 1803, off Toulon.

I was honoured with your Excellency's letters this morning of July 7th and 8th, by the Phœbe—to all which I can say little; for it is not difficult to see, if the War goes on, that the Kingdom of Naples will be lost, and its revenue appropriated to the use of Buonaparte's Troops. From my heart I wish for Peace—a solid and honourable one—but I see no prospect of such an event, unless, in addition to the evacuation of Holland and Switzerland, Malta is ceded to us. I send this letter by the Raven Brig, who waits twenty-four hours for some things for Malta, from whence she will join me. The Superb, I expect, was with you on Friday the 15th, and Captain Keats has my orders to sail the 29th. I sincerely hope that she has

---

[2] Captain Thomas Staines, who distinguished himself in command of the Cyané, in Action with a French Squadron in the Bay of Naples in June 1809 : he died a Knight Commander of the Orders of the Bath and of St. Ferdinand and Merit, in July 1830.

not been detained at Naples; for I can very ill spare the services of such a Ship. The French Squadron—seven Sail of the Line, five or six Frigates, and six or seven Corvettes—in the whole eighteen Sail, are in appearance ready for sea, every sail bent. At this moment, I am here with five Sail of the Line, and, when Monmouth goes to Naples, only four, to oppose this force. However, nothing shall induce me to neglect the personal safety of the Royal Family, and Monmouth *shall go*. Your Excellency is aware that I can send no Ship to Naples which wants re-fitting,[3] and, therefore, that parting with a perfect Ship of the Line is a serious thing. The Kent and Agincourt are gone to Malta, the Triumph to Gibraltar, and the Gibraltar wants to go into Port to refit, having sprung her mizen-mast and main-yard. I wished to have sent her to Naples; but I am obliged to keep her, and send a sound Ship. However, this state of suspense will very soon be over. I only hope that Sicily will be guarded; that the French will demand it, I am sure. I shall write fully by the Monmouth; therefore, shall only touch on another subject.

I have heard no rumours of a War with Algiers, nor do I believe a word of it; therefore I cannot begin with them. The French Fleet from St. Domingo, I think, will come to the Mediterranean—perhaps, first to Cadiz, to get the Spaniards to escort them. If so, I may have two Fleets to fight; but if I have the Ships, the more the better. Will your Excellency have the goodness to write a line to Mr. Jackson, to say that I will write him by the Monmouth? and I beg your Excellency to be assured that I am, &c.,

NELSON AND BRONTE.

TO HIS EXCELLENCY HUGH ELLIOT, ESQ.

[Autograph, in the Elliot Papers.]

Private.   July 26th, 1803.

My dear Sir,

The lad you have sent me was on board the Lion with Captain Dixon; but it is, I assure you, totally out of my power to receive the lad, or to do anything for him. I cannot afford

---

[3] As it would be in violation of the Treaty between Naples and France.

to maintain him, nor do I feel it incumbent upon me. If any Captain who goes to Naples chooses to take him, there can be no objection on my part, which is all I can do.

I am sorry that Castelcicala has taken a wrong twist against the English, who are certainly the truest friends to his Sovereign. I am glad that you stand as you [do] with the Queen and General Acton. How can it be otherwise? You have no point to gain; but to tell them and assist them in taking care of the Kingdom of Naples. We are anxiously waiting the arrival of the Victory, and news from England and Gibraltar. Not a word since we sailed. George Elliot went to the Bay of Rosas, a few days ago, and performed his mission very well, as he will do everything he is sent upon.

We are all well and happy; and I am ever, my dear Sir, your most obliged and faithful friend,

NELSON AND BRONTE.

Many thanks for the Papers, which are a great treat.

TO MAJOR-GENERAL VILLETTES, COMMANDER-IN-CHIEF AT MALTA.

[Autograph, in the possession of Josiah French, Esq.]

Off Toulon, July 26th, 1803.

My dear General,

The Phœbe sailed from Naples before the Superb, who sailed the day after Sir Richard Bickerton arrived; therefore, I have not lost a moment in sending the Raven for the money, and shall always feel pleasure in attending to your wishes in every respect. General Acton is in expectation that the Neapolitan Troops are arrived in Sicily from Malta, and as Mr. Elliot and General Acton perfectly understand one another about the possession of Messina, I can no longer object to the Neapolitan Troops leaving Malta on an idea that they might oppose our taking the Citadel of Messina; but I beg to be perfectly understood that the departure of the Neapolitan Troops from Malta will not prevent the sending of all the British force which you can spare to Messina, should that measure be desired by His Excellency Mr. Elliot, or by His Excellency General Acton. I have wrote very strongly to Government,[4] expressive of my regret at the Egyptian Army being ordered home, and urging the sending Troops not only for Sicily but for the Kingdom of Naples.

The French in Toulon are ready for sea; seven sail of the Line, five or six Frigates and six or seven Corvettes, in all eighteen sail; and I think that the St. Domingo Fleet will come to Cadiz in their way to Toulon. I have had nothing from England or Gibraltar, since I left them. Spain is yet friendly. We are looking out for the Victory. I am ever, my dear General, your most obedient and faithful servant,

NELSON AND BRONTE.

TO THE QUEEN OF NAPLES.

[From "Recollections of the Life of the Reverend Doctor Scott," p. 110.]

Madam,   Off Toulon, July 26th, 1803.

The first great object which is always nearest my heart, is the safety of the Persons of your Majesties, and of all the Royal Family. The second, so far as it is in my power, is that of the Kingdom of Naples, which is a very difficult affair.

If your Majesty were to act with all the circumspection in your power, either the French would feel themselves offended, or what is worse, if possible, their assistance would be given by force to the King, for the *preservation* of Sicily. The great wisdom of your Majesty will know all that I could allege upon this subject. I shall therefore only say, that if Sicily is lost, Europe will blame the councils of his Sicilian Majesty and Lord Nelson, for having been so weak as to pay attention to, or credit what is reported, by the Agents of the present French Government.

I have written to the English Government, declaring fully the unhappy position of the Kingdom of Naples; regretting the orders given for the return of the Army of Egypt; and setting forth with energy the necessity for sending Troops, not only to assist in the defence of Sicily, but in sufficient numbers to place garrisons in Gaeta, in the Castles of Naples, if it should be expedient; and to send a body of men into

[4] Vide p. 111, *ante.* See Lord Hobart's reply, in a subsequent page.

Calabria, to support the loyal and brave inhabitants of that
country of mountains, in case the French should be too im-
perious in their demands.

His Excellency, Mr. Elliot, will inform your Majesty of
the difficulty I have, in leaving a Ship of the Line at Naples,
considering the present state of the Enemy's Fleet at Toulon;
but I will never permit my personal feelings to weigh against
the sacred interest which I shall always take in the safety
and well-being of your Majesty and of all the Royal Family;
and I assure your Majesty that I am always your most devoted
and faithful servant,

NELSON AND BRONTE.

TO ALEXANDER DAVISON, ESQ.

[Autograph, in the possession of Colonel Davison.]

Amphion, July 27th, 1803.

My dear Davison,

What an impertinent man that Mr. Lyne must have been.
At least, my word might have been taken, that you were
appointed by unanimous consent of the Captors. Of course, I
should not have wrote so, if Captain Hardy had not authorized me. Captain Hardy did not think, on this occasion, to
name Mr. Lyne, and he has wrote to him or Mr. Tucker. I
find here that many named their own Agents, and some have
put Mr. Scott with them, but I stand independent, and shall
never solicit. I find in that correspondence, that you have sent
many letters to Plymouth, to come out with Doctor Snipe in
a Frigate; but not a thing, or a scrap of a pen, has reached
me from England since I sailed, except a line from Lady
Hamilton, inclosing your correspondence. I hope in God,
my dear Davison, that you will get over these damned prose-
cutions for the Election.[3] It has and does give me very serious
uneasiness.

We have a report through Italy of negotiations for Peace,
and changes of Administration. As for Peace, we cannot

---

[3] Mr. Davison was prosecuted for bribery at the Ilchester Election, and in April
1804, was sentenced by the Court of King's Bench to confinement for twelve
months in the Marshalsea prison.

have one but on degrading and dishonourable terms—sooner
than which, we had better spend the last shilling in resisting,
like men.   The Italian Papers mention Mr. Yorke as First
Lord of the Admiralty.   If so, what becomes of the virtuous
Sir T. T. and Tucker?   But I care not who is in or out—I
shall endeavour to do my duty to the Country.

I wish you would get me the opinion of some learned man
about the Commons, on the Bills of Lading.   I maintain that
under the description of the Bill of Lading, that the goods
are risked by the Shippers until they are received, and are,
therefore French property; and I should be glad to have
this opinion as soon as possible, as, yesterday, not less than
£40,000 worth of goods passed for Smyrna; but the Captains
were afraid to touch them.   I cannot blame them: our rules of
Admiralty have been so undecided.   I am longing for Victory;[4]
but when will she appear?   I know your goodness about my
wine, &c., from Guernsey, and that I shall have it out by some
way or other.   But tell me principally about yourself; for
believe me ever, your most obliged and faithful friend,

NELSON AND BRONTE.

TO THE RIGHT HONOURABLE HENRY ADDINGTON.

[From Clarke and M'Arthur, vol. ii. p. 320.]

27th July, 1803.

Europe seems so degraded, that I declare I would rather
die with my sword in my hand resisting, than hold any Territory by means of a degenerate guarantee.   Can a Kingdom
be said to be free, which pays contributions at the order of a
Foreign Power?   No; yet such is the state of Naples,
Tuscany, and Genoa.   General Murat demanded at Genoa a
contribution of five millions of livres on the 7th; the Government said they could only raise three; the rest must be paid
in men for the Army: 1600 men marched into Genoa on the
17th of July.   Yesterday and to-day, three Corvettes have
been trying to proceed to the Eastward: I am confident they
want to get to the Heel of Italy and the Adriatic, and it is very

[4] His Ship.

difficult to prevent their passing along shore. At Marseilles they are fitting, as reports say, eighty or ninety Gun-boats, and intend sending them, by the Canal of Languedoc, to Bordeaux; but I am sure this is not true. They are to go along shore to the Heel of Italy, and to embark and protect their Army either to Sicily or the Morea, or to both; and the Navy of Europe can hardly prevent these along-shore voyages. However, I am placing an addition to the Squadron I have already stationed upon that Coast; but from Cape St. Vincent, where it is absolutely necessary I should have a look-out for the Ships of War coming from the Mediterranean, to the Head of the Adriatic, I have only eight Frigates; which, with the service of watching Toulon, and the necessary Frigates with the Fleet, are absolutely not one half enough. I mean this as no complaint, for I am confident the Admiralty are hard pressed, and will send me more when the Service will admit it. I am, &c.,

　　　　　　　　　　　　　　　NELSON AND BRONTE.

TO SIR EVAN NEPEAN, BART., ADMIRALTY.

[Original, in the Admiralty.]

Amphion, off Toulon, 27th July, 1803.

Sir,

From the various circumstances of service attached to the Naval part of my duty in these seas, which imposes upon me a correspondence from several quarters that requires a knowledge of the different languages, I have felt it necessary to apply to the Rev. Alexander John Scott, Chaplain of His Majesty's Ship Victory, who very handsomely offered his services as Interpreter, and as this imposes upon Mr. Scott a very laborious duty, and Interpreters having been rewarded on former occasions,[5] I am, therefore, to request you will please to communicate this letter to the Lords Commissioners of the Admiralty, and move them to grant such salary to the Office as they may think proper. I am, Sir, &c.,

　　　　　　　　　　　　　　　NELSON AND BRONTE.

---

[5] Mr. Scott was allowed £100 per annum, as in former instances of an Admiral's interpreter.

TO SIR EVAN NEPEAN, BART., ADMIRALTY.

[Original, in the Admiralty.]

Amphion, off Toulon, July 30th, 1803.

Sir,

Having some days ago sent His Majesty's Sloop Termagant to the Bay of Rosas, for the purpose of ascertaining the facility of watering any of His Majesty's ships under my command, which I might find necessary to send there, and also with respect to the procuring live bullocks and other refreshments for the Fleet; You will please to acquaint the Lords Commissioners of the Admiralty, that Captain Elliot found the Spaniards very much inclined to be civil, and that any number of bullocks may at present be had there for ready money; but he found considerable difficulty in paying for three bullocks which he purchased for the Termagant's Company, and was obliged to apply to the Neapolitan Consul to take bills on the Victualling-Board for the value thereof. I only mention this as an instance, to show the necessity of Public money being supplied to the Fleet. Captain Elliot was directed not to salute the Fort of his Catholic Majesty, but upon a positive assurance of an equal number of guns being returned; finding the Governor would only return the intended salute of a Private Ship, with four guns less, the Termagant did not salute the Fort. I am, Sir, &c.,

NELSON AND BRONTE.

TO HIS EXCELLENCY HUGH ELLIOT, ESQ.

[Autograph, in the Elliot Papers.]

Amphion, July 30th, 1803.

My dear Sir,

Since I wrote to your Excellency on Tuesday the 26th July, by the Raven, I have only to inform you, that three Corvettes from Toulon have twice come out of the Harbour, and were chased back again. They were, apparently, bound to the Eastward; and, in time, the French must get a force to the Heel of Italy to attend their Army. It must be a mere chance if any of our Ships could lay hold of them from Point to Point, which is all the sea voyage these sort of gentry make.

But I must apprise you, that a much more formidable description of Vessels are *said* to be fitting at Marseilles; but this circumstance Sir John Acton ought to know from the Neapolitan Consul there. Our reports from *twenty* Vessels, all agree that a printed requisition is stuck up for obtaining eighty or ninety small Vessels of about forty tons each. Reports say that they are to be fitted as Gun-boats, and sent by the Canal of Languedoc to Bordeaux. If it is true that these Vessels are fitting out, it is perfectly clear they are destined for the *Heel of Italy*, to attend upon the Army; and I need scarcely tell you—certainly not Sir John Acton—that nothing but Vessels of similar descriptions, and with the same facilities of going into all the little Ports in bad weather, can prevent their passage alongshore—no, not *all* the Navies of Europe : therefore, if this report is true, and as yet I have no reason to doubt it, the consequences are foreseen, and we must more and more look to Sicily. I see, my dear Sir, all that will happen: so must General Acton, the Queen, and yourself. It may be a little sooner, or a little later, as may suit the convenience of the French for their other great objects, the Morea and Egypt. If we do not occupy Messina, I am free to say, that the French will not make a conquest of the whole Kingdom of Naples, because that would bar their possession of Sicily, which is their first and great object. That accomplished, *Naples falls of course;* and if not as a conquest, ten times more humiliating—the King being left as an odious Commissary to raise contributions from his unhappy Subjects for the French. For God's sake, let us reflect. I have sent an additional force to the Mouth of the Adriatic; and wherever the French possess, will, of course, not be regarded *as Neutral ground.* I have serious thoughts of notifying those Ports as blockaded, but I wish not to do anything hastily. I wish General Acton to tell me whether the City of Naples draws any, and what, supplies from those places occupied by the French; and whether a blockade, preventing any supplies going to those places, would not be attended with more advantage to the Common Cause, than receiving at Naples those supplies which the French not wanting, allow to be exported ?

I have, my dear Sir, finished stating for ever all my ideas

about Naples and Sicily. Whatever happens, I feel that I have
done all in my power to prevent misfortune; and for the
future I leave the rest to wiser heads, but to none, I assert,
more devoutly attached to the happiness and welfare of their
Sicilian Majesties, and to the real security of their Kingdoms.
Fourteen days ago, a French Seventy-four got into Cadiz from
Saint Domingo, and two French Frigates, with some Merchant-ships; but, I have kept everything here to save Italy, if
in my power; and you know I was ordered to send a Squadron
outside the Straits. What will they say at home? However,
I feel I have done right, and care not. I am ever, your
Excellency's most obedient Servant,

NELSON AND BRONTE.

TO HIS EXCELLENCY HUGH ELLIOT, ESQ.

[Autograph, in the Elliot Papers. " Saturday, 30th July. The Victory made
her number. At 10-30 bore up and made sail."—*Amphion's Log.* " 5, P.M., joined
this Ship, Captain T. M. Hardy, and superseded Captain Sutton. Hoisted Lord
Viscount Nelson's Flag."—*Victory's Log.*]

Private.   Amphion, July 30th, 1803.
My dear Sir,
Untoward events have most assuredly lost me two Sail of
the Line, and probably two Frigates; for had we been
allowed to come out in the Victory, the Jemappe would have
gone with us to Malta; and, if I had, which the Admiralty
expected, found Sir Richard Bickerton there, with his Fleet
ready for sea, two Sail of the Line would have been outside the Straits, and have taken the others. Instead of
which, finding Sir Richard at sea, short of provisions, and a
crippled Fleet, I have only been able to watch Toulon, and
to attend Naples, and send Ships into Port to be re-fitted.
The Monmouth is a very fine Sixty-four, and Captain Hart[5] a
very worthy man; before his turn is out at Naples, something
decisive must take place. The Victory is just in sight, and
Monmouth parts in the morning. I have the pleasure to tell
you that Captain Davers of the Active, from ill-health going
to England, George Elliot will to-morrow be Captain of
the Maidstone. All here are well, and desire their kindest

---

[5] Captain George Hart: he died a Rear-Admiral of the Blue in April 1812.

regards, and believe me, my dear Sir, your much obliged and faithful Servant,

NELSON AND BRONTE.

The letter you sent me for Prince Castelcicala, will go off on Monday for England.

TO LADY HAMILTON.

[Extract from " Lord Nelson's Letters to Lady Hamilton," vol. i. p. 124.]

Victory, off Toulon, August 1st, 1803.

I do not know that you will get this letter.

My dearest Emma,

Your letter of May 31, which came under cover to Mr. Noble, of Naples, inclosing Davison's correspondence with Plymouth, arrived by the Phœbe two days ago: and this is the only scrap of a pen which has been received by any person in the Fleet since we sailed from England . . . . . .

Sutton joined me yesterday, and we are all got into the Victory; and, a few days will put us in order. Everybody gives a very excellent character of Mr. Chevalier, the servant recommended by Mr. Davison; and I shall certainly live as frugal as my station will admit. I have known the pinch, and shall endeavour never to know it again. I want to send £2100 to pay off Mrs. Greaves on October 1st; but I have not received one farthing : but I hope to receive some soon. But Mr. Haslewood[7] promised to see this matter kept right for me. Hardy is now busy, hanging up your and Horatia's[8] picture ; and I trust soon to see the other two safe arrived from the Exhibition. I want no others to ornament my cabin. I can contemplate them, and find new beauties every day, and I do not want anybody else.

You will not expect much news from us. We see nothing. I have great fear, that all Naples will fall into the hands of the French; and, if Acton does not take care, Sicily also. However, I have given my final advice so fully and strongly, that, let what will happen, they cannot blame me. Captain

---

[7] His Solicitor.

[8] His daughter, now Mrs. Horatia Nelson Ward, who will be frequently mentioned.

Capel⁹ says, Mr. Elliot cannot bear Naples.   I have no doubt,
but that it is very different to your time.   The Queen, I fancy,
by the seal, has sent a letter to Castelcicala; her letter to me
is only thanks for my attention to the safety of the Kingdom.
If Dr. Scott has time, and is able, he shall write a copy for
you.   The King is very much retired.   He would not see
the French General St. Cyr, who came to Naples to settle
the contribution for the payment of the French Army.   The
Queen was ordered to give him and the French Minister a
dinner, but the King stayed at Belvidere.

I think he will give it up soon, and retire to Sicily, if the
French will allow him.   Acton has never dared give Mr.
Elliot, or one Englishman, a dinner.   The Fleet are ready to
come forth; but, they will not come for the sake of fighting
me.   I have this day made George Elliot,¹ Post; Lieutenant
Pettet, a Master and Commander; and Mr. Hindmarsh, Gunner's son, of the Bellerophon, who behaved so well this day
five years, a Lieutenant.²   I reckon to have lost two French
Seventy-fours, by my not coming out in the Victory; but I
hope they will come soon, with interest.   This goes to Gibraltar, by Sutton, in the Amphion.   I shall write the Doctor³
in a day or two.   I see, by the French Papers, that he has
kissed hands.   With kindest regards to your good mother,
and all at Merton, &c., ever yours, most faithfully and
affectionately,   NELSON AND BRONTE.

TO LIEUTENANT-GENERAL SIR THOMAS TRIGGE, K.B.

[Letter Book.]

Sir,   Victory, off Toulon, 1st August, 1803.

The Surgeon of His Majesty's Naval Hospital at Gibraltar
having stated to me the necessity of the free and entire use of

⁹ Now Vice-Admiral the Hon. Sir Thomas Bladen Capel, K.C.B.

¹ Captain, the Honourable George Elliot, was Posted from the Termagant into
the Maidstone, *vice* Moubray removed to the Active, *vice* C. S. Davers, invalided.
Captain Robert Pettet died a Commander in 1832.

² Clarke and M'Arthur state, that the following passage occurs in Lord Nelson's
Private Diary, "1st August, I have had the pleasure of rewarding merit in the
person of Mr. Hindmarsh, Gunner's son, of the Bellerophon, for his conduct this day
five years"—*i. e.*, at the Battle of the Nile.

³ His brother appears to have kissed hands on taking his degree of D.D., and
obtaining a Prebendal Stall.

one or more of the lower Wards (at present occupied by the Military) for the use and accommodation of sick and wounded Prisoners who may be sent there, and as the relinquishing these Wards by the Military was perfectly understood by Lord Keith, when it became necessary for the use of sick and wounded Seamen, &c., I am, therefore, from seeing the propriety and necessity of the Surgeon's representation, to request that you will please to give the necessary orders for one, or the whole of the Wards, at present occupied by the Military, to be relinquished and given up to the Surgeon of Gibraltar Hospital, as he may find necessary. I have the honour to be, &c.,

NELSON AND BRONTE.

TO CAPTAIN SAMUEL SUTTON, H.M. SHIP AMPHION.

[Order-Book.]

Victory, off Toulon, 1st August, 1803.

Whereas there is reason to believe that a Squadron of the Enemy's Ships of War are coming from the West Indies, or from Brest, to join the Fleet in Toulon, You are, therefore, hereby required and directed to take your route from Cape Spartel towards Madeira, from thence to Cape St. Vincent and to Cape Spartel, and use every possible endeavour to gain such intelligence of the Enemy's movements and intentions as you may judge necessary for my information, which you are to forward to me by a Sloop of War from Gibraltar; but should you fall in with an Enemy's Squadron steering for the Mediterranean, you are, in that case, to join me on my Rendezvous off Toulon without a moment's loss of time, sending a Boat into Gibraltar to acquaint any of the Squadron which may be there with such information, that if of the Line, they may join me immediately. You are to continue on this service till further orders, returning to Gibraltar at the expiration of six weeks from the time of your leaving Cape Spartel, if you should not have gained any information which might make it necessary for my being acquainted with before that time.

NELSON AND BRONTE.

TO SIR EVAN NEPEAN, BART., ADMIRALTY.

[Letter-Book.]

Victory, off Toulon, 1st August, 1803.

Sir,

I acquainted you, by letter of the 19th ult., that his Majesty's Ship Agincourt had sprung a leak, and that I had, in consequence, directed her by signal to proceed to Malta. His Majesty's Ship Victory (which joined me on the 30th ultimo) having fallen in with the Agincourt off Maretimo, Captain Briggs[4] availed himself of fhe opportunity of acquainting me thereof, and sending a copy of his log, which I herewith transmit you for the information of the Lords Commissioners of the Admiralty. Their Lordships will, I am sure, be much pleased with Captain Brigg's conduct in not requiring a Ship to attend him into Port, knowing the small force with me. I am, &c.

NELSON AND BRONTE.

TO SIR EVAN NEPEAN, BART., ADMIRALTY.

[Original, in the Admiralty.]

Victory, off Toulon, 1st August, 1803.

Sir,

You will please to acquaint the Lords Commissioners of the Admiralty, that by the last information of the Enemy's force at Toulon, there are seven Sail of Line, five or six Frigates, and six or seven Corvettes, in all eighteen Sail, apparently perfectly ready for sea : a Frigate and three Corvettes have been three times out of the harbour, but returned again. At Genoa there are three Genoese Vessels of War ready for sea, about forty sail of French Merchant Ships, and three Dutch Merchantmen ; and at Marseilles, from reports of Vessels spoke, they are putting in requisition eighty or ninety Sail of Vessels, about forty tons each, to be fitted as Gun-boats, and to proceed by the Canal of Languedoc to Bordeaux ; but I believe, if they are really fitting out, that they are destined to protect the movements of their Army in the Heel of Italy. I also understand, from a Vessel spoke by the Fleet, that a

---

[4] Now Vice-Admiral Sir Thomas Briggs, G.C.M.G.

French Line-of-Battle Ship has got into Cadiz from St. Domingo. Their Lordships will know, from the reasons set forth in my former letters, that it has been totally out of my power to send a Ship of the Line out of the Straits. I am, Sir, &c.,　　　　　NELSON AND BRONTE.

TO HIS EXCELLENCY THE COMMANDING ADMIRAL OF THE FLEET OF THE FRENCH REPUBLIC.

[Original, in the Admiralty.]

Off Toulon, August 8th, 1803.

Sir,

Your Frigates have captured the Redbridge Schooner and two Transports loaded with water. There are many French Prisoners both at Malta and Gibraltar; therefore, as it cannot be the wish of us Officers to detain those as Prisoners who can be exchanged, I therefore offer you, Sir, to send immediately as many men as you may send to me. I have the honour to be, Sir, &c.,　　　　　NELSON AND BRONTE.[5]

N.B.—Only one Transport was taken.

TO SIR EVAN NEPEAN, BART., ADMIRALTY.

[Original, in the Admiralty.]

Victory, off Toulon, August 9th, 1803.

Sir,

On Thursday morning last, as appears by the Phœbe's log sent herewith, the Redbridge Schooner[6] and a Transport, loaded with water, was captured by four Frigates and some Corvettes, which came out of Toulon in the night: having made the capture, the Frigates worked for exercise apparently between the Petit Pass and Cape Sicie, and returned into Toulon on Saturday. I have the honour to be, &c.,

NELSON AND BRONTE.

[5] On the 10th of August, Captain Moubray reported that the Officer with the Flag of Truce was desired by a sentinel to remain off Cape Sepet; a Frenchman came to him, and then another, after three hours, and said it was totally impossible Lord Nelson's letter should be received at all.

[6] Commanded by Lieutenant George Lempriere: his name is not in the Navy List of, nor after, 1805.

TO THE RIGHT HONOURABLE HENRY ADDINGTON.

[Autograph, in the Sidmouth Papers.]

Victory, off Toulon, August 10th, 1803.

My dear Sir,

I have wrote to you so fully on every occasion, and so late as the 4th, that I will not take up your time by Mr. A'Court, except to say that we are all well, and only want the French Fleet to come out to make us all happy. I am making what use I can of Spain, to get water and refreshments, and shall do so as long as they will allow us; but I suppose the French will not suffer it very long. The Spaniards are selling Vessels, taken from us by the French, at public auction. I have given Mr. A'Court the advertisement to show Mr. Frere,[7] and to carry it to England. The Kent is just joining from Malta. I wait her arrival before I close my letter. Sir Richard Bickerton is just come on board. All is well at Malta, therefore I will not detain Mr. A'Court one moment; and have only to assure you, that I am ever, my dear Sir, your most faithful and attached,

NELSON AND BRONTE.

TO CAPTAIN SIR RICHARD JOHN STRACHAN,[8] BART., H.M. SHIP DONEGAL.

[Order-Book.]

Victory, off Toulon, 10th August, 1803.

Whereas I have received information that there is a French Seventy-four and some Frigates at Cadiz, that may attempt the blocking up our Trade entering the Straits, You are, therefore, hereby required and directed to proceed immediately with his Majesty's Ship Donegal under your command, and take your station outside the Straits, in such situation as you may judge most likely to fall in with the Enemy's force above-mentioned, or any of their Privateers or Cruizers, as well as for the protection of the Trade of his Majesty's Sub-

---

[7] John Hookham Frere, Esq., Minister at Madrid.

[8] Afterwards well known, from having commanded the Squadron off Ferrol, which captured four of the French Ships that escaped at Trafalgar, for which Action he received the Red Ribbon. Sir Richard Strachan died an Admiral of the Blue, in February 1828.

jects. Having ordered the Frigates and Sloops named in the
margin[9] on the service mentioned in the copies of their orders
which accompany this, you are at liberty to take the whole,
or either of them under your command, as circumstances may
render necessary, for the more effectual execution of the services you are employed on. You are to continue on this service until relieved, or you shall receive my further orders,
returning occasionally to Gibraltar when it may be necessary
to complete your provisions and water, and afford Lieutenant-
General Sir Thomas Trigge every assistance in your power
which he may require, and you deem necessary for the good
of his Majesty's service, and the comfort and health of the
Garrison at that place—taking care to embrace every opportunity of acquainting me with your proceedings, and the orders
you may find necessary to give the Commanders of either of
the Ships before-mentioned, that I may make regulations
accordingly, paying due regard to the orders of the Medusa
and Amphion, respecting an Enemy's Fleet or Squadron,
which may appear to you steering for the Mediterranean.
You are to direct the Commander of any of his Majesty's
Ships or Vessels which you may fall in with, having dispatches
for me, or otherwise, to join me on my Rendezvous off this
place; but to approach Toulon with great caution, and not
make too free with the entrance of the harbour, and likewise
send similar orders to any Ships of War which may join me
from Gibraltar.

　　　　　　　　　　　　　　NELSON AND BRONTE.

TO SIR EVAN NEPEAN, BART., ADMIRALTY.

[Original, in the Admiralty.]

Victory, off Toulon, 10th August, 1803.

　Sir,

I herewith transmit you, for the information of the Lords
Commissioners of the Admiralty, a copy of a letter from Captain Donnelly of his Majesty's Ship Narcissus, giving an
account of the capture of the French National Brig of War
L'Alcion, together with copy of the said Brig's dimensions;

　　　　　　　　　[9] Medusa, Amphion, Bittern.

and, as she appears to be a remarkably fine Vessel and fit for
his Majesty's Service, you will please to acquaint their Lordships, that I shall give directions for her being immediately
purchased into the Service, and fitted for sea with all possible
dispatch, as I am very much in want of Vessels of that description, which I hope their Lordships will approve.   I am,
Sir, &c.,

NELSON AND BRONTE.

TO LIEUTENANT WILLIAM PEMBERTON,[1] AGENT FOR TRANS-PORTS, MALTA.

[Letter-Book.]

Victory, off Toulon, 10th August, 1803.

Sir,

I have this day received your letter of the 23rd ult., with
the Return of Transports therein mentioned, and am to observe
that your conduct in the discharge of your duty as Resident
Agent at Malta, from the testimony of every one who has
mentioned your name to me, has been such as must ever meet
my approbation.   I am, &c.

NELSON AND BRONTE.

TO THE RESPECTIVE MERCHANTS AT MALTA.

[Letter-Book.]

Victory, off Toulon, 10th August, 1803.

Gentlemen,

I have received an application for Convoy to the Ships
bound from Malta into the Archipelago, and beg to acquaint
you that a Convoy was ordered for that purpose on the 18th
of June last, and also to bring the Levant Trade from thence;
and when I think the Merchant-vessels from the Adriatic and
Archipelago are arrived at Malta, I shall appoint a Convoy to
proceed with them from thence to England.   The Merchants
of Malta and elsewhere may be assured that it will always
afford me pleasure to pay due attention to their commerce.
I am, Gentlemen, your most obedient, humble servant,

NELSON AND BRONTE.

[1] He died a Lieutenant in 1809.

TO SIR ALEXANDER JOHN BALL, BART., MALTA.

[Letter-Book.]

Victory, off Toulon, 10th August, 1803.

Sir,

Rear-Admiral Sir Richard Bickerton has communicated to me your wish that the Arab [2] could be attached to the service of the Island of Malta, under your own immediate directions; and although I am fully sensible that such a Vessel is necessary to be attached to you, as was the case with the Viceroy of Corsica, yet I do not feel myself at liberty to make such purchase without orders from the Admiralty. But if you think proper to pay the Agent what she is valued at, I will certainly, till the pleasure of the Lords Commissioners of the Admiralty is known, appoint a Lieutenant and Cutter's establishment for her, (looking to you to procure the men to man her,) to be borne as supernumeraries on some Ship's books. You must be aware that as the Agents are going to sell the said Vessel for the benefit of the Captors, that the money must be paid for her on delivery, as I do not feel myself authorized to interfere with the sale. I think it probable, from your representation to the Secretary of State, and from him to the Admiralty, that their Lordships will direct the amount of the purchase of the Vessel to be charged to the account of the Navy. I have the honour to be, &c.,

NELSON AND BRONTE.

TO LADY HAMILTON.

[Extract from " Lord Nelson's Letters to Lady Hamilton," vol. ii. p. 130.]

Victory, off Toulon, August 10th, 1803.

My dearest Emma,

I take the opportunity of Mr. A'Court's [3] going through Spain, with Mr. Elliot's dispatches for England, to send this letter; for I would not, for the world, miss any opportunity of sending you a line. By Gibraltar, I wrote you, as lately as

---

[2] A French Cutter, taken by the Maidstone, Captain Moubray, on the 14th of June.

[3] Now Lord Heytesbury, G.C.B., Lord Lieutenant of Ireland: he was then Secretary of Legation at Naples.

the 4th; but all our ways of communicating with England, are very uncertain; and, I believe, the Admiralty must have forgot us; for not a Vessel of any kind or sort has joined us since I left Spithead. News I absolutely am ignorant of; except that a Schooner belonging to me, put her nose into Toulon, and four Frigates popped out, and have taken her, and a Transport loaded with water for the Fleet. However, I hope to have an opportunity, very soon, of paying them the debt, with interest. Mr. A'Court says, at Naples, they hope that the mediation of Russia will save them; but I doubt if Russia will go to War with the French for any Kingdom; and they, poor souls! relying on a broken reed, will lose Sicily.

As for getting anything for Bronte, I cannot expect it; for the finances of Naples are worse than ever. *Patienza,* however: I will——

I see, many Bishops are dead. Is my brother tired of Canterbury? I wish I could make him a Bishop. If you see him, or write, say that I have not ten minutes to send away Mr. A'Court, who cannot be detained. I hope Lord St. Vincent has sent out Sir William Bolton. As soon as I know who is First Lord,[3] I will write him.

TO CAPTAIN WILLIAM EDWARD CRACRAFT, H.M. SHIP ANSON.

[Order-Book.]

Victory, off Toulon, 11th August, 1803.

Whereas I have received information that the French intend sending a Squadron of Frigates into the Adriatic, to protect their Army at the Heel of Italy, you are, therefore, hereby required and directed to proceed with all possible dispatch, in his Majesty's Ship Anson, under your command, off Cape Spartivento, and between that and the entrance of the Adriatic, where you will find his Majesty's Ship and Sloop named in the margin[4] cruising on the service mentioned in Captain Richardson's order of the 26th June last, and my letter to him of the

---

[3] The expected change in Administration and in the Board of Admiralty, did not take place until May 1804.

[4] Juno, Morgiana.

10th ultimo, copies of which accompany this, for your information. You are to take the said Ship and Sloop under your orders, whose Captains are directed to put themselves under your command, and cruize very diligently from the Mouth of the Archipelago along the Adriatic, as far as Ancona, for the purpose of keeping the Adriatic open to the Trade of his Majesty's Subjects; as well as to prevent the Enemy from sending any of their Cruizers, or conveying Troops across the Adriatic into the Morea, or along the Coast of Calabria, towards Reggio. You are to show yourself, or anchor occasionally at Messina, taking care to bear in view the object of my order and letter to Captain Richardson above mentioned. And whereas the French Troops have taken possession of several¯ Ports mentioned particularly in the said order, and may eventually possess themselves of more territory on the Calabrian coast, you are also hereby required and directed to take, burn, sink, or destroy, any of the Enemy's Cruizers or Trade which may avail themselves of protection in such places; and to consider every such Port or place occupied by the French, or where their flag may be flying, in any part of his Sicilian Majesty's Dominions, as entirely exempt from any protection of Neutrality. You are to continue on this service until relieved, or you shall receive my further orders, acquainting me from time to time, as opportunity may offer, with your proceedings.

NELSON AND BRONTE.

TO ABRAHAM GIBBS, ESQ., PALERMO.

[Letter-Book.]

Victory, off Toulon, 11th August, 1803.

My dear Sir,

I yesterday received your truly friendly letter of July 5th, with much pleasure, and I shall be truly thankful, if you will have the goodness to put my Bronté estate in a train, that if I cannot receive the value of it, and have done with it, that, at least, I may receive the full rental regularly; for I never will lay out another sixpence on it, but am content to pay a certain sum for the attention of some respectable person to receive the rents, and to remit them to London. As you are so good as to offer to attend to this serious concern to me, I will enter at large into the subject. I told Græfer, on first setting out, that I would give up two years' rent for fitting up a house and improving. I paid more attention to another Sovereign than my own; therefore the King of Naples' gift of Bronté to me, if it is not now settled to my advantage, and to be permanent, has cost me a fortune, and a great deal of favour which I might have enjoyed, and [much] jealousy which I should have avoided. I repine not on those accounts. I did my duty, to the Sicilifying my own conscience, and I am easy. It will be necessary, before you can take any steps beyond inquiry, to know from Sir John Acton what has been done, and what is intended. All that I beg is, that the just thing may be done immediately, and that I may have it permanent. I shall never again write an order about the estate. If the estate cannot be returned, my receiving the whole value, the income *nett* ought to be paid me, which the Hospital received, as delivered to me, was 6700 ounces on the average for seven years preceding.[5] Your kind assistance will truly oblige, my dear Sir, your very faithful, humble servant,

NELSON AND BRONTE.

TO SIR ALEXANDER JOHN BALL, BART., MALTA.

[Letter-Book.]

Private. August 12th, 1803.

My dear Ball,

I have wrote you an official letter, in order that you may send it home, which will show your reason for the purchase.[6] If you like but to man her, and put a Master in her, and consider her as not belonging to, or under the orders of the Naval Commander-in-Chief, I will still, till the orders of the Admiralty are known, bear twenty-five supernumeraries for you, although I expect they will disapprove of such an irregular

---

[5] *Sic.* This letter is very inaccurately copied in the Letter-Book: Lord Nelson probably meant, that if he could not obtain the whole rent of the estate, he ought, at least, to have the annual sum it had paid to the Hospital to which it had formerly belonged.

[6] Of the Arab.

act; but I am ready to do everything in my power to oblige you, being ever, my dear Ball, your most faithful and obliged friend, NELSON AND BRONTE.

If you wish to have a Lieutenant in her, name the person you would wish, and he shall have an order. If you have no such person, I will desire Hardy to look out for some steady man. Pray forward my packet to Gibbs at Palermo. I suppose by Girgenti is the best way.

TO CAPTAIN MOUBRAY, H.M. SHIP ACTIVE.

[Letter-Book.]

August 12, 1803.

Dear Sir,

It is not my intention to close watch Toulon, *even with Frigates;* for I see the gentlemen want one of our Frigates. When we come in sight of Sicie, join me, and I will further explain my intentions; but I beg you will not keep too close to Sepet or Sicie in the night. I am, dear Sir, your most obedient servant, NELSON AND BRONTE.

TO SIR ALEXANDER JOHN BALL, BART., MALTA.

[Letter-Book.]

August 12th, 1803.

My dear Ball,

Captain Vankempen, a Dutchman by birth, was a Captain in the French Navy, now on half-pay from us, at five shillings a-day, has a wife (you may have seen them at Sir William Hamilton's, at Naples,) and family, resides at present at Palermo, a very sensible, industrious man, set up a Store both in Palermo and Naples, but obliged to fly from his attachment to Royalty and our Cause, has begged my recommendation for some employ. He could assist the Commissary, or be useful in any department you could place him in. He is not above working for his family. Perhaps Mr. Chapman could make him useful, or the Lazaretto. In short, if you can be of service to him, send to him to Palermo, and you will make him happy, and truly oblige, my dear Ball, your affectionate, NELSON AND BRONTE.

TO SIR ALEXANDER JOHN BALL, BART., MALTA.

[Autograph, in the possession of Sir William Keith Ball, Bart.]

Victory, off Toulon, August 12th, 1803.

My dear Ball,

By Sir Richard Bickerton[5] I am favoured with your letter of July 23rd. Yours by the Redbridge, I fear the French are reading, for I dare say he never threw his dispatches overboard, although it has not been for want of caution on my part, for I charged him, when he was with me off Naples, always to have lead or plenty of shot tied to his dispatches; but he has been used to be taken like a fool, and Captain Capel, I was very near saying, had better luck in his escape than he deserved; keep this to yourself, for he is a good young man. I have to thank you for your news from the Morea and Egypt; if our Government is not on its guard, it is no fault of mine. By sending a confidential person to Messina, you will know everything, and Mr. Elliot has full confidence in the Cabinet of Naples, that they are truly sincere; therefore I should hope that even if any of the Officers who served with the French in Puglia are sent to Messina, that they are not sent for bad purposes, and that all will be smooth for our reception, which I only hope will not be delayed too long.

I am now blown off by a strong breeze; and when September sets in, I may be forced away for a week or fortnight together, and nothing ever kept the French Fleet in at Toulon or Brest, whenever they had a mind to come to sea. I have no Frigates to watch them, and must take my chance. I want to place Frigates off Cape Dell' Mell and that Coast; Cape Corse, Cape St. Sebastians; off Minorca; off the West side of the Straits of Bonafaccio; two off Toulon; and two with the Fleet. For all these indispensable services, now Phœbe is going, (what a six gun Vessel would perform, if I had one,) I have but two Frigates; therefore, my dear Ball, have a little mercy, and do not think that I have neglected the protection of the trade of Malta, when, in fact, it is the

---

[5] Rear-Admiral Sir Richard Bickerton, in the Kent, joined Lord Nelson, from Malta, on the 10th of August.

only one in my power to have attended to. First the Cyclops was ordered to carry your Trade up the Adriatic, and to bring back what you had there; the Charon went to cruize in your environs, and, by her frequently calling off the Port, could, by orders of Captain Schomberg,[6] have given protection to any Vessels going to or from Sicily, or even, if necessary, to Naples; the Juno off Cape Spartivento; two Sail to the Eastward of Malta, towards the Archipelago: in short, I considered Malta as surrounded. A one-gun Privateer in every Port in Sicily, will always take single Maltese Boats. The Blonde, as she was fitted out for one service, could have been sent for another, however it is my wish to have Vessels attached to the service of the Island and the Garrison. I have directed the Cyclops for this service till she goes to England, and orders are given for other Vessels, if she is not at Malta. I have wrote you fully respecting the Arab, and she shall either be commissioned as a Cutter, or you may do as you please about her in your Civil capacity; for although I do not feel authorized to purchase her for such a service, yet I have no doubt but that, by Lord Hobart's application to the Admiralty, money will be paid by the Navy Board, and then an Officer will be put into her. I want the Spider to carry a letter to Corfu, and bring back my answers from Constantinople. When I shall have a Vessel to send to Egypt, God only knows: at present, I have nothing with me to carry a letter. I am ever, my dear Ball, with real regard, your most obliged and faithful,

NELSON AND BRONTE.

TO MAJOR-GENERAL VILLETTES, MALTA.

[Letter-Book.]

August 12th, 1803.

My dear General,

Captain Vankempen (who, I believe, was settled at Bastia when you was there) was a Captain in the French Navy, and left Toulon with us, as Captain of the Pearl Frigate, and car-

[6] Captain Charles Marsh Schomberg, of the Madras, was for some time Senior Officer at Malta: he died a Rear-Admiral, a Companion of the Bath, and a Knight Commander of the Order of the Guelphs, in January 1835.

ried her to England under the White colours. He is on half-
pay from us, five shillings a-day. He has a wife and family.
He set up a Store at Bastia, and again at Naples, from both
which he was obliged to fly, by the circumstances of the
times. He has sent to me for my interest, to endeavour to
get him something in order to maintain his family. He is a
sensible, active man, and, what he has always been respected
for, not above doing anything, which an honest man might do,
for the benefit of his family. Can you assist this gentleman?
He is not a French, but Dutchman by birth.

            kind assistance. Perhaps Muster-
Master, or something belonging to the Lazaretto, or in the
Commissariat line. He speaks four languages. His wife is
born a gentlewoman, and he has a family. Whatever you can
do, if you knew the family, I am sure you would. It will be
a real act of charity to a worthy family, and you will also truly
oblige, my dear General, your most faithful and obliged,

                            NELSON AND BRONTE.

TO ABRAHAM GIBBS, ESQ., PALERMO.

[Letter-Book.]

Victory, off Toulon, 12th August, 1803.

. My dear Sir,

My letter about Bronté, as it will be necessary for you to
write to General Acton, you are at liberty to send him either
a copy, or extracts from it, as you may judge proper. Good,
and great good, must come to me, if you will take the business
for me. Mr. Broadbent made a sort of an offer to hire the
farm, and when I passed the Faro of Messina, I wrote him a
letter to explain himself more fully on that subject, but I have
not heard from him since. If that farm was let with its improvements, all the others are so let that a person resident in
Sicily sees in a moment what the whole lets for, and taking an
average for seven years, would probably make an offer to give
me so much a year for three, five, or seven years, as might be
agreed upon.

            pointed out that I could be useful in getting him
[employ]. I will write to Sir Alexander Ball and General
Villettes this very day to recommend him, and I will write to

Mr. Hammond, Under-Secretary of State about the Consulship of Sardinia, but I fear that is beyond my power to obtain. But I have a great respect for Captain Vankempen, as I never knew him above trying to get bread for his family in an honest way. As for yourself, I can only assure you, that whenever you want to go to England or anywhere else, only let me know as long as possible before you want to go, and I will manage that you and Miss Gibbs shall go in some good Man-of-War. Leave this to me to manage. I beg you will present my compliments to Mr. Tough, and all the Princes, Princesses, Dukes, &c., &c., at Palermo that you see, and believe me ever, my dear Gibbs, your much obliged, faithful friend,

NELSON AND BRONTE.

TO THE IMPERIAL CONSUL AT MALTA.

[Letter-Book.]

Victory, off Toulon, 13th August, 1803.

Sir,

When any Port is blockaded, I shall certainly notify it to all Ministers and Consuls. With respect to Genoa, I only beg leave to tell you that I expect orders to blockade that Port and Leghorn, of which I shall give all proper persons due notice. I have the honour to be, &c.,

NELSON AND BRONTE.

TO THE FRENCH OFFICERS, PRISONERS OF WAR, AT MALTA.

[Letter-Book.]

Victory, August 13th, 1803.

Gentlemen,

I have sent to offer the French Admiral in Toulon an exchange of Prisoners.[7] After keeping the Boat waiting three hours, a message came down that the French Admiral would receive no letter or message, and ordered the Boat to return: therefore, you must blame the cruelty of your own Admiral for keeping you Prisoners. At the same time, I shall be happy to do all in my power to render your captivity as easy as possible—always remembering, *Do as you would be done by.* I am, Gentlemen, with great respect, your most obedient servant,　　　　NELSON AND BRONTE.

[7] Vide p. 153, ante.

TO SPIRIDION FORESTI, ESQ., HIS MAJESTY'S RESIDENT MINISTER
TO THE REPUBLIC OF THE SEVEN ISLANDS.

[Letter-Book.]

Victory, off Toulon, 13th August, 1803.

Sir,

I am much obliged by your very explicit letters on all the
points which I wanted to be informed of, [and] now send the
Spider for answers from Constantinople. I sincerely hope
that the Republic of the Seven Islands will be able to maintain its Neutrality, and not suffer French Privateers to make
their Ports a home. I am sending a Squadron to the Mouth
of the Adriatic, which of course will occasionally visit Corfu.
I am, dear Sir, with great respect, &c.,

NELSON AND BRONTE.

My letter for Mr. Drummond to go by the ordinary conveyance.

TO HIS EXCELLENCY WILLIAM DRUMMOND, ESQ.,
CONSTANTINOPLE.

[Letter-Book.]

Victory, off Toulon, August 13th, 1803.

Sir,

From an intercepted letter from Odessa, I find that one of
the French Vessels there had orders to take out a Letter of
Marque, and cruise against the English in the Black Sea; if
that is the case it will be necessary for your Excellency to be
informed from the Sublime Porte, whether there is any objection to our sending Vessels of War for the protection of our
commerce in the Black Sea. I have every reason from appearances to believe that the French Fleet in Toulon is on
the eve of putting to sea, and we are perfectly ready to
give them a meeting. I am, with the greatest respect, &c.,

NELSON AND BRONTE.

TO ABRAHAM GIBBS, ESQ., PALERMO.

[Letter-Book.]

August 13th, 1803.

My dear Sir,

I wish you could get me the Arms of Bronté; for I want them for the Heralds' College. I think they could be got from the Great Hospital at Palermo, or Mr. Græfer could get them drawn at Bronté, and you would much oblige your faithful friend,

NELSON AND BRONTE.

TO SIR ALEXANDER JOHN BALL, BART., MALTA.

[Letter-Book.]

August 13th, 1803.

My dear Ball,

The French Admiral will not receive my letter, which I sent a few days ago, relative to an exchange of Prisoners. From this circumstance combined with others, I am sure they are on the eve of coming to sea; and if they have read all your letters about Sicily,[8] I should not be surprised if they push for Sicily, or they may be bound out of the Straits. I have no Vessel to send to Naples, with the account that probably the letters from Malta [have been captured] and it distresses me. Send away the Phœbe; for I am confident I shall want her very soon, to tow either an English or French Ship of the Line. Ever, my dear Ball, yours faithfully,

NELSON AND BRONTE.

TO . . . . . .

[Letter-Book. The address is not given.]

[Apparently about August, 1803.]

Sir,

I have received the honour of your letters of May 31st and 28th. My Agents, of course, are already named. You mention the Dutch Ship Orion not being addressed to any one in particular; she was addressed by all the Captors, to Alexander

---

[8] Taken in the Redbridge.

Davison, and, by their desire, I wrote him so; but, I understand an unauthorized person pretended to have received contrary orders from Captain Hardy, but which Captain Hardy declares is false—that he never saw the person who has taken possession of the Orion, nor ever gave him any order so to do. You are [aware] that the French Brig Three Consuls was taken by the Victory, then under my orders, but I believe Captain Sutton has appointed Agents for her. I am, with respect, &c.,

NELSON AND BRONTE.

TO SIR EVAN NEPEAN, BART., ADMIRALTY.

[Original, in the Admiralty.]

Sir,   Victory, off Toulon, 18th August, 1803.

You will please to acquaint the Lords Commissioners of the Admiralty, that Rear-Admiral Campbell[9] joined me yesterday off this place in His Majesty's Ship Canopus, and that I have received by him their Lordships' printed orders, &c., as particularly acknowledged by my letters of the above date which accompany this. The Seahorse and Arrow were to proceed from Gibraltar with the Convoy to Malta, the moment the wind would permit, from whence I have ordered them to join me immediately; unless any of the said Convoy should be bound up the Adriatic, or to any Port in the Archipelago; in which case, I have directed the Honourable Captain Boyle to send the Arrow with them, and join me in the Seahorse as above-mentioned. I am, &c.,

NELSON AND BRONTE.

TO CAPTAIN THE HONOURABLE COURTENAY BOYLE,[1] H.M. SHIP SEAHORSE.

["Naval Chronicle," vol. xxx. p. 34.]

Victory, off Toulon, [about 18th August, 1803.]

My dear Boyle,

I am very happy to have you in so fine a Frigate under my command, for I am ever, yours most faithfully,

NELSON AND BRONTE.

[9] Afterwards Admiral Sir George Campbell, G.C.B.: he died in January 1821.
[1] Vide vol. i. p. 108.

TO CAPTAIN THE HONOURABLE COURTENAY BOYLE, H.M. SHIP
SEAHORSE.

[Letter-Book.]

Victory, off Toulon, August 18th, 1803.

Dear Sir,

If you have any Ships with you bound into the Adriatic,
you must send the Arrow with them, and order her Captain
to bring to Malta all English and Maltese Vessels requiring
his protection. You will caution her Captain against going
into Ancona, and any other Ports, which the French may
have taken' possession of. If you have any Trade bound up
the Archipelago and they are so valuable as to require a
Convoy,——I now see by the list of your Convoy, that you
have no Vessels bound to the Levant, and Admiral Campbell
says, that probably the Vessel bound for Venice and Trieste
may have sold her cargo at Gibraltar: if so, you will bring
the Arrow with you and join me as speedily as possible; for
I am much distressed for Frigates. I am, dear Sir, your most
faithful and obedient servant,

NELSON AND BRONTE.

TO CAPTAIN JOHN STUART, H.M. SHIP KENT.

[Letter-Book.]

Victory, off Toulon, 19th August, 1803.

Sir,

I herewith transmit you a letter from Sir Evan Nepean,
dated the 20th June last, together with the Note from the
Spanish Minister at our Court therein alluded to, and am to
desire you will furnish me (for the information of the Lords
Commissioners of the Admiralty) with a particular account of
your taking the soundings of some Spanish Ports in these
seas during the time you commanded the Termagant, and
return the enclosures, and your report to, Sir, your most
obedient humble servant,

NELSON AND BRONTE.

TO REAR-ADMIRAL CAMPBELL, H. M. SHIP CANOPUS.

[Letter-Book.]

Victory, off Toulon, 21st August, 1803.

Sir,

I have just received your letter of this date, and am sorry that the Canopus should have carried away her fore-yard, but am perfectly satisfied that no blame whatever can be attached to Captain Conn[2] or the Officers of the said Ship on the occasion.   As an opportunity will soon offer for Gibraltar, I must recommend the sprung fore-yard to be sent to the Storekeeper at that place, in order that it may be made serviceable for some other Ship.   I have the honour to be, &c.,

NELSON AND BRONTE.

TO THE MARCHIONESS OF BUCKINGHAM.

[From the " Morning Herald."]

Victory, off Toulon, August 22nd, 1803.

Madam,

It is with the sincerest sorrow that I have, in return to your Ladyship's kind recommendation of your godson, Lieutenant[3] ———— , to say that he is removed from this world; but, as you will have heard, in the most honourable way in which an Officer can part with his life.   His being the son of a most valuable Brother Officer, would have ensured my kind reception of him, in addition to which your Ladyship's good wishes for his promotion would have been most cordially attended to by your Ladyship's most obedient and humble servant,

NELSON AND BRONTE.

---

   [2] Captain John Conn, before noticed.   Vide vol. iv. p. 460.
   [3] The Officer whose name was so needlessly suppressed, was evidently Lieutenant George Elliot Salter, of the Phœbe, who died on the 14th of July 1803, of wounds received in an attack, by the Boats of that Ship, on a French Privateer at Cività Vecchia.   He was the eldest son of Captain Salter who, in the Santa Margaretta, captured L'Amazone French Frigate in July 1782, to which Action Lord Nelson alludes in a letter dated on the 19th of October in that year.   Vide vol. i. p. 66.

TO LIEUTENANT LAYMAN, HIS MAJESTY'S SHIP VICTORY.

[Letter-Book.]

Victory, at Sea, 22nd August, 1803.

Sir,

I am very sorry to transmit you the copy of a letter[4] from Mr. James Cutforth, Agent Victualler at Gibraltar, to Captain Sir Robert Barlow of his Majesty's Ship Triumph, particularly as I feel myself called upon to order an inquiry into your conduct on the above occasion, which, I hope, may redound to your credit.   I am, &c.,

NELSON AND BRONTE.

TO ADMIRAL THE RIGHT HONOURABLE LORD RADSTOCK.

[Autograph, in the possession of Rear-Admiral Lord Radstock, C.B.]

Victory, off Toulon, August 22nd, 1803.

My dear Lord,

Your kind letter of July 5th, I received a few days ago by George Campbell. I have had the pleasure of making acquaintance with your son. He sent me a drawing of the Esquerques as a present. Whenever the Medusa joins I will consult with Gore as to his coming directly into the Victory; but you may rely that he shall be made as soon after he has served his time as is in my power. The sons of Brother-Officers have an undoubted claim to our protection, and when to that is added the son of a very old friend, nothing can, my dear Lord, weigh stronger with me. Your conduct *to me* on the 14th of February,[5] has proved you a *noble* man ; and I am sorry to say that I fear we have some Peers who do not answer that description. We are watching the coming out of the French Squadron: they are ready, and I do not think *Buonaparte* will allow them to remain longer in Port. Believe me ever, my dear Lord, your faithful and attached friend,

NELSON AND BRONTE.

---

[4] Lieutenant Layman, who was a favourite protégé of Lord Nelson, had charge of L'Ambuscade, the Victory's Prize, and left a thousand dollars at Gibraltar, in Mr. Cutforth's hands for security, which he said he had brought with him from England, but which gave rise to various reports. The inquiry ended satisfactorily.

[5] In the Battle of St. Vincent, in which Lord Radstock was third in command.

TO REAR-ADMIRAL HOLLOWAY.

[Autograph, in the possession of Admiral Sir Robert Otway, Bart., G.C.B.]

Victory, off Toulon, August 22nd, 1803.

My dear Holloway,

Your letter by Mr. Taylor[6] I received from Admiral Campbell—Mr. T. being gone to Malta, a place, probably, I shall never see during my command; however, I shall be happy in showing every attention to your recommendation. I am sorry that you are not employed, but I think it must come at last; for, as you observe justly, that your nerves are good, and your head I never heard disputed. Otway[7] will get a Ship, and, I hope, his Culloden; and that you may both be soon actively employed, is the sincere wish of, my dear Holloway, your obliged and faithful friend,

NELSON AND BRONTE.

Narcissus not having joined, I have not had an opportunity of seeing your nephew Lyons.[8]

TO LADY HAMILTON.

[From " Lord Nelson's Letters to Lady Hamilton," vol. ii. p. 133.]

Victory, August 24th, 1803.

My dear Lady Hamilton,

Your friend's godson arrived safe yesterday afternoon; and I shall, you know, always feel too happy in obeying your commands: for, you never ask favours, but for your friends. In short, in every point of view, from Ambassatrice to the duties of domestic life, I never saw your equal. That elegance of manner, accomplishments, and, above all, your goodness of heart, is unparalleled; and only believe, for ever, and beyond it, your faithful and devoted,

BRONTE AND NELSON.

---

[6] Apparently Mr. Nathaniel Taylor, Storekeeper in Malta Dockyard.

[7] Admiral Holloway's son-in-law, Captain, now Admiral Sir Robert Otway, Bart., G.C.B.

[8] Vide vol. iv. p. 286.

TO THE RIGHT HONOURABLE HENRY ADDINGTON.

[Autograph, in the Sidmouth Papers.]

Victory, off Toulon, August 24th, 1803.

My dear Sir,

Your time is too precious to be wasted reading unnecessarily, therefore I begin :—By the inclosed letter from the Morea, you will see the good disposition of Ali Vizir towards us. You will be the best judge, as things are at present, how he can be made most useful to us. The French will have him, if we do not. You will recollect this is the person who I ventured to recommend our Government sending a present of a handsome pair of pistols to, and you also thought it proper. I was so referred from the Treasury to other places, and at last to the Admiralty, who I knew could have nothing to do with it, that I gave it up, and had only to regret that it was not accomplished : a few hundred pounds would have made him ours for ever. I must apprise you, that General Villettes, although a most excellent Officer, will do nothing but what he receives, ' You are hereby required and directed ;' for to obey, is with him the very acme of discipline.

With respect to SICILY, I have no doubt, from what is passing at Naples and in Sicily, but that the French will have it. My former reasons for inducing General Villettes to keep the Neapolitan Troops in Malta, was to prevent what has happened; but, in a month after my back was turned, Villettes obeyed his orders, and now the Governor of Messina says we can defend it, and want no assistance. His whole conduct, I am bold to say, is either that of a traitor or a fool; and being either one or the other is the same in its effects to the poor King of Naples. Not to use every exertion to put the fortifications in repair, when a Foreign Army is in one part of the Kingdom, is nothing short of treason; and the sixteen Gunboats rotting at Messina, without a man, when they ought to be exercising in the Straits every day. I see clearly, if we have not a little Army to take it, the French will, I am sorry to say, and conclude that the mass of Sicilians wish for a change of Government. They wish for us; but if we will not go there, they will gladly, I fear, receive the French. The middle and lower class will be relieved from the oppressions of the Nobles: they love their King and English—hate the Nobles and the French.

SARDINIA.—I had a Ship from thence yesterday. The King fancies that he can point out his Neutrality. Alas, he can do nothing but what the French please! You may rely that 5000 French, or rather Corsicans, are preparing for the invasion (say conquest) of Sardinia. They are forced to enlist from particular districts—five districts, 1000 men each. All their camp equipage consists of nothing—a light linen jacket, trowsers, red cap, and a pair of shoes, is the whole expense of Government; a musket, accoutrements such as our gentlemen go shooting with, and a short sword. The plunder of the Sardinian Anglo-Sardes is held out as the reward. Not all our Navy can prevent it. Sardinia will be lost without a struggle, and yet the majority of the Sardinians would fly to receive us; but if we will not, then the French, in preference to remaining as they are—oppressed with taxes, and no protection from the Barbary States. *I need not say what a loss it will be to us.* The mode and manner of allowing us to possess the Madalena Islands, and the North part of Sardinia must be left to other heads than mine.

CORSICA—I am told, is so much oppressed by requisitions of men from that Island, that I am told they would gladly again shake off the French yoke; and this last order for the 5000 men for the conquest of Sardinia has made them outrageous. But Buonaparte cares for nothing: he sets all his engines to work. If they succeed, it is well; and if not, he is no worse than he was.

Pardon my remarks. I am looking out for the French Squadron—perhaps you may think impatiently; but I have made up my mind never to go into Port till after the Battle, if they make me wait a year, provided the Admiralty change the Ships who cannot keep the Sea in the winter, except Victory, Canopus, Donegal, and Belleisle. The Admiralty knows the state of the others, and will relieve them as soon as they can. The Triumph, Superb, Monmouth, Agincourt, Kent, Gibraltar, and Renown, are certainly amongst the very finest Ships in our Service—the best commanded, and the very best manned, yet I wish them safe in England, where they would man, filled up with landsmen, fourteen Sail of the Line, and that I had Ships not half so well manned in their

room ; for it is not a Store-Ship a week which could keep
them in repair. This day, only six men are confined to their
beds in the whole Squadron. With every good wish for your
brilliant success, and for getting us an honourable and permanent Peace, believe me, my dear Sir, with the truest esteem,
your most obliged and faithful,

NELSON AND BRONTE.

TO ALEXANDER DAVISON, ESQ.

[Autograph, in the possession of Colonel Davison.]

Victory, off Toulon, 24th August, 1803.

My dear Davison,

How can I find words to thank you for all your goodness to
me and dear Lady Hamilton ! Why, you will be ruined in
postage. I can only say, that I never shall forget it. You
have been tormented about that Mr. Lyne. Captain Hardy
never saw the man, or wrote him a word; but just before
we came afloat at Portsmouth, Hardy got a letter from
Mr. Tucker, and went into a shop and acquiesced in his
desire, little thinking that we could possibly have anything to
do with Plymouth. However, the Power of Attorney is gone
home for you, whole and sole. Respecting ‘my Secretary,
you will do as you please. I have been, am, and shall ever be
looking after the French Fleet, [so] that I have not made so
much Prize-Money as some others would have done; but if I
can score off my debts, I shall be perfectly content. You will,
of course, detain my Prize-money for the Dutchmen—two-
thirds of one-eighth. I was glad to hear, and hope it will prove
true, that your damned electioneering business will be got
quit of. It has cost me many bitter pangs; and without those
feelings for our friends, there can be no friendship. I hope,
my dear Davison, that Old England will be taken care of. If
we are true to ourselves, we need not mind Buonaparte. Every
time I look round, I see cause for thanking you. The books
and pamphlets are a treasure. I shall write a line to Lord
Moira ; but, situated as we are, I can tell him but little. It is
more to mark my respect for his Lordship, than to attempt
giving him information. I have only [to say], my dear Davison,
that no one is more truly attached to you than your most
faithful and obliged friend,　　　　NELSON AND BRONTE.

TO SIR EVAN NEPEAN BART., ADMIRALTY.

[Original, in the Admiralty.]

Victory, off Toulon, 24th August, 1803.

Sir,

I am to request you will be pleased to represent to the Lords Commissioners of the Admiralty, the situation of the Fleet under my command off this place, with respect to fuel; at present, there is not more upon an average than a month's fuel on board for each Ship, that should we be cut off from supplies of fire-wood, &c., from Sardinia, it is easy to judge the distress the Ships must naturally experience from want of fuel. I therefore beg you will suggest to their Lordships the propriety of sending out Vessels loaded with coals for the use of His Majesty's Ships under my command, together with such quantities of candles as may be deemed necessary for the supply of those Pursers who may stand in need of them, as was done during the time Earl St. Vincent and Lord Keith commanded the Fleet in these seas. I am, &c.,

NELSON AND BRONTE.

TO COMMISSIONER OTWAY, GIBRALTAR.

[Letter-Book.]

Victory, off Toulon, 25th August, 1803.

Sir,

I am to desire you will consider the Ambuscade (lately captured by the Victory) in his Majesty's Service, and give the necessary directions to the respective Officers in Gibraltar Yard to put her in a proper state for proceeding to England, (to which place she is to be sent) so soon as I shall be able to send Officers and men to take charge of her. You will please to direct that she may not be supplied with more stores than is deemed absolutely necessary for her passage to England. I am, &c.,

NELSON AND BRONTE.

TO JOHN TYSON, ESQ.

[Autograph, in the possession of Lieutenant John Edward Lane, R.N.]

My dear Tyson,　　　　*Victory, off Toulon, August 25th, 1803.*

I am very much obliged by your letter of June 26th. I have no accounts that I know of with Mr. Ross, at Gibraltar, except he owes me prize money; therefore, as Captain Murray tells me that poor Wilmot[8] took the plate at a valuation, as part of his Prize-money, the value of it is Captain Wilmot's, therefore, if you have anything of mine in your hands, be so good as to pay it to Captain W. Haire, and if you have nothing of mine, beg my Agents to pay it for me. I am very sorry to hear such an indifferent account of your health; you should keep yourself very quiet. We are here looking out for the French Fleet, which, one day or other, will put to sea. We are remarkably healthy. As to fortune-making, it is not my first object—or if I had abandoned Toulon and sent Ships off Cadiz, I might have made that money which others came on the station, and took from me. I am obliged to your friends at Constantinople. Hardy is very well; and with every good wish believe me, dear Tyson, your most faithful friend,

NELSON AND BRONTE.

I now hope that I shall get my Cause.

TO THE RIGHT HONOURABLE HENRY ADDINGTON.

[Autograph, in the Sidmouth Papers.]

My dear Sir,　　　　*Victory, off Toulon, August 25th, 1803.*

By a Vessel spoke with from Marseilles, it was with real sorrow that I read his Majesty's Message of July 28th, on the occasion of the horrid murder of Lord Kilwarden, in Dublin. The unanimity of all good Subjects will, I trust, soon bring the Rebels to justice, and certainly the more danger the more necessary for us all to put ourselves forward. I assure you, that I wish I only knew how I could serve my Country more effectually than in my present command. I attach no value

---

[8] Captain Wilmot who was killed, in command of the Alliance, at Acre, in April 1799.

to the high rank I at present hold, and if any, even the
lowest, situation is thought to be fittest for me in these times,
I should feel prouder to be so placed than in any elevation of
rank; all I ask is, to be allowed to be one of the men to be
placed in the breach to defend my King and Country. I
have but one arm, it is true, but believe my heart is in the
right trim—therefore, only consider how I can be best employed. But I trust, my dear Sir, that you know me, therefore
I will not say more, for fear it should be suspected that
I arrogate to myself more merit than, I believe, will be
found in 999 of every 1000 in the United Kingdoms. These
lines have almost involuntarily flowed from my pen as they
have done from my heart; pardon the effusion. I took the
pen for a different subject.

I yesterday told you of the intention of the French to
invade Sardinia (where no steps are taken against them). At
Marseilles, are now ready to sail—the Troops on board—a
Frigate, a Corvette and two armed Transports, with a 1000 or
1500 men under a General Ceroni, or Veroni. I believe they
are bound to Corsica, to go over with the 5000 Corsicans—if
they get to Sardinia, it is gone. I am sending two Frigates,
the only ones I have with me, to cruize off Ajaccio, in Corsica, to try and intercept them; but what I mention these
circumstances for, is, that it may be necessary to mention it
to the Russian Minister, for we may be accused of a breach
of Neutrality in Sardinia; for, being satisfied of the intention
of the French invading Sardinia, I have directed the Frigates
to pursue them, even should they chase into Sardinia, and to
take or destroy them, and also the Corsican Troops; for if
I wait till the Island is taken I should feel deserving of
reprobation. Of course, they will say that we have broken
the Neutrality, if we attack them in the Ports of Sardinia
before their conquest, and if we do not I shall be laughed at
for a fool. *Prevention is better than cure.* Many French
Vessels have been chased into Sardinia, and of course the
Neutrality respected;—L'Alcyon, Man-of-War Brig, is an instance. I mention my intention that idle reports may not be
attended to; if Russia is the guarantee of the King of
Sardinia's Dominions, let Russia look out. My station to the
Westward of Toulon, an unusual one, has been taken upon an

idea that the French Fleet is bound out of the Straits, and probably to Ireland. It is said 10,000 men are collecting at Toulon. I shall follow them to the Antipodes. You may rely on the zeal of, my dear Sir, your most faithful friend,

NELSON AND BRONTE.

TO COMMISSIONER OTWAY, AT GIBRALTAR.

[Autograph, in the possession of Rear-Admiral Inglefield, C.B.]

Victory, off Toulon, 25th August, 1803.

My dear Sir,

I feel very much obliged by your kind letter, and beg leave to return you my best thanks for your care of the box, &c., all of which are safe arrived on board the Victory, where I shall be very happy to receive you, should you ever be disposed to pay a visit to the Fleet. I suppose Malta is equally under your control as Gibraltar Yard. It is my intention to send the Ambuscade to England, and to man her from some Ship of the Line going there. With every sincere wish for your health, and a pleasant *séjour* on the Rock, I am, with great respect, &c.,

NELSON AND BRONTE.

TO SIR EVAN NEPEAN, BART., ADMIRALTY.

[Original, in the Admiralty.]

Victory, off Toulon, 25th August, 1803.

Sir,

From the Report of Survey, held this day on his Majesty's Ship Gibraltar, (transmitted herewith, together with a copy of Captain Ryves's letter,) she appears to be in such a state as to endanger her in the frequent gales of wind which happen off this place ; and as the season for more bad weather is fast approaching, it is my intention to order the Gibraltar, Monmouth, (when relieved from Naples,) and Agincourt, to Gibraltar, for the purpose of returning to England when their Captains shall receive directions from the Lords Commissioners of the Admiralty for that purpose.

I am further to acquaint you, for the information of their Lordships, that from the bad state of the Ships named in the margin,[9] I shall keep them with me off this place, that they may be in readiness to proceed to England the moment they are relieved, and their Lordships' orders arrive for that purpose, as I am well satisfied from the report of Sir Richard Bickerton and the Captains of those four Ships, that a severe gale or two would render them useless to their Country for a very considerable time, as well as be attended with a great expense in repairing them.   I am, &c.,

NELSON AND BRONTE.

TO BENJAMIN BAYNTON, ESQ.

[Autograph, in the possession of Commander Baynton, R.N.]

Victory, off Toulon, August 25th, 1803.

Sir,

Your son[1] I was sorry, to find, had been in very great distress for his chest, but Captain Sutton has been so good as to order some clothes for him at Gibraltar; and as our numbers are so great in the Victory, he has taken him with him into the Amphion.   There is, I assure you, only one voice about him,—that he is one of the very best lads ever met with: everybody seemed to love him.   His chest is arrived, and will be forwarded to him the first opportunity, with your letter.   I am, dear Sir, your most obedient servant,

NELSON AND BRONTE.

TO JOHN FALCON, ESQ. H.M. CONSUL-GENERAL AT ALGIERS.

[Letter-Book.]

Victory, off Toulon, 26th August, 1803

Sir,

I was honoured by the Triumph with your letter, inclosing one from Mr. O'Brien, American Consul, respecting some Vessels taken by the Algerine Cruizers having Malta Passes. I am not quite clear as to the regularity of these Passes; and,

---

[9] Kent, Superb, Triumph, and Renown.

[1] The present Commander Benjamin Baynton, who sailed from England with Lord Nelson, as a Midshipman of the Victory, but was removed into the Amphion. After being thirty-two years a Lieutenant, and having been severely wounded on the Coast of Catalonia, in 1810, he obtained his present rank, in November 1841.

therefore, until I receive further information from Sir Alexander Ball, I cannot take any steps about them. I am directed by the Admiralty to make inquiries into your business at Algiers, and do those things which I think most conducive to his Majesty's interest at the present time, upon consulting with you: therefore, until you come here, I can take no steps. I am, &c.

NELSON AND BRONTE.

———————

TO SIR EVAN NEPEAN, BART., ADMIRALTY.

[Autograph, in the Admiralty.]

Victory, August 26th, 1803.

Sir,

I received the honour of their Lordships' order of July 7th,[2] inclosing a letter from Lord Pelham, respecting Mr. Falcon's

———————

[2] The following is a copy of the Admiralty order referred to:—" Whereas the Right Honourable Lord Pelham, one of His Majesty's Principal Secretaries of State, hath, with his letter of the 11th instant, transmitted to us the copy of a letter, with its inclosures, which his Lordship had received from Mr. Falcon, his Majesty's Consul at Algiers, stating, that in consequence of an offence committed by his servants, without his knowledge, he had been ordered by the Dey to quit the country, almost at a moment's warning; and that, in consequence of his refusal to obey that order, he had been sent forcibly away from Algiers; and whereas his Lordship hath, at the same time, signified to us the King's pleasure, that directions should be given to the Commander of his Majesty's Fleet in the Mediterranean, to take such steps as he may deem to be most effectual for obtaining all necessary information touching the above-mentioned extraordinary transaction, and in the event of the Consul's representation being sufficiently upheld by the inquiry, to warrant further proceedings upon it, to demand satisfaction of the Dey for the insult offered to the King's Government, by requiring as that satisfaction, that Mr. Falcon should again be received and acknowledged as his Majesty's Consul; that he should be compensated for any loss he shall appear to have sustained by his unwarrantable removal; and that proper assurances should be given that his Majesty's Consul shall not be subject to a repetition of similar indignities. We send your Lordship, for your more complete information, a copy of Lord Pelham's letter abovementioned, together with the inclosures therein referred to; and in pursuance of his Majesty's pleasure therein signified, do hereby require and direct your Lordship to take such steps as you may deem most effectual for obtaining every possible information respecting the transaction represented by Mr. Falcon; and in the event of the Consul's representation being found to warrant a further proceeding upon it, to demand the satisfaction and assurances required by his Majesty, accordingly. In the event of the demand of satisfaction being refused, your Lordship is to follow up that demand in such manner as you may judge most effectual, and at the same time most consistent, under existing circumstances, with his Majesty's

business at Algiers. I have sent to desire Mr. Falcon to join me here ; for, although Mr. Falcon's treatment was scandalous and insulting to the highest degree, yet I have heard that the Dey offered to receive him again, which Mr. Falcon refused. This circumstance has been omitted in Mr. Falcon's letter to me, and must be duly considered. The crime to a Mahometan was the greatest possible—that of receiving a Turkish woman into a Christian's house, and their violence of temper knows no bounds : I believe, had it been any other Nation, that his head would have been off.

Another circumstance has also arisen, as you will see by the inclosed letter from the American Consul. This matter, if it is taken up in the way which becomes me, supposing that we are to protect Vessels bearing our Passports, will most probably bring on an Algerine War ; for assuredly I can carry through what I may demand, and, therefore, it behoves me to take care to urge no demand that is not just. It also happens that all his Cruizers are now in Port, and returning for the winter, therefore we cannot touch him in that most tender point. However, I will act with all due circumspection in this business. I wish our cut of passports was sent out to Malta ; then we must have them respected, and a letter wrote to the Barbary States to tell them of it. I have the honour to be, &c.

NELSON AND BRONTE.

TO LADY HAMILTON.

[Extract from " Lord Nelson's Letters to Lady Hamilton," vol. i. p. 136.]

August 26th, 1803.   Wrote several days past.

My dearest Emma,

By the Canopus,[3] Admiral Campbell, I have received all your truly kind and affectionate letters, from May 20th to July 3rd, with the exception of one, dated May 31st, sent to

---

interests in the Mediterranean. Your Lordship will acquaint Mr. Falcon that it is necessary he should accompany the Officer whom you may send to Algiers, in order that he may explain any part of his conduct that may require such explanation; that he may resume his station should the Dey consent to receive him. Given under our hands the 7th July, 1803.—St. VINCENT, PH. STEPHENS, JAMES ADAMS."—*Original*, in the Nelson Papers.

[3] The Canopus joined the Fleet on the 17th of August.

Naples. This is the first communication I have had with England since we sailed. . . . . . I do not think it can be a long War; and, I believe, it will be much shorter than people expect. . . . . Dr. Scott is gone with my Mission to Algiers, or I would send you a copy of the King and Queen's letter. I send you one from the Queen. Both King, Queen, and Acton, were very civil to Sir William Bolton. He dined with Acton.[4] Bolton does very well in his Brig; but he has not made a farthing of Prize money. If I knew where to send him for some, he should go; but, unless we have a Spanish War, I shall live here at a great expense, although Mr. Chevalier takes every care, and I have great reason to be satisfied. I have just asked William, who behaves very well, whether he chooses to remit any of his wages to his father? It does not appear he *does* at present. He is paid, by the King, eighteen pounds a year, as one of my retinue; therefore I have nothing to pay. I have told him, whenever he chooses to send any, to tell Mr. Scott, or Captain Hardy, and he will receive a remittance bill; so he may now act as he pleases. *Apropos* of Mr. Scott. He is very much obliged to you for your news of Mrs. Scott's being brought to bed. No letters came in the Cutter but to me, and he was very uneasy. He is a very excellent good man; and I am very fortunate in having such a one. I admire your kindness to my dear sister Bolton. I have wrote her, that certainly I will assist Tom Bolton[5] at College. It is better, as I tell her, not to promise more than I am sure I can perform. It is only doing them an injury. I tell her, if *vacancies*, please God, should happen, that my income will be much increased. With respect to Mr. Bolton,[6] everybody knows that I have no interest; nobody cares for me: but if he will point out what he wants, I will try what can be done. But, I am sure, he will not be half so well off as at present. Supposing he could get a place of a few hundreds a year, he would be a ten times poorer man than he is at present. I could convince you of it in a moment; but, if I was to begin, then it would be said, I wanted inclination to

---

[4] Sir William Bolton was not sent to Naples until the 8th of October 1803, (vide "Order-Book," and p. 238, post.) and other passages shew that if this letter was begun on the 26th of August 1803, it was not continued until long after that date.

[5] His nephew, afterwards the second Earl Nelson. [6] His brother-in-law.

render them a service. I should like to see Sir H— P—'s book.[7] I cannot conceive how a man that is reported to have been so extravagant of Government's money, to say no worse, can make a good story. . . . . . I have wrote to Dumourier; therefore, I will only trouble you to say how much I respect him. I fancy he must have suffered great distress at Altona. However, I hope he will now be comfortable for life. He is a very clever man; and beats our Generals, out and out. Don't they feel his coming? Advise him not to make *enemies*, by showing he knows more than some of us. Envy knows no bounds to its persecution. He has seen the world, and will be on his guard. I put Suckling into a Frigate, with a very good man, who has a schoolmaster; he does very well. Bulkeley[8] will be a most excellent Sea-officer; it is a pity he has not served his time. I have answered Mr. Suckling's letter. Gaetano is very well, and desires his duty. I think, sometimes, that he wishes to be left at Naples; but I am not sure. Mr. Denis's relation has been long in the Victory; but if the Admiralty will not promote my Lieutenants, they must all make a retrograde motion. But I hope they will not do such a cruel thing. I have had a very affectionate letter from Lord Minto. I hope George will be confirmed; but the Earl will not answer his application.[9] . . . . .

[7] Captain Sir Home Popham having been charged by the Navy Board with incurring unnecessary expenses in the repairs of his Ship, the Romney, in the East Indies; he printed, for private circulation, in 1803, a pamphlet, entitled "A Concise Statement of Facts, &c."

[8] Richard Bulkeley, the son of an old friend of Lord Nelson, who was with him. at St. Juan, (*vide* vol. ii. p. 445,) and from whom there are numerous letters in the Nelson Papers. Mr. Bulkeley was a Midshipman of the Victory, was wounded at Trafalgar, was made a Lieutenant in 1806, and died between 1809 and 1814.

[9] This is explained by a Letter from Lord St. Vincent to Lord Minto, in Tucker's *Memoirs* (vol. ii. p. 248), dated 2nd January 1804, whence it appears that Lord St. Vincent had desired Lord Nelson to promote Captains Durban and Hillyar, to Post vacancies, and, as Lord Nelson had not written to inform the Admiralty of his having given Captain Elliot an Acting Order in the Maidstone, Lord St. Vincent said, "I was under the necessity of waiting an explanation, before I could recommend a commission to be made out for my young friend: a satisfactory one is now arrived and the needful will be done fothwith." Captain Elliot's commission bore date on the 2nd of January 1804, instead of on the day which he received his Acting Order.

TO CAPTAIN SIR RICHARD STRACHAN, BART., H. M. SHIP
DONEGAL.

[Letter-Book.]

Victory, August 26th, 1803.

My dear Sir Richard,

You will receive an order, when the Maidstone returns
from Lisbon, (if there is no conveyance from Gibraltar to
England for my dispatches, she is to carry them to Lisbon
for the Packet,) to take her under your command; and you
already know, that if you think you want either of the other
Frigates, you are at liberty to give them orders. I have
directed the Termagant, if she has not sailed, to place herself
under your command; for you ought occasionally to have a
Sloop with [*imperfect.*]

[The following Extract from a Letter from Lord Nelson to Sir Richard Strachan,
on the 26th of August 1803, is in Clarke and M'Arthur, vol. ii. p. 323, and may
have formed part of the above.]

I wish to call your serious attention to what I am going to
mention. The French Fleet being perfectly ready for sea,
seven of the Line, six Frigates, and some Corvettes—two Sail
of the Line are now rigging in the Arsenal; I think it more
than probable that they are bound to the Westward, out of
the Mediterranean. Therefore, as I am determined to follow
them, go where they may, I wish you, in case they escape me,
to send a Frigate or Sloop after them to find out their route,
giving her a station where I may find her, and keep yourself
either at the Mouth of the Straits, or off Europa Point; for I
certainly shall not anchor at Gibraltar. You will, of course,
keep this to yourself, and I rely, my dear Sir Richard, with
full confidence on your experience, judgment, and that ardent
zeal which has ever distinguished your Public services. I
am, &c.

NELSON AND BRONTE.

TO SIR EVAN NEPEAN, BART., ADMIRALTY.

[Original, in the Admiralty.]

Victory, off Toulon, 26th August, 1803.

Sir,

I herewith transmit you, for the information of the Lords Commissioners of the Admiralty, a letter from Captain Hillyar,[9] of his Majesty's Ship Niger, giving an account of a most unjustifiable act of hostility committed against the Boats of the said Ship by a Greek Vessel; and I have to observe, for their Lordships' information, that similar acts have, and will be committed by the Grecian Ships, on their being boarded by the Boats of his Majesty's Fleet, unless severe punishment is inflicted. You will please to acquaint their Lordships, that I have represented this act of violence to his Majesty's Minister at Constantinople, and desired that he will make a regular complaint on the occasion. I have ordered the Greek Ship to be conveyed to Malta, and detained there. I am, &c.,

NELSON AND BRONTE.

P.S.—Inclosed is an extract of a letter from Captain Hillyar of the 7th instant.

TO CAPTAIN DONNELLY, NARCISSUS.

[Autograph, in the possession of the late Adam Bromilow, Esq.]

Victory, off Toulon, 26th August, 1803.

Having received information that there is an embarkation of Troops at Toulon, (or Marseilles,) intended to join the Corsicans, with a view to invade the Island of Sardinia, and as I think Ajaccio is the most likely place in Corsica for their forming such junction, You are hereby required and

[9] Captain Hillyar stated that, "On the 16th August, 1803, afternoon, Genoa bearing North 8 or 9 leagues, he sent Lieutenant Jones to examine a strange Ship bearing for Porto Fino. The Master of the Greek Ship, on being hailed, told the Boats to keep off. On approaching, a fire of guns and muskets by the Ship ensued, and Lieutenant Jones, in boarding, was mortally wounded; a seaman killed and one wounded, of the Niger; five of the Cameleon, wounded; five Greeks killed, and seven wounded. Lieutenant Jones and the Greek Captain died of their wounds. The Greek Ship was captured." In this affair, Captain Hillyar's brother, Mr. William Hillyar, so much distinguished himself, that Lord Nelson immediately promoted him into Mr. Jones' vacancy.

directed to take his Majesty's Ship named in the margin[1] under your command, (whose Captain has received my orders for that purpose,) and proceed with all possible dispatch, and take such station as you may judge most likely to intercept them, and prevent their landing or forming a junction with the Corsicans at Ajaccio, or elsewhere; but should you fall in with them at sea, you are to use your utmost endeavours to take, sink, burn, or destroy the whole of them. If, however, the Enemy should escape into any Port of the Island of Sardinia, you are to proceed and attack them wherever you may fall in with them, without paying regard to any pretended flag of Neutrality, (except under the guns of Cagliari,) or considering such Port or place entitled to the respect of Neutrality, but as an invaded Country by the Enemy. In the event of your finding them at Cagliari, that Fort being sufficient to prevent the Enemy's landing, you are to afford the Viceroy every assistance in your power to enable him to destroy the Enemy, and frustrate their designs against the Dominions of his Most Sacred Majesty the King of Sardinia. You are to return and join me on my Rendezvous off this place in fourteen days, or sooner if you should obtain any information which you may judge important for me to be acquainted with.

NELSON AND BRONTE.

TO HIS EXCELLENCY MR. DRUMMOND, CONSTANTINOPLE.

[From Clarke and M'Arthur, vol. ii. p. 323.]

27th August, 1803.

According to the reports of Vessels spoken from Marseilles and Genoa, the War is very unpopular, and I hope it will end in the destruction of that man of tyranny, Buonaparte; but I detest Europe for being so mean-spirited as to submit to the mandates of this Corsican—I blush for their meanness. In Ireland, the Militia have vied with the Regulars who should act best. If we are but true to ourselves, a fig for the great Buonaparte. I am, &c.,

NELSON AND BRONTE.

[1] Active.

TO HIS EXCELLENCY MR. DRUMMOND, CONSTANTINOPLE.

[From Clarke and M'Arthur, vol. ii. p. 323.]

27th August, 1803.

I have the honour to address your Excellency on a subject which calls loudly for redress and prevention in future. It is the acknowledged right of all lawful Cruisers to examine the Papers of Vessels hoisting Neutral Colours, in order to ascertain whether the property of Enemies, not contraband articles, be carried on board them; and it is the acknowledged Law of Nations, that resistance to such search is confiscation of Ship and Cargo, on the principle that such act of hostility makes the Ship and Crew Enemies. It has, I am sorry to say, been invariably the practice of the Greeks, whenever they fancied themselves superior, for their Vessels or Boats to fire on the English flag; and to endeavour to kill the English, who were only executing their bounden duty in examining all Ships and Vessels. When I had the command of the Agamemnon, I had sixteen men killed by these Greeks.[2] . . . I have earnestly to request that your Excellency will obtain an order to the Greek Islands that their Vessels do not fire on the English flag; for certainly the smaller the Vessel coming, the less cause for firing. I am, &c.,

NELSON AND BRONTE.

TO CAPTAIN SCHOMBERG, HIS MAJESTY'S SHIP MADRAS, MALTA.

[Letter-Book.]

Victory, off Toulon, 31st August 1803.

Sir,

I have received a letter from Mr. Schaw, Surgeon of His Majesty's Ship under your command, dated the 7th Instant, together with copy of his letter to you of the 24th ultimo, and also a letter of complaint from Major General Villettes against Mr. Schaw: the two former letters I have transmitted to the General, and as it is my intention to take an early opportunity of sending Doctor Snipe,[3] Physician of the Fleet, to Malta,

[2] Vide vol. ii. p. 76.

[3] John Snipe, Esq., M.D.: he died one of the Physicians of the Royal Naval Hospital at Plymouth, in August 1805.

with directions to inquire into the circumstance above alluded
to, I shall suspend my opinion on Mr. Schaw's conduct till
I have the Physician's report, and only observe that if Mr.
Schaw thought his professional judgment called in question
unfairly by Dr. Franklin,[4] he should have desired an inquiry to refute the statement, and not previously to have
attacked, in a private letter, the conduct of Doctor Franklin.　It is my particular directions the moment any of the
people of His Majesty's Ship under your command is attacked
with an infectious or inflammatory fever, that he is sent to the
Military General Hospital, and not be kept on board longer
than necessary.　I am, Sir, &c.,

NELSON AND BRONTE.

TO MAJOR-GENERAL VILLETTES, MALTA.

[Autograph, in the possession of Josiah French, Esq.]

Victory, off Toulon, August 29th, 1803.

My dear General,

I was favoured with your letter of August 9th, this morning.
'When Doctors differ who shall decide?' I am sure it is out
of my power. I shall answer your Public letter on the subject. If the poor man was not sent to the Hospital so soon as
he ought to have been, in that case Dr. Franklin had a right
to complain. If he was sent at a proper time, in that case
the Surgeon of the Madras would naturally feel hurt at such a
very severe letter as the one wrote by Dr. Franklin without any
inquiry from his brother Medico into the case. The one seems
too high for to look at a Surgeon in the Navy, and the other
perhaps regularly brought up, felt degraded by Dr. Franklin's
mode of procedure. I shall very soon send Dr. Snipe, Physician to the Fleet, to Malta, and I hope that he will be able to
settle this business amicably. I am, my dear General, truly
sensible of the great care and attention shown by the Medical
Gentlemen of the Hospital to our Seamen, and that they have
no reward adequate to their trouble. Sir Richard Bickerton
has told me that he is directed to give such a sum to the

---

[4] Dr., afterwards Sir William Franklin, Knight Commander of the Order of the
Guelphs : he died in October 1833.

Gentlemen of the Hospital for their trouble; but the amount
is so trifling, and in his opinion inadequate to their merits,
that he has been ashamed to offer it.   I trust that this little
asperity in a professional judgment, between two professional
men, will not prevent the reception of our Seamen in future,
and the former kindness of the Gentlemen of the Hospital towards them.   I suppose the Admiralty, if we are to keep
Malta, will establish a proper Naval Hospital.   I have sent
home a copy of Colonel Lyard's[5] report from Messina, and
have made some very strong remarks on the conduct of the
Government of Messina, and my belief that unless our
Government took a decided line of conduct with the Court of
Naples, that Sicily would be lost; but, in truth, I believe the
Court of Naples are afraid of offending the Court of Russia
by admitting us, so that 'between two stools they may fall to
the ground.'   In the present situation of England and Ireland,
I have my doubts of their sending any Troops abroad, and
therefore I most regret the sending for them home; it was a
very inconsiderate measure, to say nothing further of it.   By
Seahorse I hope you [*sic*]; much may be said about our friend
Ball's Passports.   Government at home should decide, and not
lay an Algerine War at my door; I shall be careful of beginning, but whatever on mature reflection shall be determined
upon, shall be vigorously carried into execution.   Believe me
ever, my dear General, your faithful and obliged friend,

NELSON AND BRONTE.

TO MAJOR-GENERAL VILLETTES, MALTA.

[Letter-Book.]

Victory, off Toulon, 31st August, 1803.

Sir,

I have been honoured with your letter of August 8th, enclosing a letter from Dr. Franklin to you complaining of the
conduct of Mr. Schaw, Surgeon of His Majesty's ship Madras.
I send you copies of Mr. Schaw's letter to myself and Captain
Schomberg on that occasion.   It appears to me that if Mr.

---

[5] Lieutenant-Colonel John Thomas Layard, of the 54th Regiment: he died a
Lieutenant-General, in May 1823.

Schaw did not send the poor man so soon to the Hospital as he ought to have done, that he is very blameable, for certainly in the situation of the Madras, no man ought to be kept a moment longer than is possible after an inflammatory fever was upon him. I shall take an early opportunity of sending Doctor Snipe, Physician to the Fleet, to inquire and make known to me whether the man was kept longer on board than he ought to have been. I am sorry that any reflection should be thrown out by the Medical Gentlemen, to each other. I have always heard Dr. Franklin's kindness to our Seamen spoken of in the highest terms, and I trust that he will continue it. I am free to confess that in my opinion if Mr. Schaw thought his professional judgment called in question unfairly by Doctor Franklin, he should have desired an inquiry to refute Doctor Franklin's statement, and that he had no right previously to attack, in a private letter, the conduct of Doctor Franklin; and I have so wrote Captain Schomberg, to be communicated to Mr. Schaw. I have the honour to be, &c.,

NELSON AND BRONTE.

P.S.—Inclosed is a copy of my letter to Mr. Schaw, Surgeon of the Madras.

TO SIR EVAN NEPEAN, BART., ADMIRALTY.

[Original, in the Admiralty.]

Victory, off Toulon, 2nd September, 1803.

Sir,

On the 17th ultimo, I received your letter of the 20th June last, together with a note from the Chevalier D'Anduaga, the Spanish Minister at our Court, therein mentioned, complaining of an act of violence committed on board the Spanish Xebec La Purissima Conception, by a British Frigate (whose name is unknown) on the 21st of April last, near the Island of Majorca; in answer to which, you will please to acquaint the Lords Commissioners of the Admiralty, that I have not been able to gain any information on the circumstance abovementioned, either from Rear-Admiral Sir Richard Bickerton, or any of the Captains of His Majesty's Ships at present off this place; but shall use every means in my power of obtaining a knowledge thereof, which shall be transmitted to you for their Lordships' information accordingly.   I am, &c.,

NELSON AND BRONTE.

TO HIS EXCELLENCY HUGH ELLIOT, ESQ., NAPLES.

[Autograph, in the Elliot Papers.]

Victory, September 2nd, 1803.

My dear Sir,

I have no small Vessels on this station: therefore I have no means of sending you any account of ourselves.   We are here buffeting the winds and waves, expecting one of these days that the French will put to sea.   I only wish I could know to a certainty where they are bound.   I think either to the Westward, or they will make a push at Messina, and as winter approaches, we can be sure of nothing in so short a run.

You know from Colonel Lyard and Sir Alexander Ball, and General Villettes, the state of the fortifications at Messina, and the total neglect of every means for the defence of the place.   Was any English Governor so notoriously to neglect his duty (unless he is ordered to resign to the Enemy) he would lose his head.   Instead of the sixteen Gun-boats being ready to act, and exercising every day in the Straits, they have not a man belonging to them; and from being hauled up upon the shore, and exposed to the sun, are so much out of repair, that it would take an age to prepare them for service. The Governor says, that he is ordered to make no show of preparing for defence.   If that is so, I have done.   The French will soon be there.   Surely, the best mode of keeping an Enemy out, is to convince him that you have both the means and the inclination; and from the accounts sent me from Messina, there are neither means nor inclination to prevent the French possessing themselves of it any day.   They have Privateers enough at Messina, and in Sicily, to carry men enough, where no resistance can be intended.   These conclusions are drawn from the information sent me.   I can know nothing of my own knowledge.   General Villettes also writes me, that the French are advanced to Cotrone, and that is further than they were before, and of course contrary to their promises. But I have done my duty in representing these matters, and it remains only for me to lament that it is of no avail.

Does Naples trust to Russia? I sincerely hope that Russia will go to War to defend her; but even supposing that to be the case, would not Russia be better pleased to see exertions, instead of supineness? and, I am sure, that John Bull would go any length to secure those who have spirit enough to resist the French yoke. If General Vial goes to Messina, I do not expect it will belong to Naples all this month. He will send [*query,* say] to the General—only send 500 men. Would the Neapolitan Troops fire upon them? I say, No: for if they did, they would know that their King, and the whole Kingdom of Naples, would be lost. I said before that I never would mention Sicily again; but my heart bleeds to hear what I do from Messina; and, as sure as you live, it is lost, unless other means are taken to prevent it than are followed at present.

I send you the Gibraltar, Captain Ryves, to take the Monmouth's station. If a Ship is not wanted absolutely at Naples, you will be so good as to tell Captain Ryves so in writing, that he may join me; for I have no force to spare for idleness. If it is necessary to secure the safety of the Royal Family, then it is doubly necessary to secure them a place of retreat, and Sicily will be gone if the French get to Messina. What can prevent their sending 50,000 men, if necessary, into Sicily? Then the good Sovereigns are slaves, and God only knows what else may happen.

Sardinia is on the eve of being invaded, and although all the people know it there, yet no step is taken to prevent them. However, I will not trouble you with other people's concerns; I shall write to Mr. Jackson.[4] With respect to the Barbary States, I have received such an instruction from England, that I can decide nothing about Algiers till Mr. Falcon comes up; and I fear it will turn out that his story is not quite correct. If so, it alters the whole face of the

---

[4] Minister at the Court of Sardinia.

matter. I am instructed to inquire into the circumstances,
and if his report is well-founded, to insist on his being received again. Now it turns out, that after the Dey's rage
was over, and before Mr. Falcon sailed, the Dey wished
him to remain. The Dey has since quarrelled with the
French: therefore, it is our interest to keep well with
him. Respecting the Maltese passports, our Government
should give them our *Cut*,[5] and then the Barbary States would
have no excuse for taking the poor people. However, I shall
endeavour to do all in my power. My station is here; and
here I shall remain till the French come out, if it is a year,
provided our Ships are not worn out. I can readily conceive
Sir John Acton's feelings. I shall write him a line, and I
beg of your Excellency to present my humble duty to their
Majesties, and all the Royal Family; and believe me, &c.,

                                        NELSON AND BRONTE.

I send you a letter from your brother.

TO SIR EVAN NEPEAN, BART., ADMIRALTY.

[Original, in the Admiralty.]

                              Victory, off Toulon, 2nd September, 1803.

Sir,

I herewith transmit you a copy of a letter of this date to
His Majesty's Consul-General at Sicily, which you will please
to lay before the Lords Commissioners of the Admiralty for
their information; and at the same time acquaint their Lordships, that, immediately on my arrival at Gibraltar, I ordered
the Tourterelle to take the Convoy from that place to
England, and to call off Cadiz for such Trade as might also be
there: that on my arrival at Malta I ordered the Cyclops to
proceed with the Trade from thence bound into the Adriatic,
and to bring the Merchant-Ships from the different Ports
there to Malta. I also ordered the Anson and Stately (after
cruizing on their station till the 16th July) to take the Trade
from Malta to Smyrna, with directions to bring all our Levant
Merchant-Vessels to Valette harbour; and, in passing through

----

[5] The "Mediterranean Passes," issued by our Government, were *cut* or indented
at the top.

the Faro of Messina on the 20th June last, I sent a letter to the Merchants there, acquainting them that a Convoy would soon sail from Malta to England, and enclosed them a letter to the Senior Officer at Malta, directing them to send a Ship of War to Messina for their Trade, in the event of their making application for Convoy, copies of which accompany this; that immediately on my arrival off Toulon, hearing that an English Merchant Ship was blocked up at Città Vecchia by a French Privateer, I sent the Weazel to convoy her from thence to Malta, that she might avail herself of the protection of the Blonde and Experiment, then under orders to proceed to England with the Trade; but I since understand that she left Città Vecchia with the Phœbe, and took an early opportunity of parting from her, and as she has not been heard of, I conclude she has been captured by the Enemy.

On the 2nd ultimo, I sent the Termagant Sloop to the different Spanish Ports in these Seas, to collect the Trade and convoy them to Gibraltar, for the purpose of proceeding with the first Convoy to England. I have to beg their Lordships will not impute blame to me, (as I also understand that several of the Merchant Ships in the Adriatic sailed after they heard of the War, without waiting for convoy for these Ships,) and that they may be assured every attention in my power shall be paid to the Trade of His Majesty's Subjects in these Seas. But if the Masters of Merchant Ships will act of themselves, without allowing the Commander-in-Chief to exercise his judgment and discretion in collecting the Trade from the different places, many of our Ships must inevitably fall into the hands of the Enemy. I am, &c.,

NELSON AND BRONTE.

TO JAMES TOUGH, ESQ., H.M. CONSUL-GENERAL IN SICILY.

[From a Copy in the Admiralty.]

Victory, off Toulon, 2nd September, 1803.

Sir,

A Convoy will sail from Malta on the 25th Instant, or as soon after as possible for England; and, therefore, if there are any Vessels intended to avail themselves of such protection, they must be at Malta by that time: you will please to inform the Merchants of Sicily, and desire them to acquaint the senior Naval Officer at Malta, on what day the Ships from the different Ports of Sicily will be ready, that he may send a Ship of War for them. The Merchant Ships, I understand, have been in the habit of proceeding without Convoy to England and Malta. The consequence has been that several have fallen into the hands of the Enemy; I must therefore desire you will be so good as acquaint the Merchants of Sicily, that should any of their Trade proceed without Convoy, after this public notice, I shall send an account to Lloyd's Coffee-House of the circumstance. I am, &c.,

NELSON AND BRONTE.

TO CAPTAIN CHARLES MARSH SCHOMBERG, HIS MAJESTY'S SHIP MADRAS, OR THE SENIOR OFFICER AT MALTA.

[Letter-Book.]

Victory, off Toulon, 2nd September, 1803.

Sir,

I am to desire you will please to acquaint the Merchants at Malta, that a Convoy will sail from thence for England on the 1st October, or as soon after as possible ; and you are, immediately on the receipt hereof, to employ his Majesty's Ships Cyclops and Charon, in collecting the Trade from Sicily, who are intended to proceed with the said Convoy, which you are to dispatch as early after the 1st of October, as circumstances will admit, under the escort appointed for that purpose. I am, &c.,

NELSON AND BRONTE.

TO PETER WILKIE, ESQ., AGENT VICTUALLER AT MALTA.

[Letter-Book.]

Victory, off Toulon, 6th September, 1803.

Sir,

I have received your letter of the 8th ultimo, and as the Captain of the Fleet has so fully wrote you on the subject of provisions, &c., for His Majesty's Ships under my command, it is only necessary for me to request that you will not purchase any more rice, sugar, or raisins, till you receive further orders for so doing, as sufficient supplies of those articles are coming from Gibraltar; and it being more convenient to have provisions for the Fleet off Toulon, from thence, than Malta, our principal dependence will be on that place; but it must be remembered that His Majesty's stores under your charge are sufficiently kept up for supplying the Frigates and other Cruizers in your vicinity, and to answer any exigency, which from circumstances may occur.   I am, &c.,

NELSON AND BRONTE.

TO HIS ROYAL HIGHNESS THE DUKE OF CLARENCE.

[From Clarke and M'Arthur, vol. ii. p. 323.]

[About 6th September, 1803.]

Sir,

I am happy to inform you that Captain Keats is much recovered.   I sent him to Naples for a fortnight; but having stayed only nine days, he was so anxious, knowing my inferiority in numbers to the Enemy, that he came back and joined me.[6]   I need not tell your Royal Highness, that he is amongst the very best Officers in our Service.   I have the highest respect and esteem for him.   I am, &c.,

NELSON AND BRONTE.

TO WILLIAM HASLEWOOD, ESQ., CRAVEN STREET, STRAND.

[From White's " Memoirs of Nelson," Supplement, p. 70.]

Private for yourself—and most secret.

[About 6th September, 1803.]

My dear Haslewood,

I send you home a Codicil[7] to my Will, which you will not communicate to any person breathing; as I would wish you to open, read it, and if not drawn up properly, send me a copy, and I will execute it.   It is possible that my personal estate, after the disposal of the furniture at Merton, may not amount to £4000; and sooner than this legacy, or any other, should

---

[6] " 28th August. Superb, with the Eliza Victualler, parted. . . . 5th September. H.M. Ship Superb rejoined with a Transport."—*Victory's Log.*

[7] Vide p. 259, post.

go unpaid, I would saddle Bronté, or any other estate with the legacies. I only mention this as a thing which might happen; and I want to give several other small legacies, and continue the annuity of £100 a year to poor blind Mrs. Nelson.[8] I may congratulate you on the favourable termination, (I hope,) of my law-suit.[9] You have acted not only as able lawyers, but a most friendly part through the whole business. I beg you will express my thanks to Serjeant Shepherd,[1] who has done so much justice to the cause; and be assured, I am ever, my dear Haslewood, your obliged friend,

NELSON AND BRONTE.

I have pretty near settled all my Bronté matters, and although I shall not probably at present be able to get the value of it, yet I shall secure, to be regularly paid, my £3000 a year nett.

Burn it when read.

TO HIS EXCELLENCY HUGH ELLIOT, ESQ.

[Autograph, in the Elliot Papers.]

Victory, September 8th, 1803.

My dear Sir,
I send you a letter sent to Sir Richard Bickerton; for although I do not believe that any such orders have been given, yet, as the former Neutrality of Naples only allowed four Ships of each Nation to enter their Ports, it is possible some stupid fellow may suppose her present Neutrality is the same as formerly; and, therefore, it may be very necessary to rectify any such misapprehension of orders. I am ever, my dear Sir, your faithful servant,   NELSON AND BRONTE.

TO HIS EXCELLENCY HUGH ELLIOT, ESQ.

[Autograph, in the Elliot Papers.]

Victory, off Toulon, September 8th, 1803.

My dear Sir,
George is gone down the Mediterranean, as I wish to put £10,000 in his pocket, and then I have done with him. He

---

[8] The widow of his brother, Maurice Nelson.
[9] With the Earl of St. Vincent.
[1] Afterwards Lord Chief Baron of the Exchequer in Scotland.

is an excellent young man, and a very good Officer. I had a letter lately from Lady Hamilton, wherein she says Sabatello Sabitino denies having Julia's money. He had near seventy pounds in money and valuables belonging to her, and now he refuses to pay her. Now, I know that Julia said in my presence, that Sabitino had taken her money, &c., and if he does not return it, I desire to withdraw my character of him, and so does Lady Hamilton; for he may serve others in the same manner: therefore, in behalf of a poor, injured woman, who he knows he has otherwise *injured*, I beg you will speak to him, and if he does not instantly pay the money to you to be sent home, Lady Hamilton desires not to be considered as recommending him, and I do the same; for I cannot bear such a monster of ingratitude.

We have had very severe gales of wind for seven days past: it is now fine again. Report says that 1000 or 1500 Troops sailed on the 1st from Marseilles. I have Frigates looking out for them off Corsica, where I think they are bound, in their way to Sardinia. I am ever, my dear Sir, your most faithful servant,

NELSON AND BRONTE.

I never experienced anything like the health of this Fleet. We have literally not a real sick man in it.

TO HIS EXCELLENCY HUGH ELLIOT, ESQ.

[Autograph, in the Elliot Papers.]

Victory, off Toulon, September 11th, 1803.

My dear Sir,

I have directed the Gibraltar to remain fourteen days at Naples; and if she is not wanted there, her Captain has orders to return to me: but if the Court think, or wish for her remaining, Captain Ryves has orders, on your written requisition, to remain till further orders; for I never will neglect the personal safety of those good Sovereigns. I am ever, &c.,

NELSON AND BRONTE.

TO J. B. GIBERT, ESQ., BRITISH CONSUL AT BARCELONA.

[From Clarke and M'Arthur, vol. ii. p. 324.]

13th September, 1803.

You will have the goodness to present my respectful compliments to the Captain-General, and assure him, that the return of Deserters shall be reciprocal on my part, and that I have forgiven them at his request. You will also inform his Excellency, that I have read with no small surprise, a Paper, purporting to have been given in during the year 1771, and now ordered to be put in force. I am ready to admit, that the King of Spain may order us to be refused admittance into his Ports, may refuse us, even when there, the rights of hospitality, as his Excellency has done those of civility, in not even asking Captain Whitby to sit down, although there were others in his presence seated. His Sovereign may certainly, if he pleases, go to War with us—I deny none of these rights: but I claim every indulgence which is shown to the Ships of our Enemies. The French Squadron at Corunna are acting almost as they please; the Aigle French Ship of War is not turned out of Cadiz, the French Frigate Revenge is permitted to go out of that Port, cruise, and return with Prizes, and sell them. I will not state that every Spanish Port is a home for French Privateers, for this is well known; and I am informed that even at Barcelona, English Vessels captured by the French, have been sold there. You will acquaint his Excellency, that I claim for every British Ship, or Squadron, the right of lying as long as I please in the Ports of Spain, whilst it is allowed to other Powers; that I claim the rights of hospitality and civility, and every other right which the harmony subsisting between our Sovereigns entitles us to. You will acquaint his Excellency, that I can mean no disrespect personally to himself; but that it is a British Admiral returning an answer to a Spanish Captain-General, through the same channel which conveyed the message. I am, &c.

NELSON AND BRONTE.

TO HIS EXCELLENCY JOHN HOOKHAM FRERE, MADRID.

[From Clarke and M'Arthur, vol. ii. p. 324. In transmitting the Captain-General's State Paper, with this letter, to Mr. Frere, our Envoy at Madrid, Lord Nelson
added :]

[About 13th September, 1803.]

This conduct, I suppose, indicates a War with us : I have
therefore earnestly to request, that you will send me immediate notice of such an event, that I may send to the West
Indies, and act upon it myself. If your news of War passes
through England, it will be two or three months before I
shall know it officially, and the same in the West Indies. I
would recommend to your Excellency, sending an express to
Barcelona with an order to hire a Vessel, another to the Bay
of Rosas, where our Ships of War often are, and another to
Gibraltar to the Governor and Commanding Sea-Officer;
and I only hope that your letter may be clear, whether it will
be, or is, War. I am, &c.

NELSON AND BRONTE.

TO THE RESPECTIVE CAPTAINS AND COMMANDERS OF HIS
MAJESTY'S SHIPS AND VESSELS ON THE MEDITERRANEAN
STATION.

[From a Copy in the Nelson Papers.]

Victory, off Toulon, 13th September, 1803.

When British Seamen and Marines so far degrade themselves in time of War, as to desert from the Service of their
own Country, and enter into that of Spain ; when they leave
one shilling per day, and plenty of the very best provisions,
with every comfort that can be thought of for them—for two-
pence a-day, black bread, horse-beans, and stinking oil for
their food;—when British Seamen or Marines turn Spanish
Soldiers, I blush for them : they forfeit in their own opinion,
I am sure, that character of love of their own Country,
which Foreigners are taught to admire. A Briton to put
himself under the lash of a Frenchman or Spaniard must
be more degrading to any man of spirit then any punishment I could inflict on their bodies. I shall leave the punishment to their own feelings, which, if they have any, and are
still Englishmen, must be very great. But, as they thought

proper to abandon, voluntarily, their wives, fathers, mothers, and every endearing tie, and, also, all prospect of returning to their native Country, I shall make them remain out of that Country, which they do not wish to see, and allow others, who love their Country, and are attached to their families, to return in their stead. And, as they have also thought proper to resign all their pay, I shall take care that it is not returned to them, nor their " R." taken off;[2] but it shall be noted against their names, ' Deserted to the Spaniards,' or ' Entered as a Spanish Soldier,' as the case was.

NELSON AND BRONTE.

The above Memorandum respecting the desertion of British Seamen or Marines is to be read to the respective Companies of His Majesty's Ships and Vessels under my command, and copies thereof, to be stuck up in the most public places of the Ships, in order that the magnitude of the crime may be properly impressed on their minds.

NELSON AND BRONTE.

TO MAJOR-GENERAL VILLETTES.

[Autograph, in the possession of Josiah French, Esq.]

Victory, off Toulon, September 16th, 1803.

My dear General,

I wrote you on the 29th of August; but such is my want of Small Craft, that I have had no means of sending a letter. We have had near fourteen days very blowing weather, but that is to be expected at this season of the year. The Belleisle is missing since the 14th, when I sent for her to look into Toulon. I hope the gentry did not come out in the gale, and got hold of her—that would be certainly contrary to my intentions. On the 11th, a Rear-Admiral, Chef d'Escadre, four Sail of the Line, Frigates, and Corvettes, were under sail—a Ship of the Line and Frigates were some miles outside Sepet; but they returned again, and on the 13th, they were all snug at anchor. We are now twenty leagues from Toulon, and a calm, therefore, she is, I hope, not far off. The Frigates I have are dispersed to look out, in case the French slip by me, and our little Squadron is so healthy and keen that I would

---

[2] " R."—i. e., " Run." The mark placed in the Ships' Books against the names of such as had deserted.

not recommend them to fall in with us. I am much obliged
to you for your goodness about the shells, and I have to
apologize to Colonel Bentham[2] for the trouble I am giving
him. I shall be very glad of a hundred for 12-pounders. I do
not mean to use them at sea, for that I hope to consider
burning *our own* Ships; but in case they run ashore, then a
few put into their sides will do their business. From our
communication with Spain, it looks rather hostile, she must
go to War either with France or us; and all the blame is laid
at our door because we will not bow to France, and allow the
world to be at peace. Such is the reasoning of the Spaniards
—even the Captain-General of Catalonia; but I have wrote
him a letter which will not be misunderstood, and I have sent
an express to Madrid.

I want Peace; and therefore, if we are to have more Powers
upon us, the sooner they begin the better, and not give us a
long War. Your letters, my dear General, are always so
interesting to me, that I shall ever feel much obliged by your
sending them; and believe me your most obliged and faithful
friend,

NELSON AND BRONTE.

I beg my best respects to General Oakes. As the Prévoyante goes direct for England, she will take your dispatches,
I think, perfectly safe: mine will go from Gibraltar by her.

A Swiss who was in Dillon's Regiment, came on board a
Ship at Barcelona, and, as he has been a Soldier, I send him
as a present to you. Mr. Brown, Commander of the Prévoyante will deliver him.

N. & B.

TO SIR ALEXANDER JOHN BALL, BART., MALTA.

[Autograph, in the possession of Sir William Keith Ball, Bart.]

Victory, off Toulon, September 16th, 1803.

My dear Ball,

I have had nothing to send you [since] my letter of August
29th, and we had a gale almost ever since. I bear up for every
gale. I must not, in our present state, quarrel with the North
Westers—with crazy masts and no Port or spars near us.

---

[2] Lieutenant-Colonel William Bentham, of the Royal Artillery, who died a
Lieutenant-General, about 1828 or 1829.

Indeed, in the whole station, there is not a topmast for a Seventy-four.   On the 11th, a Ship of the Line and some Frigates were outside Sepet; a Rear-Admiral, Chef d'Escadre, and another Ship of the Line, four in the whole, &c.   Eight were under Sail; but seeing Canopus stand under Sicie, they hauled their wind and worked in again.   On the 12th and 13th, they were at anchor.   That night I sent Belleisle to work off the Port, wind blowing strong out E.S.E. and S.E., which has drove us to twenty leagues West of Sicie.   I am a little anxious at her not joining; but they must have more than common luck to get hold of her.   The Squadron has health beyond what I have almost ever seen, except our going to the Nile; and I hope, if the French will give us the opportunity, that our beef and pudding will be as well applied. I should be very glad to copper the Queen Schooner for you, but I much doubt if Government send out more than is neces- sary for the Ships on the station.   If she belongs to the Government of the Island, a line from the Secretary of State to the Admiralty will produce the copper for her; therefore the Builder had better give you an account of the quantity wanted—paper, nails, &c.; and for you to write to Lord Hobart.   With respect to the Commissaryship for Prisoners, I only appointed Mr. Chapman on your recommendation; and I do not think I ought to appoint any one, much less a Foreigner, with power to draw bills on our Government; therefore, I rely that Mr. Chapman will hold it until the Transport Board appoint a proper person—be that person Mr. Vankempen,[4] or any one else.   The French Privateers in Sicily do not seem to care for Neutrality.   You and the Viceroy,[5] I take for granted, will settle this matter.   By Lieutenant Shaw's account, I never heard the equal to it, both at Girgenti and Alicati.   Your advice to Mr. Elliot will be good, and I think he will attend to it; but Diplomatic men think, of course, they know much better than any one else, and Mr. E. is the oldest Minister we have.   He has got a better appointment than any Minister ever sent to Naples: he first got £3000 for plate money, and £4500 a-year, being little [less than] Ambassador's pay—no bad hit, Mr. Elliot; and they ought, my dear Friend, to give you as much whilst you remain; but I hope to see you again afloat. I, for one of your friends, never wished you to have Malta: I had destined you in my mind for another appointment. We are all well: Murray is measuring rope and coals; Hardy rigging the main-yard on the booms; and we are caulking and refitting for a winter's cruise, unless the French will be so good as to prevent us; but I am ever, my dear Sir Alexander, most truly and faithfully yours,

NELSON AND BRONTE.

TO LIEUTENANT HARDING SHAW,[6] COMMANDING H, M, BRIG TIGER.

[Letter-Book.]

Victory, off Toulon, 16th September, 1803.

Sir,

I have received your letter of the 30th ult., together with a copy of your Log-book, and the two letters therein mentioned; and notwithstanding your conduct (in protecting the two English Merchant Ships of Girgenti from the insult, and perhaps capture, of the French Privateer laying there) appears highly praiseworthy, yet, with such information, I cannot take upon me to say that your conduct is perfectly regular, and have only to observe, that if it meets the approbation of Sir Alexander Ball, there can be no doubt of its being correct and meritorious. I am, &c., 　　　　　　NELSON AND BRONTE.

TO CAPTAIN . . . . . ., HIS MAJESTY'S SLOOP . . . . .

[Letter-Book.]

Victory, off Toulon, 16th September, 1803.

Sir,

An Officer belonging to his Majesty's Sloop . . . . . . under your command, having boarded a Vessel from Tunis, which, consequently, placed the said Sloop under the most strict Quarantine, and you having last evening, immediately after such communication, sent an Officer on board the Victory, and this morning come yourself, without previously acquainting me of such circumstance, and thereby endangering the health of the Victory's Ship's company, and that of the whole

---

[6] Lieutenant Harding Shaw was still a Lieutenant in 1809, and died before 1814.

Fleet under my command, I desire to acquaint you that such conduct is highly reprehensible and unofficerlike, and that you will hold yourself ready to answer (when called upon) for it accordingly.   I am, &c.,

NELSON AND BRONTE.

TO LADY HAMILTON.

[Autograph, in the possession of Colonel Davison.]

Victory, off Toulon, September 18th, 1803.

My dear Lady Hamilton,

The furniture and linen which was left behind at Palermo and Naples, when you came to England, is, I hope, by this time, safe at Malta.   I have desired Mr. Noble to unpack, dry them, and send you a list of the contents, which you must send to the Treasury, in order to obtain an order for their being allowed to come direct to you, without passing through the Custom-House.   I believe the cases are eighteen in number.   I have requested the favour of Mr. Brown, Commander of the Prévoyante Store-Ship, who will carry them either to Portsmouth or the Nore, to whichever place he may be ordered.   If you will apply by letter to my friend, Mr. Vansittart,[7] of the Treasury, I am sure he will send an order directly for their delivery.   Only tell me, my dear Friend, in what manner I can be useful to you in this Country, and, believe me, I shall be truly proud in obeying your commands, being for ever, your most obliged, faithful, and affectionate,

NELSON AND BRONTE.

TO SIR EVAN NEPEAN, BART., ADMIRALTY.

[Original, in the Admiralty.]

Victory, off Toulon, 21st September, 1803.

Sir,

I am to request you will be pleased to acquaint the Lords Commissioners of the Admiralty, that the Prévoyante Store Ship, which arrived here on the 21st ultimo, with stores for the Fleet under my command, has completed all their demands with much alacrity and attention, and that Mr. Brown's con-

[7] Now Lord Bexley.

duct, in the discharge of this duty, most perfectly meets my approbation.

The deficiency occasioned by issuing the small stores by retail, I have recommended the Navy Board to take into account, and allow for it accordingly. The coals which came out in the Prévoyante have been supplied to the different Ships, who are all very much in want of fuel. The Prévoyante proceeds immediately to Malta with the stores she has for that Arsenal, and afterwards proceeds to Gibraltar to dispose of the remainder, as Commissioner Otway may order; from thence she proceeds to the Nore. I am, &c.

NELSON AND BRONTE.

TO ADMIRAL THE EARL OF ST. VINCENT, K.B.

[Autograph, in the possession of Vice-Admiral Sir William Parker, Bart., G.C.B.]

Victory, off Toulon, September 21st, 1803.

My dear Lord,

I never have been better pleased than with the regularity and good order in which the stores sent out by the Prévoyante have been delivered to the Fleet; and the utility of having the Ship with us is obvious, for I never could have spared the Ships to go to Gibraltar for them. The conduct of Mr. Brown,[8] a Master in the Navy, her Commander, has been such as to induce me to wish, from the difference I have seen, that the command of the Store-ships were continued to be given to respectable Masters, or Lieutenants, as they likewise act as Storekeepers; and we know that Captains in those Ships are generally above taking care of the stores. In justice to Mr. Brown, I have wrote to the Admiralty and Navy Boards, recommending him. I am ever, my dear Lord, your most obliged and faithful,   NELSON AND BRONTE.

TO THE PRINCIPAL OFFICERS AND COMMISSIONERS OF HIS MAJESTY'S NAVY, LONDON.

[Letter-Book.]

Gentlemen,   Victory, off Toulon, 21st September, 1803.

Having by letter of the 8th July last, directed the Naval Storekeeper at Gibraltar to send the first Store-Ship which

---

[8] Mr. William Brown, Master of the Prévoyante : he died before 1806.

might arrive there, direct to the Fleet off this place, with the Clerk under whose charge the stores were entrusted, in order that the issues to the different Ships might be regular, and the receipts for the stores so issued perfectly correct, I have therefore to acquaint you that the Prévoyante Store-ship arrived here on the 21st ult., under the command of Mr. William Brown, whose care and attention to the delivery of every article of stores to the Squadron off this place, deserves every commendation I can bestow; and as the issue of nails and other small stores by retail must naturally occasion some little deficiency, I have to request you will be pleased to make allowance for it accordingly. The coals which came out in the Prévoyante have been supplied to the different Ships, being very much in want of that article. I have directed Mr. Brown to proceed to Malta with the stores he has for that place, and afterwards to return to Gibraltar, where Commissioner Otway will direct the disposal of the remainder. And as the execution of this service will make it impossible for the Prévoyante to get out of the Mediterranean before the latter end of next month, I have recommended Mr. Brown to proceed from Gibraltar to the Nore direct, agreeable to your order to him of the 27th of June, and not to go to Halifax, as mentioned in your subsequent order of the 2nd ultimo, being too late in the season, and, as such, contrary to the directions therein contained. I am, &c.

NELSON AND BRONTE.

TO HIS HIGHNESS THE BEY OF TUNIS.

(Whom God preserve.)

[From a Copy, in the possession of the late Adam Bromilow, Esq.]

His Majesty's Ship Victory, off Toulon, 23rd September, 1803.

Sir,

Reports having reached me that some Vessels who call themselves French Privateers, but who I can consider in no *other* light than as Pirates, lay under the Island Zimbra,[9] and from the top of which make their observations of Vessels passing, row out, and attack Vessels of Nations at peace and amity with your Highness, under your Flag; and that, as the

---

[9] Zimbra, at the mouth of the Gulf of Tunis.

occasion may best suit them, they are either Vessels belonging to your Highness, or pass for French Privateers; and
with this deception, I understand they have, passing for a
Cruizer belonging to your Highness, taken possession of an
English Ship, who obeyed the summons supposed to be given
by an Officer belonging to you, I have, therefore, to request
that your Highness will inquire into the truth of the assertion
made to me; and if proved, that you will order such measures
to be taken as to justice shall appertain, for the just punishment of the offenders. I send Captain Donnelly, of his
Majesty's Royal Navy, who will further explain to your Highness what may be necessary to be said upon this subject; and
I request that your Highness may give full credit to what
Captain Donnelly may say in my name; and I have the
honour to assure your Highness that I am your most obedient
and faithful humble servant,

NELSON AND BRONTE.

TO CAPTAIN ROSS DONNELLY, H.M. SHIP NARCISSUS.

[Autograph, in the possession of the late Adam Bromilow, Esq.]

Victory, off Toulon, 23rd September, 1803.

Whereas some French Privateers have, as is represented in
the Papers sent herewith, made the most unwarrantable use
of the Bey of Tunis's Port and Colours, for the capture of
an English Ship called Pomona, You are therefore hereby
required and directed to proceed, with all possible dispatch,
in his Majesty's Ship Narcissus under your command, to the
Bey of Tunis, and endeavour, in concert with Mr. Clark,
(who acts as British Consul in the absence of Mr. Magra,) to
obtain from the justice of the Bey, the restitution of the said
Ship, and any other which may have been illegally taken.
You will deliver to his Highness my letter which accompanies
this, (a copy of which is also herewith transmitted for your
information,) and you will urge, but in the most moderate
manner, the equity of our demand, and point out what would
be the consequence, if I was inclined to take a similar position; but his Highness knows that I have always respected
his Neutrality. You will also take an opportunity of acquaint-

ing his Highness, that I have received information that the French have made several purchases of oil, &c. in his Dominions, and that they are hiring Vessels belonging to Tunis, to bring it to Marseilles; and as a most particular mark of my wishing to pay every respect to his Flag, I earnestly entreat that he will order his Subjects not to hire the Ships of Tunis for any such purpose ; as if they are found with French property, or suspected French property, on board, they will be detained for trial : for although the Vessels may be *bonâ fide* belonging to Tunis, it will not protect the cargo of an Enemy.

You will, however, touch on these points with so much good humour as to leave the impression of my high respect for his Highness, and regard for the real property of his Subjects. I rely with confidence on your ability and judgment in managing these matters to my satisfaction, and to the advantage of your Country. You will, of course, receive all English Seamen who may be at Tunis; and you will get every information, what supplies of bullocks, water, wood, and onions can be furnished the Fleet, and as near as possible the prices. Having performed this service as above directed, you are to return, and join me on my rendezvous off this place, as expeditiously as possible, with an account thereof.

NELSON AND BRONTE.

TO SIR EVAN NEPEAN, BART., ADMIRALTY.[1]

[Original, in the Admiralty.]

Victory, off Toulon, 24th September, 1803.

Sir,

As it is more than probable that the Fleet under my command will be obliged to keep the seas during the whole of the winter season, for the purpose of watching the Enemy's Ships at Toulon, and as there is in the Gulf of Lyons and its vicinity, upon an average, three days' gale of severe blowing weather out of the seven, which frequently comes on suddenly, and thereby exposes the topmasts, topsail-yards and sails, to great hazard, under every care and attention; I am therefore to desire you will be pleased to communicate this circumstance

---

[1] Lord Nelson wrote a letter on the same day, and almost in the same words, to the Commissioners of the Navy.

to the Lords Commissioners of the Admiralty, and suggest to their Lordships the propriety of sending out a sufficient number of topmasts, topsail-yards, and spare sails for the Ships, they may judge necessary for the service beforementioned, as early as possible, there being none of the two former in store, either at Gibraltar or Malta. I am, &c.

NELSON AND BRONTE.

TO SIR EVAN NEPEAN, BART., ADMIRALTY.

[Original, in the Admiralty.]

Victory, off Toulon, 25th September, 1803.

Sir,

You will please to acquaint the Lords Commissioners of the Admiralty, that his Majesty's Ship Seahorse joined the Squadron off this place, yesterday forenoon, having left the Convoy, which she brought from England, at Malta. You will also please to acquaint their Lordships, that a Convoy is ordered from Malta to England, and will proceed from Valetta Harbour on the first of next month, or as soon after as the Anson and Stately have joined with the Levant trade, which I trust will be about that time: this Convoy will take under its protection the trade which may be collected at Gibraltar. I am, &c.

NELSON AND BRONTE.

TO CAPTAIN SIR RICHARD JOHN STRACHAN, BART., H. M. SHIP
DONEGAL.

[From Clarke and M'Arthur, vol. ii. p. 325.]

26th September, 1803.

The occurrences which pass every day in Spain forbode, I fancy, a speedy War with England; therefore it becomes proper for me to put you upon your guard, and advise you how to act under particular circumstances. By looking at the former line of conduct on the part of Spain, which she followed just before the commencement of the last War, we may naturally expect the same events to happen. The French Admiral Richery was in Cadiz, blocked up by Admiral

P 2

Man;[2] on August the 22nd, they came to sea, attended by the Spanish Fleet, which saw the French safe beyond St. Vincent, and returned into Cadiz. Admiral Man very properly did not choose to attack Admiral Richery under such an escort. This is a prelude to what I must request your strict attention to; at the same time, I am fully aware that you must be guided, in some measure, by actual circumstances.

I think it very probable, even before Spain breaks with us, that they may send a Ship or two of the Line to see L'Aigle round Cape St. Vincent; and that if you attack her in their presence, they may attack you; and giving them possession of the Donegal, would be more than either you or I should wish, therefore I am certain it must be very comfortable for you to know my sentiments. From what you hear in Cadiz, you will judge how far you may venture yourself in company with a Spanish Squadron; but if you are of opinion that you may trust yourself near them, keeping certainly out of gun-shot, send your Boat with a letter to the Spanish Commodore, and desire to know whether he means to defend the French Ships; and get his answer in writing, and have it as plain as possible. If it be ' yes, that he will fire at you if you attack the French under his protection,' then, if you have force enough, make your attack on the whole body, and take them all if you can; for I should consider such an answer as a perfect Declaration of War. If you are too weak for such an attack, you must desist; but you certainly are fully authorized to take the Ships of Spain whenever you meet them. Should the answer be ambiguous, you must then act as your judgment may direct you, and I am sure that will be very proper. Only recollect, that it would be much better to let the French Ships escape, than to run too great a risk of losing the Donegal, yourself, and Ship's company. I am, &c.

NELSON AND BRONTE.

[2] Vide vol. ii. p. 256.

TO LADY HAMILTON.

[From " Lord Nelson's Letters to Lady Hamilton," vol. i. p. 152.]

September 26th, 1803.

My dearest Emma,

We have had, for these fourteen days past, nothing but gales of wind, and a heavy sea. However, as our Ships have suffered no damage, I hope to be able to keep the sea all the winter. Nothing, but dire necessity, shall force me to that out of the way place, Malta. If I had depended upon that Island, for supplies for the Fleet, we must all have been knocked up, long ago; for, Sir Richard Bickerton sailed from Malta, the same day I left Portsmouth, so that we have been a pretty long cruise; and, if I had only to look to Malta for supplies, our Ships companies would have been done for long ago. However, by management, I have got supplies from Spain, and also from France; but it appears, that we are almost shut out from Spain, for they begin to be very uncivil to our Ships. However, I suppose, by this time, something is settled; but, I never hear from England. My last letters are July 6th, near three months. But, as I get French newspapers occasionally, we guess how matters are going on.

I have wrote Mr. Gibbs, again, a long history about Bronté; and, I hope, if General Acton will do nothing for me, that he will settle something : but, I know, whatever is settled, I shall be the loser. Till next year, the debt will not be paid off; how——

TO SIR EVAN NEPEAN, BART., ADMIRALTY.

[Letter-Book.]

Victory, off Toulon, 27th September, 1803.

Sir,

I herewith transmit you copy of a letter from Captain Richardson, of His Majesty's Ship Juno, giving an account of the capture of the French Bombard Privateer, Les Quatre Fils of Nice, which you will please to lay before the Lords Commissioners of the Admiralty for their information. I am, &c.,

NELSON AND BRONTE.

TO ADMIRAL THE EARL OF ST. VINCENT, K.B.

[Autograph, in the possession of Vice-Admiral Sir William Parker, Bart., G.C.B.]

Victory, off Toulon, September 27th, 1803.

My dear Lord,

It is now near three months since my last letters were dated from England; and but for a French newspaper, which hitherto we have procured through Spain from Paris, we should not have known how the world went on; and reports have so often changed the First Lord of the Admiralty, that I know not if I am now writing to him; but that does not matter; I trust I am writing to an old friend, who sincerely wishes me as well as I do him.

I have said all my say long ago on the subject of the Ships here; therefore, I shall not bore you on that subject again. The fact is this—all the Ships have expected every day before the War, to go to England; therefore, when the War came, they wanted for everything—*more especially to go to England.* However, a good deal of that fever is wore off, and we are really got to a state of health which is rarely witnessed. I have exerted myself to get all the good things we could from Spain, and latterly our cattle and onions have been procured from France; but from the apparent incivilities of the Spaniards, I suppose we are on the eve of being shut out. Our length of passage from Malta is terrible. We have not procured one single article of refreshment from thence since the Fleet sailed (May 18th;) therefore, if a Fleet here had only Malta to trust to, the Fleet must go to Malta, for the good things of Malta could never come to us; and in that case the French might do as they pleased, between here and Gibraltar, for two months together. At this moment I think the Squadron, as far as relates to me, are fit to go to Madras. Their *hulls* want docking. I hope to be able to keep the sea all the winter—in short, to stay at sea till the French choose to come to sea; and then I hope to send many of our Ships who want what I cannot give them, to England, towing a Line-of-Battle Ship. I believe we are uncommonly well disposed to give the French a thrashing, and we are keen; for I have not seen a French flag on the sea since I joined the Squadron. A fortnight ago, three or four Sail of the Line were under sail, and some had got a few miles from Sepet, but I believe it was only for an exercise. Reports say they are hard at work, fitting out two new 80-gun Ships. Their lower rigging is over the mast-heads. I wish they would make haste, for our gales of wind, Admiral Campbell says, are harder and more frequent than ever. I believe them much the same—always very violent, and a heavy sea. But it is time to finish; therefore I shall only say that I am ever, my dear Lord, your most faithful friend,

NELSON AND BRONTE.

TO THE RIGHT HONOURABLE HENRY ADDINGTON.

[Autograph, in the Sidmouth Papers.]

Victory, off Toulon, 27th September, 1803.

My dear Sir,

The French are not yet out, although they about a fortnight ago made an appearance; indeed, some of their Ships were outside the harbour, but I rather think it was to get an exercise. However, *they took wit in their anger, and returned again.* They are hard at work equipping two new Eighty-gun ships; perhaps they wait for their being ready before they give us a meeting. I hope to be able to keep up six sail of the Line; and with that force, although they will be superior in numbers, yet I have every reason to hope that we shall give a very good account of them. We are at this moment the healthiest Squadron I ever served in, for the fact is we have no sick, and are all in good humour. The Spaniards are now so very uncivil to our Ships, that I suppose we shall not be much longer friends. I have wrote to Mr. Frere, at Madrid, to entreat that he would take every possible means to give me the earliest information of hostilities; and pointed out to him the length of time which would elapse before I could know it through England, and the very great importance of my knowing it. I sent a few days ago to Minorca, but the Spaniards would not give our Ship *pratique;* but Captain Donnelly learnt, that there are three Frenchmen taking an account of the revenue and how it is raised, and making every minute inquiry. Does this portend a cession of that Island? I fear it does, and the Minorquins think so—I should be very sorry to see that happen; for, however valuable and important Malta may be in other respects, and no man rates its value more than I do, yet as a place to get refreshments from, for a Fleet off Toulon, it is useless; I always thought it, and now I know it.

Since May 18th, the day the Squadron sailed from Malta, notwithstanding that every attempt has been made, as the Victualling Board will know but too well, not one morsel of fresh beef or any vegetables have we been able to get from Malta; therefore if we had only Malta to trust to, our Fleet must go there, and leave the station for two months together, and the French to do as they please. Minorca may have its inconveniences; but its conveniences are so great, that I trust at the moment a Spanish War is certain, that we shall be able to secure it: not but I am fully aware you want all your Troops, yet I ought not to pass by what my humble opinion is. I still hope that our great plan against Spain will be able to be carried into effect, and that my Mortar rafts[2] will be used with great success: I can find no one objection to them; their effect is certain, and little or no expense. I had more to say on other subjects, but I am fearful of intruding: therefore I only beg you to be assured, that every exertion of mine shall be used to bring this just War to an honourable and successful termination; and believe me ever, my dear Sir, your most attached and faithful friend,

                                NELSON AND BRONTE.

It is near three months since we have had letters from England.

TO ALEXANDER DAVISON, ESQ.

[Autograph, in the possession of Colonel Davison.]

                                Victory, September 27th, 1803.

My dear Davison,

The Proclamation[3] is so incomprehensible to all of us, that I beg that you will desire Messrs. Booth and Haslewood to get me one or two good opinions on the questions; and if any other question should arise out of the Lawyers' answers, to get an opinion on the answer; for sending me a doubtful opinion, is leaving me as I am, in *doubt*. Cruizing as we are, but little news can come to us. Since July 6th, we have received

---

[2] Vide p. 71, ante.

[3] "A Proclamation for Granting the Distribution of Prizes," dated 7th July, 1803. A copy of it is in the "Naval Chronicle," vol. x. pp. 6-81.

nothing from England of a later date.   The Spaniards begin
to be very uncivil : I suppose this forbodes a Spanish War.   I
only hope to get early information.   Since I have joined the
Fleet we have not seen one Frenchman on the sea, but we are
waiting for the sailing of their Fleet, which we hope will not
be much longer deferred ; for we are a little impatient.   Your
kindness, my dear friend, in sending me out pamphlets and
magazines has been so uniform, that I shall only say how truly
acceptable they are.   I have only a moment to write thus
much, but only believe, my dear Davison, that I feel myself
ever your most sincere and faithful friend,

NELSON AND BRONTE.

Hardy desires his kind regards.   Make my best compliments acceptable to Lord Moira, whose character I most
highly esteem.

TO CAPTAIN RICHARD HUSSEY MOUBRAY, H.M. SHIP ACTIVE.

[Order-Book.]

Victory, off Toulon, 28th September, 1803.

Having received information that there are two of the
Enemy's Frigates to the Eastward of Toulon, You are hereby
required and directed to take his Majesty's Ship named in the
margin [4] under your command, (whose Captain is directed to
put himself under your orders,) and proceed immediately to
the Eastward of Toulon, in search of the said French Frigates,
looking into the Bay of Nice, from thence to Genoa, and
strictly examine any Bay between that and Leghorn, in which
you may judge it most likely to fall in with them.   Not finding
them at any of the before-mentioned places, you are to call at
the Island of Elba, where it is probable they may touch.
Should your endeavours be ineffectual to fall in with the
Enemy, in the course of fourteen days from the date hereof,
you are to return and join me on my Rendezvous off this place
at the expiration of that time.

NELSON AND BRONTE.

[4] Phœbe.

TO COMMISSIONER OTWAY, GIBRALTAR.

[Autograph, in the possession of Rear-Admiral Inglefield, C.B.]

Victory, off Toulon, September 29th, 1803.

My dear Sir,

The Halcyon is going to put herself under the orders of Sir Richard Strachan, but I have directed Captain Pearse[5] to carry the Gibraltar mail to Lisbon, and to bring back the mail for Gibraltar. The Monmouth I expect every day from Naples. She is to go to Gibraltar to fit out the Ambuscade, and probably to carry her home with the Convoy, which will sail from Malta about the middle of October. The Prevoyante is gone to Malta, and when she has delivered her stores, will proceed to Gibraltar. I have been expecting either the Bittern or Termagant for this month past, and also something from England, but they seem to have forgot us. I am, my dear Sir, your much obliged and faithful, humble servant,

NELSON AND BRONTE.

TO ALEXANDER DAVISON, ESQ.

[Autograph, in the possession of Colonel Davison.]

Victory, off Toulon, October 4th, 1803.

My dear Davison,

Your kind letter of August 15th, *viâ* Lisbon, I received on the 1st, and was the first line I have had from England since the first week in July. Everything relative to yourself makes me truly comfortable. The King, I hope, will make you a Baronet, or a Peer, in the stead of a simple Knight. You know my answer to such dirty dogs as wanted to pull you down—they be d——d. You are, my dear Friend, too wise a man at this time of day to run any risk of being a poor man. Recollect the epitaph, '*I was well*, but would be better.' But whatever you do, will have my sincere good wishes, and you know enough of the world not to be careful. I am truly sensible of your good wishes for my prosperity. I believe I

---

[5] Captain Henry Whitmarsh Pearse was Lord Nelson's Flag-Lieutenant, and was promoted into the Halcyon on the 12th of August, 1803: he died a Post-Captain and a Companion of the Bath, in November 1832.

attend more to the French Fleet than making captures; but what I have, I can say as old Haddock[6] said, ' it never cost a Sailor a tear, nor the Nation a farthing.' This thought is far better than Prize-money;—not that I despise money—quite the contrary, I wish I had one hundred thousand pounds this moment, and I will do everything consistent with my good name to obtain it. We are healthy beyond example, and in great good humour with ourselves; and so sharp-set, that I would not be a French Admiral in the way of any of our Ships for something. I believe we are in the right fighting trim, let them come as soon as they please. I never saw a Fleet altogether so well Officered and manned. Would to God the Ships were half as good, but they are what we call *crazy*.

You will have had the Power of Attorney for the Dutchman, and I suppose she will be given up to us. Of course, you will do what is right, and keep my Prize-money to help to pay my debt, which I am every month increasing. I do not write to Lord Moira, because I can only tell him that I am looking for the French Fleet. They must come out very soon. I was sorry to see his Lordship had a very severe fall. I hope he is perfectly recovered, and I beg that you will make my respectful compliments acceptable. I send a little parcel for Lady Hamilton, directed under cover to you. Pray, forward it to Merton, where I hope my dearest Lady Hamilton is well, comfortable, and happy. I hope next summer to be able to build the room, and I must write to Linton about the field, which I wish to have to make the new entrance, &c., &c., provided she stays to manage the improvements. I will admit no display of taste at Merton, but hers. She bought it, and I hope will continue to improve and beautify it to the day, at least, of my death. Believe me ever, dear Davison, your most faithful and affectionate friend,

NELSON AND BRONTE.

[6] Sir Richard Haddock, Admiral of the Fleet in the reign of King William the Third.

TO THE RESPECTIVE FLAG-OFFICERS, CAPTAINS, AND COM-
MANDERS OF HIS MAJESTY'S SHIPS AND VESSELS ON THE
MEDITERRANEAN STATION.

[From a Copy, in the Elliot Papers.]

Victory, at Sea, 4th October, 1803.

His Majesty having been pleased to order the Blockade of
Genoa and Port Especia,[7] You are hereby required and di-

"Downing Street, 23rd August, 1803.

[7] "My Lord,

"In consequence of the information contained in your Lordship's letter to Mr.
Addington of the 28th June—9th July, [*vide* p. 106, ante,] and confirmed by various
circumstances, it has been judged indispensably necessary for his Majesty's Service,
to give immediate orders that the Ports of Genoa and Spezzia should be placed in
a state of Blockade; and the regular notification thereof having been made to the
Ministers of the different Neutral Powers residing at this Court, your Lordship will
receive the necessary instructions for your guidance by this opportunity from the
Lords Commissioners of the Admiralty.

"The hostile conduct of the Government of Algiers towards the Maltese, since
they have been under the protection of his Majesty, renders it necessary that
your Lordship should immediately take measures for demanding that all Maltese
captured by the Algerine Cruizers during that period, should be forthwith released,
and delivered up to whomsoever you may depute to receive them; and in the
event of the Regency of Algiers refusing to comply with your demand, I am commanded by his Majesty to direct that your Lordship do adopt the most vigorous and
effectual measures for taking or destroying all Ships and Vessels belonging to the
said Regency, or to the Subjects thereof; and that you do pursue every mode of
distressing that State, until the Dey shall manifest a disposition to comply with the
just demand which your Lordship is hereby directed to make, in his Majesty's
name, on behalf of the Maltese People living under the protection of his Majesty's
Government.

"The very judicious observations contained in your Lordship's letter to Mr.
Addington upon the Political state of the South of Italy, and the opinions which
you have detailed in your correspondence with his Majesty's Minister at the Court
of Naples, have been fully considered by his Majesty's confidential servants; and I
have much satisfaction in acquainting your Lordship that the line of conduct which
you have suggested for the Court of Naples to pursue, under the critical circumstances of its present situation, has been highly approved; and Mr. Elliot will be
instructed by Lord Hawkesbury to continue to communicate with your Lordship
upon every occasion relative to that subject.

"I am likewise to desire that your Lordship's correspondence upon those, and
all other Political subjects, should be addressed to me, that I may be enabled to lay
them before the King, and to convey to you his Majesty's commands thereon. It
having been thought advisable to take measures for recruiting among the Swiss,
and Mr. Gardner having been sent to Switzerland for that purpose, I am to desire
that your Lordship will give orders to the Commanders of his Majesty's Cruizers
under your command to receive on board any such recruits, in order to their being
conveyed to the Island of Malta, or to Gibraltar. I have the honour to be, &c.,
HOBART."—*Original.*

rected, on falling in with any Merchant Ship or Vessel of whatever description or Nation, bound to either of those Ports, which may have sailed from any Port or place after such Blockade was publicly known, to detain and send them into Port for adjudication ; and you are also, on falling in with any Ship or Vessel bound to Genoa or Port Especia, whose Masters have not received information of the Blockade of those Ports, to acquaint them thereof, and to notify the same upon their bill of health, or other public paper ; and you are also to acquaint the Masters of such Ships or Vessels, that if, after this public notification, they shall be found on the West Coast to the Northward of Cape Del Melle, or on the Coast of Tuscany to the Northward of Leghorn, their Vessels and Cargoes will be sent into Port for adjudication, for a breach of Blockade.

You are also to receive from each Master of the Vessel spoke, an acknowledgment of having received such a notification. The notification is to be wrote on the bill of health, or other public paper, and the acknowledgment thereof to be kept.

NELSON AND BRONTE.

TO CAPTAIN . . . . . ., H. M. SLOOP . . . . . .

[Letter-Book.]

Victory, at Sea, October 4th, 1803.

Sir,

I have received from Mr. Falcon, his Majesty's Consul at Algiers, a letter, of which a copy is herewith enclosed, together with your correspondence with him ; and I beg leave to have your reasons in writing for throwing any impediments in his way of coming to me, more especially as you demanded of him a copy of my letter to him, which desired him to join me on His Majesty's Service. Your not bringing Mr. Falcon in his Majesty's Sloop . . . . . . under your command, is at this moment very prejudicial to His Majesty's Service. I am, &c.,

NELSON AND BRONTE.

TO COMMISSIONER OTWAY, GIBRALTAR.

[Autograph, in the possession of Rear-Admiral Inglefield, C.B.]

Victory, October 4th, 1803.

My dear Sir,

On October 1st, I was favoured with your several letters, and you will, of course, supply the Ambuscade with no more stores than is barely necessary to carry her to England; and as she will only be wanted to carry herself safe to England, I should hope that her rigging and sails taken in her will fully answer that purpose.

I have wrote, on my first arrival, recommending a Commander to be appointed to the Prison-Ship at Gibraltar. The French having at Toulon refused any communication with us, I do not think that we can liberate their Seamen. Those from Gibraltar would assist to man L'Aigle at Cadiz, and the Ships at Ferrol; but, probably, the Ship expected with dispatches for the Mediterranean will bring out some directions concerning them. If they were put in a Cartel, they would never go to England: that could not be expected; and if they were not in a Cartel, they would carry off the Ship as a good Prize. If it comes necessary to send them, it must be in a Cartel with a false destination—say Brest, and to carry them into Falmouth or Plymouth. The Master or Officer to have public and *secret* orders. We have 400 at Malta.

As I send you a very fine Brig,[6] I hope the Gut will be kept clear of French Privateers. All English seamen will, I hope, be secured for the Ships, who are between 7 and 800 short of their complements. As Captain Hart has just come from Naples, he will tell you all the Italian news. He goes to fit out, and man the Ambuscade. I am, dear Sir, with great respect and esteem, your most obedient and faithful servant,

NELSON AND BRONTE.

[6] The Halcyon, Captain Pearse.

TO ADMIRAL THE EARL OF ST. VINCENT, K.B.

[Autograph, in the possession of Vice-Admiral Sir William Parker, Bart., G.C.B.]

Victory, off Toulon, October 5th, 1803.

My dear Lord,

I have put Captain Durban, who I never saw till this day, into the Ambuscade; I trust the Admiralty will highly approve of it. His services appear to me to have been very great, and never rewarded, but his merits confessed by all.   I am—don't laugh—dreadfully sea-sick this day, and as it blows a Levanter, I must not keep the Monmouth, who joined from Naples last night.   Mr. Layman your Lordship knows very well : I have put him into the Weazle.   I am always, my dear Lord, most faithfully yours,

NELSON AND BRONTE.

TO SIR EVAN NEPEAN, BART., ADMIRALTY.

[Original, in the Admiralty.]

Victory, off Toulon, October 5th, 1803.

Sir,

I have taken no steps to commission the Ambuscade till I saw Captain Durban,[8] which was not until this morning. From the copies of letters from you, approving, by order of their Lordships, his conduct on many occasions, and from several individual letters from Members of the late and present Admiralty, I think that their Lordships will most highly approve of my embracing this opportunity of promoting so deserving an Officer.   I have appointed Lieutenant William Layman to command the Weazle, and appointed two Lieutenants to the Ambuscade.   This is all the establishment I shall give her for her passage to England, as she will be manned from his Majesty's ship Monmouth, and I hope that both will be ready to proceed to England with the next Convoy.   I have the honour to be, &c.,

NELSON AND BRONTE.

---

8 Captain William Durban. This zealous and scientific Officer, who was made an Honorary Doctor of Laws, died a Rear-Admiral of the Blue on the 9th of February 1837, a few weeks after he attained his Flag.

TO . . . . . ., MASTER OF H. M. SLOOP . . . . . .

[Letter-Book.]

Victory, off Toulon, 5th October, 1803.

Sir,

I have received your letter of the 3rd instant, requesting,
for the reasons therein mentioned, that I will order a Court-
Martial on Captain . . . . . ., Commander of his Majesty's
Sloop . . . . . . : in answer to which, I have to acquaint you,
that as you have not mentioned any particular case or instance
of Captain . . . .'s cruelty or oppression to you, I do not
feel justified in complying with your request upon such loose
charges as you allege against him in your aforesaid letter.   I
am, &c.,

NELSON AND BRONTE.

TO THE RIGHT HONOURABLE HENRY ADDINGTON.

[Autograph, in the Sidmouth Papers.]

Victory, off Toulon, October 6th, 1803.

My dear Sir,

Some of our Ships chased two Frigates into Calvi, in
Corsica, and two Corvettes have been chased into Hieres.
The French Admiral mounted yesterday morning his Sea-
Vane, a thing which a landsman would not notice; but it
gives a certainty to my mind that they wish to put to sea, and
never was a Squadron of British Ships more anxious to meet
them.   I can have no excuse, nor do I want my Country to
make any for me : if I see the Enemy, my exertions shall be
used to lay the Squadron well in, and the event, with the
blessing of Providence on a just cause, we have no reason to
fear.   Till the Battle is over I hope to write to you no more ;
whether I survive it or not, my name shall never bring a blush
on the cheeks of my friends.   May God bless you, my King
and Country, and believe me ever your most attached and
faithful friend,

NELSON AND BRONTE.

TO CAPTAIN WILLIAM LAYMAN, H. M. SLOOP WEAZLE.

[From a Copy in the Admiralty.]

Victory, off Toulon, 6th October, 1803.

Having ordered that his Majesty's Sloop Weazle, under your command, may be taken into the Mole at Gibraltar so soon as Commissioner Otway has completed the Ambuscade's defects, You are hereby required and directed to cause the utmost exertion to be used (so far as the same may depend upon you) in getting the Weazle's defects made good, and the said Ship fitted for sea with all dispatch; and, so soon as she is in all respects ready, you are to proceed and cruise very diligently in the Gut, for the purpose of keeping the communication between Gibraltar and the Coast of Barbary open, proceeding (as circumstances of information respecting the Enemy's Privateers may render necessary) for the purpose of protecting the Trade of his Majesty's Subjects, and destroying the Enemy's Privateers and Cruisers which are stationed there to intercept our commerce, attending most strictly to my order of the 30th May last, (which will be delivered to you by Captain Durban,) respecting the non-interruption of the Trade of his Catholic Majesty's Subjects, and the Neutrality to be observed with the Powers in amity with Great Britain.

You are never to exceed to the Westward of keeping the limits of Cape Spartel in sight on any account; and in the execution of this service, you are to pay due regard to such desires as Lieutenant-General Sir Thomas Trigge[9] may find necessary to require of you for the protection of the Boats employed in bringing the necessary refreshments to the Garrison, or otherwise, as his Majesty's Service may require— calling once every week on the Lieutenant-Governor to know his desires, and to receive such orders as I may find necessary to send you. You are to continue on this service till otherwise directed, acquainting me, from time to time, as opportunity may offer, with an account of your proceedings.

NELSON AND BRONTE.

N.B.—The Halcyon under similar orders.

[9] Lieutenant-Governor of Gibraltar.

TO SIR ALEXANDER JOHN BALL, BART., MALTA.

[Autograph, in the possession of Sir William Keith Ball, Bart.]

Victory, off Toulon, October 6th, 1803.

My dear Ball,

Your friendly council and advice is always most acceptable, and the wisdom of the measures you propose is undoubted, and should be followed had I the means. The state of Egypt is deplorable; and I have no doubt that the French have made a treaty with the Mamelukes, or will with the Turks. I have not only wrote it, but impressed it on Mr. Addington's mind, the necessity of his steering such a course as would neither throw the Mamelukes or Turks into the arms of France. Whether they attend at home to these things, I very much doubt and *deplore*. I hope the Capitan is, long before this, in Egypt—not that I believe the Turks will ever be what they call masters of that Country again. The wish I have of sending a small Ship now and then to Egypt is frustrated, for I have them not. I want to place a good Sloop to guard our Currant Ships, and to look about the Republic of the Seven Islands. I want also to place a Ship above Ancona. How far Captain Cracraft will be able to accomplish these things with his small Squadron, I am not sure; but he shall have a letter to attend to your wants for Convoy to both the Morea and Adriatic, for which purpose I shall add for the present the Arrow to his Squadron, and send Bittern, with 24-pounders, in the room of Troubridge's son-in-law.[1]

I had intended sending Sir Richard Bickerton to Malta to arrange these and other matters, and, amongst others, to look at the place for the Naval Hospital, and to get an estimate of the expense of fitting it up; but I believe, from appearances, that the French Fleet are so near putting to sea, that it would be cruel in me to send so excellent an Officer and friend away, at a moment we may expect so glorious a harvest. I would give a good deal for a copy of the French Admiral's orders. Report says it is Decrés, as he fought the Guillaume Tell so well. If he is a fighting man so much the better. I hope he will not run away; we may want heels to catch

---

[1] Captain Richardson, of the Juno, step-son of Sir Thomas Troubridge.

[him]—that is the only fear I have. My friend Colonel Stewart's brother is most heartily welcome, if it is at my disposal, to live in the Navy House. Apropos, Mr. Taylor has wrote to me about the houses belonging to the Naval Yard. Will you do what is proper on this occasion? If we have an Arsenal, the Officers certainly should have their houses. Mr. Elliot, I find, thinks Sicily quite safe, and Naples almost fit to bid defiance to all Buonaparte's power. I *laugh* at what I read. I know them well, and so do you. This beating off the Tunisians[2] will have a very good effect, and dispose them to resist other invaders. Again and again, only tell me your wants and wishes, and they shall be complied with as fast as my means will allow; being ever, my dear Ball—ever your faithful friend,

NELSON AND BRONTE.

TO J. B. GIBERT, ESQ., HIS BRITANNIC MAJESTY'S CONSUL AT BARCELONA.

[Letter-Book.]

Victory, off Toulon, 6th October, 1803.

Sir,

In obedience to his Majesty's orders, notified in the 'London Gazette' of the 16th August last, for the Blockade of the Ports of Genoa and Especia, I have to inform you, that I have issued to the Fleet under my command the order,[3] of which I inclose a copy, and you will have the goodness to communicate it to the Governor where you reside, and to all the Foreign Consuls, and others interested, in order that none may plead ignorance of the Blockade, or the consequences of the breach of it. I am, &c.

NELSON AND BRONTE.

---

[2] Some Ships belonging to Tunis, with which State Naples was at War, appear to have been repulsed in attempting to land in Sicily.

[3] Vide p. 219.

TO CAPTAIN SCHOMBERG, H. M. SHIP MADRAS, MALTA.

[From Clarke and M'Arthur, vol. ii. p. 327.]

Off Toulon, 7th October, 1803.

At this distance it is impossible for me to regulate every thing with exactness; therefore I can only repeat to you, Captain Cracraft, and any other your Seniors, that it is my earnest desire to give every possible expedition in getting our Trade safe to and from the Adriatic and Levant, and affording Sir Alexander Ball and General Villettes Convoys for bullocks and corn. . . We must all in our several stations exert ourselves to the utmost, and not be nonsensical in saying, ' I have an order for this, that, or the other,' if the King's service clearly marks what ought to be done : I am well convinced of your zeal. I am, &c.,

NELSON AND BRONTE.

TO LIEUTENANT WILLIAM PEMBERTON, RESIDENT AGENT OF TRANSPORTS, MALTA.

[From a Copy in the Admiralty.]

Victory, off Toulon, 7th October, 1803.

Sir,

I have received your letter of the 27th ultimo, acquainting me that a Transport had sailed to Corfu, and that two were ready to proceed to Tunis, for cattle for the Army and Island ; also, that General Villettes had expressed a wish to have two Transports, for the sole purpose of bringing cattle for the use of the Army at Malta ; I have therefore to desire that you will wait upon Sir Alexander Ball and know from him what Transports he will require for the use of the Island, and after having received his instructions on that head, you are to appropriate the number he may judge necessary for bringing cattle for the use of the Island, and also two Transports agreeably to General Villettes' desire, for the sole purpose of bringing cattle for the use of the Army. The Transports for the service of the Fleet will, eight months out of the year, be at the disposal of the General and Sir Alexander Ball ; therefore, take this into the calculation in consulting with them, which you are to acquaint General Villettes of, immediately

on receipt hereof, as it is my particular wish that the inhabitants and Army should have every necessary accommodation afforded them ; and in doing so, that Government should
not be put to undue expense, or the Transports for the above
service remain unemployed.　I am, &c.,

NELSON AND BRONTE.

TO SIR EVAN NEPEAN, BART., ADMIRALTY.

[Original, in the Admiralty.]

Victory, off Toulon, 7th October, 1803.

Sir,

I have had the honour of receiving your letter of the 27th
August, desiring me on the Ambuscade's being purchased, to
appoint Captain Durban to the rank of Post-Captain, Lieu-
tenant Yarker[4] to be Commander, and Mr. G. Greensill[5] to be
Lieutenant.　I was sorry that having waited till the 5th of
October, I then appointed Captain Durban to the Ambuscade
and Lieutenant William Layman to the Weazle, which I trust
(not knowing their Lordships' wishes respecting any other
Officers) that they will be pleased to confirm ; but their
Lordships may be assured that the very first vacancy (which
I trust will not be many days) Lieutenant Yarker and
Mr. G. Greensill shall be appointed.　As I am sure their
Lordships know the very happy consequences of a Fleet
looking up to a Commander-in-Chief for promotion, that they
will excuse my not having reduced Lieutenant Layman from
the Acting rank I had given him, as he would not have been
with me had he not been an Officer of acknowledged abilities
and merit.　I am, &c.,

NELSON AND BRONTE.

P.S.—The Commissions shall be delivered to Captain
Stuart and the Hon. Captain Elliot, and the fees received for
them as marked thereon.

---

[4] Lieutenant Robert Yarker was made a Commander in 1805, was Posted in April
1808, and died between 1816 and 1820.

[5] Lord Nelson appointed Mr. George Greensill, who was a Midshipman of the
Donegal, to be a Lieutenant of that Ship on the 10th of October 1803 : he was
promoted to Commander in February 1812, and died in that rank between 1820 and
1822.

TO NATHANIEL TAYLOR, ESQ., NAVAL STOREKEEPER, MALTA.

[Letter-Book.]

Victory, off Toulon, 7th October, 1803.

Sir,

I have received your letters of the 4th and 23rd ultimo, with the Instructions, &c., therein mentioned, and must desire whenever you may judge it necessary, consistent with the said Instructions, to muster the Crews of his Majesty's Ships and Vessels, as they arrive at Malta, that you will apply to the Captains thereof to furnish you with a Boat for that purpose, and that I do not feel justified to make any addition to your establishment of Clerks. Having so recently left England, those things ought to have been perfectly understood and settled by the Navy Board, to whom you must make application on the circumstances above mentioned. On the subject of the sails and other stores mentioned in your said letter of the 23rd ultimo, being damp, owing to the Storehouses being in bad repair, I am to desire that you will use every means necessary to put the Storehouses in a proper condition for keeping the sails, &c. dry, as serious losses and consequences may arise from their being otherwise. But in making this repair which you have represented as absolutely necessary, you are to pay the most strict regard to economy, and procure such vouchers for so doing as will satisfy the Navy Board with the correctness thereof, and that Government has not been put to any unnecessary or improper expenses. I certainly think that English weights are preferable to Maltese, and ought to be used for his Majesty's stores, provided the alteration is not attended with inconvenience to the Inhabitants who you may have occasion to deal with. I observe the propriety of the Officers of his Majesty's Yard at Malta being accommodated with houses contiguous to their duty, and have wrote Sir Alexander Ball on the subject. I am, &c.,

NELSON AND BRONTE.

TO SIR EVAN NEPEAN, BART., ADMIRALTY

[Original, in the Admiralty.]

Victory, off Toulon, 7th October, 1803.

Sir,

Yesterday evening I received their Lordships' order of the 24th August last, directing that the complements of His Majesty's Ships and Vessels under my command may be forthwith completed to the War establishment, and to enter and bear as many more men in addition to their present complements as may be necessary for that purpose. You will please to acquaint their Lordships that directions shall be given accordingly; but upon this subject I must beg to observe that there is but little probability of procuring men in this Country, as there appears no inclination in the Maltese to enter into the Navy. The means to induce them shall, however, be held out, and everything done that remains with me, for that purpose.

I enclose you for their Lordships' information, extracts of three letters from Sir Alexander Ball on this subject, together with a Proclamation issued at Malta for the purpose of procuring Maltese for the Fleet; but I am sorry to observe that there are not more than four in the Squadron at present off this place, nor is there, as their Lordships will observe, from the extracts above mentioned, any probability of procuring more Maltese for the Navy, so that the very considerable number of Seamen wanted to complete the complement of the Ships here, must be looked for from some other quarter. I am, &c.,

NELSON AND BRONTE.

TO SIR EVAN NEPEAN, BART., ADMIRALTY.

[Original, in the Admiralty.]

Victory, off Toulon, 7th October, 1803.

Sir,

I received, by the Childers, fifty-four printed Admiralty orders, dated the 30th June last, with the two additional Instructions under His Majesty's Signet and Sign Manual, dated the 24th of that month, therein mentioned, directing the Commanders of His Majesty's Ships and Privateers, not to

detain or molest any Ships or Vessels belonging to any State in
amity with His Majesty, on account of their having on board
organzine, thrown, and raw silk, the growth and produce of
Italy; or any Neutral Vessels which shall be carrying on
trade directly between the Colonies of the Enemy and the
Neutral Country to which the Vessel belongs: you will
please to acquaint the Lords Commissioners of the Admiralty
that the said orders shall be issued to the respective Flag-
Officers, Captains and Commanders of His Majesty's Ships
and Vessels under my orders.   I am, &c.,

NELSON AND BRONTE.

TO SIR EVAN NEPEAN, BART., ADMIRALTY.

[Original, in the Admiralty.]

Victory, off Toulon, 7th October, 1803.

Sir,

I yesterday received by the Childers their Lordships' order[6]
of the 26th August last, (together with copy of Lord Pelham
and Mr. Falcon's letters therein mentioned,) directing me to
send a discreet Officer to Algiers, with instructions to demand
from the Dey, in His Majesty's name, immediate restitution
of the Maltese Vessels mentioned in the said letters, together
with their cargoes and the release of their respective crews:
You will please to acquaint their Lordships that I will take

---

[6] " Whereas, the Right Honourable Lord Pelham, one of his Majesty's Principal
Secretaries of State, hath, with his letters of the 15th instant, transmitted to us a
copy of a letter with its Inclosure, which his Lordship had received from Mr.
Consul Falcon, by which it appears that several Maltese Vessels have been captured
by the Algerines, and their Crews sent into slavery; and, whereas, his Lordship
hath, at the same time, signified to us his Majesty's commands, that the necessary
instructions should be sent to the Officer commanding his Majesty's Fleet in the
Mediterranean, to demand the immediate restitution of the said Vessels, and their
Cargoes, and the release of their Crews; We send your Lordship herewith transcripts
of the said letter and its inclosure, and do hereby require and direct you (in addition
to our order of the 7th of July last) to take the first opportunity of sending one of the
Ships of your Squadron, under the command of a discreet Officer, to Algiers, with
instructions to him to demand in his Majesty's name from the Dey, the immediate
restitution of the Maltese Vessels above-mentioned, together with their Cargoes,
and the release of their respective Crews accordingly.   Your Lordship will direct
the Officer you may employ on this service to be careful, on his arrival off that
place, not to subject himself, or the Ship under his command, to the risk of capture,
in case any hostile views towards this Country should be entertained by that
Regency.   Given under our hands the 26th of August, 1803.—WM. ELLIOT, T.
TROUBRIDGE, J. MARKHAM."—*Original.*

a very early opportunity of sending a proper Officer to Algiers with instructions conformable to their orders, to demand of the Dey immediate restitution of the Maltese Vessels and cargoes, and the release of their respective Crews, and shall direct the Officer sent on this service not to subject himself or the Ship under his command to the risk of capture on his arrival off Algiers.   I am, &c.,

NELSON AND BRONTE.

TO SIR EVAN NEPEAN, BART., ADMIRALTY.

[Original, in the Admiralty.]

Victory, off Toulon, 7th October, 1803.

Sir,

I yesterday received your letter of the 13th August last, with transcript of a dispatch from Mr. A'Court, his Majesty's Chargé d'Affaires at Naples, therein mentioned, respecting two French Vessels which were attacked by the Boats of the Cyclops and Experiment in the Bay of Naples, and beg to refer you to the extracts to Sir John Acton, Bart., mentioned in my letter to you of the 8th July last; and also to request you will be pleased to acquaint their Lordships, that the other Vessel was liberated by my directions at Malta, and sent back to Naples under the authority of my protection; that the most strict orders have been issued to prevent similar proceedings; and that my marked disapprobation was signified to the Commanders of the Cyclops and Experiment, the moment I was made acquainted with their conduct.   You will also please to acquaint their Lordships that the Vessel taken by the Spider has been delivered up, and that I have very severely reprimanded Captain . . . . . . of the . . . . ., for the captures he made under the Spanish batteries; which have also been given up.   I am, &c.

NELSON AND BRONTE.

TO SIR EVAN NEPEAN, BART., ADMIRALTY.

[Original, in the Admiralty.]

Victory, off Toulon, 7th October, 1803.

Sir,

Yesterday I received their Lordships' order of the 20th August last, containing directions respecting the Ports of

Genoa and Especia; and you will please to acquaint their Lordships that I had anticipated their order, from the Gazette of the 16th of that month, and given the necessary directions to the respective Flag-Officers, Captains, and Commanders under my command, in consequence; a copy of which is herewith transmitted. The Active, Phœbe, and Childers are under orders, and will proceed from hence to-morrow to block up those Ports. You will also please to acquaint their Lordships, that I have received forty-eight printed orders, dated the 24th August, addressed to the respective Admirals, Captains, Commanders, and Commanding Officers of his Majesty's Ships and Vessels, directing them to seize and destroy all Ships and Vessels belonging to the Countries styling themselves the Italian and Ligurian Republics; which shall be issued to them respectively. I am, &c.

NELSON AND BRONTE.

TO SIR EVAN NEPEAN, BART., ADMIRALTY.

[From a Copy in the Nelson Papers.]

Victory, off Toulon, 7th October, 1803.

Sir,

You will please to acquaint their Lordships, that I have placed a Squadron outside the Straits, for the protection of the Trade of his Majesty's subjects, and destruction of the Enemy's Privateers and Cruisers; and that there are also two Sloops of War stationed between Cape Spartel and Ceuta, for protecting our commerce in the Gut. I am, &c.

NELSON AND BRONTE.

TO SIR EVAN NEPEAN, BART., ADMIRALTY.

[Original, in the Admiralty.]

Victory, off Toulon, 7th October, 1803.

Sir,

I have received their Lordships' order, dated the 16th of June last, directing me not to carry or send any Ships or Vessels which may be taken as Prizes, into the Ports of Portugal (except compelled so to do by stress of weather,) or to use any of the said Ports as Naval Stations for the purpose of carrying on from them hostilities against his Majesty's

Enemies. You will please to acquaint the Lords Commissioners of the Admiralty, that I shall give the necessary directions to the respective Captains and Commanders of his Majesty's Ships and Vessels under my orders, agreeably thereto. I am, &c.

NELSON AND BRONTE.

TO HIS EXCELLENCY MR. JACKSON, MINISTER AT TURIN.

[From Clarke and M'Arthur, vol. ii. p. 329.]

8th October, 1803.

I will write to Mr. Drake the moment the Battle is over; caution him not to believe reports: the French have taken, I suppose, an *invisible* English Frigate in the Adriatic, or the Levant, or off the Coast of Genoa; but unfortunately for their news-makers, I have lost none. I am, &c.

NELSON AND BRONTE.

TO HIS EXCELLENCY HUGH ELLIOT, ESQ.

[Original, in the Elliot Papers.]

Victory, off Toulon, 8th October, 1803.

Sir,

I herewith transmit for your information, a copy of an order of the 4th instant, issued to the Fleet under my command, for the Blockade of the Ports of Genoa and Port Especia, and request your Excellency will have the goodness to order the same to be communicated to the Foreign Ministers and Consuls at Naples, &c. I have the honour to be, &c.,

NELSON AND BRONTE.

TO NATHANIEL TAYLOR, ESQ., NAVAL STOREKEEPER AT MALTA.

[Order-Book.]

Victory, off Toulon, 8th October, 1803.

Whereas the Squadron under my command are much in want of small cordage, twine, &c., and it being judged for the benefit of his Majesty's Service, as well as a great saving to Government, to have those necessary articles made on board the respective Ships, You are hereby required and directed to send, by the first Transport coming to join the Fleet, eighty-four butts, well-packed and filled with hemp, if you have them in store. You are to prepare a Transport (if hemp cannot be purchased reasonably at Malta) to be sent up the Adriatic, for the purpose of bringing a load of hemp for his Majesty's Service, acquainting me, or Captain Schomberg, the Senior Officer at Malta, when such Transport shall be ready, that a Convoy may be ordered for her accordingly. All the cordage wanted for the Fleet, at three inches and upwards, must be made at Malta, with the hemp of this Country, (at least, what may be wanted more than the supplies from England,) which will certainly be a very great saving to Government, as well as a ready accommodation to the Ships, as they have occasion for it. You are, therefore, to turn your mind to these circumstances, that ready supplies may be had, and upon the most reasonable terms, and if it can be had cheaper than in England, to purchase a supply for Gibraltar, and even the Dockyards in England. NELSON AND BRONTE.

TO HIS EXCELLENCY HUGH ELLIOT, ESQ.

[Autograph, in the Elliot Papers.]

(1.)

My dear Sir, Victory, off Toulon, October 8th, 1803.

Your Excellency's letters by the Monmouth came to me on the 4th, at night, and I feel truly sensible of your kindness, and the trouble you have taken in detailing to me all the means of precaution, which his Excellency Sir John Acton has taken respecting Sicily, and I fully rely that those measures will be continued, and that neither Sicily nor Naples will want our assistance. God knows, we have occasion enough for our Troops without begging them to be received, and nothing but the strong order I brought out[7] would have induced General Villettes to part with a man from Malta. General Villettes writes me the same good accounts from Messina as you have done. The information of Captain Durban relative to the Tunisians, by wise precautions, has led to such a happy result, that I trust my Countrymen in Sicily will soon cruize against the Barbary States. I am sure they could soon be brought to it. However, I have been so pleased with Captain Durban

7 Vide p. 96, ante.

for this, and other wise conduct on several occasions, that I have made him a Post-Captain, and given him the command of the Ambuscade Frigate. I verily believe, my dear Sir, that you are much mistaken about Sir A. J. Ball's opinion of Sir John Acton. I believe he has the very highest one of him, and that his loss to Naples would at this moment be the ruin of the Country; but he has thought that Sir John has had difficulties to struggle with, in giving his opinions, that sometimes thwarted his wishes. I sincerely hope it is not so. Dear Sir William, who was Sir John's firm friend, against all opposition, to the day of his death, has often told me that it *was so*. I sincerely hope he has no opposition, neither in public nor *private*. The impudence of Buonaparte I am not surprised at. The Crowned Heads of Europe have to thank themselves. Our Country will ever resist; and the King of Naples is the only King who has shown any spirit. He has felt like a King. Would to God he had been as powerful as I wish him! Ever yours, faithfully,

NELSON AND BRONTE.

TO HIS EXCELLENCY HUGH ELLIOT, ESQ.

[Autograph, in the Elliot Papers.]

(2.)

My dear Sir,   Victory, October 8th, 1803.

The Childers Brig arrived from Plymouth on the 6th; and by her, I have had a full and entire approbation of my conduct, both public and private;[8] but, at the same time, I am desired to guard, and to communicate those cautions to Sir John Acton and yourself, that we are not lulled into a fatal security: therefore, notwithstanding the favourable appearances of the French withdrawing from the Kingdom of Naples, I have strengthened our Squadron in the Adriatic, and the Coast of Calabria. It now consists of the Ships as by list on the other side, under Captain Cracraft—

Anson	. . . .	44	. . . .	24-pounders.
Juno	. . . .	36	. . . .	12 do.
Arrow	. . .	22	. . . .	32 do.
Bittern	. . .	18	. . . .	24 do.
Morgiana	. . .	18	. . . .	18 do.

8 Vide p. 219, ante.

And I have recommended Captain Cracraft, if possible, to
communicate with Manfredonia, and to offer to Sir John
Acton and yourself any accommodation in his power, by
taking a Messenger, &c., for Vienna.   In short, my dear Sir,
you may rely, that whatever man can do for the safety and
comfort of the Two Sicilies, none can have more desire to do
it than myself.   You will keep the Gibraltar as long as you
want her, or until I can relieve her; and I am sure Captain
Ryves saw the Troops safe to Messina.   The English Merchants,
if any remain besides Mr. Noble, I believe, would have been
more correct in applying to me for Convoy, than through
your Excellency; but it is curious he has not sent you a
list of the English Vessels waiting for Convoy, nor have I
heard of any being at Naples.   If they find Trade, it is my
business to find Convoy; therefore, let them send a list of
Vessels to the Senior Officer at Malta, or to me.   I should
be very happy to receive authentic intelligence of the *destination* of the French Squadron—their *route,* and *time* of sailing.
Anything short of this is useless; and I assure your Excellency,
that I would not, upon any consideration, have a Frenchman
in the Fleet, except as a prisoner. I put no confidence in them.
You think yours good : the Queen thinks hers the same : I
believe they are all alike.   Whatever information you can get
me, I shall be very thankful for; but not a Frenchman comes
here.   Forgive me ; but my mother hated the French.   I am
ever, your most faithful and obliged,

                                        NELSON AND BRONTE.

TO HIS EXCELLENCY HUGH ELLIOT, ESQ.

[Autograph, in the Elliot Papers.]

(3.)

My dear Sir,   Victory, October 8th, 1803.

I am glad that your family begins to collect around you,
and that you stand a chance of seeing Mrs. Elliot.   Your
taking Harriman[9] is certainly a real act of charity ; and whatever you can do for him, I believe he will be truly grateful to
you.   By his letter he speaks of you as he ought.   He is most

_____
[9] Vide vol. ii. p. 71; and vol. iii. pp. 399, 405.

sincerely to be pitied. The remains of Lord Bristol[1] are gone in the Monmouth for England. If you will direct, agreeable to Lord Hawkesbury's desire, his effects at Naples to be collected together, and give me an idea of the quantity, I will send a Ship of War or Transport for them, and if Mr. Jackson, or Lord Bristol's factotum at Rome, will send the effects from thence to either Cività Vecchia, or Naples, and will let me know when they are at the sea-side, and ready, I will send for them.

Two French Frigates have had a narrow escape. They have been chased twice—once into Corsica with the Troops, by the Agincourt 64; and on Sunday last, by two Frigates, Active and Phœbe, into St. Tropes; but these fellows will not fight, if they can help it. Never was health equal to this Squadron. It has been within ten days of five months at sea, and we have not a man confined to his bed: therefore, if these fellows wait till we are forced into Port, they must wait some time.

May I presume to request of your Excellency to present my humble duty to the King and Queen, and assure them of my eternal attachment to their Royal persons, and to all their Family, and any other civil speeches you may be so good as to say for me. To be a Courtier is your trade, and I know myself to be a cobbler at that work. But I am ever, with all sincerity of heart, my dear Sir, your most faithful humble servant,

NELSON AND BRONTE.

This will be presented to you by my nephew, Sir William Bolton; you will be so good as to present him to Sir John Acton. He was Lieutenant of both Vanguard and Foudroyant. Do not keep the Childers; she has secret orders to execute.

N. AND B.

Your letter from Lord Minto was left behind by some mistake.

---

[1] Frederick Augustus, 4th Earl of Bristol, and Bishop of Derry, died at Naples on the 8th of July 1803. Mr. Elliot wrote to Lord Nelson, that knowing the superstitious dread of sailors of having a corpse on board their Ship, he had caused Lord Bristol's body to be packed and shipped as an antique statue !

TO CAPTAIN RYVES,[2] H. M. SHIP GIBRALTAR, NAPLES.

[Autograph, in the possession of his son, Captain George Frederick Ryves, C.B.]

Victory, October 8th, 1803.

Dear Sir,

I am much obliged by your letter of September 20th, and for the trouble you have taken about the wood at the Madalena Islands. His Excellency Mr. Elliot will request you to see the Neapolitan Troops safe to Messina; which, if not already performed, I am sure you have, or will have complied with. We have had nothing but severe gales of wind since you left us, but we get on very well. The Monmouth was only five days to Cape Sicie, but we were blown off. I am, dear Sir, with real esteem, your much obliged and obedient servant,

NELSON AND BRONTE.

The Childers is not to be detained on any account.

TO SIR JOHN ACTON, BART., NAPLES.

[From a Copy in the Nelson Papers.]

Victory, off Toulon, October 8th, 1803.

My dear Sir John,

I was honoured by your Excellency's letter of September 25th, by the Monmouth, and you will readily believe how pleased I have been with the means of precaution which you have so vigorously pursued (detailed in Mr. Elliot's letters) for the preservation of Sicily. Independent of my duty, your Excellency will give me credit for going far beyond that cold line in supporting your wise plans, and for preserving the Two Sicilies for our good Sovereigns. Only tell me how I can

---

[2] Captain George Frederick Ryves, of the Gibraltar, an Officer of reputation, had, when in the Agincourt, commanded a small Squadron sent by Lord Keith in 1802, to take possession of Corfu, and thence to the Madalena Islands, to do all in his power without using force, to prevent the French from taking possession of them. There not being any Chart of those Islands, he constructed a very accurate survey, of which Lord Nelson often spoke in his Letters in terms of high commendation. For his services to the King of Naples, His Majesty presented him with a diamond ring. Captain Ryves obtained his Flag in 1825, and died in May 1826.

most be useful to them, as a public and private man, and they and your Excellency may rely upon me. Notwithstanding some favourable appearances for the removal of the French Troops in the Kingdom, I have reinforced Captain Cracraft with two fine Vessels of thirty-two and twenty-four pounders, and I have directed him to communicate with Manfredonia, and to write to your Excellency to offer any services in his power, and to bring down the Adriatic any Messengers from Vienna which might come to Trieste or Venice. The force in the Adriatic, under Captain Cracraft, is, the Anson, 44 twenty-four pounders; Juno, 36 twelve pounders; Arrow, 22 thirty-two pounders; Bittern, 18 twenty-four pounders; Morgiana, 18 eighteen pounders; entirely independent of the Vessels appointed for the protection of Malta towards Sicily.

I have the pleasure, also, to inform your Excellency of his Majesty's most full and entire approbation of my conduct, and that he places full confidence in all my actions for the honour of his Crown, and the advantage of his faithful Friends. The testimonies of private confidence and approbation from the other Members of the Cabinet, are too flattering for me to repeat; therefore I shall only request your Excellency to lay me with all humility at the feet of the King and Queen, and assure them of my eternal fidelity and vigilance for their safety, and I am, my dear Sir John, your attached and faithful friend,

NELSON AND BRONTE.

TO CAPTAIN FOLEY.

[From Clarke and M'Arthur, vol. ii. p. 330.]

[Apparently about October, 1803.]

How little, my dear Foley, do we know who is to go first: gracious God, I am sure, to all appearance he[3] was more likely to see us pass away, than we him! My dear Foley, I only desire that you will always charge yourself in reminding

---

[3] Captain Foley's brother, Richard Foley, Esq., a Police Magistrate, who died on the 9th of July 1803. A long eulogium on his character is in the *Gentleman's Magazine*, vol. lxxiii. p. 883.

me of your nephew:[4] in whatever station I may be, I should be most ungrateful, if I could for a moment forget your public support of me in the day of Battle, or your private friendship, which I esteemed most highly; therefore, as far as relates to you, your nephew, and myself, let this letter stand against me. I was glad to see that Fremantle had got his old Ship again.[5] If you are employed, I think the Mediterranean would suit you better than the Black Rocks, North Seas, or West Indies; and I shall be truly happy to have you near me, and to have frequent opportunities of personally assuring you how much I am, my dear Foley, your faithful and affectionate friend,

NELSON AND BRONTE.

TO J. B. GIBERT, ESQ., HIS BRITANNIC MAJESTY'S CONSUL AT BARCELONA.

[Letter-Book.]

Victory, off Toulon, 10th October, 1803.

Sir,

I received by Captain Swaine your letters of the 26th ultimo; the Seaman and Boy mentioned in one of the said letters, were brought to the Fleet by the Raven. It is rather remarkable that the Vessel with wine, which you acquaint me is gone to Leghorn, should have missed the Fleet off Toulon, as we have been but little distance from that place, since the beginning of August last. I am very much obliged by your sending the Gazette and Newspapers, and will feel particularly thankful for the most early information respecting our situation with Spain, and beg you will be good enough to forward any dispatches which may arrive from Mr. Frere or Mr. Hunter for me, and to send them, as early as possible, the accompanying letter for the last-mentioned gentleman.

I shall not fail to pay due attention to the supplies you

---

[4] Mr. Richard Foley, son of Captain Foley's deceased brother. He entered the Navy as a Midshipman of the Elephant, under his uncle's command, in 1800, was afterwards in the Ambuscade, Captain Durban, was made a Lieutenant in April 1807, a Commander in May 1812, Posted in June 1814, and died on the 23rd of December, 1829.

[5] Captain Fremantle had been lately appointed to the Ganges, which Ship he had commanded at Copenhagen.

mention for the Fleet (through Neutral bottoms to Malta) in the event of a War with Spain; and shall send extracts of your proposals to the Agent Victuallers at Malta and Gibraltar, that they may avail themselves thereof, and give the preference to the most advantageous terms for Government. In case of the continuance of Peace with Spain, (which I still hope may be the case,) it would be desirable to fix the precise mode of having the Fleet under my command regularly supplied from Rosas or Alfaquez, with live bullocks, onions, and a few sheep now and then, on an average of fifty bullocks a week, taking into account the uncertainty of the weather at this season of the year, which perhaps might prevent communication with either of those places for a fortnight together. I, therefore, beg you will let me know if such supply can be had at Rosas or Alfaquez, and what the average price of the pound of beef will cost Government under the circumstances above-mentioned, for any given time, or from one month to another, during the winter season, payment thereof to be made by bills on the Victualling Board, as often as may be required; and in the event of the Fleet leaving this place unexpectedly, a reasonable allowance will be made for any live bullocks remaining on hand in consequence of the agreement which may be entered into. I am, &c.

NELSON AND BRONTE.

TO MR. D. WALSH, MERCHANT, AT BARCELONA.

[Letter-Book.]

Victory, off Toulon, 10th October, 1803.

Sir,

I have received your letters of the 29th and 30th ultimo, and have read with much attention the proposal therein contained, for supplying his Majesty's Ships and Vessels under my command with wine and brandy, under the present existing circumstances, and in the event of a War with Spain, for which I am very much obliged. The Fleet, at this moment, are perfectly complete in those articles; but I shall send copies of your letters to the Agent Victuallers at Malta and Gibraltar, that they may avail themselves of your kind offer, whenever their necessities may make it necessary. I shall be obliged by your informing me whether you can supply the Fleet with live bullocks, hay, onions, &c., at Rosas, during the present tranquillity, and also in the event of a rupture with Spain, and what terms they could be procured upon. I am, &c.

NELSON AND BRONTE.

TO ADMIRAL SIR THOMAS PASLEY, BART.

[Autograph, in the possession of William Collyns, Esq., of Kenton in Devonshire.]

Victory, off Toulon, October 13th, 1803.

My dear Sir Thomas,

I was not favoured with any letter from you, previous or since my leaving England. The conversation I had with you respecting Mr. Tailour, was at your house in Welbeck Street; and there his name stands on my list, I am sorry to say, beyond what I can form any hopes of reaching by the limited promotions allowed by the present Admiralty. They seem disposed to fill up all captured Ships, and all those Captains who go home ill. My list is full for such vacancies, and is daily adding; therefore, I only look for deaths, unless as a favour from the Admiralty, for this climate is so healthy that only two Captains died, in ten years, natural deaths. I can only say, that I have all the inclination to be useful to any friend of yours. Captain Briggs[5] I have the highest regard for, and you cannot be more anxious to promote his welfare than I am. I have received a letter from your protegé, Mr. Nairholm of the Belleisle, and I will not be unmindful of him. The taking of the French Fleet may do much for my clearing the way, but I have more than fifty to make Lieutenants. Admiral Campbell was very well when we parted. He is gone to look for water for his Ship in Sardinia; for Malta is at such an immense distance, that I can send nothing there that I may want under six or seven weeks. I am, my dear Sir Thomas, with many thanks for your good wishes, ever your much obliged, and faithful servant,

NELSON AND BRONTE.

[5] Of the Agincourt, now Vice-Admiral Sir Thomas Briggs, G.C.M.G.

TO ADMIRAL SIR PETER PARKER.

[From Clarke and M'Arthur, vol. ii. p. 330.]

14th October, 1803.

Your grandson[6] came to me, with your kind letter of
August 20th, on October 6th; nothing could be more grateful to my feelings than receiving him. I have kept him as
Lieutenant of the Victory, and shall not part with him until
I can make him a Post Captain; which you may be assured
I shall lose no time in doing. It is the only opportunity ever
offered me, of showing that my feelings of gratitude to you
are as warm and alive as when you first took me by the hand:
I owe all my Honours to you, and I am proud to acknowledge
it to all the world. Lord St. Vincent has most strongly and
kindly desired your grandson's promotion; therefore I can
only be the instrument of expediting it. Believe me ever,
my dear Sir Peter, your most grateful and sincerely attached
friend,   NELSON AND BRONTE.

TO . . . . . .

[From the "Naval Chronicle," vol. xxxix. p. 131. The blanks in this letter are
in the printed copy, and it is not in the Editor's power to fill them up.]

Victory, off Toulon, October 14th, 1803.

My dear ——,
Your letter of July 21st, came to me in the Childers, Sir
William Bolton, and I assure you that I feel very much obliged
by your kind hint, but I do not believe one word of your information: malicious liars are always travelling about doing
evil. If he comes out here, I shall be heartily glad to see
him. I *well* know his reasons for coming out; and even ——,
was he an ill-disposed man, could that hurt me? Can my
mind be turned against my King by any beings on the earth?
Besides, what is there to find out here? Only what he
knows, and every man in England and the Fleet knows—that
I will fight the French Fleet, the moment I can get at them.
I have no plans to divulge; and if I had, I should not put it

───────────────

[6] Mr. Peter Parker, before-mentioned, (vide vol. iii. p. 328,) afterwards Captain
Sir Peter Parker, Bart., who fell gallantly at the storming of an American camp,
near Baltimore, on the 30th of August, 1814.

in any man's power to give information.   In finis, I believe
the gentleman to be as loyal and attached to the King and
Country, as you or I are; if he is not, why do not Ministry
take him up?   My dear ——, some d—d backbiting rascals
are, in our turns, pulling us to pieces; you, I, him, and
others.   I shall close by my old expression—*they be damned!*

. . . .

In the Fleet I have not seen a French flag since my joining;
nor do I expect it, unless the Enemy put to sea.   Our gales
of wind are incessant; and you know that I am never well in
bad weather; but patience, I hope, will get me through it.
Sir Alexander Ball is very well, but I should rather think he
would be glad to be in the Navy again.   I am at this moment
confoundedly out of humour.   A Vessel has been spoke that
says she has seen a Fleet six days ago off Minorca; and
it is so thick that we cannot get a look into Toulon, and
blowing at this moment a Levanter.   Imagine my feelings;
but I am, my dear ——, most truly, your obliged and faithful friend,

NELSON AND BRONTE.

TO JOHN PALMER, ESQ.

[Autograph, in the possession of Mrs. Palmer.]

Victory, off Toulon, October 14th, 1803.

My dear Sir,

I was favoured with your letter of August 26th, by your
son,[7] on October 7th.   My time here has been so very short,
and you will conceive that I came out well loaded, that in
truth I do not see my way for even clearing the Victory once;
and I have upon my list twenty to be made Captains.   **Mr.
Palmer is the third recommended to me by the Duke of
Clarence**, and I sincerely wish it may be in my power to promote them all, more especially the son of an old acquaintance.
The capture of the French Fleet will make an opening for
promotion, which I shall readily embrace.   You may rely,
my dear Sir, that I will not miss an opportunity, when I am
at liberty, to be useful to your son.   I am much obliged for
your sending me the Correspondence of the Prince of Wales.

---

[7] Afterwards Captain Edmund Palmer, C.B., before mentioned.

I suppose there must be some strong reasons for not complying with his Royal Highness' gallant wishes.[8]

I think I see that the King intends to have the Prince and
his Regiment attached to his person.　As a man and as a
Soldier, there can be no reason why his Royal Highness
should not be promoted, if he wishes it; but I believe we are
now so well prepared, that the French will not venture the
attempt at landing in England.　Ireland is their object, and
Egypt.　I am ever, my dear Sir, with every good wish, your
most obedient and faithful servant,

NELSON AND BRONTE.

I have received Lord William Gordon's[9] note, enclosing Mr.
Kemble's note to Lady Hamilton; time may do much, and
I have the inclination.

TO HIS ROYAL HIGHNESS THE DUKE OF CLARENCE.

[From Clarke and M'Arthur, vol. ii. p. 330.]

Off Toulon, 15th October, 1803.

I am absolutely, Sir, beginning this letter in a fever of the
mind.　It is thick as butter-milk, and blowing a Levanter;
and the Narcissus has just spoke me to say, ' She boarded a
Vessel, and they understood that the men had seen, a few
days before, twelve Sail of Ships of War off Minorca.　It was
in the dusk, and he did not know which way they were steering.'　This is the whole story, and a lame one.　On the 8th,
the French Fleet, as counted by Captain Boyle, was eight
Sail of the Line, four Frigates, and some Corvettes.　On the
9th, it blew a tremendous storm at N.W. which lasted till the
12th, since which time, although Seahorse and Renown are
endeavouring to reconnoitre, it is so thick that I do not think
they can either see into Toulon, or find me if they do.　Your
Royal Highness will readily imagine my feelings, although I
cannot bring my mind to believe they are actually out; but
to miss them—God forbid!　They are my superior in numbers, but in everything else, I believe, I have the happiness
of commanding the finest Squadron in the world—Victory,

---

[8] The Prince of Wales' celebrated Letters to the King, soliciting higher rank in
the Army than that of Colonel.

[9] Second son of Cosmo George, third Duke of Gordon: he was Receiver-General
the Duchy of Cornwall, and died in May 1823.

Kent, Superb, Triumph, Belleisle, and Renown. Admiral Campbell is gone to Sardinia, and I have been anxiously expecting him these ten days. If I should miss these fellows, my heart will break: I am actually only now recovering the shock of missing them in 1798, when they were going to Egypt. If I miss them, I will give up the cudgels to some more fortunate Commander; God knows I only serve to fight those scoundrels; and if I cannot do that, I should be better on shore.

October 16th.—The Seahorse spoke me in the night; and made known that the Enemy were in the same state as when last reconnoitred on the 8th. I believe this was the only time in my life, that I was glad to hear the French were in Port. I think Captain Keats is very much better in his health; he is a most valuable Officer, and does honour to your friendship. Every day increases my esteem for him, both as an Officer and a man. I am, &c.

NELSON AND BRONTE.

TO THE RIGHT HONOURABLE LORD HOBART, SECRETARY OF STATE FOR THE WAR DEPARTMENT.

[Autograph, in the Colonial Office.]

Victory, off Toulon, October 16th, 1803.

My Lord,

I send you my correspondence with the Bashaw of Tripoli, and your Lordship will observe, that he is, as usual, most friendly disposed towards us. During the time of Buonaparte's greatest success in Egypt, that he gave up to me, as prisoners, the French Consul, and every Frenchman in his Dominions, amounting to fifty-seven, and that his Arsenal was always open for the supply of our Ships. I have not thought it, however, proper to notice the indirect application for gunpowder and grape-shot, on account of his War with the Americans, without the approbation of Government. Although the Bashaw is fully entitled to every act of kindness from us, yet it will strike your Lordship, as it has me, that it might give cause for a discontent on the part of the Americans, which it must be our wish to avoid. I have, &c.,

NELSON AND BRONTE.

TO THE RIGHT HONOURABLE LORD HOBART.

[Original, in the Colonial Office.]

My Lord,   Victory, off Toulon, October 16th, 1803.

On the arrival of the Childers on the 6th, the blockade of Genoa and Port Especia immediately took place, and the Southern parts of France, and the Ligurian and Italian Republics, will, I trust, severely feel the effects of it. There was certainly a difference between the situation of the poor Tuscans and those other Powers; the former will always be ready to assist us against the French, whenever they can do it with safety to themselves. By letters from Mr. Elliot and Sir John Acton, I am glad to find that some active measures are taking for the security of Sicily, and putting Messina in such a state of defence that it cannot be taken by surprise. I have told them some truths; but I am sure they are truly sensible that I have no further views in doing so, than to urge them to do what is right for the security of the Royal Family and Sicily. I will not touch on Mr. Elliot's mission. He believes that he is fully acquainted with the whole machinery which governs Naples: I own I doubt that he knows more than they wish him; but if they do what is right for their security I am content. I have always kept a Ship at Naples for the personal security of the Royal Family; and I have strengthened the Squadron which watches the French Army in the Heel of Italy, in case they should wish to cross to the Morea, which many think is their intention. What the real destination of the French Fleet may be is very difficult for me to guess. Mr. Elliot thinks they will try to have Sicily previous to their going to Egypt; others think they may go direct to cover the Army across to the Morea; others, that in the present unsettled state of Egypt, they may push with ten thousand men to Alexandria, and they may be bound outside the Mediterranean. Plausible reasons may certainly be given for every one of these plans; but I think one of the two last is their great object; and to those two points my whole attention is turned. If they put to sea, I hope to fall in with them, and then I have every reason to believe that all their plans will be frustrated. I have, &c.,

NELSON AND BRONTE.

P.S.—I have given directions for the reception of the Swiss recruits on board his Majesty's Ships.

I transmit a letter from our Consul at Minorca, and the infamous Edict decidedly against us. In short, our difficulties in the Spanish Ports are next to an exclusion—I ought rather to say, amount to an exclusion.[9]

NELSON AND BRONTE.

TO THE RIGHT HONOURABLE LORD HOBART.

[Autograph draught, in the possession of the Rev. Henry Girdlestone.]

Victory, off Toulon, 16th October, 1803.

My Lord,

I was honoured with your Lordship's letter of August 23rd, on the 6th instant, by the Childers Sloop of War: and I have sent for Mr. Falcon to come to me, that I may consult with him on the properest mode of proceeding, in order to make the Dey of Algiers conduct himself with becoming respect for his Majesty's Government, and all under his protection. Your Lordship may rest assured that I will not suffer, in the reparation I may demand, either the dignity of his Majesty to be insulted with impunity, nor those under his protection to be captured. At the same time, it will become my duty to take care that I do not rashly plunge our Country in a War with such a Power, and who, notwithstanding all which has been said, I have good reason to believe is friendly disposed towards us, and hates the French.

On the subject of Mr. Falcon (your Lordship will forgive the freedom of my remarks)—he was Secretary to the former Consul, and such persons, however elevated their rank with us, are held very low in estimation with the Moors. Therefore he never was really well received, or looked upon by the Dey; therefore I can readily believe he did not think the turning away Mr. Falcon (in the ignominious manner he did) the same as if he sent away any other Consul. The crime which was committed in Mr. Falcon's house was the very *greatest*.

Reports have reached me, that just before the Vessel's sailing with Mr. Falcon, reflection came over the Dey, and that he sent for Mr. Falcon to return. Although this

---

[9] This paragraph was added in Lord Nelson's own hand.

would not have done away the whole of the insult, yet it would have opened a door for immediate reparation; but as Mr. F. has not mentioned this circumstance—certainly very important—it may not be *true*. With respect to the reported taking of Maltese Vessels with Passports, notwithstanding the circumstances are so accurately detailed, even to the Number of the Passport, I have still very great doubts; for, notwithstanding the apparent public notoriety of the said captures, and the American Consul's letters, sent me from all quarters, even from Sir Alexander Ball, yet on my desiring of Sir Alexander Ball all the circumstances of where these Vessels were going, to whom their cargoes belong, &c. &c., all I have yet been able to obtain is the letter, of which I transmit a copy, stating —viz., 'I think it necessary to apprise your Lordship, that it has occasionally been found necessary (in consequence of the scarcity of Maltese Vessels) to grant British passports to Sicilian Vessels for *one voyage only*, for the purpose of supplying the Island; and as there is reason to believe that they have sometimes abused this privilege, by selling or otherwise misapplying these passports, it is possible that the Vessels alluded to in Mr. O'Brien's letter, may have been captured under such circumstances.' And to this day I have never heard from Sir Alexander Ball of the capture of any Maltese. I have now sent to him to demand from the Senate, who, I understand, regulate these matters, the names of the Vessels, to whom belonging, Masters' names, and the name of every man composing the crew, &c. &c. &c., that I may proceed upon strong grounds.

The orders from your Lordship, signifying the King's commands, are so perfectly clear, that if I cannot procure all the satisfaction which Mr. Falcon's case and these captures demand, hostilities will be the consequence; but if it be necessary to resort to that measure, I shall certainly not give the Dey the advantage of securing his Cruizers, which at this season are all in Port. They usually begin to fit out in February, and sail the beginning of April, returning for the winter in September; therefore I shall, if possible, not resort to actual hostilities, until I can strike a blow, the same day, on all his Vessels, from one end of the Mediterranean to the other. I have the honour to be, &c.

NELSON AND BRONTE.

TO THE REVEREND DR. NELSON, HILBOROUGH.

[Autograph, in the Nelson Papers.]

Victory, off Toulon, October 18th, 1803.

My dear Brother,

Accept my thanks for your kind letter of July   , which I received by the Childers. I sincerely hope that Canterbury will prove as profitable to you as to your predecessor last year: perhaps, if I take another French Fleet they may make you a Bishop: therefore, I shall try hard whenever they give me the opportunity. They are our superiors in numbers— they being eight to six, which is the force I can count upon being off Toulon; for one must be in turn in harbour watering, and I have Cadiz to watch with another, and one always at Naples, in case of accidents, for the security of the Royal Family; therefore, although the Admiralty may say, I have ten at my orders, the fact is I can never count upon more than six. If I am so fortunate on the day of Battle to have the seventh, I shall be very fortunate. For two days last week I was in a fever. A Frigate spoke a Spanish Vessel in the night, who said that he had seen a Fleet of twelve sail of Men-of-War off Minorca, steering to the Westward. It was thick for two days and our Frigates could not look into Toulon: however, I was relieved, for the first time in my life, by being informed the French were still in Port. They have a number of Troops ready for embarkation, but as to their destination that is a secret I am not entrusted with. The Fleet has been five months at sea this day, and in two days I [shall] have been as long, but we are remarkably healthy and in fine order to give the French a dressing. I shall try and do a little better with the Victory than Admiral Keppel.[1] We are not remarkably well manned but very well disposed people. I have wrote to Dr. Fisher[2] to congratulate him on his preferment, and if he offers his services you may be sure I will then clinch him for Mrs. Nelson's brother. I think

[1] Admiral Keppel's flag was flying in the Victory in his Action with the Count d'Orvilliers, off Brest, in July 1778; his conduct on which occasion became the subject of two celebrated Courts Martial. It would seem that Lord Nelson's opinion was unfavourable to Keppel.

[2] Dr. John Fisher was elected Bishop of Exeter in 1803: he was translated to Salisbury in 1807, and died in 1825.

this mode will be more likely to succeed than attacking him the moment of his appointment, and I assure you that I am anxious to mark my attention for good Mrs. Nelson, whose kindness I am truly sensible of. I am sorry for Mr. Rolfe: if young Mott does not do something handsome for him, he is a beast. I had wrote to Lord Hood long ago to thank him. If Sir William Fawcet had not given us his vote he would have forfeited his word, and should the Phœnix come in my way I will notice Lieutenant　　　　　, but I cannot make him a Captain. I have twenty-six on me at this moment, and sixty to make Lieutenants. It is not one French Fleet will do me service, and I shall be sure to offend more than I can oblige. However, if I take one more Fleet somebody else must take the others. With very sincere and affectionate wishes for you and yours, believe me ever, with the greatest truth, your most affectionate brother,

NELSON AND BRONTE.

TO LADY HAMILTON.

[Extract from " Lord Nelson's Letters to Lady Hamilton," vol. i. p. 156.]

Victory, off Toulon, October 18th, 1803.

My dearest Emma,

Your truly kind and affectionate letters, from July 17th, to August 24th, all arrived safe in the Childers, the 6th of this month . . . . Here I am, one day precisely like the other; except the difference of a gale of wind, or not. Since September 1st, we have not had four fine days; and, if the French do not come out soon, I fear, some of my Ships will cry out. . . . . I have just had a letter from Gibbs, of which I send you a copy. You see what interest he is taking about Bronté. I begin to think, without some assistance like his, that I never should have touched a farthing. It will be 1805, before I touch the estate. Neither principal or interest of the seven thousand ounces have been paid; and, it is now eight thousand ounces debt.

You will see, Gibbs, at last, has fixed on sending his daughter home; and I shall be glad of so good an opportunity of obliging him, as it will naturally tie him to my interest . . . . . To me, it is nothing. Thank God! there can be no tales told of my cheating; or, I hope, neglecting my duty. Whilst

I serve, I will serve well, and closely; when I want rest, I will
go to Merton. You know, my dear Emma, that I am never
well when it blows hard. Therefore, imagine what a cruize
off Toulon is; even in summer time, we have had a hard
gale every week, and two days' heavy swell . . . . . The other
day, we had a report the French were out, and seen steering
to the Westward. We were as far as Minorca, when the alarm
proved false . . . . I have received your letter, with Lord
William's and Mr. Kemble's, about Mr. Palmer:[3] he is also
recommended by the Duke of Clarence; and, he says, by
desire of the Prince of Wales. I have, without him, twenty-
six to be made Captains, and list every day increasing. It is
not *one* whole French Fleet that can get through it. I shall probably offend many more than I can oblige. Such is always the
case: like the tickets—those who get them, feel they have a
right to them; and those [who] do not get them, feel offended
for ever. But, I cannot help it: I shall endeavour to do what
is right, in every situation; and some ball may soon close all
my accounts with this world of care and vexation! . . . . The
Secretary Scott is a treasure; and I am very well mounted:
Hardy is every thing I could wish or desire. Our days pass
so much alike that, having described one, you have them all.
We now breakfast by candle-light, and all retire, at eight
o'clock, to bed. Naples, I fancy, is in a very bad way,
in regard to money. They have not, or pretend not to have,
enough to pay their Officers; and, I verily believe, if Acton
was to give up his place, that it would become a province of
France. Only think of Buonaparte's writing to the Queen,
to desire her influence to turn out Acton! She answered,
properly—at least, so says Mr. Elliot, who *knows more of
Naples* than any of us; God help him!—and General Acton
has, I believe, more power than ever.

By Gibbs's letter, I see, he has sent over about my accounts
at Bronté. He can have no interest in being unfriendly to
me. Why should he? I want no great matters from him;
and he can want nothing from me, that it is not my duty to
give his Sovereigns: therefore, why should he be against us!

---

[3] Mr. Palmer is mentioned in p. 246, ante. "Lord William," was Lord William
Gordon. Vide p. 246, ante.

For my part, my conduct will not alter, whether he is or not. Our friend, Sir Alexander, is a very great Diplomatic character; and, even an Admiral must not know what he is negotiating about : although you will scarcely believe, that the Bey of Tunis sent the man at my desire. You shall judge—viz., ' The Tunisian Envoy is still here, negotiating. He is a moderate man; and, apparently, the best disposed of any I ever did business with.' Could even the oldest Diplomatic character be drier ? I hate such parade of nonsense ! But I will turn from such stuff. Poor Mr. Este,[4] how I pity him ! but what shall I do with him ? However, if he comes, I shall show him all the kindness in my power.

October 22nd.

The Vessel is just going off. I have not a scrap of news ! Only, be assured of my most affectionate regard. Remember me kindly to Charlotte : shall always love those that are good to Horatia. I will write her by another opportunity. Remember me to Mrs. Cadogan. You may be sure, I do not forget Charles, who has not been well ; Captain Capel is very good to him. . . . .

NELSON AND BRONTE.

TO HIS EXCELLENCY COUNT WORONZOW.

[From Clarke and M'Arthur, vol. ii. p. 333.]

19th October, 1803.

The Count Mocenigo has sent me a complaint that three Vessels, one under Russian colours, and two under those of the Republic of the Seven Islands, have been taken by some English Ships, and carried into Malta, and that the only answer the Consul of Malta has obtained, was, ' The Judge of the Vice-Admiralty Court is not yet arrived.' Without entering into the merits of the case, of which I can know nothing but from the reports sent me of Ships detained or captured, whereof I send you a copy, your Excellency may rely there was great cause of suspicion that the Vessels or cargoes, or both, were belonging to Enemies, and were merely covered with Neutral papers ; and it even strikes me as odd in

---

[4] Dr. Lambton Este : who will be particularly noticed.

the complaint, they are stated as only bound to Messina, and that the other optional destination, Genoa, should be omitted : what occasion was there for concealing anything in an upright transaction? And there is another curious circumstance lately come to light, which is, I believe, that on board the Ship carrying Russian colours, the whole set of French papers have been found; however, your Excellency knows, that under such suspicious circumstances none but a Judge can decide. My orders are positive for the respect due to the Neutral Flag; and with regard to Russia, I have repeated the orders for the strict observance of the seventh Article of the Treaty signed at St. Petersburgh, the 5th (17th) of June 1801. I shall only lastly observe, that one hundred and seventy French Vessels were in the Black Sea at the commencement of hostilities, and that by *a magic touch of Merchants*, they became in a moment *Russians, Imperials, Ionians, Ragusans*, and not one French Vessel remained!—Bravo! But allow me to assure your Excellency, that I ever am, with the highest respect, your most obedient and faithful, humble servant,

NELSON AND BRONTE.

TO HIS EXCELLENCY HUGH ELLIOT, ESQ.

[Autograph, in the Elliot Papers.]

Victory, off Toulon, October 19th, 1803.

My dear Sir,

Allow me to introduce to your notice, and I may add, to your friendship, Mr. Abram Gibbs, now at Palermo. He was lately the partner of Mr. Falconet, and was always the intimate household friend of dear Sir William and Lady Hamilton, and, give me leave to add, my friend. I believe I am to call Mr. Gibbs a banker. Whatever kindness your Excellency may show him, will ever be esteemed a favour conferred upon, my dear Sir, your most faithful servant,

NELSON AND BRONTE.

TO GEORGE NAYLER,[5] ESQ., YORK HERALD.

[Autograph, in the possession of Albert William Woods, Esq., Lancaster Herald.]

Victory, off Toulon, October 19th, 1803.

My dear Sir,

You will receive herewith a letter from Sir Richard Bickerton, relative to his being gazetted for wearing the Order of the Crescent. I believe that this matter is in your line, and, therefore, recommended you to him. At the same time, I told him that Government was to pay the expenses of the warrant, &c. &c., as had been done for all the other Officers; therefore, if Government will not pay you *all* and *every* expense, do not undertake the task without a further correspondence with Sir Richard, or I shall get into a scrape. I have sent to Sicily for the Arms of Bronté, and the Herald's College there has sent for my English Arms, in order that they may be enrolled amongst those of the Sicilian Nobility; therefore, you will be so good as to send me out the same sort of thing which I sent to Germany. I very much doubt that I ever paid for that, and several other things which you have done for me; therefore, I desire (for in a man's trade there are no compliments) that you will send me out your regular bill, for I suppose you cannot live upon air; and if you are never paid, how is the pot to boil? When I take the French Fleet, which I hope to do before Christmas, I suppose there will be more alterations. I am, dear Sir, with every good wish, your most obliged and obedient servant,

NELSON AND BRONTE.

TO THE RIGHT HONOURABLE LORD HAWKESBURY, SECRETARY OF STATE FOR THE HOME DEPARTMENT.

[From Clarke and M'Arthur, vol. ii. p. 333.]

20th October, 1803.

I am happy in having anticipated your Lordship's wishes, by corresponding with Constantinople. The French Fleet from Toulon has as many destinations as there are Countries;

---

[5] Afterwards Sir George Nayler, K.H., Garter Principal King of Arms : he died in October 1831.

for it is certainly by no means sure that Buonaparte always makes War upon his Enemies. It is more to his advantage sometimes to attack his Friends, especially if they are weak, and wish to defend themselves. I have lately added to our Force, destined principally to watch the French Army in the Heel of Italy, and it is under a very intelligent Officer, Captain Cracraft,—Anson, 44; Juno, 32; Arrow, 20; Bittern, 18; Morgiana, 18. With this force, I think we have done all that is possible to save the Morea and the Seven Islands, and to prevent that Army passing to Egypt. I am, &c.,

NELSON AND BRONTE.

TO HIS EXCELLENCY JOHN HOOKHAM FRERE, MADRID.

[From Clarke and M'Arthur, vol. ii. p. 333.]

[Apparently about 20th October, 1803.]

I trust that Spain will be too wise to go to War with us. We ought, by mutual consent, to be the very best friends, and both to be ever hostile to France. . . . . . As probably this letter will be read before it gets to you, I can only tell the reader, that a British Fleet never was in higher order, health, and good humour, than the one I have the happiness to command; and if the French do not rue the day when we get alongside of them, it will not be the fault of the Captains, Officers, or Men, but must be [that] of your Excellency's most obedient servant,

NELSON AND BRONTE.

TO THE RIGHT HONOURABLE LORD HOBART, SECRETARY OF STATE FOR THE WAR DEPARTMENT.

[Autograph, in the Colonial Office.]

Victory, off Toulon, October 20th, 1803.

My Lord,

I transmit your Lordship a copy of my last letter from Corfu, which will inform you of the state of those Islands and the Morea.

I have added to the Squadron which I had already stationed to watch the French Army, two more fine Sloops of War, and

ordered Captain Cracraft, the Senior Officer, and a very able
Sea Officer, to give his attention to the Republic of the Seven
Islands, and the Mouth of the Archipelago.　His Squadron is
now composed of the

Anson	44 Guns	. . . .	24-pounders.
Juno	32 do.	. . . .	12　do.
Bittern . . .	18 do.	. . . .	24　do.
Morgiana . . .	18 do.	. . . .	24　do.
Arrow	20 do.	. . . .	24　do.

Therefore, it is clear that I have kept myself very short of
Frigates, in order that other services should not be pinched.
I have, &c.

NELSON AND BRONTE.

TO CAPTAIN SIR EDWARD BERRY.

[Autograph, in the possession of Lady Berry.]

Victory, off Toulon, October 20th, 1803.

My dear Sir Edward,

I received your kind letter, by the Childers, on the 6th
instant.　You are right to be as quiet as you can, although it
is vexing to be unemployed at such a moment; but it is useless to fret oneself to death, when the folks aloft don't care
a pin about it.　Although we have constant and very hard
gales of wind, yet this place is certainly very healthy—much
preferable for an invalid to either Channel or North Seas.
Young Forster[6] has gone with Captain Layman in the Weazle:
this Ship was too large.　The Seahorse is with me, and you may
be assured Mr. Steele[7] shall be put upon some Quarter-deck.
I will mention your wishes to Lord St. Vincent within these
two minutes: what effect it will have, time must show.　It
will have my sincere good wishes; for I am ever, my dear Sir
Edward, ever yours, faithfully,

NELSON AND BRONTE.

---

[6] Mr. William Forster, son of Thompson Forster, Esq., a Surgeon in London,
and first cousin of Sir Edward and Lady Berry: he was acting as Lieutenant in the
Colossus, at Trafalgar, and was so severely wounded that he died at Gibraltar a
week after the Battle.

[7] Mr. Steele did not enter the Navy.

TO MISS HORATIA NELSON THOMSON.

[Autograph, in the possession of Mrs. Horatia Nelson Ward.]

Victory, off Toulon, October 21st, 1803.

My dear Child,

Receive this first letter from your most affectionate Father. If I live, it will be my pride to see you virtuously brought up; but if it pleases God to call me, I trust to Himself: in that case, I have left Lady H. your guardian. I therefore charge you, my Child, on the value of a Father's blessing, to be obedient and attentive to all her kind admonitions and instructions. At this moment I have left you, in a Codicil[7] dated the 6th of September, the sum of four thousand pounds sterling, the interest of which is to be paid to your guardian for your maintenance and education. I shall only say, my dear Child, may God Almighty bless you and make you an ornament to your sex, which I am sure you will be if you attend to all Lady H.'s kind instructions; and be assured that I am, my dear Horatia, your most affectionate Father,

NELSON AND BRONTE.

TO ALEXANDER DAVISON, ESQ.

[Autograph, in the possession of Colonel Davison.]

Victory, off Toulon, October 21st, 1803.

My dear Davison,

Your original letter of the 15th of August I received by the Childers, and I have not seen a single Vessel since, that could

---

[7] The following is a copy of the remarkable Codicil to his Will, dated on the 6th of September, 1803, in which Lord Nelson made the bequest to his daughter:—

"I give and bequeath to Miss Horatia Nelson Thomson (who was baptized on the 13th day of May last, in the Parish of St. Mary-le-bone, in the County of Middlesex, by Benjamin Lawrence, Curate, and John Willock, Assistant-Clerk, and whom I acknowledge as my adopted daughter) the sum of £4000 sterling money of Great Britain, to be paid at the expiration of six months after my decease, or sooner, if possible; and I leave my dearest friend Emma Lady Hamilton, sole guardian of the said Horatia Nelson Thomson, until she shall have arrived at the age of eighteen years; and the interest of the said £4000 to be paid to Lady Hamilton for her education and maintenance. This request of guardianship I earnestly make to Lady Hamilton, knowing that she will educate my adopted child in the paths of religion and virtue, and give her those accomplishments which so much adorn herself, and I hope make her a fit wife for my dear nephew, Horatio Nelson, who I wish to marry her, if he should prove worthy, in Lady Hamilton's estimation, of such a treasure as I am sure she will be."

give me the least news. We are looking out for a Spanish
War, and for the sailing of the French Fleet, both very great
events to us. Our weather has never been good, but it is now
terrible. Such a place for storms of wind I never met with,
and I am unfortunately in bad weather, always sea-sick. We
ought to be amply repaid some day for all our toil. I trust
before next winter that we shall have Peace, and be all quiet at
home. By a Vessel just spoke from Marseilles, they report
that 40,000 Troops are marching into the South of Italy, but
we can believe nothing these Neutrals say; and yet it may be
true enough, if they intend to cross to the Morea, or Egypt.
I am ever, my dear Davison, most affectionately yours,

NELSON AND BRONTE.

Hardy desires his compliments.

TO COUNT MOCENIGO, RUSSIAN ENVOY IN THE IONIAN
ISLANDS.

[From Clarke and M'Arthur, vol. ii. p. 334.]

22nd October, 1803.

I have been honoured with your Excellency's letters respecting the detention of three Vessels, belonging, as was reported
to your Excellency, to the Republic of the Seven Isles, with
cargoes the property of Subjects of other Powers, the Vessels
being chartered; and that the Papers were not delivered to
the Consul of the Republic of the Seven Isles at Malta. I
have been positively ordered to give directions for observing,
not only the Neutrality of the Seven Isles, but, in case of
need, to assist them against the French. These orders I
notified on my first arrival; and your Excellency will believe,
that I did not fail to give the very strictest directions to his
Majesty's Fleet for their being observed.

Admitting the statement of your Excellency to be just, as
to the mode of procedure of the Captain of the Frigate, in not
delivering the Papers to the Consul of the Seven Isles at
Malta, your Excellency will, I am sure, agree with me, that
it has been, in that respect, perfectly correct; for the Captor
is obliged to make oath, that he has delivered every Paper
found, to the Commissioners appointed by the High Court of

Admiralty, and has allowed no person to have them in his
possession.   This law is so just, that not a word can be said,
and all Nations must approve of such a regulation; for, without it, Papers might be kept back, or altered for purposes
contrary to justice.

With respect to the original detention of the Vessels, that
must be deferred, on the belief that the Vessels and Cargoes
are Enemy's property, or that either the Vessel or Cargo is
Enemy's property; in either case, the necessity of carrying
the Vessel into Port is obvious.   This is a tax which Neutrals
are subject to; but if it should turn out that there was no
just cause for detention, the Vessels are liberated by the
Judge of the Admiralty Court, after a trial, and such damage
awarded as the case may require.   This Tribunal being
acknowledged by all Nations, and more particularly by our
august Sovereigns in the late Treaty of St. Petersburg,
nothing can be more regular than bringing the cause before
it as soon as possible.   I am aware it may be said, why was
not this done immediately?   To which I can only answer,
that I am very sorry the Judge of the Admiralty appointed by
his Majesty for the Island of Malta, from some cause unknown
to me, was not arrived.   It is to this circumstance that both
the Neutral Power and the Captors have equally to regret the
not being able to obtain an earlier decision.   But wherever
the fault or accident of his non-arrival may lie, your Excellency will agree with me, that it does not rest with the
Captors; and we can neither of us say, that any one has done
wrong in bringing these Vessels to adjudication, until it is
proved so.   I have every inducement, both of a public and
private nature, to wish much prosperity to the commerce of
the rising Republic, fostered under the special protection of
your august Sovereign; between whom and my Royal Master
so happily subsists such a perfect good understanding and
harmony.   I send your Excellency the report of the Captain
making the seizure, on which only I can form my judgment,
It appears, if that be correct, that there was great cause to
suspect, at least, the Cargoes being Enemy's property.   I
am, &c.,   NELSON AND BRONTE.

TO SPIRIDION FORESTI, ESQ., HIS MAJESTY'S MINISTER TO THE
REPUBLIC OF THE SEVEN ISLANDS.

[Autograph draught, in the possession of Earl Nelson.]

Sir,　　　　　　　　[Victory, off Toulon, 22nd October, 1803.]

I have been honoured with your letter of 23rd September,
enclosing one to you from the Prince President, relative to
the detention of some Vessels belonging to the Republic of
the Seven Isles.

Although I have answered Count Mocenigo fully on this
matter, yet I shall do the same to you, in order that it may
come regularly before His Excellency the Prince President.
You communicated to the Government of the Republic that
I was entrusted to aid and assist them to the utmost of my
power, in case of an attack from the French; and I gave the
very strictest order to the whole of His Majesty's Fleet under
my command, to respect their Neutrality: therefore, in those
respects, as far as related to me, I have done all which the
Republic could possibly wish or desire.

The detention of the Vessels alluded to, I am confident,
must have been made by an impression on Captain [Richardson]
that either the Vessels and Cargoes belonged to our Enemies,
or that one or other did do so; for certainly no Captain would
knowingly either risk his commission by disobedience of orders,
or ruin himself by being obliged to pay for making an illegal
seizure. I send you Captain Richardson's report of two of
the Vessels. The third, I have had no report of. I suppose,
from your letter, that she must have been taken by the Braakel,
who is stationed in the Archipelago.

From the report sent to me, of which I send you a copy, it
appears that the Parthenope and St. George belonged—
either Vessels or Cargoes, or both—to our Enemies, and
although under Ionian colours and Passes, lawful objects of
seizure; and the Cargoes being admitted by the President not
to belong to Subjects of the Republic, I cannot conceive
under what pretence he interferes for the Cargoes, whatever
he may for the Vessels. They, by his own account, he can
know nothing of, but what he is told. Captain Richardson
supposes them to belong to Genoese; and on that belief, he
was not only justifiable in sending them into Port if the

Vessels were proved to belong *bonâ fide* (and not covered for purposes contrary to Neutrality) to subjects of the Republic. I sincerely wish they had been liberated. But Captain Richardson seems to have conducted himself,—by the President's account, and no other has reached me,—in strict conformity to the laws and regulations of the High Court of Admiralty, in refusing the Ionian Consul the Papers; for it is justice, and the law of Nations, that must finally decide these matters, and not the pleasure of any individual, however high his rank. Justice presides in the British tribunals, and even the Monarch is not suffered to interfere. I trust the President will be satisfied with this information, respecting our laws; and I can only re-assure him, and the Republic, that as far as my situation will allow me to interfere, in any manner beneficial for them, it will never be omitted by, Sir, &c.

NELSON AND BRONTE.

TO HIS EXCELLENCY HUGH ELLIOT, ESQ., H. M. MINISTER PLENIPOTENTIARY AT THE COURT OF NAPLES.

[Original in the Elliot Papers.]

Victory, off Toulon, 22nd October, 1803.

Sir,

I have the honour to transmit your Excellency a letter from Captain Hillyar of his Majesty's Ship Niger, dated the 19th instant, and to mention my regret that the Ports of Sicily afford shelter to the Privateers of our Enemies, so foreign to the laws of Neutrality, by which our Trade from Malta has already materially suffered; and unless some strict prohibition is issued against the French Privateers taking our Trade from the Sicilian Ports and Shores, as mentioned in the said letter, as well as by His Majesty's Consuls, who have complained to me of similar depredations, the Trade of Malta and others passing Sicily must inevitably fall into the Enemies' hands; I therefore trust your Excellency will see the necessity of adopting such measures as may tend to prevent this serious evil. I have the honour to be, &c.,

NELSON AND BRONTE.

TO COMMISSIONER OTWAY, AT GIBRALTAR.

[Letter-Book.]

Sir,　　　　　　　　　　Victory, off Toulon, 22nd October, 1803.

Gover's Gun-carriages furnished his Majesty's Ship Narcissus some time ago, having many of them broke, and rendered the Ship almost in a state of distress for carriages, I have to request you will be pleased to consult with the Military Ordnance Store-keeper (and if necessary, Lieutenant General Sir Thomas Trigge) respecting some new ones being made, agreeable to the model sent herewith, as early as possible, for the said Ship; but if found impracticable to be done at Gibraltar, you will have the goodness to forward the model by the first opportunity to the Lords Commissioners of the Admiralty, in order that they may give the necessary directions respecting them, or the Narcissus being furnished with other Gun-carriages in their stead.　I am, &c.,

NELSON AND BRONTE.

TO J. B. GIBERT, ESQ., VICE-CONSUL, AT BARCELONA.

[Letter-Book.]

Sir,　　　　　　　　　　Victory, off Toulon, 22nd October, 1803.

Your attention in sending wine for the service of the Fleet, and refreshments, was certainly very praiseworthy; and as it ought to have been with me early in August, the Fleet never being off its station for many months, I still am at a loss to account for the conduct of the Patroons of the Vessels not coming to the Fleet: at the same time, I admit it is very hard that you should be a sufferer for such misconduct; what your recompence should be, I must leave to the Commissioners for Victualling His Majesty's Navy.　I wanted the wine and waited a month for it before I sent to other places, and it might have been on board our Ships in ten days at farthest, but that, I suppose, is no fault of yours.　I send you a letter for the Commissioners of the Victualling, which I hope will produce the desired effect, and afford you all the satisfaction the case requires.　I am, &c.,

NELSON AND BRONTE.

P.S.—I have sent the letter to the Commissioners for Victualling His Majesty's Navy under a flying seal, that you may make the proper use of it, and transmit them copies of the letters therein alluded to.

TO THE COMMISSIONERS FOR VICTUALLING HIS MAJESTY'S NAVY, LONDON.

[Letter-Book.]

Gentlemen,   Victory, off Toulon, 22nd October, 1803.

In July last, I desired Captain Gore of the Medusa, in his way to Gibraltar, to call off Barcelona, and to say to our Consul, Mr. Gregory, that a hundred tuns of good Catalonian wine, with onions and other refreshments, would be very acceptable to the Fleet. The Consul being in England, the Memorandum was delivered to Mr. Gibert, the Vice-Consul. It appears by Mr. Gibert's account, that he sent wine on the 30th of August to the Fleet, but the Vessels never came to the Fleet from that day to this. The reasons are set forth in the several letters of August 30th, September 12th and 18th, and October 7th, of which I have desired him to send you copies. Mr. Gibert feels the hardship of having shipped this wine to serve our Country, and that he is likely to be a loser by his zeal, which he certainly ought not to be. I must, Gentlemen, on your considering every circumstance, leave it to your judgment what to allow him, as I cannot possibly be a judge of these matters. His Patroons have certainly behaved very ill, for the Fleet has never been for two days together, without some one being in the sight of Toulon; but, as I observed before, Mr. Gibert, although he has been unfortunate in his selection, ought not to be a sufferer for his zeal and ready attention to my wishes. I am, &c.,

NELSON AND BRONTE.

TO J. B. GIBERT, ESQ., VICE-CONSUL, BARCELONA.

[Letter-Book.]

Sir,   Victory, off Toulon, 22nd October, 1803.

I am very much obliged by the news communicated to me in your letter of the 7th instant, and sincerely desire that Spain, for her own sake, may preserve her Neutrality; and I have also to hope that the Fleet under my command will not meet with any unnecessary impediment in getting bullocks, and other refreshments, at the different Spanish Ports or places they may be ordered to. I am, Sir, &c.,

NELSON AND BRONTE.

TO J. B. GIBERT, ESQ., VICE-CONSUL, AT BARCELONA.

[Letter Book.]

Victory, off Toulon, 22nd October, 1803.

Sir,

I have received your son's letter of the 16th instant, with the translation of an official Note from the Captain General of Barcelona therein mentioned, respecting a Catalonian Barque plundered by a Privateer under English colours : in answer to which, if the said Privateer belongs to Gibraltar, I would recommend sending the complaint to his Excellency, Lieutenant General Sir Thomas Trigge, in order that the Commander of her may be punished as the law directs. The Master's name being known, the verification can easily be made at Gibraltar. I am, &c.,

NELSON AND BRONTE.

TO J. B. GIBERT, ESQ., VICE-CONSUL, BARCELONA.

[Letter-Book.]

Victory, off Toulon, 22nd October, 1803.

Sir,

I have received your letter of the 7th instant, acquainting me with the supplies of bullocks which can be had for the Fleet under my command, at Alfaquez; but as it will not be practicable to take them from that place, there not being sufficient water to carry the Squadron there with safety for that purpose; I must, therefore, with expressing myself much obliged by your ready attention to my wishes in this respect, decline using Alfaquez for the supply of bullocks, from the reasons above mentioned, as well as the very high charge made for them. The Fleet under my command can be supplied from different quarters on much more reasonable terms. I am, &c.,   NELSON AND BRONTE.

TO THE COMMISSIONERS FOR VICTUALLING HIS MAJESTY'S NAVY, LONDON.

[Letter-Book.]

Victory, off Toulon, 22nd October, 1803.

Gentlemen,

I herewith transmit for your information, copy of my letter to your Board of this date, sent to Mr. Gibert, His Majesty's

Vice-Consul at Barcelona, together with copies and extracts of four letters from him on the subject of the wine, &c., said to be shipped for the Fleet under my command, as therein mentioned, in order that you may take the same into consideration, and make such allowance, for the losses he may have sustained, as you judge proper, which, notwithstanding what he sets forth, may not be so considerable, as it is natural to suppose men in business would have taken the precaution of insuring the safe delivery of their cargoes. Political reasons may, however, induce this last mentioned circumstance to be regarded in another point of view, and not to influence your decision against him. I am, &c.,

NELSON AND BRONTE.

TO SIR EVAN NEPEAN, BART., ADMIRALTY.

[Letter-Book.]

Victory, off Toulon, 22nd October, 1803.

Sir,

You will please to acquaint the Lord Commissioners of the Admiralty, that judging it necessary for the good of His Majesty's Service that some person should be appointed to the Ambuscade, to take charge of the provisions as Purser, I have appointed Mr. John Sullivan, late Clerk of His Majesty's Ship Belleisle, who has been upwards of six years in the Service, and recommended to me as a deserving young man. I am, Sir, &c.,

NELSON AND BRONTE.

TO THE PRINCIPAL OFFICERS AND COMMISSIONERS OF HIS MAJESTY'S NAVY, LONDON.

[Letter-Book.]

Victory, off Toulon, 22nd October, 1803.

Gentlemen,

Several Seamen having deserted from the Fleet under my command, at the Bay of Rosas, where the Ships have gone to wood and water, &c., I directed Mr. Gibert, his Majesty's Vice-Consul at Barcelona, to give forty shillings for each Deserter which might be apprehended, and acquainted him that the usual allowance of nine-pence per day would be made for their subsistence during the time they remained in custody. These sums Mr. Gibert receives from Mr. John Hunter, his Majesty's Consul-General at Madrid, who will draw upon your Board for the amount, and transmit the regular vouchers at the same time : the forty shillings will be charged against each of such Deserters, when they join their respective Ships. I am, &c.,

NELSON AND BRONTE.

TO JOHN HUNTER, ESQ., HIS MAJESTY'S CONSUL-GENERAL. MADRID.

[Letter-Book.]

Victory, off Toulon, 22nd October, 1803.

Sir,

I have received your letter of the 8th instant, and beg to observe that it is on the Navy Board you are to draw for the forty shillings allowed for apprehending each Deserter, as well as for subsisting them afterwards. I have wrote to the Commissioners of the Navy upon this subject, in order that the Bills you may have occasion to draw upon them for this service, may be duly attended to. The necessary vouchers for such disbursements must be regularly transmitted to that Board. I am, Sir, &c.,

NELSON AND BRONTE.

TO SPIRIDION FORESTI, ESQ., CORFU.

[Autograph draught, in the possession of Earl Nelson.]

Victory, off Toulon, 22nd October, 1803.

Sir,

I have received by the Niger, Captain Hillyar, duplicate of your letter of August 23rd, and triplicate of yours of July 25th, for which I am much obliged to you; and also your letter of September 23rd. In reply to the first part of your letter, I beg leave to acquaint you, that I have enlarged the Squadron destined to watch the French at Otranto, Brindisi, &c. &c., and have given Captain Cracraft, the Senior Captain, orders to call occasionally at Corfu, and to afford every assistance to the Republic of the Seven Isles, which I am sure he will do.

To the second part of your letter : You say that you would ' write to Ali Pacha, that your Lordship had transmitted his letters, &c.' I am very sorry for my omission, but I transmitted them to Mr. Ad . . . . m [Addington ?] the moment I received them, the 24th August. I am really much interested for Ali Pacha ; for he has always been a stanch friend to the English, and most particularly kind to me ; and if I ever should go to Corfu, I shall certainly, if he is within a few days' reach, go and see him. I am very happy to find that the powder and ball sent by the Arab has been seized, and some of the troublesome Greeks removed.

I have given Captain Cracraft such directions for the protection of our commerce, as cannot fail of the desired effect, unless the Republic allow the Enemy's Privateers to be sheltered in their Ports, and from thence make depredations, as has, I am sorry to say, been the case in Sicily. Your attention to every part of your duty leaves me nothing to recommend, and I only beg that you will assure the Government of the Republic of my sincere good wishes for its prosperity, and be assured I am, with the highest respect, Sir, your most obedient humble servant,   NELSON AND BRONTE.

You will be so good as to forward my letters ; and you mentioned sending the two letters from his Excellency Mr. Drummond : I only received one dated July 13th.

TO WILLIAM WILLIAMS, ESQ., PLYMOUTH DOCK.

[From a Fac-simile.]

Victory, off Toulon, October 23rd, 1803.

My dear Sir,

I return you many thanks for your kind remembrance of me, and I feel very much obliged by your present of Scilly ling, which Mr. Chapman delivered on the arrival of the Childers. I am watching and praying for the sailing of the Enemy's Fleet, and, with the Ships with me, I have no fear but we shall give a very good account of them. I sincerely condole on your loss ; but some of us are always called before the others, and we know not whose turn may be next. We none of us can escape the grim gentleman. I beg you will give my remembrances to any of our joint friends at Plymouth. I have not time to answer Captain Spicer's[7] kind letter. Believe me ever, my dear Sir, yours most faithfully,

NELSON AND BRONTE.

TO REAR-ADMIRAL MACNAMARA RUSSELL.[8]

[From Clarke and M'Arthur, vol. ii. p. 336.]

October, 1803.

Here I am, waiting the pleasure of these fellows at Toulon, and we only long to get fairly alongside of them. I dare say, there would be some spare *hats*, by the time we had done. You are a pleasant fellow at all times; and, as Commodore Johnstone said of General Meadows, 'I have no doubt but your company would be delightful on the day of Battle to your friends, but damned bad for your enemies.' I desire, my dear Russell, you will always consider me as one of the sincerest of the former. I am, &c.,

NELSON AND BRONTE.

TO HIS EXCELLENCY HUGH ELLIOT, ESQ.

[Autograph, in the Elliot Papers.]

Victory, off Toulon, October 23rd, 1803.

My dear Sir,

Be so good as to send my letter to Mr. Jackson, and answer such parts as relate to the Gibraltar, and if she can be spared for a few days to carry the Sardinian Galley with his Royal Highness over to Cagliari, I am sure Captain Ryves on being asked to do it, will perform this service with much pleasure.[9] We are all well, and ever, my dear Sir, your faithful and obedient servant,

NELSON AND BRONTE.

[7] Captain Peter Spicer, then a Post Captain, who was a Lieutenant of the Aga-memnon, and the Captain, under Lord Nelson's command. *Vide* vol. i. 300, vol. ii. 271. He died about 1830.

[8] Rear-Admiral Thomas Macnamara Russell. A Memoir of this Officer, who died an Admiral of the White in 1823 or 1824, will be found in the *Naval Chronicle*, vol. xvii.

[9] The Gibraltar did convey the Sardinian Prince to Cagliari; for which service the King of Sardinia presented Captain Ryves with a gold snuff-box.

TO CAPTAIN DONNELLY, H.M. SHIP NARCISSUS.

[Autograph, in the possession of the late Adam Bromilow, Esq.]

Victory, off Toulon, October 24th, 1803.

Sir,

I am going with the Squadron to the Madalena Islands to water, and shall return to the Rendezvous as soon as possible; but I think it will be about fourteen days from this time; you will, therefore, with the Seahorse under your command, remain off Toulon, and occasionally on the Rendezvous, till my return, taking every care in your power that the French Fleet do not put to sea without your knowing it; and, in case of their coming out, you will send the Seahorse direct to me, to let me be acquainted with it; and you will endeavour yourself to ascertain their intended route, by which time I may be able to have the Fleet ready for putting to sea. I expect the Termagant with dispatches from Gibraltar; you will, therefore, direct her Commander to come to me at the Madalena Islands, cautioning him not to entangle himself with the Islands, unless he is assured, by sending his boat on shore to the town of Madalena, or exchanging signals with the Fleet, that it is safe to approach. Should you fall in with either the Canopus or Renown, you will acquaint Admiral Campbell and Captain White[1] where I am, and of my desire for their immediate junction with me. Should certain circumstances occur, which I cannot forsee, I rely on your ability and zeal for acting in the properest manner for his Majesty's service; and I am, Sir, with great respect, your most obedient servant,

NELSON AND BRONTE.

[1] Captain John Chambers White, of the Renown: he died a Knight Commander of the Bath, Vice-Admiral of the White, and Commander-in-Chief at Sheerness, in January 1845.

PRIVATE JOURNAL,[2] FROM OCTOBER 25TH TO OCTOBER 31ST, 1803.

[From Clarke and M'Arthur, vol. ii. p. 336.]

October 25th, saw Corsica and Cape Longo Sardo; from noon to daylight next morning, we had a heavy swell with squally weather. During the whole of the 26th, lost ground

[2] This private Journal has not been found; but two small Books are preserved in which Lord Nelson daily entered, in his own hand, the state of the Barometer, Weather, and Wind twice, three times, and occasionally four, five, and even six times in every twenty-four hours, from the 24th of October 1803, to the 13th of May 1805. A few extracts from these entries may be considered interesting:—

"STATE OF THE WEATHER BY THE BAROMETER, 1803.

Week day.	Month Day.	Time taken. A.M. and P.M.	Rise & Fall of the Barometer			State of the Weather and Wind.
			Degrees.	Lines.	Tenths.	
Monday	October 24	7 A.M.	29	9	9	A heavy swell from N.W.
		Noon.	30	1	,,	Light airs. Variable.
		7 P.M.	30	1	7	Fine weather. Wind North.
Tuesday	25	7 A.M.	30	1	7	Wind E.N.E. Fine breezes and clear.
		Noon.	30	2	—	Calm, and at times fresh breezes; but very fine.
		4 P.M.	30	1	6	
		10 P.M.	30	2	2	Fresh breezes, and a swell at East.
Saturday	December 10	7 A.M.	30	1	7	Strong breezes, N.N.W.
		2 P.M.	—	—	9	Ditto weather. Anchored under Cape Tolari, in 29 fathoms water, opposite a sandy Bay, the Cape bearing W.S.W. by compass.

N.B.—From Friday morning the Barometer has been rising, and yet, for two days and one night, I never saw such a succession of heavy squalls of wind, hail, and rain.

Monday	February [1804] 23		Never so high.			
		7 A.M.	30	5	1	Fine weather. Wind E.N.E.
		7 P.M.	—	4	9	Fine weather. Wind West.
Wednesday	October 1804 31	Never rose so much in a given time.[1]				
		7 A.M.	30	0	0	Nearly calm, North.
		8 P.M.	30	0	8	Light airs, S.S.W.

[1] At 6 P.M. of the preceding day, the Barometer was 29° 7' 6".—EDITOR.

all day. The next day, we had strong breezes at E.S.E., directly through the Straits, and found we had gained two points to the Eastward in the night. Throughout the ensuing night we had strong gales, and were under reefed courses. At six o'clock the next evening, having split many sails, we found ourselves abreast of Isle Rosso. All night strong gales.

Saturday, October 29th, found ourselves about five leagues directly to leeward of the place we left last night. At daylight, made sail under close-reefed topsails and reefed courses, with a very strong current against us; but the Fleet being absolutely in distress for water, I am determined to persevere, notwithstanding all the difficulties. At one P.M., fetched Castel Sardo, a small Town in Sardinia, rounded in stays three miles from the shore: beating alongshore all night about three miles from the Coast.

October 31st.—Not being able to clear the Levisena Islands, stood towards Shark's Mouth, tacked, and fetched the Northernmost of Martha Islands. N.B. The Straits of Bonafaccio lie between the Martha and Levisena Islands, the last of which belong to Corsica. When near the Southernmost, Martha Island, we opened the little one to the Westward of the Island Spanioti, close to the ledge of rocks, and weathered them about one mile; we then tacked under Sardinia, and stood into a beautiful little bay, or rather harbour. After various tacks, and being close to the two rocks in Captain Ryves' Chart, and abreast of the rocks where he was, the whole Squadron anchored by six o'clock in the evening, without any accident, in Agincourt Sound, under the Sardinian shore.

TO HIS EXCELLENCY HUGH ELLIOT, ESQ.

[Autograph, in the Elliot Papers. "31st October, P.M.—At 3·10, came to with the best bower in Agincourt Sound, and moored Ship. November 1.—Saluted the Governor of Madalena with nine guns on coming on board."—*Victory's Log.*]

Victory, Madalena Islands, November 1st, 1803.

My dear Sir,

The Fleet being very much in want of water, I have taken the opportunity of the moonlight nights to come here, in order to obtain it, and some refreshments for our crews, who have now been upwards of five months at sea. But our health and good humour is perfection, and we only want the French Fleet out. This day week they had eight Sail of the Line ready, and a ninth fitting; so that we shall surely meet them some happy day, and I have no doubt but that we shall be amply repaid for all our cares and watchings. I have left Frigates to watch them. The Raven goes to Naples in order to obtain candles, and other things of which we stand in need, and I hope she will be favoured with the winds, and catch us here.

I have not a word of news from any quarter, and I have only to hope that all goes on well in the Two Sicilies. I should be happy, was it in my power, to communicate oftener with you, and dire necessity only obliges me to send the Raven, and I am left without a small Vessel. Pray, tell me, can I write to England through Naples with safety? How do your dispatches go? I am ever, my dear Sir, your Excellency's most faithful and obliged servant,

NELSON AND BRONTE.

Captain Murray, Hardy, and Dr. Scott, desire their compliments. My letters I send as I can, generally to Gibraltar. The other routes are uncertain, and I have no spare Vessels. I feel even parting with the Cameleon, and he has strict orders to join me as soon as possible.

TO ARCHIBALD MACNEILL, ESQ., NAPLES.

[Letter-Book.]

Victory, Madalena Islands, Sardinia, 1st November, 1803.

Sir,

By your letter of the 26th September last, you offered to supply one or two hundred head of oxen when wanted: I now beg that you will be pleased to inform me when you can have one hundred head of prime oxen either at Gaeta or Salerno, (the former place in preference, as it is a better anchorage in this season,) and fix as nearly the time they will be ready as possible, in order that the Ship I may send for them may not be delayed. It will also be necessary to have provender for the cattle for at least one month; and it would be very desirable to have twelve tons of onions for the use of the Fleet, which, with care at this season, will, I should imagine, keep perfectly good. The price and weight of the bullocks being stated in your letter of the 26th July last, it only remains for me to observe, that the Captain sent on this service will receive the bullocks, onions, and hay, and give you bills on the Commissioners for Victualling his Majesty's Navy for the amount, I am, &c.,

NELSON AND BRONTE.

TO MR. RICHARD BROMELEY, PURSER, H.M. SHIP BELLEISLE.

[Order-Book.]

Victory, Madelena Islands, 1st November, 1803.

Having judged it necessary to proceed to this place for the purpose of completing the wood and water of His Majesty's Ships named in the margin,[2] and as the health of their Companies very much depends upon as frequent supplies of fresh beef, onions, &c. as can be procured ; it is my intention that every means shall be used to effect this purpose, and to procure as many live bullocks, &c. as can be had; I shall, therefore, gladly accept of your very disinterested offer of service on this occasion. Finding, however, that it is morally impossible to purchase any kind of refreshment for the Squadron at this place without ready money, (bills on the Victualling-Board not being negotiable) Captain Hardy, of his Majesty's Ship Victory, has very handsomely offered to lend such a number of dollars as may be wanted for the above purpose : You are, therefore, hereby required and directed to purchase as many live bullocks and onions as you can procure for the use of the said Squadron, together with two hundred head of sheep for the use of the sick on board the different Ships, as I find from the Governor of Madalena (to whom I wrote this morning on the subject of supplies, and also, to afford you every facility in his power) that it will be very difficult to procure the number of bullocks wanted for the Ships on so short notice ; and as the sheep at this place are very small, meagre, and inferior in quality, you are to supply them

[2] Victory, Kent, Canopus, Superb, Belleisle, Triumph, Renown, Stately, Cameleon.

as beef, and a Memorandum will be given directing the different Pursers to charge themselves with the produce as fresh beef, and issue them to the sick, accordingly.　In making the above purchase, the strictest attention is to be paid, that the bullocks, sheep, onions, and fodder, so procured for the use of the Squadron before mentioned, are good of their kind, and fit for His Majesty's Service, and that the sum paid for them is the lowest, and the market price usually charged; for the payment thereof, you will receive hard, or Spanish dollars from Captain Hardy of the Victory, giving him a receipt for the number you may require for the said purpose.　You are to charge yourself with the whole of the bullocks, sheep, &c. so purchased, as Purser of His Majesty's Ship Belleisle, and supply them to the different Ships, agreeable to such directions as you shall receive from the Captain of the Fleet, taking the necessary receipts from the Pursers for the bullocks, sheep, &c., they may be respectively supplied with; and you are to dispose of all the bullocks' hides and sheepskins which may be slaughtered, during our stay here (if possible) to the most advantage for Government, taking care that the best possible use is made of the ready money, and that the whole and every individual article is procured on the most reasonable terms, and that the vouchers for the said purchase are regularly and correctly made out, and the prices authenticated by the Governor and other principal inhabitants at Madalena; a set of which, including the receipts from the different Ships, you will transmit to the Commissioners of the Victualling Board by the first opportunity, and two sets to me, for purposes which I may judge necessary.

NELSON AND BRONTE.

TO CAPTAIN RYVES, H. M. SHIP GIBRALTAR.

[Autograph, in the possession of Captain George Frederick Ryves, C.B.]

Victory, November 2nd, 1803.

My dear Sir,

We anchored in Agincourt Sound yesterday evening, and I assure you that I individually feel all the obligation due to you for your most correct Chart, and directions for these Islands:

We worked the Victory every foot of the way, from Asinara to this anchorage, the wind blowing from Longo Sardo, under double-reefed topsails.   I shall write to the Admiralty stating how much they ought to feel obliged to your very great skill and attention in making this Survey.   This is absolutely one of the finest harbours I have ever seen.   I am, dear Sir, your obliged and obedient servant,

NELSON AND BRONTE.

TO CAPTAIN CRACRAFT, H.M. SHIP ANSON.

[Letter-Book.]

Victory, Madalena Islands, Sardinia, 5th November, 1803.

Sir,

Although it is my sincere wish to observe the strictest Neutrality in Sicily, yet it is certainly justifiable to attack any Vessel in a place from whence she makes her attack. Two Vessels were given up at Naples on this principle, being taken by the Boats of the Cyclops and Experiment, who were sent from the anchorage.   We have shown our complaisance in giving up one Privateer, but the conduct of the French is so contrary to all Neutrality that they must be punished, and I hope that the Neapolitan Government will approve of our proceedings.   I have wrote a complaint to Mr. Elliot on the subject of the unwarrantable conduct of these Privateers, on a complaint of Captain Hillyar's.   The conduct of Captain Raynsford[3] appears from his account to have been perfectly proper, and I am very much pleased with the spirited conduct of Lieutenant Lawrence,[4] which I beg you will communicate to him.   I am, with great esteem, &c.,

NELSON AND BRONTE.

---

[3] Captain Robert Raynsford. This unfortunate Officer commanded the Athenienne, 64, when that Ship was lost on the Esquerques, in the Mediterranean, on the 27th of October 1806, and, together with 347 of her crew, perished. " I urged Captain Raynsford," said one of the surviving Officers in his Narrative, " to save himself by swimming to the Launch, but in vain ; he declaring to me that he was perfectly resigned to his fate, and was determined not to quit his post whilst a man remained."—*Naval Chronicle*, vol. xvi. p. 191.

[4] This Officer has not been identified.

TO CAPTAIN CRACRAFT, H.M. SHIP ANSON.

[Letter-Book.]

Victory, at the Madalena Islands, 5th November, 1803.

Sir,

I have just received your letter of October 6th, telling me that Captain Richardson had fallen in with an Algerine Squadron of eleven Sail. I suspect they are not Algerines but Tunisians; but as each Corsair is obliged to produce a Certificate from our Consul, the truth of who they belong to is very easily ascertained, and I wish it to be done on every occasion on falling in with these gentry. I approve very much of your going up the Adriatic, and when you call at Corfu, you will see the necessity of paying great attention to the safety of our Ships in the Currant trade. I am, with great esteem, &c.,

NELSON AND BRONTE.

TO LIEUTENANT WILLIAM PEMBERTON, RESIDENT AGENT FOR TRANSPORTS, MALTA.

[Letter-Book.]

Victory, at the Madalena Islands, Sardinia, 5th November, 1803.

Sir,

You did right to send Lieutenant M'Culloch home; he could not be wanted here. I am glad the Vessel with water is ready, and you will receive an order to load a Vessel with provisions, which I beg may be done as expeditiously as possible. The Returns of Transports, and how they have been disposed of, I have received. I am, Sir, &c.

NELSON AND BRONTE.

TO NATHANIEL TAYLOR, ESQ., NAVAL STOREKEEPER, MALTA.

[Letter-Book.]

Victory, Madalena Islands, 5th November, 1803.

Sir,

I am favoured with your letter of October 29th. The hemp in butts must be put in one of the Transports coming to the

Fleet. I am glad that you have prepared a Transport to send up the Adriatic, and I judge she is sailed before this time. With respect to the making of rope, none under three-inch is necessary to be made for the Line of Battle Ships, and we can make as far as four-inch. The rope principally to be made at Malta is upwards of four-inch, our braces are four and a half inch, and lifts the same size; the Master Attendant will teach them in a day. Our Master-Ropemaker is a child of thirteen years of age, and the best Ropemaker in the Fleet. I am glad to receive the Cameleon so completely refitted, and if the Spider is in the miserable state she is represented to me, I desire she may be surveyed by the Master-Attendant and Builder, and if found so, to be refitted. We shall be very glad of more twine and slops; for this cruizing in the Gulf of Lyons is very bad for our sails, and warm slops will be truly acceptable. Something must be done to keep the water free under the Shears. The Officers of the Yard must take care of this, and repair the Punt, and employ proper people to clear it. In the time of the Order, the sale of the mud paid, I understand, the expenses. However, it must be cleared away, and speedily; for some of us will want to go under the Shears very soon. I am, &c.,

NELSON AND BRONTE.

TO PATRICK WILKIE, ESQ., AGENT VICTUALLER, MALTA.

[Letter-Book.]

Victory, Madalena Islands, Sardinia, 5th November, 1803.

Sir,

I have received your letter of October 26th, and you will receive directions from Captain Murray, for loading a Victualler with supplies for the Fleet; and I sincerely hope that no weevily bread will be sent, as the Fleet is free from those insects at present; and I beg that every exertion may be used in loading the Transport, as far as depends upon you. I am, Sir, &c.

NELSON AND BRONTE.

TO CAPTAIN SCHOMBERG, H. M. SHIP MADRAS, MALTA.

[Letter-Book.]

Victory, Madalena Islands, Sardinia, 5th November, 1803.

Sir,

The Raven will be put particularly under your orders for the various services which may be wanted, and not to exclude her from being sent to me if you should want to send her. She must immediately convoy the two Transports to the most secret Rendezvous herewith sent, and moor them in safety under the Fort, giving directions to the Masters to take care of their Ships and wait for my further orders; and I need not tell you to keep the Raven active. She sails so fast that no Privateer can get from her, I am sure ; but you must caution Captain Swaine,[4] and very strictly, in your orders, to keep his Convoy close in passing the Faro, if you have occasion to send him to Naples.

Convoys for the Archipelago and Adriatic, I trust, Captain Cracraft will furnish; for my wish is to confine the Raven as much as possible to the service of Malta, and this you will say to Sir Alexander Ball. With respect to bearing supernumerary *Officers* and men for the Packets, I do not conceive that you can bear any Officers by *rank* for wages and victuals. The fifty desired by Sir Alexander Ball, are borne, I suppose, for wages and victuals on board the Madras, and lent from her to the Packets : farther than that, I don't believe we can do with propriety. With respect to the petition of the Maltese, it is not mentioned where the Vessels are blockaded, nor dated : I cannot understand it. If it is in the Morea, Captain Cracraft has liberated them long before this time. I congratulate you on being confirmed,[5] and when I can, compatible with my other engagements, I shall certainly be glad to put you into a good Frigate, or to do anything else in my power to serve you, being with real esteem and regard, &c.,

NELSON AND BRONTE.

[4] Captain Spelman Swaine was Posted in May 1810, and is still living.

[5] Captain Schomberg's commission as Post-Captain was dated on the 6th of August, 1803.

TO THE RIGHT HONOURABLE WILLIAM DRUMMOND, AMBASSADOR AT CONSTANTINOPLE.

[From Clarke and M'Arthur, vol. ii. p. 338.]

[Apparently about 5th November, 1803.]

The particular situation of our Country at this moment, prevents the Admiralty from furnishing me with Frigates and smaller Vessels; therefore I must equally regret with your Excellency the not being able to send any directly to Constantinople. I feel very happy that my conduct is still satisfactory to the Sublime Porte, my zeal and activity they may fully rely upon; but it may be possible, that, notwithstanding all my care and attention, the French Fleet will escape me, and get to Egypt or the Morea before I can come up with them; that they are bound there I have very little doubt: therefore I would strongly recommend the Turkish Government to be upon its guard; being at Peace with so treacherous a people as the French, is no security against an attack. The last report was, October 26th, eight Sail of the Line ready for sea, six Frigates, and five or six Corvettes: they had been pressing in every part to get men, and 5000 Troops are ready for embarkation. Every hour I expect to hear of their sailing. I am, &c.,

NELSON AND BRONTE.[6]

TO SIR ALEXANDER JOHN BALL, BART., MALTA.

[Autograph, in the possession of Sir William Keith Ball, Bart.]

Victory, Madalena Islands, November 7th, 1803.

My dear Ball,

Captain Staines delivered me your kind letter two days ago. As I expect Mr. Falcon every moment, I shall take the first opportunity of settling our business with the Dey of Algiers. The documents which I have received from you are perfectly regular. I wish we may be able to get over the Sicilian Vessels, but that I doubt being able to accomplish.

---

[6] "7th of November. I had the comfort of making an old Agamemnon, George Jones, a Gunner into the Cameleon Brig."—*Private Diary*, in Clarke and M'Arthur.

Apropos, our Vessels make so many mistakes, and call every Barbary Cruizer an Algerine, that I fear, if we should go to war with that State, that some untoward mistakes may happen. But I believe each Cruizer is obliged to produce a Certificate from our Consul of the State she belongs to; pray tell me if I am correct. I am glad to find that you are so well pleased with the Minister from Tunis. I send you an extract of my letter to Mr. Elliot, in answer to his about a coolness between you and Sir John Acton; and also an extract of a letter from Madrid, and Captain Swaine was at Barcelona on October 13th, therefore I do not think a Spanish War so near. We are more likely to go to War with Spain for her complaisance to the French; but the French can gain nothing, but be great losers, by forcing Spain to go to War with us; therefore, I never expect that the Spaniards will begin, unless Buonaparte is absolutely *mad*, as many say he is. What! he begins to find excuses! I thought he would invade England in the face of the Sun! Now he wants a three-days' fog, that never yet happened! and if it did, how is his Craft to be kept together? He will soon find more excuses or there will be an end of Buonaparte, and may the Devil take him!

Our two last reconnoiterings: Toulon has eight Sail of the Line, apparently ready for sea, five or six Frigates, and as many Corvettes—they count twenty-two Sail of Ships of War; a Seventy-four is repairing; whether they intend waiting for her I can't tell, but I expect them every hour to put to sea, and with Troops, but their destination?—is it *Ireland* or the *Levant?* That is what I want to know. However, out they will come, and, I trust, we shall meet them. The event, with God's blessing on our exertions, we ought not to doubt; I really believe that we are the ' strong pull and pull together.' With this force opposed to me, I cannot with prudence leave myself with less than six Sail of the Line, and from various circumstances, Ships going to water, &c., I am too often with only five Frigates, and Smaller Vessels I am most distressed for. However, I send the Raven to be under Captain Schomberg's particular orders, for upon every occasion I had rather leave myself bare than have my friends complain. Lord St. Vincent's words are, ' We can send you neither Ships or Men, and with the resources of your

mind, you will do without them very well.' Bravo, my Lord!
I have all the inclination in the world to send Sir Richard
Bickerton to Malta, but I dare not do it at this moment—not
so much for the want of the Ship, but from my sincere esteem
for the Admiral, and in charity to them both; for if the
Battle took place and Sir Richard absent, they would have
reason to curse me for ever. But you may assure her Ladyship [7] that I know *what* attachment is, and that the Admiral
shall be the first detached after the Battle; and if I can, on
any belief that the Enemy are not coming immediately to sea,
he shall go before the Battle. Remember me kindly to
Macaulay [8] and all our friends at Malta. I admire your Malta
Gazettes; it is the custom, and a very bad one, for the
English, never to tell their own story, and you have put it
well together. This Anchorage is certainly one of the best I
have met with for a Fleet—water, brooms, sand, onions, some
beef, plenty of sheep, and but little of aqua denta; but I suppose the French will take it now we have used it. I am
ever, my dear Ball, most sincerely and faithfully yours,

NELSON AND BRONTE.

No wonder Neutral Powers complain, when we do not
send out a Judge of the Admiralty : it is cruel both to the
Detainer, and the Neutral.

TO THE RESPECTIVE CAPTAINS AND COMMANDERS OF HIS
MAJESTY'S SHIPS AND VESSELS ON THE MEDITERRANEAN
STATION.

[From a Copy in the Nelson Papers.]

Victory, Madalena Islands, 7th November, 1803.

Memorandum.

Lord Nelson is very sorry to find that notwithstanding his
forgiveness of the men who deserted in Spain, it has failed to
have its proper effect, and that there are still men who so far
forget their duty to their King and Country, as to desert the
Service, at a time when every man in England is in arms to

---

[7] Lady Bickerton, who was then at Malta. She was Anne, daughter of James
Athill, Esq. of Antigua.

[8] Mr. Alexander Macaulay, Treasurer of Malta.

defend it against the French.   Therefore Lord Nelson desires that it may be perfectly understood, that if any man be so infamous as to desert from the Service in future, he will not only be brought to a Court-Martial, but that if the sentence should be *Death*, it will be most assuredly carried into execution.

NELSON AND BRÔNTE.

TO MAJOR-GENERAL VILLETTES, MALTA.

[From Clarke and M'Arthur, vol. ii. p. 338.]

7th November, 1803.

My dear General,

I certainly think that the Navy ought to have had a regular Hospital at Malta, and not to have thrown the trouble of attending our Seamen on the Medical skill of the Army; and whenever Sir Richard Bickerton and Dr. Snipe go to Malta, I intend they shall examine the large house on the opposite side to you, which will be a very fit place for a Marine Hospital.   I am very much obliged to you for the 100 shells, I have no doubt we shall have occasion to use them; if the Enemy run into Port, I shall not be very delicate where the place is.   Your kindness, my dear General, I have experienced on every occasion, and your readiness to serve us is acknowledged by all the Fleet. . . I agree with you, that unless Buonaparte is absolutely mad, and that the people about him are so likewise, he will not wish to throw Sicily entirely into our hands, in order to revenge himself of the King of Naples, much less force Spain into a War which must so much injure the French cause : to us it matters not being at War with Spain.   We may be forced to go to War with her for her complaisance to the French; but I never can believe, that Buonaparte's counsellors are such fools as to force Spain to begin, and of course give us all her riches and commerce. The War would not cost us one farthing more than at present. I intend to leave this anchorage on Wednesday, and get *home*[9] again : although I have two good Frigates watching them, yet I like to be at hand in case of need.   I am, &c.,

NELSON AND BRONTE.

[9] Off Toulon.

TO ARCHIBALD MACNEILL, ESQ., MALTA.

[Letter-Book. " Thursday, 10th November, 5 A.M. Weighed and made sail to the Eastward, with the Fleet in company."—*Victory's Log.*]

Victory, at Sea, November 10th, 1803.

Sir,

I have been favoured with your letters of November the 4th and 6th. I own I very much doubt the possibility of taking on board cattle from an Enemy's Coast; the French keep too good a look out. As for communicating with Mr. Grant, that will take up all the winter; but I am sure it is impossible for our Ships to go upon that Coast in the winter. I know every part of it most perfectly. When you can have the bullocks to ship at Gaeta, it may be a consideration, but I look even for that as so uncertain, that I am this day sending the Transport to Malta; but if you think you can get one hundred good bullocks for us at Gaeta, and will mention the time when they can be shipped, and will send me word by the Transports coming to the Fleet with provisions, I will send for them; but we are by no means in distress, and never was a Fleet in better health. In our very uncertain state, I cannot recommend any speculation in Sardinia: I may never go there again. I am very sorry for the trouble you have taken in writing to Tuscany. If you had asked any Seaman used to that Coast, he would have told you of the impossibility of a Ship's waiting on that part of the Coast. I have the honour to be, &c.

NELSON AND BRONTE.

TO SIR EVAN NEPEAN, BART., ADMIRALTY.

[Original, in the Admiralty. On the 13th of November, the Fleet anchored in Figaroni Roads, on the North Side of Corsica, and sailed on the 15th.]

Victory, at Sea, November 16th, 1803.

Sir,

I herewith transmit you, for the information of the Lords Commissioners of the Admiralty, a copy of a letter from Captain Cracraft, of his Majesty's Ship Anson, together with a copy of the one therein alluded to, from Captain Raynsford of the Morgiana, giving an account of the capture of a French Privateer, on the Coast of Sicily, which, under all the circumstances, I have approved of. And I am sorry to observe that the Enemy's Privateers make a very improper use of the Sicilian Ports, from whence they commit depredations on our Trade. I have wrote Mr. Elliot, his Majesty's Minister at Naples on this subject, and desired that an official complaint may be made to that Court on the occasion. I am, Sir, &c.

NELSON AND BRONTE.

TO SIR EVAN NEPEAN, BART., ADMIRALTY.

[Original, in the Admiralty. " Wednesday, 16th November, A.M. Stately in chase of a Brig, S.S.W., and the Cameleon in chase of a Schooner, S.W.; brought them to; which proved to be a French Schooner, Le Rénard, from Calvi, having the Brig under convoy, with French Troops."—*Victory's Log.*]

Victory, at Sea, November 16th, 1803.

Sir,

You will please to acquaint the Lords Commissioners of the Admiralty, that this morning the Squadron under my command captured Le Rénard, French National Schooner, mounting twelve four-pounders, with six swivels, and manned with eighty men; also Le Titus, Transport, having on board ninety-six soldiers from Corsica, bound to Toulon. The Schooner and Transport are gone to Malta under charge of the Stately. I am, Sir, &c.

NELSON AND BRONTE.[1]

[1] On the 22nd of November, the following " Memorandum," was addressed " To the respective Captains and Commanders of his Majesty's Ships and Vessels on the Mediterranean Station:"—

" If a Pendant be shown over Signal No. 36, [*i. e.*, to ' Engage the Enemy on their Starboard or Weather side,'] it signifies that Ships are to engage on the Enemy's starboard side, whether going large or upon the wind.

" If a Pendant be shown in the like manner over Signal No. 37, [*i. e.*, to ' Engage the Enemy on their Larboard or Lee side,'] it signifies that Ships are to engage on the Enemy's larboard side, whether going large or upon a wind; these additions to be noted in the Signal Book in pencil only.

" Saint George's Ensigns are to be worn by every Ship in Action.

" GEO. MURRAY."—*Order-Book.*

TO CAPTAIN CRACRAFT, H. M. SHIP ANSON.

[From a Copy, in the Nelson Papers.]

Victory, off Toulon, 23rd November, 1803.

Sir,

You will take every means in your power for the effectual protection of our Trade in the Adriatic, and in the Mouth of the Archipelago, and give such Convoys as may be wanted, not only from Malta, but also from Trieste, Venice, Fiume, Patras, Zante, &c. The French Fleet are ready for sea, but where they are bound I cannot tell you. Some reports say to the Morea, or Egypt; others out of the Mediterranean. I am, &c.

NELSON AND BRONTE.

TO SIR EVAN NEPEAN, BART., ADMIRALTY.

[Original, in the Admiralty.]

Victory, off Toulon, 24th November, 1803.

Sir,

I have received your letter of the 5th September last, together with the copy of the one therein mentioned, from Messrs. Holland and Co. of Trieste, respecting the capture of three Merchant Vessels bound from that Port to London, and signifying their Lordships' direction to make some arrangement for affording protection to the Trade in the Adriatic; in answer to which you will please to acquaint the Lords Commissioners of the Admiralty, that the strictest regard has been paid to the protection of our Commerce in the Adriatic, and every other part in these Seas, as you will observe by my letter of the 2nd September, and the Disposition of the Fleet under my command, which accompanied my letters of the 6th September, and the 8th ultimo. You will also please to acquaint their Lordships that I have directed Captain Cracraft to afford Convoy to the Trade of his Majesty's Subjects from the different Ports in the Adriatic, bound to Malta, whenever he shall learn there are any in want thereof, and on no account to suffer them (so far as it depends upon him) to sail without protection, for which and other services mentioned in the Disposition of the 8th September, the Ships and Vessels named in the margin[4] are placed under his command. But it is to be observed that the Masters of the Merchantmen frequently proceed when they judge proper, without either applying or waiting for the necessary Convoy, and I have reason to believe that the Ships alluded to in your before mentioned letter, fall under that description.

As I feel the protection of our Commerce a very essential and important part of my duty, their Lordships may be assured that everything which remains with me shall be done, to prevent any of the Trade of his Majesty's Subjects from falling into the hands of the Enemy. I am, Sir, &c.

NELSON AND BRONTE.

TO SIR EVAN NEPEAN, BART., ADMIRALTY.

[Original, in the Admiralty.]

Victory, off Toulon, 24th November, 1803.

Sir,

I yesterday received your letter of the 24th September, acquainting me that it was their Lordships' intention, in order to enable me to apply a sufficient force to watch the French Squadron at Toulon, and attend to other services, to order the Excellent to take charge of the outward-bound Convoy from Portsmouth, and to follow my orders; and that it is also their Lordships' intention to send out Line of Battle Ships with any future Convoys, to enable me to send home, in the same manner, any of the two-decked Ships under my command which, from their long continuance abroad, or other circumstances, may be rendered inefficient. You will please to acquaint the Lords Commissioners of the Admiralty, that due regard shall be paid in sending home all future Convoys under Ships of the above description, and that none shall be kept in this Country but what may be absolutely necessary for watching the Enemies' Ships in Toulon and in Cadiz, and for the protection of our Commerce in these seas. I am, Sir, your most obedient, humble servant,

NELSON AND BRONTE.

[4] Anson, Juno, Arrow, Bittern, Morgiana.

TO SIR EVAN NEPEAN, BART., ADMIRALTY.

[Original, in the Admiralty.]

Victory, off Toulon, 24th November, 1803.

Sir,

You will please to acquaint the Lords Commissioners of the Admiralty, that the Honourable Captain Boyle of the Seahorse, who reconnoitred the French Squadron at Toulon yesterday, acquainted me that there are eight Sail of the Line, eight Frigates, and five or six Corvettes in the Outer Road, all newly painted, and apparently in a perfect state of readiness for sea, with their sails bent; and that there is, in his opinion, one or two Sail of the Line in the Arsenal equipping (he judges from the distance between the topmasts). The weather being perfectly clear, Captain Boyle's account may be depended upon, particularly as it corresponds with the information formerly received. I am, Sir, &c.

NELSON AND BRONTE.

P.S.—2nd December. The Enemy's Squadron at Toulon, reconnoitred to-day, remain the same as stated above.

TO SIR EVAN NEPEAN, BART., ADMIRALTY.

[Original, in the Admiralty.]

Victory, off Toulon, 24th November, 1803.

Sir,

The Fleet being very short of wood and water, you will please to acquaint the Lords Commissioners of the Admiralty, that I judged it better to go to the Madalena Islands in order to obtain it, than to separate the Fleet, as by experience it is found almost impossible, in the continued gales of wind at this season, for any Ship to be certain of joining in any given time; I therefore left Frigates off Toulon, and proceeded to the Madalena Islands, where having procured wood and water and some refreshments, I returned to my Rendezvous. The Chart of Captain Ryves, which the Board has received, is the most correct thing I ever met with. The Fleet worked up from Asinara, with a strong East wind, to the anchorage, with perfect ease, from the Chart and directions; and Captain Ryves deserves the greatest credit for the accuracy of his Chart and remarks. The remarks I send you, and I would recommend their insertion on the Chart. I am, Sir, &c.

NELSON AND BRONTE.

TO HIS EXCELLENCY HUGH ELLIOT, ESQ., NAPLES.

[Autograph, in the Elliot Papers.]

Victory, off Toulon, November 24th, 1803.

My dear Sir,

The Raven joined from Naples, as we were weighing from the Madalena Islands; and yesterday the Excellent, seventy-four, joined from England. I send Sir John Acton's dispatches, _viâ_ Malta, to Messina, and so overland; for I have no Vessel which I can send to Naples. Your letter from Lord Minto—at least, the letter which I supposed came from him, was sent in your packet either by Gibraltar or some Vessel before her. It had 'Evan Nepean' wrote on the outside and was a short thick letter.

Lord Hobart writes me[5] in confidence that they would not

---

[5] The following is a Copy of Lord Hobart's Letter to Lord Nelson:—

"Private and Confidential.   "Downing Street, Sept. 22nd, 1803.

"My dear Lord,

"I am to acknowledge your Lordship's private letter of the 18th of July, and although I much regret that General Villettes had not felt himself at liberty to hold out the expectation of his being able, _at the time he wrote to your Lordship,_ to spare a larger force than one thousand men for the defence of Messina, I should hope it would not be very long before it might be in his power to increase it. With every deference, however, for your opinion, I cannot think I should have been justified in leaving no discretion with General Villettes in the execution of the order in question. In the course of a few days the Chasseurs Britanniques will embark from Jersey for Malta. They are rather more than four hundred and forty strong; and to that extent will add to the means of detaching from that Island, and as we gain strength at home, which we are doing very fast, we shall augment our forces in the Mediterranean.

"It would certainly have been desirable not to have brought away so large a proportion of the troops that had served in Egypt; but the state of our Army at home rendered it absolutely unavoidable. The official communication you will receive from me upon the subject of the Pacha of Yanina, if the information of Mr. Hamilton be correct, may lead to important consequences; but the management of the business will require the full exercise of all your discretion. The first object, of course, must be to ascertain how far the Port of Panormo, and the advantages it is stated to be capable of producing, be such as they are described. The next, the practica-

U 2

have drawn all the Egyptian Army from the Mediterranean, but that it was necessary in the state of England as to Troops, and the preparations of the Enemy, had they profited of the moment, but that as they get strength in England, they will send troops here. 500 are coming out, and Dillon's is to be re-established : therefore, your Son's 80 men will be a good beginning. The French force, yesterday, at two o'clock, was correctly ascertained—eight Sail of the Line, eight Frigates, and five or six Corvettes, perfectly ready, and as fine as paint can make them. A ninth Ship is visibly getting forward. I only hope in God we shall meet them. Our weather-beaten Ships, I have no fears, will make their sides like a plum-pudding. As to news, I can tell you none. We have nothing later than September 29th, from Portsmouth. I am ever, my dear Sir, your most faithful servant,

NELSON AND BRONTE.

bility of maintaining a position there, without the application of greater means than it may be in our power to furnish. Satisfied upon these points I should hope it would not be difficult for you to enable Mr. Drummond to convince the Porte that we can have no object in looking for an establishment at Panormo, but that of having it more effectually in our power to protect European Turkey against the intrigues and eventual attacks of the French. Whilst, however, the Turkish Government are thus secretly apprised of the steps we are taking, it would probably be advisable for them to appear ignorant upon the subject, as in that case, they will avoid being in any shape committed with the French, on account of the measures we may pursue with the Pacha, whose notorious independence of the Porte (though nominally subject to it) would easily exculpate that Government from the charge of being a party to the transaction. The Pacha must also be managed; and the whole business, as far as the Turkish Government can be effected, be made to appear to originate with us. You will observe that it is his wish that we should make no communication of our intentions to Constantinople.

" Our intercourse with Russia continues friendly, but it is difficult to anticipate the effect of the French intrigue, which is carried on with uncommon activity, and not without success. Mr. Frere will apprise you of the situation of things in Spain. From Lisbon, you will, I take for granted, have heard that General Lannes has obtained a complete ascendancy, and that we are to look for nothing at that Court, but implicit obedience to the dictates of France.

" I am afraid even the circumstance of some of your Ships being crippled will not induce *your friends at Toulon* to come out. It was the Port from whence they took their departure for Aboukir ; and whilst the memorable events which took place there remain impressed upon their minds, they will not encounter a Fleet under the command of Lord Nelson, if they can avoid it. With those ideas which naturally suggest themselves in the contemplation of that subject, believe me ever, my dear Lord, with the most sincere respect and regard, most faithfully yours, " HOBART.

" P.S.—Mr. Addington desires me to say he will write in a few days by another opportunity."—*Autograph.*

I have given my friend Doctor Nudi a letter of introduction to you. He is a good man, a clever man, and was a
great friend of Sir William and Lady Hamilton. Your kind
notice of him will much oblige me.

November 25th.—I send you a copy of a letter sent me,
that you may see the conduct of the French Privateers.

N. AND B.

We are in a hard gale of wind.

TO SIR JOHN ACTON, BART., NAPLES.

[From Clarke and M'Arthur, vol. ii. p. 339.]

Off Toulon, 24th November, 1803.

On the 9th, I sailed from the Madalena Islands. We have
had a very bad passage, and much blowing weather, but our
Ships have not suffered any material damage. The French
Fleet yesterday at two o'clock, was in appearance in high
feather, and as fine as paint could make them; eight Sail of
the Line, eight Frigates, and several Corvettes were ready for
sea. One Ship of the Line was fitting in the Arsenal, her
topmasts on end. This is their state; but when they may sail,
or where they will go, I am very sorry to say is a secret I am
not acquainted with. Our weather-beaten Ships, I have no
fears, will make their sides like a plum-pudding. Lord Hobart
says, as they increase in force at home, which is doing rapidly,
that they will not forget an additional one for the Mediterranean. The general orders to support the King of Naples
are repeated; and I shall only assure your Excellency, that
the defence of their Majesties and their Kingdoms is always
nearest my heart. The Excellent, 74, Captain Sotheron,[6] has
joined me from England. I am, &c.,

NELSON AND BRONTE.

---

[6] Captain Frank Sotheron, of the Excellent, has been already mentioned.
Vide vol. iv. p. 381: he died an Admiral of the White, in February 1839.

TO HIS EXCELLENCY HUGH ELLIOT, ESQ.

[Autograph, in the Elliot Papers.]

Victory, at Sea, November 24th, 1803.

My dear Sir,

I beg leave to introduce to your Excellency, Doctor Nudi, who is not *only* a good man, but a most able professional man. He is a great friend of mine, and was always so of dear Sir William and Lady Hamilton. Any kindnesses your Excellency may show him will ever be esteemed a favour conferred upon your most obliged and obedient servant,

NELSON AND BRONTE.

TO CAPTAIN CRACRAFT, H.M. SHIP ANSON.

[Letter-Book.]

Victory, off Toulon, 25th November, 1803.

Sir,

You will take every means in your power, for the effectual protection of our Trade in the Adriatic, and in the Mouth of the Archipelago, and give such Convoys as may be wanted, not only from Malta, but also, from Trieste, Venice, Fiume, Patras, Zante, &c.; the French Fleet are ready for Sea, but where they are bound I cannot tell you; some reports say to the Morea, or Egypt; others, out of the Mediterranean. I am, Sir, &c.,

NELSON AND BRONTE.

TO DOCTOR JOHN SNIPE, PHYSICIAN TO THE FLEET.

[Letter-Book.]

Victory, off Toulon, 25th November, 1803.

Sir,

The Commissioners for taking care of Sick and Hurt Seamen and Marines, having acquainted me that they had appointed Mr. John Gray to be Surgeon of a Naval Hospital intended to be established at Malta, I am, therefore, to desire you will proceed immediately, in his Majesty's Ship Narcissus, to Malta, for the purpose of examining the situation and necessary accommodations of such Hospital, previous to its being

occupied as such; and, as it has been mentioned to me by the
Admirals and Captains who have served in the Mediterranean
for some considerable time, that the situation of the former
Naval Hospital at Malta was particularly unhealthy, it is my
directions that you do not suffer that house to be received as
an Hospital, or any other which, from situation, you may judge
improper; but endeavour to procure a convenient and well-
appointed house, in an airy and healthy situation, for a Naval
Hospital *pro tempore,* until such time as Government shall
take the necessary measures for building, or otherwise providing, a convenient and proper Hospital. If such accommodations cannot at present be had, you will beg Major-General
Villettes to allow Mr. Gray the use of the Wards in the
Military Hospital at present appropriated for the Seamen,
until the necessary arrangements can be made for their reception into some other place. I am, &c.,

NELSON AND BRONTE.

P.S.—You will order Mr. Gray to transmit to the Commissioners for Sick and Wounded Seamen an account agreeable
to the letter and form herewith inclosed; also similar Returns
to be made to me for my information. The letter and form
you will bring with you, and deliver to me on your return by
the Narcissus.

TO SPIRIDION FORESTI, ESQ., CORFU.

[From Clarke and M'Arthur, vol. ii. p. 340.]

Off Toulon, November 25th, 1803.

I should wish to know whether . . . . . [7] has the power to
grant us any particular privileges in trade, and if so, what
they are? I am told he has the finest forests for building
Ships of the Line, and that vast quantities of hemp may be
grown in his Government; and I should be glad to know what
of our manufactures he could take, and to what amount. I
have desired Captain . . . . to look at the Port, and ascertain
whether it be capable of holding the Fleet under my command,
and of supplying all our wants. I am really much interested

---

[7] The names and places left blank in this letter, may be ascertained from Lord
Nelson's letter to Lord Hobart, in p. 325, post.

for . . . . : he has always been a staunch friend to the English, and most particularly kind to me ; and if I should ever go to Corfu, I shall certainly, if he be within a few days' reach, go to see him. As I have done before, so I have again written to Mr. Hammond,[8] and desired him a second time to speak to Lord Hawkesbury on the subject of at least making good your losses, and that, in my opinion, you ought to be rewarded for considerable sufferings, and for your unshaken attachment to Great Britain. Your attention to every part of your duty, leaves me nothing to recommend. I am, &c.,

NELSON AND BRONTE.

TO CAPTAIN SCHOMBERG, H.M. SHIP MADRAS, MALTA.

[Letter-Book.]

Victory, off Toulon, 25th November, 1803.

Sir,

If the Raven has not sailed with the Transports to join me, I have directed either Stately or Narcissus to take them under their Convoy, in order that the Raven may be at your disposal for the various services required of her. I have wrote to Captain Cracraft to give every facility in Convoys; and we must endeavour that our Commerce, both in the Adriatic and Levant, is kept in circulation, and protected from the French Privateers. I am, &c.

NELSON AND BRONTE.

TO CAPTAIN PARKER,[9] H.M. SHIP AMAZON.

[From a Copy, in the Nelson Papers.]

Victory, off Toulon, 25th November, 1803.

Sir,

The Jalouse will probably be wanted to see the Ship bound to Smyrna to her destination; but I hope some of Captain Cracraft's Squadron will be in the way to see our Convoy safe up the Adriatic, for I am so much in distress for Frigates that the Amazon will be a most important acquisition, espe-

---

[8] George Hammond, Esq., Under Secretary of State for Foreign Affairs, afterwards Minister Plenipotentiary in America.

[9] Now Vice-Admiral Sir William Parker, Bart., G.C.B.

cially as the French Fleet is attended by no less than eight
Frigates; therefore, I shall rejoice to see the Amazon. I
am, Sir, &c.,

NELSON AND BRONTE.

TO J. B. GIBERT, ESQ., HIS MAJESTY'S VICE-CONSUL, BARCELONA.

[Letter-Book.]

Victory, off Toulon, 25th November, 1803.

Sir,

Captain Staines of his Majesty's Sloop Cameleon, will
deliver you two letters, and three for his Excellency Mr.
Frere and Mr. Hunter, which you will be good enough to
forward by the first opportunity to Madrid. I must beg you
will be so obliging as to give me all the political news with
respect to the situation of our two Countries, which I am very
anxious to know, and hope they remain in every respect
friendly to each other. Captain Staines is good enough to
undertake the execution of some commissions for me in the
stock way, and I shall be much obliged by your friendly
assistance in procuring the several articles. I am, &c.,

NELSON AND BRONTE.

TO J. HOOKHAM FRERE, ESQ., MINISTER AT MADRID.

[From Clarke and M'Arthur, vol. ii. p. 340.]

28th November, 1803.

I have the honour to enclose, for your Excellency's information, two letters which will mark the conduct of the Spaniards
towards us, and of which I doubt not but you will seriously
complain. I trust that we shall be received in the Spanish
Ports in the same manner as the French. I am ready to
make large allowances for the miserable situation Spain has
placed herself in; but there is a certain line beyond which I
cannot submit to be treated with disrespect. We have given
up French Vessels taken within gun-shot of the Spanish shore,
and yet French Vessels are permitted to attack our Ships
from the Spanish shore. Your Excellency may assure the
Spanish Government, that in whatever place the Spaniards

allow the French to attack us, in that place I shall order the French to be attacked.   The old order of 1771, now put in force against us, is infamous; and I trust your Excellency will take proper steps, that the present mode of enforcing it be done away—it is gross partiality and not Neutrality.   I am, &c.,

NELSON AND BRONTE.

TO LIEUTENANT ————.

[From Clarke and M'Arthur, vol. ii. p. 339.]

November, 1803.

I have just received your letter, and I am truly sorry that any difference should arise between your Captain, who has the reputation of being one of the bright Officers of the Service, and yourself, a very young man, and a very young Officer, who must naturally have much to learn; therefore the chance is that you are perfectly wrong in the disagreement. However, as your present situation must be very disagreeable, I will certainly take an early opportunity of removing you, provided your conduct to your present Captain be such, that another may not refuse to receive you.   I am, &c.,

NELSON AND BRONTE.

TO HIS EXCELLENCY THE FRENCH ADMIRAL.

[Letter-Book.]

Victory, at Sea, December 4th, 1803.

Sir,

Although my Flag of Truce was treated so unkindly[9] when I wished to send you a letter relative to an Exchange of Prisoners, by being kept several hours under Sepet, and then ordered off in a very uncivil manner, which I am sure must have been unknown to you, yet, when the comfort of so many individuals is at stake, I again take this opportunity of offering an Exchange of Prisoners of War; therefore, whenever you please to send to Malta any number of English Prisoners of

[9] Vide ante.

War, I will direct as many French to be returned, and I shall be glad of this occasion of allowing of a number of your Officers to return on their parole of honour until they shall be regularly exchanged by an arrangement between our Governments. I have the honour to remain, &c.,

NELSON AND BRONTE.

TO SIR EVAN NEPEAN, BART., ADMIRALTY.

[Original, in the Admiralty.]

Victory, at Sea, 4th December, 1803.

Sir,

I herewith transmit you a Report of Survey on the main and mizen rigging belonging to his Majesty's Ship Excellent, together with a memorandum from Captain Sotheron attached to the said Report, which you will please to lay before the Lords Commissioners of the Admiralty for their information. It is much to be lamented that a Ship so recently from England, and coming direct abroad from a King's Yard, should have sailed in such a state; the Master-Attendant at Portsmouth must either have been blind to the situation of the rigging, or not have given himself trouble to discover its miserable state. I am, Sir, &c.,

NELSON AND BRONTE.

P.S.—Inclosed is a letter from Captain Conn of the Canopus, to the Captain of the Fleet, by which their Lordships will observe how bare of the necessary stores that Ship is, and that she has no shroud-hawser on board.

NELSON AND BRONTE.

TO CAPTAIN MOUBRAY, H. M. SHIP ACTIVE.

[Letter-Book.]

Victory, at Sea, 5th December, 1803.

Sir,

I have to desire that you will proceed off Toulon, with the Ships under your orders, immediately on receipt of this letter; but if you have any particular object that you may judge it necessary to keep a Frigate for a few days longer in the Gulf of Genoa, in that case you are at liberty either to stay yourself, or leave the Phœbe for that particular service. Herewith you will receive the present probable Rendezvous of the Squadron. You will find orders for your further proceedings on your arrival off Toulon, on board the Frigate watching the Enemy at that Port. I am, &c.,

NELSON AND BRONTE.

P.S.—Immediately on receipt of this, I am to desire you will dispatch Sir William Bolton, in his Majesty's Sloop Childers, to join me at St. Pierres, near the Island of Sardinia.

TO CAPTAIN MOUBRAY, H.M. SHIP ACTIVE.

[Order-Book.]

Victory, at Sea, 5th December, 1803.

Secret.

Whereas it is of the utmost importance that the Enemy's Squadron in Toulon should be most strictly watched, and that I should be made acquainted with their sailing and route with all dispatch, should they put to sea, You are therefore hereby required and directed to employ his Majesty's Ship Active, under your command, on the above service, together with the Phœbe or any other Ship which may join you from Malta; and as it is my intention to proceed with the Squadron immediately to St. Pierre's, near the Island of Sardinia, (where I shall remain till about the 14th of this month), you will instantly on receipt of this, dispatch His Majesty's Sloop Childers to join me at St. Pierre's; and as the Squadron will leave that Island as soon after the 14th as possible, and proceed direct to the Rendezvous herewith transmitted, where I shall remain, unless deemed necessary to proceed off Algiers—in which case the Squadron will not be longer absent from the enclosed Rendezvous than two or three days at furthest, should the Enemy's Squadron, or any part of it, put to sea in the meantime, or you obtain any intelligence necessary for my immediate information, you are to dispatch a Frigate to St. Pierres, near the Island of Sardinia, with an account thereof, where instructions will be left for her Commander where to find me, should I have quitted that anchorage. And you are also to proceed immediately in the Active to the enclosed

Rendezvous, where the Squadron will be found, unless, as is before-mentioned, it should become necessary for me to make my appearance off Algiers for a day or two. You are only to keep the Active and another Frigate for this service, and dispatch any other Ship or Vessel which may join you off Toulon, to St. Pierres, or to the Rendezvous which accompanies this, should you judge that I have left the former place. You are to continue on this service until relieved, or you receive my orders for your further proceedings.   I have directed the Honourable Captain Boyle to join me at St. Pierres, the moment he is relieved from watching the Enemy at Toulon.

NELSON AND BRONTE.

N.B.—The Rendezvous, No 97, alluded to in the above order, is transmitted to you in my letter of this date.

TO COMMISSIONER OTWAY, AT GIBRALTAR.

[Letter-Book.]

Victory, at Sea, 6th December, 1803.

Sir,

I have received your letters of the 2nd ultimo, on the subject of the scarcity of stores at Gibraltar Yard, which I am very well aware must be the case; but before any could be returned you in the William, Store-Ship, from Malta, the Hindostan will have arrived from England, when you must take a small quantity of such articles of cordage, &c., as may be wanted for the use of His Majesty's Ships in your vicinity; and as the Ships watching the Enemy off Toulon are much in want of spars and sails, the Hindostan must be held in readiness to join me off that place, or on such other Rendezvous as I may find expedient.   The Convoy sent for her will have my instructions on that head.   I am, &c.,

NELSON AND BRONTE.

TO SIR EVAN NEPEAN, BART., ADMIRALTY.

[Original, in the Admiralty.]

Victory, at Sea, 6th December, 1803.

Sir,

I herewith transmit you a letter from Mr. Joseph King,[1] Boatswain of the Guerrier, Sheer-hulk at Gibraltar, dated the 3rd ultimo, requesting for the reasons therein set forth, that I would appoint him Boatswain of the Dock-Yard at that place, which you will please to lay before the Lords Commissioners of the Admiralty for their consideration ; and to say that I believe Mr. King to be a very deserving good man. I am, &c.,

NELSON AND BRONTE.

TO HIS ROYAL HIGHNESS THE DUKE OF CLARENCE.

[From Clarke and M'Arthur, vol. ii. p. 341.]

Off Toulon, December 7th, 1803.

The French Fleet keep us waiting for them during a long and severe winter's cruise; and such a place as all the Gulf of Lyons, for gales of wind from the N.W. to N.E., I never saw ; but by always going away large, we generally lose much of their force and the heavy sea of the gulf. However, by the great care and attention of every Captain, we have suffered much less than could have been expected. I hope now to be allowed to call Keats my friend. He is very much recovered, and cheerful; he is a treasure to the Service. By the French Papers, which we have to November 19th, we are in momentary expectation of Buonaparte's descent upon England ; and although I can have no fears for the event, yet there is, I hope, a natural anxiety to hear what is passing at so critical a moment, when everything we hold dear in this world is at stake. I trust in God, Buonaparte will be destroyed, and that then the French may be brought, if the Powers of Europe have either spirit or honour, to reasonable terms of Peace : that this may be soon, and with honour to our Country, is my fervent prayer, and shall ever be my most ardent endeavour. I am, &c.,   NELSON AND BRONTE.

[1] Vide vol. i. p. 257.

TO SIR EVAN NEPEAN, BART., ADMIRALTY.

[Original, in the Admiralty.]

Victory, at Sea, 10th December, 1803.

Sir,

Having judged it necessary to proceed with the Squadron to the Madalena Islands, in order to complete the wood and water of the respective Ships, and to procure such refreshments for their Companies as the place would afford, you will please to acquaint the Lords Commissioners of the Admiralty, that, from the very handsome supply of dollars from Captain Hardy, of the Victory, and the disinterested services of Mr. Richard Bromley, Purser of the Belleisle, the Companies of the Ships named in the margin [2] were supplied with as many bullocks, (sheep for the use of the sick,) and onions, as our short stay would admit of, under the circumstances which they were to be procured. I feel much indebted to Captain Hardy for supplying money for that purpose, (bills on the Victualling-Board not being negotiable,) and particularly so to Mr. Bromley, whose trouble on the occasion has only been rewarded by my approbation; I therefore take the liberty of mentioning him as very deserving of promotion, and hope their Lordships will bear him in recollection as a candidate for a First or Second Rate.

Complete vouchers for the whole of this purchase are gone to the Commissioners of Victualling, who will no doubt signify their approbation of the transaction. I am, Sir, &c.,

NELSON AND BRONTE.

TO THE RESPECTIVE CAPTAINS AND COMMANDERS OF H. M. SHIPS AND VESSELS ON THE MEDITERRANEAN STATION.

[Order-Book.]

Victory, at Sea, 10th December, 1803.

Whereas, Robert Dwyer, a Private Marine belonging to His Majesty's Ship Belleisle was, by the sentence of a Court-Martial held on him the 4th ultimo, to receive 500 lashes for

[2] Victory, Kent, Canopus, Superb, Belleisle, Triumph, Renown, Stately, Cameleon.

disobedience of orders and insolence to his Superior Officer,
crimes of the most serious nature, and for which the delinquent
no doubt looked forward to the awful sentence of death being
pronounced upon him, instead of the corporal punishment
above-mentioned: and, although the said Robert Dwyer has
received only part of his punishment, yet it being the first
offence of a public nature which has been brought to trial
since my taking upon me the command of His Majesty's Fleet
in the Mediterranean, and the respective Captains having particularly mentioned to me the very orderly conduct and good
behaviour of their Ships' Companies, I am, therefore, induced
from these circumstances to remit the remainder of the said
Robert Dwyer's punishment; but I must desire it to be perfectly understood, and to warn the respective Ships' Companies
against the commission of crimes of a similar or any other
nature, as well as against the shameful disgraceful crime of
Desertion, as the sentence of the Court-Martial for either of
these offences, be it death or otherwise, will most certainly be
inflicted without mitigation.

NELSON AND BRONTE.

TO THE CAPTAIN OF ANY OF HIS MAJESTY'S SHIPS WHO MAY
BE IN SEARCH OF ME.

[Letter-Book. " Saturday, 10th December. At 3·15 P.M. the Fleet anchored in
Tolare Roads, on the South side of Sardinia.]

Victory, Gulf of Palma, December 11th, 1803.

Sir,

I am at anchor in the Gulf of Palma, which I prefer to St.
Pierres: indeed, we were not able to get in for the bad
weather. In your passage round you must not pass between
the Vacca and Antioco, but may safely pass between Toro
and Vacca. I am Sir, &c.,

NELSON AND BRONTE.

N.B.—If you have intelligence of importance to communicate, a Boat can come through the bridge of Antioco, at the
North end. The Boat must be a small one.

To be put under a cover and left for any other Ship which
may come to St. Pierres in search of me.

TO ALEXANDER DAVISON, ESQ.

[Autograph, in the possession of Colonel Davison.]

Victory, Gulf of Palma, December 12th, 1803.

My dear Davison,

By the Excellent I received all your truly kind and friendly letters, and duplicate of one by Lisbon, with all your kind present of pamphlets, &c., for which I am truly obliged to you; and I only wish I had the power of returning your continued kindness in any manner, but that is impossible. I rejoice to hear such good accounts of your new House,[3] and I wish I could pass fifty thousand pounds through it. However, my name shall stand in it, if only for £10, and I sincerely hope every success will attend it. You deserve everything which your most sincere friends can wish you. Your letter of July 13th only arrived in the Excellent, with a packet of newspapers sent to Plymouth. I have signed the Proxy for Lord Moira, and in doing it, I have broke through a resolution I made, never to give a Proxy; nor could anything have induced me to swerve from it, but to such a man as Lord Moira. Whether he is in or out of Office, my opinion of him is formed for ability, honour, and strict integrity, which nothing can shake, even should ever we unfortunately differ on any particular point.

I wish, my dear Davison, that I had the power, as I have the inclination, to have named you Agent for the Prizes taken by the Victory, but they all know my wishes; and if they will not, I cannot help it. It has fretted me not a little. My Secretary, Mr. Scott, who is a good man, perfectly understands that if we take any part of the French Fleet, and I am offered to name the Agent, which I do not expect, that I shall name you, and that although his name will not appear in the Agency, that I had settled with you that a part of the Agency, such as I thought just, should go to him for his trouble in this Country; and if he was satisfied to do all the business in this Country, that the Agency being five per cent. on the nett proceeds, two per cent. should go to him for his trouble, and three per cent. to you for making the distribution, and that sum

---

[3] The Banking House of Alexander Davison, Noel, Templer, Middleton, Johnson, and Wedgwood, 34, Pall Mall.

you would pay him, with which he seemed perfectly satisfied, and so I hope will you; but I assure you I do not expect any offer of the kind will be made me. They are all nearly strangers to me, and have their own friends and connexions.

Dear Lady Hamilton tells me of all your kindness to her, and I am truly sensible of it. I shall not enlarge on that topic; you know what I must feel. I wish I could be useful to Mr. Lucas, who Mr. Sparrow has recommended, but the Sceptre is gone to the East Indies: so finishes that matter.

You will remember me kindly to Nepean. I hope your news from that quarter is correct. My crazy Fleet are getting in a very indifferent state, and others will soon follow. The finest Ships in the Service will soon be destroyed. I know well enough that if I was to go into Malta, I should save the Ships during this bad season; but if I am to watch the French, I must be at sea, and if at sea, must have bad weather; and if the Ships are not fit to stand bad-weather, they are useless. I do not say much; but I do not believe that Lord St. Vincent would have kept the sea with such Ships. But my time of service is nearly over. A natural anxiety, of course, must attend my station; but, my dear friend, my eyesight fails me most dreadfully. I firmly believe that, in a very few years, I shall be stone-blind. It is this only, of all my maladies, that makes me unhappy; but God's will be done.

If I am successful against the French, I shall ask my retreat; and if I am not, I hope I shall never live to see it; for no personal exertion on my part shall be spared. I can only again and again thank you for all your kindness; and to beg you to believe me for ever, with the sincerest friendship, yours most faithfully,　　　　NELSON AND BRONTE.

Be so good as to order my account to be made up, that I may know what I am in your debt.

TO ADMIRAL THE EARL OF ST. VINCENT, K.B.

[Autograph, in the possession of Vice-Admiral Sir William Parker, Bart., G.C.B.]

Victory, Gulf of Palma, December 12th, 1803.

My dear Lord,

I have received your kind letters by the Excellent, who joined me on the 24th of November, Captain Sotheron having very properly, when off Minorca, left the Convoy to join me. I shall only say, that all your wishes respecting Officers shall be complied with, and, occasionally, I hope to be allowed to put in some of my followers; for as to deaths in this country, they cannot be expected; and dismissals by Court Martials, I hope never to experience. The station I chose to the Westward of Sicie, was to answer two important purposes: one to prevent the junction of a Spanish Fleet from the Westward; and the other, to be to windward, so as to enable me, if the Northerly gale came on to the N.N.W. or N.N.E., to take shelter in a few hours either under the Hières Islands or Cape St. Sebastian; and I have hitherto found the advantage of the position. Now Spain, having settled her Neutrality, I am taking my winter's station under St. Sebastian, to avoid the heavy seas in the Gulf, and keep Frigates off Toulon. From September, we have experienced such a series of bad weather that is rarely met with; and I am sorry to say, that all the Ships which have been from England in the late War, severely feel it. I had ordered the Transports, with provisions, to meet me at St. Pierre's, but as yet they have not made their appearance; and although this day we average three months' provisions, yet I wish to keep them complete to near five months. You will see by the Admiral's[4] letter that the Kent has suffered so severely that she is going to Malta, and I much doubt our getting her to sea again under six weeks or two months, and the passage from Malta is hardly to be made with any Ship. The Amazon, who I have not seen but heard of, was three weeks from Malta as far as Minorca. In short, my dear Lord, if I was to allow this Fleet to get into such a Port as Malta, they had better be at Spithead. I know no way of watching the Enemy but to be at sea, and therefore good Ships are necessary. The Superb is in a very weak state; but her Captain[5] is so superior to any difficulties, that I hear but little from her. Triumph and Renown complain a good deal. The next Convoy will probably be the Braakel and Agincourt. The Donegal I am ordering to join me, and the French L'Aigle[6] must take her chance till I can get something more about me. However,

---

[4] Rear-Admiral Sir Richard Bickerton.　　　[5] Keats.　　　[6] At Cadiz.

you may rely that all which can be done by Ships and men shall be done; whilst it pleases God to give me strength of health, all will do well, and when that fails, I shall give the cudgels to some stouter man; but I hope to last till the Battle is over, and if I do that, it is all I can hope for, or in reason expect. Sir Richard Bickerton is a very steady, good Officer, and fully to be relied upon; George Campbell you know; and I am ever, my dear Lord, with the greatest regard, most faithfully yours,   NELSON AND BRONTE.

TO JOHN TYSON, ESQ.

[Autograph, in the possession of Edwin Beedell, Esq.]

Victory, Gulf of Palma, December 12th, 1803.

My dear Tyson,

I am very much obliged by your kind attention. The things you was so good as to send me are all arrived safe. I only beg that you will regularly debit me with the amount; and on those conditions only I shall accept your kind offer of service. I have to thank you for my account of what has been paid for the Guillaume Tell and Généreux; and I beg you will, as soon as convenient, let me know how my account stands with you.

Mr. Tucker's account to you I can put no credit in. His conduct towards me has been illiberal in the greatest degree, for I can never suppose it to have been Lord St. Vincent's orders. As for Digby's[7] claiming, he may whistle. I suppose Mr. Tucker has put him upon it. With respect to Lord Bridport,[8] that is a distinct consideration, and I shall be very careful how I get involved in another lawsuit. But the new Proclamation is so involved in doubt, that it is impossible to comprehend it; but to prevent disputes, Sir Richard Bickerton and myself agreed in writing, that I should share from the 30th May, the day I passed Cape Finisterre, and he shares with me for all Prizes taken by my orders to the day I joined him, which was July 8th.

[7] Captain Henry Digby, apparently as Captain of the Alcmene : he commanded the Africa, 64, at Trafalgar, and died an Admiral of the Blue and Knight Grand Cross of the Bath, in August 1842.

[8] Admiral Lord Bridport became Commander-in-Chief of the Squadron off Brest, in April 1799.

Buonaparte has, I think, certainly attempted a landing before this time, and, I trust in God, been cut off, and this will give us Peace. At Toulon, the Enemy are perfectly ready to put to sea, and they must soon come out; but who shall [say] where they are bound. My opinion is, certainly, out of the Mediterranean.[9] Malta is useless to me, and when I am forced to send a Ship there, I never see her under two months. I am sure Toulon would be better watched from St. Helen's than from Malta. Our Ships are not in very good plight, and we want sails and spars for topmasts for Seventy-fours: there is not, I believe, one in this country.

The William is gone to Malta, and, therefore, I know not her cargo; but our weather has been so bad that sails cannot stand it, more especially with the very bad canvas made at present for the Navy. I have my usual luck about Prize-money: if I pay my expenses it is as much as I expect; but the French Fleet will, I trust, repay me for all my toil and trouble. Captains Hardy and Murray are both very well, and desire their remembrances; and believe me ever, my dear Tyson, your much obliged and sincere friend,

NELSON AND BRONTE.

TO JAMES CUTFORTH, ESQ., AGENT VICTUALLER, GIBRALTAR.

[Letter-Book.]

Victory, Gulf of Palma, 13th December, 1803.

Sir,

As rice and sugar are but poor substitutes for butter and cheese, and, in general, not much liked by the Ships' Companies, I am to desire you will (if the price does not exceed that of rice and sugar) purchase cocoa and sugar, in lieu of butter and cheese, for the Fleet under my command—at least, for occasional supplies, and provided the stores under your

---

[9] Mons. Thiers says, in his " History of the Consulate and the Empire," that " to deceive Nelson was quite possible, for that great Seaman, full of the genius of Battle, had not always a perfectly correct judgment; and, moreover, his mind was continually disturbed with the remembrance of Egypt:" and he represents him as being so " constantly engrossed" with the idea that Egypt was the destination of the French Fleet, as to have had no conception that it was intended to leave the Mediterranean!—*Forbes' Translation*, vol. v. pp. 97, 98.

charge are not over-stocked with rice, in which case you will submit my letter to the Commissioners of the Victualling for their direction. I am, &c.,

NELSON AND BRONTE.

TO MR. J. DALTON,[1] ON BOARD THE RENOWN.

[From Clarke and M'Arthur, vol. ii. p. 342.]

December 14th, 1803.

As Mrs. Lutwidge[2] sends me word, that you have admired some of my Naval Battles, I think that you will like to receive from me a Medal, which was struck by the partiality of my friends in remembrance of one of those Actions: at least, it will serve to remind you, that on the 13th December 1803, I had first the pleasure of being known to you. A wish to imitate successful Battles, is the sure road, by exertion, to surpass them, which that you may do, for your own honour, and the advantage of your Country, is my sincere wish. I am, &c.,   NELSON AND BRONTE.

TO MR. CHARLES CONNOR, H. M. SHIP NIGER.

[From Clarke and M'Arthur, vol. ii. p. 342.]

[Apparently December, 1803.]

Dear Charles,

As Captain Hillyar has been so good as to say he would rate you Mid., I sincerely hope that your conduct will ever continue to deserve his kind notice and protection, by a strict and very active attention to your duty. If you deserve well, you are sure of my assistance. Mr. Scott will furnish you with money to begin your mess, and I shall allow you thirty pounds a year, if it be necessary, which Captain Hillyar will supply you with. And as you from this day start in the world as a man, I trust that your future conduct in life will prove you both an Officer and a Gentleman. Recollect that

---

[1] Query, if the present Retired Post Captain James Robert Dalton, who was made a Lieutenant in November 1806, and a Commander in April 1810? The Medal was probably one of those struck by Mr. Davison to commemorate the Battle of the Nile.

[2] Wife of his friend, Admiral Skeffington Lutwidge, so often mentioned.

you must be a Seaman to be an Officer, and also, that you cannot be a good Officer without being a Gentleman. I am always, with most sincere good wishes, your true friend,

NELSON AND BRONTE.

TO THE REVEREND DR. NELSON.

[Autograph, in the Nelson Papers.]

Victory, December 14th, 1803.

My dear Brother,

Your letter of September 23rd I received November 24th from Captain Strachey,[3] who wants to be made a Post-Captain. I thank you much for your letter, and am always sure of your unalterable regard and affection. Most certainly, if you send out Charles Brown, I will, (if he has served his Time during my stay here,) if opportunity offers, promote him ; but next Christmas, please God, I shall be at Merton ; for, by that time, with all the anxiety attendant on such a Command as this, I shall be done up. The mind and body both wear out, and my eye is every month visibly getting worse, and, I much fear, it will end in total blindness. The moment the Battle is over, if I am victorious, I shall ask for my retreat—if, unfortunately, the contrary, I hope never to live to see it. In that case, you will get an early Seat in the House of Lords. If Mr. Addington does not give me the same Pension as Government gave to the rich Lord St. Vincent and Duncan, I shall consider no great favour done me, and the Country never could avoid giving the Pension to you : therefore, unless the other is tacked to it, I would not give thanks or sixpence to have it brought before Parliament to benefit Lord St. Vincent's heirs, and certainly, from circumstances, not mine. The putting the stone over poor Maurice[4] was well done, and I approve very much. I do not know that you owe me anything respecting Hilborough ; but if you do, I fully acquit you of the debt, and so let it be considered.

The Ministers ought to have done more for you ; but if you are made more comfortable, that is well. I have wrote

------

[3] Captain Christopher Strachey, who was made a Commander in April 1802 : he was not Posted until June 1814.

[4] Their eldest brother. Vide vol. iv. pp. 378.

to Horace[5] at Eton, as I suppose his holidays will be over before this letter gets to Canterbury. I desire my kindest regards to Mrs. Nelson; and believe me ever your most affectionate brother,

NELSON AND BRONTE.

TO SIR EVAN NEPEAN, BART., ADMIRALTY.

[Original, in the Admiralty.]

Victory, in the Gulf of Palma, 14th December, 1803.

Sir,

Having frequently since my arrival in this Country as Commander-in-Chief, had occasion to forward dispatches by express, and otherwise to disburse sums of money for particular services, I am to request you will please to communicate the same to the Lords Commissioners of the Admiralty, that such a sum of money may be ordered me, for the above and other various purposes, (which the Service may occasionally demand,) as their Lordships may judge proper, and which may have been furnished Commanders-in-Chief in these Seas for their contingent expenses. I am, Sir, &c.

NELSON AND BRONTE.

TO THE COMMANDERS OF HIS MAJESTY'S SHIPS STATELY, NARCISSUS, AND TERMAGANT, ON THEIR ARRIVAL AT ST. PIERRES.

[Letter-Book.]

Victory, Gulf of Palma, 17th December, 1803.

Sir,

I am very much disappointed at the Transports from Malta not having arrived before this at St. Pierres, and as I judge it necessary to proceed with the Squadron from hence, I am to desire you will, immediately on receipt of this, make the best of your way, with his Majesty's Ship under your command, together with the Transports which may be under your protection, off Cape St. Sebastian, where you will find the Squadron, or instructions for your proceedings. But should you from circumstances of bad weather, be unable to

---

[5] Dr. Nelson's only son, afterwards Viscount Trafalgar.

proceed off that place, you will make the best of your way to the Madalena Islands, where you will remain with the Transports till you receive further orders, sending to me an account of your arrival by any Vessel of War which you may fall in with; but you are on no consideration whatever to leave the Transports or Victuallers unprotected.　I am, &c.

NELSON AND BRONTE.

N.B.—Should it so happen that before you can get so far to the Northward as Asinara, you are overtaken by a gale of wind from the Northward, in that case you are to anchor in the Gulf of Palma, sending to St. Pierres (to the care of the English Vice-Consul) a letter for me, which will be forwarded by any Vessel of War looking for me.

N. & B.

N.B.—The Commander of either of his Majesty's Ships before mentioned, is hereby directed to take a copy of this letter, and leave the original, unless he shall be satisfied that the others are gone to join me, in which case he will take this letter with him, and proceed with the Transports as therein directed.　　　　　　　　　　　　　　N. & B.

TO CAPTAIN JOHN WHITBY, H. M. SHIP BELLEISLE.

[Letter-Book.]

Victory, Gulf of Palma, 17th December, 1803.

Sir,

I have received your letter of yesterday's date, together with a list of men who are considered to require the benefit of the Hospital, and a letter from Doctor Felix, submitting the propriety of an infusion of bark in wine or spirits being given to the people sent on the watering duty; in answer to which I am to desire you will refer Doctor Felix to the 29th Article of his Instructions, which, in my opinion, cannot be considered as literally implying an additional quantity of wine to be given men sent on watering parties in Tropical Climates, but as their daily allowance; and therefore (as you must be the best judge of the number of men sent on those occasions, and the necessity of administering bark in their wine or spirits previous thereto) I request that you will also be governed by the said Article; and further desire to observe

on Doctor Felix's letter, that it is not usual or proper to
supply wine to the sick, in addition to their daily allowance,
except when beer is constantly issued, a pint of wine being
sufficient for almost any sick or convalescent person. I
am, &c.

NELSON AND BRONTE.

N.B.—The four men mentioned in the list before alluded
to, are to be sent on board the Kent, when the Captain of the
Fleet gives directions for that purpose.

TO THE COMMANDERS OF HIS MAJESTY'S SLOOPS CAMELEON AND CHILDERS.

[Letter Book.]

Victory, Gulf of Palma, 17th December, 1803.

Sir,

Not having been joined by his Majesty's Sloop under your
command, at St. Pierres, and judging it necessary to proceed
from hence with the Squadron, I am to desire you will make
the best of your way, and join me with the said Sloop, immediately on receipt of this, off Cape St. Sebastian's, as directed
in my secret Rendezvous, No. 97, dated the 4th instant, which
I perceive has been delivered to you by Captain Moubray of
the Active. I am, &c.

NELSON AND BRONTE.

N.B.—If the above Sloops do not arrive together, the Captain who first anchors at St. Pierres, is to take a copy of this
letter, and leave the original for the other, with a note in the
margin that he has done so.

MEMORANDUM FOR SIR RICHARD BICKERTON TO CARRY INTO EXECUTION AT MALTA.

[Order-Book.]

Victory, Gulf of Palma, 17th December, 1803.

The Braakel is intended to go home with the next Convoy,
and the Agincourt to join her at Gibraltar; therefore the
Ships from the Levant, the Currant Ships from Patrass and
Zante, the Trade from the Adriatic and Sicily, are to be col-

lected as soon as possible. As the Agincourt will not go to Malta, a Sloop of War must be appointed to attend the Convoy to Gibraltar, and then directed to return and join me on the Rendezvous. Sir Richard Bickerton will give all the necessary orders for carrying the Convoy to England, and for Captain Briggs to put himself under his command, and proceed with the Convoy; and also write a letter to the Senior Officer at Gibraltar to see the Convoy, not only safe through the Gut, but also twenty-five leagues to the Westward of Cape Spartel. Sir Richard is desired during his stay to give all the assistance in his power to our Trade, and, in particular, to take care that the Fish Ships are not delayed for want of Convoy.

I wrote some time ago to Captain Cracraft, that if he could spare the Juno, I wanted her, being much distressed for Frigates, and if it is necessary, the Jalouse Sloop must be left in her room; but should Sir Richard meet with Captain Cracraft, and he wishes for a change of station, in that case Sir Richard Bickerton is at liberty to transfer the command of Captain Cracraft's Squadron to Captain Richardson of the Juno, and to send the Anson directly to me. Should the Renard be judged fit for the Service, and Maltese got to enter for her, the Kent is to fit her for sea, and the ten men belonging to the Victory are to be left for her, on board the Madras, till her Commander arrives; and you will receive herewith an order to be delivered to the Officers of the Yard.

The bread from Malta being very much infested with weevils, Sir Richard Bickerton is requested to inquire into the reason, and to take such steps as may, in some measure, prevent so great a destruction of that species of provisions, by either housing it in clean Store-houses, or putting it up in clean Transports. You will receive a copy of my orders for the regulation of the Victuallers, should you meet them, to come to me under St. Sebastians; if to the Northward of Asinara, to go to the Madalena Islands; if to the Southward, to come here, and to take the best means in the Commanders' power to let me know his anchorage, and not to abandon the Transports; and Sir Richard is desired to make inquiry what could have occasioned the non-arrival of the Transports long before this period.

NELSON AND BRONTE.

TO REAR-ADMIRAL SIR RICHARD BICKERTON, BART.

[Letter-Book.]

Victory, the Gulf of Palma, 18th December, 1803.

Sir,

The state of his Majesty's Ship Kent, bearing your Flag, having rendered it expedient to send her immediately to Malta, I herewith transmit you an order to Captain Stuart for that purpose, and have to request you will be pleased to proceed with her to that place, and on your arrival give such directions to the Officers of his Majesty's Yard at Malta, as you may find necessary to get the Kent put in a state for service. But should it be found impracticable to make good her defects at Malta, so as to render her an effective Ship for the present, or, from other circumstances, you should judge it proper to join me previous thereto, you are at liberty to hoist your Flag on board any Ship coming to the Fleet, and join me on my Secret Rendezvous off Toulon, or on No. 97, dated the 4th instant, under Cape St. Sebastian's, as from the state of the weather you may think proper. I have the honour to be, &c.

NELSON AND BRONTE.

P.S.—I am to desire you will be pleased to order a survey to be held at Malta Hospital, on such Seamen, &c. as may be represented fit objects for invaliding, and order them a passage to England in the Braakel. Enclosed is an order for a survey on the remains of medicines, &c. at Malta Hospital, which you will order to be carried into effect.

N. & B.

TO SIR EVAN NEPEAN, BART., ADMIRALTY.

[Letter-Book. " Monday, 19th December. At 6, weighed and made sail out of the Gulf of Palma, as did the Squadron : left the Kent at anchor, and parted company. Narcissus and Transports from Malta, joined the Squadron."—*Victory's Log.*]

Victory, at Sea, 19th December, 1803.

Sir,

Having ordered a Transport and Victualler from Malta to rendezvous at St. Pierres, near the Island of Sardinia, you will please to acquaint the Lords Commissioners of the Admiralty, that I bore up for that place with the Squadron, the 6th instant; but finding it impracticable, from the excessive bad weather, to gain that anchorage, I proceeded to the Gulf of Palma, and arrived there the 11th. It is a most excellent and commodious Bay, with good and safe anchorage for any number of Ships; and having communicated with St. Pierres, and finding the Transport and Victualler had not arrived, I remained in the Gulf of Palma till the 19th instant, when I got under weigh, and was joined by the Narcissus from Malta, with the Transport and Victualler before mentioned, which will nearly complete our provisions, and in some measure supply our wants of stores. The Squadron was only enabled to procure bullocks for ready money, which was done as far as private individuals could contribute, but not sufficiently, although there was great abundance of cattle, and to be had upon reasonable terms. Finding from the Cameleon, which has just joined me, that the Enemy's Ships at Toulon are still in Port, I shall proceed to the Madalena Islands for a few days, to clear the Transports and complete our water, and immediately after return off Toulon. I am, &c.

NELSON AND BRONTE.

TO SIR EVAN NEPEAN, BART., ADMIRALTY.

[Original, in the Admiralty.]

Victory, at Sea, 20th December, 1803.

Sir,

Dr. Snipe, Physician of the Fleet under my command, and Inspector of Hospitals, having returned from Malta (where he went for the purpose mentioned in my letter to you of the 24th ultimo,) I herewith transmit you for the information of the Lords Commissioners of the Admiralty, his several letters from Number one to five, on the subject of the Naval Hospital at Malta, together with copy of a contract which he has entered into with a Mr. William Higgins, merchant at Valetta, for victualling the Seamen and Marines that may be sent to that Hospital, which appears to be done very consistently for the interest of Government and for the comfort of the sick and convalescent people. I have, therefore, approved the said contract and returned it to Malta to be carried into effect,

which I trust will meet their Lordships' approbation. It is
only to be observed that Bughay [?] is the fittest situation at
Malta for a Naval Hospital.   I am, Sir, &c.,

NELSON AND BRONTE.

TO THE RESPECTIVE CAPTAINS AND COMMANDERS OF HIS
MAJESTY'S SHIPS AND VESSELS ON THE MEDITERRANEAN
STATION.

[From a Copy, in the Admiralty.]

Victory, at Sea, 21st December, 1803.

Whereas, Doctor Snipe, Physician to the Fleet, under my
command, has represented to me by letter of this date, the
very great danger attending the health of the Seamen sent in
wooding and watering parties, either on the Island of Sardinia
or the Madalena Islands, which abound with marshes; and as
a preventive against the effects of disease which the men are
subject to on these occasions, at the places above-mentioned,
has recommended that a dose of Peruvian-bark, in a preparation of good sound wine or spirits, be given to each man in
the morning, previous to his going on shore on either of the
above services, and the same in the evening after his return on
board, and has, at the same time, stated that two gills of wine,
or one gill of spirits mixed with an equal quantity of water,
in addition to the usual allowance, is all that is necessary:
And as the preservation of the health of the Seamen is on all
occasions (more particularly on the present) of the utmost
consequence and importance to the Country, You are, therefore, hereby required and directed, whenever His Majesty's
Ship under your command, goes into either the Island of
Sardinia, or the Madalena Islands, to order the Purser to
supply the Surgeon with two gills of wine, or one gill of
spirits per day, for each of the men sent on shore on wooding
or watering parties, to be mixed with Peruvian bark, and given
to the men in the manner before-mentioned.

Great care is to be taken by the Captain that no improper
use is made of this order, and that none but those who are
actually sent on either of the services before-mentioned, are
supplied with wine or spirits; the Commanding-Officer is
therefore to deliver a list of the men's names who are to be

sent on these services to the Surgeon, regularly signed, whose
receipt, approved by the Captain, shall be a sufficient voucher
to the Purser.   And on the Ship's being completed in wood
and water, an account of the quantity of wine or spirits issued
to the men as above, in addition to their allowance, is to be
sent to me for my information, together with the Surgeon's
observations on its effects to the Physician of the Fleet.

                                        NELSON AND BRONTE.

TO CAPTAIN SIR THOMAS TROUBRIDGE, ADMIRALTY.

[From Clarke and M'Arthur, vol. ii. p. 343.]

Off Corsica, 21st December, 1803.

Were I, my dear Troubridge, to begin describing *all* the
complaints and wants of this Fleet, it would be exactly the
same, I dare say, as you receive from all other Stations; but
as it can be attended with no good effect, I shall save myself
the trouble of writing, and you of reading them.   The
Storekeeper has sent two Ships to the Adriatic to land [query,
ship] hemp, and therefore I hope that we shall in time get
rope to supply our wants.   Every bit of twice-laid stuff belonging to the Canopus is condemned, and all the running-
rigging in the Fleet, except the Victory's.   We have fitted the
Excellent with new main and mizen rigging; it was shameful
for the Dock-yard to send a Ship to sea with such rigging.
The Kent is gone to Malta, fit only for a summer's passage.
They are still under such alarm at Naples, that I cannot withdraw the Gibraltar.   I have submitted to Sir Richard Strachan,
whether the state of the French Ships at Cadiz would allow
of his coming to me for six weeks? for although I have no
fears of the event of a Battle with six to their eight, yet
if I can have eight to their eight, I shall not despise the
equality.

    We are not stoutly, or in any manner, well-manned in the
Victory, but she is in very excellent order, thanks to Hardy;
and I think, woe be to the Frenchman she gets alongside of.
I have just been to the Southern end of Sardinia, having
ordered the Transports with provisions to meet me at St.
Pierres; but it blew such a tremendous storm, that we could

not get in. It, however, turned out fortunate, for after the
gale we got into the Gulf of Palma, which is without exception the finest open Roadstead I ever saw. I shall send
you the plan of it, and soundings taken by the Master of the
Victory,[5] an *elève* of Hallowell's ; I have him here, to make him
a Lieutenant. Lemon-juice we are getting, and much better
than we procure from England ; but the difficulty is coming
at the price ; and at this distance it is not all our letters that
can rectify incorrectness. I have directed Sir Richard Bickerton, who is gone in the Kent, to make inquiries into this department : there is no such thing as stopping the baking of
bread, although I have accounts of abundance coming from
England ; but they like to buy, and so they may ; I will, however, give no order. You will see the reports respecting a
Naval Hospital at Malta. It is curious that in a place taken
by the close blockade of the Navy, and when the only reason
for keeping it was to have a Naval Station, that no spot has
been allotted for a Naval Hospital ; and we are upon suffer-
ance from day to day. Bughay[?] is certainly the only proper
place, as it stands insulated with grounds, and has every means
of comfort ; but to complete it for 150 men would cost, besides
the purchase of house and grounds, 1000*l.*, and 2000*l.* more
to put it in order. Ball says 5000*l.* would do the whole ; but
I say for 5, read 10,000*l.* I have six Frigates and Sloops
watching the French Army in the Adriatic, and at the Mouth
of the Archipelago. I am, &c.,

NELSON AND BRONTE.

TO CAPTAIN DONNELLY, H.M. SHIP NARCISSUS.

[Autograph, in the possession of the late Adam Bromilow, Esq.]

Victory, at Sea, December 21st, 1803.

Sir,

Being obliged to go into the Madalena Islands for water,
and being very anxious to know if the Enemy's Fleet are
still in Toulon, I have to desire that you will immediately
proceed off that Port, and either by looking in or speaking
any of the Frigates stationed off there, ascertain whether the

---

[5] Mr. Atkinson, afterwards Master-Attendant at Portsmouth Dock Yard.

Enemy are in or out of Port. It is probable, supposing the wind Westerly, that I shall not be able to leave Madalena until Monday the 26th, and you will therefore regulate your movements according to circumstances; and you will direct every Vessel of War which you may fall in with to join me without loss of time: from Madalena I shall proceed directly under Cape St. Sebastians. The Amazon, Seahorse, Termagant and Niger, are the Vessels you are most likely to fall in with. I am, Sir, &c.,

NELSON AND BRONTE.

TO SIR EVAN NEPEAN, BART., ADMIRALTY.

[Original, in the Admiralty.]

Victory, at Sea, 21st December, 1803.

Sir,

The French National Schooner Le Renard, captured by the Squadron under my command on the 16th ultimo, as mentioned in my letter to you of that date, having been found upon survey, by the Officers at Malta Yard, fit for his Majesty's Service, and Vessels of that description being very much wanted, you will please to acquaint the Lords Commissioners of the Admiralty, that I have ordered her to be taken into his Majesty's Service by the same name, and have directed the respective Officers at Malta to fit her for sea with all dispatch, with a complement of sixty men, including two boys to be borne on the third class. I have appointed Lieutenant Richard Spencer,[5] late of the Cameleon, (who has been for some time in the Triumph,) to command the Renard, and have placed her immediately under the directions of Sir Alexander Ball for the protection of the commerce at Malta, and the various other services of that Island; consequently, have desired Lieutenant Spencer to apply to Sir Alexander for his assistance in procuring Maltese to man the said Schooner, which I hope will meet their Lordships' approbation. I am, Sir, &c.,

NELSON AND BRONTE.

---

[5] Afterwards Captain Sir Richard Spencer, C.B, K.C.H.: he died Governor of Western Australia, in July 1839.

TO THE RESPECTIVE ADMIRALS, CAPTAINS, AND COMMANDERS
OF HIS MAJESTY'S SHIPS AND VESSELS ON THE MEDITERRA-
NEAN STATION.

[Order-Book.]

Victory, at Sea, 21st December, 1803.

Having placed His Majesty's Schooner the Renard under
the immediate directions of Sir Alexander John Ball, Bart.,
to be employed for the protection of the commerce of the
Island of Malta, or on such other service as the Governor may
think proper, You are therefore, hereby required and directed
on no account to interfere with the said Schooner, or to give
her Commander any order whatever, unless upon consulting
with Sir Alexander Ball, you find her service for the time
being can be dispensed with, and the urgency of the case
shall require it.

NELSON AND BRONTE.

TO LIEUTENANT WILLIAM PEMBERTON, LATE RESIDENT AGENT
OF TRANSPORTS AT MALTA, HEREBY APPOINTED GOVERNOR
OF THE NAVAL HOSPITAL AT MALTA.

[From a Copy, in the Admiralty.]

Victory, at Sea, 21st December, 1803.

Whereas I judge it necessary, for the good of his Majesty's
Service, that a Governor, or Superintendant Officer should be
appointed to the Naval Hospital established at Malta, (by the
Lords Commissioners of the Admiralty,) under the charge of
Mr. John Gray, Surgeon, You are therefore hereby required
and directed to take upon you the charge and employment of
Governor of the said Naval Hospital, paying very strict and
particular attention to the cleanliness and comfort of the
Patients in their different apartments, so far as you may
judge necessary, and the Surgeon recommend for their good;
also to use every means to prevent desertions and irregularities
of every description, for which purpose you are to apply to
the Commanding or Senior Officer in Valette Harbour whenever you find his interference necessary to carry the same into
effect.

You are to transmit to the said Senior Officer, a list of such

Seamen and Marines as the Surgeon may deem fit objects for invaliding, previous to the sailing of any Ship or Vessel of War for England, in order that a survey may be held upon them, and sent home by such opportunity; but strict regard is to be paid to this circumstance, and none put on the list for invaliding but such as cannot recover in this Country; regular lists of which, and the state of the sick in the said Hospital, you are to transmit to me monthly, and direct the Surgeon to send an account to the Sick and Hurt Board of the number of Seamen and Marines which may have been received into the Military Hospital, agreeable to the form and instructions left by Dr. Snipe. You are to continue in the employment of Governor of the said Naval Hospital until the pleasure of the Lords Commissioners of the Admiralty shall be known, with such an allowance for yourself and servant as is usual on similar occasions; and, for so doing this shall be your order.

NELSON AND BRONTE.

TO SIR EVAN NEPEAN, BART., ADMIRALTY.

[Original, in the Admiralty.]

Victory, at Sea, 21st December, 1803.

Sir,

Judging it for the good of his Majesty's Service, that a Governor or Superintending Officer should be appointed to the Naval Hospital at Malta, as has been customary in this Country, you will please to acquaint the Lords Commissioners of the Admiralty, that I have appointed Lieutenant William Pemberton (late Agent for Transports at Malta) to be Governor of the Naval Hospital at that place, until their Lordships' pleasure shall be known, which I hope they will approve and be pleased to confirm. Lieutenant Pemberton, from his late situation, requires no recommendation, and it only remains for me to observe, that he is an old Officer, and, in my opinion, very deserving of their Lordships' notice. Inclosed is a copy of his Order, for their information. I am, Sir, &c.

NELSON AND BRONTE.

TO SIR ALEXANDER JOHN BALL, BART., MALTA.

[Autograph, in the possession of Sir William Keith Ball, Bart.   A Fragment.]

[About 21st December, 1803.]

I have to thank you very much for a number of baskets of very fine Malta oranges; and in the proper season, if you have people that pack them in paper, I wish they should pack some for me, and send the account; for I insist, as the only terms on which I shall take them, that, at least, you, my good friend, are put to no expense.   By the Cameleon, who has just joined,[5] I find that a Cutter from England is hunting for me with dispatches; and the Niger is also off Toulon, with a mail for Malta.   You shall have them as soon as possible, and every other assistance in the power of, my dear Sir Alexander, your most faithful and affectionate friend,

NELSON AND BRONTE.

You will see how Mr. Stone calls out.   I have now before me Captain Raynsford's letter, assuring me that there is not a Privateer on that Coast, from whence he is just returned, dated December 6th.

December 28th, Madalena.   We put in here to water and clear the Transports, and are this day moving out.   I send you a complete list of the French Fleet, found among the papers of the Renard.

_____

TO LIEUTENANT WILLIAM PEMBERTON, MALTA.

[Letter-Book.]

Victory, at Sea, 22nd December, 1803.

Sir,

I have received your letter of the 6th instant, and herewith transmit you an Order to act as Governor or Superintendent of the Naval Hospital established at Malta, agreeable to your wish, and have also wrote the Lords Commissioners of the Admiralty, requesting that you may be confirmed in the appointment; but, I would at the same time recommend your immediate application to their Lordships on the subject, and

[5] " December 21st. Cameleon rejoined."—*Victory's Log.*

sincerely hope you may succeed.   Mr. Gray, Surgeon of the Hospital, is directed to enter you and servant on the Hospital Books for wages and victuals.   I am, Sir, &c.,

NELSON AND BRONTE.

TO MR. JOHN GRAY, SURGEON OF THE NAVAL HOSPITAL
AT MALTA.

[Letter-Book.]

Sir,   Victory, at Sea, 22nd December, 1803.

Having approved the contract made by Doctor Snipe, Physician of the Fleet under my command, and Inspector of Hospitals, I herewith return it to you, and desire it may be fully and strictly complied with, and that the Seamen and Marines who are received into the Hospital under your charge, may on all occasions derive the comforts of the said contract; and in case of any failure or non-compliance therewith on the part of Mr. Higgins, that you will immediately acquaint me, that such steps may be taken as the nature of the case shall require.   I have appointed Lieutenant William Pemberton, Governor, and Mr. John William Ellice, Surgeon's Mate or Assistant, to the said Hospital under your charge, and desire you will enter them together with Lieutenant Pemberton's Servant, upon the Hospital Books for wages and victuals accordingly.   I am, &c.,

NELSON AND BRONTE.

TO THE RIGHT HONOURABLE LORD HOBART, SECRETARY OF
STATE FOR THE WAR DEPARTMENT.

[Autograph, in the Colonial Office.]

Victory, off Toulon, December 22nd, 1803.

My Lord,

Your letter of September 23rd, I received by the Excellent, November 24th, and I immediately wrote to Captain Cracraft, the Senior Captain in the Adriatic, to proceed to Panormo, and, in secret instructions, charged him to examine the Country, its resources, &c., as your Lordship directed; and I likewise directed him, if the Pasha of Yannina sent to desire a conference with him, that he would go and hear what he had to say; and I wrote to the Pasha in his cipher, to say that Captain C. was gone to Panormo, if he wished to have any conversation with him; and I have no doubt but Captain Cracraft will execute his mission to your Lordship's satisfaction.

With respect to raising the Corsican Corps, I shall give every facility in my power, and have on board two Officers to be landed at Madalena; some of the Corsican conscripts taken in their passage to France, have entered into the Corps, and we have picked up some of Dillon's, which I have sent to Malta. Messina, should it be entrusted to our care, shall, you may rely, be well guarded by a Naval defence. I have, &c.

NELSON AND BRONTE.

TO THE RIGHT HONOURABLE LORD HOBART.

[From Clarke and M'Arthur, vol. ii. p. 344.]

December 22nd, 1803.

My dear Lord,

In presuming to give my opinion on any subject, I venture not at infallibility, and more particular information may convince me that opinion is wrong. But as my observations on what I see are not unacceptable, I shall state them as they strike me at the moment of writing. God knows, if we could possess one Island, Sardinia, we should want neither Malta, nor any other: this, which is the finest Island in the Mediterranean, possesses Harbours fit for Arsenals, and of a capacity to hold our Navy, within twenty-four hours' sail of Toulon. Bays to ride our Fleets in, and to watch both Italy and Toulon, no Fleet could pass to the Eastward between Sicily and the Coast of Barbary, nor through the Faro of Messina: Malta, in point of position, is not to be named the same year with Sardinia. All the fine Ports of Sicily are situated on the Eastern side of the Island, consequently of no use to watch anything but the Faro of Messina. And, my Lord, I venture to predict, that if we do not—from delicacy, or commiseration of the lot of the unfortunate King of Sardinia—the French will, get possession of that Island. Sardinia is very little known. It was the policy of Piedmont to keep it in the background, and whoever it has belonged to, it seems to have been their maxim to rule the Inhabitants with severity, in loading its produce with such duties as prevented the growth. I will only mention one circumstance as a proof: half a cheese was seized, because the poor man was selling it to our Boats, and it had not paid the duty. Fowls, eggs, beef, and every article, are most heavily taxed. The Coast [Court?] of Sardinia certainly wants every penny to maintain itself; and yet I am told, after the wretched establishment of the Island is paid, that the King does not receive £5000 sterling a-year. The Country is fruitful beyond idea, and abounds in cattle and sheep—and would in corn, wine, and oil. It has no manufactories. In the hands of a liberal Government, and freed from the dread of the Barbary States, there is no telling what its produce would not amount to. It is worth any money to obtain, and I pledge my existence it could be held for as little as Malta in its establishment, and produce a large revenue. I have done; perhaps you will think it time: I will not venture to give an opinion on the state of the Turkish Empire, although I have a strong one; but that would be too bad. I am, &c.,   NELSON AND BRONTE.

TO CAPTAIN SCHOMBERG, H.M. SHIP MADRAS, MALTA.

[Letter-Book.]

Victory, at Sea, 22nd December, 1803.

Sir,

By the Narcissus I received your letter of the 30th ultimo, acquainting me with the steps you had taken to forward the provisions and stores for the Squadron, and that the residue on demand should be sent by the first opportunity; that you had ordered scuttles to be cut in the Raven, so as to enable her to use her sweeps with effect; that the Spider was completely refitted; that, in order to enable the Yard Officers to caulk the Juno, it became necessary to remove a great part of the stores on board the William Store Ship, to get at the pitch, and that, in consequence, it was advisable to unload her: in answer to which, I beg to observe, that the whole of your conduct, in the above particulars of service, meets my entire approbation. I am, &c.,

NELSON AND BRONTE.

TO NATHANIEL TAYLOR, ESQ., NAVAL STOREKEEPER AT MALTA.

[Letter-Book.]

Victory, at Sea, 22nd December, 1803.

Sir,

By the Narcissus I received your letter of the 5th instant, acknowledging my several letters, &c. and requesting, for the reasons therein mentioned, that your instructions may be returned; that you had forwarded by the Eliza and Ellice an additional supply of slops, hemp, &c.; that the Yard punts were repaired, the Cracker hauled up for that purpose, and two new ones agreed for; that the Thomas and Mary Transport proceeded to Trieste, under protection of the Jalouse, for hemp, which you had desired might be taken from the person in charge of Government hemp and other stores; and that you had drawn on the Navy Board for £10,200 sterling, for the payment thereof, and sent the bills to be negotiated on the best terms for Government. In answer to which, I herewith return your instructions, and am glad that the slops, hemp, and other stores are arrived, the Squadron being very much in want of them. I approve of the Cracker's being hauled up for repairs, and two others agreed for, as you mention; also of the measures you have taken to procure hemp for the Fleet, and other Naval stores, should they be wanted. I hope supplies of the stores you may soon be in want of, will arrive from England in the Hindostan, time enough to answer your necessities, as purchases must, on all occasions, be avoided as much as possible. I am, &c.

NELSON AND BRONTE.

TO HIS EXCELLENCY HUGH ELLIOT, ESQ.

[Autograph, in the Elliot Papers. " Saturday, 24th December. At 9·50, anchored in Agincourt Sound, Madalena Islands, with the Squadron and Transports." —*Victory's Log.*]

Private.   Victory, December 25th, 1803.

My dear Sir,

I congratulate you most cordially on the near approach of Mrs. Elliot and your fine family, who I hope arrived at the time you expected, in perfect health. I suppose some Ships will come out to relieve the crippled ones of this station, but I do not believe they will increase my numbers. I do not credit a word of our taking Guadaloupe.

I am sorry that good Mr. Falconet should get into any scrape upon my account, and I never considered the buying a few candles with my money would be construed into supplying the Fleet: however, I will be more careful in future. I wish you had employed Nudi for the sake of your family. He has the only good medicines in Naples, and he does not torment his patients with physic. I enclosed Acton a list of the French Fleet. Numerous as they are, I only wish them out. We should have sailed this morning but for a hard gale of Westerly wind. With respectful compliments to Mrs. Elliot, I am ever, my dear Sir, your much obliged and faithful,

NELSON AND BRONTE.

TO SIR EVAN NEPEAN, BART., ADMIRALTY.

[Original, in the Admiralty.]

Victory, at the Madalena Islands, Sardinia, 26th December, 1803.

Sir,

Mr. Atkinson, Master of his Majesty's Ship Victory, having with much care and attention, in company with Mr. Charles Royer,[6] surveyed the Bay or Gulf of Palma, and taken the particular soundings, as mentioned in a Chart which has been done by the said Mr. Charles Royer, a Midshipman belonging to the Victory; and as I judge it to be a very correct and well-executed Plan of the said Bay, I herewith transmit it to you for their Lordships' information; and beg leave to say, that as Mr. Royer has no friend to bring him forward in the Service, and being a very deserving young man, I mean to take an early opportunity of promoting him to the rank of Lieutenant, which I trust will meet their Lordships' approbation. I am, Sir, &c.

NELSON AND BRONTE.

---

[6] Mr. Charles Royer was made a Lieutenant, in November 1804, and obtained his present rank of Retired Commander in February 1838.

TO CAPTAIN THE HONOURABLE THOMAS BLADEN CAPEL,
H. M. SHIP PHŒBE.

[Order-Book.]

Victory, Madalena Islands, 26th December, 1803.

You are hereby required and directed to proceed immediately with His Majesty's Ship Phœbe, under your command, to my Rendezvous No 97, under Cape St. Sebastians, and cruize there till you shall fall in with any of the Squadron; upon your doing so, you are to communicate to them where I am, at this moment, and that the first change of wind after Wednesday next, the 28th instant, I shall proceed immediately to the said Rendezvous, under Cape St. Sebastians. Should you on your way to that place fall in with either the Seahorse, Niger, or Termagant, on their passage to this place, you are not to order their return to the Rendezvous, but direct their Commanders to proceed to this anchorage with the utmost dispatch. Having performed this service you are to land the Spanish recruits on board the Phœbe, either at Barcelona, or any other place more convenient, and write a letter to the Captain General, impressing upon his mind your great attention to His Catholic Majesty's Subjects, in not sending them to Malta, being taken in an Enemy's Vessel; and also state very particularly the conduct of the party which fired upon the English Boats. You are immediately (after having landed the Spanish recruits as above) to proceed to Gibraltar, and deliver my dispatches for the Admiralty to Commissioner Otway, and those also bearing his address, and use every possible exertion in refitting His Majesty's Ship Phœbe, and in completing her stores, provisions, &c. to the usual time; having so done, you are to return and join me on my Rendezvous No. 97, under Cape St. Sebastians, with all dispatch; and as, it is probable, the Hindostan Storeship may have arrived from England, and being very much distressed for stores, you are to take her under your protection, and bring her with you to the Squadron on the Rendezvous abovementioned.

NELSON AND BRONTE.

TO JAMES CUTFORTH, ESQ., AGENT VICTUALLER, GIBRALTAR.

[Letter-Book.]

Victory, Madalena Islands, 26th December, 1803.

Sir,

As provisions will soon be wanted for the Fleet under my command off Toulon, I am to desire you will load a proper Transport with a proportion of bread for 5600 men, for two months, about six weeks' beef and pork, with every species of provisions in proportion to the bread, except wine, of which a small quantity only will be wanting, as supplies of that article can be had from Rosas, upon more reasonable terms for Government than from your stores. The Victualler to be loaded immediately, and to be held in readiness to join me by the Phœbe, or the first Man-of-War coming to the Fleet. I am, &c.

NELSON AND BRONTE.

N.B.—The provisions to be all put in one Transport or Victualler, that the Convoy bringing her may take her in tow; the wine, therefore, to be excepted, if it cannot be stowed.

NELSON AND BRONTE.

TO HIS MAJESTY THE KING OF THE TWO SICILIES.

[From a Copy.]

Victory, 26th December, 1803.

Sire,

I presume to address your Majesty on the return of this season of the Nativity, and to express my wishes for your Majesty's health, and every felicity which Divine Providence can bestow. I also feel pleasure in renewing my sincere and devoted attachment to your Majesty and your august Family, and to assure you that the last drop of my blood is at your disposal. I have wrote to General Acton respecting the Gibraltar's joining me, yet your Majesty and Family are the great objects of my care and attention; and although she would be acceptable on the day of Battle, yet I trust, with the blessing of God on our just Cause, that we shall give a very good account of the Enemy without her. Therefore, whether

the Ship comes or not, entirely depends upon your Majesty's
pleasure. I hope that the French have not yet invaded your
Capital; but with such a Nation as the French, who can be
sure of them for a moment? With most respectful and sincere attachment, I am for ever, your Majesty's most devoted
servant,

NELSON AND BRONTE.

TO HER MAJESTY THE QUEEN OF THE TWO SICILIES.

[From a Copy.]

Victory, December 26th, 1803.

Madam,

I know your Majesty's heart so well, that whatever is well
meant will be favourably received; therefore I presume at
this season of festivity, to renew to your Majesty my assurances of the most devoted attachment to your august person
and family, and that I feel all the warmth of the obligations I
owe you, for all your goodness to me. Never, as long as I
draw breath, will my exertions cease for the comfort of your
Majesty, and I only wish that they may be attended with the
desired effect. I have sent General Acton a list of the French
Fleet, and of ours, and I leave it to the King's pleasure to send
the Gibraltar for the Battle or not. The safety of your Royal
Family is one of the objects nearest my heart, and the destruction of the French Fleet, in my opinion, more certainly assures
that safety which is so dear to me. With every sentiment of
the most respectful attachment and devotion, and with my
prayers for your Majesty's health and felicity, and that of
all your family, I am your Majesty's most dutiful servant,

NELSON AND BRONTE.

TO HIS EXCELLENCY HUGH ELLIOT, ESQ.

[Autograph, in the Elliot Papers.]

Victory, Madalena, December 27th, 1803.

My dear Sir,

The Kent being done up, and gone to Malta, has reduced
me from seven Sail of the Line to ten, therefore, I have left it
to the King's pleasure to send me the Gibraltar or not; and

so entirely do I wish it to be left to the King, that I request your Excellency will not urge it, as you might naturally be supposed to do, when the superiority is looked at; but the safety of the Royal Family shall not be risked one moment by me.

We have had a most terrible winter: it has almost knocked me up. I have been very ill, and am now far from recovered; but I hope to hold out till the Battle is over, when I must recruit myself for some future exertion. I hear there is a Cutter from England looking for me with dispatches: she left Portsmouth the end of November. I have not a scrap of news to tell you; for we have none. I am ever, my dear Sir, your Excellency's most obedient and obliged,

NELSON AND BRONTE.

Doctor Scott is very well: perhaps he will go to Naples.

TO GEORGE NOBLE, ESQ.

[Autograph, in the Elliot Papers.]

Victory, December 27th, 1803.

Dear Sir,

Your letter of October 17th, by the Childers only reached me two days ago. You will find that your idea has been anticipated of a Ship of War being stationed at Naples, by the continuance of the Gibraltar; and she had been at Naples within three days of a month when you suggest the propriety of a Ship being stationed for the general protection of the British, should the French advance to the Capital. It is my duty, and I have the satisfaction of knowing that it has been in my power, to take care of all our Commerce in the Mediterranean. I am, Sir, &c.,

NELSON AND BRONTE.

TO CAPTAIN RYVES, H. M. SHIP GIBRALTAR.

[Autograph, in the possession of Captain George Frederic Ryves, C.B.]

My dear Sir,　　　　　Victory, December 28th, 1803.

The Cameleon merely goes to Naples to inquire how all goes on in that Kingdom. I came here to clear out Trans-

ports from Malta and to complete our water, and am now un-
mooring. Your old Ship[6] goes home the next Convoy, and I
hope, in March I shall be able to send the Gibraltar, which I
fancy will not be displeasing to you. We have had a dreadful
winter. The Kent is almost done for, and she is going to Malta
merely for a passage in the summer. Stately is obliged to
have her lower-deck guns taken out, she is so very weak. I
now hope that we shall get a little better weather, but we are
all in good health, and I hope the air, &c. at Naples, has produced no maladies in the Gibraltar. I am, my dear Sir,
with every good wish, your most obedient and obliged Servant,

NELSON AND BRONTE.

TO MR. THOMAS LONGSTAFF, MASTER OF HIS MAJESTY'S HIRED
TRANSPORT ELLICE.

[Letter-Book.]

Victory, Madalena Islands, 28th December, 1803.

Sir,

In answer to your letter of this date, to the Captain of the
Fleet, representing that you had every species of provisions
necessary for victualling the supernumeraries sent on board
his Majesty's Hired Transport under your command, for a
passage to Malta—except wine; I am therefore to desire you
will immediately purchase such a quantity of wine at this
place, as may be necessary for the said supernumeraries during
their continuance on board the Ellice, which will be re-
imbursed your Owners, with the other species of provisions
in the manner mentioned to you in my order of this date. I
am, &c.,

NELSON AND BRONTE.

N.B.—The wine will be purchased about nine-pence per
gallon, and, very probably, considerably under.

---

[6] The Agincourt.

TO NATHANIEL TAYLOR, ESQ., NAVAL STOREKEEPER, MALTA.

[Letter-Book.]

Victory, Madalena Islands, 28th December, 1803.

Sir,

I herewith transmit you copies of two Reports of Survey held on board the Ships named in the margin,[7] on slops received from the Ellice Transport, by which you will observe the considerable deficiency of shoes,—I must, therefore, desire to recommend the most strict attention to all future supplies of slops, and that the cases of shoes, &c. are particularly examined, previous to their being shipped on board the Transport, in order to avoid unnecessary trouble to the Service, as well as to prevent fraud or abuses after they are so shipped. I am, &c.

NELSON AND BRONTE.

TO HIS EXCELLENCY HUGH ELLIOT, ESQ.

[Autograph, in the Elliot Papers.]

Victory, Madalena, December 29th, 1803.

My dear Sir,

Your kind letters of December 10th, and also your private letters of the 10th and 11th, arrived at nine o'clock last night. Your news, every part of it, is so interesting, that I read it over and over; and I am sorry that I cannot send you news in return, of the sailing of the French Fleet—our meeting, fighting, and beating them; but, as yet they have not come out: therefore, I can only thank you for your letters. A Cutter sailed from Portsmouth November 27th, came on my Rendezvous this day fortnight; but not finding me, has, instead of remaining, run after me, and I know not where she is gone. She sailed without notice, and has only dispatches. The dispatches, the Commander states, (but he can know nothing,) are of great importance. He has fell in with many of our Frigates, who are now with me.

With respect to Sardinia, I have not the smallest doubt but if we do not, that the French will possess it before two months,

[7] Superb, Canopus.

and the invasion of Sicily is not difficult from Sardinia. The
Viceroy of Sardinia has no means to prevent a descent: he
could not send a hundred men here. I have stated my
opinion fully to Lord Hobart. If we possessed this Island, it
would save Sicily—perhaps Italy, certainly Turkey and
Egypt. But we shall never point out to the King of Sardinia
that he will lose it, until the French have it. I can be of
little use in having a Vessel cruising in these Straits. It is
only ten miles from Bonifaccio; and either a calm or a gale
of wind renders all our efforts useless.

The good King of Naples has, under the advice of Sir
John Acton, always supported his honour and dignity; and if
other Powers, more powerful, had done the same, they would
not now have become degraded by great sacrifices. The
Queen is a great woman, and, I think, would hardly commit
herself in communicating secrets to a Frenchman.[8] We have
had the French papers to December 5th, and the King's
speech I sent to Malta. Windham spoke violently on the
Address, but there was no opposition to it. The moment
I get the Cutter, if there are any dispatches for your Excellency, they shall be instantly forwarded; and I am, my dear
Sir, most faithfully yours,   NELSON AND BRONTE.

TO HIS EXCELLENCY MR. JACKSON, MINISTER AT TURIN.

[From Clarke and M'Arthur, vol. ii. p. 345.]

Madalena Islands, 29th December, 1803.

I anchored here to clear my Transports with provisions,
and was going to sea this morning, but I am prevented from a
heavy gale of Westerly wind. By letters from Mr. Elliot,
of December 11th, received last night, I find apprehensions
are renewed of the invasion of Sardinia from Corsica. The
King may be assured, that as far as I am able, I should be
happy in preventing it; but a Vessel cruising in the Straits
of Bonifaccio would not have the desired effect; for either a
calm, a gale of wind, or even a night, would preclude any use
from such a Cruiser. I only hope that the King will not be

[8] The Queen of Naples was suspected of giving too much confidence to a French
Officer, Colonel St. Clair.

alarmed. The Sardinians, generally speaking, are attached to us; yet there are French intriguers amongst them, and I understand they hope to bring about a revolt before this invasion. In whatever I can be useful to their Majesties, they may command me; but the destroying of the French Fleet is the greatest service I can render to them, to Europe, and our own Country. The Chart of Sardinia which you sent me, is a most excellent one. I am, &c.

NELSON AND BRONTE.

TO SIR JOHN ACTON, BART., NAPLES.

[From Clarke and M'Arthur, vol. ii. p. 345.]

29th December, 1803.

I am much obliged for all the news you are so good as to tell me, but the assurances of the present French Government are not to be depended upon: their system is to lull those whom they wish to destroy into a fatal security. In no other light can they wish for the disarming of the Calabrians; they would then have an open road to the Coast opposite to Sicily; and as I am touching upon this subject, should unhappily the King find it proper to quit Naples, although the Court and the greater part of the Royal Family should go to Palermo, yet the Head-quarters with the King ought to be at Messina, in order to communicate freely with the Kingdom of Naples. So much advantage would arise from it, that I am sure it will strike your Excellency; and with the Calabrians in arms, what good effects may not be expected! I am fully aware, my dear Sir John, of the delicacy of touching upon this subject, but my heart is with you, and I could not resist it. I observe what your Excellency says respecting the European Powers; it was a desire of aggrandizement in some of the great ones that lost them everything, even much of their own possessions. I have my fears that Russia will not come forward as she ought; but if she and the Emperor were to join, I think Buonaparte would tumble from his station, and Europe get an honourable Peace. That the French should hate you, is the highest compliment they can pay: if you had advised the King to degrade himself, they would have despised you, and his honour would have been lost, which now, thanks to your Excellency, is preserved entire. . . . . I shall conclude by merely repeating, that you are sure of me in time of need; and I hope to be more at my ease after the Battle with the French Fleet. I think they cannot much longer remain in Port, and it would be a very dangerous experiment to leave them, on the presumption that they would not come to sea. I am, &c.

NELSON AND BRONTE.

TO THE QUEEN OF NAPLES.

[From " Recollections of the Life of the Reverend Dr. Scott," p. 113.]

Victory, December 29th, 1803.

Madam,

Yesterday evening I had the honour of receiving your Majesty's gracious and flattering letter of the 10th December; and it is only possible for me to repeat my assurances, that my orders for the safety of the Two Sicilies will be always exactly executed, and to this end my whole soul goes in unison with my orders. The Gibraltar shall not be sent away; for I would rather fight twice our number of forces, than risk for a moment the seeing your Royal person and Family fall into the hands of the French. I see no hope of a permanent Peace for Europe, during the life of Buonaparte. I ardently wish, therefore, that it would please God to take him from the world.

Your Majesty's letter to my dear and good Lady Hamilton shall set out by the first opportunity. Her attachment to your Majesty is as lively as ever. Her heart is incapable of the slightest change; and whether in prosperity, or in adversity, she is always your devoted servant; and such, permit me to say, remains your faithful,

NELSON AND BRONTE.

I beg to be allowed to present my humble respects to the Princesses and to Prince Leopold.

TO CAPTAIN ROSS DONNELLY, H. M. SHIP NARCISSUS.

[Order-Book.]

Victory, Madalena Islands, 29th December, 1803.

You are hereby required and directed to proceed with all possible expedition in His Majesty's Ship under your command, off the harbour of Toulon, in order to ascertain whether the Enemy's Ships are still in Port, and immediately after join me on my rendezvous No 97, under Cape St. Sebastians, with an account thereof; unless, from the state of the weather, you should judge that the Squadron has not been able to obtain that situation, in which case, you will stand over to Asinara, and endeavour to effect a communication with me. Should you fall in with any of His Majesty's Ships, you will acquaint their Commanders with my present anchorage, and that I shall leave this the moment a change of wind takes place, and proceed to Rendezvous No. 97, before mentioned, a copy of which you will give to any of the Captains who may not have received it.

NELSON AND BRONTE.

TO HIS EXCELLENCY ADMIRAL SIR JOHN WARREN, K.B., AMBASSADOR AT PETERSBURG.

[From Clarke and M'Arthur, vol. ii. p. 346.]

[About the end of December, 1803.]

It would be so much for the honour of Russia to go to War with the Corsican, that I hope the Emperor has decided upon it long before this time. If he does not, his protegés, Naples and Sardinia, will be lost. I am, &c.

NELSON AND BRONTE.

TO CAPTAIN WILLIAM PARKER, H.M. SHIP AMAZON.

[Letter-Book.]

Victory, Madalena Islands, 30th December, 1803.

Sir,

I have this moment received a set of vouchers for five live bullocks, 300 pounds of onions, and six bags of hay, procured

z 2

for the Company of his Majesty's Ship Amazon, under your command; and I must desire to acquaint you that the onions ought not to have been purchased without my particular orders for so doing; and I see no reason for the purchase of hay for bullocks which have been killed so immediately. I am, &c.

NELSON AND BRONTE.

TO MAJOR-GENERAL VILLETTES, MALTA.

[From Clarke and M'Arthur, vol. ii. p. 347. " On the 31st of December, 1803, in an official letter to General Villettes, Lord Nelson expressed a wish to know whether, if the French should possess themselves of those Islands, the General could send a number of men, not exceeding 1000, to retake them, which the Admiral was of opinion would be an easy thing, with such assistance as he could give from the Fleet, if it were done before the French had a sufficient length of time to fortify themselves, or to induce the inhabitants to co-operate. And this was supported on the same day by the following private letter :"]

31st December, 1803.

In the request I have made for more Troops, in case the French from Corsica should take possession of these Islands, in order to deprive us of the harbour, I have thought it better to make it entirely official, that it may not be misunderstood. If you think you can with propriety spare the Troops for such a service, you will of course have them ready for embarkation at the shortest notice; but I hope that the French will remain quiet. They have, however threatened the Sardinians if they do not shut their Ports to us. I am, &c.

NELSON AND BRONTE.

TO LIEUTENANT-GENERAL SIR THOMAS TRIGGE, K.B., LIEUTENANT-GOVERNOR OF GIBRALTAR.

[From Clarke and M'Arthur, vol. ii. p. 347.]

[About 31st December, 1803.]

I am sorry to be obliged to take Donegal from your vicinity for a few weeks, but the absence of Kent, Stately, and Gibraltar, which are never likely to be of any service again in this Country, renders it absolutely necessary, with the present Fleet of the Enemy. They are now ten to our seven, and, although I have no fears for the result of a Battle, with our present force, yet if I could have more, and had not, I should consider myself very reprehensible. The conduct of the French Privateers from Algiers and Tariffa is very blameable, and calls loudly for reformation. I am, &c.

NELSON AND BRONTE.[8]

TO CAPTAIN FREMANTLE.[9]

[From Clarke and M'Arthur, vol. ii. p. 354.]

About the beginning of January, 1804.

I trust, my dear Fremantle, in God and in English valour. We are enough in England, if true to ourselves. He may by chance injure us, but can never conquer a determined people. It would be well if the generality of Englishmen would remember that they who know the whole machine, can better keep it going than we who only see a very small part. Although I am naturally anxious for the issue of the attempt, yet I cannot doubt of the final event—it will be the ruin of that infamous Buonaparte, and give us an honourable Peace. I should most assuredly rejoice to have you here, but we none of us see the inside of a Port : I have twice taken shelter under the Madalena Islands on the North end of Sardinia, which form a very fine anchorage. The Village, I am told, for I have not set my foot out of the Victory, contains forty or fifty small houses. As to Malta, it is a perfectly useless place for Great Britain ; and as a Naval Port to refit in, I would much sooner undertake to answer for the Toulon Fleet from St. Helens, than from Malta ; I never dare venture to carry the Fleet there. I know your friends think differently from me, but they talk of what they know nothing about in that respect, and I know it from dear-bought experience. During the winter, generally

[8] " List of the British and French Fleets in the Mediterranean at the close of 1803, as sent by Lord Nelson:—FRENCH (as given in a list found on board a captured French schooner): Neptune, 80; Formidable, 80; Indomptable, 80; Mont Blanc, 74; Scipion, 74; Intrepide, 74; Atlas, 74; Hannibal, 74; Swiftsure, 74; Berwick, 74.—BRITISH: Victory, 100; Canopus, 80; Superb, 74; Belleisle, 74; Excellent, 74; Triumph, 74; Renown, 74. Early in the ensuing year, the Royal Sovereign, for the Flag of Sir Richard Bickerton, and the Leviathan, were sent to the Mediterranean."—*Clarke and M'Arthur*, vol. ii. p. 347.

[9] Afterwards Vice-Admiral Sir Thomas Francis Fremantle, who has been so often mentioned.

speaking, I cannot get even a Frigate from Malta, the Westerly winds are so prevalent; and as they approach the Gulf of Lyons, they are blown to the South end of Sardinia. Perseverance has done much for us, but flesh and blood can hardly stand it. I have managed to get some fresh provisions from Rosas in Spain, which with onions and lemons have kept us remarkably healthy. We are longing for the French Fleet, which is to finish our hard fate. I am, &c.

NELSON AND BRONTE.

TO CAPTAIN PHILIP LAMB, AGENT OF TRANSPORTS, MALTA.

[Letter-Book.]

Victory, Madalena Islands, 1st January, 1804.

Sir,

Having ordered the Agent Victualler at Malta to ship provisions immediately, on board the largest of the Transports named in the margin,[9] for the Fleet under my command, and it being of the utmost consequence to have it all sent in one Vessel, in order that the Convoy which I shall appoint may take her in tow, I am to desire you will particularly inspect the state of their ballast, as I am of opinion the Ellice has a great deal too much on board, as she appears at this moment deeply laden. You will also examine their other accommodations that no space may be lost, and render every facility in your power to get this Transport ready. I must also desire your particular attention on all future occasions to the ready dispatch of the Transports or Victuallers employed for the Fleet. I am, &c.

NELSON AND BRONTE.

TO PATRICK WILKIE, AGENT VICTUALLER, MALTA.

[Letter-Book.]

Madalena Islands, 1st January, 1804.

Sir,

I am to desire you will immediately cause to be shipped on board the largest of the Transports named in the margin,[1] a

---

[9] Ellice and Eliza.   [1] Id.

proportion of bread for 5600 men for two months, with every other species of provisions to six weeks, except wine, of which none is wanted; and should there not be a sufficient quantity of sugar in store for the above purpose, you are not to purchase, but send what remains. And as it is of great consequence to have all the provisions in one Transport, in order that the Vessel of War which convoys her may take her in tow, you will endeavour to have the provisions all put into one Transport: and, therefore, if it cannot be stowed in such Victualler, you will only send a month's beef and pork, instead of six weeks', as our little supplies of fresh beef will, in some measure, make up the deficiency. You will send me an account of the provisions which you may ship, as before directed, by the first opportunity, as well as a regular account of the remains of every species in store, by any of his Majesty's Ships joining me from Malta, that I may on all occasions know what supplies can be drawn from the stores under your charge. I am, &c.

NELSON AND BRONTE.

TO CAPTAIN JOHN WHITBY, H.M. SHIP BELLEISLE.

[Letter-Book. "Monday, 2nd January, 1804. Weighed and made sail out of Agincourt Sound, as did the Squadron. P.M. At 1, carried away the jib-boom in the cap; bore up for Agincourt Sound, and at 2, anchored.'—*Victory's Log.*]

Victory, Madalena Islands, 3rd January, 1804.

Sir,

I have received your letter of yesterday's date, acquainting me that Thomas Carrol, Quarter-Gunner, belonging to his Majesty's Ship Belleisle, under your command, had given himself up as a deserter from the Peterel Sloop, having entered for that Vessel previous to her being paid off; in answer to which I am to desire you will, whenever the Belleisle meets the Peterel, if he entered on board her since her being paid off, deliver him up: and you will warn the said Thomas Carrol of the punishment which he merits, and that it is only by his extraordinary good conduct in the Belleisle from this time, that [he] can lessen the punishment which a Court-martial may inflict; and that if ever he deserts again, he can expect nothing less than to suffer death. I am, &c.

NELSON AND BRONTE.

TO THE RIGHT HONOURABLE LORD HOBART, SECRETARY OF STATE FOR THE WAR DEPARTMENT.

[Autograph, in Colonial Office. " Wednesday, 4th January, weighed and made sail out of Madalena, as did the Squadron."—*Victory's Log*.]

Victory, at Sea, January 4th, 1804.

My Lord,

Short as my force is of the Enemy's Fleet, which I enclose you a list of, and from the absence of the Kent, I wished to draw the temporary assistance of the Gibraltar, who is stationed at Naples for the protection of the Royal Family, yet receiving from their Sicilian Majesties the enclosed letters, and one from his Excellency Sir John Acton, and from Mr. Elliot, stating the very critical situation of that Kingdom, from the recent insolent threats of Buonaparte, and declaring that they look up in their distress to his Majesty's Fleet, and requesting that I would not withdraw the Gibraltar from their protection,—what, my Lord, could I do? I have ordered the Gibraltar to remain, and my determination never to abandon those faithful Allies of our Sovereign, and sooner than withdraw the Gibraltar from Naples, to fight double our force. My heart, my Lord, is warm, my head is firm, but my body is unequal to my wishes. I am visibly shook; but as long as I can hold out, I shall never abandon my truly honourable post. I am, &c.

NELSON AND BRONTE.

TO CAPTAIN PARKER, H. M. SHIP AMAZON.

[From Clarke and M'Arthur, vol. ii. p. 348.]

4th January, 1804.

An invasion of Sardinia is intended immediately on our departure, by the French from Corsica; it is therefore my direction that you remain at your present anchorage, and use your utmost endeavours in preventing the invasion of the French, and give every aid and assistance in your power to the Inhabitants, should it be attempted. The Cameleon will give similar orders to Captain Staines, and direct him to remain on this service till further instructions; and you will get under weigh occasionally, as you may think proper.

NELSON AND BRONTE.

TO THE RIGHT HONOURABLE LORD HOBART.

[Autograph, in the Colonial Office.]

Victory, at Sea, January 6th, 1804.

My Lord,

Herewith I transmit two letters which were taken in the mail from Antibes to Çorsica, which, with many other circumstances, assure me that an early invasion of Sardinia is intended, of which I have transmitted my belief to his Royal Highness the Duke de Génévois,[1] the Viceroy, and offered him all the assistance in my power, consistent with the other important objects of my instructions.

I also send you two letters from the Commandants of Madalena and Longo Sardo to my Chaplain and Interpreter.[2] I have, therefore, left a Frigate for their present protection; for however [great] my distress is, and greater it cannot well be, for Frigates and Sloops, yet I could not allow the most important Island and Naval Station in the Mediterranean to fall, whilst I have any means of preventing it; and under the keeping of Providence and my own mind, I hope I do all which the warmest wishes of my Country can expect from me. I have, &c.   NELSON AND BRONTE.

Not having Ships for the Blockade of Genoa, I have been obliged to leave it, till the Admiralty can give me more Vessels, for more important services.

TO CAPTAIN RICHARD GOODWIN KEATS, H.M. SHIP SUPERB.

[Autograph Draught, in the possession of J. Young, Esq., of Wells, and Copies in the Admiralty, and in the Order-Book.]

Victory, off Cape St. Sebastians, 9th January, 1804.

Having received directions[3] to send a discreet Officer to Algiers with Mr. Falcon, his Majesty's Agent and Consul-General at that place, and to carry into effect the orders and instructions respecting him (as well as the capture and detention of several Maltese Vessels, Cargoes, and Crews,) which

---

[1] Prince Charles Felix Joseph, Duke of Génévois, (in Savoy,) fourth son of Victor Amadeus, King of Sardinia.
[2] The Rev. Alexander Scott.   [3] Vide p. 232, ante.

accompany this, You are, therefore, hereby required and directed to receive the said Mr. Falcon on board his Majesty's Ship Superb, under your command, and proceed with him to Algiers with all possible dispatch. And whereas the Dey of Algiers having, some time ago, by force, sent Mr. Falcon from that place, and since then, his Cruizers having taken several Maltese Vessels and their Crews, being Vessels considered as belonging to his Majesty's Subjects; and the Algerine Cruizers having also taken several Vessels, which, although under Neapolitan colours, yet were under English Passes for the voyage, and carrying provisions belonging to, and for the use of his Majesty's Maltese Subjects, (for as such they must be considered from the time of our possessing the Island, in September 1798,) you will, therefore, in consequence of these hostile acts, anchor his Majesty's Ship under your command, out of reach of their batteries, and neither give or receive any mark of honour or kindness from the Dey, until he has made full and complete reparation for the indignity offered his Majesty, in sending away Mr. Falcon, his Representative and Consul-General at Algiers. You will herewith receive a letter from me to his Highness the Dey, which you will either send to him by an Officer, and desire him to appoint a time when you can have a conference, in order to the receiving full satisfaction for the acts of hostility against his Majesty and his Subjects. The reparation which you are to insist upon in his Majesty's name for the indignity shown to his Representative and Consul-General, must be a written declaration of sorrow for having committed such an act, and an assurance that it shall never happen again; and on no other terms is the Consul to be landed.

When this matter is settled, you are to enter upon the hostile act of his Cruizers having taken Maltese Vessels and their Crews, being in every respect Vessels and Crews belonging to his Majesty's Subjects, and you are to insist on the immediate restitution of the Vessels and Crews, and also (if found possible) pecuniary compensation for the damages sustained by this hostile act; and, although you will accept the Vessels, Cargoes, and Crews, yet you are not to consider the matter as settled, but that great injustice has been done to his Majesty's Maltese Subjects. With respect to the seizure of Sicilian Vessels with

English Passports, carrying English cargoes of provisions for his Majesty's distressed Maltese Subjects—their taking these Vessels is a most unfriendly act, and you are to use every means of persuasion for their being restored. In order that you may be fully prepared to meet the Dey of Algiers upon the various important subjects of your instructions, I herewith transmit, for your information, copies of two Admiralty orders, dated the 7th of July and 26th of August last, also an extract of a letter from the Right Honourable Lord Hobart, dated the 23rd of August, together with a Memorandum, dated the 9th of January instant, for your general guidance on topics of conversation with the Dey, and also the several letters and papers referred to in the orders, &c., above mentioned, from No. 1 to No. 4, which you will return to me, with the result of your mission to Algiers. Having completed (if practicable) the object of your said instructions, you will join me without a moment's loss of time, on my rendezvous, No. 97, under Cape St. Sebastians.

NELSON AND BRONTE.

TO HIS HIGHNESS THE DEY OF ALGIERS.

[Autograph Draught, in the possession of James Young, Esq. of Wells, and a Copy in the Admiralty.]

His Britannic Majesty's Ship Victory, January 9th, 1804.

Sir,

When I arrived in last June at Gibraltar, to take upon me the command of his Majesty's Fleet in the Mediterranean, it was with the utmost surprise and sorrow that I found Mr. Falcon, his Majesty's Agent and Consul-General to Algiers, at that place, and that I understood from him that he had been sent from Algiers by force, and in the most indecent manner, by order of your Highness. This insult to the person of his Majesty's Representative, I judged of too great a magnitude for my interference, and therefore the statement of Mr. Falcon was sent to England, in order to be laid before the King.

I need not, I am sure, point out to your Highness, that Mr. Falcon, as Representative of his Majesty, could commit no act in his private capacity, which could subject his Majesty's Representative to receive the smallest insult from the Government of Algiers, and that any insult shown to him, is, in fact, an insult to his Royal Master; and whether he was or was not privy to receiving (although I am satisfied he was not) the Moorish women into his house, is not a matter of which I can take notice, until reparation be made in the fullest manner to his Majesty for the insult offered to him in the person of his Representative.

This reparation for the indignity offered his Majesty, I am directed to demand of your Highness; and I trust from the good sense of your Highness, and from the amity which has always subsisted between his Majesty and your Highness, that you will find no difficulty in giving his Majesty full and complete reparation for the indignity offered him in the person of his Representative, Mr. Falcon, and also assurances that a similar insult shall never be offered again. And as it is my intention to mark, by every means in my power, my former regard and respect for your Highness, I annex the words which are the least exceptionable which you can offer, or I accept, for the insult done his Majesty; and it must be delivered in writing, before Mr. Falcon, his Majesty's Agent and Consul-General, can be landed. For this purpose, I have sent my right trusty friend Richard Goodwin Keats, Esq., Captain of his Majesty's Ship Superb, to your Highness, to settle this matter in the most proper manner; and whatever he shall state in my name, I beg your Highness to consider as coming from me.

I sincerely hope that this disagreeable business will be settled in the most amicable manner, and it will give me the very highest satisfaction to convey to my Royal Master the sentiments of real friendship of your Highness. And I assure your Highness that I am, with the greatest respect, your most obedient, humble servant,

NELSON AND BRONTE.

The least exceptionable apology which will be accepted from his Highness the Dey of Algiers, for the insult offered his Majesty :—

NELSON AND BRONTE.

' I am most exceedingly sorry that, in an unguarded moment of anger, I should have ordered out of the State of Algiers, the Agent and Consul-General of my great Friend his Britannic Majesty; and I declare, upon my faith and word as a Prince, that I will never offer such an insult again to his Britannic Majesty, and will with pleasure receive Mr. Falcon.'

TO HIS HIGHNESS THE DEY OF ALGIERS.

[Autograph Draught, in the possession of James Young, Esq., and a Copy in the Admiralty.]

His Britannic Majesty's Ship Victory, January 9th, 1804.

Sir,

It has been with the sincerest sorrow and surprise that I find that the Cruizers of your Highness have taken several Vessels belonging to the Island of Malta, which is, with its Inhabitants, under the Protection and Sovereignty of his Majesty; and, of course, every Maltese Vessel and Inhabitant is as much British as if owned or born in London.

The giving up of these Vessels and Crews, and making ample reparation for the damages they may have sustained, is so just, that I will not allow myself to suppose that your Highness will hesitate one moment; and I also trust that your Highness will direct orders to be given, that all the Vessels which were chartered by the British Government at Malta, to carry provisions for his Subjects in Malta, be restored. The judgment of your Highness will clearly mark the distinction between these Vessels being actually belonging to your Enemies, and being for that voyage, in fact, belonging to the British Government, and the Cargoes being *bonâ fide* British property; and your Cruizers could not have met with them, but for the protection granted them by British Officers. I have the honour to be, &c.

NELSON AND BRONTE.

MEMORANDUMS FOR THE GUIDANCE OF CAPTAIN KEATS IN HIS TRANSACTIONS WITH THE DEY OF ALGIERS.

[From a Copy in the Admiralty.]

Victory, off Cape St. Sebastians, 9th January, 1804.

Should the Dey refuse to receive you, unless you return his salute, *you will not do it;* and acquaint him by letter that you will sail in twenty-four hours; and you will not receive any letter from the Dey to me, as that would open a negotiation which could never end. In your first conversation with the Dey, every sorrow is to be expressed that his Highness should commit such an insult to his Majesty as sending away his Representative, and taking his Maltese Subjects prisoners. To whatever the Dey may urge, and endeavour to turn the conversation to any complaints of his own, *you are never to reply*, but always to answer by telling him that you were come for reparation of an insult, and not to attend to his complaints, which he had sent to England and settled. Although you will never give up the reparation due to his Majesty, yet if he sends off the Maltese, you will receive them; but you will never recede a tittle from your original demands.

The Dey will probably, if you are parting with only part of your Mission accomplished, ask you repeatedly, ' *Well, are we now at Peace?*' To which, unless you completely succeed, only reply, that you will communicate with me what of our just demands have not been complied with, and that is the only answer you will give. Never appear satisfied with what has been granted, but demand what has not; and leave the question of Peace or War entirely open, so that it may hang over his head. If the Consul is not received, I shall never send again to Algiers; and more reparation will be demanded if he even wishes to receive the offer *now made him*. Should the Dey (which I am told is often the case) rise up in a passion and retire, you will signify to him by letter, that you will not submit to be so treated, and that you will never come into his presence again to be insulted; nor, unless you receive his word of honour, that all your just demands shall be satisfied and finished if you go again to him, and that you will sail in twenty-four hours.

The Dey may, to our demand for the Sicilian Vessels, reply by asking, 'If one of my Subjects, on my account, freight a French Ship, will you allow her to pass?' The answer would be, 'Yes, under similar circumstances. If your Highness were driven out of Algiers, and all your Vessels destroyed —that you were with your Subjects besieging it, or having obtained it, as was the case with Maltese and British, and you freighted a Vessel with provisions to keep you from perishing,

Great Britain would not take an Enemy's Vessel under those circumstances. It would be the most cruel thing in nature to attempt starving our friends on any such pretence ; yet your Highness's Cruizers attempted to starve his Britannic Majesty's Subjects under these circumstances.'

NELSON AND BRONTE.

TO CAPTAIN ROSS DONNELLY, H. M. SHIP NARCISSUS.

[Original, in the possession of the late Adam Bromilow, Esq., and Order-Book.]

Victory, off Cape St. Sebastian's, 9th January, 1804.

Secret.

You are hereby required and directed to take his Majesty's Ship named in the margin[4] under you command; and after having waited forty-eight hours on the present Rendezvous, from the receipt hereof, for the purpose of falling in with his Majesty's Ship Amazon, (whose Captain you will order to join me immediately off Algiers, with the intelligence he may have to communicate; but should Captain Parker not find the Squadron or Superb at anchor off Algiers, he is to return immediately to Rendezvous No. 97, under Cape St. Sebastians, and wait my arrival,) you will proceed to the Bay of Rosas, for the purposes mentioned in my letter to you of this date; which, having accomplished, you will take a convenient opportunity of reconnoitring the Enemy's force at Toulon, and of ascertaining whether they are still in Port. You will, immediately after having performed this service, return to Rendezvous No. 97, under Cape St. Sebastians, where you will remain till my return, unless the Enemy's Squadron has put to sea; in which case, you will make the best of your way off Algiers, and endeavour to join me with an account thereof. You will inform any of his Majesty's Ships who may be in search of the Squadron, where I am gone, and that I shall not be absent from Rendezvous No. 97, more than ten days from the date hereof.

NELSON AND BRONTE.

[4] Active.

TO CAPTAIN ROSS DONNELLY, H.M. SHIP NARCISSUS.

[Letter-Book.]

Victory, off Cape St. Sebastians, 9th January, 1804.

Sir,

I am to desire you will deliver the letter which accompanies this to Mr. Edward Gayner, Merchant at Rosas, who has been, some time ago, directed to purchase twenty tons of onions, and one hundred head of oxen, for the Fleet under my command. If the onions before-mentioned are perfectly ready, you will receive them on board for the use of the Squadron; and if the one hundred oxen are purchased, you will direct Mr. Gayner to have them ready for shipping at a moment's notice; and you will take such a number of the said hundred oxen as you may judge proper, for the use of your Ship's Company, giving the proper and necessary vouchers for the onions and oxen you may so receive. And it having been mentioned to me, that a Quarantine of fifteen days must be performed by any of his Majesty's Ships going to Rosas, I am to desire you will make particular inquiry respecting this very extraordinary circumstance, and demand of the Governor whether he has orders to prevent our receiving water and refreshments at Rosas? I am, &c.,

NELSON AND BRONTE.

TO J. B. GIBERT, H.M. VICE-CONSUL, BARCELONA.

[Letter-Book.]

Victory, off Cape St. Sebastians, 9th January, 1804.

Sir,

I have this moment received your letter of the 24th December last, with its enclosures, for which I am much obliged. On the subject of the eighty pipes of wine at Rosas, the original price so far exceeds any wine purchased for the Fleet under my command, that I do not feel justified in putting Government to such an additional expense. With respect to a duplicate and triplicate of my letter to the Commissioners for victualling his Majesty's Navy, as requested in your said letter, I have to observe that a copy thereof has been already transmitted to them; and I shall, by the first opportunity, send another, and also one to you, in case that any accident should happen to the original, which you have received. I am, &c.

NELSON AND BRONTE.

TO EDWARD POWNALL, ESQ., NAVAL STOREKEEPER, GIBRALTAR.

[Letter-Book.]

Victory, at Sea, 10th January, 1804.

Sir,

I am to desire you will immediately on the arrival of any of his Majesty's Ships or Vessels at Gibraltar, muster their Companies very strictly agreeably to your instructions on that head, and that you will weekly (or oftener, as it may be deemed necessary) muster any Ship or Vessel which may remain there; and you are to be particularly strict in mustering all the Hired Armed Cutters in his Majesty's Service which may arrive at Gibraltar, that it may be known whether the Officers commanding them cause strict compliance with their Charter Parties, and that the said Hired Vessels are complete in their Crews, and found in provisions, &c., agreeably thereto, which you will transmit to me through Commissioner Otway. I am, &c.,

NELSON AND BRONTE.

TO THE PRINCIPAL OFFICERS AND COMMISSIONERS OF HIS MAJESTY'S NAVY, LONDON.

[Letter-Book.]

Victory, at Sea, 10th January, 1804.

Gentlemen,

I yesterday received your letter of the 21st October last, acquainting me with the directions you had given the Naval Storekeepers on the several Foreign Stations respecting their transmitting to your Board their periodical Returns of the remains of stores in the magazines under their charge, and, also, their demands for replenishing the same, in due time, throughout the War, together with every other informa-

tion in their power for enabling you to send out timely and
proper supplies for the respective Squadrons, requesting also,
that I will from time to time communicate to you the present
or expected want of stores for his Majesty's Ships and Vessels
under my command. In answer to which, I have to observe,
that the Ships in general, at present under my command, are
very much in want of cordage, sails, and other stores, and that
the temporary supplies which have hitherto arrived from
England, are by no means adequate to their indispensable
necessities. Commissioner Otway informs me, that they are
so bare of stores at Gibraltar as to be unable to supply the
Ships cruizing in that vicinity, who are consequently much
distressed for almost every article. I am fully aware of the
large demand for stores from all quarters; and, therefore, have
to observe, that the utmost care and attention shall be paid to
the preservation of every description of Naval stores, and as
far as is practicable, I shall acquaint you with the probable wants
of the Squadron; but as the Admiralty, who are aware of the
force which may be wanted for the service of this Country, are
consequently the best judges of the necessary stores to be deposited in the magazines at Gibraltar and Malta—the latter place,
from the Storekeeper's account, is equally bare as the former.

I must here desire to mention, in justice to the Storekeepers
at Gibraltar and Malta, that blame is not imputable to them on
that account, as the Ships that were in this Country previous to
and during the short interval of Peace, being now obliged to
keep the sea, have entirely eat up the stores, and their *real*
wants not half complied with. I have applications from the
different Line of Battle Ships for surveys on most of their sails
and running rigging, which cannot be complied with, as there
is neither cordage nor sails to replace the unserviceable stores,
and, therefore, the evil must be combated in the best manner
possible. I have some time ago directed the Naval Storekeeper
at Malta to purchase a quantity of hemp in the Adriatic for
the purpose of making cordage, which shall be done as far as
is practicable. I herewith transmit for your information an
extract of a letter from Captain Gore of the Medusa, respecting the miserable state of that Ship's sails, running rigging,
&c., which has obliged him to purchase these stores at
Lisbon. I am, &c.,

NELSON AND BRONTE.

TO COMMISSIONER OTWAY, GIBRALTAR.

[Letter Book.]

Victory, at Sea, 10th January, 1804.

Sir,

I am very much obliged by your letter of the 20th November, transmitting me an account of the arrival and sailing of his Majesty's Ships and Vessels and Transports to and from Gibraltar, since the 20th October last: also, by your letter of this date acquainting me that it was necessary, for the reasons therein mentioned, to heave down the Ambuscade to come at the leak in the hudding ends, which was effectually stopped by heaving out only one side, and that she was perfectly ready for sea. I am very glad the Ambuscade's bottom and timbers were found sound and good, and much pleased with your exertions on the occasion, as well as by the ready dispatch the Weazle has met with in refitting, under the present scarcity of stores, and hope she will prove an effective and useful Vessel for the destruction of the Enemy in your neighbourhood. I am, &c.,

NELSON AND BRONTE.

TO COMMISSIONER OTWAY, GIBRALTAR.

[Letter-Book.]

Victory, at Sea, 10th January, 1804.

Sir,

I have received your letter of the 26th November, returning the vouchers for the payment of the Caulkers employed in caulking the Victory, which accompanied my letter to you of the 22nd October last; and as the Carpenter of the Victory (who is a very good, intelligent man) informs me, that he was paid for caulking the Culloden, off Cadiz, by Commissioner Coffin, I shall transmit the said vouchers to the Navy Board, and request the Admiralty to give the necessary orders for their being paid, if such was usual during Lord St. Vincent's command in these seas. I am informed that Mr. Carey, the Builder at Gibraltar, was paid five shillings a day for superintending the caulking of the Ships off Cadiz, when he was Carpenter of the Victory; and, therefore, consider him reprehensible for not having made you acquainted with such circumstance. I am, &c., NELSON AND BRONTE.

TO THE RESPECTIVE CAPTAINS AND COMMANDERS OF ANY OF
HIS MAJESTY'S SHIPS, VESSELS, OR HIRED ARMED CUTTERS,
WHICH MAY ARRIVE AT GIBRALTAR.

[Letter-Book.]

Victory, at Sea, 10th January, 1804.

Memorandum.

It is my particular directions that you afford the Naval
Storekeeper at Gibraltar every assistance in mustering the
Crews of his Majesty's Ships or Vessels under your command,
on their arrival at that place, or at such time as he may judge
proper, agreeably to the rules of the Service; and it is my
most positive directions that the Lieutenants or Commanders
of any of his Majesty's Hired Armed Cutters or Tenders who
shall arrive at Gibraltar, do strictly attend to this Memorandum, that it may appear on mustering their Crews whether their Vessels are found agreeably to their Charter Parties,
which they are hereby directed to produce to Commissioner
Otway and the Storekeeper on mustering them.

NELSON AND BRONTE.

TO THE COMMANDERS OF HIS MAJESTY'S SLOOPS HALCYON
AND WEAZLE, OR ANY OTHERS WHICH MAY HEREAFTER BE
STATIONED AT GIBRALTAR.

[Letter-Book.]

Victory, at Sea, 10th January, 1804.

Sir,

As the most active service against the Enemy's Privateers
in the Straits of Gibraltar, as well as for the protection of our
Trade and the comforts of the Garrison at that place, is expected of his Majesty's Sloop under your command, and
Commissioner Otway being perfectly able to advise you on
many points of service, which the present situation of affairs
with Spain may render necessary, I am to desire that you
will on all such occasions consult with the said Commissioner,
as well as receive his advice, respecting any temporary refit
the Sloop under your command shall require, which I expect
will be seldom, and that when you are taken into the Mole
for such purpose, the utmost exertion will be used to repair

your defects, in order that you may proceed to sea with all dispatch. I have further to observe, that Commissioner Otway's opinion of your conduct, will have great weight with me, and I shall feel exceedingly obliged by his kind attention to my wishes. I am, &c.,

NELSON AND BRONTE.

N.B.—This letter to remain in the possession of Commissioner Otway.

TO SIR EVAN NEPEAN, BART., ADMIRALTY.

[From a Copy, in the Nelson Papers.]

Victory, at Sea, 10th January, 1804.

Sir,

I yesterday received your duplicate letter of the 9th November last, with copy of the letter therein mentioned from the Prince of Castelcicala, the Neapolitan Minister at our Court, complaining of the conduct of one of his Majesty's Brigs, and two English Merchant-Ships, in entering the Port of Girgenti, in Sicily, and capturing three English Merchant-ships, which had been taken by two French Privateers and carried into that Port ; signifying at the same time their Lordships' directions to me, to lose no time in inquiring very minutely into the circumstances therein stated, and report the same to you for their information.

In answer to which, I herewith transmit you the copy of a letter from Lieutenant Shaw of his Majesty's Brig Spider, dated the 30th August last, together with copies of the two letters therein referred to, and also, a copy of my letter of the 16th September in answer thereto ;[5] and beg further to acquaint you for their Lordships' information, that I have heard no more of this business, nor any complaint against the conduct of his Majesty's Cruisers; but, on the contrary, have received many complaints respecting the reception the French Privateers meet with in the Sicilian Ports, which have been transmitted to our Minister at Naples. I shall, however, in further obedience to their Lordships' directions, transmit to Rear-Admiral Sir Richard Bickerton (who is now at Malta, refitting the

[5] Vide p. 205, ante.

Kent) a copy of your said duplicate letter and enclosures therein mentioned, and shall instruct him to make a further inquiry into the circumstances of Lieutenant Shaw's conduct on that occasion, which shall be transmitted to you for their Lordships' information, agreeable to your request.   I am, &c.,

NELSON AND BRONTE.

TO SIR EVAN NEPEAN, BART., ADMIRALTY.

[Original, in the Admiralty.]

Sir,   Victory, at Sea, 10th January, 1804.

I yesterday received your most secret letter, dated the 21st of November last, communicating to me their Lordships' opinion on the Report of Survey upon the Gibraltar's defects; also that there was no immediate probability of their being enabled to relieve the Ships named in the margin,[6] but that Line-of-Battle Ships should be sent out with the Convoys, (when the Public Service would admit of it,) to enable me to send home any Ship of that description whose condition may render such measure absolutely necessary, signifying at the same time, the service appointed to the Monmouth and Agincourt;[7] and acquainting me that it is their Lordships' directions, in the event of those Ships not being able to bring the whole of the arms from Trieste, to make some arrangement for the removal of the remainder; and also to send home such of the said arms as may, by the Commanders of those last-mentioned Ships, be deposited at Malta.

In answer to which, you will please to acquaint the Lords Commissioners of the Admiralty, that their directions respect-

---

[6] Kent, Superb, Triumph, Renown.

[7] On the 23rd of November 1803, the Admiralty issued a "most secret" order to Captain George Hart of the Monmouth, stating that measures had been taken for procuring a supply of arms from the Austrian Dominions for his Majesty's Service, and that it was expected about 4000 chests, each chest containing twenty-five muskets, would be sent to Trieste for that purpose; and directing Captain Hart to take the Agincourt, Captain Schomberg, under his command, and after putting out the lower-deck guns of those Ships, to go to Trieste, take on board the said arms, and proceed with them to Spithead.   Instructions, founded on the expediency which existed of immediately removing as many muskets as possible from the Austrian Dominions, were then added for Captain Hart's guidance, in case the Ships could not take on board the whole of the arms.   The effort to obtain arms from Austria entirely failed.

ing the Gibraltar shall be duly attended to ; and I shall rejoice exceedingly, if the stores sent from England, will enable Commissioner Otway to make her an efficient Ship: and it shall be my particular object to preserve the Ships under my command, as much as possible, from being exposed to unnecessary damages in their hulls, masts, rigging, sails, &c., and that the greatest care of every description of Naval stores shall be taken.

It gives me infinite satisfaction that the Monmouth had not sailed for England with the Convoy, and that she and the Agincourt were at Gibraltar, ready to execute their Lordships' orders of the 21st of November last, (copies of which are in my possession.) Strict regard shall be paid to the important service those Ships are ordered upon, and a very early opportunity taken of bringing away any of the arms*which may remain at Trieste, and of sending them, together with those which Captain Hart may find necessary to deposit at Malta, to England, agreeably to their Lordships' direction contained in your said letter. I am Sir, &c.

NELSON AND BRONTE.

TO SIR EVAN NEPEAN, BART., ADMIRALTY.

[Original, in the Admiralty.]

Victory, at Sea, 10th January, 1804.

Sir,

You will please to acquaint the Lords Commissioners of the Admiralty, that on my return yesterday from the Madalena Islands, (where the Squadron went to complete their water, as mentioned in my letter to you of the 19th ult.,) I was joined by the Hired Armed Cutter, British Fair, on my Rendezvous off Cape St. Sebastians, and received their Lordships' dispatches brought from England by that Vessel, from the Honourable Captain Boyle, who had fallen in with the said Cutter, and taken them from Lieutenant Price, for greater security. I am, Sir, &c.

NELSON AND BRONTE.

TO SIR EVAN NEPEAN, BART., ADMIRALTY.

[Original, in the Admiralty.]

Victory, at Sea, 10th January, 1804.

Sir,

I herewith transmit you, for the information of the Lords Commissioners of the Admiralty, a copy of my letter of this date to the Commissioners of the Navy, together with a voucher, and copies of the two letters therein mentioned, and request you will be pleased to move their Lordships to give the necessary directions for the Carpenter of the Victory,[8] and Caulkers who were employed in caulking that Ship, being paid as early as possible.

It is not necessary to observe that the Victory left England without being caulked; and if great exertion had not been used in having it done at sea, the service of that Ship would have been lost for some considerable time. The propriety of their being paid, therefore, more evidently appears; and I further beg to observe that the Superintending Carpenter and Caulkers employed on similar occasions in this Country, during Lord St. Vincent's command, were regularly paid, and it appears to me a very proper and necessary measure for the good of his Majesty's Service. I am, Sir, &c.

NELSON AND BRONTE.

————————

TO SIR EVAN NEPEAN, BART., ADMIRALTY.

[Original, in the Admiralty.]

Victory, at Sea, 10th January, 1804.

Sir,

I have received your letter of the 24th November last, together with a copy of the one therein mentioned, from the Chairman of the Committee of Merchants concerned in the Trade to Gibraltar and the Mediterranean, respecting the depredations committed by the French Row-Boats that rendezvous at Tariffa and Ceuta, acquainting me, by their Lordships' direction, that it is of great importance that some arrangement should be made for the protection of our Trade on its entering

[8] Mr. Bunce.

the Straits, and to make such a disposition as may, in my opinion, be best adapted for that purpose. In answer thereto, I have to request you will be pleased to acquaint the Lords Commissioners of the Admiralty, that I am perfectly aware of the danger our Trade is exposed to on entering the Straits, from the Enemy's Row-Boats and Privateers, as very justly stated in the inclosure which accompanied your said letter. My first object, therefore, on my arrival at Gibraltar, on the 3rd of June last, was to remedy this evil as much as possible, and for that purpose stationed the Bittern between Gibraltar and Ceuta; and as soon as I was enabled to afford more protection to our Trade coming into the Straits, the Halcyon and Weazle were sent to relieve the Bittern on that important service, and the most strict orders given to Sir Richard Strachan, the Senior Officer of the Squadron outside the Straits, to afford our Trade, on its entry into the Gut, every protection in his power, and to use the utmost exertion in destroying the Enemy's Row-Boats and Privateers which infest that Coast, and from the Spanish Ports commit the most unprincipled acts of piracy. I, however, trust that the Halcyon and Weazle will keep them in check, with the joint exertions of our Cruizers in that vicinity; and the moment I am enabled to afford more protection to that important service, it shall be done.

I herewith transmit you, for their Lordships' information, a copy of the orders which the Sloops before mentioned are under, together with a copy of a letter from Captain Gore of the Medusa, and extract of one from Captain Hart,[9] giving an account of the capture of L'Esperance, French Privateer, and the destruction of Le Sorcier, on the 8th ult., and beg leave to express the very high opinion I entertain of Captain Gore's conduct, in putting to sea immediately on the appearance of these Vessels, and his very able manœuvres in capturing and destroying them. I am, Sir, &c.

NELSON AND BRONTE.

---

[9] These Letters were published in the "London Gazette" of February 1804, together with the last paragraph of Lord Nelson's letter.

TO SIR EVAN NEPEAN, BART., ADMIRALTY.

[Original, in the Admiralty.]

Victory, at Sea, 10th January, 1804.

Sir,

You will please to acquaint the Lords Commissioners of the Admiralty, that the Enemy's Squadron at Toulon is still in Port, and that by Captain Donnelly's account, who reconnoitred them on the 6th Instant, they are apparently ready for sea; their force nine Sail of the Line and Frigates, the same as when last reported to you. From the information I have received, there is every reason to believe that the Enemy intend sending a force from Corsica, to take possession of the Madalena Islands, with a view to prevent us from using that place as an anchorage. I have, therefore, left the Amazon to bring me an account of their proceedings, and have ordered the Cameleon to proceed there and remain for the protection of the Inhabitants, and endeavour, if possible, to frustrate the Enemy's intention of landing. I am, Sir, &c.

NELSON AND BRONTE.

TO THE COMMISSIONERS OF THE TRANSPORT BOARD, LONDON.

[Original, in the Record Office, in the Tower of London.]

Victory, at Sea, 10th January, 1804.

Gentlemen,

I yesterday received your letter of the 16th September last, acquainting me that you had appointed Captain Philip Lamb, of the Navy, to be Agent for Prisoners of War at Malta, and that you had directed him to communicate his Warrant of appointment and instructions to me immediately on his arrival; that his Warrant appoints him generally as the Agent of your Board; and that he is also authorized to act as Resident Agent for Transports at Malta, as well as Agent for Prisoners of War at that place. I have also received your printed instructions to Agents for Prisoners of War abroad, together, with copies of a Contract which you have entered into with Mr. William Webb, for victualling the Prisoners of War in health at Malta and at Gibraltar. I cannot allow

Lieutenant Pemberton to be withdrawn from his late situation as Resident Agent for Transports at Malta, without express-ing my full and entire approbation of his conduct. I am, &c.

NELSON AND BRONTE.

TO MRS. BOLTON.

[Autograph, in the possession of James Young, Esq., of Wells.]

Victory, January 11th, 1804.

My dear Sister,

Your kind letter of October 9th, is just arrived; and you may rest assured that, although I may not write or make all sorts of professions, which I might never have the power of accomplishing, yet I am not less anxious for your and Mr. Bolton's interest in every respect. Sir William Bolton has not yet been fortunate; and if I knew where to place him in fortune's way, he should go. If a Spanish War comes on, he is sure of one, or he must be truly unlucky. With respect to Tom,[1] although I do not know if it be absolutely in my power to say I will entirely keep him at College, yet you may be sure of my assistance; and when poor blindy[2] goes the way of all flesh, and please God some other vacancies which at present drain my pocket very deeply, I shall be more at my ease in pecuniary matters, and, of course, better able to afford permanent assistance. You know, my dear Sister, how I have teazed and teazed for that paltry Prebendary,[3] and I really believe no Minister would give me a place of £50 a-year; but if I know what Mr. Bolton looks to, I shall then know how to act. My sincere friendship for him, independent of his relationship, would induce me to do everything in my power to meet his wishes, and that, I trust, he is sure of; but he knows I have had, in reality, not an atom of interest. The French having no trade in the Mediterranean, but very little has been done in the Prize way; indeed, I am afraid my pur-suit lays another way. I never did, or could, turn my thoughts to money-making. With most affectionate regards to Mr.

---

[1] His nephew, afterwards second Earl Nelson.

[2] The widow of his brother, Maurice Nelson.

[3] At Canterbury, for his brother, Dr. Nelson.

Bolton and all your family, believe me ever, my dear Sister, your most affectionate brother,

NELSON AND BRONTE.

I am glad [to hear] such a good account of Mr. Suckling of Wootton. He is most perfectly right to keep his carriage and live comfortably. Remember me kindly to him, and assure him that no person rejoices more at his comfortable situation than myself.

TO ADMIRAL THE EARL OF ST. VINCENT, K.B.

[From Clarke and M'Arthur, vol. ii. p. 352.]

11th January, 1804.

I had not, my dear Lord, forgot to notice the son of Lord Duncan. I consider the near relations of Brother Officers, as legacies to the Service. On the subject of promotions, I beg leave to say a few words, because I feel now exactly as you have felt in a similar situation to mine; and I rejoice that you, my dear Lord, are not only alive, but in Office to bear witness to the truth of my words, which I should have quoted, even if you had not been in Office, ' that it was absolutely necessary merit should be rewarded on the moment; and that the Officers of the Fleet should look up to the Commander-in-Chief for their reward: for that otherwise the good or bad opinion of the Commander-in-Chief would be of no consequence.' You always promoted meritorious Officers out of the Victory, and Ville de Paris, and many private Ships, for their merit. The good effect was, that whatever was undertaken, succeeded. I, myself, stand in that situation, and Hardy, rewarded by you as Commander-in-Chief. You know, my dear Lord, there is nothing you can desire me to do that I shall not do with pleasure; and if I had known the intentions of the Admiralty respecting the Lieutenant mentioned, he would certainly have been appointed; but having appointed a very gallant and meritorious Officer, who had in a most particular manner distinguished himself on board the Isis at Copenhagen,[4] it would have lowered me in the Fleet, that my follower, who had performed gallant services under my eye, should be displaced.

---

[4] Lieutenant William Layman.

I trust you will be so good as to state, what you thought proper for the benefit of the Service to the Admiralty, and be my friend at the Board. I have said enough for any friend to act upon, and I rely on your kind support. I shall certainly endeavour to imitate you, when you commanded here with so much advantage to your Country. I shall not trouble you with complaints of Ships, the Board shall be answered. Thank God, the health of the Fleet has been wonderful, and I wish I could add my own; however, I hope to hold out to meet the French Fleet, and after that I believe my career will finish. In addition to my other cares, Sardinia must be guarded; the French most assuredly mean to invade it, first, I suppose, under a pretext for keeping us out of it; and then they will have it ceded to them. I have written to Lord Hobart on the importance of Sardinia, it is worth a hundred Maltas in position, and has the finest Man of War harbour in Europe; they tell me it is superior to Beerhaven—in short, it has nothing but advantages; the mode of getting it is to be considered by Ministers, but money will do anything in these days. To keep it, could not in the first instance cost half so much as Malta. I can have no reserves—I venture my opinion, Ministers are not bound to follow it: I can have no views, but to benefit my Country by telling all I know of situations, and how far they can be useful.[5] I am, &c.

NELSON AND BRONTE.

TO THE RIGHT HONOURABLE LORD MINTO.

[Autograph, in the Minto Papers.]

Victory, at Sea, January 11th, 1804.

My dear Lord,

You have allowed the effusion of your good heart to go too far, but I own it was grateful to my feelings; now, I desire you will never mention any obligation to me again; I assure you on my word of honour that George Elliot is at this moment, for his standing, one of the very best Officers in our Service, and his Ship in high order. I placed him under Sir Richard Strachan's command, off Cadiz, and he does nothing but praise him in every letter; I hope yet he will make

---

[5] Vide the Note in page 367, post.

£10,000, and then I have done with him ; if Lord St. Vincent does not confirm him[4] it will be the cruellest thing in the world, but I cannot bring myself to believe it, and I hope he has got his Commission long since. I beg you will present my respects to Admiral Elliot ;[5] I have had the honour of being introduced to him twenty-two years ago, but never had the pleasure of serving with him; but his action with Thurot will stand the test with any of our modern Victories.

Your speech,[6] my dear Lord, was yourself, and there is not a tittle that every man who loves his Country must not subscribe to. I have not heard very lately from Naples, but I expect a Vessel from thence every hour—their situation is very critical —Buonaparte threatening that if the King does not disarm his Subjects, he will march another Army into his Kingdom ; the King has positively refused. I have letters both from the King and Queen, reposing the greatest confidence in our Country: of my services they are sure. Sardinia, if we do not take it very soon, the French will have it, and then we lose the most important Island, as a Naval and Military station, in the Mediterranean. It possesses at the Northern end, the finest harbour in the world; it equals Trincomalee. It is twenty-four hours sail from Toulon; it covers Italy; it is a position that the wind which carries the French to the Westward is fair for you to follow. In passing to the Southward they go close to you. In short, it covers Egypt, Italy, and Turkey. Malta must not be mentioned in the same century. I delivered my opinion on the inutility of Malta as a Naval station for watching Toulon. A Fleet would sooner pass from St. Helens to Toulon than from Malta. If I lose Sardinia I lose the French Fleet; and to keep it, it could not,

---

[4] Vide p. 184, ante.

[5] John Elliot, then an Admiral of the White, uncle of Lord Minto. On the 29th of February, 1760, when Captain of the Æolus of 32 Guns, and having under his orders the Pallas and Brilliant, he attacked and captured, after a gallant action off the Isle of Man, the Marshal Belleisle of 48 guns, commanded by the celebrated Monsieur Thurot, who was killed; La Blonde of 36 guns, and La Terpsichore of 26 guns. A memoir of this veteran Officer, who died an Admiral of the Red, on the 20th of September 1808, and an account of Monsieur Thurot, will be found in the 'Naval Chronicle,' vol. ix. p. 426, et seq.

[6] No speech is attributed to Lord Minto in the "Parliamentary History" of that period.

in the first instance, cost half so much as Malta, and be of all
the use of Malta, and ten thousand times as much.　I have
told Lord Hobart fully my opinion on this subject.　I can have
no reserves.　I venture my opinion.　Ministers are not bound
to follow it.　I can have no views but to benefit my Country
by telling all I know of situations, and how far they can be
useful.

The Turk calls to me might and main, so does Naples, Sardinia, (and Malta for to guard Egypt,) but[7] my course is steady,
and I hope some day, very soon, to fulfil the warmest wishes
of my Country and expectations of my friends, amongst whom,
in the first rate quality, I rate you, my old and sincere friend
—and I only hope you may be able, at some debate, to say, as
your partiality has said before, 'Nelson has done more than
he has done before;' I can assure you it shall be a stimulus
to my exertion on the day of Battle.　I have seven, the
French ten, Spaniards sixteen at Cadiz, and going there
easily from Carthagena.　I am now on my way to settle a
little account with the Dey of Algiers; we had better be at
open War than insulted as we have been.　Government have
reposed great confidence in me, and I hope my conduct will
meet their approbation; but, my dear friend, after all, this
almost boasting—what is man? a child of the day,—and you
will scarcely credit, after all I have wrote, that the Medical
gentlemen are wanting to survey me, and to send me to *Bristol*
for the re-establishment of my health; but, whatever happens,
I have run a glorious race, and I shall be for ever your most
attached and affectionate friend,

　　　　　　　　　　　NELSON AND BRONTE.

The 20th of this month I have been eight months at sea—
do not mention my health (it is my concern) I beg of you.

---

[7] The words from ' My course,' to ' debate to say,' are given by Clarke and
M'Arthur as the conclusion of the ' *unfinished*' letter to the Earl of St. Vincent,
in p. 365, and those words do not occur in their imperfect copy of the above letter
to Lord Minto, of which they certainly formed part.

TO REAR-ADMIRAL SIR RICHARD BICKERTON, BART., MALTA.

[Letter-Book.]

Victory, at Sea, 12th January, 1804.

Sir,

I herewith transmit you a duplicate Admiralty letter, dated the 9th November last, together with a copy of the one from the Prince of Castelcicala, the Neapolitan Minister at our Court, therein mentioned, complaining of the conduct of the Commander of one of his Majesty's Brigs, and two English Merchant Ships, in entering the Port of Girgenti, in Sicily, and capturing three English Merchant Ships, which had been taken by two French Privateers, and carried into that Port; and, in order that the most minute inquiry may be made into this circumstance, I also enclose for your information a copy of a letter from Lieutenant Harding Shaw, commanding his Majesty's Brig Spider, together with copies of the letters therein referred to; and desire you will be pleased to call upon the said Lieutenant for a clear and correct statement of the whole of his conduct in this transaction, as well as to beg of Sir Alexander Ball (who is privy to the business) to furnish you with the particulars, as far as may come within his knowledge, which you will transmit to me by the first opportunity, with the said duplicate Admiralty letter and papers therein mentioned, for their Lordships' information. I have the honour to be, &c.

NELSON AND BRONTE.

TO NATHANIEL TAYLOR, ESQ., NAVAL STOREKEEPER, MALTA.

[Letter Book.]

Victory, at Sea, 12th January, 1804.

Sir,

I have just received your letter of the 15th ultimo, transmitting an account of the Renard's ordnance stores, together with copy of the agreement and plan for building two new punts, which you acquaint me have been approved of by Sir Alexander Ball; communicating to me also that the middle buoy in the entrance of Valetta Harbour had broke loose, (but afterwards found,) and that the outer buoy had likewise broke loose, and drifted away, owing to the late tempestuous weather. On the subject of Pilotage, mentioned in your said letter, I conceive it a very proper reward to those who pilot such of his Majesty's Ships in and out of harbour as have never been at Malta; but I am of opinion that the Masters of Ships making frequent use of that harbour ought to be their own Pilots, and save Government at least half of the pilotage. This I desire you will acquaint the respective Captains with, and at the same time inform the Navy Board, that you may, in this, act under their authority and approbation. I have further to desire for your immediate government, that you will consult with Rear-Admiral Sir Richard Bickerton and Sir Alexander Ball, as I have not a sufficient knowledge of the ingress or egress to and from that harbour to judge of the propriety of continuing or disallowing this practice. On your letter of the 19th November, I have to observe, that there could have been no objection to your sending the William Store-Ship up the Adriatic for a cargo of hemp; but the lapse of time is now so great, and Store-Ships being much wanted in England, that I do not consider it advisable to send her on that service, and therefore she must go home with the next Convoy. I am, &c.

NELSON AND BRONTE.

TO CAPTAIN CHARLES MARSH SCHOMBERG, HIS MAJESTY'S SHIP MADRAS.

[Letter-Book.]

Victory, at Sea, 12th January, 1804.

Sir,

I have just received your letter of the 20th November last, acquainting me with the various Naval occurrences at Malta, amongst others, that the Tender belonging to the Madras was captured by two heavy Privateers, and that a Mate and two men were killed on the occasion. In answer to which, I am sorry for the loss of the Mate and two men mentioned in your said letter. I am, &c.

NELSON AND BRONTE.

TO ALEXANDER DAVISON, ESQ.

[Autograph, in the possession of Colonel Davison.]

Victory, January 13th, 1804.

My dear Davison,

The Cutter brought me your kind letter of the 24th November, on the 9th; and as I do not know hardly where to begin thanking you, it's almost as well to say nothing. But your kindness to my dear, good Lady Hamilton, is what I never shall forget. Your packages will come out safely in the Convoy. That every person in Government or out, should know you, is not to be wondered at, and knowing you, not to esteem you, both as a public and private man. I am sure you felt all which the sincerest friendship could do, that justice had triumphed. This event[9] will put me out of debt, and, I hope, build my room at Merton, and leave my income, whatever it may be, unclogged. I suppose my Agents will receive it. They will do what is right. As Mr. Matcham[1] is buying an estate out of the Kingdom, perhaps he will want his £4000. No; upon reconsideration, it is trust-money. What a speculation he is going upon! I have no fears for Old England, whilst we are true to ourselves; and in that belief I send your Banking-house a Bill for £1000. I do not know that it will all be mine, but it will serve to open an account.

Apropos of money; Hardy desires me to ask you what has been done about the Dutchman: whether you petition as the

---

[9] The successful termination of his Lawsuit with the Earl of St. Vincent on the 14th of November 1803, which is thus reported in the 'Naval Chronicle,' vol. x. p. 432:—" Court of King's Bench, November 14. Lord Nelson *v.* Tucker. The Court pronounced judgment in this cause, the particulars of which have been long before the public. It was an action in the Common Pleas nominally against the defendant, Agent for the Prizes taken by the Mediterranean Fleet, in October 1799, but the real defendant was the Earl of St. Vincent. It was to recover £13,000, one-eighth share of the Prizes taken by Captain Digby, of Lord St. Vincent's Squadron, after his Lordship had left his station and returned to England, and when Lord Nelson had the command. Judgment was given for Lord St. Vincent in the Court below; but upon Writ of Error, Lord Ellenborough delivered it as the opinion of the Court, that the moment a Superior Officer left his station, the right of the next Flag Officer commenced; and, consequently, that Lord St Vincent having returned to England, the enterprise and conduct of the Fleet devolved on Lord Nelson. Judgment was, accordingly, given in favour of Lord Nelson, who thereby becomes entitled to the whole of the Admiral's share of the Prize-money."

[1] His brother-in-law.

Agent, or whether the Captors must petition? and if so, to send them a form. There is another Dutchman in the same situation at Malta, only laden with wine and brandy.

I am glad you are known to Mr. Addington: he is a good man. I began a correspondence, or rather ventured an opinion on the state of affairs in this Country,[2] but he had not time to answer me, and turned me over to Lord Hobart, who I now write to occasionally; but, in fact, I have nothing to write about. That the French are rascals, every one knows; and that they want Naples, Sicily, Sardinia, and Turkey, and Egypt, and Malta—by the way, to write this is no news; nor that I long most ardently to meet the French Fleet. I think they cannot remain much longer in Port. If they do, they might as well have no Fleet. Whenever you write to Lord Moira, you will not fail to remember me most kindly. I have entrusted him with what I did not believe I would entrust any man;[3] and I hope he will be a firm supporter of Mr.

[2] Vide pp. 106, 220, ante.

[3] His Proxy. Vide p. 305, ante. Lord Nelson attached the greatest importance to the use of his Proxy, and gave it very unwillingly, even to Lord Moira. For the following anecdote on the subject, the Editor is indebted to Mr. Haslewood, Lord Nelson's Solicitor:—

"A few days before Lord Nelson last left England, in September 1805, Mr. Haslewood accompanied his Lordship to the door of Mr. Pitt's house in Downing-place. Lord Nelson appeared thoughtful, and said, abruptly—'I wish I had never given a Proxy to Lord Moira;—not that I can complain of his having used it improperly; he is a distinguished Officer, an enlightened Statesman, and a man of too much honour to abuse so sacred a confidence; but I ought to have considered that partiality will cloud the judgment, and that Lord Moira was, or might become, attached to a Party.'

"The next day, Lord Nelson called on Mr. Haslewood; and almost immediately said—'I was so full of the subject we were speaking of yesterday, as to continue it in my interview with Mr. Pitt. I gave some specimen of a Sailor's politics by frankly telling him, that not having been bred in Courts, I could not pretend to a nice discrimination between use and abuse of Parties; and, therefore, must not be expected to range myself under the Political banners of any man, in place or out of place; that England's welfare was the sole object of my pursuit; and where the tendency of any measure to promote or to defeat that object seemed clear, I should vote accordingly, without regard to other circumstances; that in matters where my judgment wavered, or to the full scope of which I might feel unequal, I should be silent, as I could not reconcile to my mind the giving a vote, without full conviction of its propriety. Mr. Pitt listened to me with patience and good humour; indeed, paid me some compliments; and observed, that he wished every Officer in the Service would entertain similar sentiments.'

"Lord Nelson afterwards declared more than once, with reference to the above conversation, that 'he felt his mind at ease,' and expressed himself highly pleased with the liberal conduct and language of the Minister."

Addington's Administration. You know, my dear friend, that I could not get a Ship with me ; no, not even the Victory. Captain Sothern[4] I never saw but once ; therefore I could not ask for him. Nothing, Sir Andrew ought to know, would give me more sincere pleasure than to have, not merely the Plantagenet, but Captain Hamond.[5] It must be desirable to have our friends round us. I am with perfect strangers, although I believe very good men. For Heaven's sake, do not let him think that I neglect him for a moment, or that I should not, upon every occasion be happy to meet his wishes, upon every subject. Pray explain that I have no influence. *It is most true.* But never mind : we shall all have our day.

I do not think we shall have a Spanish War, although they are fitting sixteen or eighteen Sail of the Line at Cadiz. Prizes I never sought for, and I hope never shall. All my object and wish is to meet the Enemy's Fleet, and then I hope to get a little rest ; for I am really fagged—always tossed about, and always sea-sick.

I wish you would get rid of the gout. You will never be able to run after Buonaparte. Are Colonels[6] allowed to ride ? But as sure as he would have come, had we not been prepared, so sure he will not come, now we are. If he does, his destruction will give us an honourable Peace.

I am truly sorry to hear that my friend Nepean[7] has been ill. I hope, from my heart, that he will, far away, weather all his enemies, or false friends. With every sincere good wish for your health and happiness, believe me for ever your most obliged and faithful friend,

NELSON AND BRONTE.

---

[4] Query, if Captain Frank Sotheron. Vide iv. p. 381.

[5] Now Vice-Admiral Sir Graham Eden Hamond, Bart., K.C.B., son of Sir Andrew Snape Hamond, Bart.

[6] Mr. Davison was appointed Lieutenant-Colonel of the Loyal Britons, a Westminster Volunteer Corps, on the 12th of August 1803.

[7] Sir Evan Nepean, Bart., Secretary to the Admiralty.

TO SIR ALEXANDER JOHN BALL, BART., MALTA.

[Autograph, in the possession of Sir William Keith Ball, Bart.]

Victory, January 16th, 1804.

My dear Ball,

I have nothing in the shape of a small Vessel, or your letters for Egypt should have been sent from the Fleet. The orders for the Cutter's[8] return to England were most peremptory, and I cannot bring myself to believe very civil. However, the Vessel was useless; she sailed so ill that she was always in tow. The Childers carried my letters to Gibraltar, for I could not trust them in the Cutter. Either Spider or Renard can go to Egypt; and their Commanders have secret orders, not to be opened till the Vessel arrives at a certain place. I feel very much my inability to comply with your wishes in sending a Vessel to Egypt, but I cannot help myself. With respect to a Convoy to Odessa, no Ship of War is to go into the *Black Sea,* but as there will most probably be Ships in the Convoy, more certainly expected to go up the Levant, the same Ship of War can convoy to the entrance of the Dardanelles the Vessels for the Black Sea; and if the time can be nearly fixed when they will arrive at the entrance of the Dardanelles on their return, a Vessel of War shall certainly be ready to bring them to Malta. The Convoys bound to and from Smyrna, must give and take a little time each with the Malta trade; therefore, I hope your Vessels will be ready to proceed with the Smyrna trade. The Admiralty think I have a great many Vessels to the Eastward of Sicily. Your interrogatories respecting Quarantine have been given out, and a Memorandum to enforce it. The French Fleet being safe, the 5th, I judged it a most convenient moment to stand over to Algiers, to support Keats, who, I expect, arrived there yesterday, with the appearance of the Fleet. My mind is prepared for either alternative. I have left but little to negotiate upon: my demands are as moderate as is possible, considering how we have been insulted, and never will be receded from in the smallest degree; and I am sure Captain Keats will conduct himself to my satisfaction. Mr. Falcon has nothing to say in the business till he is reinstated.

[8] The Hired Armed Cutter, British Fair, Lieutenant Price.

It is difficult to say what may be the destination of the Toulon Fleet. Circumstances may even make it necessary to alter its destination by Buonaparte; Egypt or Ireland, and I rather lean to the latter destination. Sardinia is to be taken; but that will be done from Corsica. Narcissus and Active are off Toulon, and my present distance is nothing, be the Enemy bound either to the Southward or out of the Mediterranean. I do not believe you will get a single man to garrison Alexandria from our Government. It is not difficult to see, and I wrote Mr. A.[9] so in June, that the Mamelukes going to England will get them into a cleft stick, and it will require much address to keep clear of offending either Turks or Mamelukes. I do not know Mr. Drummond, but I am told he is not likely to make the Porte understand the intended purity of our Cabinet. My dear Ball, you are fit to govern; and when we get Sardinia (and if we do not the French will) they ought to make you Viceroy. When we have that Island, we shall hold a fine footing in the Mediterranean. I hope we shall not in another Treaty abandon it; we suffered enough by it in the Treaty of Amiens. The Spaniards are fitting sixteen Sail of the Line at Cadiz—rather say assembling; six are gone from Carthagena, and some from Ferrol. I thank you for your papers, which I have turned over to good Captain Hardy. Your caricatures Murray will return. I have no doubt but the circulation of Leibnitz's Memoir[1] will assist in opening the eyes of Europe; but they are blindfolded, and dare not pull off the bandage. I shall detach the Niger the moment I can guess at the result of my first [visit?] to Algiers: she has two mails, and is full of stores for the Fleet, which we have not had an opportunity of taking out. I have to thank you again and again for your kind present of oranges, which are very fine. Ever, my dear Ball, yours most faithfully,

NELSON AND BRONTE.

---

[9] Mr. Addington. Vide p. 111, ante.

[1] Apparently an account, then lately published in England, of the Memoir addressed by the celebrated German philosopher, Leibnitz, to Louis XIV., recommending to that Monarch, the conquest of Egypt as conducive to the establishment of supreme authority over the Governments of Europe.

January 19th, 1804.

The Dey is violent, and will yield no one point; therefore I have no further business here. Time and opportunity will make him repent.

N. AND B.

As the letters from Constantinople may relate to the Greek Vessel taken by Captain Hillyar, or some other interesting topic, you have my full permission to read them, and then forward them to me. Ever yours truly,

NELSON AND BRONTE.

January 19th, 1804.

TO THE RESPECTIVE FLAG OFFICERS, CAPTAINS, AND COMMANDERS, OF HIS MAJESTY'S SHIPS AND VESSELS ON THE MEDITERRANEAN STATION.

[Order-Book.]

Memorandum.

Victory, at Sea, 16th January, 1804.

The Lords Commissioners of the Admiralty having resolved that a change of the Numeral Flags described in page 14, of the Day Signal-Book, shall immediately take place, I have it in command from their Lordships to send you a painted copy of the Flags as now altered, and to desire that you will paste the same on the 14th page of the day Signal-Book in your possession, and to use the altered Numeral Flags instead of the Numeral Flags at present in use, until you receive further orders. And their Lordships having reason to apprehend that Officers under the rank of Commanders have been permitted to take, or have otherwise obtained, copies of the Signals described in the Day and Night Signal-Books above mentioned, direct me to give the strictest injunctions that such improper proceedings may not take place in future, and that you recal such copies of the said Signal-Books as may be in the possession of Officers for whom they are not intended. I am, therefore, to desire you will pay the most implicit obedience to their Lordships' direction before recited.

NELSON AND BRONTE.

TO CAPTAIN KEATS, H.M. SHIP SUPERB.

[From a Copy, in the Admiralty. "Tuesday, 17th January, A.M. At 6·30 the extremes of the Coast of Barbary, from S.E. to W. b. S. At 8, Cape Caxine bore S.S.W., distance six leagues."—*Victory's Log.*]

Victory, ½ past 8 A.M., 17th January, 1804.

My dear Sir,

We just see you, although not near enough to communicate; therefore I put down two or three things as they occur. You will not bring out any person for me to send to England from the Dey, upon any account, nor any letter to England, which may tend to prolong the business. All must now be settled, and if so, you may take a letter for England, or myself. If you do not think that the presence of the Fleet is longer necessary, I am anxious with this wind to return under St. Sebastians.

You will settle all matters as far as is possible, and leave nothing for any pretence of sending messages to me. You have my confidence. The Consul being received according to my instructions, the collecting all the Maltese together may be a work of some time, which Mr. Falcon can do, if the principle of restitution is agreed upon. It blows so strong at 9 o'clock, that we can see nothing; therefore I send the Niger with this letter. You need only say, 'We go on well or ill; stay off here, or you may go.' The Dey will not know but every day we may re-appear. I beg my compliments to Mr. Falcon; there were no letters for him on board the Seahorse. I am ever, my dear Sir, your most faithful servant,

NELSON AND BRONTE.

TO CAPTAIN KEATS, H.M. SHIP SUPERB.

[From a Copy in the Admiralty. "Noon, Tuesday, 17th January. The Light House on the Mole Head of Algiers bore S.S.W. ¼ W., distance four or five leagues; Squadron in Company."—*Victory's Log.*]

Victory, off Algiers, January 17th, 1804.

My dear Sir,

I approve very much of all your conduct; but with respect to Mr. Falcon's not being received, that is a point I can never give up; for if that is given up, he will always remove any Consul who does not please. I can appoint no other: at the same time, if Mr. Falcon either does not choose to land, or the Dey still refuse to receive him, and yet give up the Maltese, you will receive them, and comply with that part of your instructions—viz., not telling him whether we are at Peace or War; but that you will inform me that his Highness has not given satisfaction for the insult done his Majesty in sending away his Representative.

If you could make him understand, he might complain of Mr. Falcon after receiving him, and it is possible his Majesty, as a mark of his friendship, might remove him, you will act properly; and if nothing can be done, you must come away, but bring nothing to me unless he gives up the Maltese. I am ever, my dear Sir, your most obedient and faithful servant,

NELSON AND BRONTE.

TO CAPTAIN KEATS, H.M. SHIP SUPERB.

[From a Copy, in the Admiralty.]

January 17th, 1804.

My dear Sir,

If the Minister of the Marine is to send you out a Boat with any message, you can stand in, and to any message send the *ultimatum*,—all our demands must be complied with. If not likely to end to your wishes, do not condescend to go to him, but leave Algiers in doubt of the event. I am ever yours faithfully,

NELSON AND BRONTE.

TO CAPTAIN KEATS, H.M. SHIP SUPERB.

[From a Copy, in the Admiralty.]

Victory, January 17th, 1804, 7 P.M.

My dear Sir,

If you think it may be of any use to stand in to-morrow morning, do so; if not, join me. I will not give up an *iota* of my original moderate demand; I should betray my trust if I did. But leave the question of absolute War, for the reasons you know, undetermined. I will have all the claimed Maltese delivered, and Mr. Falcon received. I am, dear Sir, yours faithfully,

NELSON AND BRONTE.

TO THE RIGHT HONOURABLE LORD HOBART.

[Autograph, in the Colonial Office. On the 19th of January, the Victory and Squadron were lying to, off and on, off Algiers; in the afternoon, they made sail for their station off Cape St. Sebastians, and arrived there about noon on the 22nd.]

Victory, at Sea, January 19th, 1804.

My Lord,

In obedience to His Majesty's commands, signified to me through the Admiralty of July 7th and August 26th, and through your Lordship òn August 23rd, I lost not a moment after the arrival of Mr. Falcon, his Majesty's Agent and Consul-General, to detach His Majesty's Ship Superb, commanded by a most excellent Officer and sensible man, Captain Keats, to Algiers, with the Instructions No. 1, and Memorandum No. 2, together with every Paper necessary for his guidance; and, as I thought the appearance of the Squadron might add weight to the Mission (and the French Fleet being in Toulon on the 6th), I stood over to Algiers, and made my appearance on the 17th. By Captain Keats' letters your Lordship will observe that the Dey was immovable, both as to receiving Mr. Falcon, or giving up those persons the Government of Malta claimed as Maltese; therefore, I have apprised both Sir Alexander Ball at Malta, and Sir Thomas Trigge at Gibraltar, of the failure of our Mission, by the enclosed Memorandum.

The insolence of the Dey is only to be checked (with due submission to whatever His Majesty may please to direct) by blockading Algiers, and his other Ports of Bona and Oran, and to capture his Cruizers; for the more that is given up to him the more he will demand with insolence in future. Therefore, I should propose, that, on the 28th day of April next, when, if he means to send his Cruizers to sea, they will be out, that, on that day, every Ship under my command should have strict orders (to open on that day) to take, sink, burn, and destroy every Algerine, and that, on that day, the Ports of Algiers should be declared in a state of Blockade. Thus, the Dey could get neither commerce, presents, or plunder; and, although the other Powers may rejoice at the War with us, yet, my Lord, I am firmly persuaded that it will be most advantageous to us (and humiliating to the other Powers whom he will squeeze) for the next one hundred years.

If I should find his Cruizers at sea before that time, in consequence of what has passed, I shall, of course, take them, but my wish is to make a grand *coup*. I have, &c.,

NELSON AND BRONTE.

P.S.—I am so very unwell, that I have wrote very incorrectly, which I must request your Lordship to excuse, for I could not write another letter.

GENERAL MEMORANDUM.

[From a Copy in the Admiralty.]

Victory, at Sea, 19th January, 1804.

The Dey of Algiers having refused to receive the British Consul, all Ships are cautioned to beware how they approach the Coast of Algiers, or permit themselves to be boarded by the Algerine Cruizers.

NELSON AND BRONTE.

TO ADMIRAL THE EARL OF ST. VINCENT, K.B.

[Autograph, in the possession of Vice-Admiral Sir William Parker, Bart., G.C.B.]

Victory, January 19th, 1804.

My dear Lord,

As the wind is Easterly, I hope the Frigate[1] which I send with the result of our Mission to Algiers, will catch the Cutter[2] at Gibraltar, where I was obliged to send her to clean her bottom, and repair her mast, and to send my letters by the Childers. All the time the Cutter was with us, she was obliged to be towed. She sailed worse than any Ship in the Fleet.

Before the summer is out, I dare say the Dey of Algiers will be sick of his insolence, and perhaps have his head cut off. I have recommended Mr. Falcon to go to England, and then he will be able to explain every part of his conduct; but it appears to me that Mr. Falcon's conduct has been spirited, but perfectly correct; and that the two women found in his house was greedily seized as the pretext for getting rid of a clear-headed, spirited man. I should do great injustice to my

---

[1] The Seahorse.　　　[2] The British Fair.

own feelings, if I did not state my opinion to your Lordship, and other his Majesty's Ministers. I have only a few hours to write all my letters, as the wind is Easterly, and you know that is not to be lost; but I am ever yours most faithfully,

NELSON AND BRONTE.

TO CAPTAIN KEATS, H. M. SHIP SUPERB.

[Letter-Book.]

Victory, at Sea, 19th January, 1804.

Sir,

Having with much attention read over your several letters communicating to me the purport of your conference with the Dey of Algiers, on the subject of his receiving Mr. Falcon, his Majesty's Agent and Consul-General to that place, whom he had so indecently turned out of his Dominions, as well as the several circumstances which you judged necessary to state to him by letter, in farther obedience to the instructions you received from me, I beg leave to express my full and entire approbation of the whole of your conduct, which appears to have embraced every proper and conciliating measure for the purpose of accomplishing the object of your mission to Algiers, and that everything has been done on your part consistent with the honour and interest of his Majesty's Government to bring the Dey of Algiers to a right understanding, which I have communicated to the Lords Commissioners of the Admiralty and his Majesty's Ministers. I have the honour to be, &c.,

NELSON AND BRONTE.

TO CAPTAIN THE HONOURABLE COURTENAY BOYLE, H. M. SHIP SEAHORSE.

[Order-Book.]

Victory, at Sea, 20th January, 1804.

You are hereby required and directed to receive Mr. Falcon, his Majesty's Consul, Secretary, and Suite, on board his Majesty's Ship Seahorse under your command, and give them a passage to Gibraltar; and immediately on your arrival at that place, you will deliver the Public dispatches which you

will herewith receive, to Commissioner Otway, to be forwarded to England, as mentioned in my order to the Senior
Officer, which accompanies this. You are to use the utmost
exertion in completing the provisions, water, and necessaries
of the said Ship to the usual time : having so done, you will
join me, with all possible expedition, on my Rendezvous
No. 97, under Cape St. Sebastians.

NELSON AND BRONTE.

TO THE CAPTAIN OR COMMANDER OF ANY OF HIS MAJESTY'S
SHIPS OR VESSELS AT GIBRALTAR, BOUND TO LISBON.

[Order-Book.]

Victory, at Sea, 20th January, 1804.

Whereas it is my intention that Mr. Falcon, his Majesty's
Consul-General at Algiers, shall proceed, with as much expedition as possible to Lisbon, in any of his Majesty's Ships or
Vessels bound to that place, You are therefore hereby required and directed to receive the said Mr. Falcon on board
his Majesty's Ship or Vessel under your command, together
with his Secretary, suite, and baggage, and give them a passage to Lisbon, (with every necessary accommodation,) should
the communication between us be open. You will also, in
the event of my Public dispatches, forwarded by the Seahorse,
being too late to go to England in the British Fair, Hired
Armed Cutter, receive them on board, and on your arrival in
the Tagus you will deliver them to the Post-Master at that
place, taking his receipt for the same : having so done, pursue
the object of your former instructions.

NELSON AND BRONTE.

TO THE RIGHT HONOURABLE LORD HOBART.

[Autograph, in the Colonial Office.]

Victory, January 20th, 1804.

My dear Lord,

I have had much conversation with Captain Keats, but the
whole of the conference with the Dey, if such a meeting can
be called a conference, was nothing but rage and violence on
the part of the Dey, and firmness on the part of Captain Keats,

the stamp of whose character (if it was not so well known by his actions) is clearly marked by his sensible, clear letters. Amongst other questions, and his swearing that he never would receive Mr. Falcon, he was asked, ' What complaint have you?' his answer was, 'Women in his house.' Captain K., ' That we can prove he was not privy to.' Answer, ' Well, they were in his house and he is answerable; besides, two years ago, his servant rode over a Moor and killed him.' I merely mention this part of the conversation to show your Lordship, as I am now convinced, that Mr. Falcon has committed no impropriety, but that he is disagreeable by his spirited conduct. Your Lordship will find him a very sensible, clear-headed man.

After what has passed, it is not for me to suggest any mode, short of hostilities, to the wisdom of His Majesty's Ministers; the only thing to be done short of hostilities, and even that is in some measure giving up the point, is a declaration that His Majesty will never to this Dey send another Consul to be liable to insult, and to demand what we can prove by name were taken in Maltese Vessels. Mediterranean Passes should be sent out to Malta, as was done to Minorca.

I shall be very anxious to receive His Majesty's commands, and I will endeavour to withhold from hostilities till they arrive, which, if sent as soon as possible, may be in March. I shall give Mr. Falcon a letter of introduction to your Lordship; and, I have, &c.,

NELSON AND BRONTE.

TO SIR EVAN NEPEAN, BART., ADMIRALTY.

[Original in the Admiralty.]

Victory, at Sea, 20th January, 1804.

Sir,

Mr. Falcon, his Majesty's Agent and Consul-General at Algiers having joined me, I detached Captain Keats in the Superb to Algiers, and supported his Mission by showing the Squadron off Algiers on the 17th Instant; but, as their Lordships will perceive by the enclosed papers, nothing can be done with the Dey at present, by anything but humiliation, which I shall never assent to; for, if we do, he will treat us in future (as he has often threatened) like the Danes and Swedes. As all his Cruizers are in Port, I have left the business of declaring to the Algerines hostilities, until a more favourable opportunity offers of giving his Marine, which has been allowed to get too powerful, a most severe blow. I have apprised both Sir Alexander Ball and Sir Thomas Trigge, by the enclosed notice, to warn our Commerce.

I am sure the conduct of Captain Keats has been such as will merit the increased esteem of their Lordships as it has done of, Sir, &c.,   NELSON AND BRONTE.

TO COMMISSIONER OTWAY, GIBRALTAR.

[Letter-Book.]

Victory, at Sea, 20th January, 1804.

Sir,

As great circumspection is necessary to prevent our Trade from falling into the hands of the Algerines, in case they should be hostile to us (as you will observe by the enclosed Notice) I am to desire you will be pleased to acquaint the Commanders of all *future* Convoys bound up the Mediterranean to pass, if convenient, to the Northward of Ivica and Majorca; but should that not be practicable, to pass close to the Southward of Ivica and Majorca, unless under the protection of a Ship of the Line. I am, &c.,

NELSON AND BRONTE.

TO THE RIGHT HONOURABLE LORD HOBART.

[Autograph, in the Colonial Office.]

January 20th, 1804.

My dear Lord,

I send you the Queen of Naples and General Acton's last letters. Mr. Elliot's are in the same strain of doubt as to the lot of Naples. I am, &c.,

NELSON AND BRONTE.

TO SIR ANDREW SNAPE HAMOND, BART.

[Autograph, in the possession of Vice-Admiral Sir Graham Eden Hamond, Bart., K.C.B.]

Victory, January 20th, 1804.

My dear Sir Andrew,

I received yesterday a packet from our friend Mr. Falconet, at Naples, for you. I should have been truly happy to have been useful to so good a man in any manner in my power, but from the Neutrality of his Country, and having the finding money for the French Troops, nothing is in my power to offer, or his to accept; but Mr. and Mrs. Falconet are every day executing commissions for me at Naples, as my private wants require. I hear of you occasionally from our friend Davison. I hope Captain Hamond has sufficiently recovered to join his Ship again : I think he would have been better in this Country. The weather is certainly not so raw as a Channel cruize, and I need not say what pleasure it would give me to have him here on the day of Battle, which cannot be much longer deferred. I am ever, my dear Sir Andrew, with the sincerest attachment, your most obliged and faithful friend,

NELSON AND BRONTE.

TO ADMIRAL THE EARL OF ST. VINCENT, K.B.

[From Clarke and M'Arthur, vol. ii. p. 355.]

20th January, 1804.

Captain Hillyar is most truly deserving of all your Lordship can do for him, and, in addition to his Public merits, has a claim upon us. At twenty-four years of age he maintained his mother and sisters, and a brother,[3] until I made him a Lieutenant for his bravery a short time ago. For these reasons he declined the Ambuscade, which was offered him; because, although he might thus get his Rank, yet if he were put upon Half-pay, his family would be the sufferers. From all these circumstances, so honourable to Captain Hillyar, independent of his services, which every one thought would have obtained him promotion in the late War, I beg leave to submit, as an act of the greatest kindness, that as the Niger is a very fine fast-sailing Frigate, well-manned, and in most excellent condition, she may be fitted with the Madras's 32 carronades, which are not so heavy as her present nine-pounders, and that your Lordship would recommend her being considered as a Post Ship,[4] either a thirty-two or twenty-eight. Captain Hillyar's activity would soon complete the additional number

---

[3] Vide p. 186, ante.

[4] In consequence of this application, the Niger was established as a Post Ship, and a Commission sent out for Captain Hillyar to command her.

of men, and she would be an efficient Frigate. I will not venture to say more; I am sensible of your attention to merit. I am, &c.,

NELSON AND BRONTE.

TO ALEXANDER DAVISON, ESQ.

[Autograph, in the possession of Colonel Davison.]

January 20th, 1804.

My dear Davison,

I have nothing new to tell you, since I wrote you a few days ago. I enclose a list of a few things Mr. Chevalier[5] wants, which I will thank you to order from Burgess for my account. I find Mr. Chevalier everything which you recommended, and I wonder he has not set up some hotel.

The French Fleet I expect every hour, and that will do me good; for if I beat them, there can be no objection to my getting a little rest: I have not been very stout. Perhaps you may tumble upon Mr. Falcon, our Consul at Algiers. He is going home by this opportunity—the Dey objecting to receive him again. He is a clever man, but too spirited for such a beast, whom the Powers of Europe, to their disgrace, bow down to. I am ever, my dear Davison, with the sincerest friendship, yours most faithfully,

NELSON AND BRONTE.

TO ADMIRAL . . . . . .

[From Clarke and M'Arthur, vol. ii. p. 356. In reply to a letter from an Admiral, (whose name is not given,) a friend of Admiral Sir John Borlase Warren, requesting Lord Nelson's intercession on behalf of a young Officer who had behaved improperly to his Captain, and who was, in consequence, to be brought to a Court-Martial.]

[About January, 1804.]

We would all do everything in our power, to oblige so gallant and good an Officer as our friend Warren; but what would he do, if he were here? exactly what I have done, and am still willing to do. The young man must write such a letter of contrition as would be an acknowledgment of his

---

[5] His Steward.

great fault, and with a sincere promise, if his Captain will
intercede to prevent the impending Court-Martial, never to
so misbehave again.   On his Captain's enclosing me such a
letter, with a request to cancel the order for the Trial, I might
be induced to do it ; but the letters and reprimand will be given
in the Public Order-Book of the Fleet, and read to all the
Officers.   The young man has pushed himself forward to
notice, and he must take the consequence.   We must recollect, my dear Admiral, it was upon the Quarter-deck, in
the face of the Ship's Company, that he treated his Captain
with contempt; and I am in duty bound to support the
authority and consequence of every Officer under my command.   A poor ignorant Seaman is for ever punished for contempt to *his* superior.   I am, &c.,

                                NELSON AND BRONTE.

TO CAPTAIN WILLIAM PARKER, H. M. SHIP AMAZON.

[Order-Book.]

Victory, off Cape St. Sebastians, 22nd January, 1804.

You are hereby required and directed to proceed immediately in his Majesty's Ship Amazon, under your command,
off St. Pierres, near the Island of Sardinia, and send your
Boats in for the purpose of bringing out the Transport, (left
there by the Termagant) which you are to take in tow, and
proceed with her to the Madalena Islands with all possible
dispatch, leaving the accompanying letter with the English
Consul, for any of his Majesty's Ships or Vessels which may
arrive there, and bring with you the letters which were left at
that place when the Squadron was left in the Gulf of Palma.
Should you fall in with the Termagant, unaccompanied by
any Transport or Victualler, you will direct her Commander
to proceed to the enclosed Rendezvous No. 97, under Cape
St. Sebastians, where he will find orders for his further proceedings.   But if the Termagant is accompanied with the
Transport from St. Pierres, or any Victualler from Malta, you
will take her and such Victuallers under your charge, and
bring them with you to the Madalena Islands as before directed,
without proceeding to St. Pierres, unless Captain Pettet

should acquaint you that the Victualler, which he brought from Gibraltar, is still at the former place.　In the event of your falling in with any other of his Majesty's Ships, you will acquaint their Commanders that I am on my way to the Madalena Islands, and recommend their approaching that place with caution, unless they are satisfied of my arrival there, as it is probable the Enemy may have taken possession of them.

NELSON AND BRONTE.

TO THE CAPTAIN OR COMMANDER OF ANY OF HIS MAJESTY'S SHIPS OR VESSELS WHICH MAY ARRIVE AT ST. PIERRES.

[Letter-Book.]

Victory, at Sea, 22nd January, 1804.

Sir,

I am on my way with the Squadron to Rendezvous No. 60, where I am to desire you will join me in his Majesty's Ship under your command, without a moment's loss of time, together with any Transport or Victualler which may be under your charge; and as it is probable the Enemy may have taken possession of the Port to which the above Rendezvous alludes, you will approach it with great caution, unless you learn that I have gained that anchorage.　I am, &c.

NELSON AND BRONTE.

TO HIS EXCELLENCY JOHN HOOKHAM FRERE, ESQ., MADRID.

[From Clarke and M'Arthur, vol. ii. p. 356.]

23rd January, 1804.

If this goes on,[6] you may acquaint them that I will anchor in Rosas with the Squadron, and receive our daily supplies, which will offend the French much more than our staying at sea.　Refreshments we have a right to as long as we remain at Peace.　I am, &c.

NELSON AND BRONTE.

---

[6] The refusal of the Spanish Governors to supply the Fleet with refreshments.

TO HIS EXCELLENCY JOHN HOOKHAM FRERE, MADRID.

[From a Copy, in the State Paper Office.]

Victory, January 23rd, 1804.

Sir,

I have just received information that leads me to believe that the French Fleet is either put to sea, or on the eve of it, and bound to the Eastward, towards Naples and Sicily. I am this moment making sail in the direction I think most likely to intercept them. His Majesty's Fleet is in high health, and the event of a meeting ought not to be doubted. I am, &c.

NELSON AND BRONTE.

TO CAPTAIN ROSS DONNELLY, H.M. SHIP NARCISSUS.

[Autograph, in the possession of the late Adam Bromilow, Esq., and Order-Book.]

Victory, off Cape St. Sebastians, 23rd January, 1804.

You are hereby required and directed to proceed immediately, with his Majesty's Ship Narcissus under your command, into the Bay of Rosas, and endeavour to communicate with the shore, for the purpose of obtaining the latest and most correct information of what is passing in France. Having so done, you will make the best of your way off the entrance of Toulon Harbour, to ascertain the state of the Enemy's Squadron in that place; and if their Fleet is in Port, you will proceed off the Harbour of Ajaccio in Corsica, and reconnoitre the Enemy's force in that place, and afterwards use your utmost endeavours to join me at the Madalena Islands with the information you may have obtained from the above-mentioned places.

NELSON AND BRONTE.

TO CAPTAIN RICHARD HUSSEY MOUBRAY, H.M. SHIP ACTIVE.

[Order-Book.]

Victory, off Cape St. Sebastians, 23rd January, 1804.

Whereas, it is my intention to proceed immediately with the Squadron to the Madalena Islands, You are hereby required and directed to remain on the present Rendezvous, No. 97, under Cape St. Sebastians, with his Majesty's Ship Active, under your command, for the purpose of acquainting any of his Majesty's Ships which may come on the above Rendezvous, that I am gone to the Madalena Islands, and to direct their Commanders to proceed and join me there with the utmost possible expedition. You are to continue on this Service till further orders, and upon no account to quit it in chase of any Vessel; but should you get any positive information of the sailing of the Enemy's Fleet, you are to join me at Madalena, without one moment's loss of time. If the Termagant or Childers join, to direct them, if to be done without much loss of time, to look into either Barcelona, or Rosas, for letters; and in the course of a week, I have no objection to the Active's calling off Barcelona for any letters, but by no means to anchor.

NELSON AND BRONTE.

TO CAPTAIN RICHARD BUDD VINCENT, H.M. SLOOP ARROW.

[Letter Book.]

Victory, at Sea, January 24th, 1804.

Sir,

By the Termagant I received your letter of the 19th ult., giving me an account of your proceedings with the Trade from Malta up the Adriatic, and the protection afforded them from thence to Valetta Harbour; also transmitting me copies of the several letters, &c. therein referred to, together with a Log of your proceedings, and a list of the Convoy under your charge. In answer to which, I very much approve of the whole of your conduct on this occasion, and am much pleased with your attention to the Government concerns up the Adriatic, under the direction of Mr. Leard,[1] who has communicated to me the object of his being there; and transmitted bills of lading of the stores sent in the Mentor, Giuro, and Imperial Schooner Hungary, which last mentioned Vessel I hope may arrive safe at Malta, as the stores she has on board are more particularly wanted than any of the others. I am, Sir, &c.

NELSON AND BRONTE.

---

[1] Vice-Consul at Ragusa.

TO CAPTAIN JOHN GORE, H. M. SHIP MEDUSA.

[From a Copy, in the Nelson Papers.]

Victory, at Sea, 24th January, 1804.

Sir,

I have this day received your letter of the 27th August by the Termagant, and very much approve of the exertion used in heaving down his Majesty's Ship Medusa under your command, as well as of the precaution taken for preserving the health of your Seamen, by issuing an additional half-pint of wine to each man; but I would recommend your acquainting the Admiralty with the circumstance, that you may have their Lordships' sanction for so doing; otherwise the Victualling-Board will most certainly impress your Account for the wine so issued.

I have received copies of the several orders you found necessary as Senior Officer at Gibraltar to issue, which very fully meet my approbation, as well as the arrangement you proposed making with Commissioner Otway, for the reception of British Seamen as they arrive from Spain. I am, &c.

NELSON AND BRONTE.

TO J. B. GIBERT, ESQ., HIS MAJESTY'S CONSUL AT BARCELONA.

[Letter-Book.]

Victory, at Sea, 24th January, 1804.

Sir,

I have received your letter of the 5th instant, together with the enclosures from Madrid, therein mentioned, and also your duplicate letter of the 24th ultimo, with the one from Mr. Frere, acting Consul-General at Madrid, therein alluded to. I am very much obliged by your intentions of sending me the earliest information of any political news respecting our two Countries. Agreeably to your request, I herewith transmit a copy of my letter to the Victualling Board. I am, &c.

NELSON AND BRONTE.

TO REAR-ADMIRAL SIR RICHARD BICKERTON, BART.

[Letter-Book.]

Victory, at Sea, 24th January, 1804.

Sir,

This morning I received your letter of the 27th ultimo, with copy of one from Mr. Woodhead, Agent to the Naval Hospital at Malta, requesting, for the reasons therein mentioned, that you would give your sanction and directions for his having a Clerk. In answer thereto, I perfectly approve of the temporary Assistant-Clerk which you recommended that gentleman to employ, but shall certainly not give my sanction to his having a Clerk allowed him, and therefore have desired him to apply to the Sick and Hurt Board for such Assistant. I have the honour to be, &c.

NELSON AND BRONTE.

TO MR. WILLIAM BEND, SURGEON OF HIS MAJESTY'S NAVAL HOSPITAL, GIBRALTAR.

[Letter-Book.]

Victory, at Sea, 24th January, 1804.

Sir,

I have this day received your letter of the 20th October last, (with the statement of the Hospital therein mentioned,) acquainting me, that you had, in consequence of Doctor Snipe's directions, visited the prisoners on board the Guerrier Prison-Ship, and removed such of them as were confined to bed, to the Hospital, to prevent contagion being generated. I am to desire you will, with all future Returns of the Hospital under your charge, transmit me a regular list of the Officers and Men who may die at the said Hospital, stating the Ships they belong to, when received, and the time of their death, that the respective Captains may be made acquainted therewith, and regulate their Books accordingly. I approve of the orders Doctor Snipe gave respecting your visiting the Prisoners on board the Guerrier, and your conduct in consequence. You will bear in mind my directions respecting a Porter for the Hospital gate, and apply to Commissioner Otway to recommend a proper person for that purpose. I am, &c.

NELSON AND BRONTE.

TO CAPTAIN WILLIAM EDWARD CRACRAFT, H.M. SHIP ANSON.

[Letter Book.]

Victory, at Sea, 24th January, 1804.

Sir,

I have this day received your letter of the 13th ultimo, with a copy of the one therein mentioned from Captain Corbett of his Majesty's Sloop Bittern, giving an account of his having run on shore a large Ship near Brindisi, and of his having set fire to her, owing to his not being able to get her off. In answer thereto, from the circumstances mentioned in Captain Corbett's said letter, his conduct appears to have been perfectly correct, and that the Ship in question, from her suspicious manœuvres, was, most probably, Enemy's property. I am, &c.,

NELSON AND BRONTE.

TO MR. JOHN WOODHEAD, AGENT TO THE NAVAL HOSPITAL, MALTA.

[Letter-Book.]

Victory, at Sea, 24th January, 1804.

Sir,

I have received a copy of your letter of the 27th ultimo to Rear-Admiral Sir Richard Bickerton, representing the necessity of your having the assistance of a Clerk, and requesting, for the reasons therein mentioned, that he would give his sanction and directions to that effect. In answer thereto, I do not feel justified to comply with your request, as the Commissioners of the Sick and Hurt Board must certainly have known at the time they appointed you, that it was probable upwards of two hundred men might be in the Naval Hospital at Malta at once, (on several occasions,) and, therefore, desire you will apply to the said Commissioners for a person of the description you mention. I am, &c.,

NELSON AND BRONTE.

TO CHARLES STUART, ESQ.,[7] SECRETARY OF LEGATION AT THE COURT OF VIENNA.

[Letter-Book.]

Victory, at Sea, 24th January, 1804.

Sir,

I have received your letter of the 1st September last, acquainting me that every possible reparation has been made by the Austrian Minister for the outrage against the British Flag, and that you had transmitted to Government copies of the several papers which passed between Captain Fyffe and the Commandant of Venice, on the occasion. I am very glad the Austrian Government have seen Captain Fyffe's conduct in its proper light, and that the necessary reparation has been made, as I was perfectly satisfied with the correctness of that Officer's proceedings on the above occasion. I am, &c.

NELSON AND BRONTE.

TO CAPTAIN SAMUEL SUTTON, H.M. SHIP AMPHION.

[Letter-Book.]

Victory, at Sea, 24th January, 1804.

Sir,

I have this day received your letter of the 16th October last, acquainting me, for the reasons therein mentioned, of your having gone to Lisbon, and also that, in consequence of the inclosure from Lord Robert Fitz-Gerald, his Majesty's Minister at Lisbon, which accompanied your said letter, you had brought the Duke de Coigny from that place to Gibraltar, in order to his proceeding by the first Frigate to England. In answer to which, I approve of your having gone to Lisbon under the circumstances you represent, and also of your having brought the Duke de Coigny to Gibraltar. I am, &c.,

NELSON AND BRONTE.

P.S.—I have received your letter of the 16th October, with the Amphion's state and condition, together with the log therein mentioned.

[7] Afterwards Lord Stuart de Rothsay, G.C.B.: he died on the 5th of November, 1845.

TO CAPTAIN JOHN GORE, H.M. SHIP MEDUSA.

[Letter-Book.]

Victory, at Sea, 24th January, 1804.

Sir,

I have this day received your letter of the 9th October last, together with one from the Captain of the American Sloop of War Siren, dated the 7th of that month, and your answer thereto respecting the three British Subjects named in the margin,[8] who had returned to their duty and allegiance from the said Sloop, on board his Majesty's Ship under your command. In answer thereto, as the Officers of the said Sloop of War declare they knew them to be British Subjects at the time they entered for the Service of the United States, I very much approve of your not having delivered them up, and also of the orders you gave Lieutenant Williams of the Victory, to receive all British Seamen in Gibraltar for the Service of their Country. I am, &c.

NELSON AND BRONTE.

TO CAPTAIN THOMAS STAINES, COMMANDING HIS MAJESTY'S SLOOP CAMELEON.

[Order-Book. Thursday, 26th January. " P.M. Standing into Agincourt Sound. At 5, came to with the small bower, in 10 fathoms."—*Victory's Log.*]

Victory, Madalena Islands, Sardinia, 26th January, 1804.

Whereas, it is probable, from the information I have received, that the Enemy's Fleet may be at Sea, or that some of their Frigates, with Transports, having Troops on board, may be coming this way, You are therefore hereby required and directed to proceed immediately with his Majesty's Sloop Cameleon, under your command, off Monte Christo, and between that and the Mainland, and use your utmost endeavour to speak every Merchant-Vessel which you may be able to fall in with, for the purpose of gaining intelligence of any of the Enemy's Ships or Vessels which may be coming that way from Genoa, or the Island of Elba, either accompanied by Transports or otherwise; and upon gaining such information, you are to join me at this anchorage without a

---

[8] James Dunbervan, James Pearce, John Cox.

moment's loss of time. The Termagant will proceed and join you to-morrow on the above service, in the execution of which you will continue three or four days; but upon gaining any intelligence, you are to send the Termagant or join me yourself, with an account thereof, without a moment's loss of time. NELSON AND BRONTE.

TO HIS EXCELLENCY HUGH ELLIOT, ESQ.

[Autograph, in the Elliot Papers.]

My dear Sir, *Victory, Madalena, January 30th, 1804.*

The non-appearance of the Gibraltar tells me what the answer of Buonaparte has been. Nothing but insolence could be expected from him. My movements are regulated as my intelligence and fancy lead me to suppose the French Fleet will [come] out. Sardinia is certainly to be taken by the French, and I do not believe that I can prevent it. The French Fleet were to have sailed on Friday the 20th, and it was then put off to Wednesday the 25th, but they had not sailed the 27th. I go from here in a few days, and all my hopes are to meet them.

By your letter No. 2, I am glad to find that your dispatches from England have been so agreeable to yourself and where you are placed. No. 3.—I have no Vessel to send to Naples. I am kept in great distress for Frigates and smaller Vessels at this critical moment. I want ten more than I have, in order to watch that the French should not escape me. I shall keep this letter till an opportunity offers, of which I see no prospect at present. I have talked to Captain Hardy about your son, and as we have no schoolmaster in the Victory, and the greater part of our youngsters dispersed, we have asked Captain Parker of the Amazon to take him, which he has kindly promised to do. He could be nowhere so well placed on every account: therefore, you may send him when you please. A good Schoolmaster is also in that Frigate.

I observe what you say in No. 5, and shall pay great attention to it. I hope to hold out till the French Fleet are taken, burnt, or sunk; and that they shall be, will be the exertion of, my dear Sir, your most obliged friend and servant,

NELSON AND BRONTE.

Doctor Scott is very well.

TO SIR JOHN ACTON, BART., NAPLES.

[From Clarke and M'Arthur, vol. ii. p. 357.]

30th January, 1804.

I am distressed for Frigates, which are the eyes of a Fleet;
for the terrible winter we have had has obliged me to send
three into Port to be refitted: however, I trust we shall
fall in with the Enemy, and do the business. Your Excellency
knows, that with all the care and attention possible, it has
happened that Fleets have passed each other; therefore I
need not apprise you, how necessary it is to keep a good look-
out for them.   I am, &c.,

NELSON AND BRONTE.

TO CAPTAIN ROSS DONNELLY, H. M. SHIP NARCISSUS.

[Autograph, in the possession of the late Adam Bromilow, Esq., and Order-Book.]

Victory, at the Madalena Islands, 30th January, 1804.

Secret.

Having received information that the Enemy intend sending Troops from Ville Franche to the Island of Corsica, and
it being of the utmost importance that they should be intercepted, You are hereby required and directed to take his
Majesty's Ship named* in the margin[9] under your command,
and proceed with all possible dispatch off Cape Revallata, on
the West side of Corsica, where you will take such station as
you may judge most likely to fall in with the Enemy, as above
mentioned; and, on doing so, use every means in your power
to take or destroy them. It may, therefore, be advisable,
under favourable circumstances, first to attack and destroy the
Transports with the Troops on board, and afterwards engage
the Ships or Vessels of War which may accompany them.

You will continue on this service for the space of fourteen
days from this date, and at the expiration thereof, (should you
not fall in with the Enemy,) return without loss of time to
this anchorage, where you will find me, or orders for your
further proceedings.

NELSON AND BRONTE.

[b] Juno.

TO CAPTAIN ROSS DONNELLY, H.M. SHIP NARCISSUS.

[Autograph, in the possession of the late Adam Bromilow, Esq.]

Victory, at the Madalena Islands, Sardinia, 30th January, 1804.
Secret.
Sir,

In the event of your falling in with and capturing the Enemy's Ships, with Troops on board, expected from Ville Franche, as mentioned in my order to you of this date, I am to desire you will bring them to this anchorage; and after having taken the whole of their arms, use every means to secure them on board their respective Vessels and Transports, till such time as an opportunity offers of sending them to Malta, as the service of the Ship you command cannot, at this important season, be spared to accompany them there. I am, &c.   NELSON AND BRONTE.

TO REAR-ADMIRAL GEORGE CAMPBELL, H. M. SHIP CANOPUS.

[From a Copy in the Admiralty.]

Victory, at the Madalena Islands, Sardinia, 30th January, 1804.
Sir,

The two Ships named in the margin[1] being wanted for immediate service, I delivered orders for their proceedings to Captain Donnelly, immediately on his coming on board here after the Court[2] broke up. I have, therefore, to desire you will be pleased to communicate to the Members composing the Court, that circumstances of the most important nature to the Country require the immediate service of those two Frigates. I have the honour to be, &c.

NELSON AND BRONTE.

TO REAR-ADMIRAL GEORGE CAMPBELL.

[Letter-Book.]

Victory, Madalena Islands, Sardinia, 30th January, 1804.
Sir,

As his Majesty's Ships named in the margin[1] will proceed to sea to-morrow, on secret and important service, if the

---

[1] Narcissus, Juno.   [2] A Court-Martial on Lieutenant Wales, of the Renown.

weather will permit, (which will be officially announced to
you,) I am to desire you will be pleased to order the Judge-
Advocate to acquaint the prisoner thereof, in case he should
desire to have the evidence of Lieutenant Thompson of the
Narcissus, or any person belonging to either of those Frigates,
that they may be summoned to-night, and left behind accordingly.   I have the honour to be, &c.,

NELSON AND BRONTE.

TO THE CAPTAIN OR COMMANDER OF ANY OF HIS MAJESTY'S
SHIPS OR VESSELS WHO MAY ARRIVE AT THE MADALENA
ISLANDS IN SEARCH OF THE SQUADRON.

[Letter Book.]

Victory, Madalena Islands, Sardinia, 30th January, 1804.

Sir,

I am to desire you will proceed immediately with the Ship
or Vessel under your command to a station from twelve to
fifteen leagues West of Rendezvous No. 70, and cruize there
for the space of seven days, for the purpose of joining the
Squadron; but should you not fall in with it, or gain any
intelligence thereof, I am to desire, at the expiration of the
above time, that you will proceed to Rendezvous No. 60, where
you will find me, or orders for your further proceedings.   This
letter to be sealed up and left with the Governor under the
same address.   I am, &c.

NELSON AND BRONTE.

TO CAPTAIN THOMAS STAINES, H. M. SLOOP CAMELÉON.

[Order-Book.]

Victory, at the Madalena Islands, Sardinia, 31st January, 1804.

You are hereby required and directed to proceed immediately with his Majesty's Sloop under your command, and
cruize off the North end of Asinara, for the purpose of
acquainting any of his Majesty's Ships or Vessels that the
Squadron is gone to a station twelve or fifteen leagues West
of Rendezvous No. 70.   You will also recommend them to
cruize for the space of seven days on the said station, and in
the event of not gaining any intelligence of me to proceed to

Rendezvous No 60, where they will find the Squadron, or orders for their further proceedings.

NELSON AND BRONTE.

Should any Transport arrive off Asinara, I think she could be securely moored in the snug Cove, in the S.E. part of the Island, and would be safe under the protection of your cruizing, until I shall come, or send for her.

TO CAPTAIN ROBERT PETTET, H. M. SHIP TERMAGANT.

[Order-Book.]

Victory, Madalena Islands, Sardinia, 31st January, 1804.

Secret.

Whereas I judge it necessary that his Majesty's Sloop Termagant, under your command, should remain at this anchorage, for the protection of such Transports, or Victuallers, as may arrive for the Fleet, You are hereby required and directed to remain with the said Sloop, in the N.W. part of the Bay, at single anchor, and take the Transport which the Amazon may accompany to this place, or any other that may arrive from Malta or Gibraltar, taking care to moor them close to the Termagant, and remain here till you receive my further orders. And as it is probable the French may send Troops from Corsica to take possession of these Islands, you are to cause a look-out to be kept by day on the height immediately to the N.W. of your anchorage, for the purpose of discovering the approach of the Enemy, should they make an attempt; and you will order an Officer to row guard constantly during the night, round the Transports or Victuallers under your charge, that on the least appearance of danger, or capture by a superior force, you may take the necessary measures for their safety, and proceed to sea with them.

NELSON AND BRONTE.

P.S.—Keep a strict watch during the night, and have your guns loaded with grape.[1]

---

[1] To this Order, the following addition was made by Lord Nelson's Secretary:—" Lord Nelson desires you will give it out at Madalena, that you not only wait here for the protection of the Transports, but also to acquaint the Gibraltar, expected from Naples, and others of his Majesty's Ships from Malta and Gibraltar, where his Lordship is gone with the Squadron.—JOHN SCOTT."

TO SIR EVAN NEPEAN, BART., ADMIRALTY.

[Copy, in the Admiralty. Wednesday, 1st February. "A.M. At 7, weighed and made sail; Squadron in company."—*Victory's Log.*]

Sir,   Victory, at Sea, 1st February, 1804.

I herewith transmit the sentence of a Court-Martial on Lieutenant Richard Wales,[4] of his Majesty's ship Renown, and request you will be pleased to lay it before the Lords Commissioners of the Admiralty for their information; and, at the same time, acquaint their Lordships that in consequence of my having received information that the Enemy had embarked troops at Ville Franche, which were to proceed immediately to St. Fiorenzo, in Corsica, for the purpose of taking possession of the Island of Sardinia, I ordered the Narcissus and Juno, who arrived in the afternoon of the 29th ult. (in a heavy gale of wind) to complete their water, &c., with the utmost dispatch, which, from its blowing so excessively hard was found impracticable, till early on the 30th, when the Juno (who was in want of every description of provisions) completed from the Line of Battle Ships. Conceiving, therefore, that the Court-Martial, which was ordered for the 30th, on the said Lieutenant, would be over in the course of that day (and before the Juno was ready for sea) I suffered it to assemble, under the most perfect conviction that it would so terminate; and the instant the signal was hauled down on board the Canopus, Captain Donnelly came on board the Victory, and received his orders to proceed with the before-mentioned Frigates off Cape Revellata, for the purpose of preventing the Enemy from landing in Corsica, and of capturing or destroying them on their coming on that Coast. Impressed with the importance of this service and the necessity of preventing the Enemy from landing their Troops in Corsica, I felt justified, although the Trial was not over, in ordering the Frigates to proceed immediately, without risking the delay of a moment, or subjecting their Captains to detention by the Court; and, therefore, wrote a letter to the President[5] (a copy of which accompanies this) communicating the necessary absence of those Frigates, which I trust will meet their Lordships' approbation.

I am, &c.,   NELSON AND BRONTE.

---

[4] He was tried for having behaved himself with contempt and disobedience to his Captain.   [5] Vide p. 397, ante.

TO CAPTAIN PARKER, H.M. SHIP AMAZON.

[Order Book.]

Victory, at Sea, 7th February, 1804.

Having been prevented by the late blowing weather from reconnoitring the Enemy at Toulon, You are hereby required and directed to proceed, without a moment's loss of time, in his Majesty's Ship Amazon,[2] under your command, off the entrance of Toulon Harbour, for the purpose of ascertaining whether the Enemy's Ships are still in Port, and return and join the Squadron at the Madalena Islands with the utmost possible expedition, with an account thereof, where you will find me, or orders for your further proceedings.

NELSON AND BRONTE.

TO CAPTAIN WILLIAM PARKER, H.M. SHIP AMAZON.

[Letter-Book.]

Victory, at Sea, 8th February, 1804.

Sir,

When the signal No. 122[3] is made for the Amazon to part company, I am to desire you will proceed with the utmost dispatch off the North end of Asinara, where you will find his Majesty's Sloop Cameleon, and on joining her, deliver Captain Staines the letter you will herewith receive, bearing his address. In the event of not falling in with the said Sloop immediately on her Rendezvous, as above, you are to proceed with all dispatch, and put in execution my order to you of yesterday's date, which also accompanies this. I would recommend you, in standing over to Toulon, not to keep more to the Northward than N.W. b N., as the wind at this season hangs very much to the North-West, which prevented the Squadron from reconnoitring the Enemy in that harbour, in our late attempt. You will acquaint any of his Majesty's Ships or Vessels which you may fall in with, that I am gone with the Squadron to the Madalena Islands, where they will find me, or orders for their proceedings. I am, &c.,

NELSON AND BRONTE.

---

[2] The Amazon and Donegal joined the Squadron in the afternoon of the 7th of February.

[3] "Permission is given to part company."

TO CAPTAIN THOMAS STAINES, H. M. SLOOP CAMELEON.

[Letter-Book.]

Victory, at Sea, 8th February, 1804.

Sir,

I am to desire you will join the Squadron immediately in his Majesty's Sloop Cameleon under your command, at the Madalena Islands, where you will find me, or orders for your further proceedings. You will bring with you any Victualler which may be under your charge to the said anchorage with the utmost dispatch, and acquaint any of his Majesty's Ships or Vessels which you may fall in with, that I am gone to the Madalena Islands. I am, &c.,

NELSON AND BRONTE.

PRIVATE JOURNAL.

[From Clarke and M'Arthur, vol. ii. p. 358. "Wednesday, 8th February. A.M. At ½ past 11, shortened sail, and came to with the best bower," in the Madalena Islands.]

8th February, 1804.

The Fleet ran in [the Madalena Islands] under reefed foresails, through the Eastern passage, which looked tremendous from the number of rocks, and the heavy sea breaking over them; but it is perfectly safe when once known. Captain Ryves' mark of the Pedestal Rock can never be mistaken.

TO CAPTAIN CHARLES WILLIAM ADAIR, OF THE ROYAL MARINES, H. M. SHIP VICTORY, HEREBY APPOINTED INSPECTING OFFICER OF RECRUITS TO BE RAISED FOR THE ABOVE SERVICE.

[Order-Book.]

Victory, at Sea, 9th February,[2] 1804.

Whereas I have this day received a letter from Sir Evan Nepean, Bart., dated the 29th November last, acquainting me

---

[2] *Sic*, but as it occurs in the Order-Book among Orders dated early in *March*, and as it is dated "*At Sea*," whereas on the 9th of February 1804, the Victory was at Anchor in the Madalena Islands, the 9th of *March* is probably the correct date of this Order.

that notwithstanding all the exertions of the Recruiting-parties, it has been found impossible to complete the Royal Marines to the number voted by Parliament, and signifying to me their Lordships' direction to authorize the enlisting of any men, natives of any Country excepting France, who may be disposed to enter, and may be found in all respects fit for his Majesty's Marine Service, causing them to be paid the usual bounty on their being attested, and letting them know that they will be discharged at the end of the War, and be sent back to the Mediterranean, if they should desire it—acquainting me also, that the sum of five guineas is to be paid to each recruit upon his being approved of and attested as beforementioned, and to cause bills to be drawn upon the Honourable George Villiers, Paymaster of the Royal Marines, for the amount.

And, whereas, I judge it necessary for the more effectually carrying their Lordships' instructions into immediate execution, and to prevent imposition of every description, that some person should have the charge of inspecting the Recruits which may be raised, previous to their being paid the bounty, as well as to be answerable to Government for the money drawn for that purpose; You are, therefore, hereby appointed, Inspecting Officer of Recruits to be raised for the Royal Marine Service, under the before-mentioned instructions— who, I shall order to be sent on board His Majesty's Ship Victory for that purpose, and if they are found in every respect fit for the said service, you are to pay each Recruit the sum of five guineas upon his being attested, and to enable you to do so, you are to draw bills (which are to be approved of by me) upon the Honourable George Villiers, Paymaster of the Royal Marines, for such sums of money as you may from time to time find necessary, taking care to acquaint him thereof, and transmit regular vouchers and documents for the disbursement to the said Paymaster, and also, to me for my information. You are to pay the most strict regard to this service, and take every means in your power (in addition to the Public Order which I shall give the respective Captains of the Fleet, under my command) for raising recruits for the Royal Marine Service.

NELSON AND BRONTE.

TO SIR RICHARD BICKERTON, BART., REAR-ADMIRAL OF THE WHITE, AND SECOND OFFICER IN THE COMMAND OF HIS MAJESTY'S SHIPS AND VESSELS ON THE MEDITERRANEAN STATION.

[Order-Book. Numerous Orders to the same effect as the following, which is inserted to show the form of assembling Courts-Martial, occur in the Order-Book. All the Orders printed in this work commence and end in similar words to those here given.]

By the Right Honourable Lord Viscount Nelson, K.B., &c. &c. &c.

Whereas you have, with your letter of the 13th ultimo, transmitted me one which you had received from Spelman Swaine, Esq., Commander of his Majesty's late Sloop Raven, dated the 8th day of January last, giving an account of the loss of his Majesty's said late Sloop, having run on shore near Mazzara, in Sicily, at about eleven o'clock on the night of the 5th of that month, and was totally wrecked; and whereas I think fit that the said Captain Spelman Swaine, the Officers, and Company of his Majesty's late Sloop Raven, shall be tried by a Court-Martial, for the loss of the same, I send you herewith your before-mentioned letter, together with the one from Captain Swaine, therein alluded to, dated the 8th ultimo; and do hereby require and direct you to assemble a Court-Martial as soon as conveniently may be, which Court (you being President thereof) is hereby required and directed to try the said Captain Spelman Swaine, the Officers, and Ship's Company, for the loss of his Majesty's late Sloop Raven, on the night of the 5th of January 1804, as mentioned in his letter of the 8th of that month; and also to inquire into and try the said Captain Swaine, the Officers, and Sloop's Company for their conduct after the loss of his Majesty's said late Sloop Raven accordingly.

Given under my hand, on board his Majesty's Ship Victory, at the Madalena Islands, Sardinia, the 9th of February 1804. NELSON AND BRONTE.

By Command of the Vice-Admiral. JOHN SCOTT.

TO PATRICK WILKIE, ESQ., AGENT VICTUALLER, MALTA.

[Letter-Book.]

Victory, Madalena Islands, February 10th, 1804.

Sir,

I have received from Rear-Admiral Sir Richard Bickerton, the offers made you for supplying wine and fresh beef, which, he acquaints me, you have accepted, provided the proposals meet my approbation. In answer to which, and to your letter of the 13th ultimo, on that subject, I approve of the offers therein mentioned, under a conviction that the Contract entered into is upon the lowest and most reasonable terms for Government, and that you have maturely weighed the propriety thereof, previous to your accepting the conditions. I, however, desire you will communicate the said Contract to the Commissioners of the Victualling, that you may act under the sanction of their authority on the occasion. I am, &c.,

NELSON AND BRONTE.

TO HIS EXCELLENCY THOMAS JACKSON, ESQ., MINISTER PLENI-
POTENTIARY AT THE COURT OF SARDINIA.

[From a Copy, in the Elliot Papers.]

My dear Sir,   Victory, February 10th, 1804, Madalena.

I was honoured on the 8th, on my arrival here, with your letter of January 6th. The storm is brewing, and there can be little doubt but that Sardinia is one of the first objects of its violence. Apropos—We have a report that the visit of Lucien Buonaparte is to effect an amicable exchange of Sardinia for Parma and Piacenza. This must not take place, or Sicily, Malta, Egypt, &c. &c., is lost, sooner or later. What I can do to ward off the blow shall be done, as I have already assured His Royal Highness the Viceroy. From Marseilles and Nice there are not less than 30,000 men ready for embarkation. Should Russia go to war with France, from that moment I consider the mask as being thrown off, with respect to any Neutrality of his Sardinian Majesty: therefore, if that should be the case, would the King consent to two or three hundred British Troops taking post upon the Madalena? It would be a momentary check against an invasion from Corsica; and enable us to assist the Northern part of Sardinia. You will touch upon this matter in the way you think most prudent, or entirely omit it.   But there is only this choice—to lose the whole of Sardinia, or to allow a small body of friendly Troops to hold a post at the Northern end of the Island.   We may prevent: we cannot retake.   Sardinia is the most important post in the Mediterranean: it covers Naples, Sicily, Malta, Egypt, and all the Turkish Dominions ; it blockades Toulon ; the wind which would carry a French Fleet to the Westward is fair from Sardinia ; and Madalena is the most important station in this most important Island.   I am told that the revenues, after paying the expenses of the Island, do not give the King £5000 sterling, a year.   If it is so, I would give him £500,000 to cede it, which would give him £25,000 a year for ever.   This is only my conversation, and not to be noticed—but the King cannot long hold Sardinia.

With respect to the King's desire for me to have a Vessel ready to receive him from some part of the Roman Coast, I can only say, that if I knew the exact *time* and *place* of such embarkation, a Vessel should certainly be there to the day and the hour.   As the mention stands, it is too indeterminate to answer, except that nothing shall be wanting on my part to meet the wishes of his Sardinian Majesty, as far as is possible.

With respect to the history about the French Privateers from Ancona, and the conduct of the English Privateers at Fuimesino, I believe you are correct, but our Enemies never adhere to it.   They go in and out of the Spanish and Sicilian Ports, at all times, night and day—in short, to examine all Vessels passing.   But all Privateers are very incorrect, and I sincerely wish there was no such Vessels allowed.   They are only one degree removed from Pirates : but, I believe, an English Armed-Vessel never yet trusted his cause to any Court but an English Court of Admiralty.   However, I have no power over them.   But, certainly, if the custom of the Port of Fuimesino has invariably been not to allow any Corsair to sail out of the Port until the twenty-four hours after the sailing of a Neutral, then our Privateer ought to have been forced to conform.   But, I dare say, the French go in and out of Ancona as they please ; and if so, the Court of Rome has no great cause of complaint.   I can only again repeat, that over Privateers I have no control.   I am ever, my dear Sir, yours most faithfully,   NELSON AND BRONTE.

TO MR. RICHARD FORD, AGENT FOR VICTUALLING HIS
MAJESTY'S FLEET ON THE MEDITERRANEAN STATION.

[Order-Book.]

Victory, Madalena Islands, 10th February, 1804.

The Commissioners for Victualling his Majesty's Navy
having, in consequence of instructions from the Lords Commissioners of the Admiralty, directed their Agent at Gibraltar
to supply me with such sums of money as might be necessary
for the purchase of provisions for the Ships under my command, till such time as an Agent should be attached to
the Fleet, and Mr. Cutforth[5] having forwarded to me some
time ago, six thousand hard, or Spanish dollars, for the purpose above mentioned, the greater part of which is expended,
You are therefore hereby required and directed, in order that
the whole receipt and disbursement of the Public money may
appear upon the face of one account, to charge yourself with the
said six thousand dollars, and to grant me a general receipt for
the number supplied the Captains of his Majesty's Ships named
in the margin, agreeable to their receipts, from No. 1 to 9, being
four thousand nine hundred and fifty dollars, and also, for the
residue of the said sum, being one thousand and fifty dollars.
And you are also hereby directed to charge yourself with all
future sums of money, which may be sent from Mr. Cutforth
for the use of the Fleet under my command, and grant him
the necessary receipts for the same, taking care to have constantly a sufficient number of dollars in your possession to
answer the purpose of your situation, that Government by the
use of ready money, may receive the benefit resulting there-
from, and that the Fleet may at all times, when fresh beef,
&c., can be procured, be well and duly supplied, for which
porpose, you are hereby directed to purchase such live bullocks, &c., as can be procured for the use of the Fleet on the
present occasion, and also, such a number of sheep for the use
of the sick and convalescent Seamen and Marines, on board
the different Ships, as the Captain of the Fleet may judge
proper, which, as the price is little more than that of fresh
beef, and the quality so inferior to English mutton, you are

[5] Agent Victualler at Gibraltar.

to issue to the respective Pursers, pound for pound, the same as beef; and as Frigates are frequently detached from the Squadron to the different places in these seas, where fresh provisions can be had upon much more reasonable terms for ready money, than by bills of exchange, it is also my directions that you supply their Captains with such a number of dollars as I may think proper to order, taking proper receipts for the same.

NELSON AND BRONTE.

TO THE PRINCIPAL OFFICERS AND COMMISSIONERS OF HIS MAJESTY'S NAVY, LONDON.

[Letter-Book.]

Victory, Madalena Islands, 10th February, 1804.

Gentlemen,

I have this day received your letter of the 9th September last, communicating to me the directions you had given the Naval Storekeeper at Malta, respecting the Cordage lately made at that place, and his means for making it, and whether any articles are wanted for the purpose of making cables and cordage, and likewise to let you know what supplies of other Naval Stores can be procured in that neighbourhood, and to what extent, &c. In answer thereto, I have some time ago directed the Naval Officer at Malta, to use every means in his power for making Cordage, &c., with the hemp lately purchased up the Adriatic; but, I very much suspect, from Mr. Taylor's account of the transaction, that our purchases and supplies from that quarter will be very limited. I have, however, transmitted him an account of the prices of Cordage and other Naval Stores to be procured at Smyrna, in the event of our being obliged to have recourse to that quarter for any future supply. I am, &c.,

NELSON AND BRONTE.

TO MR. JOHN GRAY, SURGEON OF HIS MAJESTY'S NAVAL
HOSPITAL, MALTA.

[Letter-Book.]

Victory, Madalena Islands, 10th February, 1804.

Sir,

I have received from Rear-Admiral Sir Richard Bickerton
your letter of the 21st January last, with the one from Mr.
Higgins, Contractor for Victualling the Naval Hospital therein
mentioned, on the subject of supplying milk to the Patients in
their tea, morning and evening; and as it appears that article
has not been provided for in the Contract entered into by the
said Mr. Higgins, I am to desire you will request him to
supply the necessary quantity of milk for the purpose above-
mentioned, and so soon as Doctor Snipe, Physician to the
Fleet, has returned from Gibraltar, I shall direct him to take
the same into consideration, and make such allowance for it
as shall by him and the said Contractor be deemed equal to
the additional expense incurred by such supply. I am, &c.,

NELSON AND BRONTE.

TO HIS EXCELLENCY HUGH ELLIOT, ESQ., NAPLES.

[Autograph, in the Elliot Papers.]

Victory, February 10th, 1804.

My dear Sir,

I have had no opportunity of sending my letter of the
30th ultimo. We have been off Toulon, in most terrible
weather, and are drove in here. My accounts from Gibraltar
lead me to suppose that the Ferrol Squadron is destined for
the Mediterranean. The L'Aigle 74 at Cadiz is ready to join
them. But I hope to intercept them; and if they join, which
is very possible—for I dare not go so far from Toulon to take
a proper station for intercepting them—we must look them in
the face.

I received on my arrival here, on the 8th, your Excellency's
letter of January 18th, which is very interesting. I only hope
that the French Army in Naples will not act until the arrival
of the Russians; but the Northern Powers are slow, and I
would rather see a Russian Army than a Russian Fleet in Italy.

Your story of Lucien Buonaparte is curious. Reports say, that he is come into Italy to negotiate with the King of Sardinia for an exchange of Sardinia for Parma and Piacenza. If the French get Sardinia it requires not the gift of prophecy to say, that sooner or later Sicily will belong likewise to France : therefore, no countenance must be given to such an exchange. I hope the Galleys will be stationed here—it may be useful; but when you talk of the Militia acting in Sardinia, and a body of Infantry, I recollect there are no Troops in the Island worth mentioning, and no *money* to put any Militia, if they were inclined to move, in activity. *Entre nous*, it is not the interest of the Sardinians to remain as they are. The Peasantry are oppressed with small taxes, and the Nobles are detested. I shall answer Mr. Jackson's letter, and send it open for your perusal; and I shall only repeat that I am ever, my dear Sir, your most obliged friend,

NELSON AND BRONTE.

TO NATHANIEL TAYLOR, ESQ., NAVAL STOREKEEPER, MALTA.

[Letter-Book.]

Victory, Madalena Islands, 10th February, 1804.

Sir,

I have received your letter of the 23rd ult., together with the several papers and documents from Mr. Leard, forwarded by the Kent, as therein mentioned, which I shall give due consideration to; but I am hopeful, as the summer season is approaching, that supplies from the Adriatic will not be wanted : at least, for this considerable time, and trust the Hungarian Schooner with the cordage and tar for the stores under your charge, will soon arrive. I herewith transmit you an account of the prices of cordage and other Naval stores at Smyrna, and desire you will compare it with the prices paid for the like articles in the Adriatic, and send me your remarks thereupon. I am, &c.,

NELSON AND BRONTE.

TO CAPTAIN RYVES, H. M. SHIP GIBRALTAR.

[Autograph, in the possession of his son, Captain George Frederic Ryves, C.B.]

Victory, Madalena, February 10th, 1804.

My dear Sir,

It is with the sincerest sorrow that I am to be the bearer of such news[6] as will distress you very much, but, for the sake of your dear children, you must bear up against the heavy misfortune. To attempt consolation at such a time is, I know, out of the question : therefore, I can only assure you of my sincere condolence, and that I am, your most faithful friend,

NELSON AND BRONTE.

TO HIS EXCELLENCY SIR JOHN ACTON.

[From a Copy in the Elliot Papers.]

My dear Sir John,　　Victory, Madalena, February 10th, 1804.

Since my letter of January 30th (which has never left the Ship) I have been off Toulon, but it blew such a violent storm of wind and snow, that I was obliged to bear up, and passing round Cape Corse, was glad to get here again, and shall sail the 13th at furthest.

I am now rather led to believe that the Ferrol Squadron of French Ships will push for the Mediterranean. The French Ship at Cadiz[7] is ready to join them. I shall try to intercept them, but I cannot go so far to the Westward as is necessary ; for I will not lose sight of the Toulon Fleet. What a most zealous man can do to meet all points of difficulty, shall be done. My Squadron is the finest for its numbers in the world, and much may be expected from it ; and should superior numbers join, we must look it in the face. Nil desperandum! God is good, and our cause is just. The assemblage of Troops at Nice is going on ; and, although Sardinia, Naples, and Sicily, may be some of the objects, yet I have no doubt but Egypt is the favourite and ultimate object of the Corsican tyrant. I beg you will assure their

---

[6] The death of Admiral Ryves's first wife, Catherine Elizabeth, youngest daughter of the Hon. James Everard Arundell, third son of Henry, sixth Lord Arundell of Wardour. She died on the 27th of December 1803.

[7] L'Aigle.

Majesties that Nelson is Nelson still, and most zealously attached to their service; and I am, my dear Sir John, your Excellency's most faithful friend,

NELSON AND BRONTE.

P.S.—I send two letters from Dumourier. Your Excellency will judge from his character whether he could at any period be useful to Naples: I have a very high opinion of his *abilities.* I had, to December 29th, letters from Lady Hamilton, who desires me to present her best compliments to your Excellency, and to Lady Acton.   N. AND B.

TO WILLIAM LAWSON, ESQ., MASTER-ATTENDANT, MALTA.

[From a Copy in the Nelson Papers.]

Victory, Madalena Islands, 10th February, 1804.

Sir,

Rear-Admiral Sir Richard Bickerton having transmitted to me your letter to him of the 11th ultimo, acquainting him that the five and six-inch rope, sent out in the Ellice Transport, for the Fleet under my command, was not manufactured at Malta, but at Trieste, and sent from the last-mentioned place in June last, by Mr. Leard, to the stores under your charge. I am very glad to find that the rope above-mentioned was not manufactured at Malta, and also, much pleased with the improvement you are making in the manufacture of cordage at that Yard, as stated in Sir Richard Bickerton's letter on the subject. I am, &c.,

NELSON AND BRONTE.

TO REAR-ADMIRAL SIR RICHARD BICKERTON, BART.

[From a Copy in the Nelson Papers.]

Victory, Madalena Islands, 10th February, 1804.

Sir,

His Majesty's Ship Juno being ordered upon very important service, and must not on any account be detained from carrying the object of my instructions into execution, I am, therefore, to desire, if the accidental circumstance of her being for the moment forced to her present anchorage, interferes with the Court-Martial ordered upon the four Seamen belonging to the Victory, that it is put off till she has proceeded to sea, as Captain Richardson cannot divert from the immediate prosecution of my orders. I have the honour to be, &c.,

NELSON AND BRONTE.

TO SIR ALEXANDER JOHN BALL, BART., MALTA.

[Autograph, in the possession of Sir William Keith Ball, Bart.]

Victory, February 11th, 1804.

Private.

My dear Ball,

Many, many thanks for your kind letters, oranges, &c., &c., as Hallowell[7] has been with you he will tell you all the English news, therefore, I have little to say, except that now all my force, except Gibraltar, is united, and for our numbers none better can be. If the Ferrol Squadron joins the Toulon, they will much outnumber us; but in that case I shall never lose sight of them, and Sir Edward Pellew[8] will soon be after them. The loss of the Raven is very great, and the Admiralty seem determined not to increase my force. I, at this moment, want ten Frigates or Sloops, when I believe neither the Ferrol or Toulon Squadron could escape me; the Diana is ordered home from Gibraltar—it is shameful: Lord St. Vincent was not treated so. The moment I can possibly part with a Vessel, you shall have another in the room of the Raven. We are, my dear friend, on the eve of great events; the sooner they come the better; 12,000 men are ready for embarkation at Toulon, and 16,000 at Nice, and as they have not Transports, they must naturally expect more Ships of War; the Admiralty tells me nothing, they know nothing; but my private letters say, that the Brest Squadron, as well as Ferrol, is bound here—if so, we shall have work enough upon our hands. But, I am sure of my present force as far as it will go; we shall come

---

[7] Captain, afterwards Admiral Sir Benjamin Hallowell Carew, G.C.B. (vide vol. ii. p. 90) who joined the Mediterranean Fleet in the Argo, but soon after returned to England. Vide p. 416, post.

[8] Captain Sir Edward Pellew (afterwards Admiral Viscount Exmouth, G.C.B.) then commanded the Tonnant, with a small Squadron under his orders.

to no harm. I send a packet for Mr. Drummond; when opportunity offers, pray send it to Patras, Corfu, or Smyrna, and ever believe me, dear Ball, yours most truly and faithfully,

NELSON AND BRONTE.

We are all well.

TO THE GRAND VIZIR.

[From Clarke and M'Arthur, vol. ii. p. 358.]

11th February, 1804.

If the French unite their Fleets outside of the Mediterranean with that at Toulon, it is not the Sublime Porte's being at peace with Buonaparte, that will prevent an invasion of both the Morea and Egypt: your Highness knows them too well to put any confidence in what they say. Buonaparte's tongue is that of a serpent oiled. Nothing shall be wanting on my part to frustrate the designs of this common disturber of the human race. I am, &c.,

NELSON AND BRONTE.

TO HIS HIGHNESS THE CAPITAN PASHA.

[From Clarke and M'Arthur, vol. ii. p. 358.]

11th February, 1804.

My letters inform me that you are appointed, by the Grand Seignor, Capitan Pasha, in the room of his late Highness, on which high honour allow an old friend most sincerely to congratulate you; and to wish that you may long live to enjoy it, and increase the splendour of the Ottoman Arms. Your Highness will soon have to fight the French; for the perfidious Buonaparte will certainly, if he can, attack some part of the Ottoman Empire. You have my sincere prayers for a complete victory over them. I am, &c.,

NELSON AND BRONTE.

TO THE MARQUIS OF HERTFORD.

[From Clarke and M'Arthur, vol. ii. p. 353.]

[About the 11th of February, 1804.]

I was honoured with your Lordship's letter by Mr. Seymour,[9] the son of my oldest friend; who would at this moment, if it had pleased God to save his life, have most essentially served his King and Country. I am very much pleased with Seymour, and have given him the first Commission which has fallen since his arrival. I am, &c.

NELSON AND BRONTE.

TO MR. THOMAS FOTHERINGHAM, MASTER OF HIS MAJESTY'S HIRED TRANSPORT ELIZA.

[Order-Book.]

Victory, at the Madalena Islands, 12th February, 1804.

Having directed the Commander of his Majesty's Sloop Termagant to escort you to the South end of Sardinia, or further, if he shall, from circumstances, deem it necessary, You are hereby required and directed to proceed to sea with the Transport under your charge, in company with the said Sloop, and make all possible dispatch to Valetta Harbour, taking care, after parting with the Termagant, to keep company with the Sea-Nymph, and on no account to separate; but use your utmost endeavours, if attacked by a Privateer, to defend your Vessels against the Enemy. You are to receive Captain Swaine, the Officers, &c., of his Majesty's late Sloop Raven, together with the eleven recruits named in the margin, on board the Eliza, for a passage to Malta; victualling the former at whole allowance of all species of Provisions, and the Recruits at two-thirds only, during their continuance on board. You will obtain a certificate from the

---

[9] Mr., now Rear-Admiral Sir George Francis Seymour, G.C.H. and C.B., Commander-in-Chief in the Pacific, eldest son of Admiral Lord Hugh Seymour, and nephew of Francis, second Marquis of Hertford, to whom this letter was addressed. Lord Nelson promoted Mr. Seymour to a Lieutenancy, in the Madras, on the 11th of February 1804.

Senior Officer at Malta for the number of days you may have
victualled the said people, that the Transport Board may
allow for it accordingly,   NELSON AND BRONTE.

TO CAPTAIN HALLOWELL, H.M. SHIP ARGO.

[Autograph, in the possession of Rear-Admiral Inglefield, C.B.]

Victory, February 12th, 1804.
My dear Hallowell,
Many thanks for your kind letter, and for your goodness
in bringing out so many good things for me. I wish on your
return you could join the Fleet for a day, to take my letters.
You know me enough, to be sure, that I will not keep you
from getting to the new Swiftsure, in which Ship I shall rejoice to have you here. I expect to retake your old Ship[2]
before February expires, and believe me ever, my dear Hallowell, your most faithful friend,

NELSON AND BRONTE.

TO JOHN WILLIAM MAGNON, ESQ., HIS MAJESTY'S CONSUL, CAGLIARI.

[Letter-Book.]

Victory, Madalena Islands, 14th February, 1804.
Sir,
I have sent his Majesty's Sloop Termagant for the Midshipman and Seaman belonging to the Phœbe, and also to bring
such Deserters from the Fleet under my command, as may have
been apprehended at Cagliari, and request you will be so
good as to deliver them to Captain Pettet,[3] who will grant a
receipt for them; and if you will send me an account of the
number of days each of the said men has been victualled, I
will order the sum of 9d. sterling per day to be paid for their
maintenance, in addition to 40s. for apprehending each of
them, to any person you may think proper at this place, or
otherwise if more convenient. I am, &c.

NELSON AND BRONTE.

[2] The Swiftsure, 74, which, while commanded by Captain Hallowell, was taken
by a French Squadron, under the command of Vice-Admiral Gantheaume, off the
Coast of Barbary, on the 24th of June 1801, after a very gallant defence.

[3] Captain Robert Pettet, of the Termagant, was made a Commander in 1804, and
died in that rank in November 1833.

TO CAPTAIN JOHN GORE, H.M. SHIP MEDUSA.

[Letter Book.]

Victory, Madalena Islands, 14th February, 1804.

Sir,

I have received your letter of the 14th ultimo, acquainting me of the arrival of his Majesty's Ship Medusa, under your command, at Gibraltar, with the Portuguese Merchant-Ship Lassa, and also with your having ordered the Weazle to examine several Vessels going through the Gut, one of which Captain Layman brought in, as mentioned in the list which accompanied your said letter, and which you had detained for a breach of blockade. I presume the latter will be condemned to the captors, but the former appears a doubtful case. I, however, hope it may prove otherwise, and am, Sir, your most obedient servant,

NELSON AND BRONTE.

TO CAPTAIN SAMUEL SUTTON, H.M. SHIP AMPHION.

[Letter-Book.]

Victory, Madalena Islands, 14th February, 1804.

Sir,

I have received your letter of the 3rd ultimo, giving me an account of your having seen the English Convoy clear of Cape St. Vincent, agreeably to Captain Sir Richard Strachan's directions, and also with your having fallen in with a large Ship off Cape St. Mary's, dismasted and abandoned by her Crew, which you had carried into Gibraltar. In answer to which, I am very much pleased with your having seen our Convoy in safety past Cape St. Vincent, and with the circumstance of your having fallen in with the Merchant-Ship above mentioned, and convoying her in safety to Gibraltar. The list of her cargo, which accompanied your said letter, has also been received. I am, &c.

NELSON AND BRONTE.

TO JAMES CUTFORTH, ESQ., AGENT VICTUALLER, GIBRALTAR.

[Letter-Book.]

Victory, Madalena Islands, 14th February, 1804.

Sir,

I have received your letter of the 1st instant, acquainting me with the arrival of the Victuallers named in the margin,[2] at Gibraltar, and that three others are said to have gone to Lisbon with the Sophie ; also that the Nestor and Lady Shaw Stewart wait my orders. In answer thereto, I desire to acquaint you that the Chatham and Latona have completed the victualling of the Ships at present with me, to five months; and are gone to Malta with some small remains of their cargoes to be deposited there, and afterwards to proceed under the first Convoy to Gibraltar. You will, therefore, order the Nestor and Lady Shaw Stewart to proceed to Malta with the first Convoy, and also one of the three Victuallers expected from Lisbon, in order that the Stores under the charge of Mr. Wilkie, may be equal to the exigency of any future service. I am, &c.

NELSON AND BRONTE.

TO EDWARD POWNALL, ESQ.,[3] NAVAL OFFICER, GIBRALTAR.

[Letter-Book.]

Sir,   Victory, Madalena Islands, 14th February, 1804.

I have received your letters of the 2nd instant and 23rd ultimo, enclosing an account of the twine put on board the Childers by Commissioner Otway's directions, for the use of the Fleet under my command ; also an account of the stores put on board the Donegal, together with a copy of a bill of lading of sails brought out in his Majesty's Ship Diana, which, from their being landed in so very wet and bad a state, you judged it necessary to keep them to dry and repair. I have also received your letter of the 30th ultimo, and from the difficulties you have experienced in mustering the Companies of his Majesty's Ships which have hitherto arrived at Gibral-

---

[2] Thetis, Latona, Nestor, Lady Shaw Stewart.

[3] Mr. Pownall was afterwards Clerk of the Cheque at Sheerness, and died on the 26th of February, 1829.

tar, as stated in your letter to Commissioner Otway, of the 19th December, I have judged it necessary to transmit an additional Memorandum on that subject to the Commissioner, which I trust will obviate the evils you so justly complain of. I am, &c.

NELSON AND BRONTE.

MEMORANDUM TO THE RESPECTIVE CAPTAINS AND COMMANDERS OF HIS MAJESTY'S SHIPS AND VESSELS WHICH MAY ARRIVE AT GIBRALTAR.

[From a Copy in the Admiralty.]

Victory, at the Madalena Islands, Sardinia, 14th February, 1804.

In addition to my Memorandum of the 10th ult.,[4] respecting the mustering his Majesty's Ships and Vessels at Gibraltar, it is my most positive directions that the Commanding Officer of the Ship which the Naval Officer may go on board to muster, immediately turn the people up for that purpose, (meal times excepted) and that he is not delayed by the *frivolous excuse of the Clerk being on shore,* or on any pretence whatever; and I am also to desire that the Captain or Commander of any of his Majesty's Ships or Vessels arriving at Gibraltar, do furnish the Naval Officer with a copy of their Complete Book, including all the Officers, Widows' Men, and Ship's Company, which may be actually borne upon such Book, with their entries and ratings complete, which is to be signed by all the Signing Officers.

NELSON AND BRONTE.

N.B.—This Memorandum to remain in Commissioner Otway's possession.

TO ADMIRAL LORD RADSTOCK.

[Autograph, in the possession of Rear-Admiral Lord Radstock, C.B.]

Victory, February 14th, 1804.

My dear Lord,

Granville[5] is with me. You may rely that I shall be happy in an opportunity of placing him in a vacancy. Many

---

[4] Vide p. 356, ante.　　　[5] Now Rear-Admiral Lord Radstock, C.B.

thanks for your papers and good wishes : some day very soon
we shall want all the wishes of our friends ; for out the Enemy
must come, and that they shall go to Spithead, no exertion
shall be wanting by, my dear Lord, your old and sincere
friend,

NELSON AND BRONTE.

TO ADMIRAL THE EARL OF ST. VINCENT, K.B.

[From a Fac-simile in Tucker's " Memoirs of Earl St. Vincent," vol. ii. p. 248.]

Victory, February 14th, 1804.

Most cordially do I hail and congratulate you on the return
of St. Valentine ; and may you, my dear Lord, live in health
to receive them for many, many years. This morning also
your nephew, Captain Parker, has very much pleased [me,] (as
indeed he always does.) On Sunday, the 12th, I sent him to
look into Toulon : as he was reconnoitring under Sepet, he
saw a Frigate rounding Porquerolle, the wind was right out of
the harbour at North. At first the Frigate seemed desirous
to bring him to action ; but the determined approach of the
Amazon made him fly with every rag of sail : he ran through
the Grand Pass, and got under Bregançon ; some of the Ships
hoisted their yards up. I am rather glad that Parker did not
bring her to action, for I think they must have come out and
taken him ; but I admire his spirit and resolution to attack
her under all the disadvantages of situation ; and such conduct will, some happy day, meet its reward.

A Lieutenant belonging to the Madras being invalided, I
have put Mr. Seymour[6] into it, but will change him for a more
active Ship, the moment the Battle is over, which cannot be
much longer deferred. This thought keeps me up under a
nasty cough, and which I have always been subject to ; but
I am always, my dear Lord, your faithful friend,

NELSON AND BRONTE.

We have not a sick man in the Fleet, except Kent, who
has been to Malta.

---

[6] Vide p. 314, ante

TO CAPTAIN JOHN GORE, H.M. SHIP MEDUSA.

[Letter-Book.]

Victory, Madalena Islands, 14th February, 1804.

Sir,

I have received your letter of the 23rd ultimo, together with a log of your proceedings from the 22nd July to the 23rd January last, and also copies of your orders to the Master of the Boyne Transport, and to the Senior Officer of his Majesty's Ships at Gibraltar, enforcing the instructions contained in the Admiralty letter of the 4th November last, a copy of which also accompanied your aforesaid letter. I have also received a copy of your letter of the 24th ultimo, to the Hon. Captain Capel of the Phœbe, and very much approve of the orders and directions you have given as above mentioned; but apprehend your letter to Captain Capel has, by some mistake been forwarded to me, as there is a large packet addressed to him from the Medusa, with your name in the corner. I am, &c.,

NELSON AND BRONTE.

TO CAPTAIN HENRY RICHARDSON, H.M. SHIP JUNO.

[Order-Book.]

Victory, Madalena Islands, 15th February, 1804.

Whereas, it is my intention to put to sea with the Squadron the moment the wind comes to the Eastward, and proceed direct from hence to Rendezvous No. 97, under Cape St. Sebastians, You are therefore hereby required and directed to proceed immediately, in his Majesty's Ship Juno, under your command, and make the best of your way off the entrance of Toulon Harbour, for the purpose of ascertaining whether the Enemy's Squadron is still in Port, and join me with an account thereof, on the above Rendezvous, with all dispatch; but should the wind be to the Westward, the Squadron will proceed on the East side of Corsica, round Cape Corse. You will, therefore, under the above probable chances of the wind, judge where to find me, with any intelligence you may have to communicate.

NELSON AND BRONTE.

TO CAPTAIN SIR WILLIAM BOLTON, H. M. SLOOP CHILDERS.

[Order-Book.]

Victory, Madalena Islands, 16th February, 1804.

In order that the French Fleet may not pass without information thereof being communicated to me, You are hereby required and directed to proceed off Monte Christo immediately, in his Majesty's Sloop under your command, for the purpose of falling in with the Enemy's Squadron, or of gaining intelligence of them; and, upon meeting with two or more Frigates, or Ships of the Line, you are to return to this place with an account thereof, without a moment's loss of time, and on no consideration suffer their approach, so as to endanger the Childers to capture. You are not to be absent on this service longer than three days from the date hereof; but, at the expiration of the above time, return to this anchorage, where you will find me, or orders with the Governor at the Madalena Islands for your further proceedings.

NELSON AND BRONTE.

TO CAPTAIN SIR WILLIAM BOLTON, H.M. SLOOP CHILDERS.

[Letter Book.]

Victory, Madalena Islands, 17th February, 1804.

Dear Bolton,

I shall stand to the N.W., towards Toulon, and from thence towards St. Sebastians. If you have a good opportunity, approach near Ajaccio to see if the French Fleet are there, but do not get near enough to endanger being taken yourself. Ever yours faithfully,

NELSON AND BRONTE.

TO CAPTAIN GORE, H. M. SHIP MEDUSA.

[From Clarke and M'Arthur, vol. ii. p. 359.]

17th February, 1804.

The Admiralty seem to think that the Spaniards may be hostile to us, and therefore have put me on my guard. Do not let it escape your lips—I am determined to have the first blow; even if they come with their whole eighteen, they shall not join the French. If they come up the Mediterranean, and you have a mind for a shooting party, come with your Frigates. Every part of your conduct is like yourself, perfect. Your letters will be answered formally. I am, &c.

NELSON AND BRONTE.

***

TO MAJOR LOWE.[7]

[Autograph, in the possession of Josiah French, Esq.]

Victory, February 17th, 1804.

Dear Sir,

I am just favoured with your letter of the 5th, from Cagliari; poor King and Princes! they have neither money or Troops. That Sardinia will be invaded I am sure of; and I only hope that we shall fall in with the French Fleet, and I may reasonably suppose that we shall frustrate their plans. As you are coming here, I shall probably, after the Battle, have the pleasure of seeing you. Your Officers here are very attentive. Some Recruits are gone to Malta with Colonel Phillips, who sailed on the 15th. I am, dear Sir, &c.

NELSON AND BRONTE.

***

TO LIEUTENANT ROBERT LLOYD, COMMANDING HIS MAJESTY'S PRISON-SHIP GUERRIER.

[Letter-Book.]

Victory, Madalena Islands, 18th February, 1804.

Sir,

In answer to your letter of the 5th December last, I herewith transmit you an order to bear twenty Seamen, including two Midshipmen, on the Books of the Guerrier Prison-Ship, under your command, which I trust will enable you to carry on the duty of your situation till their Lordships shall think

---

[7] Afterwards Lieutenant-General Sir Hudson Lowe, G.C.M.G. K.C.B. He was then employed in Sardinia to raise recruits; and was desired by Mr. Elliot, Minister at Naples, to ascertain the means which that Island possessed of resisting an invasion of the French, and to report on the expediency of assisting the Sardinian Government with money. This zealous and intelligent, but ill-treated Officer, so well known as Governor of St. Helena, died on the 10th of January 1844.

proper to send you the establishment of the said Ship. I am very much pleased with your conduct in keeping the Guerrier so perfectly clean, as well as with your exertions in assisting the Merchant-Ships coming into Gibraltar in distress, and also with your ready endeavours to prevent their being captured by the Enemy, and hope you may soon be enabled to render them more effectual service. I am, &c.

NELSON AND BRONTE.

P.S.—I desire to recommend your applying to the Admiralty for the establishment of the Guerrier.

TO CAPTAIN WILLIAM PARKER, H. M. SHIP AMAZON.

[Order-Book.]

Victory, Madalena Islands, 18th February, 1804.

Whereas it is of the utmost importance that I should be acquainted with the movements of the Enemy's Squadron, You are hereby required and directed to proceed, without a moment's loss of time, in his Majesty's Ship under your command, from twenty to twenty-five leagues due W. N. W. of Asinara, where it is probable, if they are bound to the Southward, you may be fortunate enough to fall in with them. And as it is my intention to put to sea with the Squadron the moment the wind will allow me to do so, and proceed to Rendezvous No. 97, under Cape St. Sebastians, the movements of the Amazon must be governed from circumstances of wind and weather, as you, upon due consideration thereof, may judge proper. But should the wind continue to blow so hard from the Eastward as to prevent the Squadron from putting to sea, and you gain intelligence of the Enemy's motions, you will land an express at Castel Sardo or Porto di Torres, with directions to proceed with an account thereof to me, at this anchorage, with the utmost dispatch; or send a Boat from the Amazon, if you judge that to be the most expeditious way of communication. You are to continue on this service for the space of three days, or longer, if you think the Squadron is not able to proceed from this anchorage, and afterwards join me on my Rendezvous No. 97, as before-mentioned.

NELSON AND BRONTE.

TO CAPTAIN JOHN WHITBY, H.M. SHIP BELLEISLE.

[Letter-Book. " Sunday, 19th February. A.M. At 6·40, weighed and made sail, as did the Squadron, through Agincourt Sound to the Westward."—*Victory's Log.*]

Victory, Madalena Islands, 19th February, 1804.

Memorandum.

As an anchor and cable is of great importance, it is my directions that you remain and weigh the anchor, which his Majesty's Ship under your command parted from in the night of the 17th Instant; and after having done so, you are to proceed after the Squadron with the utmost possible dispatch, to Rendezvous No. 97, under Cape St. Sebastians, where you will find me, or orders for your further proceedings.

NELSON AND BRONTE.

The Childers will be in to-day. You will not suffer her to anchor, but acquaint Captain Sir William Bolton that he will find a Private letter with the Governor at Madalena, from me, which he will open, and proceed accordingly. The Public one is not meant for him, and therefore desire he will not open it.

TO SIR EVAN NEPEAN, BART., ADMIRALTY.

[Letter-Book.]

Victory, at Sea, 20th February, 1804.

Sir,

I have received your letter of the 19th December last, together with a copy of the orders which have been given to Captain Hallowell of the Argo, as also a copy of a secret letter to that Officer; and you will please to acquaint the Lords Commissioners of the Admiralty that Captain Hallowell shall be permitted to return to England, agreeable to their Lordships' directions, communicated to me in your said letter. I am, &c.,

NELSON AND BRONTE.

TO SIR EVAN NEPEAN, BART., ADMIRALTY.

[From a Copy in the Admiralty.]

Victory, at Sea, 20th February, 1804.

Sir,

I have received your letter of the 9th November last, with a copy of the one therein mentioned from Mr. James Douglas, Master of the Ship Mentor, respecting the depredations committed by the Enemy's Privateers in the Adriatic. In answer thereto, I beg to transmit you, for the information of the Lords Commissioners of the Admiralty, duplicate of my letter of the 24th November last, and to acquaint you, for their information, that the utmost possible attention has been paid to the protection of our Trade in the Adriatic, as far as the force under my command has enabled me, and, I may add, to a greater extent than comes within my knowledge on any former occasion. I am, &c.

NELSON AND BRONTE.

TO SIR EVAN NEPEAN, BART., ADMIRALTY.

[From a Copy in the Admiralty.]

Victory, at Sea, 20th February, 1804.

Sir,

Lieutenant Robert Lloyd, commanding his Majesty's Prison-Ship Guerrier, at Gibraltar, having, with his letter of the 5th December, transmitted me a copy of their Lordships' instructions of the 27th September last, and at the same time requested permission to bear a sufficient number of men to enable him to carry the said instructions into execution, till such time as the Guerrier's establishment shall be sent to him, you will be pleased to acquaint the Lords Commissioners of the Admiralty, that I have directed Lieutenant Lloyd to enter twenty Seamen, including two Midshipmen, and to bear them upon a supernumerary list for wages and victuals, till such time as their Lordships shall think proper to furnish the said Lieutenant with the Guerrier's establishment. I have also directed him to enter as part of the said number, any Seamen who may be invalided at Gibraltar Hospital, as unfit for active service in this Country.

It is but justice to observe that the Guerrier, when visited by Doctor Snipe, was found most perfectly clean and in good order, and also that Lieutenant Lloyd's active exertions in going to the assistance of any Vessel in distress, or in danger of capture by the Enemy's Gun-boats, deserve commendation. I am, Sir, &c.

NELSON AND BRONTE.

TO NATHANIEL TAYLOR, ESQ., NAVAL OFFICER, MALTA.

[Letter-Book.]

Victory, at Sea, 20th February, 1804.

Sir,

The Commissioners of his Majesty's Navy, having by their letter of the 17th November last, acquainted me that there are superfluous quantities of some species of Slops [6] at Malta, according to your opinion, and requested that I will order such part thereof to be sent to Gibraltar as may be judged proper, I am therefore, to desire you will send by the first Transport or Ship of War going from Malta to Gibraltar, such superfluous Slops as you may consider unnecessary to be kept in his Majesty's stores under your charge, and that are not likely to be wanted in this Country; but I desire to recommend you on no account to send to Gibraltar any article of Slops which may be wanted for the Companies of his Majesty's Ships on this station, and that you do also transmit me a list of such Slops as you may send to Gibraltar. I am, &c.,

NELSON AND BRONTE.

---

[6] *Slops* mean every kind of clothing, hats, shoes, stockings, &c., supplied to Seamen by the Purser, the cost of which are charged against their wages. The word is usually defined to mean trowsers; but a kind of shoe was called a slop, and the term was also applied to some other articles of dress. Palsgrave, in his "L'esclaircissement de la langue Francoyse," printed in 1530, translates "sloppes, hosyn," by "*brayes à marinier*." See a Note on the word in the "Privy Purse Expenses of Elizabeth of York," p. 256.

TO CAPTAIN HENRY RICHARDSON, H.M. SHIP JUNO.

[Order-Book.]

Victory, off Cape St. Sebastians, 25th February, 1804.

Whereas it is my intention to proceed immediately with the Squadron to the station mentioned in the accompanying Secret Memorandum, You are hereby required and directed to remain on the present Rendezvous No. 97, under Cape St. Sebastians, with his Majesty's Ship Juno under your command,. for the purpose of acquainting any of his Majesty's Ships or Vessels which may come on the above Rendezvous where I am gone, and to direct their Commanders to proceed and join me, with the utmost possible expedition. You are to continue on this service till further orders, and upon no account to quit it in chase of any Vessel; but should you obtain positive information of the sailing of the Enemy's Fleet from Toulon, you are to join me on the above station with the utmost expedition. You will deliver my orders (herewith transmitted) to the Ships and Vessels named in the margin,[6] agreeable to their address, the moment they join, and also deliver the present intended station of the Squadron, which accompanies this, to the Captains of his Majesty's Ships Belleisle, Seahorse, Phœbe, and Niger, who may be hourly expected to arrive at this place, and acquaint them that it is my directions they join me, agreeably thereto, without loss of time.

NELSON AND BRONTE.

TO CAPTAIN THOMAS STAINES, H. M. SLOOP CAMELEON.

[Order-Book.]

Victory, off Cape St. Sebastians, 25th February, 1804.

You are hereby required and directed to proceed immediately with his Majesty's Sloop Cameleon, under your command, to the Bay of Rosas, and communicate with Mr. Edward Gayner of that place, or his partner in his absence,

_____

[6] Active, Narcissus, Amazon, Cameleon, Childers,

for the purpose of obtaining any intelligence of the Enemy's
Fleet at Toulon, or of the line of conduct which Spain is likely
to pursue, with any other information which you may deem
necessary, and join me with an account thereof, on the present
intended station of the Squadron, (herewith transmitted,) with
the utmost dispatch, bringing with you any letters, &c., which
Mr. Gayner may have for me.

NELSON AND BRONTE.

TO ADMIRAL THE EARL OF ST. VINCENT, K.B.

[Autograph, in the possession of Vice-Admiral Sir William Parker, Bart., G.C.B.]

Victory, February 26th, 1804.

My dear Lord,

I feel confident that there is not an Officer in the Service
that bows with more respect to the orders of the Admiralty
than myself; but I am sure you will agree with me, that if I
form plans for the sending home our Convoys, and the clearing the different parts of the station from Privateers, and the
other services requisite, and that the Admiralty in some
respects makes their arrangements, we must clash. For instance, I judged it necessary, from the force of the Enemy in
Toulon, to call the Donegal from watching L'Aigle at Cadiz,
and I directed Captain Gore to take the Agincourt, and with
her to attend to the French Ship; for although the Agincourt
could not catch her in running, yet she would protect the
Trade coming to and from the Mediterranean; but being
taken away, I admit on an important service, has left L'Aigle
at liberty, although Gore has collected the three Frigates,
Medusa, Amphion, and Maidstone, and means to attack her
if she puts to sea. But this laudable purpose interferes with
the protection it is necessary to give to the Mouth of the
Tagus; and I much fear the Amphion, who was ordered to
Lisbon, not going, has exposed our commerce to the depredations of a large French Privateer. Lord Robert Fitz-Gerald
calls out, but I have not the means of doing all that is necessary. Having also given credit for the Diana's coming to this
station, I had ordered the Braakel and Stately home with the
Convoy. Had I known she was going back again, I should
have saved the Braakel for the next Convoy, in May. The

Gibraltar and the worst of the Sloops were intended for that Convoy, but the orders of the Admiralty relative to that Ship will prevent her going home; so that, in fact, I have not at present any further arrangement to make relative to Convoys. I have been anxious to get all the Troop-Ships home, knowing they must be wanted. I hope the Gibraltar when fitted will answer the Board's expectation; but I firmly believe, when done, she will only be fit for a summer's passage to England. I shall send her to Otway,[8] when she can be spared from Naples. She is a very fine Ship, and in excellent order. My letter to Sir Evan Nepean, on my first arrival, I find every day was perfectly correct. The Kent is under jurymasts. I had rather have bestowed new masts upon her than the other. However, we must very soon have a Battle, and then we shall all want new masts, &c. I have done. All my wishes are to meet the intentions of the Admiralty as far as I can.

I am, my dear Lord, happy to hear from Dr. Baird that you are not only well, but your health improved. I wish I could say the same; but I hope to hold out till after the Battle, when, if successful, I shall probably ask for rest. We have had a most terrible long winter, and from the 26th of January, we have not been twenty-four hours without a gale of wind. The Fleet is healthy beyond anything I have seen; and if we meet the French, I trust we shall give a very good account of them. With every kind wish, I am ever, my dear Lord, yours most sincerely,

NELSON AND BRONTE.

Captain Murray has been laid up with a bad leg; but Hardy is well, and equal to everything.

TO SIR EVAN NEPEAN, BART., ADMIRALTY.

[From a Copy in the Admiralty.]

Victory, at Sea, 27th February, 1804.

Sir,

I herewith transmit you an extract of a letter from Major-General Villettes, together with a copy of a letter from Doc-

---

[8] Commissioner Otway, at Gibraltar.

tor Franklin, therein alluded to, which I request you will be
pleased to lay before the Lords Commissioners of the Admiralty, that such direction may be given thereupon as their
Lordships shall judge proper. It only remains for me to
observe that much credit is due to the Military Medical gentlemen, for their great care and attention to Naval patients at
Malta, and that they are certainly entitled to some remunera-
tion. I am, &c.

NELSON AND BRONTE.

P.S.—Sir Richard Bickerton acquaints me that the Medical
gentlemen before alluded to, were paid up to the 24th February
1803; it is, therefore, to be presumed that they want the
payment to be continued from that time till the removal of
our Seamen from the Military Hospital, on the 1st January
1804.

NELSON AND BRONTE.

TO CAPTAIN HENRY RICHARDSON, H. M. SHIP JUNO.

[Order-Book.]

Victory, off Cape St. Sebastians, 27th February, 1804.

You are hereby required and directed to proceed immediately in his Majesty's Ship Juno, under your command, to
Barcelona, and send a Boat with an Officer on shore to Mr.
Gibert, his Majesty's Consul at that place, with my dispatches,
and for any letters or intelligence which he may have for me.
You are not to anchor, but stand off and on till your Boat returns
from the shore, and immediately after, join the Squadron on
its present Rendezvous. But should circumstances render
my leaving this necessary, previous to your return, you will
remain on your station, and put my order of the 25th instant
into execution; and if you receive any information from Mr.
Gibert, you will forward it to me by any of the Ships which
you may fall in with, and cancel the order to Sir William
Bolton. But in the event of the Consul's absence, or you
should not be able to procure any intelligence, the Childers,
in that case, will proceed to Barcelona, in the execution of
my orders to her Commander.

NELSON AND BRONTE.

TO RICHARD FORD, ESQ., AGENT VICTUALLER TO THE
MEDITERRANEAN FLEET.

[Order-Book.]

Victory, at Sea, 27th February, 1804.

In order that it may be exactly ascertained what supplies
of different species of provisions, wine, and other refreshments
can be had for the Fleet under my command at Barcelona and
in the neighbourhood of that place, You are hereby required
and directed to proceed to Barcelona, and make the most strict
inquiry with respect to what supplies of provisions and refreshments can be had for the respective Ships' Companies, and upon
what terms they are to be procured, the time required for that
purpose, and to what extent? After having obtained such information upon this subject as you may judge necessary to
enable you to procure supplies with expedition, you are to
proceed to Rosas (where frequent purchases of bullocks, wine,
onions, &c., have hitherto been procured for the Squadron),
and make the same necessary inquiry on the subject above-
mentioned, in order that we may, on all future occasions, know
what supplies can be drawn from those places, and to what
extent; and as wine is wanted for the Ships you will purchase
two hundred pipes, together with thirty thousand oranges, and
twenty tons of onions for the respective Ships' Companies, and
also, fifty good sheep for the use of the sick and convalescent
Seamen of the Squadron, paying for the whole either by bills
on the Victualling-Board, or ready money, as you may find
most to the interest of Government, which I must desire you
will bear constantly in mind on all occasions of purchases and
disbursement of the Public money.

NELSON AND BRONTE.

TO EDWARD GAYNER, ESQ., MERCHANT, ROSAS.

[Letter-Book.]

Victory, off Cape St. Sebastians, 28th February, 1804.

Sir,

I have this moment received your letter of the 10th, and
note of the 12th instant, and from the circumstance you

mention of onions vegetating at this season of the year, I recommend your not purchasing any more for the Fleet. I trust the Court of Spain will not prevent the Squadron under my command from having a reasonable number of bullocks for its consumption, with every other refreshment necessary for the Seamen, which the Peace subsisting between our Countries entitles me to expect and demand. I have sent you a letter to Dr. Scott, who you will soon see, accompanied by Mr. Richard Ford, the Agent-Victualler appointed by Government to the Fleet, who will enter upon the subject of supplying wine for the Squadron from Rosas, and of course arrange the business with you as to the quantity and time required to procure it. If you will be so good as to make out an account of the abatement, which has been made by the Spanish Government, for our former supplies, and also, of the omission in the Superb's voucher, as mentioned in your said letter, Mr. Ford will settle it with you as well as for all future supplies for the Fleet. I am very much obliged for the information communicated in your said letter. I am, Sir, &c.,

NELSON AND BRONTE.

TO THE CAPTAINS OF EITHER OF HIS MAJESTY'S SHIPS ABOVE [UNDER] MENTIONED, WHICH MAY FIRST JOIN COMPANY WITH THE JUNO.

[Order-Book.]

Memorandum.

Victory, at Sea, 28th February, 1804.

It is my directions that the Captain of either of his Majesty's Ships named in the Margin,[9] which may first join company with the Juno, in addition to my order of the 25th instant, transmitted to you on that day, proceed off the entrance of Toulon Harbour, for the purpose of ascertaining whether the Enemy's Squadron is still in Port, and afterwards join me, with an account thereof, on the station of the Squadron mentioned in the said order.

NELSON AND BRONTE.

[9] Active, Narcissus, Amazon, Phœbe, Seahorse.

TO MR. RICHARD FORD, AGENT VICTUALLER TO THE FLEET.

[Letter-Book.]

Victory, at Sea, 2nd March, 1804.

Sir,

As wine will soon be wanted for the Fleet under my command, I am to desire you will enter upon the subject with Mr. Edward Gayner, Merchant at Rosas, and endeavour to settle with him for a hundred tuns of good Catalonian wine, upon the most reasonable and advantageous terms for Government; and I am also to desire you will acquaint Mr. Gayner that casks will be wanted for the said wine, and to take care that they are good, well-conditioned, and in proper order, that no loss may happen to Government or the individual, from the wine's leaking out, as it is impossible at this uncertain season to send casks from the different Ships. I am, &c.,

NELSON AND BRONTE.

P.S.—As soon as it can be done, the wine casks will be returned. I suppose Mr. Gayner can have no objections to receiving them. You will settle some little error with Mr. Gayner in the Superb's former vouchers, as mentioned in my letter of the 28th ultimo to him.

TO HENRY CLARKE, ESQ., BRITISH PROCONSUL AT TUNIS.

[From a Copy in the Colonial Office.]

Victory, March 2nd, 1804.

Sir,

The Bey has asked me for one or two Passports for some Vessel or Vessels which are coming from Holland with his presents, (I suppose from the Batavian Republic.) The request seems to me so reasonable that, if the Vessels had been in the Mediterranean, I should have granted the Passports without the smallest difficulty. Luckily, within two hours after the arrival of the Bey's letter, I was sending a Vessel for England, and I enclosed it to Lord Hobart, strongly recommending the granting the Passports. The only difficulty which can occur is Lord Hobart's not knowing how either to describe the Vessels, or to know who to deliver them to; therefore, I

would immediately recommend to his Highness to send to
England or Holland for his Agent to communicate with Lord
Hobart, for I am anxious that his Highness should be gratified
as expeditiously as possible.

You will also take this opportunity of assuring his Highness
of my earnest wish to do everything in my power to accelerate
the arrival of the articles from Holland; and also assure him
of my high esteem for his person and character.　I am, &c.,

NELSON AND BRONTE.

TO CAPTAIN HENRY RICHARDSON, H.M. SHIP JUNO.

[Letter-Book.]

Sir,　　　　　　　　　　　　Victory, at Sea, 2nd March, 1804.

Being particularly anxious that his Majesty's Ships in search
of the Squadron should be immediately informed where it is
gone to, I am to desire you will most strictly keep His
Majesty's Ship Juno on Rendezvous No. 97, about ten leagues
due South of Cape St. Sebastians; and I am to desire in
addition to my Memorandum of the 28th ultimo, that you
acquaint the Captains of his Majesty's Ships named in the
margin [1] (who I understand are together) that it is my directions
they proceed off Toulon in company, for the purpose mentioned in the said Memorandum, in their way to join me.　I
am, &c.,

NELSON AND BRONTE.

TO CAPTAIN DONNELLY, H.M. SHIP NARCISSUS.

[Autograph, in the possession of the late Adam Bromilow, Esq.]

Victory, at Sea, 4th March, 1804.

You are hereby required and directed to proceed immediately with his Majesty's Ship Narcissus, under your
command, off Cape Corse, and cruize very diligently between
that and Port Especia, for the purpose of obtaining information of the Enemy's movements and expeditions fitting out at
Leghorn and Genoa, and also, of their Fleet at Toulon, should
it put to sea.　Upon your gaining any intelligence which you

---

[1] Narcissus, Active.

may deem necessary for my immediate information, you will proceed to Rendezvous No. 100, herewith delivered, where you will find me, or instructions where the Squadron may have gone. You will continue on this service till further orders.

NELSON AND BRONTE.

TO CAPTAIN FRANK SOTHERON, H.M. SHIP EXCELLENT.

[Letter-Book.]

Victory, at Sea, 7th March, 1804.

Sir,

I have received your letter of the 28th February, enclosing one from the Purser of his Majesty's Ship Excellent, under your command, dated the 16th of that month, respecting a hogshead of tobacco, which, after issue, was found two hundred and eleven pounds short of its contents. In answer thereto, I am rather surprised, as the hogshead of tobacco in question, when opened, appeared to want six inches of being full, that the Purser did not immediately represent the circumstance to you, that it might have been weighed in the presence of the proper Officers, and the real deficiency ascertained previous to any issue. I shall, however, transmit the before-mentioned letters to the Commissioners for Victualling, for their consideration. I am, &c.,

NELSON AND BRONTE.

TO CAPTAIN MOUBRAY, H. M. SHIP ACTIVE.

[Order-Book.]

Victory, at Sea, 8th March, 1804.

You are hereby required and directed to proceed immediately with his Majesty's Ship Active, under your command, to the Bay of Rosas or Barcelona, as may be found most convenient, in order to afford your Ship's Company every necessary refreshment for the benefit of their health, for which purpose you are to remain at either of the said places for the space of seven days, and during that time you are to cause your people to be supplied with fresh beef every day, with as many onions, in addition to the quantity allowed by the purser, as you and the Surgeon may deem necessary to remove any taint of the scurvy which may have introduced itself among them. You are, during your stay at the Bay of Rosas, or Barcelona, as before mentioned, to purchase fifty head of good sheep for the use of the sick on board the different Ships, with a sufficient quantity of corn and fodder to last them for a month ; and if it is possible to procure thirty thousand good oranges for the Fleet, with onions, or any other vegetables, that will keep about eight or ten days, you will also purchase them, together with as many live bullocks for the Ships' Companies as you can conveniently stow, with fodder to last them during your passage. Having remained the above-mentioned time at anchor, and complied with the purport of this order, you are to return and join the Fleet on its present Rendezvous No. 100, with the utmost expedition, where you will find me, or orders for your further proceedings. You are to acquaint any of his Majesty's Ships or Vessels which you may fall in with where I am to be found. You are to bring a sufficient quantity of good fresh vegetables for the Active's Company to serve them a fortnight at sea, after your leaving the anchorage.

NELSON AND BRONTE.

N.B.—In the event of your going to the Bay of Rosas, you will call upon Mr. Gayner, who was commissioned by Captain Staines to procure ten chords of wood for the Victory, and bring the whole of that quantity with you, or such part thereof as the Cameleon may have left, and you can conveniently stow.

TO DOCTOR MOSELEY, CHELSEA HOSPITAL.

[From Harrison's " Life of Nelson," vol. ii. p. 418.]

Victory, 11th March, 1804.

My dear Dr. Moseley,

Yesterday, I received the favour of the fourth edition of your invaluable work on Tropical diseases, &c.,[4] and with it your most kind letter ; and though I know myself not equal to your praises, yet I feel that my honest intentions for the

---

[4] Vide vol. i. p. 7.

good of the Service have ever been the same; and as I rise in rank, so do my exertions. The great thing in all Military Service is health; and you will agree with me, that it is easier for an Officer to keep men healthy, than for a Physician to cure them. Situated as this Fleet has been, without a friendly Port, where we could get all the things so necessary for us, yet I have, by changing the cruizing ground, not allowed the sameness of prospect to satiate the mind — sometimes by looking at Toulon, Ville Franche, Barcelona, and Rosas; then running round Minorca, Majorca, Sardinia, and Corsica; and two or three times anchoring for a few days, and sending a Ship to the last place for *onions*, which I find the best thing that can be given to Seamen; having always good mutton for the sick, cattle when we can get them, and plenty of fresh water. In the winter it is the best plan to give half the allowance of grog, instead of all wine. These things are for the Commander-in-Chief to look to; but shut very nearly out from Spain, and only getting refreshments by stealth from other places, my Command has been an arduous one.

Cornwallis[5] has great merit for his persevering cruise, but he has everything sent him: we have nothing. We seem forgotten by the great folks at home. Our men's minds, however, are always kept up with the daily hopes of meeting the Enemy. I send you, as a curiosity, an account of our deaths, and sent to the Hospital, out of six thousand men. The Fleet put to sea on the 18th of May 1803, and is still at sea; not a Ship has been refitted, or recruited, excepting what has been done at sea. You will readily believe that all this must have shaken me. My sight is getting very bad; but *I* must not be sick until after the French Fleet is taken. Then, I shall soon hope to take you by the hand, and have further recourse to your skill for my eye.

I am always glad to hear good accounts of our dear Lady Hamilton. That she is beloved wherever she is known, does not surprise me: the contrary would, very much. I am sure she feels most sincerely all your kindness. Believe me for ever, my dear Doctor, your much obliged friend,

NELSON AND BRONTE.

[5] His old friend (vide vol. i. p. 30) Admiral the Honourable William Cornwallis, then commanded the Squadron off Ushant.

TO THE RESPECTIVE CAPTAINS AND COMMANDERS OF HIS
MAJESTY'S SHIPS AND VESSELS ON THE MEDITERRANEAN
STATION.

[Order-Book.]

Memorandum.

Victory, at Sea, 13th March, 1804.

When any of his Majesty's Ships and Vessels under my
command is ordered to return to England, it is my most particular directions that they do not take away with them a
greater proportion of provisions, or stores of any description,
than may be necessary for the passage.

NELSON AND BRONTE.

———————

TO LADY HAMILTON.

[From "Lord Nelson's Letters to Lady Hamilton," vol. ii. p. 10.]

Victory, March 14th, [1804,] off Toulon.

Young Faddy,[6] my dearest Emma, brought me, two days
ago, your dear and most kind letter of November 26th, and
you are sure that I shall take a very early opportunity of
promoting him; and he appears to be grown a fine young
man, but vacancies do not happen very frequently in this
station. However, if he behaves well, he may be sure of me.
With respect to Mr. Jefferson, I can [neither] say nor do
anything. The Surgeon of the Victory[7] is a very able, excellent man, and the Ship is kept in the most perfect state of
health; and, I would not, if I could—but, thank [God] I
cannot—do such an unjust act, as to remove him. He is my
own asking for; and, I have every reason to be perfectly
content. Mr. Jefferson got on, by my help; and, by his own
misconduct, he got out of a good employ, and has seen another
person, at Malta Hospital, put over his head. He must now
begin again; and act with much more attention and sobriety,
than he has done, to ever get forward again: but, time may
do much; and, I shall rejoice to hear of his reformation . . . .
A thousand pounds a year will not go far; and, we need be

———

[6] Son of Captain Faddy, of the Vanguard, who was killed at the Battle of the
Nile. Vide vol. iii. pp. 54, 59, 127.

[7] Mr. Magrath, now Doctor Sir George Magrath, K.H. Vide vol. ii. p. 443.

great economists, to make both ends meet, and to carry on
the little improvements. As for making one farthing more
Prize-money, I do not expect it, except by taking the
French Fleet: and, the event of that day, who can foresee?
With respect to Mrs. Græfer—what she has done, God and
herself knows; but I have made up my mind, that Gibbs
will propose an hundred pounds a year for her: if so, I shall
grant it, and have done. I send you Mrs. Græfer's last letter.
Whilst I am upon the subject of Bronté I have one word more
—and your good, dear, kind heart, must not think that I shall
die one hour the sooner; on the contrary, my mind has been
more content ever since I have done [it] : I have left you a
part of the rental of Bronté, to be first paid every half-year,
and in advance. It is but common justice; and, whether Mr.
Addington gives you anything, or not, you will want it.

I would not have you lay out more than is necessary, at
Merton. The rooms, and the new entrance, will take a great
deal of money. The entrance by the corner I would have
certainly done ; a common white gate will do for the present ;
and one of the cottages, which is in the barn, can be put up,
as a temporary lodge. The road can be made to a temporary
bridge ; for that part of the Nile, one day, shall be filled up.
Downing's canvas awning will do for a passage. For the
winter, the carriage can be put in the barn ; and, giving up
Mr. Bennett's premises, will save fifty pounds a year: and,
another year, we can fit up the coach-house and stables, which
are in the barn.

The foot-path should be turned. I did show Mr. Haslewood the way I wished it done ; and Mr.   will
have no objections, if we make it better than ever it has been :
and, I also beg, as my dear Horatia is to be at Merton, that a
strong netting, about three feet high, may be placed round
the Nile, that the little thing may not tumble in; and, then,
you may have ducks again in it. I forget, at what place we
saw the netting; and either Mr. Perry, or Mr. Goldsmid,
told us where it was to be bought. I shall be very anxious
until I know this is done. I have had no very late opportunities of sending to Naples: but, *viâ* Malta, I wrote to Gibbs, to
desire he would send over and purchase the *amorins*. They
will arrive in time. I hope the watch is arrived safe. The

British Fair Cutter, I hope, is arrived safe. She has three packets, from me, to England. The expenses of the alterations at Merton you are not to pay from the income. Let it all be put to a separate account, and I will provide a fund for the payment . . . . All I long for, just now, is to hear that you are *perfectly* recovered; and, then, I care for nothing : all my hopes are, to see you, and be happy, at dear Merton, again ; but, I fear, this miscarriage of Pichegru's in France, will prolong the War. It has kept the French Fleet in Port, which we are all sorry for.

Sir William Bolton was on board yesterday. He looks thin. The fag in a Brig is very great; and I see no prospect of his either making Prize-money, or being made Post, at present : but, I shall omit no opportunity. I wrote to Mrs. Bolton a few months ago; and I gave her letter, yesterday, to Bolton. He conducts himself very well, indeed. Although, I cannot well afford it, yet I could not bear that poor blind Mrs. Nelson should be in want in her old days, and sell her plate ; therefore, if you will find out what are her debts, if they come within my power, I will certainly pay them. Many, I dare say, if they had commanded here, would have made money ; but, I can assure you, for Prizes taken within the Mediterranean, I have not more than paid my expenses. However, I would rather pinch myself, than she, poor soul, should want. Your good, angelic heart, my dearest beloved Emma, will fully agree with me, everything is very expensive ; and, even we find it, and will be obliged to economise, if we assist our friends : and, I am sure, we shall feel more comfort in it than in loaded tables, and entertaining a set of people who care not for us. An account is this moment brought me, that a small sum is payable to me, for some Neutral taken off Cadiz in May 1800; so that I shall not be poorer for my gift. It is odd, is it not ?

I shall, when I come home, settle four thousand pounds in trustees' hands, for Horatia ; for I will not put it in my own power to have her left destitute : for she would want friends, if we left her in this world. She shall be independent of any smiles or frowns. I am glad you are going to take her home ; and, if you will take the trouble with Eliza and Ann,[8]

---

[8] His nieces and nephew, children of his sister, Mrs. Bolton.

I am the very last to object. Tom, I shall certainly assist at
College; and, I am sure, the Doctor expects that I should do
the same for Horace: but I must make my arrangements, so
as not to run in debt.

April 9th.—I have wrote to the Duke; but, by your account, I fear he is not alive. I write because you wish me,
and because I like the Duke, and hope he will leave you
some money. But for myself, I can have no right to expect
a farthing; nor would I be a legacy-hunter for the world: I
never knew any good come from it. I send you a letter from
Mr. Falconet. I am afraid they have made a jumble about
the *amorins* . . . .

NELSON AND BRONTE.

TO SIR EVAN NEPEAN, BART., ADMIRALTY.

[From a Copy in the Admiralty.]

Victory, at Sea, 15th March, 1804.

Sir,

I have received your most secret duplicate letter of the 13th
January, with a copy of the private letter from Mr. Eaton
therein mentioned, acquainting me that he had purchased in
the Russian Dominions, a certain quantity of Naval stores
and provisions for the use of the Fleet on the Mediterranean
station, and that he had made his arrangements for embarking a part of that supply at Odessa, and signifying to me their
Lordships' direction to send two coppered Transports, in the
charge of an Agent, under the protection of a Frigate or
Sloop, to the above-mentioned place, for the purpose of bringing away the articles which may have been so purchased by
Mr. Eaton.

In answer to which, you will please to acquaint the Lords
Commissioners of the Admiralty, that a Convoy has just
sailed from Valetta Harbour with Ships for Odessa, to bring
corn to Malta, which they were ordered to leave at Constantinople, in consequence of a Proclamation from the Emperor
of Russia, prohibiting all Armed Vessels from entering the
Black Sea, as communicated to me in the enclosures from
Count Woronzow, the Russian Minister, and from Count
Alexander Woronzow, which accompanied your letter to me of

the 28th September last. I shall, as early ás possible, send two coppered Transports, under the charge of Lieutenant Woodman,[7] to Odessa, escorted by a Frigate or Sloop of War to Constantinople, for such articles of stores and provisions as Mr. Eaton may have procured at the former place, and shall direct a proper Convoy to be in waiting to bring them from Constantinople, on their return there, to Malta.

Lieutenant Pemberton, the late Agent of Transports at Malta, having been some time ago superseded, and ordered by the Transport Board to return to England, was appointed Governor of the Naval Hospital at Malta, as mentioned in my letter to you of the 21st December last, and therefore I judge it expedient to send Lieutenant Woodman (who I understand is a very sensible, intelligent Officer,) to Odessa, in his room. Lieutenant Pemberton is certainly a worthy, as well as an old and experienced Officer, whose services I trust their Lordships for the present will reward by a confirmation of his appointment, until something more to his advantage shall offer. I am, &c.

                                        NELSON AND BRONTE.

TO SIR EVAN NEPEAN, BART., ADMIRALTY.

[Original, in the Admiralty.]

Victory, at Sea, 15th March, 1804.

Sir,

I have this day received your duplicate most secret letter of the 13th January last, acquainting me, that in consequence of the hostile preparations which are now making in the different Ports of Spain, it has been deemed expedient to re-inforce the Squadron under my command with the Royal Sovereign, and that the Leviathan is to follow her with the Mediterranean Convoy, appointed to sail on the 10th of last month; and as it is probable Sir Richard Bickerton would be desirous of shifting his flag to the Royal Sovereign, their Lordships conceive it a mark of attention due to his rank and services, that he should be allowed to do so.

In answer to which, you will please to acquaint the Lords

---

[5] Lieutenant Henry Frederick Woodman: he died a Lieutenant about 1811.

Commissioners of the Admiralty, that Sir Richard Bickerton is to shift his flag to the Royal Sovereign, the moment the weather and other circumstances will admit, and that I shall appoint Captain Malcolm to the Kent, agreeably to their direction. And in further obedience to their Lordships' instructions, communicated in your said letter, the strictest regard shall be paid to the conduct of Spain; and I have the pleasure to acquaint you that the Squadron under my command is all collected, except the Gibraltar, complete in their provisions and stores to near five months, and in a perfect state of readiness to act as the exigency of the moment shall render necessary. I am, &c.

NELSON AND BRONTE.

TO CAPTAIN ROSS DONNELLY, H.M. SHIP NARCISSUS,

[Letter-Book.]

Victory, at Sea, 15th March, 1804.

Sir,

Having directed the Commander of his Majesty's Ship Cameleon to proceed off Cape Corse, and on falling in with the Narcissus, put himself under your command, I am, therefore to desire you will take him and the said Sloop under your command, and employ her in such manner as you may judge best for the service you are ordered upon. Should you obtain any intelligence of the Enemy's movements or intentions necessary for me to be acquainted with, I am to desire you will join me with the utmost expedition, with an account thereof on Rendezvous No. 100, where you will find me, or information where the Squadron may have gone to. You are to continue on this service for the space of one month from this date; and at the expiration thereof, join me on the above Rendezvous; or, in the event of not finding the Squadron there, you will proceed to Rendezvous 97, under Cape St. Sebastian. I am, &c.,

NELSON AND BRONTE.

TO JAMES CUTFORTH, ESQ., AGENT VICTUALLER, GIBRALTAR.

[Letter-Book.]

Victory, at Sea, 15th March, 1804.

Sir,

I have received your letter of the 23rd ultimo, together with a copy of the one therein-mentioned from the Commissioners of the Victualling, respecting the further sum of £10,000 being sent me in specie, for the general use of the Fleet under my command; and also directing you to supply me with such further sums of money as I may find necessary for the above purpose. In answer to which, I have to acquaint you, that the 18,000 hard dollars mentioned in your said letter have been received by the Royal Sovereign, and that Mr. Ford, the Agent-Victualler, will grant a receipt for the same, as mentioned in my letter to you of the 10th ultimo on that subject. I approve of your taking advantage of the exchange being under par for procuring the necessary sum of dollars for the future use of the Fleet, and which you will forward in such sums as the Agent-Victualler may find necessary to call for, and take his receipts for it, as before mentioned. I am, &c.,

NELSON AND BRONTE.

TO CAPTAIN GORE, H.M. SHIP MEDUSA.

[Letter-Book.]

Victory, at Sea, 15th March, 1804.

Sir,

I have this day received your letter of the 18th ultimo, together with copies of the orders therein mentioned; and under the circumstances of information which you received from his Excellency Mr. Frere, his Majesty's Minister at Madrid, I very much approve of the judicious arrangements you have made of his Majesty's Ships named in the margin,[8] and also of your having detained the sailing of the Diana and Convoy. But I have extremely to regret that Mr. Frere should have put such a construction on my letter,[9] and inter-

---

[8] Medusa, Amphion, Maidstone.　　　[9] Of the 23rd of January. Vide p. 387.

preted what only amounted to a belief, into a positive certainty. The intention, no doubt, was well meant. The Enemy are still in Port, and there can be little doubt of their intentions of putting to sea the moment they are in all respects ready, and a favourable opportunity offers for that purpose; but I trust the season of the year will enable me to watch them so closely as to fall in with them soon after their leaving Toulon. I am, &c.,

NELSON AND BRONTE.

TO SIR EVAN NEPEAN, BART., ADMIRALTY.

[Letter-Book.]

Victory, at Sea, 15th March, 1804.

Sir,

In further compliance with their Lordships' direction, communicated to me in your duplicate letter of the 9th November last, I herewith transmit you copy of my letter of 12th January, to Rear-Admiral Sir Richard Bickerton, who I had directed to inquire into the circumstances of Lieutenant Shaw's conduct, in entering the Port of Girgenti, in Sicily, and capturing three English Merchant Ships, which had been taken by two French Privateers, and carried into that Port. The Rear-Admiral, not having received my letter above mentioned till after his leaving Malta, sent it to Captain Cracraft of the Anson. I am, therefore, not enabled to send their Lordships the particulars on this subject so fully at present as was my intention; but I conceive it proper to transmit you, for their information, a copy of a letter from Lieutenant Shaw, and, also, a copy of one from Mr. Edmund Noble, a respectable Merchant at Malta, and to acquaint you that the most early opportunity shall be taken of further investigating into this circumstance. It is but justice to mention that the conduct of our Cruizers in these seas, under the particular circumstances they have experienced by the Enemy's Privateers claiming the protection of Neutrality at the different Ports, from whence they have committed unwarrantable depredations on our Trade, has been actuated from the best motives, although perhaps, in some instances, not so perfectly correct. I am, &c.,

NELSON AND BRONTE.

TO SIR EVAN NEPEAN, BART., ADMIRALTY.

[Original, in the Admiralty.]

Victory, at Sea, 15th March, 1804.

Sir,

You will please to acquaint the Lords Commissioners of the Admiralty that I have received their order of the 11th January last, and agreeably to the instructions therein contained, shall give the most strict orders to `the Captains and Commanders of his Majesty's Ships and Vessels under my command, whenever they are in want of stores, to apply, if it can be done, to the Naval Officers at Gibraltar and Malta for a supply thereof, and not to purchase any article of stores whatever at Lisbon, unless such purchase shall be absolutely and unavoidably necessary.

I have every reason to believe that Captain Gore's purchase at Lisbon, mentioned in the extract of his letter of the 4th December last, which accompanies this, was absolutely necessary, as, by Commissioner Otway's letters of the 2nd and 30th November, the Magazines at Gibraltar were almost bare of every necessary article of stores. In my letter of the 10th January last, I transmitted the Navy-Board an extract of Captain Gore's before-mentioned letter on the subject of the purchase of stores at Lisbon. I am, Sir, &c.,

NELSON AND BRONTE.

TO SIR EVAN NEPEAN, BART.. ADMIRALTY.

[Original, in the Admiralty.]

Victory, at Sea, 15th March, 1804.

Sir,

I herewith transmit you a copy of a letter from Captain Cracraft of his Majesty's Ship Anson, together with a copy of the one therein mentioned from Captain Raynsford of the Morgiana, giving an account of his having taken possession of the French Privateer L'Intrepide, at the Island of Milo, which you will please to lay before the Lords Commissioners of the Admiralty, for their information. I am, Sir, &c.,

NELSON AND BRONTE.

TO REAR-ADMIRAL SIR RICHARD BICKERTON, BART.

[Order Book.]

Victory, at Sea, 15th March, 1804.

Pursuant to instructions from the Lords Commissioners of the Admiralty, you are hereby required and directed to strike your Flag on board his Majesty's Ship Kent, and hoist it on board his Majesty's Ship Royal Sovereign, as soon as conveniently may be.

NELSON AND BRONTE.

TO CAPTAIN DANVERS, ROYAL MARINES, H.M. SHIP BELLEISLE.

[Letter-Book.]

Victory, at Sea, 16th March, 1804.

Sir,

I have received your letter of the 14th instant, respecting the monthly Returns of the different detachments of Marines, on board the Ships of the Squadron, being made to you, for the purposes therein mentioned. In answer to which as it has hitherto been customary for the Commanding Marine Officers of the different Ships to send their monthly Returns to the Admiralty, I do not wish to make any alteration unless such should appear to their Lordships as necessary, and ordered by them in consequence. I am, &c.,

NELSON AND BRONTE.

TO THE RUSSIAN GENTLEMEN ON BOARD HIS MAJESTY'S SHIP ROYAL SOVEREIGN.

[Letter-Book.]

Victory, at Sea, 16th March, 1804.

Gentlemen,

Far removed from your Country and relations, and placed to serve in the Fleet under my command, I desire that you will, on every occasion, both in public and private concerns, consult with me, and let me know your wants and wishes, and always consider me as your sincere friend,

NELSON AND BRONTE.

TO ALEXANDER DAVISON, ESQ.

[Autograph, in the possession of Colonel Davison.]

Victory, March 17th, [1804.]

My dear Friend,

I cannot sufficiently thank you for all your kindness to me, and to my dearest friend Lady Hamilton; and thanks is all which I can give you. So our friend Nepean[1] is gone from the Admiralty at last; it will be play, any other station, and I sincerely hope his health will be re-established. All the things you ordered from Turner, at Portsmouth, are safe arrived. We are waiting impatiently for the French sailing; but the unexpected arrival of the Royal Sovereign[2] may keep them still in Port. A Spanish War seems very uncertain. I hardly think it possible, but I am prepared for all events. My friends need not to fear that I shall be taken napping. I am much pressed for time; for a new Captain has this morning joined for the Belleisle, and Captain Whitby is ordered to be expedited home to join Admiral Cornwallis. Mr. Marsden will, I dare say, receive my letters, and do the kind things about my letters, &c., as good Nepean did. When you write Nepean, make my kind regards, and also to Lord Moira; and believe me ever, for ever, whether I write or not, your much obliged friend,　　　　　　　　NELSON AND BRONTE.

TO THE RIGHT HONOURABLE LORD HOBART, SECRETARY OF STATE FOR THE WAR DEPARTMENT.[3]

[Original, in the Colonial Office.]

Victory, March 17th, 1804.

My Lord,

In obedience to your wishes to be informed of the state of the Sea-ports in the Pachalick of Ali Vizir, I sent a most

[1] Sir Evan Nepean had retired from the Secretaryship to the Admiralty, and was succeeded by William Marsden, Esq.

[2] Lord Nelson's Squadron was reinforced, on the 14th of March, by the arrival of the Royal Sovereign, of 100 guns, Captain Pulteney Malcolm, afterwards Vice-Admiral Sir Pulteney Malcolm, G.C.B., G.C.M.G., who died on the 20th of July 1838.

[3] Lord Nelson had then just received the following Letter from Lord Hobart:—
"My Lord,　　　　　　　　"Downing Street, 7th January, 1804.
"I am to acknowledge the receipt of your Lordship's dispatches of the 16th and

intelligent Officer, Captain Cracraft, upon that service. I send you his account of the Port of Panormo, and also how the Country appeared to him. His Ship running on shore, obliged him to return to Malta. I send an extract of Mr. Foresti's letter, by which your Lordship will observe that he thinks there are many Ports which could contain in safety a number of Ships of War, and that the Country abounds

20th October, (vide pp. 248, 258, ante,) all of which, with their respective enclosures, I have had the honour to lay before the King.

"The vigilant and zealous attention therein manifested for the Public interests has afforded much satisfaction to his Majesty, and I am particularly commanded to express his Majesty's most gracious approbation of the line of conduct which, under the circumstances represented in your letter of the 16th of October, you have deemed it advisable to pursue towards the Regency of Algiers, and especially of your intention, at all events, not to commence hostilities until you can strike an effectual blow against the Cruizers belonging to that Power. It is, however, without doubt, of the greatest consequence, at the present moment, to obviate the necessity of resorting to measures of force against the Barbary States, provided forbearance can be maintained without detriment to the dignity of his Majesty's Crown, or to the security of those who are placed under the protection of his Government; and as some of the Vessels which have been captured by the Algerine Cruizers, may have been taken with passports whose dates had expired, as is suggested by Sir Alexander Ball, I entertain the strongest hope, that by means of explanation between your Lordship and his Majesty's Civil Commissioner at Malta, and subsequent communication with the Algerine Government, the ground of future complaint will be obviated. If, on the other hand, it should be found absolutely necessary, after such explanation and communication, to establish the authority of the Passports granted in the name of his Majesty, by active measures, I place the most complete dependence upon your Lordship's discretion, energy, and vigour for carrying his Majesty's former instructions of the 23rd of August, into full effect.

"I am also to convey his Majesty's approbation of your Lordship's correspondence, and the system you have in consequence pursued with respect to the Bashaw of Tripoli. The critical situation of the Island of Corfu, and the whole of the Morea, cannot too strongly claim your Lordship's attention, for the defence of which important countries you have already made so excellent a disposition of your Cruizers. Whatever may prove to be the real object of the French Fleet, should it, by any circumstances of wind and weather, be freed from the blockade in which it is held by the Squadron under your Lordship's command, I still entertain the most sanguine expectation, that the measures you make take, upon your apprehension of its probable destination, will enable you to justify the confidence you express of frustrating all its plans.

"I entirely concur in the propriety of keeping a Vessel at Naples for the personal security of the Royal Family, lest the progress of events should render their retreat from thence indispensable: and I depend much upon the execution of your Lordship's instructions, to receive Recruits on board his Majesty's Ships, for overcoming the difficulties which the activity of the Agents of France have opposed to the progress of the Recruiting Service in Switzerland. I have the honour o be, &c., HOBART."—*Autograph*, in the Nelson Papers.

with Ship-timber, and everything else. Our communication with Ali Vizir had, I am of opinion, better be in future carried on through him : he is a very intelligent man, and, I believe, fully to be trusted.

Sardinia will be in the hands of the French, either by compact, exchange, or insurrection. It is the *summum bonum* of everything which is valuable for us in the Mediterranean. The more I know of it, the more I am convinced of its inestimable value, from position, Naval Port, and resources of all kinds. I am rather led to believe that the French are negotiating very hard for an exchange. Sir Alexander Ball thinks the French are destined for Egypt, and every Power thinks they are destined against them; but whatever the French may intend to do, I trust, and with confidence, they are destined for *Spithead*. I am afraid Mr. Frere has created some little alarm that the French Fleet has escaped us. My letter to him[4] was intended to do away any such fears. I beg leave, in justice to myself, to send your Lordship a copy of it. I shall not take up more of your time than to say that I believe the King of Naples, Sardinia, and the Porte, place confidence in us to save them from the French. I am, &c.,

NELSON AND BRONTE.

TO CAPTAIN GORE, H. M. SHIP MEDUSA.

[Letter-Book.]

Victory, at Sea, 17th March, 1804.

Sir,

I have just received your letter of the 5th ultimo, together with the several inclosures therein mentioned, and very much approve of every part of your conduct. I regret that I did not know of the Diana's being ordered to England with the Trade, as I would have detained the Braakel to have assisted in the blockade of L'Aigle. Your intentions of attacking that Ship with the small Squadron under your command are certainly very laudable; but I do not consider your force by any means equal to it. I must, however, leave your judgment to determine upon this point, as well as with regard to the future

---

[4] Vide p. 387, ante.

arrangement of the Ships under your orders; and only observe that the protection of our Commerce, and the destruction of the Enemy's Privateers and Cruizers, are most essential objects for your consideration. I must desire to refer you to my secret letter of yesterday's date, with respect to the Spaniards, and that you will furnish me with the most early intelligence of the Enemy's Ships, should they escape from Ferrol and be bound into the Mediterranean. I am, &c.,

NELSON AND BRONTE.

TO CAPTAIN SUTTON, H.M. SHIP AMPHION.

[Autograph, in the possession of Captain Ives Sutton.]

March 17th, 1804.

My dear Sutton,

Many thanks for your letter of February 9th, and I assure you that I shall always rejoice in your success, whether I may be benefited or not. The French Fleet will some day or other put to sea, and it shall go hard but that some of them shall visit Spithead. I am ever, dear Sutton, your much obliged friend,

NELSON AND BRONTE.

Hardy writes you.

TO ADMIRAL THE EARL OF ST. VINCENT, K.B.

[From Clarke and M'Arthur, vol. ii. p. 359.]

March 17th, 1804.

My dear Lord,

Whilst I have your support, and the Officers of the Fleet look up to me, I can do anything which the number of Ships can allow the warmest wishes of my friends to anticipate. Take that from me, and I am nothing. I am the child of opinion, and the Admiralty can with their breath destroy it. But I rely with confidence upon you, my dear Lord, and that alone keeps me up. My general health, I think, within this last fortnight is better; but my sight is much fallen off,—I have always thought I should be blind. If I can but meet the French Fleet, and do the thing well, I shall certainly ask for rest; it is necessary for me. I have sent your nephew[5]

---

[5] Captain Parker, of the Amazon.

this morning, to see if he can lay salt upon the tail of a French Frigate; I every day see new and excellent traits in him. Hardy is his great pattern about his Ship, and a better he could not have. I have only to hope the restless animal, Buonaparte, will be upset by Frenchmen, and then we may have some quiet. I am, &c.,

NELSON AND BRONTE.

TO CAPTAIN SIR THOMAS TROUBRIDGE, BART., ADMIRALTY.

[From Clarke and M'Arthur, vol. ii. p. 360.]

17th March, 1804.

My dear Troubridge,

You must have reading enough, and your letters convey to you only complaints and misery, of Ships and Men. I have none to make: we are all cheerful and healthy, and our expenditure of stores has been, comparatively speaking, nothing. The French want to get out, and we want them out. Yesterday two of their Frigates were outside Hieres, peeping to know if we were gone to the Devil. Ball is sure they are going to Egypt; the Turks are sure they are going to the Morea; Mr. Elliot at Naples, to Sicily; and the King of Sardinia, to his only spot. Your son[6] cannot be anywhere so well placed as with Donnelly. I am, &c.,

NELSON AND BRONTE.

TO HIS ROYAL HIGHNESS THE DUKE OF CLARENCE.

[From Clarke and M'Arthur, vol. ii. p. 360, who state that, "at the conclusion of a long and most interesting Letter to his Royal Highness, in which Nelson pointed out how very erroneous the opinions of some of our ablest Ministers, and even of the French themselves, had been, respecting a thorough knowledge of the Mediterranean," he added:]

[Query, March, 1804.]

I have often sat and smiled to hear grave and eminent Senators expatiate on the importance of a place,[7] which I well knew was of no importance to us. I think I have told your Royal Highness enough, to induce you at all times to steer clear of possessing it. I am, &c.,

NELSON AND BRONTE.

---

[6] Now Rear-Admiral Sir Edward Thomas Troubridge, Bart., C.B.
[7] Query, Malta?

TO CAPTAIN RYVES, H.M. SHIP GIBRALTAR.

[Letter-Book.]

Victory, at Sea, 18th March, 1804.

Sir,

I have this day transmitted an order to his Excellency Sir John Acton, Bart., directing the return of his Majesty's Ship under your command to join me on the Rendezvous No. 100, as therein mentioned, the moment he shall signify that his Majesty the King of Naples has no further occasion for the services of the Gibraltar. You will herewith receive a List of Rendezvous from No. 97 to No. 101, issued to the Squadron since you left it, together with the Order of Battle and of Sailing. I am, &c.,

NELSON AND BRONTE.

TO ALEXANDER DAVISON, ESQ.

[Autograph, in the possession of Colonel Davison.]

Victory, March 18th, 1803.

My dear Davison,

I have not only personal obligations to you out of number, but also a load of pecuniary debt. This latter I must manage and pay off; therefore, I beg that you will let me know how the account stands. We hope the Dutch Ship will be given us; for it will be very hard that those taken before June 13th should not be given to the Captors. We were equally at War. We all look to you, as our Agent, for having petitioned, or done whatever is proper, in order to obtain it; and if it is given up, you will, of course, keep my proportion, two-thirds of one-eighth, in your hands, and place it to my credit, as also that of Copenhagen, and every day I am asked why it is not paid? At all events, a portion might be reserved for the Army; but I should think Mr. Falkner could easily get this settled, and Sir Hyde might write [?] about it. At all events, I must try and get out of your debt for money. There is not one farthing of Prize-money stirring here. Except at the first start, I have not got enough to pay my expenses. You will place the £200 sent Mr. Bolton to my account. She[8] is

---

[8] Query, Lady Hamilton.

generous beyond her means, and, therefore, she should not be asked for what is not in her power to spare. I much doubt whether the Pension[9] will ever be given—more shame for them!

I am sorry to hear you have not been well, which has grieved me very much. Take care of yourself; for what signifies all the riches of this world! I am ever, my dear Davison, most faithfully yours,

NELSON AND BRONTE.

TO HIS EXCELLENCY HUGH ELLIOT, ESQ.

[Autograph, in the Elliot Papers.]

Victory, March 18th, 1803.

My dear Sir,

The Royal Sovereign has joined me, and the Admiralty, unless our Enemies increase by the Spaniards, will order a Ship to England in lieu of her; therefore, as the Gibraltar is ordered to be refitted at Gibraltar, I must request that she may leave Naples whenever the King has no further commands for her. I have sent orders to Captain Ryves, and shall write to his Excellency Sir John Acton; for, however displeased the Admiralty may be with me for keeping a Ship of the Line constantly at Naples, yet I have always considered, and do still consider the preservation of the Royal Family a most particular part of my duty. I have no doubts but that the French Fleet would long ago have sailed from Toulon, but for the commotions in France.

Your Excellency's two packets of January . . . , and February 14th, arrived the same day—one by Cagliari, the other by the Cameleon. Nothing but Troops can save Sardinia; and if Russia does not send them, she only misleads the King of Sardinia. I believe they are jealous of our doing anything, and will do nothing themselves.

I have been but very indifferent, but I am much recovered, and I hope to hold out a few months longer, when I shall lay down my Office, which, whoever may take up, however they may carry on the service with greater ability, will never do it with more zeal than, my dear Sir, your faithful and obliged,

NELSON AND BRONTE.

My eyesight is very, very bad.

---

[9] Apparently, to Lady Hamilton.

TO THE RIGHT HONOURABLE LORD HOBART.

[Original, in the Colonial Office.]

Victory, March 19th, 1804.

My Lord,

I send a letter which I have just received from the Bey of
Tunis, and I am sure that your Lordship will think it right to
pay attention to his request, but not knowing the name of the
Neutral Vessel or Vessels may create some little difficulty ; but
I shall assure his Highness of the readiness of his Majesty's
Ministers to meet his wishes, and that the moment I receive
the passports, they shall be sent to him.   I am, &c.,

NELSON AND BRONTE.

TO SIR EVAN NEPEAN, BART., ADMIRALTY.

[Letter-Book.]

Victory, at Sea, 19th March, 1804.

Sir,

You will please to acquaint the Lords Commissioners of the
Admiralty, that the Enemy's Fleet at Toulon is still in Port,
but in a perfect state of readiness to proceed to sea.   The
Seahorse reconnoitred them on the 17th instant—eight Sail
of the Line are in the outer Road, and two in the inner.
Their Frigates and Corvettes are, apparently, all perfectly
equipped.   I am, &c.,

NELSON AND BRONTE.

TO CAPTAIN RICHARDSON, H. M. SHIP JUNO.

[Letter-Book.]

Most Secret.   Victory, at Sea, 19th March, 1804.

Sir,

As it is probable from the recent accounts I have received
from the Lords Commissioners of the Admiralty that a rupture with Spain may soon take place, I am to desire you will
communicate weekly with Mr. Gibert, His Majesty's Consul
at Barcelona, in order to obtain the most early information of
the intentions of Spain towards our Country ; but, I must

request that you will on no account suffer the least hint of this to escape. In communicating with Barcelona, I must desire you will keep His Majesty's Ship Juno, under your command, well out of reach of shot from the Spanish Forts or Batteries, and send an Officer on shore to Mr. Gibert, to obtain the news and such intelligence as he may have to transmit to me, and if you judge it necessary for my immediate information, you will join me on my present Rendezvous, No. 100, herewith enclosed, without a moment's loss of time. I am, &c.,

NELSON AND BRONTE.

N.B.—It is to be remembered that Mr. Gibert is a Spaniard; and, therefore, only request him to send any letters which may arrive from Madrid for me, with any Newspapers or other circumstances he may have to communicate.

TO CAPTAIN LAYMAN, H.M. SLOOP WEAZLE.

[Letter Book.]

Victory, at Sea, 19th March, 1804.

Sir,

It is my direction that you omit no opportunity of raising good men for the Victory as she is very much in want of them, and bear them on a supernumerary list; and you will produce this order, that no Senior Officer may presume to take them from the Weazle. I am, Sir, &c.,

NELSON AND BRONTE.

You will send them every opportunity.

TO CAPTAIN LAYMAN, H.M. SLOOP WEAZLE.

[Letter-Book.]

Victory, at Sea, 19th March, 1804.

Sir,

In answer to your letter of the 20th October last, respecting the complement of His Majesty's Sloop under your command, I am to desire you will increase the complement of the said Sloop to the number it was last War; and with respect to the

other parts of your letter, the Weazle must strictly execute
the orders she is under from me, and such as the Senior
Officer may find necessary, from time to time, to give in addition.   I am, &c.,

NELSON AND BRONTE.

TO CAPTAIN PHILIP LEWIS ROSENHAGEN, H.M. SLOOP
LA SOPHIE.

[Order-Book.]

Victory, at Sea, 19th March, 1804.

You are hereby required and directed to proceed immediately with his Majesty's Sloop La Sophie under your command to Rendezvous No. 97, under Cape St. Sebastians,
where you will find his Majesty's Ship Juno, and on doing
so, you will deliver my most secret letter, which accompanies
this, to Captain Richardson; but should you not fall in with
the Juno after cruizing on the above Rendezvous with the
utmost activity for the space of forty-eight hours, you are to
proceed to Gibraltar, and deliver the whole of my Public
dispatches, which you will herewith receive, to Commissioner
Otway at that place.   After having so done, you will remain
at Gibraltar forty-eight hours for such dispatches as Lieutenant-General Sir Thomas Trigge and Commissioner Otway
may have to send to me, and afterwards proceed, without loss
of time, to Rendezvous No. 97, where you will find me, or
orders for your further proceedings.   In the event of your
falling in with a Spanish Fleet or Squadron, either in your
way to Gibraltar, or on your return, you are to be very careful
in not approaching too near them, and instantly return to
me with an account thereof on the above Rendezvous, No.
97.   You are to receive Captain Whitby, late of the Belleisle,
his servant, baggage, &c., with any other person he may have
to take with him, and give them a passage to Gibraltar,
victualling them, on a supernumerary list, the same as your
Sloop's Company during their continuance on board.

NELSON AND BRONTE.

TO REAR-ADMIRAL SIR JOHN DUCKWORTH, K.B.

[From Clarke and M'Arthur, vol. ii. p. 360.]

19th March, 1804.

There is not a man in the world, that rejoices more at the happy conclusion you have given to the French Expedition to St. Domingo,[5] than myself, and for all your well-earned successes: your perseverance deserves to be amply rewarded. Now, you have done with the French, unless you can get hold by agreement with the *sold* Spaniards, of their part of St. Domingo, (for I hope in God we shall never attempt to possess any portion of the other part of that Island,) although I see all the danger of a Black Republic, yet I trust we shall be very particular in making a treaty of commerce with them. It is a nice game to play; but if you are contented, I am sure it is in good and able hands. I hope to hold out, to beat your friend Admiral la Touche Tréville,[6] who took the

---

[5] Rear-Admiral Sir John Thomas Duckworth, K.B., Commander-in-Chief at Jamaica, concluded, in December, 1803, a negotiation with General Rochambeau, the Commander of the French forces at St. Domingo, by which that Officer and his Troops surrendered as Prisoners of War. "From General Rochambeau's extraordinary conduct on the public service," says Captain Loring, in his Dispatch, "neither Captain Bligh nor myself have had anything to say to him further than complying with his wishes in allowing him to remain on board the Surveillante until her arrival at Jamaica, which I very readily agreed to, as also the Commodore."—*London Gazette*, 7th February, 1804.

[6] Vice-Admiral la Touche Tréville, Commander-in-Chief of the French Fleet, has become a person of historical importance from the assertion of Monsieur Thiers, that the death of that gallant Officer, in August 1804, saved England from Invasion! He is again frequently mentioned by Nelson, to whom, on the 14th of February 1804, he wrote the following letter in reply to his letter to the French Admiral, dated on the 10th of December, 1803, in p. 298, ante. Instead, however, of imitating Lord Nelson's example by sending this letter direct, by a Flag of Truce, Admiral la Touche Tréville directed it to *Malta*, and forwarded it through the French Post Office, so that it did not reach Nelson's hands until the end of May or beginning of June :

"A bord du V^au le Bucentaure en Rade de Toulon le 28 pluviose, (18 Fevrier, 1804) an 12e de la République Francaise.

"Le Vice-Amiral la Touche-Tréville, de la Légion d'Honneur, Commandant en Chef une Escadre dans la Méditerranée,

"A Son Excellence Lord Nelson, Duc de Bronté, Commandant en Chef les Forces Navales de S. M. Britannique dans la Méditerranée.

"Monsieur,

"J'ai reçu la lettre que votre Excellence a adressée au Commandant de l'Armée Navale à Toulon, sous la date du 4 X^bre dernier. N'ayant pris que depuis peu le Commandement de cette armée, je n'ai point eu connaissance de l'objet de vos reproches, sur lesquels par consequent je ne suis pas fondé à repondre.

"Je me suis empressé de faire part à mon Gouvernement de ce qui concerne

command at Toulon the moment of his arrival there. He was sent for on purpose, as *he beat me* at Boulogne, to beat me again ; but he seems very loth to try. I am, &c.,

NELSON AND BRONTE.

TO SIR EVAN NEPEAN, BART., ADMIRALTY.

[Original, in the Admiralty.]

Sir, Victory, at Sea, 19th March, 1804.

I herewith transmit you, for the information of the Lords Commissioners of the Admiralty, a letter from Captain Hardy of His Majesty's Ship Victory, respecting Mr. . . . . , the Purser of the said Ship, not having joined; and, I request you will communicate to their Lordships the great distress Captain Hardy has been subject to, in the purchase of neces-

l'échange que vous proposez ; aussitot que ses intentions me seront connues, je ne manquerai pas d'avoir l'honneur de les participer à votre Excellence, et de prendre tous les moyens qui sont en mon pouvoir pour satisfaire au desir qu'elle témoigne, et aux sentimens d'humanité qui les lui a inspirés. J'ai l'honneur d'être de votre Excellence le très obeïssant serviteur, LA TOUCHE TREVILLE."—*Autograph*, in the Nelson Papers.

Vice-Admiral la Touche Tréville communicated the decision of his Government respecting the proposed exchange of Prisoners, in the following Letter, dated on the 22nd of March, which, like the preceding one, he sent, *via Paris*, directed to Lord Nelson at *Malta!*

"A bord du Vaisseau de la Republiqué Francaise le Bucentaure, en rade de Toulon le 1er germinal de l'an 12 (22 Mars, 1804.)

"A Son Excellence Lord Nelson, Duc de Bronté, Commandant en Chef les Forces Navales de S. M. Britannique dans la Meditérranée.

"Monsieur,

"J'ai l'honneur de faire connaitre à Votre Excellence les intentions de mon Gouvernement sur ce qui fesait l'objet de la lettre que vous avez adressée au Commandant des Forces Navales à Toulon, et dont j'ai eu celui de vous accuser reception.

"Il me charge de mander à votre Excellence que tout échange de prisonniers entre les deux Puissances, est devenu impossible par les conditions inadmissibles que S. M. Britannique a voulu imposer à l'etablissement d'un Cartel ; et que pour éviter les inconveniéns attachés à l'admission des parlementaires dans un port uniquement consacré aux operations militaires et navales, il avait affecté specialement le port de la Ciotat sur la Mediterranée à les recevoir. C'est donc par ce seul port que je pourrai recevoir les communications dont il plairait à Votre Excellence de m'honorer. J'ai l'honneur d'etre, de Votre Excellence le très obeissant serviteur, LA TOUCHE TREVILLE, Vice-Amiral, Commandant en Chef les Forces Navales de la République Française dans la Mediterranée."—*Autograph*, in the Nelson Papers.

saries, and that if it had not been for Mr. Bromley, Purser of the Belleisle, who has on all occasions purchased beef, &c., for the Victory's Company, the Service must have suffered materially.

I feel much indebted to Mr. Bromley for his attention to these particulars, and certainly consider Mr. . . . . .'s conduct not only reprehensible, but that he ought not to have any employment in the Service : almost twelvemonths since his appointment, and not yet joined, or any account of him ! I am, Sir, &c.,　　　　　　　　NELSON AND BRONTE.

TO VICE-ADMIRAL BLIGH.

[From " Marshall's Naval Biography," Supplement, Part I. p. 431.]

Victory, March 19th, 1804.

My dear Admiral,

Your son is a very good young man, and I sincerely hope that, now your Flag is up,[7] you will be able to promote him. It would give me great pleasure to do it, but I see no prospect, unless we capture the whole French Fleet in Toulon ; therefore, do you consider about him. You are sure of my regard, but I cannot kill people ; and, I am more likely to go off myself than any one about me. I have many thanks to give you . . . . . I am, &c.,

NELSON AND BRONTE.

TO DR. BAIRD.

[From " The Athenæum."]

My dear Sir,　　　　　　　　March 19th, 1804.

Many thanks for your kind letter of 30th October. I am sure no man is more able to place our Hospitals in a proper state than yourself, and that you always bear in mind not to

---

[7] Vice-Admiral, afterwards Admiral Sir Richard Rodney Bligh, G.C.B., had then lately hoisted his Flag as Commander-in-Chief on the Coast of Scotland. His defence of the Alexander 74, for two hours, against three French Sail of the Line, in November 1794, was one of the most gallant actions of the War: he died an Admiral of the Red in April 1821. His son mentioned in this letter was Mr. George Miller Bligh, at that time a Lieutenant of the Victory, who was dangerously wounded in that Ship at Trafalgar: he was made a Commander in January 1806 ; Posted in December 1808, and died about 1834.

be penny-wise and pound-foolish. A small sum, well laid out, will keep Fleets healthy; but it requires large sums to make a sickly Fleet healthy, besides the immense loss of personal services. Health cannot be dearly bought at any price —if the Fleet is never sickly. By general exertions, we have done well; but we have not a place that we can be sure of supplies from. Spain will not give us a live animal; Naples dare not; and Sardinia ought not: but that is the only place we have a chance for fresh provisions. God knows how many days—it will not be many—that Island will be out of the hands of the French.

I hope to hold out till after the Battle; but, as you know, mine is a wretched constitution, and my sight is getting very, very bad. I rejoice to hear the Earl[8] is so well. Believe me ever, yours faithfully and obliged,

NELSON AND BRONTE.

TO SIR JOHN ACTON, BART., NAPLES.

[From Clarke and M'Arthur, vol. ii. p. 361.]

March, 1804.

Will Russia come forth as she ought, or are her plans only preparative to the taking possession of Greece, and of course Constantinople? This is a subject I have no business at present to enter into, although it is seriously in my mind. I am, &c.,   NELSON AND BRONTE.

TO SPIRIDION FORESTI, ESQ., CORFU.

[From Clarke and M'Arthur, vol. ii. p. 361.]

March, 1804.

The ultimate views of Russia become every hour more distinct; how long the mask may be kept on I cannot say, but sooner or later the Morea will belong by conquest to Russia. What part Great Britain may take, the connexions which Russia may form will point out. However, we are at present on the most friendly terms with the Emperor, and I hope we shall always continue so. I have said enough to so sensible a man as yourself. I am, &c.,

NELSON AND BRONTE.

8 Earl St. Vincent.

TO CAPTAIN PHILIP LAMB, AGENT FOR PRISONERS OF WAR
AND TRANSPORTS, MALTA.

[From a Copy in the Admiralty.]

Victory, at Sea, 20th March, 1804.

Sir,

I have received your letter of the 28th ultimo, together with
the state of the Transports and Prisoners of War at Malta, and
I have to desire that you will prepare two coppered Transports,
and have them in momentary readiness to proceed to Odessa,
for the purpose of bringing stores and provisions from thence
to Malta, under the charge of Lieutenant Woodman, whenever I shall deem proper to order a Convoy for that purpose.
The said Transports are to be as commodious as possible, and
in every respect complete for the service they are to be employed on. With respect to the others that are not wanted
for the service of the Island of Malta and the Fleet under my
command, I must desire you will hold them in readiness to
proceed to England with the first Convoy; and on the subject of the number necessary to be kept for those purposes, I
desire to refer you to the copy of my letter of the 7th October
last, to Lieutenant Pemberton (then Resident Agent of Transports) herewith transmitted, and to which you will pay most
implicit obedience, in order that no more Transports may be
kept in this Country than what may be absolutely necessary
for the services before mentioned. I am, &c.

NELSON AND BRONTE.

TO WILLIAM MARSDEN, ESQ., ADMIRALTY.

[Original, in the Admiralty.]

Victory, at Sea, 20th March, 1804.

Sir,

I have to request you will be pleased to acquaint the Lords
Commissioners of the Admiralty, that in consequence of Lieutenant William Miller (2nd)[1] of the Triumph being appointed
an Agent of Transports, and ordered to England by the Commissioners of that Board, I have given Mr. William Faddy,[2]

----

[1] He became a Retired Commander in July 1839, and died early in 1844.
[2] Mr. William Faddy died a Lieutenant, about 1811.

Midshipman of the Victory, a Commission in his room, (a copy of which is herewith transmitted,) and trust their Lordships will order the appointment to be confirmed. I am satisfied when I call to their Lordships' recollection, that this deserving young man is son to the late Captain of the Marines who was killed on board the Vanguard, in the Battle of the Nile, they will feel as much pleasure in confirming the appointment, as I do in making the request on his behalf. I beg leave also to observe that his widowed mother is alive, with the charge of a large family unprovided for, and naturally looks up to him for assistance. I am, Sir, &c.

NELSON AND BRONTE.

[Added, in Lord Nelson's own hand:]

Mr. Faddy was a Mid. in the Vanguard, when his father was killed.

TO CAPTAIN CRACRAFT, H.M. SHIP ANSON.

[Letter-Book.]

Victory, at Sea, 20th March, 1804.

Sir,

I have received your letter of the 23rd January last, together with the one therein mentioned from Captain Raynsford, of his Majesty's Sloop Morgiana, giving an account of his having taken possession of the French Privateer L'Intrepide, which, under the circumstances stated in Captain Raynsford's said letter, I very much approve of, and trust that he brought a sufficient number of her crew with him to Malta, to answer the necessary interrogatories by the Vice-Admiralty Court at that place. I have also to acknowledge your letters of 8th and 10th ultimo, acquainting me that the false keel and copper were the only parts of the Anson that had received any damage by her having been on shore, and with the orders you had given his Majesty's Sloops named in the margin,[2] which also meet my approbation, as I take it for granted that you have directed Captain Vincent[3] to bring all the Trade with him from Smyrna, and the different Ports in the Levant, to Malta. I am, &c.

NELSON AND BRONTE.

[2] Arrow, Morgiana, Bittern.   [3] Of the Arrow.

TO NATHANIEL TAYLOR, ESQ., NAVAL OFFICER, MALTA.

[Letter-Book.]

Victory, at Sea, 20th March, 1804.

Sir,

I have received your letter of the 10th ultimo, on the subject of the stores you had found necessary to purchase for the indispensable repairs of his Majesty's Ships at Malta, and requesting an order to pay the Bills, and to enable you to pass your accounts at the Navy-Board. In answer to which I herewith transmit you an order for the purpose above-mentioned, satisfied that you would not have made the purchases in question, but under the most pressing and absolute necessity. It is not necessary to repeat my instructions respecting purchases, as I trust none will be made but upon occasions of the most indispensable necessity; more particularly so as the stores under your charge have lately been recruited from England. I have to acknowledge the receipt of your letter of the 26th, ultimo, with the extract therein mentioned, and am very glad to find the Imperial Schooner Hungaria, with the cordage and tar, is safe arrived at Malta. I am, &c.

NELSON AND BRONTE.

MEMORANDA.

[Autograph in the possession of the Reverend Henry Girdlestone.]

[About 20th March, 1804.]

To Captain Schomberg, or Senior Captain at Malta:—

The Trade from Naples, Sicily, and the Adriatic to be collected by the middle of April, that they may be ready to proceed to England when the Levant Ships arrive, under convoy of the Monmouth, or Argo, or both.

A Letter to the Senior Captain at Malta:—

Should the Agincourt be left in Egypt by Captain H., the Reynard Schooner, or some other fast sailing Vessel, to be sent here with my letter.

TO CAPTAIN SCHOMBERG, H.M. SHIP MADRAS, MALTA.

[Letter-Book.]

Victory, at Sea, 20th March, 1804.

Sir,

Rear-Admiral Sir Richard Bickerton having left Malta previous to his receiving my letter of the 12th January, and paper therein referred to, I herewith transmit you the said letter, and papers therein mentioned, and desire you will consider it as addressed to yourself, and comply with it accordingly. Lieutenant Shaw has sent me his own statement of the circumstances, together with a Letter from Mr. Noble, Merchant at Malta; but I wish a more particular account from the Senior Officer, and also Sir Alexander Ball's opinion on the occasion, in order that Lieutenant Shaw may be perfectly clear of any blame. You will please to return the several papers with your report to, Sir, your most obedient humble servant,

NELSON AND BRONTE.

TO CAPTAIN GEORGE HART, H.M. SHIP MONMOUTH.

[Order-Book, and Autograph Memorandum in the possession of the Reverend Henry Girdlestone.]

Victory, at Sea, 20th March, 1804.

Whereas it is my intention that his Majesty's Ship Monmouth, under your command, shall convoy all the Trade which may be collected at Malta by the time the Merchant Ships arrive from Smyrna, which I expect the Arrow is ordered to bring down on her return from Constantinople, You are therefore hereby required and directed to remain in Valetta Harbour until the arrival of the Arrow and Trade from the Levant, when you will make the Signal for, and take under your convoy and protection, the whole of the Trade which shall be collected at Malta, together with the Ships brought from the Levant by the Arrow, and proceed with them as soon as possible to Gibraltar, where you will also take under your convoy all the Merchant Ships from Malaga and Cadiz which may be ready, and whose Masters are desirous to avail themselves of your protection, and proceed with the whole of them to England as expeditiously as possible, consistent with their safety.   On your arrival off Plymouth, you will be governed with respect to their future protection as circumstances shall render expedient, and proceed with the Monmouth to Spithead, together with such of the Convoy as are bound to the Eastward, dropping them in your way up Channel as they arrive off their respective destinations.   You are to pay the most strict attention to the safety and protection of the Trade under your charge, that none of them may separate from you, or fall into the hands of the Enemy.   You are, until the arrival of the Arrow from Smyrna, as before mentioned, to employ the Monmouth in any manner you judge best for collecting the Trade; and in the event of Captain Vincent's not having brought the Trade with him from the Levant, you are hereby directed to proceed immediately, with his Majesty's Ship under your command, to Smyrna, and the different Ports in the Levant, for the purpose of collecting the Trade, and bring them with you to Malta; and on your arrival there, proceed with the whole, as before directed.   In order to enable you the more effectually to perform this service, I have directed Captain Hallowell of the Argo to put himself under your command.   You will, therefore, take him and the said Ship under your orders accordingly.   On the Monmouth's arrival off Spithead, you will acquaint the Secretary of the Admiralty thereof, and transmit an account of your proceedings for their Lordships' information.[4]

NELSON AND BRONTE.

TO CAPTAIN BENJAMIN HALLOWELL, H. M. SHIP ARGO.

[Order-Book, and Autograph Memorandum.]

Victory, at Sea, 20th March, 1804.

Whereas I consider the protection of our Trade the most essential service that can be performed, You are, therefore,

---

[4] " Should it happen that the Monmouth has left Malta for England, then this order is to be put in full and entire execution by Captain Benjamin Hallowell, of his Majesty's Ship Argo; for in no manner must the Trade of Great Britain be neglected."—*Autograph Memorandum.*

hereby required and directed, in the event of the Monmouth's having proceeded from Malta without the Convoy for England, to open the letter directed to Captain Hart, (which is also, in such case, intended for you, as mentioned in the said letter in the possession of the Senior Officer,) and consider the order it contains[5] as addressed to yourself, and most strictly and punctually put it into execution. But should the Monmouth be at Malta on your return from Alexandria, you are hereby directed to put yourself under the command of Captain Hart, and follow his orders for your further proceedings.

NELSON AND BRONTE.

TO CAPTAIN THOMAS BRIGGS, H. M. SHIP AGINCOURT.

[Order-Book, and Autograph Memorandum.]

Victory, at Sea, 20th March, 1804.

Whereas I judge proper that his Majesty's Ship Agincourt, under your command, shall proceed to Gibraltar and take in her lower-deck Guns,[6] You are (notwithstanding my orders to the contrary) hereby required and directed to proceed, without a moment's loss of time, in his Majesty's said Ship to Gibraltar, and after having received your lower-deck Guns on board, (which you will cause to be done with the utmost dispatch,) put yourself under the command of Captain Gore of the Medusa, or the Senior Officer at that place, and follow his orders for your further proceeding. But should no Senior Officer be at Gibraltar, you will proceed, the moment the Agincourt is ready, outside the Straits, and cruize there for the protection of our Commerce, and the destruction of the Enemy's Privateers and Cruizers. You are to continue on this service till further orders, and endeavour as early as possible to communicate with Captain Gore, or the Senior Officer, and be governed in your future proceedings agreeable to the instructions you may receive from him.

NELSON AND BRONTE.

[5] Vide p. 466, ante.   [6] Vide p. 358, ante, note.

TO CAPTAIN SCHOMBERG, H.M. SHIP MADRAS, MALTA.

[Letter-Book.]

Victory, at Sea, 20th March, 1804.

Sir,

I have received your letter of the 26th ultimo, acquainting me that you had ordered the Morgiana up the Adriatic with the Fish Ships, that the Sophie Sloop was to join me, and that the only Merchant-ship bound to England (the Hero) sails so well, and is so well armed, as to be able to run it.[7] In answer to which, I approve of your having sent the Morgiana up the Adriatic with the Fish Ships, and take it for granted that you have ordered Captain Raynsford to collect and bring with him all the Trade for Malta and England. I must desire in future that you will order the Captains proceeding with Convoys to send you a regular list of the Ships they may have under their charge, to and from Malta, which you will transmit to me as opportunity offers, for my information. On the subject of the Hero's sailing for England without convoy, I cannot give my approbation, and would recommend to you great care in furnishing the Masters of such Ships with certificates under any circumstance. In the event of the Ship in question getting safe to her destination, it will be all very well; otherwise, the Under-writers will certainly attach blame for sanctioning her sailing. I am, &c.,

NELSON AND BRONTE.

CERTIFICATE.

[Letter-Book.]

Victory, at Sea, 20th March, 1804.

These are to certify that I have no objections to the Greeks belonging to a Ship of that Nation, which was taken by his Majesty's Ship Niger, being liberated; provided the Proctor of the Vice-Admiralty Court at Malta deems it proper, under the circumstances of their having fired upon the Boats of his Majesty's said Ship, and killed an Officer and one or more of her people. NELSON AND BRONTE.

[7] i. e., To proceed without the protection of a Ship of War.

TO LIEUTENANT HENRY FREDERICK WOODMAN, AGENT FOR
TRANSPORTS AT MALTA.

[Letter-Book.]

Victory, at Sea, 21st March, 1804.

Most Secret.

Sir,

Admiral Holloway having acquainted me by letter of your
arrival in this Country as an Agent of Transports, and also of
your being very equal to any important service, from your
intelligence and observation; and the Lords Commissioners
of the Admiralty having recommended me to send an Officer
of that description in charge of the Transports, I have, therefore, thought proper to send You, and must recommend to
your serious attention the circumstances in general that are
passing in the Black Sea on the part of Russia, who, it is said,
is forming an Armament to a very considerable extent; and
although there is not the most distant idea that this Armament will direct its operations against the interests of Great
Britain, yet it is essentially necessary that its real intentions
should be discovered as early as possible, and, therefore, you
will let no opportunity escape you of obtaining all the information you may be able to collect on this important subject.

And I must desire you will endeavour to gain a particular
account of the Naval Force which Russia may have at
Sebastapol and Cherson, (their two principal Naval Ports in
the Black Sea,) and to what extent they are arming there.
You will likewise endeavour to obtain a knowledge of their
Fortifications, and what number of guns is mounted on their
different Batteries, and whether they are able to protect
their Trade. It will be advisable to ascertain whether these
Armaments are with a view to check and oppose the measures
of the French, should they attempt to possess themselves of
the Morea. You will also endeavour to gain information of
the trade and manufactures carried on by the Russians in the
Ports above mentioned—what supplies of provisions and Naval
stores might be drawn from that Country, and upon what
terms. In order to obtain a perfect knowledge of the local
situation of the Russian Territory in the Black Sea, you are to
procure a Chart of their Country, which will assist you in

forming a more clear idea of the places of principal importance, and endeavour, by every means, to obtain information of their present and future intentions with regard to England, transmitting me a very full and correct account of your observations, &c., on your return to Malta, for the information of the Lords Commissioners of the Admiralty.　I am, &c.,

NELSON AND BRONTE.

MEMORANDA.

[Autograph draught in the possession of Earl Nelson.]

[About 22nd March, 1804.]

The Fleet to proceed to Palma, where they will remain as few days as possible ; and when they sail, a letter will be left with the Consul at St. Pierres.

Orders for Active to take Seahorse, Phœbe, and Amazon under his orders, to look into Toulon every two or three days at furthest ; and in the event of the Enemy's putting to sea, to detach a Frigate to me ; and as it will be of the very utmost importance my being acquainted with it, should the wind prove contrary when on the Coast of Sardinia, an intelligent active Officer to be sent to me in a Boat, which will probably get along shore faster than the Frigate.

The Phœbe is expected every hour from Gibraltar.

Captain Moubray must calculate about the time of the Fleet's return, and keep a good look-out for me.

Seahorse being in want of wood, to be ordered, when Phœbe joins, to the Island of Asinara, to cut wood, for which purpose she may remain forty-eight hours.　In much less time, I am informed the Victory could be wooded.

To call at Cagliari for two English Ships, and to take them to Malta.

Niger to proceed to Malta, deliver the stores she has on board, and to return and join me on Rendezvous 100, without a moment's loss of time.

Is it necessary to give an order for the Invalids to be sent to England in the first Ship of War ?

TO CAPTAIN MOUBRAY, H. M. SHIP ACTIVE.

[Order-Book.]

Victory, at Sea, 22nd March, 1804.

Whereas I judge it necessary to proceed with the Squadron to the Gulf of Palma, for the purpose of completing their wood and water, which will only require a few days, You are hereby required and directed to take his Majesty's Ships named in the margin[7] under your command, and remain on the present Rendezvous No. 100, employing the said Frigates, during my absence, in watching the motions of the Enemy's Fleet at Toulon, by sending one or two of them off the entrance of that Harbour every two or three days, for the purpose of ascertaining whether their Squadron still remains in Port; and in the event of its putting to sea, you will detach a Frigate to me with an account thereof, directing the Captain to use the utmost exertion to join me; and as it is of the utmost importance that I should be immediately acquainted with it, you will order the Captain of the Frigate sent on this service, should the wind prove contrary when he arrives on the coast of Sardinia, to dispatch an intelligent, active Officer to me in a Boat, which will probably get alongshore much quicker than the Frigate. You must take into account the circumstances of weather, and calculate the probable time of the Fleet's return from Palma to the present Rendezvous, No. 100, and keep a good look out, that you may join me the moment I arrive upon the said Rendezvous. His Majesty's Ship Phœbe is hourly expected from Gibraltar; you will, therefore, the moment she joins, deliver the accompanying order to the Hon. Captain Boyle of the Seahorse, and direct him to proceed in the execution of it accordingly.

NELSON AND BRONTE.

TO HIS EXCELLENCY HUGH ELLIOT, ESQ.

[Autograph, in the Elliot Papers.]

Victory, March 23rd, 1804.

My dear Sir,

Yesterday I received a letter from Mr. Frere of March 9th, in which, after having put us so much upon our guard that we

[7] Seahorse, Phœbe, Amazon.

expected a Spanish War every day, the name of Spain is not mentioned : therefore, I must suppose his alarm is gone off, or we may be lulled, by his neglect to say anything, into a fatal security. To me it matters not : I am prepared for all events.

The King, Mr. Frere says, by advices from London of February 26th, is fast recovering. I wish it may be so, but I fear very much the contrary. I believe the Prince will be sole Regent ; and I see, through the French papers—' London News, February 7th'—that Lord Grenville had been three hours with Mr. Fox, supposed forming a new Administration. Georges, I see, is also arrested, and he and Pichegru are to be tried by Military Tribunals. The Invasion must be over before this time, which I still hope will overturn Buonaparte's despotic Government. My reports say that the French have taken up at Leghorn a number of Greek Vessels as Transports. If they leave Leghorn without Troops, it is natural to suppose they are destined to take the French Troops from the Coast of the Adriatic. If so, they must either be destined for the Morea or Egypt. Information upon these points is so important, to enable me to form a probable guess at the destination of the Toulon Fleet, that no money or trouble ought to be spared to obtain it. At eight o'clock yesterday morning, our Frigates saw the French Fleet quite safe. I am going to Madalena to get some refreshments ; for I am sorry to say the scurvy has made its appearance in several Ships.

The Belleisle will stay four days at Naples ; and if the Gibraltar is sent away, I may occasionally, to relieve each other, send Ships : but of this the King shall judge ; for I never will deprive him of the protection and services of an English Ship. Yesterday, I received from Major Lowe a copy of his letter to your Excellency. There will be no resistance in Sardinia worth mentioning, should the French land in any force. Major Lowe is probably with you by this time.

Captain Hargood[8] of the Belleisle has just joined her from

---

[8] Afterwards Admiral Sir William Hargood, G.C.B. : he was a Midshipman of the Bristol in 1778 and 1779, when Nelson was a Lieutenant of that Ship. A memoir of this gallant Officer, who distinguished himself in the command of the Belleisle at Trafalgar, and died on the 12th of December, 1839, was privately printed by his widow.

England, in the room of Captain Whitby, gone home to be Admiral Cornwallis's Captain. Captain Hargood is a very old acquaintance and Ship-mate of mine, and an *elève* of the Duke of Clarence, and, what is better than all, a very good man. I am ever, my dear Sir, your most obedient, faithful servant, NELSON AND BRONTE.

I have heard nothing from 888.

TO CAPTAIN SIR WILLIAM BOLTON, H. M. SLOOP CHILDERS.

[Order-Book. The Victory and Squadron anchored at the Madalena Islands about Noon on the 25th of March 1804.]

Victory, at the Madalena Islands, 25th March, 1804.

You are hereby required and directed to receive the Master of the Victory on board his Majesty's Ship Childers, under your command, and proceed immediately to Terranova, on the South East end of Sardinia, for the purpose of surveying and ascertaining the anchorage of that place, the number of Ships which may ride there in safety, the different soundings and marks for going into the said Bay, what refreshments— such as live bullocks, sheep, poultry, onions, &c.—are to be had there, and the time required to procure them : also if it is well supplied with wood and water, and what time might be required to complete a Ship of the Line or Squadron with both. You are to remain on this service for the space of three days, and at the expiration thereof, return and join me at this anchorage ; but should I have sailed, you will proceed to Rendezvous No. 100, where you will find the Squadron, or orders for your further proceedings.

NELSON AND BRONTE.

TO CAPTAIN FRANK SOTHERON, H. M. SHIP EXCELLENT.

[Order-Book.]

Victory, at the Madalena Islands, 26th March, 1804.

You are hereby required and directed to proceed immediately with his Majesty's Ship Excellent, under your command, to Rendezvous No. 100, where you will find Captain Moubray of his Majesty's Ship Active, agreeable to my order to him, dated the 22nd instant, a copy of which is herewith inclosed, (together with copy of the one therein alluded to,) which you will consider as addressed to yourself, and execute it accordingly.　And in the event of your obtaining any information of the sailing of the Enemy's Fleet from Toulon, you will send a Frigate to me at this anchorage with an account thereof, (instead of the Gulf of Palma, as directed in Captain Moubray's said order,) bearing in mind that the Squadron will proceed from hence about Monday next, the 2nd of April; and if the wind is from the Westward, will proceed up the East side of Corsica; but if from the Eastward, the Squadron will proceed on the West side of that Island to the said Rendezvous, No. 100, so that any Ship coming to me must have this clearly in view, and be governed accordingly.

NELSON AND BRONTE.

TO ALEXANDER DAVISON, ESQ.

[Autograph, in the possession of Colonel Davison.]

Victory, March 28th, 1804.

My dear Davison,

Last night, to my surprise, Mr. Chevalier[9] sent to speak to me, and said—'I beg pardon, my Lord, but I find myself so disagreeably situated in the Ship, that I beg of your Lordship to send me to England by the first opportunity.'　To which I answered, 'Certainly, Mr. Chevalier.'　I can have no conception to what this is owing.　I never said a harsh thing to him, nor any one else, I am sure.　He is very much respected, and an excellent servant.　He is his own master in all his department; but was he, if possible, a better servant, I never would ask a servant to stay.　It is some *vagary* or *other*: so he must follow his own fancy.　So much for that.

Day by day, my dear friend, I am expecting the French Fleet to put to sea—every day, hour, and moment; and you may rely that if it is within the power of man to get at them, it shall be done; and, I am sure, that all my brethren look to that day as the finish of our laborious cruize.　The event no man can say exactly, but I must think, or render great

---

[9] His Steward.

injustice to those under me, that let the Battle be when it may, it will never have been surpassed. My shattered frame, if I survive that day, will require rest, and that is all I shall ask for. If I fall on such a glorious occasion, it shall be my pride to take care that my friends shall not blush for me. These things are in the hands of a wise and just Providence, and His Will be done. I have got some trifle, thank God, to leave those I hold most dear, and I have taken *care* not to neglect it. Do not think I am low-spirited on this account, or fancy anything is to happen to me. Quite the contrary: my mind is calm, and I have only to think of destroying our inveterate foe.

April 7th.—A Frigate has just brought me an account that she saw the French Fleet outside Toulon thirty-four hours ago, and she does not know that they are returned. I have two Frigates gone for more information, and we all hope for a meeting with the Enemy. Nothing can be finer than the Fleet under my command. Whatever be the event, believe me ever, my dear Davison, your most obliged and sincere friend,　　　　　　　　　　　NELSON AND BRONTE.

TO ALEXANDER DAVISON, ESQ.

[Autograph, in the possession of Colonel Davison.]

[Apparently, about 28th March, 1804.]

My dear Davison,

Since my last, I have received your kind letters by the Thisbe, and the Lawyer's opinion, which is very clear, and there end my inquiries; and, if ever I command the Channel Fleet, it will be my turn to make money. I [neither] want nor wish for any man's money, but justice is all I ask. I have nothing later than December from you; but, I am truly sorry to hear from Lady Hamilton that you have been laid up with the gout. Your reports are true about the poor King. I suppose there will be a change of Ministry, and then I shall expect to see you Paymaster-General, if you like the Office, and with a Title; and I shall, if it pleases God to spare my life, certainly take you by the hand before next Christmas. I wish the intended Invasion was over; for if the thing is always to hang over the Country, we shall ever be in hot water. I wish the thing decided: I am in no fears for the event.

Hardy sends you the power of attorney for the Rising Sun, but Captain Sutton must sign, and he may send it, perhaps, to his relation, Mr. Martin. I do not think it was very kind to me. Apropos, if you can be of any use to Captain Layman, I beg that you will, whether it is to get him confirmed, or to get him a good Sloop. He has not made any Prize-money since his appointment, which I am sorry for, upon his account. If I can, my dear friend, but make enough to pay my debt of money to you, I shall be fully content. Your other favours I can never repay, but I must ever feel myself your much obliged and sincere friend,

NELSON AND BRONTE.

Poor old blind Mrs. Nelson, is, I hear, something in debt. If the sum is not very large, I intend to pay it for her. I have desired dear Lady Hamilton to inquire: therefore, if within bounds, pay it for me.

N. AND B.

TO HIS EXCELLENCY HUGH ELLIOT, ESQ.

[Autograph in the Elliot Papers.]

Victory, March 29th, 1804.

My dear Sir,

Major Lowe being so completely master of everything which can inform your mind respecting the Island of Sardinia, its resources, and the probable means it has of resisting the French, it would be idle and presumptuous in me to say a word. I only sigh, and wish it belonged to Great Britain. The advantages of its position must strike every one who looks upon the Map, and its resources, called forth by a protecting Power, are certainly very great; and there is only this certainty, fixed as fate, in my mind, that if it does not belong to England, it will to France; for the present system cannot last one year, nor, I believe, half that time.

I shall sail from hence on Monday, wind and weather permitting, and shall very soon hope to meet the Enemy. I am ever, my dear Sir, your most obliged humble servant,

NELSON AND BRONTE.

P.S.—What a pack of nonsense about Sardinia! It could not be likely that I could wish to commit Sardinia, and, God knows, I have no Troops to throw away, where they are not acceptable! I rather believe a friend of mine wants me to send some troops to Alexandria, but I will neither do that, nor give my sanction to their being sent there. They are entrusted to me to defend Sicily, and to that object they shall be kept till the Court of Naples say, 'We do not want your help.' Then it is time enough to think of other things.

N. AND B.

TO THE REVEREND DR. NELSON.

[Autograph, in the Nelson Papers.]

Victory, March 29th, 1804.

My dear Brother,

I received with much pleasure your kind letter of December 30th, which, I was too much pressed for time to answer with my last dispatches. If Mr. Charles Brown[9] has served his time, and passed, you may send him out, and when opportunity offers he shall certainly be promoted; but I doubt very much that any such opportunity will offer during my command, for my health will require a few months' rest, next winter: however, you may be sure I shall do my best to serve him.

With respect to Horace, you know so much better than I how to educate him that I can say nothing; and as to what mode of life he is to follow, that must be a matter for future consideration, as events may turn out. A good education and languages fit him for anything. The Corps Diplomatique, as far as I have seen, is the road to ruin. I never knew or heard of any one who made a fortune in it, and it is very easy to spend one: indeed, without much more prudence than is considered right, a Minister cannot exist upon his salary. We must not judge, because perhaps, Lord Elgin at a particular moment got money at Constantinople, and even a Scotchman I dare say would have been richer with his interest if he had set up as a master-tailor. But, you may be sure, that in any

---

[9] As his name has not been found on the List of Lieutenants, he was probably never promoted.

way that I can be useful to Horace, whom I really love, nothing will be wanting on my part, as far as is within the the reach of my abilities. I am glad you like Canterbury, and if we may judge of the difficulty of getting there, we cannot expect it very easy to get a removal, but time and chance happeneth to all. I wish the Invasion was over, for until the trial is made our Country never can be at rest. Let who will rule in France, England will always be the object of hatred.

April 7th.—Accounts are just brought me that thirty-four hours ago the French Fleet were outside the harbour of Toulon, and we do not know they are returned, so that a meeting may be expected. The result we ought not to doubt, but I think everything good and great may be expected. I beg my kind regards to good Mrs. Nelson, and believe me ever, your most affectionate Brother,

NELSON AND BRONTE.

TO HIS EXCELLENCY HUGH ELLIOT, ESQ.

[Autograph, in the Elliot Papers.]

Victory, March 30th, 1804.

My dear Sir,

I beg leave to introduce to your Excellency's notice Doctor John Snipe, Physician to the Fleet under my command. He is not only a very able Professional gentleman, but a man of most excellent private character. He is naturally anxious to see Naples, Pompeii, Herculaneum, and the Museum of Portici; as his stay will be short, I will thank you to obtain for him speedily the orders for seeing Portici. I am ever, my dear Sir, with the sincerest good wishes for you, Mrs. Elliot, and your family, your much obliged,

NELSON AND BRONTE.

TO CAPTAIN SIR WILLIAM BOLTON, H. M. SLOOP CHILDERS.

[Order-Book.]

Victory, Madalena Islands, Sardinia, 30th March, 1804.

Doctor Snipe, Physician to the Fleet under my command, having represented to me the necessity of supplying the sick and convalescent Seamen on board the different Ships with some nutritive food in addition to the necessaries allowed by Government, and at the same time recommended Maccaroni as a light, wholesome, and nourishing food, and whereas I am perfectly satisfied of the necessity of adopting every measure for restoring the health of the sick and convalescent Seamen on board the different Ships, You are hereby required and directed to proceed immediately with his Majesty's Sloop Childers, under your command, to Naples; and on your arrival there, you will order the Purser of the said Sloop to purchase a thousand pounds of the best large pipe Maccaroni for the use of the sick and convalescent Seamen on board the different Ships—taking care that the said purchase is made upon the best and most reasonable terms for Government; for the payment of which you will direct the Purser to draw Bills upon the Commissioners for taking care of the Sick and Wounded Seamen, London, and to procure the necessary vouchers for such purchase, authenticated in the same manner as those for provisions—one of which, with a copy of this order, you will transmit to their Board by the first opportunity, and another to me on your return, for my information. You will also certify at the bottom of the Purser's bill for the amount of the Maccaroni, that it was drawn for that purpose, for the use of the sick and convalescent Seamen, and by my order. After having completed this service, you will return and join the Squadron with all possible expedition on Rendezvous No. 100, where you will find me, or orders for your further proceedings.

NELSON AND BRONTE.

TO WILLIAM MARSDEN, ESQ., ADMIRALTY.

[Original, in the Admiralty.]

Victory, Madalena Islands, Sardinia, 1st April, 1804.

Sir,

I herewith transmit you a copy of a letter from Captain Layman, giving an account of the loss of His Majesty's late Sloop Weazle,[1] under his command, on the night of the 29th

[1] The Weazle, Captain Layman, was lost by striking on a rock off Cabretta Point, near Gibraltar, on the 29th of February, 1804, in thick foggy weather.

February last, together with a letter from Lieutenant General Sir Thomas Trigge, and the paper from the Merchants at Gibraltar therein referred to: also, an extract of a letter from Captain Gore, of his Majesty's Ship Medusa, communicating to me the very high opinion he entertained of Captain Layman's conduct, which I request you will lay before the Lords Commissioners of the Admiralty for their information, and, at the same time, to acquaint their Lordships, that from the constant information I have received of Captain Layman's great exertions for the protection of our trade in the Gut of Gibraltar, I consider his appointment to another Sloop on this service would be very beneficial to the Commercial interest.   I am, &c.

NELSON AND BRONTE.

TO THE CAPTAIN OR COMMANDER OF ANY OF HIS MAJESTY'S SHIPS, VESSELS, OR TRANSPORTS, ARRIVING AT MADALENA IN SEARCH OF THE SQUADRON.

[Letter-Book.]

Victory, Madalena Islands, 2nd April, 1804.

Sir,

The Squadron is proceeding to Rendezvous No. 100, (passing Rendezvous No. 70,) where you will find me, or orders for your proceedings.   I am, &c.

NELSON AND BRONTE.

N.B.—This letter to be sealed up, and left with the Governor at Madalena.   N.B.—If the Thetis arrives, she is to remain at this anchorage; but if the Hindostan arrives, she is to proceed immediately to Malta, and deliver the stores she has on board for that Arsenal, and those for Gibraltar to be kept on board, and wait at Malta my orders.

TO CAPTAIN . . . . . ., H.M. SLOOP . . . .

[Letter-Book.]

Victory, Madalena Islands, 2nd April, 1804.

Sir,

The Agent Victualler having acquainted me that you had been making purchases of wine and vegetables for the

. . . .'s Company, which he has paid; I am, therefore, to
acquaint you that such purchase was excessively improper,
and to desire that you will on no consideration, in future, purchase wine or vegetables for the Sloop's Company under your
command : and as the wine might have been had from any of
the Ships, previous to your leaving the Squadron, and is more
than threepence per gallon dearer than what is purchased for
the Fleet by the Agent Victualler, I think it's more than probable the Victualling Board will charge the difference to your
account, and also the vegetables, as none are allowed by Government, except to Ships after a long cruize, the Pursers
being obliged to find what may be deemed necessary to Ships
in Port, or those using harbours frequently.   I am, &c.

NELSON AND BRONTE.

TO CAPTAIN ROBERT PETTET, H. M. SLOOP TERMAGANT.

[Order-Book.]

Victory, Madalena Islands, 2nd April, 1804.

You are hereby required and directed to put to sea immediately with His Majesty's Sloop Termagant, under your
command, and if the wind is from the Westward, you will
proceed on the East side of Sardinia, and on your arrival off
Tavolara, you will open the Secret letter which is herewith
transmitted, and act agreeably to the directions therein contained, but if the wind is from the Eastward, you will proceed
on the West side of Sardinia, and when you arrive off
Asinara, you will open the Secret letter, and proceed as
before mentioned.

NELSON AND BRONTE.

TO WILLIAM MARSDEN, ESQ., ADMIRALTY.

[Original, in the Admiralty. "Monday, 2nd April.—At 2·15 P.M., weighed
and made sail out of Agincourt Sound into the Eastern anchorage. At 3, shortened
sail and anchored. Donegal and Kent at anchor here. Tuesday, 3rd April. At
7 A.M., weighed and made sail through the Eastern passage. Left H. M. Ships
Canopus, Superb, and Phœbe, at anchor in Agincourt Sound. Termagant rejoined.
Noon, strong gales."—Victory's Log.]

Sir,　　　　　　　　　　　Victory at Sea, 3rd April, 1804.

I have received Sir Evan Nepean's letter of the 22nd December last, together with the inclosures 'from Mr. Arbuthnot therein mentioned, respecting a Russian Vessel having been detained by Captain Clarke,[2] of the Braakel, under the plea of her not being navigated by the stipulated proportion of Russian Seamen, her crew being habited in the Grecian dress; and signifying their Lordship's direction to make a most particular inquiry into the circumstances therein referred to, and also, to give instructions to the Captains and Commanders of His Majesty's Ships and Vessels under my orders, not to detain any Vessel bearing the Russian Flag, under the pretext assumed by Captain Clarke, if they should be otherwise regularly navigated according to the Convention.

In answer thereto, you will please to acquaint the Lords Commissioners of the Admiralty, that His Majesty's Ship Braakel has some time ago left this Country with Convoy for England, and that I shall, agreeably to their direction, give the necessary instructions to the respective Captains under my orders not to detain any Vessel under the Russian Flag upon a similar pretence.　I am, &c.,

NELSON AND BRONTE.

―――――――――

TO CAPTAIN . . . . . ., H. M. SLOOP . . . . . .

[Letter-Book.]

Sir,　　　　　　　　　　　Victory, at Sea, 3rd April, 1804.

I have received your letter of the 4th February last, together with the Report of Survey therein mentioned, and am sorry that any circumstance whatever should have detained the . . . . . so long at Lisbon, and left our Trade so much exposed to the Enemy's Privateers and Cruizers in the Gut; and I must desire that you will most strictly attend to the object of my orders, and on no account whatever remain in Port longer than may be absolutely necessary.　I am, &c.

NELSON AND BRONTE.

―――――――――

[2] Captain George Clarke, of the Braakel.　He was accidentally drowned by the upsetting of a Boat in Woolwich Reach, on the 1st of October 1805.　A notice of Captain Clarke will be found in the *Naval Chronicle* for that year, vol. xiv. p. 287.

TO WILLIAM MARSDEN, ESQ., ADMIRALTY.

[From a Copy at the Admiralty.]

Victory, at Sea, 3rd April, 1804.

Sir,

By his Majesty's Ship Phœbe, which joined on the evening of the 31st ultimo from Gibraltar, I have received your printed letter of the 19th December, (together with the several letters and orders acknowledged under this date,) signifying to me their Lordships' direction not to allow any Tenders in future to be employed by any Ship or Vessel under my command, and if any Tenders should be now employed, to cause them to be instantly discharged, and their Crews to be taken on board their respective Ships ; and also to apprise the Captains of the penalties they will be subject to, in case of their failing to pay immediate attention to the orders on this subject.

In answer to which, you will please to acquaint the Lords Commissioners of the Admiralty that their instructions shall be duly attended to, and the necessary orders issued to the respective Captains and Commanders in consequence. I am, Sir, &c.

NELSON AND BRONTE.

TO CAPTAIN GORE, H.M. SHIP MEDUSA.

[Letter-Book.]

Victory, at Sea, 3rd April, 1804.

Sir,

I have received your letter of the 20th February last, together with a Log of your proceedings, and list of Vessels spoke with, as therein mentioned, acquainting me, also, that you had, for the reason stated in your said letter, given up the object of watching the Straits of Gibraltar, for the purpose of attending to L'Aigle,[3] in order to render the approach of the Hindostan's Convoy secure. In answer to which, I very much approve of your cruizing off Cadiz, for the purpose of attending to L'Aigle, and securing the approach of our Con-

[3] L'Aigle of 74 Guns was a French Line-of-Battle Ship in Cadiz, and formed part of the Fleet at Trafalgar, on the 21st of October 1805, when she was wrecked near Rota.

voy, as well as of all the arrangements you have made with your little Squadron, which entitle you to much credit, and fully meet my approbation. With respect to your attacking L'Aigle, I must desire to refer you to my letter of the 17th ultimo.[4] I am, &c.

NELSON AND BRONTE.

___

TO CAPTAIN GORE, H.M. SHIP MEDUSA.

[Letter-Book.]

Victory, at Sea, 3rd April, 1804.

Sir,

I have received your letter of the 19th ultimo, together with the Report of Survey, and copies of the orders you have given the Amphion and Maidstone, and also the paper of intelligence from Mr. Duff.[4] I approve of the orders given the Ships above mentioned, and am exceedingly pleased with Captain Elliot's conduct and exertions in keeping the sea with the Maidstone in her present bad state, and request you will be so good as to tell him so. The loss of the Weazle will, no doubt, be much felt at Gibraltar, but I am glad to find that Captain Layman's conduct has so fully met your approbation. I have ordered the Agincourt to proceed and join you from Malta; and it is my intention, the moment the Sophie returns from Gibraltar, to order her on the late Weazle's station, and trust the exertions of Captain Rosenhagen,[5] with the assistance of the Halcyon, will keep the Gut perfectly clear of Privateers, and secure our Trade a safe passage through it. It will then become your object to direct the three Frigates to cruize very diligently outside the Straits, within the limits of the Mediterranean Station, for the protection of our Commerce, and destruction of the Enemy's Privateers and Cruizers, which, I understand, are particularly destructive to our Trade passing the skirts of the station ; and you will direct Captain Briggs, upon the Agincourt's joining, to cruize off Cape Spartel, in order to cover and protect our Commerce on its entrance into the Straits. The watching

___

[4] Vide p. 450, ante.

[4] Mr., afterwards Sir James Duff, British Consul at Cadiz. Vide vol. ii. p. 469.

[5] Captain Philip L. Rosenhagen: he was Posted in 1806, and died in April 1813.

L'Aigle, except to furnish me with the most early intelligence of her sailing, cannot be of consideration, as the whole of your force is certainly by no means equal to attack her with effect. I am fully satisfied with your endeavours to destroy the French Privateer mentioned in your said letter, and am well aware that no one can act with more zeal for the Service than yourself. I approve of your returning to Gibraltar, and hope the stores in that Arsenal will enable you to refit the Medusa and Amphion with effect. I do not hear of the Halcyon: I hope Captain Pearse is kept on the alert. Do not suffer that Sloop to be a moment inactive, and acquaint me of her proceedings. I am, &c.

NELSON AND BRONTE.

TO WILLIAM MARSDEN, ESQ., ADMIRALTY.

[Original, in the Admiralty.]

Victory, at Sea, 3rd April, 1804.

Sir,

I have received Sir Evan Nepean's letter of the 24th December last, together with a copy of a letter from Mr. Secretary Yorke[6] therein mentioned, suggesting that a notification should be made by me to our Consuls at the several Barbary States, of his Majesty's expectation that the Vessels furnished with the new Mediterranean Papers should be respected, and signifying their Lordships' direction to me to do as therein proposed. In answer to which, you will please to acquaint the Lords Commissioners of the Admiralty that, in obedience to their Lordships' direction, I have dispatched the Termagant to Tunis, with a notification to our Consul at that place, agreeably to the instructions above mentioned, and also one to be forwarded by him to his Majesty's Consul-General at Tripoli; but I have not, for the present, deemed it proper to make any notification to the Dey of Algiers. I am, &c.

NELSON AND BRONTE.

---

[6] Mr. Yorke succeeded Lord Pelham as Secretary of State for the Home Departmnte, in August 1803.

TO ADMIRAL THE EARL OF ST. VINCENT, K.B.

[Autograph, in the possession of Vice-Admiral Sir William Parker, Bart., G.C.B.]

Victory, April 6th, 1804.

My dear Lord,

I cannot allow Captain Layman[7] to present himself before you without bearing my testimony to his abilities and active conduct during his command of the Weazle; and I am sure his re-appointment to the Gibraltar station would give general satisfaction to the Rock, which you have always (and I continue it) endeavoured to please. I am always, my dear Lord, most affectionately yours,

NELSON AND BRONTE.

TO REAR-ADMIRAL SIR RICHARD BICKERTON, BART.

[From Clarke and M'Arthur, vol. ii. p. 360.]

7th April, 1804.

As the Enemy's Fleet has been out,[9] and may still be at sea, and as I should be very sorry to baulk their inclinations of a Battle by your superiority of numbers, You will, therefore, whenever I make the signal, haul from us to the Southward, furl your top-gallant sails so as not to be discovered from the shore, and just keep sight of us from the masthead; and make

[7] Captain Layman having been acquitted by a Court-Martial of all blame for the loss of the Weazle, he was soon after appointed to command the Raven Sloop, as will appear from subsequent letters. In the Memoir of that Officer in Marshall's "Naval Biography" (vol. iii. p. 327) is the following passage:—"On the 2nd of April 1804, Nelson, then unaware of the disaster which had befallen his protegé, wrote to a mutual friend, as follows: 'I hope the Admiralty will confirm Layman; for he is not only attached to me, but is, indeed, a very active Officer. It was his venturing to know more about India than Troubridge did, that made them look shy upon him. His tongue runs too fast. I often tell him neither to talk nor write so much.'"

[9] In his letter to Mr. Rose, written on the 8th April, (vide p. 488,) Lord Nelson said, that, in the preceding week, two Sail of the Line came outside Toulon, and that on Thursday the 5th, in the afternoon, they all came out. On that day the Victory was off Cape Corse, on her way to her station off Toulon, and Lord Nelson appears to have been informed of the circumstance on the morning of the 7th, when he was rejoined by the Superb, Canopus, and Active. Clarke and M'Arthur (vol. ii. p. 360) say that Lord Nelson, when informing Mr. Frere of these movements of the French Fleet, added—"If they go on playing out and in, we shall some day get at them."

the signal for your Division, (except Excellent, who is going towards Toulon,) and do you call in Belleisle, unless I should call her by signal to me.   I am, &c.,

NELSON AND BRONTE.

TO THE REVEREND ROBERT ROLFE.

[Autograph, in the possession of the Reverend Robert Rolfe.]

Victory, April 7th, 1804.

My dear Mr. Rolfe,

I am just favoured with your kind letter of January 5th, and you may be assured that if it is in my power, I will most assuredly promote Mr. Bedingfeld;[1] and if it should not, that I will leave him as a legacy to my successor.   I must apprise you that we have no deaths in this fine climate, and the French Fleet will not give us an opportunity of being *killed* off.   I am well aware of your obligations to Sir R. Bedingfeld, and of the pleasure it must afford to show your goodness of heart.   I will not say all which I could on this subject.   Remember me most kindly to your good mother, my Aunt;[2] and believe [me] ever, my dear Rolfe, your most affectionate cousin,

NELSON AND BRONTE.

TO THE RIGHT HONOURABLE GEORGE ROSE.

[Autograph, in the possession of the Right Honourable Sir George Rose, G.C.H,]

Victory, April 8th, 1804.

My dear Sir,

I was favoured with your kind letter of December 15th, a few days ago.   I have not as yet heard a word of the entailing the English pension; and if common justice is done me, Parliament ought to give me the £1000 a-year that your Administration gave to Lords St. Vincent and Duncan; but, if our reports are true about the King, very great alterations must take place.

[1] Mr. Thomas William Bedingfeld, second son of Frank Bedingfeld, Esq., was distantly related to Sir Richard Bedingfeld, Bart.   He was wounded in the hand in an attack made by the Boats of the Narcissus, Seahorse, and Maidstone, on some French Vessels in Hières Bay, in the night of the 11th of July 1804; was immediately made a Lieutenant, and died in July 1811.

[2] Vide vol. i. pp. 17, 18.

We are on the eve of great events. Last week, at different times, two Sail of the Line put their heads outside Toulon; and on Thursday the 5th, in the afternoon, they all came out. We have had a gale of wind and calm since; therefore, I do not know whether they are returned to Port or have kept the sea. I have only to wish to get alongside of them with the present Fleet under my command; so highly officered and manned, the event ought not to be doubted. That event shall, if possible, be useful to your recommendation, Captain Strachey, who I shall be glad of an opportunity of promoting. With many thanks for your obliging offers of service, for which I hope to thank you soon in London, believe me ever, my dear Sir, your much obliged friend,

NELSON AND BRONTE.

TO CAPTAIN SOTHERON, H.M. SHIP EXCELLENT.

[Letter-Book. "Monday, 9th April. At Noon, Cape Sicie bore N.W., distant five leagues. P.M. Amazon took possession of a French Merchant brig between Cape Sepet and Porquerolle. Observed the batteries at Sepet firing at the Amazon, and that three Frigates came out of Toulon, and stood for the Amazon and her Prize. Donegal's and Active's signals made to close the Amazon. Observed four more of the Enemy's Ships coming out of Toulon round Sepet; the Prize standing off the land for the Squadron. At 6·30, the Enemy's Ships tacked, and stood into Toulon. Superb closed the Donegal, Active, and Amazon."—Victory's Log.]

Victory, off Toulon, 9th April, 1804.

Sir,

I am to desire you will proceed immediately with his Majesty's Ship Excellent, under your command, (taking with you the Frigates named in the margin,[3]) to Rendezvous No. 100, where you will remain until I shall join you with the Squadron, which will most probably be in three or four days from this date. You will detain the Argo, Agincourt, or any other Vessel of War or Transport which may come on the said Rendezvous, till my arrival; and every two days, or as often as you may, from circumstances or information, judge necessary, send two of the Frigates to reconnoitre the Enemy at Toulon. I am, &c.,

NELSON AND BRONTE.

[3] Active, Phœbe, Seahorse, Amazon.

TO J. B. GIBERT, ESQ., HIS BRITANNIC MAJESTY'S CONSUL, BARCELONA.

[Letter-Book.]

Victory, at Sea, 10th April, 1804.

Sir,

I have received your letter of the 24th ultimo, together with the one therein alluded to, transmitting a packet from Mr. Frere, and am very much obliged by your sending me the several French and Spanish Papers, with the four copies of the Courier de Londres, which have all been received safe. I am aware that a Bill of Health is required from his Majesty's Ships and Vessels using either Barcelona or Rosas, and am sorry to observe that every difficulty and impediment is thrown in the way of our procuring the small supplies of bullocks and refreshments for the Fleet under my command, very unusual between two Nations in peace and amity. I trust, however, that Mr. Frere's remonstrance with the Court of Madrid may do away the necessity of such Bill of Health, and also procure us more liberal supplies of bullocks, &c., free from the immense duties imposed on them. I enclose a letter to the Captain-General on the subject of the Captain of any of his Majesty's Ships giving his word of honour, that his people are in perfect health and pratique, and ought to be received as such. You will, therefore, have the goodness to explain to the Captain-General, that the word of honour of the Captain of a British Man-of-War is as sacred as a Monarch's, and equal to any Bill of Health from me. I am, with much respect, &c.,

NELSON AND BRONTE.

TO WILLIAM MARSDEN, ESQ., ADMIRALTY.

[Original, in the Admiralty.]

Victory, off Toulon, 10th April, 1804.

Sir,

I herewith transmit you, for the information of the Lords Commissioners of the Admiralty, a copy of the Active's log on the 6th instant, and request you will be pleased to acquaint their Lordships that yesterday forenoon the Squadron under my command stood close in with the entrance of Toulon Harbour and reconnoitred the Enemy's force, the same as mentioned in my letter to Sir Evan Nepean of the 19th ultimo. They are certainly, however, upon the alert, as an Admiral, with four Sail of the Line and three Frigates, came out in the evening, in order to recapture a small Coasting-Vessel taken by the Amazon close under their batteries; but finding her covered by the Donegal, Superb, and Excellent, they returned into Port. I am, &c.,

NELSON AND BRONTE.

TO LADY HAMILTON.

[Extracts from " Lord Nelson's Letters to Lady Hamilton," vol. ii. p. 26.]

Victory, off Toulon, April 10th, 1804.

. . . . . The *amorins* will go under the care of Captain Layman; who, unfortunately, lost his Sloop: but, with much credit to himself, he has been acquitted of all blame. I rejoice that dear Horatia is got well; and, also, that you, my dearest Emma, are recovered of your severe indisposition. In our present situation with Spain, this letter, probably, may never reach you. I have wrote fully; and intend to send them by the Argus, who I expect to ' join every minute. Elfi Bey, I hear, has had all his fine things taken from him. He escaped into the Desert, and is pursued; probably, his head is off, long before this time. The French Fleet came out on the 5th, but went in again the next morning. Yesterday, a Rear-Admiral and seven Sail of Ships, including Frigates, put their nose outside the harbour. If they go on playing this game, some day we shall lay salt upon their tails; and so end the campaign of, my dearest Emma, your most faithful and affectionate.

I am glad to hear that you are going to take my dear Horatia, to educate her. She must turn out an angel, if she minds what you say to her; and Eliza and Ann[4] will never forget your goodness. My health is *so so!* I shall get through

---

[4] His nieces, daughters of his sister, Mrs. Bolton. The former married the Reverend Henry Girdlestone, and the latter died unmarried in October 1830.

the summer; and, in the winter, shall go home. You will readily fancy all I would say, and do think. My kind love to all friends.

TO THOMAS BOLTON, ESQ.

[Autograph, in the possession of James Young, Esq., of Wells.]

My dear Sir, Victory, April 11th, 1804.

Your letter of October 23rd has only just reached me. Your letter for Sir William[5] shall be delivered when he joins the Fleet: he is now on his return from Naples. His conduct is such as not only merits my esteem, but also, that of all the Officers in the Fleet. If I knew where to place him to get some money, I should most gladly do it. I have given him his choice of station, but he rather wishes to keep at hand, in case of something turning up. As to vacancies, unless the French Fleet come out, I see no prospect of promotion; but time and chance happeneth to all, and so it will to him, if he looks out sharp for good fortune. We have various reports here of the King's illness; of the Invasion having been attempted, and failed, &c. &c. We shall never have a solid Peace until the Invasion is tried and found to fail. My state of health will certainly oblige me to return to England before next Christmas, and I shall always be happy in taking you by the hand, being ever, my dear Sir, your much obliged friend,

NELSON AND BRONTE.

TO CAPTAIN JOHN GORE, H. M. SHIP MEDUSA, OR THE SENIOR OFFICER AT GIBRALTAR.

[Order-Book.]

Victory, at Sea, 12th April, 1804.

Whereas it is a well known custom in the Service, that after the loss of a Ship or Vessel of War, the Captain, Officers, and Men (who survive) are always considered answerable for their conduct, and cannot be employed until they have been tried by a Court-Martial; and, whereas, the four men named

---

[5] Captain Sir William Bolton, of the Childers, nephew and son-in-law of Mr. Bolton, to whom this letter was written.

in the margin, have been very improperly detained on board the Amphion, You are hereby required and directed to cause the said four men to be discharged from the Amphion, and sent to the Victory by the very first opportunity; and should either of the men named on the other side hereof be on board the Amphion, or any other of his Majesty's Ships under your orders, you will also cause them to be discharged, and sent to the Victory in the manner above-mentioned, and also the seven men belonging to the late Weazle Sloop (who were sent to the Hospital), on their recovery.

NELSON AND BRONTE.

TO CAPTAIN SAMUEL SUTTON, H.M. SHIP AMPHION.

[Letter-Book.]

Victory, at Sea, 12th April, 1804.

Dear Sir,

As the people belonging to His Majesty's late Sloop Weazle ought to have been sent up for Trial with the others, I have sent an order to the Senior Officer at Gibraltar to direct their discharge from the Amphion, that they may be sent to the Victory by the very first opportunity. I am &c.,

NELSON AND BRONTE.

P.S.—Should the order above-mentioned come to you, as Senior Officer, at Gibraltar, you will of course comply with it immediately.

TO WILLIAM MARSDEN, ESQ., ADMIRALTY.

[Letter-Book.]

Victory, at Sea, 13th April, 1804.

Sir,

I herewith transmit you for the information of the Lords Commissioners of the Admiralty, a copy of my order of yesterday's date, for the survey of Lieutenant Robert Stupart,[6] of His Majesty's Ship Triumph, together with a report of that Officer's health in consequence; and I am to request you will

---

[6] Lieutenant Robert Stupart died between 1805 and 1807.

please to acquaint their Lordships, that as Lieutenant Askew[7]
has not yet joined the Triumph, Mr. Faddy continues acting
in the room of Lieutenant Miller, as mentioned in my letter
to you of the 20th ultimo, and as soon as Lieutenant Askew
joins, I have given Mr. William Faddy an order to act in the
room of Lieutenant Stupart, a copy of which, is herewith
transmitted for their Lordships information, and trust, from a
consideration of the circumstances stated in my said letter,
respecting Mr. Faddy, their Lordships will be pleased to give
him a Commission. I am, &c.,

NELSON AND BRONTE.

TO MISS HORATIA NELSON THOMSON.

[From "Lord Nelson's Letters to Lady Hamilton," vol. ii. p. 107.]

Victory, April 13th, 1804.

My dear Horatia,
I send you twelve books of Spanish dresses, which you will
let your Guardian Angel, Lady Hamilton, keep for you, when
you are tired of looking at them. I am very glad to hear, that
you are perfectly recovered; and, that you are a very good
child. I beg, my dear Horatia, that you will always continue
so; which will be a great comfort to your most affectionate,

NELSON AND BRONTE.

TO CAPTAIN BENJAMIN HALLOWELL, H. M. SHIP ARGO.

[Order-Book.]

Victory, at Sea, 14th April, 1804.

You are hereby required and directed on your arrival at
Gibraltar, to make the signal for, and take under your
convoy and protection, all the Trade bound from thence to
any part of the United Kingdom, and proceed with them as
expeditiously as possible, consistent with their safety, off
Cadiz, where you will also take under your convoy and
protection all the Merchant-Ships at that place, bound for

[7] Lieutenant William Askew died in December 1805: he was a brother of the
present Lieutenant-General Sir Henry Askew, K.C.B., and of Captain Christopher
Crakenthorp Askew, R.N.—*Vide* Burke's "History of the Landed Gentry," p. 29.

England, and make the best of your way with them to their
destination; and, in order that the Convoy under your Command may be sufficiently strengthened against L'Aigle, or
any of the Enemy's Cruizers, You are hereby directed to order
the Captain of the Agincourt to proceed in company with
you from Gibraltar, and escort you twenty or twenty-five
leagues to the Westward of Cadiz; and afterwards to return
to Gibraltar, and follow my orders of the 20th ultimo, which
he will find with Commissioner Otway at that place. You will
also receive such money on board his Majesty's Ship Argo,
under your command, as the Merchants at Gibraltar and
Cadiz may have to send to England; but in receiving the
money from the last-mentioned place, I must recommend
great caution, and desire that you will take such measures for
that purpose as may be perfectly consistent with the safety
of the Trade which may be under your protection from
Gibraltar. It may, therefore, be advisable to proceed in the
Argo to Cadiz for the purpose above-mentioned, as well as
for the bringing the Trade with you from that place, and leave
the Agincourt to take the Convoy from Gibraltar off Cadiz,
in order to its being joined by the Argo, on its appearance
off Cadiz, and then proceed as before directed.

NELSON AND BRONTE.

TO WILLIAM MARSDEN, ESQ., ADMIRALTY.

[Original, in the Admiralty.]

Victory, at Sea, 14th April, 1804.

Sir,

I request you will be pleased to acquaint the Lords Commissioners of the Admiralty, that I have charged Captain
Layman, of his Majesty's late Sloop Weazle, with my Public
dispatches for the Admiralty, and beg to recommend him to
their Lordships as an Officer very deserving their patronage
and protection. I am, Sir, &c.,

NELSON AND BRONTE.

MEMORANDUM.

[The following Paper was written by Captain Layman, late of the Weazle Sloop, and transmitted to the Admiralty by Lord Nelson on the 14th of April, 1804. "The importance of a Cruizer in the Gut of Gibraltar, in a Naval and Commercial point of view, as well as the consideration of obtaining supplies for the Garrison, seems to require a particular description of Vessel to keep her station in a Channel confined to the space of eight miles, in which, exclusive of the wind and sea being often boisterous and turbulent, there are four strong tides, besides the current; and, as to effect turning to the westward, against the wind, some tacks do not exceed one mile. It is presumed that a fast-sailing Brig is the best description of Vessel for this service, and as she ought not only to be able to repulse but to take anything in the shape of a Privateer, some of which have from twenty-two to twenty-six guns, with from one hundred and fifty to two hundred men, it would require her to be of such dimensions as to be armed with eighteen 32-pounder carronades, with sufficient space, abaft and forward, to mount a long 18-pounder to fire in all directions; and the better to prevent her being annoyed in a calm, and to enable her to pursue Privateers or Gun-boats, she should be fitted so as to pull thirty-eight sweeps and two skulls, the advantages of which were evinced in the Weazle.—H. M. Ship Victory, April 13th, 1804, W. LAYMAN."—*From a Copy in the Admiralty.*]

[Autograph on the above Paper.]

Victory, April 14th, 1804.

I agree most perfectly in the propriety of having Vessels of the aforementioned description, stationed in the Straits of Gibraltar; and I know no man so fit to command one of them as Captain Layman.

NELSON AND BRONTE.

TO THE MASTERS OF THE MERCHANT SHIPS ZEPHYR, COURIER, OAK, AND HOPE, AT GIBRALTAR.

[Letter-Book.]

Victory, at Sea, 14th April, 1804.

Gentlemen,

I have received your Petition, dated at Gibraltar the 6th instant, stating, that you had for some time past been detained in the said Bay for want of Convoy; in answer to which, I am to acquaint you that Captain Hallowell, of his Majesty's Ship Argo, is directed to take the Ships you respectively command, and any others at Gibraltar, under his protection and convoy, and proceed with them to England as early as possible; but I cannot, at the same time, help expressing my

astonishment at your detention at Gibraltar for want of Convoy,
particularly as his Majesty's Ship Monmouth sailed from that
place on the 1st ultimo for England, and I am persuaded
Captain Hart would have taken any Trade bound for the United
Kingdom under his protection.　I am, &c.,

NELSON AND BRONTE.

TO THE SENIOR OFFICER OF HIS MAJESTY'S SHIPS AND
VESSELS AT GIBRALTAR.

[Letter-Book.]

Victory, at Sea, 14th April, 1804.

Sir,

As I wish my Public dispatches in the charge of Captain
Layman, of his Majesty's late Sloop Weazle, to be forwarded
to Government as early as possible, I am to desire you will
(in case the Argo is sailed from England) immediately send
a Vessel of War to Lisbon, with Captain Layman and the said
dispatches; or in the event of none being at Gibraltar on his
arrival, you will receive Captain Layman on board the Ship
you command and proceed to Lisbon with him, with as much
expedition as possible.　Having so done, pursue the object of
your former orders.　I am, &c.,

NELSON AND BRONTE.

TO CAPTAIN GORE, H.M. SHIP MEDUSA, OR THE SENIOR OFFICER
OF HIS MAJESTY'S SHIPS AND VESSELS AT GIBRALTAR.

[Letter-Book.]

Victory, at Sea, 15th April, 1804.

Sir,

As the Rendezvous of the Squadron under my command
is particularly uncertain, and must ever depend upon circumstances, I must desire that you will acquaint the Captains or
Commanders of any of his Majesty's Ships, Vessels, or Transports ordered to join me, that they are to come to Rendezvous
No. 97, under Cape St. Sebastians, mentioned on the inclosed
Sheet of Rendezvous, where they will meet a Ship of War
stationed for the purpose of falling in with Ships in search of
me ; and you will acquaint them that they are on no account

or consideration to leave the said Rendezvous No. 97, but remain there for my further orders.   I am, &c.,

NELSON AND BRONTE.

N.B.—A letter of the same tenor and date as the above, inclosing a sheet of Rendezvous, sent to Commissioner Otway, Gibraltar.

TO THE RIGHT HONOURABLE LORD HOBART, SECRETARY OF STATE FOR THE WAR DEPARTMENT.

[Autograph, in the Colonial Office.]

Victory, April 16th, 1804.

My Lord,

I have been honoured with your letter of January 7th, and it has given me most sincere pleasure that my whole conduct in my Command here has been such as to meet his Majesty's approbation, and which it shall always be my study to deserve.

Your Lordship will probably hear something of Sardinia through Mr. Elliot at Naples, and Mr. Jackson at Rome.   I send your Lordship a copy of my last letter to Mr. Jackson. My line of conduct, in obedience to the spirit of his Majesty's instructions communicated through your Lordship, has been simply this,—to conciliate all, to protect all from French rapacity,—and I have the satisfaction to think that I have completely succeeded.

My eye is constantly fixed upon Toulon; and I have no great reason to believe that the French will escape me, whatever may be their destination : and it is with real pleasure I can state to your Lordship, and request you will state it to the King, that no Fleet ever was in higher discipline, and health, and good humour, than the one I have the honour to command ; and whenever we fall in with the Enemy's Fleet, (if I do my duty,) the happiest result will, I may venture to say, accrue.   I have the honour to be, &c.,

NELSON AND BRONTE.

The French Fleet safe in Toulon this day at noon.

TO THE RIGHT HONOURABLE LORD HOBART.

[Autograph, in the Colonial Office.]

Victory, April 16th, 1804.

My Lord,

I have the honour to transmit your Lordship two letters from Ali Vizir, Pacha of Yanina. Captain Cracraft or Mr. Foresti have most probably seen him before this time. With respect to the Vessel, there must be some mistake in his Italian writer; but with regard to the Artillery-men, there can be none. Your Lordship will judge how far it would be proper to send them. I shall write to the Pacha about the Vessel. I think he can only mean a small handsome Vessel. Your Lordship is, I dare say, fully aware of the sort of independence this Pacha holds himself of the Porte, and that it has always been considered, that whenever he could get possession of the Suliotes, he would declare his independence. He has now accomplished his object, and could hold the Morea in spite of all the power of the Porte; but the times are also changed, and what he could have done easily ten years past, may now be difficult. The Russians, I fancy, resist any Power holding the Morea and European Turkey except themselves.

Your Lordship will judge of the Pacha's present intentions, and whether he looks to us for support. I shall write him word that I have referred his letter to your Lordship. Of this we may be sure, that if we do not give him the two Artillerymen and the Vessel, the French will. I am, &c.,

NELSON AND BRONTE.

TO CAPTAIN LEWIS SHEPHEARD, H. M. SHIP THISBE.

[Letter-Book.]

Victory, at Sea, 17th April, 1804.

Sir,

I have received your letter of the 31st ultimo, acquainting me that you had detained a Greek Polacca Ship from Smyrna bound to Amsterdam, and that you had carried her into Valetta Harbour, under an idea that her cargo was Dutch property, which, I hope may prove so, to exonerate the detention. I have also to acknowledge the receipt of your letter of the 1st instant, acquainting me, that all the Convoy under your charge had arrived safe, except an armed Polacca belonging to Gibraltar. I am, &c.,

NELSON AND BRONTE.

TO CAPTAIN SCHOMBERG, H. M. SHIP MADRAS, MALTA.

[Letter-Book.]

Victory, at Sea, 17th April, 1804.

Sir,

I have received your letter of the 17th ultimo, acquainting me, that Lieutenant Cantelo, of the Bombay Marine, had arrived at Malta, with dispatches for England, and that you had sent him on board the Agincourt to proceed to Gibraltar: also, that several Transports had arrived in the last Convoy from England, that are fit (with a little alteration) to receive Troops, that you had ordered them to victual and water for two months for their respective complements of Troops, and that embarkation for at least one thousand four hundred men is ready at a moment's notice. In answer to which, I very much approve of every part of your conduct on this occasion; but trust this arrangement has not interfered with the sailing of the two coppered Transports to the Black Sea, under the charge of Lieutenant Woodman, as mentioned in my letter to Captain Lamb, of the 20th March last, and order, to Lieutenant Woodman, of that date. I am, also, to desire you will use every possible exertion in your power, to collect all the Trade from the Levant and Adriatic, in order to proceed to England under the protection of the Agincourt and Thisbe, the moment the former shall arrive at Malta from Gibraltar, where I have sent her to take in her lower-deck guns, previous to her proceeding on this service. The Thisbe is for the moment directed to follow the orders of Captain Donnelly, to bring out Transports to the Fleet, and will return immediately. I have received information that there are three French Privateers (two of them Brigs) who have taken their station off Tunis, for the purpose of intercepting stragglers from

Convoys, or Runners.　I must, therefore, desire that you will pay all the attention to the destruction of these Privateers, which may be in your power, and at the same time communicate this circumstance to Captain Cracraft of the Anson, that he may also turn his mind to their capture.　I am, &c.,

NELSON AND BRONTE.

TO CAPTAIN SCHOMBERG, H.M. SHIP MADRAS.

[Letter-Book.]

Victory, at Sea, 17th April, 1804.

Sir,

I have received your letter of the 31st ultimo, acquainting me with the arrival of the Thisbe, with the Convoy from England mentioned on the list which accompanied your said letter, and that you had in consequence of directions from the Admiralty, communicated in Sir Evan Nepean's letter of the 21st December, ordered the Jalouse up the Adriatic with the Trade, and directed Captain Strachey to use his utmost exertions to collect the Ships left by the Morgiana, that they might arrive at Malta time enough to proceed with the Convoy for England; acquainting me, also, that a great part of the guns and stores belonging to his Majesty's late Sloop Raven, had been saved by Mr. Tough,[8] and that you had recommended to him not to dispose of them, and that you should take the necessary steps to convey them to Malta.　In answer to which, I very much approve of your sending the Jalouse with the Trade up the Adriatic, and also, with the measures you have taken respecting the conveyance of the stores saved from the late Raven Sloop to Malta, when I shall direct the Naval Officer to value them, and make the usual salvage for saving them.　I approve of your having sent the Thisbe to pick up her straggled Convoy, and am glad to hear from Captain Shepheard[9] that they have arrived safe.　I am, &c.,

NELSON AND BRONTE.

[8] British Consul at Palermo.

[9] Captain Lewis Shepheard of the Thisbe was Posted in October 1810, and died about 1831.

TO LIEUTENANT ROBERT CORNER.[1]

[Autograph, in the possession of Peter Smith, Esq.]

Victory, April 18th, 1804.

Sir,

If you are the gentleman who was Second of the Terrible, and afterwards in the Victory, I remember you most perfectly. I am not aware of any opportunity offering for your removal into more active employ; but, if you can effect an exchange into any Ship here, I can have no objections. I am, Sir, &c.,

NELSON AND BRONTE.

TO NATHANIEL TAYLOR, ESQ., NAVAL STOREKEEPER, MALTA.

[Letter-Book.]

Victory, April 18th, 1804.

Sir,

Perhaps the hawser-laid rope of six and a half, six, five and a half, five, four and a half, and four, may if the hemp is **good** be relaid and made serviceable in our present **great** want of stores. I wish to talk to Mr. Lawson about it, and if it can be done, it will be very desirable. I am, &c.

NELSON AND BRONTE.

TO CAPTAIN HENRY RICHARDSON, H. M. SHIP JUNO.

[Letter-Book.]

Victory, at Sea, 19th April, 1804.

Sir,

Although nothing can be greater than the necessity of his Majesty's Ship Juno, under your command, keeping constantly on Rendezvous No. 97 ; and, although, in the absence of the said Ship, the Swift Cutter,[2] with dispatches from the

---

[1] Lieutenant Robert Corner, who obtained that rank in 1779: he died a Lieutenant about 1820.

[2] The Swift Hired Cutter, of eight four pounders and twenty-three men, under the command of Lieutenant William Martin Leake, who was killed in the Action, was captured by the French Xebec Privateer L'Esperance, of ten Guns and fifty-four men, in the Mediterranean, on the 3rd of April 1804. James says, ("Naval His-

Admiralty, has been captured by the Enemy, without being able to save them, I cannot but approve of your conduct in quitting your station, and proceeding to the Bay of Rosas, to assist the Officers and people of the late Hindostan;[3] but, I must recommend the strictest attention being had to keep the Juno on the said Rendezvous, to protect any Victualler, Transport, &c. from capture by the Enemy. I enclose you Rendezvous No. 102, being the present station of the Fleet, and am to desire you will acquaint any of his Majesty's Ships or Vessels in search of the Squadron, that they will find me there, or orders for their further proceedings. I am, &c.,

NELSON AND BRONTE.

TO ALEXANDER DAVISON, ESQ.

[Autograph, in the possession of Colonel Davison.]

Victory, April 19th, 1804.

My dear Davison,

Whatever I might have had in the Hindostan is gone, and also all our letters in the Swift Cutter. She was taken the 5th, and all our dispatches, letters, &c. &c., are gone to Paris. I have only had two dispatches sent me since my leaving England. One, the British Fair, was very near taken in the Gut. The Swift, of the force of *twenty-three* men and boys, is taken by a thing of fifty-three men and boys. How Government can think of sending Papers of consequence in such a Vessel I cannot imagine. I suppose we shall have a Book of intercepted correspondence,[4] with such additions as

tory," vol. iii. p. 263)—" The Swift, it appears, was carrying dispatches to Vice-Admiral Lord Nelson off Toulon, but which, we rather think, for very few, if any, particulars have been published, were thrown overboard previously to the Cutter's capture ;" and adds, that " it seems strange that important dispatches should be forwarded by a Vessel not equal to a Frigate's Launch, when armed with her carronade and proper complement of men."

[7] The Hindostan Store-Ship, Captain (or more properly Commander) John Le Gros, caught fire, and was totally destroyed in the Bay of Rosas, on the 2nd of April 1804. Captain Le Gros was " honourably acquitted of any blame, and the Court-Martial gave him great credit for his conduct in smothering the fire at a distance of twelve leagues from the shore, which saved the lives of the Crew." He died at Jersey, in 1807.

[4] Lord Nelson evidently alluded to an octavo volume which was published in London in 1798, entitled, " Copies of Original Letters from the Army of General Buonaparte in Egypt, intercepted by the Fleet under the command of Admiral Lord Nelson."

the ingenious head of a Frenchman can invent. Lieutenant Askew is safe on board the Triumph: he was fortunate to come up in the Thisbe. I see no prospect of my being useful to any one. I shall only repeat that I am ever, my dear Davison, your most obliged friend,

NELSON AND BRONTE.

I have wrote to you before respecting paying poor blind Mrs. Nelson's debts, if within the bounds of reason, and my fortune.

TO ADMIRAL THE EARL OF ST. VINCENT, K.B.

[Autograph, in the possession of Vice-Admiral Sir William Parker, Bart., G.C.B.]

Victory, April 19th, 1804.

My dear Lord,

The loss of the Hindostan has been great; but from our care and attention, I may truly say, of every Captain in the Fleet, we shall get on for the summer. It is an accident, such a Ship must be liable to; and if Captain Le Gros' account is correct (he is now on his Trial) he had great merit in the order in which the Ship was kept, and it must have arose from either some of the Medicine-Chests breaking, or from wet getting down, which caused things to heat. The preservation of the Crew seems little short of a miracle: I never read such a Journal of exertions.

Misfortunes seldom come alone. The Juno very properly, hearing of the accident, quitted her station off Cape St. Sebastians the very day the Swift was taken, or that would have been prevented. I send the account I have of that event to the Admiralty. I only hope that no dispatches of any consequence were entrusted in such a Vessel. Whatever they are, they are this day before Buonaparte. Every Jack in Diplomatic affairs is intrusted with a cipher, but an Admiral Commander-in-Chief is not. It will now be corrected. I am ever, my dear Lord, most affectionately yours,

NELSON AND BRONTE.

TO LADY HAMILTON.

[From " Lord Nelson's Letters to Lady Hamilton," vol. ii. p. 29.]

Victory, April 19th, 1804.

My dearest Emma,

I had wrote you a line, intended for the Swift Cutter; but, instead of her joining me, I had the mortification, not only to hear that she was taken, but that *all* the dispatches and let-ters had fallen into the hands of the Enemy; a very pretty piece of work! I am not surprised at the capture, but am very much so that any dispatches should be sent in a Vessel with twenty-three men, not equal to cope with any Row-boat Privateer. As I do not know what letters of yours are in her, I cannot guess what will be said. I suppose, there will be a publication. The loss of the Hindostan, was great enough; but, for importance, it is lost, in comparison to the probable knowledge the Enemy will obtain of our connexions with Foreign Countries! Foreigners for ever say, and it is true —' We dare not trust England; one way or other, we are sure to be committed!' However, it is now too late to launch out on this subject. Not a thing has been saved out of the Hin-dostan, not a second shirt for any one; and it has been by extraordinary exertions, that the people's lives were saved.

Captain Hallowell is so good as to take home for me, wine as by the enclosed list; and, if I can, some honey. The Spanish honey is so precious, that if [any one has] a cut, or sore throat, it is used to cure it. I mention this, in case you should wish to give the Duke a jar. The smell is wonderful! It is produced nowhere but in the mountains near Rosas. The Cyprus wine—one hogshead, was for Buonaparte,—I would recommend the wine-cooper drawing it off: and you can send a few dozens to the Duke; who, I know, takes a glass every day at two o'clock. I wish I had anything else to send you; but, my dearest Emma, you must take the will for the deed. I am pleased with Charlotte's letter; and, as she loves my dear Horatia, I shall always like her. What hearts those must have, who do not! But, thank God, she shall not be dependent on any of them.

Your letter of February 12th, through Mr. Falconet, I have

received. I know they are all read; therefore, never sign your name. I shall continue to write through Spain; but never say a word that can convey any information—except, of eternal attachment and affection for you; and that I care not who knows; for I am, &c.

NELSON AND BRONTE.

Poor Captain Le Gros had your Note to him in his pocket-book, and that was all he saved.

Mr. Este[4] left him at Gibraltar, and went to Malta in the Thisbe. Captain Le Gros is now Trying. I think it will turn out that every person is obliged to his conduct for saving their lives. She took fire thirteen leagues from the land.

· · · · · · · · ·

TO MISS CHARLOTTE NELSON.[5]

[From " Lord Nelson's Letters to Lady Hamilton," vol. ii. p. 109.]

Victory, April 19th, 1804.

My dear Charlotte,
    I thank you very much for your kind letters of January 3rd and 4th; and I feel truly sensible of your kind regard for that dear little orphan, Horatia. Although her parents are lost, yet she is not without a fortune; and I shall cherish her to the last moment of my life, and *curse* them who *curse* her, and Heaven *bless* them who *bless* her! Dear innocent! she can have injured no one. I am glad to hear that she is attached to you; and, if she takes after her parents, so she will to those who are kind to her. I am ever, dear Charlotte, your affectionate uncle,

NELSON AND BRONTE.

---

    [4] Now Dr. Lambton Este, who has been, and will again be mentioned.
    [5] His niece, only daughter of the Reverend Doctor Nelson, afterwards Earl Nelson. Miss Nelson married, on the 3rd of July 1801, the Honourable Samuel Hood, now Lord Bridport.

TO THE RIGHT HONOURABLE LORD HOBART.

[Autograph, in the Colonial Office.]

Victory, April 19th, 1804.

Private.

My dear Lord,

I rely with confidence that, although the Admiralty for ever send their dispatches, of whatever consequence, without the use of cipher, and trust to their being thrown overboard in case of capture, yet, as I know the other Departments of Government always use cipher if of importance, and although Admirals are never entrusted with ciphers, yet I rely that your Lordship would not trust any dispatch of consequence in a Vessel with twenty-three men, much less commit the interests and schemes of other Powers to such a conveyance. This is the only consolation I derive from all the dispatches being this day read by the First Consul; I wish they were in his throat. I think a great deal on this matter, but it may be prudent to hold my tongue, except to say, I am, &c.,

NELSON AND BRONTE.

TO WILLIAM MARSDEN, ESQ., ADMIRALTY.

[From a Copy in the Admiralty.]

Victory, at Sea, 19th April, 1804.

Sir,

I herewith transmit you the sentence of a Court-Martial held this day, on board his Majesty's Ship Royal Sovereign, for the trial of Captain Le Gros, and the Officers and Company of his Majesty's late Ship Hindostan,[6] which you will please to lay before the Lords Commissioners of the Admiralty, for their information; and at the same time acquaint their Lordships, that, from every information which I have received, the exertions of Captain Le Gros, his Officers, and Ship's Company, in the late unfortunate business, deserve great commendation, and that to the cool and collected con-

---

[6] Captain Le Gros, his Officers, and Ship's Company were honourably acquitted. Vide p. 498, ante.

duct of Captain Le Gros, is to be attributed the preservation of their lives. I am, Sir, &c.

NELSON AND BRONTE.

P.S.—Inclosed is a letter from Rear-Admiral Sir Richard Bickerton, (at the request of the Court,) respecting the conduct of Mr. Banks, Acting-Lieutenant of his Majesty's late Ship Hindostan, which I request you to lay before their Lordships, with a hope that they will grant him a Commission for his very meritorious conduct, as there set forth.[7]

NELSON AND BRONTE.

TO THE PRINCIPAL OFFICERS AND COMMISSIONERS OF HIS MAJESTY'S NAVY, LONDON.

[Letter-Book.]

Victory, at Sea, 19th April, 1804.

Gentlemen,

The two Artificers named in the margin,[8] having been detained to attend as Evidence at the Court-Martial on Captain Le Gros, the Officers and Company of his Majesty's late Ship Hindostan, are consequently prevented from proceeding to Malta with the others; and understanding that the Artificers are entitled to certain privileges on their entering upon duty in that Yard, I am to acquaint you that I have ordered the Naval Officer at Malta to consider the said two men as arriving with the others, and pay them the sum they would be entitled to in consequence, and request you will be pleased to give the necessary directions to the Naval Officer accordingly. The conduct of all the Artificers on the late Hindostan's accident, was very meritorious, and met the entire approbation of the Court-Martial, particularly the two men above mentioned, whose exertions were very exemplary. I am, &c.

NELSON AND BRONTE.

---

[7] In reply to this recommendation, Lord Nelson was informed that Mr. Banks " will be considered when an opportunity offers." Mr. Thomas Banks was made a Lieutenant on the 23rd of June, 1804 and died about 1810.

[8] Samuel Follett, Thomas Rogers.

TO CAPTAIN THOMAS BRIGGS, H. M. SHIP AGINCOURT.

[Order-Book.]

Victory, at Sea, 19th April, 1804.

You are hereby required and directed to return immediately with his Majesty's Ship Agincourt, under your command, to Gibraltar, and on your arrival at that place, you will take such Trade as may be there ready to accompany you to Malta, and proceed with them, with all possible dispatch, consistent with their safety; and on your arrival at Valetta Harbour, you will make the signal for, and take under your convoy and protection, all our Trade which may be collected there, from the Levant and Adriatic, and proceed with them as expeditiously after as possible, consistent with their safety, to Gibraltar, where you will also take all the Merchant-Ships bound to any part of the United Kingdom under your convoy, and proceed with them to England without delay: and as the Thisbe will be ordered also on this service, you will take that Ship under your command at Malta; and in the event of any of your Convoy being destined for Ireland, you will order Captain Shepheard (when it shall be deemed proper to part company) to proceed with the Trade bound to Cork and the Bristol Channel; and after having seen them in safety to their destination, you will direct the Thisbe to proceed to Plymouth or Portsmouth, as may be most expedient, and continue on yourself, with the rest of the Convoy, to Spithead, dropping such as are bound to Ports in the Channel on your way up; and on your arrival there, you will acquaint the Secretary of the Admiralty thereof, and transmit an account of your proceedings for their Lordships' information. The protection of our Commerce being an object of great importance, you are to pay the utmost attention to every Ship under your convoy, and on no account leave them exposed to the Enemy's Privateers or Cruizers.

NELSON AND BRONTE.

TO WILLIAM MARSDEN, ESQ., ADMIRALTY.

[Letter-Book.]

Victory, at Sea, 20th April, 1804.

Sir,

In consequence of his Majesty's Ship Kent having been reported to me in too leaky and unsafe a state to keep the sea in bad weather, I ordered the Captains of the Ships named in the margin,[9] together with their respective Carpenters, to proceed on board the Kent, and strictly examine into the state of her hull, beams, topsides, &c., in order to ascertain the real state and situation of that Ship. And I herewith transmit you the Report made to me yesterday in consequence, which I request you will lay before the Lords Commissioners of the Admiralty, for their information; and at the same time, acquaint their Lordships that she this day proceeded to Naples, where I have directed her Captain to remain till further orders. The Gibraltar being greatly in want of cordage for running rigging, &c., I have directed Captain Ryves to purchase what may be absolutely necessary to put that Ship in a state for sea; having so done, to join me immediately, and I shall, as soon after as may be expedient, order her to Gibraltar to get the repairs their Lordships have directed, and hope by that time stores will have arrived from England for this purpose. I am, &c.,

NELSON AND BRONTE.

TO ADMIRAL LORD RADSTOCK.

[Autograph, in the possession of Rear Admiral Lord Radstock, C.B.]

Victory, April 20th, 1804.

My dear Lord,

I have just received your kind note of February 2nd, saved from the Hindostan, and also your packet of Patriotic papers.[1] &c., which you have been so good as to send me by Mr.

---

[9] Superb, Victory, Canopus.

[1] This was probably a new edition of a small volume, called "The British Flag Triumphant," which Lord Radstock had caused to be printed, at his own expense, in 1797, and circulated throughout the Fleet, containing the Dispatches announcing all our great Naval Victories.

Morier,[2] who fortunately went up in the Thisbe (I suppose) to Malta. You and your friends, my dear Lord, have certainly the greatest merit in turning the minds of the people to a proper and true way of thinking. Without that precaution, arming them might turn to our destruction instead of preservation. I wish, on every account, I could announce to you the promotion of your son. If the Admiralty will allow me to follow my intentions, Granville[3] will be promoted next but one, and that *one* is Mr. Faddy, who was a child in the Vanguard when his father was killed. I have protected him ever since, and he served his time and passed last October. Your excellent heart will, I am sure, accord in this respect with mine.

I expect the French Ships from Ferrol, if they can escape our Squadron, and then, probably, they will fight us. Till then they will only try to escape this Squadron—certainly, I believe, the finest we have at sea. You will have heard they have been playing in and out of Toulon. They may carry their play further some day than they intend; and that it may be soon (before I am done up) is the sincere wish of, my dear Lord and friend, your ever most faithful and obliged,

Granville has passed.   NELSON AND BRONTE.

---

[2] John Philip Morier, Esq., who, in December 1803, had been appointed Consul-General in Albania and the Morea.

[3] On the 25th of April, five days after the date of this letter, the Honourable Granville George Waldegrave (now Rear-Admiral Lord Radstock, C.B.,) was appointed Acting-Lieutenant of the Victory, vice Lieutenant Lackey, invalided, and who died in October following. As Mr. Faddy had been appointed a Lieutenant of the Triumph on the 13th of April, in the room of an Officer who had been invalided, and as Lord Nelson was not sure of his being confirmed by the Admiralty, he meant that he should reserve the first vacancy by death, or Court-Martial, which he had the right of filling up, for Mr. Faddy, if necessary. To Lord Nelson's letter announcing Mr. Waldegrave's appointment, (which, from a delicacy perhaps mistaken, however honourable to its present possessor, has not been communicated by him to the Editor,) Lord Radstock thus feelingly replied, on the 23rd of July 1804:

"The Board behaved very handsomely on this occasion, as a Commission was directed to be made out for my son the very day that your order made its appearance. But I cannot, my dear friend, pass over in silence what you say of my son. Great as my joy was at your notification of his advancement, it was comparatively nothing to the delight I experienced on reading what you say of him, both as an Officer and a Man. Such commendation from such a man as yourself, is of that value, that no pen can describe. It will not only be an everlasting spur to himself, but the sight of your letter (for it shall never perish in the family, if I can help it) shall fill the breast even of his son's son with that noble fire, which can alone lead to glorious and immortal actions."—*Autograph*, in the Nelson Papers.

TO WILLIAM MARSDEN, ESQ., ADMIRALTY.

[Original, in the Admiralty.]

Sir,   Victory, at Sea, 20th April, 1804.

You will please to acquaint the Lords Commissioners of
the Admiralty, that, in obedience to their direction, communicated to me in Sir Evan Nepean's letter, dated the 13th
December last, I shall give a Commission to Mr. Silas Hiscutt
Paddon,[4] to be a Lieutenant of his Majesty's Sloop Halcyon ;
but I have to express a wish that their Lordships had, at the
same time, signified which of the Lieutenants of that Sloop
Mr. Paddon was to supersede, as it leaves this very unpleasant
business for me to determine.   I shall, however, transfer that
duty to the Commander of the said Sloop.   I am, &c.,

NELSON AND BRONTE.

TO ADMIRAL THE EARL OF ST. VINCENT, K.B.

[Autograph, in the possession of Vice-Admiral Sir William Parker, Bart., G.C.B.]

My dear Lord,   Victory, April 21st, 1804.

Mr. James,[5] Lord Camden's nephew, has delivered me
your letter; but, from his total loss of clothes in the Hindostan, he has desired to go to England, and upon consulting
Captain Capel, who he has been with, I have consented, and
have so wrote to Lord Camden.

I have, in obedience to Admiralty order, signed a Commission for Mr. [Paddon] for the Halcyon, but I wish it

---

[4] Mr. Silas Hiscutt Paddon had greatly distinguished himself in July 1800, when
Midshipman of the Viper Cutter, in her Boat, with only 12 hands, under Lieutenant
Coghlan, in boarding and capturing the French Gun-brig Cerbère, with a crew of
87 men, when he received *six* wounds.   An account of that affair, the intrepidity
of which induced Lord St. Vincent to present Lieutenant Coghlan (who died a
Post Captain, and a Companion of the Bath) with a handsome sword, will be found
in James's "Naval History," vol. iii. p. 45.   Mr. Paddon was confirmed as a
Lieutenant on the 20th April, 1804 ; but that gallant and zealous Officer, though
often actively employed, (*Ibid.*, vol. v. p. 26,) did not obtain his present rank of
Commander until March 1826.

[5] Mr. John James, second son of Sir Walter James James, Bart., by Lady Jane
Pratt, youngest daughter of Charles first Earl Camden.   Mr. James's ill health
obliged him to leave the Navy, and he was afterwards Secretary of Embassy and
Minister Plenipotentiary at the Court of the Netherlands.   He died in June 1814,
leaving a son, now Sir Walter James, Bart.; and his widow, Lady Emily, daughter
of Robert first Marquis of Londonderry, married, secondly, in 1821, the Right
Honourable Sir Henry Hardinge, G.C.B., the present Governor-General of India.

had been mentioned which Lieutenant he was to supersede. One is an elève of the Duke of Clarence, the other a very meritorious Officer, Nephew to Captain Donnelly of the Narcissus. I am ever, my dear Lord, yours faithfully,

NELSON AND BRONTE.

We have now had a forty-eight hours' gale, and no signs of its abating.

TO WILLIAM MARSDEN, ESQ., ADMIRALTY.

[Original, in the Admiralty.]

Sir,   Victory, at Sea, 22nd April, 1804.

I herewith transmit you a letter from Captain Le Gros of his Majesty's late Ship Hindostan, which I request you will please to communicate to the Lords Commissioners of the Admiralty, and, at the same time, acquaint their Lordships that, in addition to Mr. Edward Gayner's honest and honourable dealings in supplying the Fleet with wine and other necessary refreshments, which can be procured from no other person at Rosas, every Officer in the Squadron is infinitely indebted to him for his great care and attention in executing their private commissions as well as their public transactions; and it is but justice to state, that Mr. Gayner has on every occasion furnished us with articles prohibited by the Spanish Government, without a motive of pecuniary reward, from want of which the Ships' Companies would have felt a severe loss: therefore beg to mention him to their Lordships as a person very deserving of some consideration for his great exertions for the Public service.[6]   I am, &c.,

NELSON AND BRONTE.

TO LADY HAMILTON.

[From "Lord Nelson's Letters to Lady Hamilton," vol. ii. p. 34. On the 23rd of April, St. George's day, 1804, a promotion of Admirals took place, when Lord Nelson became a Vice-Admiral of the White—the highest rank he ever attained.]

My dearest Emma,   Victory, April 23rd, 1804.

Hallowell has promised me, if the Admiralty will give him leave to go to London, that he will call at Merton. His spirit

---

[6] The Lords of the Admiralty consequently presented Mr. Gayner with a silver Cup, value one hundred guineas.

is certainly more independent than almost any man's I ever
knew; but, I believe, he is attached to me. I am sure he
has no reason to be so to either Troubridge, or any one at the
Admiralty. I have sent, last night, a box of Maraschino
veritabile of Zara, which I got Jemmy Anderson to buy for
me, and twelve bottles of Tokay. I have none for myself—
being better pleased that you should have it. I am, &c.

NELSON AND BRONTE.

Hallowell parted last night; but, being in sight, I am sending a Frigate with a letter to the Admiralty.

May God Almighty bless you, and send us a happy meeting.

TO CAPTAIN RYVES, H. M. SHIP GIBRALTAR, AT NAPLES.

[Letter-Book.]

Sir,   Victory, at Sea, 26th April, 1804.

As Seamen's beds and hammocks are very much wanted for
the Fleet, and as, from the loss of the late Hindostan, a supply
from England cannot be expected for many months, I am to
request you will use every means to find out whether beds
can be procured at Naples, the price and quality thereof, and
also, upon what notice any number, from one to two thousand
beds, may he had. You will also make inquiry if any cotton,
&c., can be purchased for hammocks—the price per yard,
and what quantity may be had for this purpose. It would,
therefore, be advisable to bring a bed complete, with a sample
of the cotton. The price of the former, I think, ought not to
exceed fourteen or sixteen shillings each. I am, &c.,

NELSON AND BRONTE.

TO HIS EXCELLENCY HUGH ELLIOT, ESQ.

[Autograph, in the Elliot Papers.]

Victory, April 26th, 1804.

My dear Sir,
I have been duly honoured with your Excellency's letters by
the Belleisle and Childers, and feel very much obliged by
your communication of the very interesting news from the

various Powers on the Continent. It must, if they are induced to move, be for our advantage—that is, I mean against France, and for their own future peace and quietness. If Austria and Russia submit to the invasion of the German Territory,[7] the two young Emperors deserve the worst which can happen. You will be sorry to hear of the loss of the Hindostan with all our stores; but this being an accident which no human precaution could prevent, I must turn my mind to do without them, and I dare say I shall do tolerably the summer. But the capture of the Swift Cutter of four or six guns and twenty-three men, with all the Dispatches, is a loss which ages cannot do away. I only hope, but I have my *great fears*, that not only the secrets of our own Country are exposed, but that perhaps Naples, Russia, Sardinia, and Egypt may be mentioned. How the Admiralty could send out such a Vessel is astonishing! I wish it to be known at Petersburg and Constantinople, in case any plan has been agreed upon by our Courts, for the French will, of course, strike a blow instantly. Naples will keep on her guard, for we must prepare for the worst which may have happened. It has made me very uneasy and unwell.

The Gibraltar is ordered by the Admiralty to be refitted, and, therefore, I have sent the Kent, who is to go home in July, being unable any longer to encounter our dreadful weather off Toulon. As you will see, she is a very fine Ship, and fully equal to convey any *important* freight to Sicily. I send your Excellency a secret order in case of need.

The Argo is just sailed for England. You know she is from Egypt. Captain Hallowell thinks the French are destined for that Country. I have not heard from England officially since January, and I only wish they had kept their letters instead of trusting them in such a Vessel. You will find Captain Malcolm a very intelligent, good Officer. I am ever, my dear Sir, your most faithful and obedient servant,

NELSON AND BRONTE.

---

[7] Vide p. 518, post.

TO HIS EXCELLENCY HUGH ELLIOT, ESQ.

[Original, in the Elliot Papers.]

Victory, 26th April, 1804.

Lord Nelson presents his compliments to Mr. Elliot, and transmits herewith an order to Captain Malcolm of the Kent, or the Senior Officer of his Majesty's Ships in the Bay of Naples, which Mr. Elliot will have the goodness to deliver, should it become necessary; and also, to forward the accompanying letter to Mr. Jackson at Rome.

TO CAPTAIN PULTENEY MALCOLM, H. M. SHIP KENT, OR THE SENIOR OFFICER OF HIS MAJESTY'S SHIPS IN THE BAY OF NAPLES.

[Original, in the Elliot Papers.]

Victory, at Sea, 26th April, 1804.

Most Secret and Confidential.

You are hereby required and directed, on this order being delivered to you, to receive on board, or to convoy them if they embark on board their own Ships, the King, Queen, and Royal Family of Naples, to Palermo, or such other place as the King may choose to proceed to, and you will afford every protection and assistance to all those who may wish to follow their Majesties (and that they approve of).

And you will also receive his Majesty's Minister and Suite, and afford such other protection as in your power to all British subjects and their property, as the urgency of the case may require.

NELSON AND BRONTE.

TO HIS EXCELLENCY HUGH ELLIOT, ESQ.

[Autograph, in the Elliot Papers.]

My dear Sir,   Victory, April 26th, 1804.

I am obliged by your suggestions relative to supplying the Fleet with bullocks and vegetables, but the distance is too great to render such a supply certain. It could not be by

Neutrals; for they would soon be taken, and the expense would be enormous. I must do as well as I can. I want small Vessels; but instead of the Admiralty increasing my numbers, they are daily diminishing. It would be most desirable to hear from you every week; for events of great importance may be expected every day to arise; but I have them not. I must finish; for a gale of wind is coming on, and the Kent must part company. I do not think I can possibly write Mr. Jackson at Rome. Pray, say so for me ; and that the King of Sardinia need not fear I shall force Troops upon his Territory. Ever, my dear Sir, yours faithfully,

NELSON AND BRONTE.

TO J. B. GIBERT, ESQ., HIS MAJESTY'S VICE-CONSUL, BARCELONA.

[Letter-Book.]

Victory, at Sea, 26th April, 1804.

Sir,

I have received your letter of the 7th instant, acquainting me with the capture of the Swift Cutter by the French Privateer Esperance, and trust, as the French prisoner landed from the Seahorse, at Rosas, was insisted upon by the Spanish Governor, as free from that moment, that you have, in like manner, insisted upon and obtained the freedom of the Swift Cutter's Crew, (in the event of their having been landed,) and put them on board his Majesty's Ship Juno, as the sending Seamen to Gibraltar is not only attended with great inconvenience, but contrary to my wish respecting them. I have also to acknowledge your letter of the fifth instant, with the circular one, therein mentioned, from Mr. Hunter, forbidding the sale of English Vessels (captured by the French) in any of the Ports of Spain, together with the French Papers which accompanied your said letter, for which I am very much obliged, as well as by the information respecting the King's recovery, and the political circumstances of news from Paris. I am, &c.,

NELSON AND BRONTE.

TO EDWARD GAYNER, ESQ., ROSAS.

[Letter-Book.]

Sir, Victory, at Sea, 26th April, 1804.

I have received your letter of the 4th instant, sent by Lieutenant Tailour,[8] of his Majesty's late Ship Hindostan, giving an account of the total loss of that Ship by fire, that you propose examining the remains of that Ship to see whether anything can be got out, and that, from the exertions and assistance of Neapolitan divers, several articles of stores might be recovered, upon allowing them a salvage upon what they deliver; and also acquainting me that you had agreed to pay Pera Marti the sum of two hundred Spanish hard dollars for bringing Captain Le Gros's letter, and other intelligence to the Fleet. In answer to which, I am very much obliged by the kind attention you have paid to Captain Le Gros, the Officers and Company of the late Hindostan, and very much approve of every means being tried to save any article of stores belonging to the said late Ship, for which such salvage shall be made as may be judged proper. I must beg you will be good enough to make up and transmit me your account of the said two hundred dollars, with any other expense which you may have been at on this late occasion, that I may order it to be immediately paid. I am, &c.,

NELSON AND BRONTE.

TO SIR JOHN ACTON, BART., NAPLES.

[From Clarke and M'Arthur, vol. ii. p. 361.]

26th April, 1804.

The Emperor of Russia will, I hope, get his Troops into Italy. The insult offered his Father-in-Law, cannot, if there is any spirit in a young Emperor, be overlooked;[9] and I should

---

[8] Lieutenant John Tailour was First Lieutenant of the Hindostan. He was made a Commander for his gallant services, in November 1809, became a Post Captain in October 1813, and died on the 1st of May 1820.

[9] On the 15th of March 1804, the Duke d'Enghien was seized by a body of French Cavalry at Ettenheim, in the Electorate of Baden, taken to Paris, tried by a Military Commission, and shot. The Emperor Alexander having married a daughter of Charles Lewis, eldest son of Charles Lewis Frederic, Elector of Baden, the insult was offered, not to his father-in law, but to the father of that personage.

also hope the Austrian eagle is not humbled. If the Emperor submits, it is not difficult to see that the Imperial diadem will be removed from that family. I am, &c.,

NELSON AND BRONTE.

TO THE RESPECTIVE CAPTAINS.

[Autograph draught in the possession of James Young, Esq., of Wells, and from a Copy in the Nelson Papers.]

Victory, at Sea, 28th April, 1804.

Memorandum.

As it is my determination to attack the French Fleet in any place where there is a reasonable prospect of getting fairly alongside of them, and as I think that in Hières Bay, Gourjean Bay, Port Especia, Leghorn Roads, Ajaccio, and many other places, opportunities may offer of attacking them, I therefore recommend that every Captain will make himself, by inquiries, as fully acquainted with the above-mentioned places as possible—viz., for Hières Bay, the Petite Passe, Grande Passe, and Passage from the Eastward; Gourjean Bay, (of which I send a Chart from the latest surveys made,) Port Especia, and, in particular, the Northern Passage into Leghorn Roads, from which side it is only, in my opinion, possible to attack an Enemy's Fleet to advantage; and with the Gulf of Ajaccio.

In going in to attack an Enemy's Fleet, it is recommended, if possible, to have the Launch out, and hawsers and stream-anchors in her; and, with any other Boats, to lay out of gun-shot, ready to act as circumstances may require. Ships, in bringing up, will anchor as the Captains may think best, from circumstances of wind and weather, and the position of the Enemy; but I would recommend strongly having the *four* large anchors clear for letting go; because I know, from experience, the great difficulty, with crippled masts and yards, getting an anchor over the side; and it is probable that it may be necessary to remove the Ship after an Action, and to leave some of her anchors behind. The Ships will anchor in such a manner as to give each other mutual support for the destruction of the Enemy.

NELSON AND BRONTE.

A Chart of Gourjean Bay to be delivered to each Line-of-Battle Ship.

TO . . . .

[Autograph, in the possession of James Young, Esq., of Wells. Neither the name of the Officer to whom this letter was written, nor its date, has been ascertained. It is inserted in this place, from its appearing to relate to the previous Memorandum, though it may perhaps have been written at a different time.]

My dear Sir,

I scrawl this from recollection : but you may rely upon it I have beat [in], in the Captain in the Night, and gone in, in gales of Westerly wind. The approaching Leghorn must be regulated by what may call our attention. If the French Fleet is in the Southern anchorage you can certainly get within gun-shot of them, and perhaps if they are anchored amongst the Knowls alongside of them ; and at all events you secure a safe retreat for our crippled Ships, for it would be impossible for a crippled Ship with the wind at W.S.W. or even West to clear the shore to the Southward of Leghorn, and if you are sure of passing over the Knowls after an Action, you are sure of a safe and smooth anchorage. Be so good as to return me this paper when copied, as I may add something to it, and at all events it will save me the trouble of writing another. Ever yours faithfully,

NELSON AND BRONTE.

DIRECTIONS FOR LEGHORN ROADS.

[Autograph in the possession of James Young, Esq., of Wells.]

The Knowls are shifting in a space of a mile (at least) from the Mazocco to the Malora.

The whole shoal of the Malora is surrounded with Knowls, particularly to the South and North ends : therefore, must be approached with caution. You have from twelve fathoms to five at one cast of the lead, and from nine fathoms I have known Ships strike.

The mark for being clear of the Malora North end is the Guard-House on the Beach, (which has one window to the Westward), on with the last hillock of the nearest ridge of mountains.

If the weather is hazy and the mountains cannot be seen,

bring the Guard-House called Mezzo Spiago to bear E.S.E. by Compass, which will clear you of the North end of the Malora.

If the weather is so hazy that the Guard-House cannot be made out, you may steer with safety towards the Mouth of the Arno: there is no danger in approaching the shore, and you will naturally in such weather haul to the Southward, or approach the shore with caution.

The leading mark for running in, is the Light-House, on with the further point of Monte Nero, as laid down in the Chart.

In working in, if you can make out the Church of Monte Nero, which is difficult for a stranger, as it has no steeple and looks like a long Barn in a clump of trees, the mark is perfectly safe in standing towards the Malora. In standing to the shore to the Northward of the Knowls and the Mazocco (a high white building exactly resembling a Light-House) you may safely stand in until the Light-House forms an *Island*, but the soundings are towards the shore so gradual that you may trust to your lead.

TO CAPTAIN FRANK SOTHERON, H. M. SHIP EXCELLENT.

[Order-Book.]

Victory, at Sea, 28th April, 1804.

Having ordered the Honourable Captain Capel to cruize with the Ship and Sloops named in the margin,[7] between the Levant Islands, and the head of the Gulf of Frejus, you are hereby required and directed to proceed immediately in his Majesty's Ship Excellent, under your command, towards the Gulf of Frejus, where you will fall in with some of the said Vessels; and on doing so, you will direct the whole to join you immediately on Rendezvous No. 102, where you will continue till the return of the Squadron from Rendezvous No. 97, under Cape St. Sebastians, to which place I shall proceed this evening, in order to receive the Thetis Transport with wine from Rosas, and immediately after return to the first mentioned Rendezvous. Should the wind come from the

---

[7] Phœbe, Niger, Childers, Termagant.

Eastward, the Cameleon may soon be expected to join ; You
will, therefore, send the Childers and Cameleon to me with
all dispatch, off St. Sebastians, as they are wanted for particular service, and also any other Vessel which may join you
in search of the Squadron. If the wind is Westerly, the Ships
and Vessels which may join you are to remain on Rendezvous
No. 102, as my absence from that place will be but for as short
a time as possible. As the Active, Amazon, and Narcissus, are
ordered to join on Rendezvous No. 102, you will, so soon as
you have a sufficient force of Frigates, order Toulon to be
reconnoitred as often as, from circumstances of the Enemy's
motions, you may find necessary.; and in the event of their
sailing from Toulon, you will use every effort to communicate
the same to me as early as possible, and join me in the
Excellent without delay, leaving some Vessel of War on
Rendezvous No. 102, for the purpose of acquainting any
Ship in search of me with an account of the Enemy's sailing,
and where it is probable they may find me.

                                        NELSON AND BRONTE.

TO RICHARD FORD, ESQ., AGENT VICTUALLER TO THE FLEET.

[Letter-Book.]

                                Victory, at Sea, 28th April, 1804.

Sir,

In answer to your letter of the 16th instant, I have ordered
120 empty wine-pipes from the different Ships, and sent them
by the Seahorse for the purpose of holding the remainder of
the last 200 pipes contracted for from Mr. Gayner, which you
will order to be filled as early as possible, that they may be in
readiness to come by the next Vessel sent for the brandy. As
I take it for granted that you have the 290 pipes of wine on
board the Thetis, I have ordered her to join me without a
moment's loss of time ; and must desire, as the Squadron may
soon go where fresh provisions can be had, that you will join
me in the Seahorse, which convoys the Thetis to the Fleet, as
they cannot be supplied with the necessary refreshments without your being on the spot. I am, &c.,

                                        NELSON AND BRONTE.

TO WILLIAM MARSDEN, ESQ., ADMIRALTY.

[Letter-Book.]

Victory, at Sea, 29th April, 1804.

Sir,

I herewith transmit you, for the information of the Lords Commissioners of the Admiralty, a letter from Captain White, of his Majesty's Ship Renown, together with the list of Proctors' fees, charged in the Vice-Admiralty Court of Malta, on the condemnation of La Babienne, a French Bombard; and request you will be pleased to move their Lordships to lay the said letter and inclosure before the Admiralty Solicitor, in order that it may be correctly ascertained whether the half fees[8] of the Vice-Admiralty Court at Malta, upon so small an amount, are consistent with the charges, on similar occasions, in the Admiralty Court of England, and transmit the same to me, for the information of Captain White, and the other Commanders of his Majesty's Ships upon this station, who consider these charges as very high and exorbitant.   I am, &c.,

NELSON AND BRONTE.

[8] *Sic.*   Query, *heavy* fees ?

END OF VOL. V.